DATABASE PROCESSING

Fundamentals, Design & Implementation

Seventh Edition

David M. Kroenke

PRENTICE HALL INTERNATIONAL, INC.

Acquisitions Editor: David Alexander
Editorial Assistant: Keith Kryszczun
Assistant Editor: Lori Cerreto
Managing Editor: Lucinda Gatch
Editor-in-Chief: Mickey Cox
Director of Strategic Marketing: Nancy Evans
Production Editor: Marc Oliver
Manufacturing Buyer: Lisa DiMaulo
Senior Manufacturing Supervisor: Paul Smolenski
Senior Manufacturing/Prepress Manager: Vincent Scelta
Senior Designer: Cheryl Asherman
Design Manager: Patricia Smythe
Interior/Cover Design: Jill Little
Cover Illustration/Photo: Wassily Kandinsky (1866–1944) Russian,
"Improvisation 34." Museum of art, Kazan, Russia/Superstock, Inc. © 1999
Artists Rights Society (ARS), New York/ADAGP, Paris
Composition: UG / GGS Information Services, Inc.

ISBN 0-13-085212-0

Prentice-Hall International (UK) Limited, London
Prentice-Hall of Australia Pty. Limited, Sydney
Prentice-Hall Canada, Inc., Toronto
Prentice-Hall Hispanoamericana, S.A., Mexico
Prentice-Hall of India Private Limited, New Delhi
Prentice-Hall of Japan, Inc., Tokyo
Pearson Education Asia Pte. Ltd., Singapore
Editora Prentice-Hall do Brasil, Ltda., Rio de Janeiro
Prentice-Hall, Upper Saddle River, New Jersey

Printed in the United States of America

10 9 8 7 6 5 4 3 2

BRIEF CONTENTS

TABLE OF CONTENTS

PREFACE

In 1983, the popularity of the IBM personal computer prompted one industry pundit to write, "After years of explosive growth, the computer industry has finally reached its infancy." Today, the same statement can be made about the Internet: After years of explosive growth, the Internet has finally reached its infancy.

True enough, but why does the Internet matter to database processing? Part of the answer is that the Internet tremendously amplifies the importance of database technology, knowledge, and skills. Chapter 13 shows how to call Active Data Objects from script code in Microsoft IIS Active Server Pages for the purpose of listing a table. Basically, the example wraps a straightforward SQL SELECT statement with Internet technology to perform a task that was simple many years ago. This isn't particularly special except that, as of December, 1998, 153 million people worldwide can view that table with software that is already in place on their computer!

The Internet (and organizational intranets) need database technology to move from brochure publishing to application publishing. We know the stories of Amazon.com, Dell Computer, and other well-known "e-tailers." Database applications are, of course, critically important to those companies. Lesser known are smaller companies like the yacht broker in Seattle who used a database application to sell a boat located in Hawaii to a customer living in North Carolina. The broker never met the buyer nor saw the boat. The contract was negotiated over the Web, the buyer flew to Hawaii to inspect the boat, and the deal was done. The net was $4700 to the broker for basically an Internet information service.

The Internet is important to database processing not only as amplifier, however, but also because of the new technologies being developed. I believe that XML (see Chapter 11) is the most important development for database processing since the relational model. What justifies such a dramatic statement? By separating structure, content, and materialization, XML is the perfect protocol for exchanging database views. Because it is extensible in a standardized way, and because it readily represents arbitrary hierarchical structures, XML provides a superior means for organizations to exchange database views. In time, XML will revolutionize electronic data interchange.

Now, before we all run off to our offices shrieking in panic about the amount of new technology to be learned, consider this perspective: Internet technology provides a wrapper around the fundamentals we have always taught. Thus, I believe we need first to teach data modeling, normalization, database design, database application design, and then follow that by teaching the application of these fundamentals for the Internet and organizational intranets. Hence, in this text, the first 10 chapters address fundamentals; it is only the next three that concern Internet technologies.

One last note on important new developments—with Office 2000, Microsoft will place its Pivot Table Service on the desktops of the world. This service is a desktop version of its OLAP server and, indeed, it can process not only local OLAP cubes, but also those stored on remote computers providing OLAP services for large databases. Hence, this edition augments the data warehousing material in Chapter 14 with a substantial discussion of OLAP.

MICROSOFT ACCESS AND SQL SERVER AND WALL DATA'S DBAPP

I have used Access 2000 to illustrate discussion points throughout the text. This is done primarily to give form and substance to otherwise ethereal ideas. Also, since Access is the world's most popular database management system (DBMS), it is the product students are most likely to have now and to encounter later in their careers.

In addition to Access, the Microsoft Corporation agreed to license the Evaluation Edition of SQL Server 7.0 to users of this text, free of charge. A copy of this software is shrink-wrapped with this text. This version of SQL Server 7.0 can be run on Windows 95, Windows 98, Windows NT, and Windows 2000. It requires a 166 MHz or higher Pentium processor, 32 megabytes of RAM, and from 65–180 MB of disk storage. The license for this software lasts for 120 days from the date of installation, which should be more than adequate for student use in your course. Installation and use of SQL Server is described in Appendix B.

Appendix C presents Wall Data's DBApp. This software, which is available for free to students from the Prentice Hall Web site (**www.prenhall.com/kroenke**), can be used to create semantic object data models, to generate both Access and SQL Server database schemas, and to create .asp pages for publishing database views on the Web. DBApp will also reverse engineer existing databases and create semantic object models from them. See Appendix C for more information.

ORGANIZATION OF THIS BOOK

This text is organized into seven parts. Part I provides an introduction. A number of different types of databases and applications are presented in Chapter 1, along with important definitions and a brief history of database processing. Chapter 2 illustrates the components of a DBMS and provides an overview of the process of building a database and related applications.

The focus of Part II is on data modeling. Chapter 3 explains the concepts and constructs of the entity-relationship model and illustrates its use. Chapter 4 presents the semantic object model in a similar way. Either of these models can be used to express the users' data requirements.

Part III discusses the transformation of data models into relational database designs. Chapter 5 sets the stage by discussing the relational model and normalization. Normalization techniques are then used in Chapter 6 to explain the transformation of entity-relationship data models into relational designs and in Chapter 7 to explain the transformation of semantic object models into relational designs.

The implementation of relational databases is presented in Part IV. Chapter 8 discusses the foundations of relational implementation and relational algebra. Chapter 9 then presents SQL in a DBMS-independent manner. Chapter 10 concludes Part IV by discussing the design of database applications. This chapter sets the stage for the next three chapters by making a clear distinction between database views and materializations on database views. It also discusses application roles in the enforcement of constraints and business rules.

Part V concerns database processing using Internet technologies. Chapter 11 introduces basic Web concepts and describes the three-tier processing architecture. Web-oriented programming languages like JavaScript, VBScript, and Java are described and the features and functions of DHTML and XML are discussed. The chapter concludes with an explanation of the role and purpose of Active Server Pages. Chapter 12 then focuses on the database server tier. Concurrency control, transaction management, backup and recovery, and security are all addressed.

Finally, Chapter 13 describes standards for accessing Web databases including ODBC, OLE DB, and ADO.

Enterprise database processing is addressed in Part VI. Chapter 14 discusses enterprise database system architectures, describes the processing of downloaded data, and surveys OLAP. It concludes with a discussion of data warehousing and data administration. Chapter 15 then presents a case example of DB2 and Chapter 16 discusses the hierarchical and network data models. Both of these models are old but have come back into prominence because of the need to fix Y2K problems as well as the need to find some way to put their data on the Web. OLE DB will give new importance to IMS to our students.

Chapter 17, the sole chapter in Part VII, addresses object-oriented DBMS technology. While such databases are of conceptual interest, they play, at most, a minor role in commercial database processing. This chapter therefore presents basic concepts so that students will be familiar with the important ODBMS terminology and standards.

ACKNOWLEDGEMENTS

I would like to thank the following reviewers who provided most useful guidance and many helpful comments:

David Overbye, Keller Graduate School of Management
William J. Stratton, The Rochester Institute of Technology
Mark W. Smith, Trident Technical College
Maureen Thommes, Bemidji State University
Lisa Friedrichsen, Keller Graduate School of Management

Also, a special thanks to David Alexander, who saw the importance of Internet technology and agreed to push for a two-year revision of this text, and to his always helpful and cheerful assistant Keith Kryszczun. Thanks as well to Marc Oliver, who managed the production of this edition and now has had a key role in two revisions of this text.

Thanks to the Microsoft Corporation for the complementary license to readers of this text for SQL Server 7.0. I am especially grateful to John Wall and the executive team at Wall Data for the complementary license to use DBApp and also for their continuous support of the educational community since 1992. Many of the ideas in this text arose from delightful and interesting conversations with Wall Data employees and especially with Ted Carroll, Lee Eggebrotten, Ed Fogard, Mike Gardner, Pat Hammack, Kenji Kawai, Michael Miller, Nick Nichols, Chris Olds, Charles Porter, Danny Rosenthal, and Cathy Stanford. I am most grateful to all of them for their time, their thoughts, and their consideration. Finally, a special thanks to Lynda, whose delightful presence has been not only an inspiration but also a steadfast support through thick and thin.

The computer industry is as exciting and interesting today as at any time since I entered it in 1967. I sincerely hope that readers of this text will have as much fun with this technology as I have had. If they have even half as much, they will truly be blessed.

David Kroenke
Seattle, Washington

DATABASE PROCESSING

INTRODUCTION

The two chapters in Part I introduce the topic of database processing. Chapter 1 describes four typical database applications and discusses the advantages of databases over earlier file-processing systems. It also defines the term *database* and surveys the history of database processing. Chapter 2 then summarizes the tasks necessary to develop a database and related applications. It also describes the elements of a database and surveys the functions of the DBMS as well.

This part provides an overview of the need for databases and the nature of the components of databases and their related applications. Its purpose is to set the stage for your study of the details of database technology in subsequent chapters.

CHAPTER 1

Introduction to Database Processing

Database processing has always been an important topic in the study of information systems. In recent years, however, the explosion of the World Wide Web (WWW) and the dramatic development of new technology for the Internet has made knowledge of database technology one of the hottest career paths. Database technology enables Internet applications to step beyond the simple brochure publishing that characterized early applications. At the same time, Internet technology provides a standardized and readily accessible means of publishing database content to users. None of these new developments takes away from the need for classical database applications that were vital to business interests prior to the rise of the Internet. They simply amplify the importance of database knowledge.

Many students find this subject enjoyable and interesting, even though it can be challenging. Database design and development involve both art and engineering. Understanding user requirements and translating them into effective database designs is an artistic process. Transforming those designs into physical databases with functionally complete, high performance applications is an engineering process. Both aspects are full of challenging and enjoyable intellectual puzzles.

Because of the immense need for database technology, the skills you develop and the knowledge you gain in this course will be in great demand. The goal of this text is to provide a solid foundation in the fundamentals of database technology so that you can begin a successful career in this field if you choose to do so.

➤ FOUR DATABASE EXAMPLES

The purpose of a database is to help people keep track of things. The classical database applications concern the tracking of items like orders, customers, jobs, employees, phone calls, or other items of interest to a business person. Recently, as databases have become more readily available, database technology has been applied to new areas such as databases for the Internet or for organizational intranets. Also, databases are increasingly used to create and maintain multimedia applications. Consider several typical examples.

MARY RICHARDS HOUSEPAINTING

Mary Richards is a professional housepainter who owns and operates a small company consisting of herself, another professional painter, and, when needed, part-time painters. Mary has been in business for ten years and has earned a reputation as a high-quality painter who works for a reasonable rate. Mary gets most of her work through repeat business from customers who hire her to paint their houses and also from their word-of-mouth referrals. In addition, Mary gets some work from building contractors and professional interior designers.

Customers remember Mary far better than she remembers them. Indeed, sometimes she is embarrassed when a customer calls and says something like, "Hi Mary, this is John Maples. You painted my house three years ago." Mary knows she is supposed to remember the caller and the work she did for him, but since she paints more than fifty houses a year, it usually is difficult for her to do so. This situation becomes worse when the customer says something like, "My neighbor liked the job you did on our house and would like something similar done to her house."

In order to help her memory and to keep better track of her business records, Mary had a consultant develop a database and database application that she uses on her personal computer. The database stores records regarding customers, jobs, and sources in the form of tables, as shown in the example in Figure 1-1.

It is the job of a program called a database management system (DBMS) to store and retrieve the data in these tables. Unfortunately, when such data are in the form of tables, they are not very useful to Mary. Rather, she would like to know how customers and jobs and referrals relate to one another, for example, what jobs she has done for a particular customer or what customers have been referred by a particular person.

To provide this capability, Mary's consultant created a database application that processes data entry forms and produces reports. Consider the example form in Figure 1-2. Here, Mary keys in data about customers such as name, phone, and address. She also links the customer to a particular referral source and keys in data about jobs performed for the customer. This data can then be displayed in

> ➤ FIGURE 1-1

Tables of Data for Mary Richards Housepainting

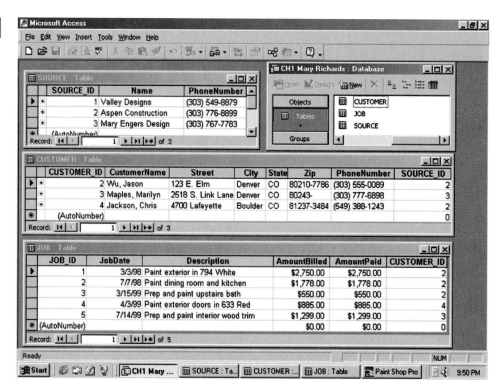

➤ FIGURE 1-2

Example Data Entry Form for Mary Richards Housepainting

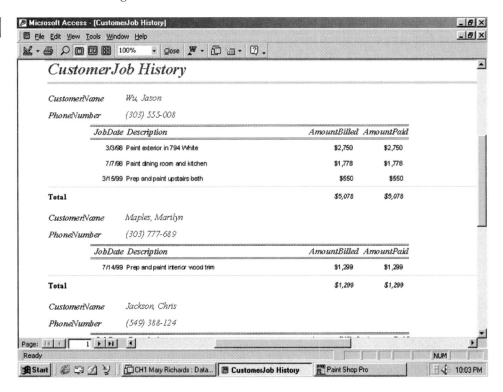

reports like the one shown in Figure 1-3. Other uses of the database include recording bid estimates, tracking referral sources, and producing mailing labels for the direct sales literature that Mary sends out from time to time.

The database application and the DBMS process the form and store the data that are entered into tables like those in Figure 1-1. Similarly, the application and DBMS extract data from tables like those in Figure 1-1 to create a report like the one in Figure 1-3.

Consider again the data in Figure 1-1, and notice that the rows in the tables cross-reference and are linked to one another. Each JOB contains the CUSTOMER_ID of the CUSTOMER who purchased that JOB, and each CUSTOMER contains the SOURCE_ID of the person who referred that customer. These references are used to combine the data to produce forms and reports like those shown in Figures 1-2 and 1-3.

➤ FIGURE 1-3

Example Report for Mary Richards Housepainting

As you can imagine, Mary is unlikely to know how to design the tables in Figure 1-1, how to use a DBMS to create those tables, and how to develop the application to create the forms and reports. But by the time you have finished this course, you should know how to use database technology to create this database and its application. You should also know how to design and manipulate tables to create forms and reports of greater complexity.

TREBLE CLEF MUSIC

Mary Richards's database is called a *single-user* database because only one user accesses the database at a given time. In some cases, this limitation is too restrictive; multiple people need to access the database simultaneously from multiple computers. Such *multi-user* databases are more complicated because the DBMS and the application must keep one user's work from interfering with another's.

Treble Clef Music uses a database application to keep track of musical instruments that it rents. It needs a multi-user database application because, during busy periods, several salespeople may rent musical instruments at the same time. Also, the store manager needs to access the rental database to determine when to order more instruments of a given type. She does not want to interrupt the rental process when she does this.

The Treble Clef store has a local area network that connects several microcomputers to a server computer that holds the rental database as shown in Figure 1-4. Each clerk has access to a database application that has the three forms illustrated in Figure 1-5. The Customer form is used to maintain customer data, the Rental Agreement form is used to track the instruments that have been rented and whether or not they have been returned, and the Instrument form is used to show instrument data and rental history.

To understand the problems that must be overcome in a multi-user database, consider what happens when two customers attempt to rent the same B-flat clarinet at the same time. The DBMS and the application programs must somehow detect that this situation is occurring and inform one of the clerks that he or she must choose a different instrument.

STATE LICENSING AND VEHICLE REGISTRATION BUREAU

Now consider an even larger application of database technology. This example is of a state licensing and auto registration bureau. It has 52 centers that conduct drivers' tests and issue and renew drivers' licenses and also 37 offices that sell vehicle registrations.

➤ FIGURE 1-4

Local Area Network with Database Server Used by Treble Clef Music

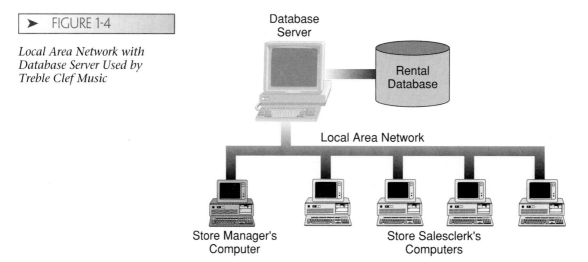

➤ FIGURE 1-5

*Three Forms Used by Treble Clef Music:
(a) Customer Form,
(b) Rental Agreement Form, and
(c) Instrument Form*

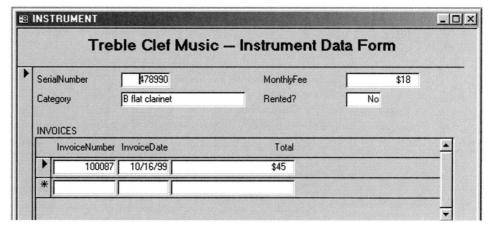

(a)

(b)

(c)

The personnel in these offices access a database to perform their jobs. Before people can be issued or can renew their driver's licenses, their records in the database are checked for traffic violations, accidents, or arrests. This data are used to determine whether the license can be renewed and, if so, whether it should carry any limitations. Similarly, personnel in the auto registration department access the database to determine whether an auto has been registered before and, if so, to whom, and whether there are any outstanding matters that should prohibit the registration.

This database has hundreds of users, including not only the license and registration personnel but also the people in the state department of revenue and in law enforcement. Not surprisingly, the database is large and complex, with more than 40 different tables of data, several of which contain hundreds of thousands of rows of data.

Large organizational databases like the Licensing and Registration Bureau were the first applications of database technology. These systems have been in existence for 20 or 30 years and have been modified to meet changing requirements over that period. Because of their age and complexity, these systems were the most challenging to modify for Y2K compliance (ensuring that no undesirable behavior occurs when the year changed to 2000). Other examples of organizational databases concern account processing at banks and financial institutions, production and material supply systems at large manufacturers, medical records processing at hospitals and insurance companies, and governmental agencies.

CALVERT ISLAND RESERVATIONS CENTRE

Calvert Island is a little known, beautiful island on the west coast of Canada. To promote tourism to a worldwide market, the Calvert Island Chamber of Commerce has developed a Web site with three purposes:

➤ To promote the beauty and recreational opportunities on Calvert Island

➤ To obtain and store name and address data of Web site visitors for follow-up postal promotions

➤ To obtain and store reservation requests for hotels, lodges, and tourist services and communicate those requests to the appropriate vendors

Two databases are used to support this Web site. The first, the promotional database, stores data, photos, video clips, and sound bites of places, events, and facilities on Calvert Island. This database has two types of user. Normal users access this database in read-only mode. Using standard browsers, these users can point and click around the Web site to view activities and facilities in which they have an interest. Behind the scenes, a database application is extracting data and multimedia elements from the promotional database (See Fig. 1-6).

The second type of user of the promotional database is an employee of the Chamber of Commerce who maintains the site. Employees add, change, and delete data and multi media files in the database as promotions change, vendors enter and leave the program, and in response to user requests.

In addition to the promotional database, applications at the Web site process a customer and reservation database. This database stores data entered when Web site visitors complete a customer survey form and when they request a reservation. Customer name, postal and e-mail addresses, interests, preferences, and reservation requests are maintained in this database. When a reservation request is entered, the database application forwards it to the appropriate vendor via e-mail. Periodically, summary reservation reports are prepared and e-mailed to vendors for follow-up and other management purposes.

Three primary characteristics of the Calvert Island database differentiate it from the other applications we have discussed. First, a large portion of the first database contains not only structured data like vendor names and addresses, but also nonstructured bit streams of multimedia files. Second, application content is delivered to the user via a standardized browser. The forms used for Mary Richards, Treble Clef, and the driver's license bureau are fixed in format by the designer and change only when the application is modified. In contrast, Calvert Island users see the form in a format that is determined not only by the application but also by the brand, version, and local options used in their browsers.

The third differentiating characteristic of the Calvert Island application is that standardized Web-oriented technology is used to transfer the data between the browser and the application and database. **Hypertext transfer protocol (HTTP), dynamic hypertext markup language (DHTML),** and **extensible markup language (XML)** are all used. Use of these standards means that any users who have a browser can access this application. No software must be pre-installed on their computers. Consequently, use of this application is virtually unlimited. We will discuss the role of HTTP, DHTML, and XML for database applications in Chapter 11. (See Fig. 1-7).

FIGURE 1-6

Calvert Island Reservation Centre Web Page

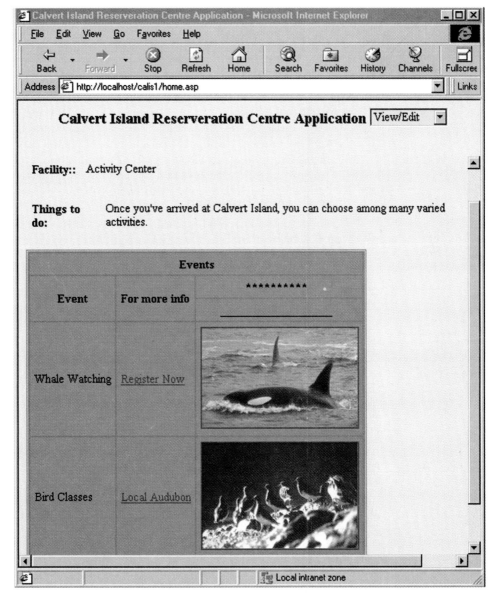

*Characteristics of
Internet Technology
Applications*

- Include both structured data and multimedia data.

- Forms and reports displayed via a standard browser.

- Data transfer via Internet standards such as HTTP, DHTML, and XML.

COMPARISON OF DATABASE APPLICATIONS

These examples represent a sampling of the uses of database technology. Hundreds of thousands of databases are like the one used by Mary Richards House Painting, single-user databases with a relatively small amount of data—say, less than ten megabytes. The forms and reports for these are generally simple and straightforward.

Other databases are like the one used by Treble Clef Music; they have more than one user but usually fewer than 20 or 30 users all together. They contain a moderate amount of data, say, 50 or a 100 megabytes. The forms and reports need to be complex enough to support several different business functions.

The largest databases are like those in the auto registration case, which have hundreds of users and trillions of bytes of data. Many different applications are in use, each application having its own forms and reports. Finally, some databases involve use of Internet technology and process both character and multimedia data such as pictures, sounds, animations, movies, and the like. The characteristics of these types of databases are summarized in Figure 1-8.

When you finish this book, you should be able to design and create databases and database applications like those used by Mary Richards and Treble Clef. You will probably not be able to create one as large and complicated as the vehicle registration database, but you will be able to serve as an effective member of a team that does design and create such a database. You should also be able to create a small to medium database using Internet technology.

Characteristics of Different Types of Databases

Type	Example	Typical Number of Concurrent Users	Typical Size of Database
Personal	Mary Richards House Painting	1	<10 Megabytes
Workgroup	Treble Clef Music	<25	<100 Megabytes
Organizational	Licensing and Registration	Hundreds	>1 Trillion Bytes
Internet Technology	Calvert Island Reservations	Possibly Hundreds	Any

➤ THE RELATIONSHIP OF APPLICATION PROGRAMS AND THE DBMS

All of the preceding examples and, indeed, all database applications have the general structure shown in Figure 1-9: The user interacts with a database application, which in turn interfaces with the DBMS, which accesses the database data.

At one time, the boundary between the application program and the DBMS was clearly defined. Applications were written in third-generation languages like COBOL, and those applications called on the DBMS for data management services. In fact, this still is done, most frequently on large mainframe databases.

Today, however, the features and functions of many DBMS products have grown to the point that the DBMS itself can process sizable portions of the application. For example, most DBMS products contain report writers and form generators that can be integrated into an application. This fact is important to us for two reasons. First, although the bulk of this text considers the design and development of databases, we will often refer to the design and development of database applications. After all, no user wants just a database. Instead, users want forms, reports, and queries that are based on their data.

Second, from time to time you will note an overlap between the material discussed in this class and that discussed in your systems development class because developing effective database applications requires many of the skills that you have learned or will learn in your systems development class. Likewise, most systems development classes today also include the design of databases. The difference between the two courses is one of emphasis. Here, our emphasis is on the design and construction of the database. In a systems class, the emphasis is on the development of information systems, most of which use database technology.

➤ FILE-PROCESSING SYSTEMS

The best way to understand the general nature and characteristics of databases today is to look at the characteristics of systems that predated the use of database technology. These systems reveal the problems that database technology has solved.

➤ FIGURE 1-9

Relationships of Users, Database Applications, DBMS, and Database

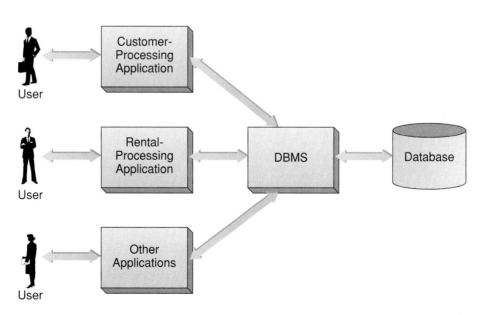

The first business information systems stored groups of records in separate files and were called **file-processing systems.** Figure 1-10, for example, depicts two file-processing systems that Treble Clef could use. One system processes CUSTOMER data, and the other one processes RENTAL data.

Although file-processing systems are a great improvement over manual record-keeping systems, they have important limitations:

➤ Data are separated and isolated.

➤ Data are often duplicated.

➤ Application programs are dependent on file formats.

➤ Files are often incompatible with one another.

➤ It is difficult to represent data in the users' perspectives.

SEPARATED AND ISOLATED DATA

The salespeople at Treble Clef need to relate their customers to the instruments that they rent. For the system in Figure 1-10, the data need to be extracted somehow from CUSTOMER and RENTAL files and combined into a single file. With file-processing, this is difficult. First, systems analysts and computer programmers must determine which parts of each of the files are needed; then they must decide how the files are related to one another; last, they must coordinate the processing of the files so that the correct data are extracted. Coordinating two files is difficult enough, but imagine the task of coordinating 10 or more of them!

DATA DUPLICATION

In the Treble Clef example, a customer's name, address, and other data may be stored many times. That is, the data are stored once for CUSTOMER and again for each RENTAL agreement the customer has. Although these duplicate data waste file space, that is not the most serious problem; rather, the most serious problem with duplicated data concerns **data integrity.**

A collection of data has integrity if the data are logically consistent. Poor data integrity often results when data are duplicated. For example, if a customer changes his or her name or address, then all the files containing that data must be updated, but the danger is that all of the files might *not* be updated, causing discrepancies among them. In the Treble Clef example, the customer might have one address for one RENTAL record and a different address for a second RENTAL record.

Data integrity problems are serious. If data items differ, they will produce inconsistent results and uncertainty. If a report from one application disagrees with

➤ FIGURE 1-10

Two File-Processing Systems

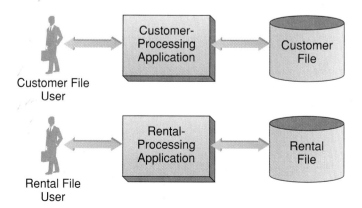

a report from another application, who will be able to tell which one is correct? When results are inconsistent, the credibility of the stored data, and even the MIS function itself, comes into question.

APPLICATION PROGRAM DEPENDENCY

With file processing, application programs depend on the file formats. Usually in file-processing systems the physical formats of files and records are part of the application code. In COBOL, for example, file formats are written in the DATA DIVISION. The problem with this arrangement is that when changes are made in the file formats, the application programs also must be changed.

For example, if the customer record is modified to expand the ZIP code field from five to nine digits, all programs using that customer record must be modified, even if they do not use the ZIP code field. Because there might be 20 programs that process the customer file, such a change means that a programmer has to identify all the affected programs, modify them, and then retest them—all time-consuming and error-prone tasks. Also, requiring programmers to modify programs that do not use the field whose format has changed is a waste of money.

INCOMPATIBLE FILES

One of the consequences of program data dependency is that file formats depend on the language or product used to generate them. Thus, the format of a file processed by a COBOL program is different from the format of a file processed by a Visual Basic program, which is different still from the format of a file processed by a C program.

As a result, files cannot be readily combined or compared. Suppose, for example, FILE-A contains CUSTOMER data that includes CustomerNumber, and FILE-B contains RENTAL data that also includes CustomerNumber. Suppose an application requires that we combine records that have matching CustomerNumbers. If FILE-A were processed by a COBOL program and FILE-B were processed by a C program, we would need to convert both files to a common structure before we could combine the records. This would be time consuming and sometimes difficult. Such problems grow worse as the number of files to be combined increases.

THE DIFFICULTY OF REPRESENTING DATA IN THE USERS' PERSPECTIVES

It is difficult to represent file-processing data in a form that seems natural to users. Users want to see RENTAL data in a format like that in Figure 1-5(b). But in order to show the data in this way, several different files need to be extracted, combined, and presented together. This difficulty arises because with file processing, relationships among records are not readily represented or processed. Since a file-processing system cannot quickly determine which CUSTOMERs have rented which instruments, producing a form showing CUSTOMER preferences is quite difficult.

➤ DATABASE PROCESSING SYSTEMS

Database technology was developed largely to overcome the limitations of file-processing systems. To understand how, compare the file-processing system in Figure 1-10 with the database system in Figure 1-9. File-processing programs directly access files of stored data. In contrast, database-processing programs call the DBMS to access the stored data. This difference is significant because it makes application programming easier; that is, application programmers do not have to be concerned with the ways in which data are physically stored. Rather, they are free to concentrate on matters important to the user instead of matters important to the computer system.

INTEGRATED DATA

In a database system, all the application data is stored in a single facility called the **database.** An application program can ask the DBMS to access customer data or sales data or both. If both are needed, the application programmer specifies only how the data are to be combined, and the DBMS performs the necessary operations to do it. Thus, the programmer is not responsible for writing programs to consolidate the files, as must be done for the system in Figure 1-10.

REDUCED DATA DUPLICATION

With database processing, the duplication of data is minimal. For example, in Treble Clef's database, the customer's number, name, and address are stored only once. Whenever these data are needed, the DBMS can retrieve them, and when they are modified, only one update is necessary. Because data are stored in only one place, data integrity problems are less common—there is less opportunity for discrepancies among multiple copies of the same data item.

PROGRAM/DATA INDEPENDENCE

Database processing reduces the dependency of programs on file formats. All record formats are stored in the database itself (along with the data), and they are accessed by the DBMS, not by application programs. Unlike file-processing programs, database application programs need not include the format of all the files and records they process. Instead, application programs must contain only a definition (the length and data type) of each of the data items they need from the database. The DBMS maps the data items into records and handles other similar transformations.

Program/data independence minimizes the impact of data format changes on application programs. Format changes are input into the DBMS, which in turn updates the data it maintains concerning the structure of the database. For the most part, application programs are unaware that the format has changed. This also means that whenever data items are added, changed, or deleted from the database, only those programs that use these particular data items have to be modified. For applications consisting of dozens of programs, this can be a considerable savings of time.

EASIER REPRESENTATION OF THE USERS' PERSPECTIVES

As you will discover throughout this text, database technology makes it possible to represent, in a straightforward fashion, the objects found in the user's world. The forms in Figure 1-5 can readily be produced from a database because the relationships among the records of data are stored as part of the database.

➤ DEFINITION OF A DATABASE

The term *database* suffers from many different interpretations. It has been used to refer to everything from a collection of index cards to the volumes and volumes of data that a government collects about its citizens. In this text, we use this term with a specific meaning: *A database is a self-describing collection of integrated records.* It is important to understand each part of this definition.

A Database Is Self-Describing

A database is self-describing: It contains, in addition to the user's source data, a description of its own structure. This description is called a **data dictionary** (also called a **data directory** or **metadata**).

In this sense, a database is similar to a library, which can be thought of as a self-describing collection of books. In addition to the books, the library contains a card catalog describing them. In the same way, the data dictionary (which is part of the database, just as the card catalog is part of the library) describes the data contained in the database.

Why is this self-describing characteristic of a database so important? First, it promotes program–data independence. That is, it makes it possible to determine the structure and content of the database by examining the database itself. We do not need to guess what the database contains, nor do we need to maintain external documentation of the file and record formats (as is done in file-processing systems).

Second, if we change the structure of the data in the database (such as adding new data items to an existing record), we enter only that change in the data dictionary. Few, if any, programs will need to be changed. In most cases, only those programs that process the altered data items must be changed.

If you are familiar with COBOL, you know that the structure of the data for file-processing programs is described in the DATA DIVISION. Compared with database processing, this practice is inefficient. It is like putting a copy of your library's card catalog in the home or office of every library user. Then when the library buys a new book, the card catalog has to be changed in dozens or hundreds of places!

You may have learned in your COBOL or other programming courses that it is good practice to store the files' structure in a copy library and extract this structure from the library when the files are compiled. A similar strategy is used with databases. The structure of the database is extracted from the database and loaded into the program before the program is compiled.

A Database Is a Collection of Integrated Records

The standard hierarchy of data is as follows: Bits are aggregated into bytes or characters; characters are aggregated into fields; fields are aggregated into records; and records are aggregated into files [see Fig. 1-11(a)]. It is tempting to follow the pattern of that statement and say that files are aggregated into databases. Although this statement is true, it does not go far enough.

A database does include files of user data, but it also contains more. As we mentioned earlier, a database contains a description of itself in metadata. In addition, a database includes **indexes** that are used to represent relationships among the data and also to improve the performance of database applications. Finally, the database often contains data about the applications that use the database. The structure of a data entry form, or a report, is sometimes part of the database. This last category of data we call **application metadata.** Thus a database contains the four types of data shown in Figure 1-11(b): files of user data, metadata, indexes, and application metadata.

A Database Is a Model of a Model

A database is a model. It is tempting to say that a database is a model of reality or of some portion of reality as it relates to a business. This, however, is not true. A database does not model reality or some portion thereof. Instead, a database is a model of the *users' model.* For example, Mary Richards's database is a model of

➤ FIGURE 1-11

Hierarchy of Data Elements in (a) File-Processing Systems and (b) Database Systems

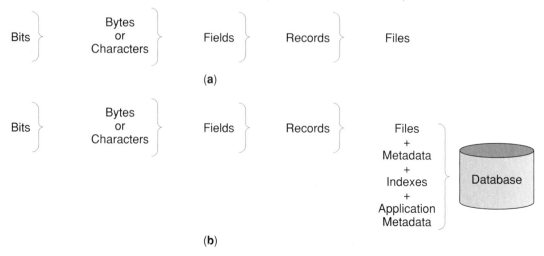

(a)

(b)

the way in which Mary Richards views her business. As she sees it, her business has customers, jobs, and referrals. Her database, therefore, contains representations of facts concerning those entities. The names and addresses of customers, the dates and descriptions of her jobs, and the names of her referral sources all are measurements that are important to her view of her business.

Databases vary in their level of detail. Some are simple and crude. A list of customers and the amounts they owe is an approximate representation of Mary's mental model. A more detailed representation includes jobs, referrals, and the trips made for each job. And a very detailed representation contains the amount and type of paint used on each job, the number of paintbrushes required, and the hours of labor on specific job tasks such as taping, painting woodwork, painting walls, cleanup, and the like.

The degree of detail that should be incorporated into a database depends on the information desired. Clearly, the more information that is wanted, the more detail the database must have. Deciding on the appropriate amount of detail is an important part of the job of designing a database. As you will discover, the principal criterion is the level of detail that exists in the minds of the users.

The database model must be dynamic because businesses change. People come and go. Products are introduced and phased out. Money is earned and spent. As these changes occur, the data that represents the business also must be altered. If not, the data will become outdated and inaccurately represent the business.

Transactions are representations of events. When events take place, the transactions for the events must be processed against the database. To do this, someone (a data entry clerk, a salesperson, or a teller, for example) activates a transaction-processing program and enters the transaction data. The program then calls on the DBMS to alter the database. Transaction-processing programs usually produce displays or print responses such as order confirmations or receipts.

➤ THE HISTORY OF DATABASE PROCESSING

Database processing was originally used in major corporations and large organizations as the basis of large transaction-processing systems. An example is the licensing and vehicle registration example considered earlier. Later, as microcomputers gained popularity, database technology migrated to micros and was used for single-user, personal database applications like that described for Mary Richards. Next, as micros were connected together in work groups, database technology moved to the workgroup setting such as in the Treble Clef example. Finally, databases are being used today for Internet and intranet applications.

THE ORGANIZATIONAL CONTEXT

The initial application of database technology was to resolve problems with the file-processing systems discussed earlier in this chapter. In the mid-1960s, large corporations were producing data at phenomenal rates in file-processing systems, but the data were becoming difficult to manage, and new systems were becoming increasingly difficult to develop. Furthermore, management wanted to be able to relate the data in one file system to those in another.

The limitations of file processing prevented the easy integration of data. Database technology, however, held out the promise of a solution to these problems, and so large companies began to develop organizational databases. Companies centralized their operational data, such as orders, inventory, and accounting data, in these databases. The applications were primarily organization-wide, transaction-processing systems.

At first, when the technology was new, database applications were difficult to develop, and there were many failures. Even those applications that were successful were slow and unreliable: The computer hardware could not handle the volume of transactions quickly; the developers had not yet discovered more efficient ways to store and retrieve data; and the programmers were still new at accessing databases, and sometimes their programs did not work correctly.

Companies found another disadvantage of database processing: vulnerability. If a file-processing system fails, only that particular application will be out of commission. But if the database fails, all of its dependent applications will be out of commission.

Gradually, the situation improved. Hardware and software engineers learned how to build systems powerful enough to support many concurrent users and fast enough to keep up with the daily workload of transactions. New ways of controlling, protecting, and backing up the database were devised. Standard procedures for database processing evolved, and programmers learned how to write more efficient and more maintainable code. By the mid-1970s, databases could efficiently and reliably process organizational applications. Many of those applications are still running today, more than 25 years after their creation!

THE RELATIONAL MODEL

In 1970, E. F. Codd published a landmark paper[1] in which he applied concepts from a branch of mathematics called relational algebra to the problem of storing large amounts of data. Codd's paper started a movement in the database community that in a few years led to the definition of the **relational database model.** This model is a particular way of structuring and processing a database, and we discuss it at length in Chapters 5 and 9 through 13.

BENEFITS OF THE RELATIONAL MODEL   The advantage of the relational model is that data are stored in a way that minimizes duplicated data and eliminates certain types of processing errors that can occur when data are stored in other ways. Data are stored as tables, with rows and columns, like the data in Figure 1-1.

---

[1]E. F. Codd, "A Relational Model of Data for Large Shared Databanks," *Communications of the ACM,* June 1970, pp. 377–387.

According to the relational model, not all tables are equally desirable. Using a process called *normalization,* a table that is not desirable can be changed into two or more that are. You will learn about the normalization process in detail in Chapter 5.

Another key advantage of the relational model is that columns contain data that relate one row to another. For example, in Figure 1-1, CUSTOMER_ID in the JOB table relates to CUSTOMER_ID in the CUSTOMER table. This makes the relationships among rows visible to the user.

At first, it was thought that the relational model would enable users to obtain information from databases without the assistance of MIS professionals. Part of the rationale of this idea was that tables are simple constructs that are intuitively understandable. Additionally, since the relationships are stored in the data, the users would be able to combine rows when necessary. For example, to access a RENTAL record, a user at Treble Clef would be able to combine a row of the CUSTOMER table with rows of a RENTAL table.

It turned out that this process was too difficult for most users. Hence, the promise of the relational model as a means for nonspecialists to access a database was never realized. In retrospect, the key benefit of the relational model has turned out to be that it provides a standard way for specialists (like you!) to structure and process a database.

RESISTANCE TO THE RELATIONAL MODEL   Initially the relational model encountered a good deal of resistance. Relational database systems require more computer resources, and so at first they were much slower than the systems based on earlier database models. Although they were easier to use, the slow response time was often unacceptable. To some extent, relational DBMS products were impractical until the 1980s, when faster computer hardware was developed and the price–performance ratio of computers fell dramatically.

The relational model also seemed foreign to many programmers, who were accustomed to writing programs in which they processed data one record at a time. But relational DBMS products process data most naturally an entire table at a time. Accordingly, programmers had to learn a new way to think about data processing.

Because of these problems, even though the relational model had many advantages, it did not gain true popularity until computers became more powerful. In particular, as microcomputers entered the scene, more and more CPU cycles could be devoted to a single user. Such power was a boon to relational DBMS products and set the stage for the next major database development.

MICROCOMPUTER DBMS PRODUCTS

In 1979, a small company called Ashton-Tate introduced a microcomputer product, dBase II (pronounced "d base two"), and called it a relational DBMS. In an exceedingly successful promotional tactic, Ashton-Tate distributed—nearly free of charge—more than 100,000 copies of its product to purchasers of the then-new Osborne microcomputers. Many of the people who bought these computers were pioneers in the microcomputer industry. They began to invent microcomputer applications using dBase, and the number of dBase applications grew quickly. As a result, Ashton-Tate became one of the first major corporations in the microcomputer industry. Later, Ashton-Tate was purchased by Borland, which now sells the dBase line of products.

The success of this product, however, confused and confounded the subject of database processing. The problem was this: According to the definition prevalent in the late 1970s, dBase II was neither a DBMS nor relational. In fact, it was a programming language with generalized file-processing (not database-processing) capabilities. The systems that were developed with dBase II appeared much more like those in Figure 1-10 than the ones in Figure 1-9. The million or so users of dBase II thought they were using a relational DBMS when, in fact, they were not.

Thus, the terms *database management system* and *relational database* were used loosely at the start of the microcomputer boom. Most of the people who were processing a microcomputer database were really managing files and were not receiving the benefits of database processing, although they did not realize it. Today, the situation has changed as the microcomputer marketplace has become more mature and sophisticated. dBase IV and the dBase products that followed it are truly *relational* DBMS products.

Although dBase did pioneer the application of database technology on microcomputers, at the same time other vendors began to move their products from the mainframe to the microcomputer. Oracle, Focus, and Ingress are three examples of DBMS products that were ported down to microcomputers. They are truly DBMS programs, and most would agree that they are truly relational as well. In addition, other vendors developed new relational DBMS products especially for micros. Paradox, Revelation, MDBS, Helix, and a number of other products fall into this category.

One impact of the move of database technology to the micro was the dramatic improvement in DBMS user interfaces. Users of microcomputer systems are generally not MIS professionals, and they will not put up with the clumsy and awkward user interfaces common on mainframe DBMS products. Thus, as DBMS products were devised for micros, user interfaces had to be simplified and made easier to use. This was possible because micro DBMS products operate on dedicated computers and because more computer power was available to process the user interface. Today, DBMS products are rich and robust with graphical user interfaces such as Microsoft Windows.

The combination of microcomputers, the relational model, and vastly improved user interfaces enabled database technology to move from an organizational context to a personal-computing context. When this occurred, the number of sites that used database technology exploded. In 1980 there were about 10,000 sites using DBMS products in the United States. Today there are well over 20 million such sites!

CLIENT–SERVER DATABASE APPLICATIONS

In the middle to late 1980s, end users began to connect their separated microcomputers using local area networks (LANs). These networks enabled computers to send data to one another at previously unimaginable rates. The first applications of this technology shared peripherals, such as large-capacity fast disks, expensive printers and plotters, and facilitated intercomputer communication via electronic mail. In time, however, end users wanted to share their databases as well, which led to the development of multi-user database applications on LANs.

The LAN-based multi-user architecture is considerably different from the multi-user architecture used on mainframe databases. With a mainframe, only one CPU is involved in database application processing, but with LAN systems, many CPUs can be simultaneously involved. Because this situation was both advantageous (greater performance) and more problematic (coordinating the actions of independent CPUs), it led to a new style of multi-user database processing called the **client–server database architecture.**

Not all database processing on a LAN is client–server processing. A simple, but less robust, mode of processing is called **file-sharing architecture.** A company like Treble Clef could most likely use either type since it is a small organization with modest processing requirements. Larger workgroups, however, would require client–server processing. We will describe these approaches and discuss them in detail in Chapter 14.

Databases Using Internet Technology

As shown in the Calvert Island Reservations Centre example, database technology is being used in conjunction with Internet technology to publish database data on the WWW. This same technology is used to publish applications over corporate and organizational intranets. Some experts believe that, in time, all database applications will be delivered using HTTP, XML, and related technologies—even personal databases that are "published" to a single person.

Because many database applications will use Internet technology to publish databases on organizational intranets and department LANs, it is incorrect to refer to this category of application as *Internet databases*. Rather, this text will employ the phrase *databases using Internet technology* instead.

This category stands on the leading edge of database technology today. As will be described in Chapter 11, XML in particular serves the needs of database applications exceptionally well, and it will likely be the basis of many new database products and services.

Distributed Database Processing

Before concluding this survey of the history of database processing, we need to discuss two aspects of database technology that are important in theory but have not been, at least so far, widely adopted. The first is distributed database processing, and the second is object-oriented databases. We discuss these topics in more detail in Chapters 13 and 17, respectively.

Organizational database applications solve the problems of file processing and allow more integrated processing of organizational data. Personal and workgroup database systems bring database technology even closer to the user by allowing him or her access to locally managed databases. **Distributed databases** combine these types of database processing by allowing personal, workgroup, and organizational databases to be combined into integrated but distributed systems. As such, in theory, they offer even more flexible data access and processing, but they also unfortunately pose many unsolved problems.

The essence of distributed databases is that all of the organization's data are spread over many computers—micros, LAN servers, and mainframes—that communicate with one another as they process the database. The goals of distributed database systems are to make it appear to each user that he or she is the only user of the organization's data and to provide the same consistency, accuracy, and timeliness that he or she would have if no one else were using the distributed database.

Among the more pressing problems with distributed databases are those of security and control. Enabling so many users to access the database (there can be hundreds of concurrent users) and controlling what they do to that distributed database are complicated tasks.

Coordinating and synchronizing processing can be difficult. If one user group downloads and updates part of the database and then transmits the changed data back to the mainframe, how does the system prevent, in the meantime, another user from attempting to use the version of the data it finds on the mainframe? Imagine this problem involving dozens of files and hundreds of users using scores of pieces of computer equipment.

Whereas the transitions from organizational to personal to workgroup database processing were relatively easy, the difficulties facing the database designers and engineers of the distributed DBMS are monumental. In truth, even though work on distributed database systems has been underway for more than 25 years, significant problems remain. Microsoft has defined and is building a distributed processing architecture and set of supporting products called the **Microsoft Transaction Server (MTS).** While MTS has promise and, of all companies, Microsoft has the resources to develop and market such a system, it is still unknown whether truly distributed databases can meet the needs of day-to-day organizational processing. See the discussion of OLE DB in Chapter 13 for more on this topic.

OBJECT-ORIENTED DBMS (ODBMS)

In the late 1980s a new style of programming called *object-oriented programming* (OOP) began to be used, which has a substantially different orientation from that of traditional programming, as is explained in Chapter 17. In brief, the data structures processed with OOP are considerably more complex than those processed with traditional languages. These data structures also are difficult to store in existing relational DBMS products. As a consequence, a new category of DBMS products called *object-oriented database systems* is evolving to store and process OOP data structures.

For a variety of reasons, OOP has not yet been widely used for business information systems. First, it is difficult to use, and it is very expensive to develop OOP applications. Second, most organizations have millions or billions of bytes of data already organized in relational databases, and they are unwilling to bear the cost and risk required to convert those databases to an ODBMS format. Finally, most ODBMS have been developed to support engineering applications, and they do not have features and functions that are appropriate or readily adaptable to business information applications.

Consequently, for the foreseeable future, ODBMS are likely to occupy a niche in commercial information systems applications. We will discuss OOP and object-oriented databases in Chapter 17, but the bulk of the discussion in this text will concern the relational model, since it concerns technologies that you are likely to use in the first five years of your career.

➤ SUMMARY

Database processing is one of the most important courses in the information systems curriculum. Database skill and knowledge is in high demand not only for traditional applications but also for applications that use Internet technology for public and private networks.

Database technology is used in a variety of applications. Some serve only a single user on a single computer; others are used by work groups of 20 or 30 people on a LAN; still others are used by hundreds of users and involve trillions of bytes of data. Recently, database technology has been combined with Internet technology to support multimedia applications over public and private networks.

The components of a database application are the database, the database management systems (DBMS), and application programs. Sometimes the application programs are entirely separate from the DBMS; other times substantial portions of the application are provided by features and functions of the DBMS.

File-processing systems store data in separate files, each of which contains a different type of data. File-processing systems have several limitations. With separated files, it is difficult to combine data stored in separate files, as the data are often duplicated among files, leading to data integrity problems. Application programs are dependent on file formats, causing maintenance problems when the formats change and the files become incompatible, requiring file conversions. And it is difficult to represent data from the users' perspectives.

Database-processing systems were developed to overcome these limitations. In the database environment, the DBMS is the interface between application programs and the database. The data are integrated, and their duplication is reduced. Only the DBMS is affected by changes in the physical formats of stored data. And if data items are changed, added, or deleted, few application programs will require maintenance. With database technology, it is easier to represent objects in the users' environments.

A database is a self-describing collection of integrated records. It is self-describing because it contains a description of itself in a data dictionary. A data dictionary is also known as a data directory or metadata. A database is a collection of integrated records because the relationships among the records are stored in the database. This arrangement enables the DBMS to construct even complicated objects by combining data on the basis of the stored relationships. Relationships are often stored in overhead data. Thus, the three parts of a database are the application data, the data dictionary, and the overhead data.

Database technology developed in several stages. Early databases focused on the transaction processing of organizational data. Then, the relational model, together with the microcomputer, led to the use of personal database applications. With the advent of LANs, departments began to implement workgroup client–server databases. Today, multimedia and traditional database applications are being delivered using Internet technology. Distributed processing and object-oriented databases are important topics in database processing. To date, however, neither has been commercially successful or seen widespread use in business applications.

➤ GROUP I QUESTIONS

1.1 Why is database processing an important subject?

1.2 Describe the nature and characteristics of a single-user database application used by an individual like Mary Richards.

1.3 Describe the nature and characteristics of a database application used by a workgroup like Treble Clef Music.

1.4 Describe the nature and characteristics of a database application used by an organization like the state's driver's licensing and vehicle registration bureau.

1.5 Describe the nature and characteristics of a database application used by an organization like the Calvert Island Reservation Centre.

1.6 Explain the nature and function of each of the components of Figure 1-9.

1.7 How is the relationship between application programs and the DBMS changing over time?

1.8 List the limitations of file-processing systems as described in this chapter.

1.9 Explain how database technology overcomes the limitations you listed in your answer to Question 1.8.

1.10 Define the term *database*.

1.11 What are metadata? What are indexes? What are application metadata?

1.12 Explain why a database is a model. Describe the difference between a model of reality and a model of a user's model of reality. Why is this difference important?

1.13 Give an example, other than one in this chapter, of a personal database application.

1.14 Give an example, other than one in this chapter, of a workgroup database application.

1.15 Give an example, other than one in this chapter, of a large-enterprise database application.

1.16 What were some of the weaknesses of early organizational database applications?

1.17 What are the two primary advantages of the relational model?

1.18 Why was the relational model initially resisted?

1.19 Summarize the events in the development of microcomputer DBMS products.

1.20 What was the major factor that gave rise to workgroup database applications?

1.21 How does the client–server architecture differ from mainframe multi-user architectures?

1.22 Explain the general nature of distributed processing. What are some of the difficult problems to be faced?

1.23 Describe the purpose of an object-oriented database. Why have such databases not been more accepted for information systems applications?

➤ PROJECTS

A. Access the Web site of a computer manufacturer such as Dell (www.dell.com). Use the Web site to determine which model of laptop computer you would recommend for under $2500. Do you think one or more databases are used to support this site? If so, which features and functions of the Web site do you think would be most helped by database technology, keeping in mind both the definition of a database and the advantages of database processing?

B. Access the Web site of a retail bookseller such as Amazon (www.amazon.com). Use the Web site to locate the most recently published biography of William Wordsworth. Do you think one or more databases are used to support this site? If so, which features and functions of the Web site do you think would be most helped by database technology, keeping in mind both the definition of a database and the advantages of database processing?

CHAPTER 2

Introduction to Database Development

This chapter presents a broad overview of the development of a database and a database application. We begin with a description of the elements of a database and a discussion of the features and functions of a DBMS. Next we illustrate the creation of a database and a database application. Finally, we discuss common strategies of database development. The goal of this chapter is to create a perspective for the detailed descriptions of the technology in following chapters.

➤ THE DATABASE

Figure 2-1 shows the main components of a database system. The **database** is processed by the **DBMS,** which is used by both developers and users, who can access the DBMS either directly or indirectly via **application programs.** We discuss the database in this section and the DBMS and applications in subsequent sections.

As described in Chapter 1, a database contains four main elements: user data, metadata, indexes, and application metadata.

USER DATA

Today, most databases represent user data as relations. We formally define the term relation in Chapter 5. For now, consider a relation to be a table of data. The columns of the table contain fields or attributes, and the rows of the table contain records for particular entities in the business environment.

Not all relations are equally desirable; some relations are better structured than others. Chapter 5 describes a process called normalization that is used to create well-structured relations. To get an idea of the difference between poorly structured and well-structured relations, consider the relation R1 (StudentName, StudentPhone, AdviserName, AdviserPhone) with the following data:

StudentName	StudentPhone	AdviserName	AdviserPhone
Baker, Rex	232-8897	Parks	236-0098
Charles, Mary	232-0099	Parks	236-0098
Johnson, Beth	232-4487	Jones	236-0110
Scott, Glenn	232-4444	Parks	236-0098
Zylog, Frita	232-5588	Jones	236-0110

The problem with this relation is that it has data concerning two different topics, students and advisers. A relation structured in this way presents a number of problems when it is updated. For example, if adviser Parks changes his or her telephone number, three rows of data must be changed. For this reason, the data would be better represented by the two relations R2 (StudentName, StudentPhone, AdviserName) with data

StudentName	StudentPhone	AdviserName
Baker, Rex	232-8897	Parks
Charles, Mary	232-0099	Parks
Johnson, Beth	232-4487	Jones
Scott, Glenn	232-4444	Parks
Zylog, Frita	232-5588	Jones

➤ FIGURE 2-1

Components of Database Systems

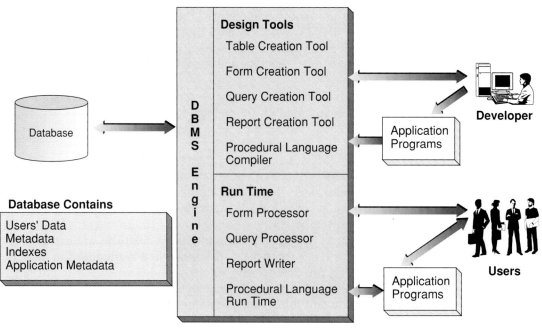

and R3 (AdviserName, AdviserPhone) with data

AdviserName	AdviserPhone
Parks	236-0098
Jones	236-0110

Now if an adviser changes his or her phone, only one row of R3 has to be changed. Of course, to produce a report that shows the names of students along with their advisers' phone numbers, the rows of these two tables will need to be combined. It turns out, however, that it is far better to store the relations separately and combine them when producing a report than to store them as one combined table.

METADATA

As defined in Chapter 1, a database is self-describing, which means that it contains a description of its structure as part of itself. This description of the structure is called **metadata.** Since DBMS products are designed to store and manipulate tables, most products store the metadata in the form of tables, sometimes called **system tables.**

Figure 2-2 shows an example of metadata stored in two system tables. The first stores a list of tables that are in the database, indicating how many columns are in each table and what column(s) is the primary key. Such a column is the unique identifier of a row. The second table stores a list of columns in each table and the data type and length of each column. These two tables are typical of system tables; other such tables store lists of indexes, keys, rules, and other portions of the database structure.

➤ FIGURE 2-2

Examples of Metadata

SysTables Table

Table Name	Number of Columns	Primary Key
Student	4	StudentNumber
Adviser	3	AdviserName
Course	3	ReferenceNumber
Enrollment	3	{StudentNumber, ReferenceNumber}

SysColumns Table

Column Name	Table Name	Data Type	Length*
StudentNumber	Student	Integer	4
FirstName	Student	Text	20
LastName	Student	Text	30
Major	Student	Text	10
AdviserName	Adviser	Text	25
Phone	Adviser	Text	12
Department	Adviser	Text	15
ReferenceNumber	Course	Integer	4
Title	Course	Text	10
NumberHours	Course	Decimal	4
StudentNumber	Enrollment	Integer	4
ReferenceNumber	Enrollment	Integer	4
Grade	Enrollment	Text	2

* Lengths are stated in bytes, which are the same as characters of text data.

Storing metadata in tables is not only efficient for the DBMS; it is also convenient for users because they can use the same query tools for metadata as they do for user data. Thus, once a user learns how to use the DBMS's query facility to query a user table, he or she can use that same facility to query system tables. Later in this book we discuss a language called SQL (pronounced "sequel") that is used to query and update tables for both metadata and user data.

As an example of how you might use SQL for this purpose, suppose that you have developed a database with 15 tables and 200 columns. You remember that several of the columns have the data type *currency*, but you cannot remember which ones. By using SQL, you can access the SysColumns Table to find out which columns have that data type.

INDEXES

A third type of database data improves the performance and accessibility of the database. These data, which are sometimes called **overhead data,** consist principally of indexes, although other types of data structures, such as linked lists, are sometimes used (see Appendix A for a discussion of indexes and linked lists).

Figure 2-3 shows a table of student data and two indexes. To demonstrate the necessity of having these indexes, suppose that the data are stored on disk in ascending order of StudentNumber and that the user wants to print a report of student data sorted by LastName. To do this, all of the data could be extracted from the source table and sorted, but unless the table is small, this is a time-consuming process. Alternatively, an index like the LastName index in Figure 2-3 could be created. The entries in this index are sorted by value of LastName, so the entries of the index can be read and used to access the student data in sorted order.

➤ FIGURE 2-3

Examples of Database Indexes

Example STUDENT Table

Student Number	FirstName	LastName	Major
100	James	Baker	Accounting
200	Mary	Abernathy	Info Systems
300	Beth	Jackson	Accounting
400	Eldridge	Johnson	Marketing
500	Chris	Tufte	Accounting
600	John	Smathers	Info Systems
700	Michael	Johnson	Accounting

LastName Index

LastName	StudentNumber
Abernathy	200
Baker	100
Jackson	300
Johnson	400, 700
Smathers	600
Tufte	500

Major Index

Major	StudentNumber
Accounting	100, 300, 500, 700
Info Systems	200, 600
Marketing	400

Now suppose that student data must also be printed in order of student major. Again, the data could be extracted from the source table and sorted, or an index like the Major index could be constructed and used as just described.

Indexes are used not only for sorting but also for quick access to data. For example, a user wants to access only those students who have the value "Info Systems" for Major. Without an index, the entire source table must be searched. But with the index, the index entry can be found and used to find all of the qualifying rows. Although indexes are not needed for a table with as few rows as the STUDENT table in Figure 2-3, consider a table that has 10,000 or 20,000 rows of data. In that case, sorting or searching the entire table would be very slow.

Indexes are helpful for sorting and searching operations, but at a cost. Every time a row in the STUDENT table is updated, the indexes must also be updated. This is not necessarily bad; it just means that indexes are not free and so should be reserved for cases in which they are needed.

APPLICATION METADATA

The fourth and final type of data that is stored in the database is **application metadata,** which is used to store the structure and format of user forms, reports, queries, and other application components. Not all DBMS products support application components and, of those products that do, not all store the structure of those components as application metadata in the database. However, most of the modern DBMS products do store such data as part of the database. In general, neither the database developers nor the users access the application metadata directly. Instead, they use tools in the DBMS to process it.

➤ THE DBMS

DBMS products vary considerably in the features and functions that they provide. The first such products were developed for use on mainframes in the late 1960s, and they had very primitive features. Since then, DBMS products have been continually enhanced and improved not only to process database data better but also to incorporate features that facilitate the creation of database applications.

In this chapter we use Microsoft Access 2000 to illustrate the capabilities of DBMS products. This is done because Access 2000 provides features and functions that typify the characteristics of a modern DBMS. Access 2000 is not, however, the only such DBMS, and our selecting it is not meant to be an endorsement of it over other, similar products, such as Lotus Approach.

As shown in Figure 2-1, the features and functions of a DBMS can be divided into three subsystems: the design tools subsystem, the run-time subsystem, and the DBMS engine.

THE DESIGN TOOLS SUBSYSTEM

The design tools subsystem has a set of tools to facilitate the design and creation of the database and its applications. It typically includes tools for creating tables, forms, queries, and reports. DBMS products also provide programming languages and interfaces to programming languages. For example, Access has two languages, a macro language that does not require in-depth programming knowledge and a version of BASIC called Visual Basic.

RUN-TIME SUBSYSTEM

The run-time subsystem[1] processes the application components that are developed using the design tools. For example, Access 2000 has a run-time facility that materializes forms and connects form elements with table data. For example, a form has been defined that includes a text box to display the value of StudentNumber of the STUDENT table. During execution, when the form is opened, the form run-time processor extracts the value of StudentNumber from the current STUDENT row and displays it in the form. All of this is automatic; neither the user nor the developer need do anything once the form is created. Other run-time processors answer queries and print reports. In addition, there is a run-time component that processes application program requests for reading and writing database data.

Although not shown in Figure 2-1, DBMS products must also provide an application program interface for standard languages such as COBOL, C++, and ANSI BASIC. Some type of subprogram call library or a similar facility enables programs written in standard languages to read table data, to add and update data, and even to define new tables and queries.

THE DBMS ENGINE

The third component of the DBMS is the DBMS engine, which is the intermediary between the design tools and run-time subsystems and the data. The DBMS engine receives requests from the other two components—stated in terms of tables, rows, and columns—and translates those requests into commands to the operating system to read and write data on physical media.

The DBMS engine is also involved with transaction management, locking, and backup and recovery. As we show in Chapter 12, actions against the database often must be made as a complete unit. When processing an order, for example, changes in the CUSTOMER, ORDER, and INVENTORY tables should be made as a group: Either all of them should be made, or none of them should be made. The DBMS engine helps coordinate the activities to ensure that either all of the group or none of the group is applied.

Microsoft provides two different engines for Access 2000: the Jet Engine and SQL Server. The Jet Engine is used for smaller personal and workgroup databases. SQL Server, which is an independent Microsoft product, is used for larger departmental and small to medium-size organizational databases. When you create a database using the native Access 2000 table generation capabilities (databases stored with the suffix .mdb), you are using the Jet Engine. When you create Access 2000 projects (with suffix .adp), you are creating an application interface to the SQL Server engine.

➤ CREATING THE DATABASE

A *database schema* defines a database's structure, its tables, relationships, domains, and business rules. A database schema is a design, the foundation on which the database and the applications are built.

---

[1]Do not confuse the term *run-time subsystem* with the term *run-time product*. Some vendors use the term *run-time product* to refer to a product that includes the run-time and DBMS engine components but not the design tools subsystem. Such a product can be used to process an application that has already been developed. The purpose of run-time products is to reduce the cost of the application to the end user. Normally, the run-time product is much less expensive (sometimes free) than the full DBMS product. Hence, only the developer buys the full product that includes the design tools subsystem; the end users buy only the run-time product.

AN EXAMPLE OF A SCHEMA

To illustrate a schema and why it is important, consider an example. Highline College is a small liberal arts college in the Midwest. Its student activities department sponsors intramural athletic leagues, but it has a problem keeping track of the athletic equipment that has been checked out to various team captains. The following schema components are used for this system:

TABLES   The database contains two tables[2]:

CAPTAIN (CaptainName, Phone, Street, City, State, Zip)

and

ITEM (Quantity, Description, DateOut, DateIn)

where the table names are shown outside the parentheses and the column names are shown inside the parentheses.

Neither CaptainName nor Description is necessarily a unique name, as two captains could easily be named 'Mary Smith' and there certainly are many items called 'Soccer Balls.' In order to make sure that each row can be identified (the importance of this will be made clearer in later chapters), we add two columns of unique numbers to these tables, as follows:

CAPTAIN (CAPTAIN_ID, CaptainName, Phone, Street, City, State, Zip)

ITEM (ITEM_ID, Quantity, Description, DateOut, DateIn)

RELATIONSHIPS   The relationship between these two tables is as follows: One row of CAPTAIN relates to many rows of ITEM, but a row of ITEM relates to one, and only one, row of CAPTAIN. The general notation for a relationship like this is **1:N** and is pronounced "one to N" or "one to many." The term 1:N means that one row of the first table is related to many rows of the second.

For the tables shown here, there is no way to tell which row of CAPTAIN relates to which rows of ITEM. Therefore, to show that relationship, we add CAPTAIN_ID to ITEM. The complete structure of the two tables is as follows:

CAPTAIN (CAPTAIN_ID, CaptainName, Phone, Street, City, State, Zip)

ITEM (ITEM_ID, Quantity, Description, DateOut, DateIn, CAPTAIN_ID)

With this structure, it is easy to determine which captain has checked out a given ITEM. For example, to find out who has checked out item 1234, we examine the row for item 1234 and find the value of CAPTAIN_ID stored in that row. We can then use that value to determine the name and phone number of that captain.

DOMAINS   A domain[3] is a set of values that a column may have. Consider the domains for the columns of ITEM. Suppose that both ITEM_ID and Quantity have the domain of integer numbers, that Description is text of length 25, that both DateOut and DateIn have the domain of date, and that CAPTAIN_ID also has the domain of integer numbers. In addition to the physical format, we also need to decide whether any of the domains are to be unique to the table. For our example, we want ITEM_ID to be unique and so must specify its domain in that way. Since a captain may have more than one ITEM checked out, CAPTAIN_ID is not unique to the ITEM table.

---

[2]As we show in Chapters 3 through 7, the most important and difficult task in database development is designing the table structure. By starting this example with the tables already defined, we have skipped a major portion of the project.

[3]This discussion is simplified considerably so as to focus on the components of a database system. A more complete discussion of domains appears in Chapter 4.

The domains of the columns of CAPTAIN also must be specified. CAPTAIN_ID is integer, and all the rest of the columns are text of different lengths. CAPTAIN_ID must be unique in the CAPTAIN table.

BUSINESS RULES   The last element of a database schema is business rules, which are restrictions on the business's activities that need to be reflected in the database and database applications. The following are examples of business rules for Highline College:

1. In order to check out any equipment, a captain must have a local phone number.

2. No captain may have more than seven soccer balls checked out at any one time.

3. Captains must return all equipment within five days after the end of each semester.

4. No captain may check out more equipment if he or she has any overdue.

Business rules are an important part of the schema because they specify the constraints on allowed data values that must be enforced no matter how the data changes reach the DBMS engine. Regardless of whether the request for a data change comes from the user of a form, a query/update request, or from an application program, the DBMS must ensure that the change violates no rules.

Unfortunately, business rules are enforced in different ways by different DBMS products. With Access 2000, some rules can be defined in the schema and enforced automatically. With products like SQL Server and ORACLE, additional business rules are enforced via a facility called *stored procedures*. In some cases, the DBMS product does not have the capability to enforce the necessary business rules and they must be coded into application programs. We will discuss this topic in greater detail in Chapter 10.

CREATING TABLES

Once the schema has been designed, the next step is creating the database tables using the DBMS's table creation tools. Figure 2-4 shows the form used with Microsoft Access to create the ITEM table. Each table column name is typed in the Field Name form column, and the data type of the column is specified in the Data Type column. Additional data about the column—such as text length, field format, caption, and other data—are specified in the entry fields in the lower left-hand column of the form.

In Figure 2-4, the focus is on the ITEM_ID column. Observe that the indexed property at the bottom of the form has been set to Yes (No Duplicates), which means that an index of unique values is to be created for the ITEM_ID column. To complete the database definition, the CAPTAIN table is created in a similar way.

DEFINING RELATIONSHIPS

The relationship between CAPTAIN and ITEM is 1:N, which we represent in the schema by placing the key of CAPTAIN in ITEM. In Figure 2-4, we place CAPTAIN_ID in the ITEM table. A column like CAPTAIN_ID in the ITEM table is sometimes called a **foreign key** because it is the key of a table that is foreign to the table in which it resides. When creating forms, queries, and reports, the DBMS can provide more services and help to the developer if it knows that CAPTAIN_ID in ITEM is a foreign key of CAPTAIN.

DBMS products vary in the way that they declare this status. With Microsoft Access, the declaration is made by drawing the relationship between the key and the foreign key, as shown in Figure 2-5. CAPTAIN_ID of the primary table (CAPTAIN) is set equal to CAPTAIN_ID of the related table (ITEM).

► FIGURE 2-4

Creating a Table with Microsoft Access 2000

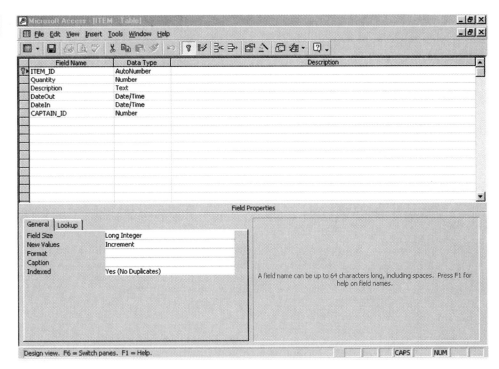

► FIGURE 2-5

Declaring a Relationship with Microsoft Access 2000

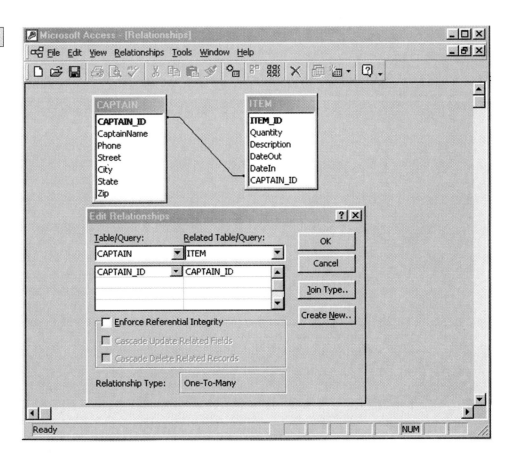

One of the advantages of declaring a relationship to the DBMS is that whenever columns from the two tables are placed in a form, query, or report, the DBMS will know how to relate the rows of the tables. Although this can be declared each time for each form, query, or report, declaring it once saves time and reduces the chance of errors. For now, ignore other elements in the Edit Relationships window. You will learn about them as we proceed. Once the tables, columns, and relationships have been defined, the next step is to build the application components.

➤ COMPONENTS OF APPLICATIONS

A database application consists of forms, queries, reports, menus, and application programs. As shown in Figure 2-1, the forms, queries, and reports can be defined using tools supplied with the DBMS. Application programs must be written in either a language that is part of the DBMS or a standardized language and connected to the database through the DBMS.

FORMS

Figure 2-6 shows three different presentations of the data in the CAPTAIN and ITEM tables. In Figure 2-6(a), the data is shown in spreadsheet or tabular format. The user can click on the plus sign at the start of each row to display the ITEM records that are related to a particular CAPTAIN row. This has been done for the data for Abernathy in the second row in this figure. Observe that two ITEM rows are related to Abernathy.

Figure 2-6(b) shows a second presentation using a data entry form. This form displays the data for a single captain at a time. Untrained users will most likely find it easier to use than the tabular format.

The Captain Registration Page shown in Figure 2-6(c) can be used over the Internet or the university's intranet and can be accessed via Microsoft's Internet Explorer. Such use will require it to be stored on a Web server like the Internet Information Server. You will learn more about this in Chapters 11, 12, and 13. For now, just realize that the Access 2000 form tool can be used to create such forms.

Access 2000 automatically generates the tabular form for each table defined in the database. Data entry forms, however, must be created using form generation tools. Figure 2-7 shows one way of creating such a form. Here, a new form has been created using the form design tool. The source of data for the form has been set to the CAPTAIN table (not shown in Fig. 2-7). Access then shows a window, called a *field list*, that displays the columns of the CAPTAIN table. In this figure, the user has dragged and dropped CaptainName from the field list onto the form. In response, Access creates a label control with the caption CaptainName and a textbox control that will be used to enter and display values for CaptainName. At this point, the textbox is said to be *bound to* the CaptainName column of the CAPTAIN table. Other columns are bound in the same way; columns from the ITEM table are bound to the form using a facility called a subform. Access also has a form design wizard that can be used to create forms like the one in Figure 2-6(b).

Neither of these forms displays the CAPTAIN_ID or ITEM_ID columns. Such IDs have been hidden from the user. Behind the scenes, however, the DBMS automatically assigns new values whenever the user causes a new CAPTAIN or ITEM row to be created. Thus, when the user opens a blank form, the DBMS automatically creates a new row in CAPTAIN and assigns a value for CAPTAIN_ID. When

► FIGURE 2-6

*Presentations of
CAPTAIN and ITEM
Data*

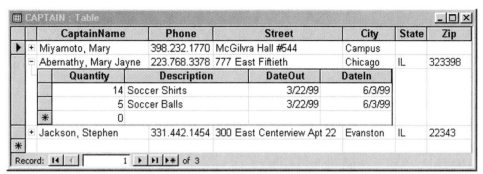

(a) Tabular Form

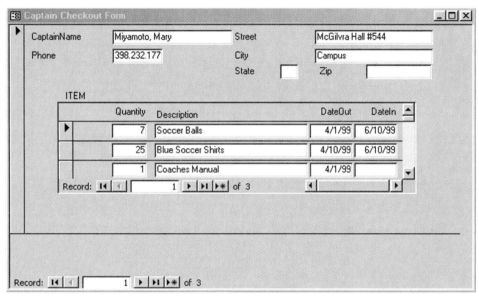

(b) Data Entry Form

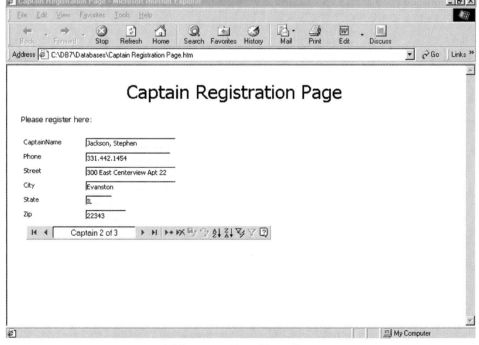

(c) Browser Data Entry Form

FIGURE 2-7

Creating a Form with Microsoft Access 2000

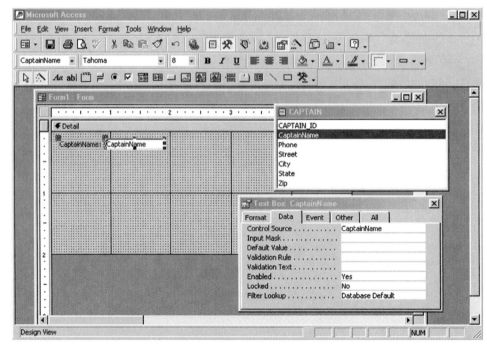

the user then adds new ITEM rows for that captain, the DBMS creates new values of ITEM_ID for each new ITEM row and places the current value of CAPTAIN_ID in the CAPTAIN_ID column in the ITEM row. Examine Figure 2-4 again. The data type of ITEM_ID has been set to AutoNumber. This instructs Access to assign values to ITEM_ID when new rows are created. When the CAPTAIN table was created (not shown), a similar setting was given to CAPTAIN_ID. Note, however, that CAPTAIN_ID in the ITEM table is not set to AutoNumber. This is because the value of CAPTAIN_ID is created when the CAPTAIN row is created; that value is then copied into the CAPTAIN_ID field in the ITEM table when an ITEM row is connected to a particular captain.

Why are these IDs hidden? The reason is that they have no meaning to the users. Highline does not assign IDs to captains or to particular items that are checked out. If they did, then these IDs would be used and made visible. Instead, these IDs have been created only so that each row of each table will be uniquely identifiable to Access. Since these IDs have no meaning to the user, they are hidden.

QUERIES

From time to time, users want to query the data to answer questions or to identify problems or particular situations. For example, suppose that at the start of the fall semester, 1999, one of the users wants to know whether any equipment that was checked out before September 1, 1999, has not yet been checked back in. If it has not, the user wants to know the name of the captain, his or her phone number, and the quantity and description of the items checked out.

There are a number of ways that such a query can be expressed. One is to use the data access language SQL, which is explained in Chapter 9. Another way is to use **query by example (QBE).** Figure 2-8 shows the creation of this query using QBE in Microsoft Access. To create a query, the user places into the query window the names of the tables that are to be queried. This has already been done in the upper section of the form shown in Figure 2-8. Since the relationship

*Creating a Query
with Microsoft Access
2000*

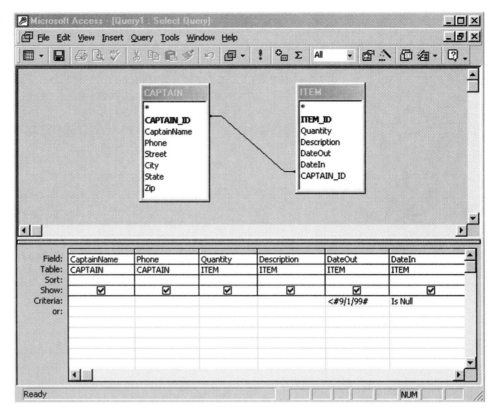

between CAPTAIN and ITEM has already been defined for Access (in Figure 2-5), Access knows that the two tables are linked by CAPTAIN_ID, as shown by the line drawn between CAPTAIN_ID in the two table boxes in Figure 2-8.

Next the query creator indicates which columns of data are to be returned by the query. With Access, this is done by dragging and dropping the names of the columns from the table boxes into the grid in the bottom half of the form. In Figure 2-8, the columns CaptainName, Phone, Quantity, Description, DateOut, and DateIn have been placed into the query. Then the query criteria are specified in the row labeled Criteria. These criteria are that data must be before (<) 9/1/99. (In Access, dates are surrounded by pound signs [#].) Also, the value of DateIn is to be equal to null, which means that no value for DateIn has been specified. The result of this query for sample data is shown in Figure 2-9. Note that all of the equipment shown was checked out before 9/1/99, as was required in the query definition.

With Access and most other DBMS products, queries can be saved as part of the application so that they can be rerun as necessary. In addition, queries can be parameterized, meaning that they can be constructed so as to accept criteria values at the time they are run. For example, the query in Figure 2-8 can be parameterized so that the user enters the value of DateOut when the query is run. Any items that were checked out before that date but that have not yet been checked back in will be shown.

➤ FIGURE 2-9

*Result of Example
Query in Figure 2-8*

	CaptainName	Phone	Quantity	Description	DateOut	DateIn
▶	Miyamoto, Mary	398.232.1770	1	Coaches Manual	4/1/99	
*						

Record: ◄◄ ◄ | 1 | ► ►► ►* | of 1

A third type of query, one that is easier for users, is called **query by form.** With it, the user types query constraints on a data entry form and presses the search button. The DBMS finds all instances that meet the given constraints. For the example query, for the form in Figure 2-6, the user would enter <#9/1/1998# in the DateOut field and Is Null in the DateIn field and press the QueryByForm button. The DBMS would find the records for all captains who meet the query constraints. Query by form is a newer and more modern way to query data than query by example and is likely to replace query by example in many applications.

REPORTS

A report is a formatted display of database data. The report in Figure 2-10 contains a section for each team captain and a list of the items checked out by that captain in the section. For example, the items checked out by captain 'Miyamoto Mary' are shown in the first section of the report.

Developing a report is similar to developing a data entry form, although in some ways it is easier because a report is used only for displaying data. In other ways, constructing a report is more difficult because reports often have a more complicated structure than forms do.

Figure 2-11 shows the display of the Access 2000 report definition for the report shown in Figure 2-10. This is an example of a **banded report writer**; it is called that because the report is divided into sections or bands. As shown, there are header bands, a detail band, and footer bands. The report header band displays the name of the report and the report footer band shows the time the report was printed, the page number and the total number of pages. The page header is empty, but the CAPTAIN_ID header has captain data and labels for the detail section. The detail section shows the items checked out by a captain.

There is a problem with this report in that the two date fields are separated from each other. A better report would be to move DateOut between Description and DateIn. This can readily be done by dragging and dropping the labels and text boxes and is typical of the kinds of changes made using such tools.

In general, reports can have many sections. In a more complex example, say course/student enrollment, a report could be grouped by COLLEGE, by DEPARTMENT, by COURSE, and by STUDENT. In this case the report would have three header sections and a detail line.

➤ FIGURE 2-10

Example Report for Highline College

Captain Equipment Report

CaptainName	Miyamoto, Mary			
Phone	398.232.1770			

DateOut	Quantity	Description	DateIn
4/1/99	1	Coaches Manual	
4/1/99	7	Soccer Balls	6/10/99
4/10/99	25	Blue Soccer Shirts	6/10/99

CaptainName	Abernathy, Mary Jayne			
Phone	223.768.3378			

DateOut	Quantity	Description	DateIn
3/22/99	5	Soccer Balls	6/3/99
3/22/99	14	Soccer Shirts	6/3/99

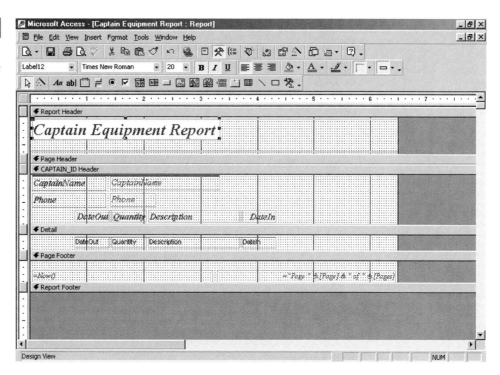

► FIGURE 2-11

Developing a Report with Microsoft Access 2000

MENUS

Menus are used to organize the application components so as to make them more accessible to the end user and to provide control over the user's activities. Figure 2-12 shows an example menu for the Highline application. The line across the top of the form presents the highest-level options: File, Forms, Queries, Reports, and Help. The underlined letters represent keyboard shortcut keys. If the user types ⟨Alt⟩ plus the underlined letter, the submenu choices will be displayed.

In Figure 2-12, the user has keyed ⟨Alt⟩ plus the letter *S*. The submenu choices are Select All Records, Select by Name, and Select by Phone. Again, keyboard shortcut keys can be used to select one of these items by typing ⟨Alt⟩ and the underlined letter of the choice. Menus make the application more accessible to the user by showing what options are available and helping the users select those actions they want performed. Menus can also be used to control user access to forms, reports, and programs. Some applications take advantage of this by dynamically changing menu items after the user signs on.

► FIGURE 2-12

Example Menu

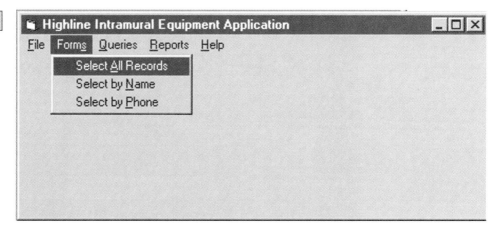

APPLICATION PROGRAMS

The final component of a database application is application programs. As we mentioned earlier, such programs can be written in a language that is specific to the DBMS or in a standard language that interfaces with the DBMS through a predefined program interface. Here we will use Microsoft Visual Basic in conjunction with Access 2000.

Suppose that Highline has a business rule that captains who live off campus cannot checkout a coach's manual. We do not know the reason for this rule; perhaps the manual contains secret instructions that give Highline teams a competitive advantage and Highline is attempting to control the distribution of the manuals. Maybe the manuals are expensive and students who live on campus are easier to bill if a manual is lost. For whatever reason, Highline wants the database application to enforce this rule.

There are many ways to do this. One way, shown in Figure 2-13, is to trap the change event on the Description textbox in the Item subform of the Captain Checkout Form and to insert code to enforce the rule whenever the Description changes. In Figure 2-13, the developer has opened the properties for the Description textbox and set the On Change event to Event Procedure. When this was done, Access opened the coding window shown in Figure 2-14.

The developer wrote a section of Visual Basic that will be run when the change event occurs. The code first determines if the value of City is not equal to the string "Campus." If so, then the InStr function is called to determine if the contents of the textbox (Description.Text) contains the string "Coaches Manual." If so, a beep is issued, a message box is generated, and the Description textbox is set to blank.

This code is executed whenever the user changes the value of the Description textbox. Other, more efficient means of enforcing this rule exist, but the point here is just to show you how application code can be integrated with database forms.

Of course, it is also possible to write code that runs independently of any form or report. Programs can be written to read and update database data in the

 FIGURE 2-13

Trapping an Event on the Captain Checkout Form

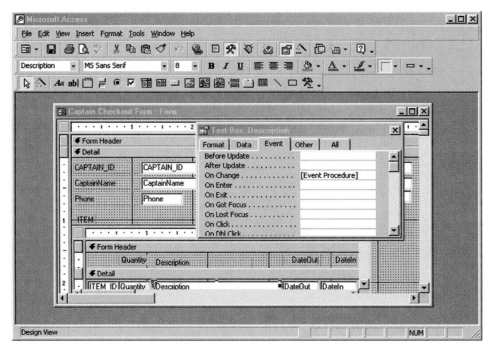

FIGURE 2-14

Visual Basic Code to Enforce Business Rule

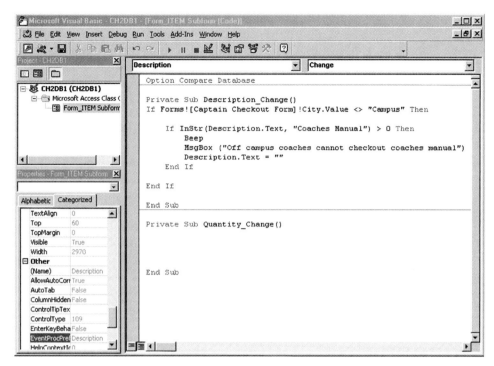

same sense that they read and update other types of files. You will see examples of this later in this text, particularly in Chapter 13 where we show the use of Microsoft ADO to read and update data from a Web server.

➤ DATABASE DEVELOPMENT PROCESSES

Volumes and volumes have been written on the development of information systems in general and on the development of database applications in particular. Therefore, we do not need to discuss here systems development processes in any depth, but we will conclude this chapter with an overview of the processes used to develop databases and database applications.

GENERAL STRATEGIES

A database is a model of the users' model of their business activities. Therefore, in order to build an effective database and related applications, the development team must thoroughly understand the users' model. To do this, the team builds a data model that identifies the things to be stored in the database and defines their structure and the relationships among them. This understanding must be obtained early in the development process, by interviewing the users and building a statement of requirements. Most such statements include the use of **prototypes,** which are sample databases and applications that represent various aspects of the system to be created.

There are two general strategies for developing a database: top-down and bottom-up. **Top-down development** proceeds from the general to the specific. It begins with a study of the strategic goals of the organization, the means by which those goals can be accomplished, the information requirements that must be satisfied to reach those goals, and the systems necessary to provide that information. From such a study, an abstract data model is constructed.

Using this high-level model, the development team progressively works downward toward more and more detailed descriptions and models. Intermediate-level models also are expanded with more detail until the particular databases and related applications can be identified. One or more of these applications is then selected for development. Over time, the entire high-level data model is transformed into lower-level models, and all of the indicated systems, databases, and applications are created.

Bottom-up development operates in the reverse order of abstraction, by beginning with the need to develop a specific system. The means of selecting the first system vary from organization to organization. In some organizations, a steering committee chooses the application; in others, the users may choose it themselves; in still others, the loudest voice in the executive office wins out.

By whatever means, a particular system is selected for development. The development team then obtains statements of requirements by considering the outputs and inputs of any existing computer-based systems, by analyzing the forms and reports for existing manual systems, and by interviewing the users to find out their need for new reports, forms, queries, and other requirements. From all of this, the team develops the information system. If the system involves a database, the team uses the requirement specifications to build a data model, and from the model, it designs and implements the database. When this system is finished, other projects are started in order to build additional information systems.

Proponents of the top-down approach claim that it is superior to the bottom-up approach because the data models (and subsequent systems) are constructed with a global perspective. They believe that such systems have better interfaces to one another, are more consistent, and require far less rework and modification.

Proponents of the bottom-up approach claim that it is superior to top-down because it is faster and less risky. They assert that top-down modeling results in many studies that are difficult to complete and that the planning process often ends in analysis paralysis. Although bottom-up modeling does not necessarily produce the best set of systems, it does produce useful systems quickly. The benefits of these systems begin accruing much faster than with top-down modeling, and they can more than compensate for any rework or modification that will need to be done to adjust the system to a global perspective.

This text explains the tools and techniques that can be used with either style of systems development. For example, although both entity-relationship modeling (Chapter 3) and semantic object modeling (Chapter 4) work with either top-down or bottom-up development, the entity-relationship approach is particularly effective with top-down development, and the semantic object approach is particularly effective with bottom-up development.

Data Modeling

As we stated, the most important goal of the requirements phase is creating a model of the users' data. Whether this is done in top-down or bottom-up fashion, it involves interviewing users, documenting requirements, and, from those requirements, building the data model and prototypes. Such a model identifies what is to be stored in the database and defines their structure and the relationships among them.

For example, consider Figure 2-15(a), a list of orders made by a salesperson during a specific period of time. For this report to be produced by a database application, the database must contain the data shown, so the database developers need to examine the report and work backward to the data that must be stored in the database. In this case, there must be data concerning salespeople (name and region) and data concerning orders (company, order date, and amount).

Database development is complicated by the fact that there is not just one requirement but many and that the requirements usually overlap. The report in

Salesperson Order List
14-Jun-96

Name	Region	CompanyName	OrderDate	Amount
Kevin Dougherty	Western			
		Cabo Controls	9/12/1998	$2,349.88
				$2,349.88
Mary B. Wu	Western			
		Ajax Electric	9/17/1998	$23,445.00
		American Maxell	9/24/1998	$17,339.44
				$40,784.44
			Grand Total:	$43,134.32

(a)

Salesperson Commission Check Report
14-Jun-96

Name	LocalNumber	CheckDate	CType	CAmount
Kevin Dougherty	232-9988			
		9/30/1998	XZ	$487.38
				$487.38
Mary B. Wu	232-9987			
		9/30/1998	C	$237.44
		9/30/1998	A	$1,785.39
				$2,022.83
			Grand Total:	$2,510.21

(b)

➤ FIGURE 2-15

Examples of Two Related Reports: (a) Sample SALES Report and (b) Sample COMMISSION Report

Figure 2-15(b) is also about salespeople, but, instead of orders, it lists commission checks. From this report, we can surmise that there are different types of orders and that each type has a different commission rate.

The orders implied by the report in Figure 2-15(b) somehow relate to the orders listed in Figure 2-15(a), but how they do so is not entirely clear. The development team must determine this relationship by inference from reports and forms, from interviews with users, from the team's knowledge of the subject matter, and from other sources.

DATA MODELING AS INFERENCING   When the users say they need forms and reports with specific data and structures, their statement implies a model that the users have of the things in their world. The users may not, however, be able to describe exactly what that model is. If a developer were to ask the typical user, "What is the structure of the data model in your brain regarding salespeople?" the user would, at best, look quizzical, because most users do not think in that way.

Instead, the developers must infer, from the users' statements about forms and reports, the structure and relationships of the things to be stored in the database. The developers then record these inferences in a data model that is transformed into a database design, and that design is implemented using a DBMS. Applications that produce the reports and forms for the users are then constructed.

Building a data model is thus a process of inference. Reports and forms are like shadows projected on a wall. The users can describe the shadows, but they cannot describe the shapes that give rise to the shadows. Therefore the developers must infer, work backward, and reverse-engineer the structures and relationships of those shapes from the shadows.

This inferencing process is, unfortunately, more art than science. It is possible to learn the tools and techniques for data modeling; in fact, such tools and techniques are the subject of the next two chapters, but using those tools and techniques is an art that requires experience guided by intuition.

The quality of the model is important. If the documented data model accurately reflects the data model in the users' minds, there is an excellent chance that the resulting applications will be close to the users' needs. But if the documented data model inaccurately reflects this data model, it is unlikely that the application to be produced will be close to what the users really want.

MODELING IN MULTI-USER SYSTEMS   The data modeling process becomes even more complicated for multi-user workgroup and organizational databases, because many users may envision many different data models. Occasionally these data models are inconsistent, although sometimes the inconsistencies can be resolved. For example, the users may be employing the same term for different things or different terms for the same things.

Sometimes, however, the differences cannot be reconciled. In such cases, the database developer must document the differences and help the users resolve them, and this usually means that some people have to change the way they view their world.

An even greater challenge is presented by large systems in which no single user has a model of the complete structure. Each user understands some of the work-group's or organization's data model, but no single user understands all of it. In such cases, the database becomes the logical union of the pieces of the work-group's or organization's model, and the developers must document that logical union in the data model. And this can be quite difficult.

CONFUSION ABOUT THE TERM *MODEL*   The next two chapters present two alternative tools for building data models: the entity-relationship model and the semantic object model. Both models are structures for describing and documenting users' data requirements. To avoid confusion, note the different uses of the term *model*. The development team analyzes the requirements and builds a *users' data model* or a *requirements data model*. This model is a representation of the structure and relationships of what needs to be in the database to support the users' requirements. To create the users' data model, the development team uses tools called entity-relationship and the semantic object data models, which consist of language and diagramming standards for representing the users' data model. Their role in database development is similar to that of flowcharting and pseudocode in programming.

➤ SUMMARY

The components of a database system are the database, the DBMS, and application programs, which are used by both developers and users. A database contains data, metadata, indexes, and application metadata. Most databases today represent data as relations or tables, although not all relations are equally desirable. Undesirable relations can be improved through a process called normalization. Metadata is often stored in special tables called system tables.

A DBMS's features and functions can be grouped into three subsystems. The design tools subsystem defines the database and the structure of applications or application components. The functions of the run-time subsystem are to materialize the forms, reports, and queries by reading or writing database data. The DBMS engine is the intermediary between the other two subsystems and the operating system. It receives requests stated in terms of tables and rows and columns and translates those requests into read and write requests.

A schema is a description of the structure of a database and includes descriptions of tables, relationships, domains, and business rules. The rows of one table can be related to the rows of other tables. This chapter illustrated a 1:N relationship between table rows; there are other relationship types as well, as we will discuss in the next chapter.

A domain is a set of values that a column may have. We must specify a domain for each column of each table.

Finally, business rules are restrictions on the business's activities that must be reflected in the database and database applications.

The facilities of the DBMS are used to create table structures, to define relationships, and to create forms, reports, queries, and menus. DBMS products also include facilities for interacting with application programs written in either DBMS-specific languages or standard languages like COBOL.

Since a database is a model of the users' model of the business, database development begins by learning and recording this model. Sometimes it is expressed in prototypes of the application or application components to be constructed.

The two general styles of development are top-down development, which proceeds from the general to the specific, and bottom-up development, which proceeds from the specific to the general. With top-down, applications are developed with a global perspective; with bottom-up, applications are developed more quickly. Sometimes a combination of the two approaches is used.

Data models are constructed by a process that involves inferencing from users' statements. Forms, reports, and queries are gathered, and the developers work backward to infer the structures that the users envision. This is necessary because most users cannot describe their data models directly. Data modeling can be especially difficult and challenging in multi-user applications, in which the users' views may contradict one another's and no single user can visualize the entire view of the business activity.

The term *data model* is used in two ways, to refer to a model of the users' view of their data and to refer to the tools used to define the users' view of their data.

➤ GROUP I QUESTIONS

2.1 Name the major components of a database system, and briefly explain the function of each.

2.2 Give an example, other than the one in this chapter, of a relation that is likely to have problems when it is updated. Use relation R1 as an example.

2.3 Transpose the relation in your answer to Question 2.2 into two or more relations that do not have update problems. Use relations R2 and R3 as examples.

2.4 Explain the roles of metadata and system tables.

2.5 What is the function of indexes? When are they desirable, and what is their cost?

2.6   What is the function of application metadata? How does it differ from metadata?

2.7   Explain the features and functions of the design tools subsystem of a DBMS.

2.8   Describe the features and functions of a DBMS's run-time subsystem.

2.9   Explain the features and functions of the DBMS engine.

2.10   What is a database schema? List its components.

2.11   How are relationships represented in a relational database design? Give an example of two tables with a 1:N relationship, and explain how the relationship is expressed in the data.

2.12   What is a domain, and why is it important?

2.13   What are business rules? Give an example of possible business rules for the relations in your answer to Question 2.11.

2.14   What is a foreign key? Which column(s) in your answer to Question 2.11 is a foreign key?

2.15   Explain the purpose of forms, reports, queries, and menus.

2.16   Explain the difference between query by example and query by form.

2.17   What is the first important task in developing a database and related applications?

2.18   What is the role of a prototype?

2.19   Describe top-down development. What are its advantages and disadvantages?

2.20   Describe bottom-up development. What are its advantages and disadvantages?

2.21   Explain the two different meanings of the term *data model.*

➤ GROUP II QUESTIONS

2.22   Implement a database with the relations CAPTAIN and ITEM in any DBMS to which you can gain access. Use one of the DBMS products facilities to enter data into each of these relations. Create and process a query to use the DBMS's facility to process a query that identifies those items checked out before September 1, 1999, that have not yet been checked back in. Print the name of the captain, his or her phone number, and the quantity and description of any such items.

2.23   Interview a professional database application developer, and find out the process that this person uses to develop databases. Is this top-down development, bottom-up development, or some other strategy? How does this developer build data models and with what tools? What are the biggest problems usually encountered in developing a database?

2.24   Consider the statement "A database is a model of the users' model of reality." How does it differ from "A database is a model of reality"? Suppose two developers disagree about a data model, and one of them asserts, "My model is a better representation of reality." What does this person really mean? What differences are likely to result when a developer believes the first statement more than the second statement?

DATA MODELING

Data modeling is the process of creating a logical representation of the structure of a database. To be correct, the data model must support all of the users' views of the data. Data modeling is the most important task in the development of effective database applications. If the data model incorrectly represents the users' view of the data, the users will find the applications difficult to use, incomplete, and very frustrating. Data modeling is the basis for all subsequent work in the development of databases and their applications.

Part II describes two different data modeling tools: Chapter 3 considers the entity-relationship model, which was introduced in 1976 and has a considerable following among CASE vendors and others, and Chapter 4 describes the semantic-object model, which was introduced in 1988. As the newer model, it has a smaller following, but some consider it to be richer and easier to use than the E-R model.

These models provide a language to express the structure of data and relationships in the users' environment. Data modeling expresses a logical data design just as flowcharting expresses a logical program design.

CHAPTER 3

The Entity-Relationship Model

This chapter describes and illustrates the use of the **entity-relationship model (E-R model)** which was introduced by Peter Chen in 1976.[1] In this paper, Chen set out the foundation of the model, which has since been extended and modified by Chen and many others.[2] In addition, the E-R model has been made part of a number of CASE tools, which also have modified it. Today, there is no single, generally accepted standard E-R model but, instead, a set of common constructs from which most of the E-R variants are derived. This chapter describes these common constructs and shows how they are used. Be aware, however, that during your career you may encounter variants of the approach presented here.[3] In addition, the symbols used to express the E-R model differ considerably. Those used here are typical and popular, but they are by no means the only symbols that you will encounter.

➤ ELEMENTS OF THE ENTITY-RELATIONSHIP MODEL

Key elements of the E-R model are entities, attributes, identifiers, and relationships. Consider each of these in turn.

ENTITIES

An **entity** is something that can be identified in the users' work environment, something that the users want to track. Example entities are EMPLOYEE Mary Doe, CUSTOMER 12345, SALES-ORDER 1000, SALESPERSON John Smith, and

---

[1]P. P. Chen, "The Entity-Relationship Model—Towards a Unified View of Data," *ACM Transactions on Database Systems*, January 1976, pp. 9–36.

[2]T. J Teorey, D. Yang, and J. P. Fry, "A Logical Design Methodology for Relational Databases Using the Extended Entity-Relationship Model," *ACM Computing Surveys*, June 1986, pp. 197–222.

[3]Thomas A. Bruce, *Designing Quality Databases with IDEF1X Information Models* (New York: Dorset House Publishing, 1992).

➤ FIGURE 3-1

*CUSTOMER: An Example of
an Entity*

```
CUSTOMER
entity contains:
    CustNumber
    CustName
    Address
    City
    State
    Zip
    ContactName
    PhoneNumber

Two instances of CUSTOMER:

12345                           67890
Ajax Manufacturing              Jefferson Dance Club
123 Elm St                      345-10th Avenue
Memphis                         Boston
TN                              MA
32455                           01234
P. Schwartz                     Frita Bellingsley
223-5567                        210-8896
```

PRODUCT A4200. Entities of a given type are grouped into **entity classes.** Thus, the EMPLOYEE entity class is the collection of all EMPLOYEE entities. In this text, entity classes are printed in capital letters.

It is important to understand the differences between an entity class and an entity instance. An *entity class* is a collection of entities and is described by the structure or format of the entities in that class. An *instance* of an entity class is the representation of a particular entity, such as CUSTOMER 12345; it is described by the values of attributes of the entity. There are usually many instances of an entity in an entity class. For example, within the class CUSTOMER, there are many instances—one for each customer represented in the database. An entity class and two of its instances are shown in Figure 3-1.

ATTRIBUTES

Entities have **attributes** or, as they are sometimes called, **properties** that describe the entity's characteristics. Examples of attributes are EmployeeName, DateOfHire, and JobSkillCode. In this text, attributes are printed in both uppercase and lowercase letters. The E-R model assumes that all instances of a given entity class have the same attributes.

The original E-R model definition includes both composite and multi-value attributes. An example of a composite attribute is Address which consists of the group of attributes {Street, City, State/Province, Zip/PostalCode}. An example of a multi-value attribute is ContactName in CUSTOMER, where more than one person's name is associated with a given Customer. An attribute can be both multi-value and composite; for example, the composite attribute Phone {AreaCode, Number} could be multi-value to allow for multiple phone numbers. Most implementations of the E-R model ignore single-value composite attributes. They require multi-value attributes (whether composite or not) to be transformed into entities as will be shown below.

IDENTIFIERS

Entity instances have **identifiers,** which are attributes that name, or identify, entity instances. For example, EMPLOYEE instances could be identified by SocialSecurityNumber, EmployeeNumber, or EmployeeName. EMPLOYEE instances are not likely to be identified by attributes like Salary or DateOfHire because normally these attributes are not used in a naming role. Similarly, CUSTOMERs could be identified by CustomerNumber or CustomerName, and SALES-ORDERs could be identified by OrderNumber.

The identifier of an entity instance consists of one or more of the entity's attributes. An identifier may be either **unique** or **nonunique.** If it is unique, its value will identify one, and only one, entity instance. If it is nonunique, the value will identify a set of instances. EmployeeNumber is most likely a unique identifier, while EmployeeName is most likely a nonunique identifier (there may be many John Smiths, for example).

Identifiers that consist of two or more attributes are called **composite identifiers.** Examples are {AreaCode, LocalNumber}, {ProjectName, TaskName}, and {FirstName, LastName, PhoneExtension}.

RELATIONSHIPS

Entities can be associated with one another in **relationships.** The E-R model contains both relationship classes and relationship instances. *Relationship classes* are associations among entity classes, and *relationship instances* are associations among entity instances. Relationships can have attributes.

As defined in the original E-R model, a relationship can include many entities; the number of entities in a relationship is the **degree** of the relationship. In Figure 3-2(a), the SP-ORDER relationship is of degree 2 because each instance of the relationship involves two entity instances: a SALESPERSON entity instance and an ORDER entity instance.[4] In Figure 3-2(b), the PARENT relationship is of degree 3, since each instance involves three entities: MOTHER, FATHER, and CHILD. Relationships of degree 2 are very common and are often referred to by the term **binary relationships.**

THREE TYPES OF BINARY RELATIONSHIPS   Figure 3-3 shows the three types of binary relationships. In a 1:1 (read "one-to-one") relationship, a single-entity instance of one type is related to a single-entity instance of another type. In Figure 3-3(a), the AUTO-ASSIGNMENT relationship associates a single EMPLOYEE with a single AUTO. According to this diagram, no employee has more than one automobile assigned, and no automobile is assigned to more than one employee.

Figure 3-3(b) shows the second type of relationship, 1:N (read "one to N" or "one to many"). In this relationship, called a DORM-OCCUPANT relationship, a single instance of DORMITORY relates to many instances of STUDENT. According to this sketch, a dormitory has many students, but a student has only one dormitory.

The positions of the 1 and the N are significant. The 1 is close to the line connecting DORMITORY, which means that the 1 refers to the DORMITORY side of the relationship, and the N is close to the line connecting STUDENT, which means that the N refers to the STUDENT side of the relationship. If the 1 and the

➤ FIGURE 3-2

Relationships of Different Degrees: (a) Example Relationship of Degree 2 and (b) Example Relationship of Degree 3

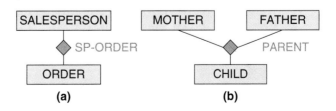

---

[4]For brevity, we sometimes drop the word *instance* when the context makes it clear that an instance rather than an entity class is involved.

Three Types of Binary Relationships: (a) 1:1 Binary Relationship, (b) 1:N Binary Relationship, (c) N:M Binary Relationship, and (d) Relationship Representation with Crow's Feet

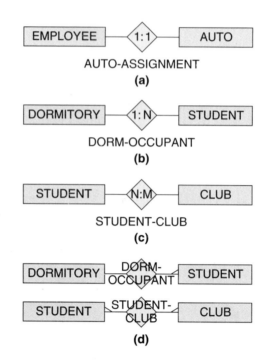

N were reversed and the relationship were written N:1, a DORMITORY would have one STUDENT, and a STUDENT would have many DORMITORIES. This is not, of course, the case.

Figure 3-3(c) shows the third type of binary relationship, N:M (read "N to M" or "many to many"). This relationship is named STUDENT-CLUB, and it relates instances of STUDENT to instances of CLUB. A student can join more than one club, and a club can have many students as members.

The numbers inside the relationship diamond show the maximum number of entities that can occur on one side of the relationship. Such constraints are called the relationship's **maximum cardinality.** The relationship in Figure 3-3(b), for example, is said to have a maximum cardinality of 1:N. But the cardinalities are not restricted to the values shown here. It is possible, for example, for the maximum cardinality to be other than 1 and N. The relationship between BASKETBALL-TEAM and PLAYER, for example, could be 1:5, indicating that a basketball team has at most five players.

Relationships of the types shown in Figure 3-3 are sometimes called **HAS-A relationships.** This term is used because an entity *has a* relationship with another entity. For example, an EMPLOYEE has an AUTO; a STUDENT has a DORMITORY; and a CLUB has STUDENTs.

ENTITY-RELATIONSHIP DIAGRAMS   The sketches in Figure 3-3 are called **entity-relationship** or **E-R diagrams**. Such diagrams are standardized, but only loosely. According to this standard, entity classes are shown by rectangles, relationships are shown by diamonds, and the maximum cardinality of the relationship is shown inside the diamond.[5] The name of the entity is shown inside the rectangle, and the name of the relationship is shown near the diamond.

---

[5]The graphical symbols that originated with the model (which are the symbols described here) are not the best ones for displaying a model in a Graphical User Interface (GUI) system such as the Macintosh or Microsoft Windows. In fact, the E-R model was developed long before any GUI system was popular. Consequently, as vendors developed GUI CASE tools, they chose to invent new symbols for presenting their designs. The result is that an E-R CASE tool may use symbols different from these. This kind of problem is common in the information systems industry: Standards must be extended as technology evolves.

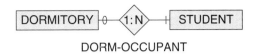

DORM-OCCUPANT

*Relationship with Minimum
Cardinality Shown*

Although in some E-R diagrams the name of the relationship is shown inside the diamond, this can make the diagram look awkward, since the diamonds may have to be large and out of scale in order to include the relationship name. To avoid this, relationship names are sometimes written over the diamond. When the name is placed inside or on top of the diamond, the relationship cardinality is shown by placing crow's feet on the lines connecting to the entity(ies) on the many side of the relationship. Figure 3-3(d) shows the DORM-OCCUPANT and STUDENT-CLUB relationships with such crow's feet.

As we stated, the maximum cardinality indicates the maximum number of entities that can be involved in a relationship. The diagrams do not indicate the minimum. For example, Figure 3-3(b) shows that a student is related, at maximum, to one dormitory, but it does not show whether a student *must be* related to a dormitory instance.

A number of different ways are used to show **minimum cardinality.** One way, illustrated in Figure 3-4, is to place a hash mark across the relationship line to indicate that an entity must exist in the relationship and to place an oval across the relationship line to indicate that there may or may not be an entity in the relationship. Accordingly, Figure 3-4 shows that a DORMITORY must have a relationship with at least one STUDENT but that a STUDENT is not required to have a relationship with a DORMITORY. The complete relationship restrictions are that a DORMITORY has a minimum cardinality of one and a maximum cardinality of many STUDENT entities. A STUDENT has a minimum cardinality of zero and a maximum cardinality of one DORMITORY entity.

A relationship may exist among entities of the same class. For example, the relationship ROOMS-WITH could be defined on the entity STUDENT. Figure 3-5(a) shows such a relationship, and Figure 3-5(b) shows instances of entities that conform to this relationship. Relationships among entities of a single class are sometimes called **recursive relationships.**

SHOWING ATTRIBUTES IN ENTITY-RELATIONSHIP DIAGRAMS   In some versions of E-R diagrams, the attributes are shown in ellipses and are connected to the entity or relationship to which they belong. Figure 3-6(a) shows the

Recursive Relationship

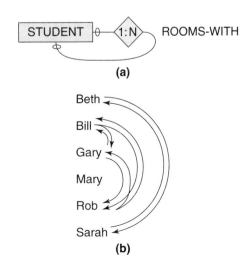

Showing Properties in Entity-Relationship Diagrams: (a) Entity-Relationship Diagram with Properties Shown and (b) Entity-Relationship Diagram with Properties Listed Separately

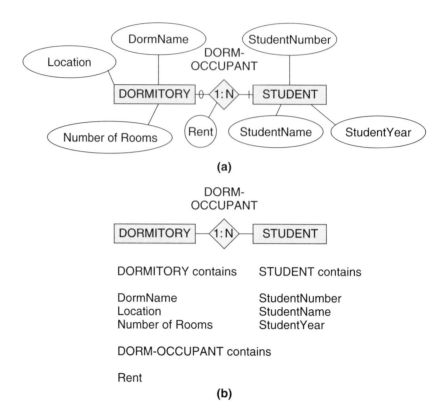

DORMITORY and STUDENT entities and the DORM-OCCUPANT relationship with the attributes. As shown, DORMITORY has DormName, Location, and NumberOfRooms attributes, and STUDENT has StudentNumber, StudentName, and StudentYear attributes. The relationship DORM-OCCUPANT has the attribute Rent, which shows the amount of rent paid by a particular student in a particular dorm.

If an entity has many attributes, listing them in this way on the E-R diagram may make the diagram cluttered and difficult to interpret. In these cases, entity attributes are listed separately, as shown in Figure 3-6(b). Many CASE tools show such attributes in pop-up windows.

WEAK ENTITIES

The entity-relationship model defines a special type of entity called a **weak entity.** Such entities are those that cannot exist in the database unless another type of entity also exists in the database. An entity that is not weak is called a **strong entity.**

To understand weak entities, consider a human resource database with EMPLOYEE and DEPENDENT entity classes. Suppose the business has a rule that an EMPLOYEE instance *can exist* without having a relationship to any DEPENDENT entity, but a DEPENDENT entity *cannot exist* without having a relationship to a particular EMPLOYEE entity. In such a case, DEPENDENT is a weak entity. This means that DEPENDENT data can be stored in the database only if the DEPENDENT has a relationship with an EMPLOYEE entity.

As shown in Figure 3-7(a), weak entities are signified by rounding the corners of the entity rectangle. In addition, the relationship on which the entity depends for its existence is shown in a diamond with rounded corners. Alternatively, in some E-R diagrams (not shown here), weak entities are depicted by using a double line for the boundary of the weak entity rectangle and double diamonds for the relationship on which the entity depends.

FIGURE 3-7

Weak Entities: (a) Example
of a Weak Entity and
(b) ID-Dependent Entity

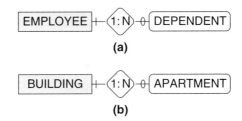

The E-R model includes a special type of weak entity called an **ID-depen-dent entity.** Such an entity is one in which the identifier of one entity in-cludes the identifier of another entity. Consider the entities BUILDING and APARTMENT. Suppose the identifier of BUILDING is BuildingName, and the identifier of APARTMENT is the composite identifier {BuildingName, ApartmentNumber}. Since the identifier of APARTMENT contains the identifier of BUILDING (BuildingName), then APARTMENT is ID-dependent on BUILD-ING. Contrast Figure 3-7(b) with Figure 3-7(a). Another way to think of this is that, both logically and physically, an APARTMENT cannot exist unless a BUILDING exists.

ID-dependent entities are common. Another example is the entity VERSION in the relationship between PRODUCT and VERSION, where PRODUCT is a soft-ware product and VERSION is a release of that software product. The identifier of PRODUCT is ProductName, and the identifier of VERSION is {ProductName, ReleaseNumber}. A third example is EDITION in the relationship between TEXT-BOOK and EDITION. The identifier of TEXTBOOK is Title, and the identifier of EDITION is {Title, EditionNumber}.

Unfortunately, there is an ambiguity hidden in the definition of weak entity, and this ambiguity is interpreted differently by different database designers (as well as different textbook authors). The ambiguity is this: In a strict sense, if a weak entity is defined as any entity whose presence in the database depends on another entity, then any entity that participates in a relationship having a mini-mum cardinality of 1 to a second entity is a weak entity. Thus, in an academic database, if a STUDENT must have an ADVISOR, then STUDENT is a weak entity, because a STUDENT entity cannot be stored without an ADVISOR. This interpre-tation, however, seems too broad to some people. A STUDENT is not physically dependent on an ADVISOR (unlike APARTMENTs and BUILDINGs), and a STU-DENT is not logically dependent on an ADVISOR (in spite of how it might appear to either the student or the advisor!); therefore, a STUDENT should be considered a strong entity.

To avoid such situations, some people interpret the definition of weak entity more narrowly. To be a weak entity, an entity must *logically* depend on another entity. According to this definition, both DEPENDENT and APARTMENT would be considered weak entities, but STUDENT would not. A DEPENDENT cannot be a dependent unless it has someone to depend on, and an APARTMENT cannot exist without a BUILDING to reside in. A STUDENT, however, can logically exist without an ADVISOR, even if a business rule requires it.

To illustrate this interpretation, consider several examples. Suppose a data model includes the relationship between an ORDER and a SALESPERSON [Figure 3-8(a)]. While we might say that an ORDER must have a SALESPERSON, it does not necessarily require one for its existence (the ORDER could be a cash sale in which the salesperson is not recorded). Hence, the minimum cardinality of 1 arises from a business rule, not from logical necessity. Thus, ORDER requires a SALESPERSON but is not existence-dependent on it, and ORDER would be con-sidered a strong entity.

FIGURE 3-8

Examples of Required Entities

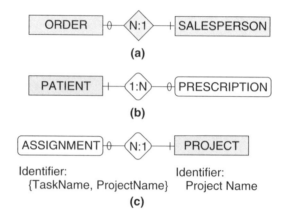

(a)

(b)

Identifier: Identifier:
    {TaskName, ProjectName}   Project Name

(c)

Now, however, consider the relationship of PATIENT and PRESCRIPTION in Figure 3-8(b). Here, a PRESCRIPTION cannot logically exist without a PATIENT. Hence, not only is the minimum cardinality 1, but also, the PRESCRIPTION is existence dependent on PATIENT. PRESCRIPTION is thus a weak entity. Finally, consider ASSIGNMENT in Figure 3-8(c), where the identifier of ASSIGNMENT contains the identifier of PROJECT. Here, not only does ASSIGNMENT have a minimum cardinality of 1, and not only is ASSIGNMENT existence-dependent on PROJECT, but it is also ID-dependent on PROJECT, since its key includes the key of another entity. Thus, ASSIGNMENT is a weak entity.

In this text we will assume that weak entities must logically depend on another entity. Hence, not all entities that have a minimum cardinality of 1 in relationship to another entity are weak. Only those that are logically dependent are termed weak. This definition also means that all ID-dependent entities are weak. Additionally, every weak entity has a minimum cardinality of 1 on the entity on which it depends, but every entity that has a minimum cardinality of 1 need not necessarily be weak.[6]

REPRESENTING MULTI-VALUE ATTRIBUTES WITH WEAK ENTITIES
Multi-value attributes are represented in the E-R by creating a new weak entity to represent the multi-value attribute and constructing a one-to-many relationship. For example, Figure 3-9(a) shows the representation of the multi-value attribute ContactName in CUSTOMER. A new weak entity called CONTACTNAME is created with a single attribute ContactName. The relationship between CUSTOMER and CONTACTNAME is one-to-many. The constructed entity must be weak because it is logically dependent on the entity that had the multi-value attribute.

Figure 3-9(b) shows the representation of the multi-value composite attribute Address. The new weak entity ADDRESS contains all of the attributes of the composite, namely, Street, City, State/Province, Zip/PostalCode.

SUBTYPE ENTITIES

Some entities contain optional sets of attributes; these entities are often represented using subtypes.[7] Consider, for example, CLIENT, with attributes ClientNumber, ClientName, and AmountDue. Suppose that a CLIENT can be

---

[6]This discussion omits the cases in which the minimum cardinality is greater than 1. The logic is similar, but the entity depends on a set of entities.
[7]Subtypes were added to the E-R model after the publication of Chen's initial paper, and they are part of what is called the *extended E-R model*.

FIGURE 3-9

Representing Multi-value Attributes with Weak Entities

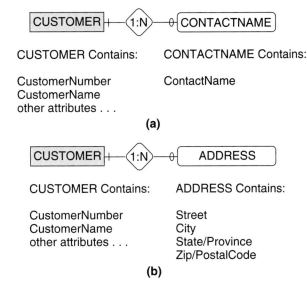

an individual, a partnership, or a corporation and that additional data are to be stored depending on the type. Assume that these additional data are as follows:

INDIVIDUAL-CLIENT:
Address, SocialSecurityNumber
PARTNERSHIP-CLIENT:
ManagingPartnerName, Address, TaxIdentificationNumber
CORPORATE-CLIENT:
ContactPerson, Phone, TaxIdentificationNumber

One possibility is to allocate all of these attributes to the entity CLIENT, as shown in Figure 3-10(a). In this case, some of the attributes are not applicable. ManagingPartnerName has no meaning for an individual or corporate client, and so it cannot have a value.

A closer-fitting model would instead define three subtype entities, as shown in Figure 3-10(b). Here the INDIVIDUAL-CLIENT, PARTNERSHIP-CLIENT, and CORPORATE-CLIENT entities are shown as **subtypes** of CLIENT. CLIENT, in turn, is a **supertype** of the INDIVIDUAL-CLIENT, PARTNERSHIP-CLIENT, and CORPORATE-CLIENT entities.

The ∈ next to the relationship lines indicates that INDIVIDUAL-CLIENT, PARTNERSHIP-CLIENT, and CORPORATE-CLIENT are subtypes of CLIENT. Each subtype entity must belong to the supertype CLIENT. The curved line with a 1 next to it indicates that a CLIENT entity must belong to one, and only one, subtype. It means that the subtypes are exclusive and that one of them is required.

Subtypes are not always mutually exclusive, however, nor are they always required. Figure 3-10(c) shows the CLIENT-USING subtypes within CLIENT. The *m* indicates that CLIENT may belong to from zero to many CLIENT-USING subtypes.

Structures of subtypes and supertypes are sometimes called **generalization hierarchies** because CLIENT is a generalization of the three subtypes. Sometimes, too, this relationship type is called an **IS-A relationship,** since, in Figure 3-10(b), INDIVIDUAL-CLIENT *is a* CLIENT, just as PARTNERSHIP-CLIENT and CORPORATE-CLIENT also are CLIENTs.

FIGURE 3-10

Subtype Entities: (a) CLIENT Without Subtype Entities, (b) CLIENT with Subtype Entities, and (c) Nonexclusive Subtypes with Optional Supertype

CLIENT Contains

ClientNumber
ClientName
AmountDue
Address
SocialSecurityNumber
ManagingPartnerName
TaxIdentificationNumber
ContactPerson
Phone

(a)

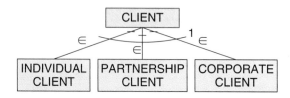

CLIENT Contains

ClientNumber
ClientName
AmountDue

INDIVIDUAL-CLIENT Contains

Address
SocialSecurityNumber

PARTNERSHIP-CLIENT Contains

ManagingPartnerName
Address
TaxIdentificationNumber

CORPORATE-CLIENT Contains

ContactPerson
Phone
TaxIdentificationNumber

(b)

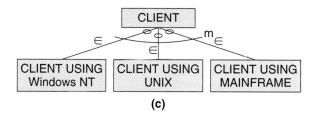

(c)

Entities with an *IS-A* relationship should have the same identifier since they represent different aspects of the same thing. In this case, that identifier is Client Number. Contrast this situation with the HAS-A relationships shown in Figure 3-3.

Generalization hierarchies have a special characteristic called **inheritance,** which means that the entities in subtypes inherit attributes of the supertype entity class. PARTNERSHIP-CLIENT, for example, inherits ClientName and AmountDue from CLIENT.

EXAMPLE E-R DIAGRAM

Figure 3-11 is an example E-R diagram that contains all of the elements of the E-R model that we have been discussing. It shows the entities and relationships for an engineering consulting company that analyzes the construction and condition of houses and other buildings and facilities.

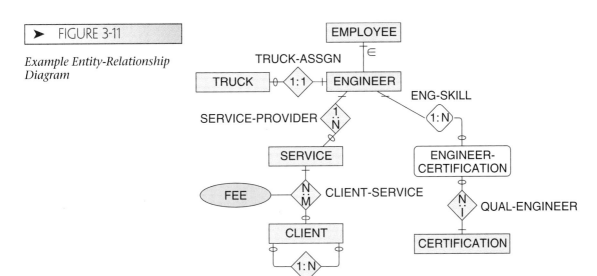

FIGURE 3-11

Example Entity-Relationship Diagram

There is an entity class for the company's employees. Because some EMPLOYEEs are ENGINEERs, there is a subtype relationship between EMPLOYEE and ENGINEER. Every ENGINEER must be an EMPLOYEE; ENGINEER has a 1:1 relationship to TRUCK; and each TRUCK must be assigned to an ENGINEER, but not all ENGINEERs have a TRUCK.

ENGINEERs provide SERVICEs to CLIENTs. An ENGINEER can provide from zero to many services, but a given SERVICE must be provided by an ENGINEER and can be provided by only that ENGINEER. CLIENTs have many SERVICEs, and a SERVICE can be requested by many CLIENTs. A CLIENT must have purchased at least one SERVICE, but SERVICE need not have any CLIENTs. The CLIENT-SERVICE relationship has an attribute Fee, which shows the amount that a particular client paid for a particular SERVICE. (Other attributes of entities and relationships are not shown in this diagram.)

Sometimes CLIENTs refer one another, which is indicated by the recursive relationship REFERRED-BY. A given CLIENT can refer one or more other CLIENTs. A CLIENT may or may not have been referred by another client, but a CLIENT may be referred by only one other CLIENT.

The ENGINEER-CERTIFICATION entity shows that a given ENGINEER has completed the education and testing required to earn a particular certificate. An ENGINEER may have earned CERTIFICATIONs. ENGINEER-CERTIFICATION's existence is dependent on ENGINEER through the relationship ENG-SKILL. CERTIFICATION is the entity that describes a particular certification.

DOCUMENTATION OF BUSINESS RULES

Chapter 2 defined a database schema as consisting of tables, relationships, domains, and business rules. We can obtain or infer the first three of these from an E-R model, but we cannot obtain business rules from the model. Thus, these rules are sometimes added to the E-R model during the data modeling stage.

The E-R model is developed from an analysis of requirements obtained from users. During this analysis, business rules often are brought up, and, indeed, systems analysts should make it a point to ask about them.

Consider the entities TRUCK and ENGINEER in Figure 3-11. Does the business have rules concerning who is assigned a TRUCK? If there are not enough TRUCKs for one to be assigned to every ENGINEER, what rules determine who gets a

TRUCK? It might be that the database application is to assign trucks on the basis of which ENGINEER has the most number of SERVICEs scheduled during some period of time, the most number of SERVICEs out of the office, or some other rule.

Another example concerns the allocation of ENGINEERs to SERVICEs. There probably are rules concerning the type of ENGINEERING-CERTIFICATION that an ENGINEER must have in order to be assigned to particular types of SERVICE. To inspect an apartment building, for example, the ENGINEER may need to be licensed as a professional ENGINEER. Even if there is no law that dictates this rule, it may be the policy of the company to enforce it.

Business rules may or may not be enforced by the DBMS or by the application program. Sometimes business rules are written in manual procedures that the users of the database application are to follow. At this point, the way in which the rules are to be enforced is not important. What is important is to document these rules so that they become part of the system's requirements.

THE ENTITY-RELATIONSHIP MODEL AND CASE TOOLS

Developing a data model using the entity-relationship model has become easier in recent years, because the tools for building E-R diagrams are included in many popular CASE products. Products such as IEW, IEF, DEFT, ER-WIN, and Visio have drawing and diagramming facilities to create E-R diagrams. Such products also integrate entities with the database relations that represent them, which can facilitate the administration, management, and maintenance of the database.

We do not assume the use of a CASE tool for the discussions in this text. But if your university has such a tool, by all means use it to create E-R diagrams for exercises you are assigned. The E-R diagrams created using these tools are generally more visually pleasing, and they are far easier to change and adapt.

➤ EXAMPLES

The best way to gain proficiency with any modeling tool is to study examples and to use the tool to make your own models. The remainder of this chapter presents two case applications to help you with the first task. After working through these examples, you should then work the example problems at the end of the chapter.

EXAMPLE 1: THE JEFFERSON DANCE CLUB

The Jefferson Dance Club teaches social dancing and offers both private and group lessons. Jefferson charges $45 per hour per student (or couple) for a private lesson and $6 per hour per student for a group lesson. Private lessons are offered throughout the day, from noon until 10 P.M., six days a week. Group lessons are offered in the evenings.

Jefferson employs two types of instructor: full-time salaried instructors and part-time teachers. The full-time instructors are paid a fixed amount per week, and the part-time instructors are paid either a set amount for an evening or a set amount for teaching a particular class.

In addition to the lessons, Jefferson sponsors two weekly social dances featuring recorded music. The admission charge is $5 per person. The Friday night dance is the more popular and averages around 80 people; the Sunday night dance attracts about 30 attendees. The purpose of the dances is to give the students a place in which to practice their skills. No food or drinks are served.

Jefferson would like to develop an information system to keep track of students and the classes they have taken. Jefferson's managers would also like to know how many and which types of lessons each teacher has taught and to be able to compute the average cost per lesson for each of their instructors.

ENTITIES

The best way to begin an entity-relationship model is to determine potential entities. Entities are usually represented by nouns (places, persons, concepts, events, equipment, and so on) in documents or interviews. A search of the previous example for important nouns that relate to the information system reveals the following list:

➤ Private lesson

➤ Group lesson

➤ Teacher

➤ Full-time teacher

➤ Part-time teacher

➤ Dance

➤ Customer

Clearly, the nouns *private lesson* and *group lesson* have something in common, as do the nouns *teacher, full-time teacher,* and *part-time teacher.* One solution is to define an entity LESSON, with subtypes PRIVATE-LESSON and GROUP-LESSON, and another entity TEACHER, with subtypes FULL-TIME-TEACHER and PART-TIME-TEACHER. Additional entities are DANCE and CUSTOMER.

As stated in Chapter 2, data modeling is as much art as it is science. The solution just described is one of several feasible solutions. A second solution is to eliminate LESSON and TEACHER from the list in the preceding paragraph and to eliminate all subtypes. A third solution is to eliminate LESSON (since lesson was never mentioned by itself as a noun) but to keep TEACHER and its subtypes. Here we choose the third case because it seems to be the best fit for the information we have. Thus, the list of entities is PRIVATE-LESSON, GROUP-LESSON, TEACHER, FULL-TIME-TEACHER, PART-TIME-TEACHER, DANCE, and CUSTOMER.

Choosing among these alternatives requires analyzing the requirements and considering the design implications of each of them. Sometimes it helps to consider the attributes of the entities. If, for example, the entity LESSON has no attributes other than its identifier, then it is not necessary.

RELATIONSHIPS

To begin, TEACHER has two subtype entities, FULL-TIME-TEACHER and PART-TIME-TEACHER. A given teacher must be one or the other, so the subtypes are mutually exclusive.

Consider next the relationships between TEACHER and PRIVATE-LESSON and GROUP-LESSON. A TEACHER can teach many PRIVATE-LESSONs, and normally a PRIVATE-LESSON is taught by a single TEACHER. However, further discussion with Jefferson's management reveals that for advanced dancers, especially those preparing for competitions, sometimes two teachers are involved in a private lesson. Therefore the relationship between TEACHER and PRIVATE-LESSON must be many to many. Assume, however, that only one teacher is involved in a group lesson. The relationships just described are shown in Figure 3-12.

CUSTOMERs can take either PRIVATE-LESSONs or GROUP-LESSONs. Sometimes a lesson is taken by an individual and sometimes by a couple. There are two ways in which this situation can be modeled. An entity COUPLE can be defined as having a one-to-two relationship with CUSTOMER, or either CUS-

Initial E-R Diagram for the Jefferson Dance Club

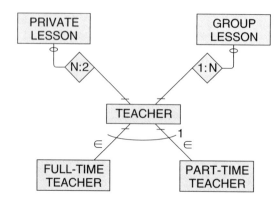

TOMER or COUPLE can have a relationship with PRIVATE-LESSON. We assume that couples do not take group lessons or that if they do, it is not important to store that fact in the database. This alternative is shown in Figure 3-13(a).

PRIVATE-LESSON's existence is dependent on CUSTOMER or COUPLE. That is, a lesson cannot exist unless it is given to either a CUSTOMER or a COUPLE. The 1 next to the horizontal line underneath CUSTOMER and COUPLE indicates that PRIVATE-LESSON must have at least one CUSTOMER or one COUPLE, which makes sense, since PRIVATE-LESSON is dependent on them.

Another alternative is not to represent couples but, instead, to model the relationship between CUSTOMER and PRIVATE-LESSON as many to many. More precisely, this relationship is one or two to many and is shown in Figure 3-13(b). Although the model is not as detailed as that in Figure 3-13(a), it may very well suffice for Jefferson's purposes.

The last relationship possibility is that between DANCE and other entities. Both customers and teachers attend dances, and the developers must decide whether it is important to store these relationships. Does Jefferson really need to know which customers attended which dances? Do Jefferson's managers really

Alternatives for Representing CUSTOMER: (a) E-R Diagram Showing COUPLE Entity and (b) E-R Diagram Without Couples

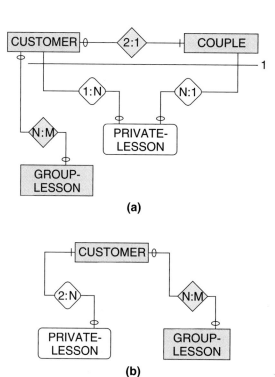

want to record attendance in a computer-based information system as customers enter the door? Do the customers want that fact recorded? Most likely, this is not a relationship that need or should be stored in the database.

The situation between DANCE and TEACHER is different. Jefferson likes some of its teachers to be present at each dance. In order to be fair about this requirement, Jefferson's management has drawn up a schedule for the teachers' attendance at dances. Developing and recording this schedule requires that the database contain the DANCE-TEACHER relationship, which is many to many.

FINAL E-R DIAGRAM FOR THE JEFFERSON DANCE CLUB

Figure 3-14 shows an E-R diagram for the model described in this section. We have not named the relationships in this diagram. Although doing so would make the diagrams more true to form, for our data, naming relationships would add little.

PRIVATE-LESSON's existence is dependent on CUSTOMER, but GROUP-LESSON's is not, because group lessons are scheduled long before any customer signs up, and they will be held even if no customers show up. This situation is not true, however, for private lessons, as they are scheduled only at the customer's request. Also notice that this model does not represent couples.

Once a model such as this is developed, its accuracy and completeness in regard to the requirements should be verified. Usually this is done with the users.

EVALUATING THE E-R DATA MODEL

It is easier and cheaper to correct errors early in the database development process rather than later. For example, changing the maximum cardinality of a relationship from 1:N to N:M in the data modeling stage is simply a matter of recording the change in the E-R diagram. But once the database has been designed and loaded with data and application programs written to process the database, making such a change requires considerable rework, possibly even weeks of labor. It is important, therefore, to evaluate the data model before designing it.

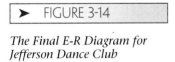

➤ FIGURE 3-14

The Final E-R Diagram for Jefferson Dance Club

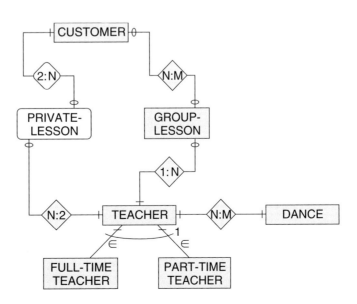

One evaluation technique is to consider the E-R data model in the context of possible queries that might be posed to a database with the structure implied by the model. For example, look at the diagram in Figure 3-14. What questions could be answered from a database that was implemented according to this design?

➤ Who has taught which private lessons?
➤ Which customers have taken a private lesson from Jack?
➤ Who are the full-time teachers?
➤ Which teachers are scheduled to attend the dance on Friday?

When evaluating an E-R data model, you can construct such questions and show them to the users, who can then be asked to draw up their own list of questions. Their questions can then be posed against the design in order to check its appropriateness. For example, suppose that the users asked which customers attended last week's Friday night dance. The designers of the data model in Figure 3-14 would conclude that their design was not correct, because it is not possible to answer this question using their E-R model. If it must be answered, a relationship between CUSTOMER and DANCE must be constructed.

Clearly, such an informal and loosely structured process cannot be used to *prove* that a design is correct. It is, however, a pragmatic technique that can be used to verify the potential correctness of a design. And it is far better than no evaluation at all!

EXAMPLE 2: SAN JUAN SAILBOAT CHARTERS

San Juan Sailboat Charters is an agent that leases sailboats to customers for a fee. San Juan does not own any sailboats but instead leases them on behalf of boat owners who wish to earn income when they are not using their boats. San Juan charges a fee for its service. San Juan specializes in boats that can be used for multi-day or weekly charters—the smallest sailboat in their inventory is 28 feet and the largest is 51 feet.

Each sailboat is fully equipped at the time it is leased. Most of the equipment is provided by the owners, but some is added by San Juan. The owner-provided equipment includes what is fixed on the boat, such as radios, compasses, depth indicators and other instrumentation, stoves, and refrigerators. Other owner-provided equipment is not installed as part of the boat. Such equipment includes sails, lines, anchors, dinghies, life preservers, and, in the cabin, dishes, silverware, cooking utensils, bedding, and the like. San Juan provides consumable equipment, which could also be considered supplies, such as charts, navigation books, tide and current tables, soap, dish towels, toilet paper, and similar items.

An important part of San Juan's responsibilities is keeping track of the equipment on the boat. Much of it is expensive, and some of it, particularly what is not attached to the boat, can easily be lost or stolen. Customers are responsible for all equipment during the period of their charter.

San Juan likes to keep accurate records of its customers and the charters, not only for marketing but also for recording the trips that customers have taken. Some itineraries and weather conditions are more dangerous than others, and so San Juan likes to know which customers have what experience.

Most of San Juan's business is bare-boat chartering, which means that no skipper or other crew is provided. In some cases, however, customers request the services of a skipper or other crew member, and so San Juan hires such personnel on a part-time basis.

Sailboats often need maintenance. San Juan is required by its contracts with the boat owners to keep accurate records of all maintenance activities and costs, including normal activities, such as cleaning or engine-oil changes, and unscheduled repairs. In some cases, repairs are necessary during a charter. A boat engine, for example, might fail while the boat is far away from San Juan's facility. In this case, the customers radio the San Juan dispatcher, who determines the best facility to make the repair and sends the facility's personnel to the disabled boat. To make these decisions, the dispatchers need information about repair facilities as well as past histories of repair quality and costs.

Before you continue reading, try to produce an entity-relationship diagram on your own. Examine the preceding statements and look for nouns that seem important to the design. Then check the possible relationships among the entities. Finally, list the likely attributes for each entity or relationship.

ENTITIES

The data model required for San Juan Charters is more complicated than that for the Jefferson Dance Club. Potential entities are shown in Figure 3-15(a).

Consider first the equipment-related entities. There are a number of different kinds of equipment, and this fact suggests the possibility of modeling subtypes. However, why does San Juan care about equipment? It does not really want to know the characteristics of each item—the chain length on each anchor, for ex-

➤ FIGURE 3-15

Entities for San Juan Charters

```
LEASE
BOAT
CUSTOMER
OWNER
EQUIPMENT
OWNER-PROVIDED-EQUIPMENT
FIXED OWNER-EQUIPMENT
REMOVABLE OWNER-EQUIPMENT
SAN-JUAN-PROVIDED-EQUIPMENT
ITINERARY/WEATHER
CHARTER
PART-TIME-CREW
SCHEDULED-MAINTENANCE
UNSCHEDULED-MAINTENANCE
REPAIRS
REPAIR-FACILITY

(a) Possible entities for San Juan Charters

LEASE or CHARTER(synonyms)
BOAT
CUSTOMER
OWNER
EQUIPMENT
ITINERARY/WEATHER
PART-TIME-CREW
SCHEDULED-MAINTENANCE
REPAIR or UNSCHEDULED-MAINTENANCE(synonyms)
REPAIR-FACILITY

(b) Entities selected for the E-R design
```

ample. Instead, its goal is to keep track of the items and their type so that it can determine if any has been lost or damaged. This can be done without keeping detailed records of the particular subtypes of equipment. Thus, for this design, we place all types of equipment into the entity EQUIPMENT.

Ownership of equipment is established by defining a relationship between EQUIPMENT and OWNER. If San Juan Charters is allowed to be an instance of OWNER, all of the equipment that it owns can be carried by this relationship. Similarly, from the case description, there is no reason to define the equipment that is attached to the boat differently from that not attached. An accurate list can be produced without this division. Figure 3-15(b) shows the final list of entities. Note that LEASE and CHARTER are synonyms; they refer to the same transaction. We show both names here so that they can be related to the case description.

It is possible that SCHEDULED-MAINTENANCE should be combined with UNSCHEDULED-MAINTENANCE. One way to decide is to examine the attributes of each of these entities. If they are the same, the two entity classes should be merged into one. Also observe that REPAIR and UNSCHEDULED-MAINTENANCE are defined as synonyms.

RELATIONSHIPS

Figure 3-16 is an entity-relationship diagram for San Juan Charters. For the most part, the relationships in this diagram are straightforward, but the relationship between EQUIPMENT and LEASE is arguable. One might say that EQUIPMENT should be related to BOAT and not to LEASE or that some EQUIPMENT should be related to BOAT (the equipment that stays with the boat) and the other equipment should be related to LEASE. These changes would be feasible alternatives to the design shown in Figure 3-16.

Notice, too, that SCHEDULED-MAINTENANCE is related to BOAT but that REPAIR (UNSCHEDULED-MAINTENANCE) is related to LEASE. This implies that no repair action is required when the boat is not being leased. Perhaps this is unrealistic.

Finally, LEASE and ITINERARY-WEATHER have a 1:1 relationship, and they also have the same identifying attributes. Therefore, it would be possible, and might even be preferable, to combine them into one entity class.

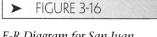

➤ FIGURE 3-16

E-R Diagram for San Juan Charters

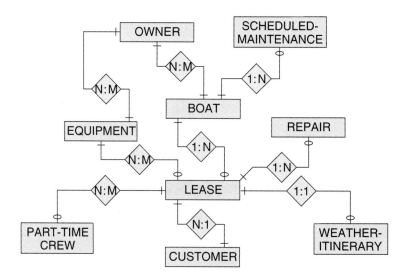

➤ DATABASES AS MODELS OF MODELS

As you can see, there are many different ways of modeling a business situation, and the variety becomes even greater as the application grows more complex. Often, dozens of models are feasible, and it can be difficult to choose among them.

Sometimes when evaluating alternatives, project team members discuss and argue about which data model best represents the real world. These discussions are misguided. Databases do not model the real world, although it is a common misconception that they do. Rather, databases are models of the users' models of the world (or, more to the point, of their business world). The question to ask when evaluating alternative data models is not "Does this design accurately represent the real world?" but, rather, "Does this design accurately represent the users' model of his or her environment?" The goal is to develop a design that fits the users' mental conception.

In fact, Immanuel Kant and other philosophers argued that it is impossible for humans to build models of what actually exists, claiming that the essence of things is forever unknowable by humans.[8] Extending this line of argument to computer systems, Winograd and Flores stated that in societies, humans construct systems of tokens that enable them to operate successfully in the world. A series of tokens is not a model of the infinitude of reality but, rather, only a social system that enables users to coordinate their activities successfully, and nothing more can be said.[9]

Computer systems therefore need to model and represent their users' communications with one another. They do not model anything other than that system of tokens and communications. So learn to ask these questions of yourself: "Does this model accurately reflect the users' perceptions and mental models of their world? Will it help the users respond consistently and successfully with one another and with their customers?" It is pointless for one analyst to claim that his or her model is a better representation of reality. Instead, the point is to develop a model that well represents the user's model of his or her business environment.

➤ SUMMARY

The entity-relationship model was developed by Peter Chen. With this model, entities—which are identifiable things of importance to the users—are defined. All of the entities of a given type form an entity class. A particular entity is called an instance. Entities have attributes that describe their characteristics, and one or more attributes identify an entity.

Relationships are associations among entities. The E-R model explicitly defines relationships; each relationship has a name; and there are relationship classes as well as relationship instances. Relationships may have attributes.

---

[8]"We cannot, indeed, beyond all possible experience, form a definitive concept of what things in themselves may be. Yet we are not at liberty to abstain entirely from inquiring into them; for experience never satisfies reason fully, but, in answering questions, refers us further and further back and leaves us dissatisfied with regard to the complete solution." Immanuel Kant, *Prolegomena to Any Future Metaphysics* (Indianapolis: Bobbs-Merrill, 1950), p. 100.
[9]Terry Winograd and F. Flores, *Understanding Computers and Cognition* (Reading, MA: Addison-Wesley, 1986).

The degree of the relationship is the number of entities participating in the relationship. Most relationships are binary. The three types of binary relationships are 1:1, 1:N, and N:M.

In entity-relationship diagrams, the entities are shown in rectangles, and the relationships are shown in diamonds. The maximum cardinality of the relationship is shown inside the diamond. The minimum cardinality is indicated by a hash mark or an oval. Relationships that connect entity instances of the same class are recursive. Attributes can be shown in an E-R diagram in ellipses or in a separate table.

A weak entity is one whose existence depends on another entity; an entity that is not weak is called a strong entity. Weak entities are shown in rectangles with rounded corners, and the relationship on which the entity depends is indicated by a diamond with rounded corners. In this text, we further define a weak entity to be an entity that logically depends on another entity. An entity can have a minimum cardinality of 1 in a relationship with another entity and not necessarily be a weak entity. Multi-value attributes are represented with weak entities.

Some entities have subtypes that define subsets of similar entities. Subtypes inherit attributes from their parent, the supertype. HAS-A relationships connect entities of different types, and the identifiers of the entities are different. IS-A relationships are subtypes, and the identifiers of the entities are the same.

Once a data model is developed, the designers should consider business rules that may restrict processing against entities. Each entity in the model should be evaluated in light of possible data additions, changes, and deletions. Deletions, in particular, often are the source of important processing restrictions. When business rules are discovered, they should be documented in the data model.

The E-R model is an important part of many CASE products. These products provide tools for constructing and storing E-R diagrams. Some CASE tools integrate the E-R constructs with data constructs in the CASE repository.

Once they are completed, E-R models should be evaluated. One technique is to list queries that could be answered using the data model. This list is then shown to the users, who are asked to think of additional questions. The design is then evaluated against these questions to ensure that the model can answer them.

Databases do not model the real world but instead model the users' model of their business world. The appropriate criterion for judging a data model is whether the model fits the users' model. Arguing about which model best fits the real world is pointless.

➤ GROUP I QUESTIONS

3.1 Define *entity* and give an example.

3.2 Explain the difference between an entity class and an entity instance.

3.3 Define *attribute* and give examples for the entity you described in Question 1.

3.4 Explain what a composite attribute is and give an example.

3.5 Which attribute defined in your answer to Question 3.3 identifies the entity?

3.6 Define *relationship* and give an example.

3.7 Explain the difference between a relationship class and a relationship instance.

3.8 Define *degree of relationship*. Give an example, other than the one in this text, of a relationship greater than degree 2.

3.9 List and give an example of the three types of binary relationships. Draw an E-R diagram for each.

3.10 Define the terms *maximum cardinality* and *minimum cardinality.*

3.11 Name and sketch the symbols used in entity-relationship diagrams for (a) entity, (b) relationship, (c) weak entity and its relationship, (d) recursive relationship, and (e) subtype entity.

3.12 Give an example E-R diagram for the entities DEPARTMENT and EMPLOYEE, which have a 1:N relationship. Assume that a DEPARTMENT does not need to have any EMPLOYEE but that every EMPLOYEE does have a DEPARTMENT.

3.13 Give an example of a recursive relationship and show it in an E-R diagram.

3.14 Show example attributes for DEPARTMENT and EMPLOYEE (from Question 3.12). Describe the two ways that attributes can appear on or with E-R diagrams.

3.15 Define the term *weak entity* and give an example other than the one in this text.

3.16 Explain the ambiguity in the definition of the term *weak entity.* Explain how this text interprets this term. Give examples, other than those in this text, of each type of weak entity.

3.17 Define the term *ID-dependent entity* and give an example other than one in this text.

3.18 Show how to use a weak entity to represent the multi-value attribute Skill in an EMPLOYEE entity. Indicate both the maximum and minimum cardinalities on both sides of the relationship.

3.19 Show how to use a weak entity to represent the multi-value composite attribute Phone that contains the single-value attributes AreaCode, PhoneNumber. Assume Phone appears in an entity called SALESPERSON. Indicate both the maximum and minimum cardinalities on both sides of the relationship.

3.20 Describe subtype entities and give an example other than those in this text.

3.21 Explain the term *inheritance* and show how it applies to your answer to Question 3.20.

3.22 Explain the difference between a HAS-A relationship and an IS-A relationship, and give an example of each.

3.23 How are business rules treated in an E-R model?

3.24 Describe why it is important to evaluate a data model once it has been created. Summarize one technique for evaluating a data model, and explain how that technique could be used to evaluate the data model in Figure 3-16.

➤ GROUP II QUESTIONS

3.25 Change the E-R diagram in Figure 3-14 to include an entity LESSON. Let PRIVATE-LESSON and GROUP-LESSON be subtypes of LESSON. Modify the relationships as necessary.

3.26 Change the E-R diagram in Figure 3-14 to exclude TEACHER. Modify the relationships as necessary.

3.27 Which of the models in Figure 3-14 and in your answers to Questions 3.25 and 3.26 do you prefer? Explain the reason for your preference.

3.28 Change the E-R diagram in Figure 3-16 to include subtypes of equipment. Assume that the equipment owned by San Juan Charters pertains to LEASE and that other equipment pertains to BOAT. Model the differences between the BOAT-related EQUIPMENT that is fixed on the boats and the BOAT-related EQUIPMENT that is not fixed. What benefits does the added complexity of this model bring?

➤ PROJECTS

A. Develop an E-R diagram for a database to support the tracking needs of the following organization: The Metropolitan Housing Agency (MHA) is a nonprofit organization that advocates the development and improvement of low-income housing. The MHA operates in a metropolitan area of approximately 2.2 million people in a midwestern city.

The MHA maintains data about the location, availability, and condition of low-income housing in 11 different census tracts in the metropolitan area. Within the boundaries of these tracts are approximately 250 different buildings that provide low-income housing. On average, each building contains 25 apartments or other units.

The MHA keeps data about each census tract, including geographic boundaries, median income of the population, elected officials, principal businesses, principal investors involved in attributes in that tract, and other demographic and economic data. It also maintains a limited amount of data about crime. For each building, the MHA stores the name, address, size, owner(s)'s name and address, mortgagor(s)'s name and address, renovations and repairs, and availability of facilities for handicapped people. In addition, the MHA keeps a list of each of the units within each building, including the type of unit, size, number of bedrooms, number of baths, kitchen and dining facilities, location in the building, and any special remarks. The MHA would like to maintain data regarding the average occupancy rates for each unit, but, to date, it has been unable to collect or store such data. The MHA does, however, keep data about whether a given unit is occupied.

The MHA serves as an information clearinghouse and offers three basic services. First, it works with politicians, lobbyists, and advocacy groups to support legislation that encourages the development of low-income housing through tax incentives, developmental zoning preferences, and other legislative inducements. To accomplish this, the MHA provides information about low-income housing to state, county, and city governments. Second, through speeches, seminars, displays at conventions, and other public relations activities, the MHA officials strive to raise the community's consciousness about the need for low-income housing. Finally, the MHA provides information about the availability of low-income housing to other agencies that work with the low-income and homeless populations.

B. Access the World Wide Web site for a computer manufacturer such as Dell (www.dell.com). Use the Web site to determine which laptop computer you would buy for a power user who has a budget of $10,000. As you use the Web site, think about the structure of a possible database of computer systems and subsystems to support this site.

Develop an E-R diagram of computer system and subsystem database for this Web site. Show all entities and relationships and at least two or three attributes per entity. Indicate minimum and maximum cardinalities for both sides of each relationship. Possible entities are BASE-SYSTEM, MEMORY-OPTION, VIDEO-CARD, and PRINTER. Of course there are many more possible entities. Model any multi-value attributes as shown in the text. Use subtypes where appropriate. To keep this project from exploding in size, constrain your design to the needs of someone who is making a purchase decision.

 C. Access the Web site for a bookseller such as Amazon (www.amazon.com). Use the Web site to determine the three best books on XML (Extended Markup Language) for someone who is just learning that subject. As you use the Web site, think about the structure of a possible database of books, authors, subjects, and related topics.

Develop an E-R diagram of a book database for this for this Web site. Show all entities and relationships and at least two or three attributes per entity. Indicate minimum and maximum cardinalities for both sides of each relationship. Possible entities are TITLE, AUTHOR, PUBLISHER, COPY, and SUBJECT. Of course there are many more possible entities. Model any multi-value attributes as shown in the text. Use subtypes where appropriate. To keep this project from exploding in size, assume that only books are to be tracked. Further, constrain your design to the needs of someone who is looking for books to purchase. Do not consider customer ordering, order fulfillment, purchase ordering, and other such business processes.

CHAPTER 4

The Semantic Object Model

This chapter discusses the semantic object model, which, like the E-R model discussed in Chapter 3, is used to create data models. As shown in Figure 4-1, the development team interviews users; analyzes the users' reports, forms, and queries; and from these constructs a model of the users' data. This data model is later transformed into a database design.

The particular form of the data model depends on the constructs used to build it. If an E-R model is used, the model will have entities, relationships, and the like. If a semantic model is used, the model will have semantic objects and related constructs, which are discussed in this chapter.

The E-R model and the semantic object model are like lenses through which the database developers look when studying and documenting the users' data. Both lenses work, and they both ultimately result in a database design. They use different lenses to form that design, however, and because the lenses create different images, the designs they produce may not be exactly the same. When developing a database, you must decide which approach to use, just as a photographer needs to decide which lens to use. Each approach has strengths and weaknesses, which we discuss at the end of this chapter.

The semantic object model was first presented in the third edition of this text, in 1988. It is based on concepts that were developed and published by Codd and by Hammer and McLeod.[1] The semantic object model is a data model. It is different from **object-oriented database processing**, which we

---

[1]E. F. Codd, "Extending the Relational Model to Capture More Meaning," *ACM Transactions on Database Systems*, December 1976, pp. 397–424; and Michael Hammer and Dennis McLeod, "Database Description with SDM: A Semantic Database Model," *ACM Transactions on Database Systems*, September 1981, pp. 351–86.

> FIGURE 4-1

Using Different Data Models for Database Designs

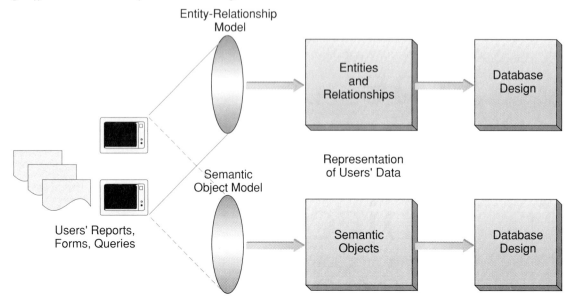

will discuss in Chapter 17. There you will learn how the purposes, features, and constructs of semantic object modeling differ from object-oriented database processing.

> SEMANTIC OBJECTS

The purpose of a database application is to provide forms, reports, and queries so that the users can track entities or objects important to their work. The goals of the early stages of database development are to determine the things to be represented in the database, to specify the characteristics of those things, and to establish the relationships among them.

In Chapter 3, we referred to these things as entities. In this chapter, we refer to them as **semantic objects**, or sometimes as just objects. The word *semantic* means meaning, and a semantic object is one that models, in part, the meaning of the users' data. Semantic objects model the users' perceptions more closely than does the E-R model. We use the adjective *semantic* with the word *object* to distinguish the objects discussed in this chapter from the objects defined in object-oriented programming (OOP) languages.

DEFINING SEMANTIC OBJECTS

Entities and objects are similar in some ways, and they are different in other ways. We begin with the similarities. A semantic object is a representation of some identifiable thing in the users' work environment. More formally, a semantic object is a *named collection of attributes that sufficiently describes a distinct identity*.

Like entities, semantic objects are grouped into classes. An object class has a *name* that distinguishes it from other classes and that corresponds to the names of the things it represents. Thus, a database that supports users who work with student records has an object class called STUDENT. Note that object class names, like entity class names, are spelled with capital letters. A particular semantic object is an instance of the class. Thus, 'William Jones' is an instance of the STUDENT class, and 'Accounting' is an instance of the DEPARTMENT class.

Like entities, an object has a *collection of attributes*. Each attribute represents a characteristic of the identity being represented. For instance, the STUDENT object could have attributes like Name, HomeAddress, CampusAddress, DateOfBirth, DateOfGraduation, and Major. This collection of attributes also is a *sufficient description*, which means that the attributes represent all of the characteristics that the users need in order to do their work. As we stated at the end of Chapter 3, things in the world have an infinite set of characteristics; we cannot represent all of them. Instead, we represent those necessary for the users to satisfy their information needs so that they can successfully perform their jobs. Sufficient description also means that the objects are complete in themselves. All of the data required about a CUSTOMER, for example, is located in the CUSTOMER object, so we need not look anywhere else to find data about CUSTOMERs.

Objects represent *distinct identities*; that is, they are something that users recognize as independent and separate and that users want to track and report. These identities are the nouns about which the information is to be produced. To understand better the term *distinct identity*, recall that there is a difference between objects and object instances. CUSTOMER is the name of an object, and 'CUSTOMER 12345' is the name of an instance of an object. When we say that an object represents a distinct identity, we mean that users consider each *instance* of an object to be unique and identifiable in its own right.

Finally, note that the identities that the objects represent may or may not have a physical existence. For example, EMPLOYEEs physically exist, but ORDERs do not. Orders are, themselves, models of a contractual agreement to provide certain goods or services under certain terms and conditions. They are not physical things but, rather, representations of agreements. Thus, something need not be physical in order to be considered an object; it need only be identifiable in its own right in the minds of the users.

ATTRIBUTES

Semantic objects have attributes that define their characteristics. There are three types of attributes. **Simple attributes** have a single value. Examples are DateOfHire, InvoiceNumber, and SalesTotal. **Group attributes** are composites of other attributes. One example is Address, which contains the attributes {Street, City, State, Zip}; another example is FullName, which contains the attributes {FirstName, MiddleInitial, LastName}. **Semantic object attributes** are attributes that establish a relationship between one semantic object and another.

To understand these statements better, look at Figure 4-2(a), which is an example of a **semantic object diagram**, or **object diagram.** Such diagrams are used by development teams to summarize the structures of objects and to present them visually. Objects are shown in portrait-oriented rectangles. The name of the object appears at the top, and attributes are written in order after the object name.

The DEPARTMENT object contains an example of each of the three types of attributes. DepartmentName, PhoneNumber, and FaxPhoneNumber are simple attributes, each of which represents a single data element. CampusAddress is a group attribute containing the simple attributes Building and OfficeNumber. Finally, COLLEGE, PROFESSOR, and STUDENT each are semantic object attributes, which means that those objects are connected to and logically contained in DEPARTMENT.

The object attributes, or **object links** as they are sometimes called, mean that when a user thinks about a DEPARTMENT, he or she thinks not only about

DEPARTMENT Object Diagram: (a) DEPARTMENT Object and (b) DEPARTMENT Object with Cardinalities

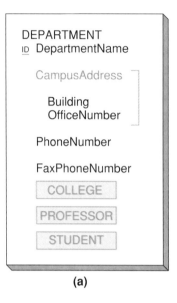

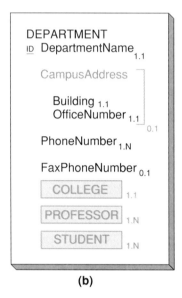

(a)　　　　　　　　　　　(b)

DepartmentName, CampusAddress, PhoneNumber, and FaxPhoneNumber but also about the COLLEGE, PROFESSORs, and STUDENTs who are related to that department. Since COLLEGE, PROFESSOR, and STUDENT also are objects, the complete data model contains object diagrams for them, too. The COLLEGE object contains attributes of the college; the PROFESSOR object contains attributes of the faculty; and the STUDENT object contains attributes of the students.

ATTRIBUTE CARDINALITY Each attribute in a semantic object has both a minimum cardinality and a maximum cardinality. The minimum cardinality indicates the number of instances of the attribute that must exist in order for the object to be valid. Usually this number is either 0 or 1. If it is 0, the attribute is not required to have a value. If it is 1, the attribute must have a value. Although it is unusual, the minimum cardinality can sometimes be larger than 1. For example, the attribute PLAYER in an object called BASKETBALL-TEAM might have a minimum cardinality of 5, since this is the smallest number of players required to make up a basketball team.

The maximum cardinality indicates the maximum number of instances of the attribute that the object may have. It is usually either 1 or N. If it is 1, the attribute can have no more than one instance; if it is N, the attribute can have many values, and the absolute number is not specified. Sometimes the maximum cardinality is a specific number such as 5, meaning the object can contain no more than exactly five instances of the attribute. For example, the attribute PLAYER in BASKETBALL-TEAM might have a maximum cardinality of 15, which would indicate that no more than 15 players could be assigned to a team's roster.

Cardinalities are shown as subscripts of attributes in the format **N.M,** where N is the minimum cardinality and M is the maximum. In Figure 4-2(b), the minimum cardinality of DepartmentName is 1 and the maximum is also 1, which means that exactly one value of DepartmentName is required. The cardinality of PhoneNumber is 1.N, meaning that a DEPARTMENT is required to have at least one PhoneNumber but may have many. The cardinality of 0.1 in FaxPhoneNumber means that a DEPARTMENT may have either zero or one FaxPhoneNumber.

The cardinalities of groups and the attributes in groups can be subtle. Consider the attribute CampusAddress. Its cardinalities are 0.1, meaning a DEPARTMENT need not have an address and has at most one. Now examine the attributes inside CampusAddress. Both Building and OfficeNumber have the cardinalities 1.1. You might be wondering how a group can be optional if the attributes in that group are required. The answer is that the cardinalities operate only between the attribute and the container of that attribute. The minimum cardinality of CampusAddress indicates that there need not be a value for address in DEPARTMENT. But the minimum cardinalities of OfficeNumber and Building indicate that both OfficeNumber and Building must exist in CampusAddress. Thus a CampusAddress group need not appear, but if one does, it must have a value for both OfficeNumber and Building.

OBJECT INSTANCES   The object diagrams for DEPARTMENT shown in Figure 4-2 are a format, or general structure, that can be used for any department. An instance of the DEPARTMENT object is shown in Figure 4-3, with each attribute's value for a particular department. The DepartmentName is Information Systems, and it is located in Room 213 of the Social Science Building. Observe that there are three values for PhoneNumber—the Information Systems Department has three phone lines in its office. Other departments may have fewer or more, but every department has at least one.

Furthermore, there is one instance of COLLEGE, the College of Business, and there are multiple values for the PROFESSOR and STUDENT object attributes. Each of these object attributes is a complete object; each has all the attributes defined for an object of that type. To keep this diagram simple, only the identifying names are shown for each of the instances of object attribute.

An object diagram is a picture of the user's perception of an object in the work environment. Thus, in the user's mind, the DEPARTMENT object includes all of this data. A DEPARTMENT logically contains data about the COLLEGE in which it resides, as well as the PROFESSORs and STUDENTs who are related to that department.

PAIRED ATTRIBUTES   The semantic object model has no one-way object relationships. If an object contains another object, the second object will contain the first. For example, if DEPARTMENT contains the object attribute COLLEGE, then COLLEGE will contain the matching object attribute DEPARTMENT. These object attributes are called **paired attributes**, since they always occur as a pair.

Why must object attributes be paired? The answer lies in the way in which human beings think about relationships. If Object A has a relationship with Object B, then Object B will have a relationship with Object A. At the least, B is related to A in the relationship of "things that are related to B." If this argument seems obscure, try to envision a one-way relationship between two objects. It cannot be done.

An Instance of the DEPARTMENT Object in Figure 4-2

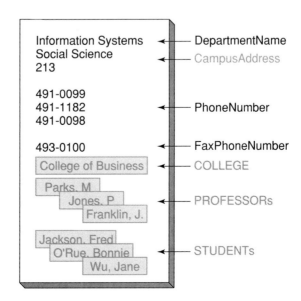

OBJECT IDENTIFIERS

An **object identifier** is one or more object attributes that the users employ to identify object instances. Such identifiers are potential names for a semantic object. In CUSTOMER, for example, possible identifiers are CustomerID and CustomerName. Each of these are attributes that users consider to be valid names of CUSTOMER instances. Compare these identifiers with attributes like DateOfFirstOrder, StockPrice, and NumberOfEmployees. Such attributes are not identifiers because the users do not think of them as names of CUSTOMER instances.

A **group identifier** is an identifier that has more than one attribute. Examples are {FirstName, LastName}, {FirstName, PhoneNumber} and {State, License Number}.

Object identifiers may or may not be unique, depending on how the users view their data. For example, InvoiceNumber is a unique identifier for ORDER, but StudentName is not a unique identifier for STUDENT. There may, for example, be two students named 'Mary Smith.' If so, the users will employ StudentName to identify a group of one or more students and then, if necessary, use values of other attributes to identify a particular member of that set.

In semantic object diagrams, object identifiers are denoted by the letters *ID* in front of the attribute. If the identifier is unique, these letters will be underlined. In Figure 4-2(b), for example, the attribute DepartmentName is a unique identifier of DEPARTMENT.

Normally, if an attribute is to be used as an identifier, its value is required. Also, generally there is no more than one value of an identifier attribute for a given object. In most cases, therefore, the cardinality of an ID attribute is 1.1, and so we use this value as a default.

There are (relatively few) cases, however, in which the cardinality of an identifier is other than 1.1. Consider, for example, the attribute Alias in the semantic object PERSON. A person need not have an alias, or he or she may have several aliases. Hence, the cardinality of Alias would be 0.N.

Showing the subscripts of all attributes clutters the semantic object diagram. To simplify, we will assume the cardinalities of simple-value identifier attributes are 1.1 and the cardinalities of other simple-value attributes are 0.1. If the cardinality of the simple-value attribute is other than these assumptions, we will show it on the diagram. Otherwise subscripts on simple-value attributes will be omitted.

ATTRIBUTE DOMAINS

The **domain** of an attribute is a description of an attribute's possible values. The characteristics of a domain depend on the type of the attribute. The domain of a simple attribute consists of both a physical and a semantic description. The physical description indicates the type of data (for example, numeric versus string), the length of the data, and other restrictions or constraints (such as the first character must be alphabetic, or the value must not exceed 9999.99). The semantic description indicates the function or purpose of the attribute—it distinguishes this attribute from other attributes that might have the same physical description.

For example, the domain of DepartmentName could be defined as "the set of strings of up to seven characters that represent names of departments at Highline University." The phrase *strings of up to seven characteristics* is the physical description of the domain, and the phrase *that represent names of departments at Highline University* is the semantic description. The semantic description differentiates strings of seven characters that represent names of departments from similar strings that represent, say, names of courses or buildings or some other attribute.

In some cases, the physical description of a simple attribute domain is an **enumerated list,** the set of an attribute's specific values. The domain of the attribute PartColor, for example, might be the enumerated list {'Blue', 'Yellow', 'Red'}.

The domain of a group attribute also has a physical and a semantic description. The physical description is a list of all of the attributes in the group and the order of those attributes. The semantic description is the function or purpose of the group. Thus the physical domain description of CampusAddress (in Figure 4-2) is the list {OfficeNumber, Building}; the semantic description is *the location of an office at Highline University.*

The domain of an object attribute is the set of object instances of that type. In Figure 4-2, for example, the domain of the PROFESSOR object attribute is the set of all PROFESSOR object instances in the database. The domain of the COLLEGE object is the set of all COLLEGEs in the database. In a sense, the domain of an object attribute is a dynamically enumerated list; the list contains all of the object instances of a particular type.

SEMANTIC OBJECT VIEWS

Users access the values of object attributes through database applications that provide data entry forms, reports, and queries. In most cases, such forms, reports, and queries do not require access to all of an object's attributes. For example, Figure 4-4 shows two application views of DEPARTMENT. Some attributes of DEPARTMENT (its DepartmentName, for example) are visible in both application views. Other attributes are visible in only one. For example, STUDENT is seen only in the StudentListing View, but PROFESSOR is visible in only the Staff View.

The portion of an object that is visible to a particular application is called the **semantic object view** or simply the **view.** A view consists of the name of the object plus a list of all of the attributes visible from that view.

Views are used in two ways. When you are developing a database, you can use them to develop the data model. Look at Figure 4-1 again. As shown, when developing the data model, the database and application developers work backward. That is, they begin with the forms, reports, and queries that the users say they need and then work backward to the database design. To do this, the team selects a required form, report, or query and determines the view that must exist in order for the form, report, or query to be created. Then the team selects the next form, report, or query and does the same. These two views are then integrated. This process is repeated until the structure of the entire database has been created.

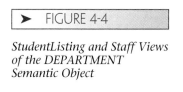

StudentListing and Staff Views of the DEPARTMENT Semantic Object

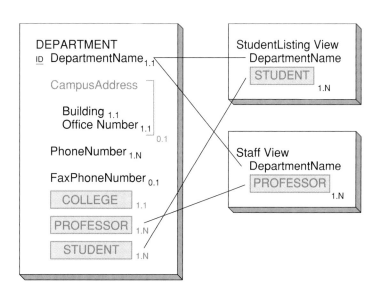

The second way in which views are used occurs after the database structure has been created. At this point, views are constructed to support new forms, reports, and queries based on the existing database structure. Examples of this second use are shown in Part IV when we discuss database implementation.

➤ CREATING DATA MODELS WITH SEMANTIC OBJECTS

This section illustrates a process for developing semantic objects in which the developers examine the application interface—forms, reports, and queries—and work backward (or reverse-engineer) to derive the object structure. For example, to model the structure of a DEPARTMENT object, we first gather all of the reports, forms, and queries based on DEPARTMENT. From them, we define a DEPARTMENT object that enables those reports, forms, and queries to be constructed.

For a totally new application, however, there will be no computer-based reports, forms, or queries to examine. In this case, the developers begin by determining what objects the users need to track. Then through interviews with the users, the team finds out what object attributes are important. From this, prototypes of forms and reports can be constructed that are then used to refine the data model.

AN EXAMPLE: THE HIGHLINE UNIVERSITY ADMINISTRATION DATABASE

Suppose that the administration at Highline University wants to keep track of department, faculty, and student major data. Suppose further that the application needs to produce four reports (Figures 4–5, 4–7, 4–9, and 4–11). Our goal is to examine these reports and, using reverse engineering, determine the objects and attributes that must be stored in the database.

THE COLLEGE OBJECT   The example report in Figure 4-5 is about a college—specifically, the College of Business. This example is only one instance of the report; Highline University has similar reports about other colleges, such as the College of Arts and Sciences and the College of Social Sciences. When creating a data model, it is important to gather enough examples to form a representative sample of all of the college reports. Here we assume that the report in Figure 4-5 is representative.

In examining the report, we find data specific to the college—such as the name, dean, telephone number, and campus address—and also facts about each of the departments within the college. This *suggests* that the database might contain COLLEGE and DEPARTMENT objects, with a relationship between the two.

➤ FIGURE 4-5

Example COLLEGE Report

College of Business
Mary B. Jefferson, Dean

Phone: 232-1187

Campus Address:
Business Building, Room 100

Department	Chairperson	Phone	Total Majors
Accounting	Jackson, Seymour P.	232-1841	318
Finance	HeuTeng, Susan	232-1414	211
Info Systems	Brammer, Nathaniel D.	236-0011	247
Management	Tuttle, Christine A.	236-9988	184
Production	Barnes, Jack T.	236-1184	212

➤ FIGURE 4-6

First Version of COLLEGE and
DEPARTMENT Objects

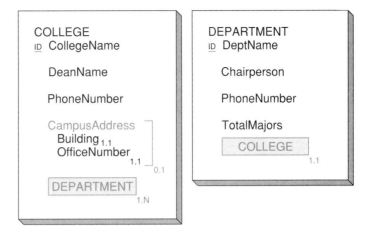

These preliminary findings are documented in the object diagrams in Figure 4-6. Notice that we have omitted cardinalities from simple attributes having a cardinality of 0.1.

The cardinality of DEPARTMENT within COLLEGE is 1.N, indicating that a COLLEGE must have at least one DEPARTMENT and that it may have many. This minimum cardinality cannot be deduced from the report in Figure 4-5; rather, it was obtained by asking the users whether or not a college could exist with no departments. Their answer was no.

Also note that the structure of DEPARTMENT is inferred from the data shown in Figure 4-5. Since object attributes are always paired, COLLEGE is shown in DEPARTMENT, even though, strictly speaking, this fact cannot be determined from Figure 4-5. As with the DEPARTMENT attribute in COLLEGE, the users were asked to determine the cardinalities of the COLLEGE attribute. They are 1.1, meaning that a DEPARTMENT must be related to one, and only one, COLLEGE.

As an aside, we have interpreted the report in Figure 4-5 to mean that the groups of repeating data refer to DEPARTMENT as an independent object. In fact, such repeating groups are often a signal that another object exists. *This is not always the case, however.* The repeating group can also be a group attribute that happens to have several values.

You may be wondering how to tell the difference between repeating-object data and repeating-group data. There is no hard and fast rule, because the answer depends on the ways that the users view their world. Consequently, the best approach is to consult the users about the semantics of the data. Ask whether these repeating-group data are only a part of the college or whether they refer to something else that stands on its own. If the former, they constitute a group attribute; if the latter, a semantic object. Also, look for other reports (or forms or queries). Do the users have one for departments? If so, then the assumption that DEPARTMENT is a semantic object would be confirmed. In fact, the personnel at Highline use two reports regarding DEPARTMENTs. This fact further substantiates the notion that a DEPARTMENT object must be defined.

Also, groups of attributes that represent an independent object generally have obvious identifying attribute(s). Automobiles have a VINNumber or LicenseNumber; products have a ProductNumber or SKU. Orders have an OrderNumber. However, the group of attributes {DateOfMeasure, TirePressure} does not have an obvious identifier. When you ask a user about that group's identifier, he or she will say something like "Tire pressure of what?" It will be tire pressure of a car or a truck or a trailer or some vehicle. Hence, such a group would be a group attribute within another object—the object that is the answer to the "of what" question.

*Example DEPARTMENT
Report*

**Information Systems Department
College of Business**

Chairperson: Brammer, Nathaniel D
Phone: 236-0011
Campus Address: Social Science Building, Room 213

Professor	Office	Phone
Jones, Paul D.	Social Science, 219	232-7713
Parks, Mary B	Social Science, 308	232-5791
Wu, Elizabeth	Social Science, 207	232-9112

THE DEPARTMENT OBJECT   The department report shown in Figure 4-7 contains departmental data, along with a list of the professors who are assigned to those departments. Note that this report contains data concerning the department's campus address. Since these data do not appear in the object in Figure 4-6, we need to add them to the DEPARTMENT object, as has been done in Figure 4-8. This adjustment is typical of the data modeling process. That is, the semantic objects are continually adjusted as new reports, forms, and queries are identified and analyzed.

THE PROFESSOR OBJECT   The report in Figure 4-7 not only indicates that a DEPARTMENT object needs to be modeled but also, it suggests that another object may be needed to represent professor data. Accordingly, a PROFESSOR object was added to the model, as shown in Figure 4-8. The ID of PROFESSOR, which is ProfessorName, is not unique; this is denoted by not underlining the ID in Figure 4-8.

According to the object diagrams in Figure 4-8, a DEPARTMENT must have at least one PROFESSOR and may have several, but a PROFESSOR must have one, and only one, DEPARTMENT. Thus, according to this model, joint appointments are prohibited. This restriction is part of the business rules that must be obtained from interviews with the users.

Figure 4-9 shows a second report about a department. This one concerns a department and the students who major in that area. Having two reports about an object is typical; they are simply documenting different views of the same thing. Moreover, the existence of this second report strengthens the notion that department is an object in the minds of the users.

THE STUDENT OBJECT   The report in Figure 4-9 gives data about students who major in a department's area, implying that students are also an object.

*Adjusted DEPARTMENT and
New PROFESSOR Objects*

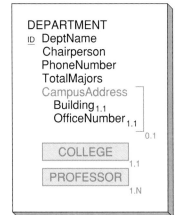

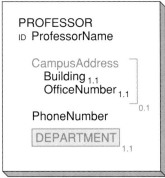

➤ FIGURE 4-9

*Second Example
DEPARTMENT Report*

**Student Major List
Information Systems Department**

Chairperson: Brammer, Nathaniel D   Phone: 236-0011

Major's Name	Student Number	Phone
Jackson, Robin R.	12345	237-8713
Lincoln, Fred J.	48127	237-8713
Madison, Janice A.	37512	237-8713

Therefore the DEPARTMENT object must contain a STUDENT object as well as a PROFESSOR object, as in Figure 4-10.

The STUDENT object in Figure 4-10 contains the attributes StudentName, StudentNumber, and PhoneNumber, the attributes listed on the report in Figure 4-9. Note that both StudentName and StudentNumber are identifiers. StudentNames are not unique, but StudentNumbers are.

Figure 4-11 is an example of another report about a student—the acceptance letter that Highline sends to its incoming students. Even though this is a letter, it is also a report; the letter was probably produced using mail merge with a word-processing program.

Those data items in the letter that should be stored in the database are shown in boldface type. In addition to data regarding the student, the letter also contains data regarding the student's major DEPARTMENT and the student's adviser. Since an adviser is a PROFESSOR, this letter substantiates the need for a separate PROFESSOR object. Object diagrams from the revised PROFESSOR and STUDENT objects are shown in Figure 4-12. According to the STUDENT object, both DEPARTMENT and PROFESSOR are single value (they have a maximum cardinality of 1). Hence, a student at this university has, at most, one major department and one adviser and is required to have both.

The STUDENT object in Figure 4-12 corresponds to the data shown in the letter in Figure 4-11. It may turn out, however, that the student actually has more than one major, in which case both PROFESSOR and STUDENT would be multivalue. This fact cannot be determined from this single form letter, so additional letters and interviews are needed to find out whether multiple majors are permitted. Here we assume that only one major is allowed.

➤ FIGURE 4-10

*Adjusted DEPARTMENT and
New STUDENT Objects*

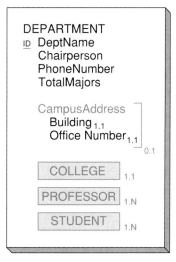

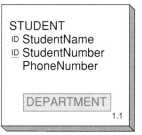

Acceptance Letter

Mr. Fred Parks
123 Elm Street
Los Angeles, CA 98002

Dear **Mr. Parks**:

You have been admitted as a major in the **Accounting** Department at Highline University, starting in the **Fall Semester**, **2000**. The office of the Accounting Department is located in the **Business** Building, Room **210**.

Your adviser is professor **Elizabeth Johnson**, whose telephone number is **232-8740** and whose office is located in the **Business** building, Room **227**. Please schedule an appointment with your adviser as soon as you arrive on campus.

Congratulations and welcome to Highline University!

Sincerely,

Jan P. Smathers
President

JPS/rkp

The format of the student's name is given first in the format *first name last name* at the top of the letter and then in the format *last name* in the salutation. If presenting names in this format is a requirement, then the single attribute StudentName (in Figure 4-10) will not suffice, and instead the group FirstName, LastName must be defined. This has been done in Figure 4-12. Note also that the adviser's name is in the format {first name, last name}, which means that the name of PROFESSOR should be changed as well.

In addition, this letter indicates that names in addresses and salutations must be preceded by the title 'Mr.' or 'Ms.' If this is to be done, an additional attribute must be placed in STUDENT. One alternative is to record the gender of the stu-

➤ FIGURE 4-12

Adjusted PROFESSOR and STUDENT Objects

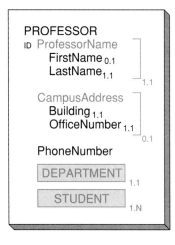

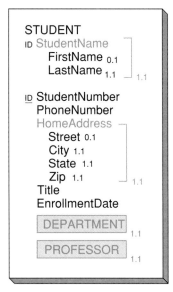

dent and to select the title based on this attribute. Another alternative is to store the title itself. The advantage of this second alternative is that titles other than 'Mr.' and 'Ms.', such as 'Dr.', can be stored.

As currently documented, the model does not require a title other than Mr. or Ms. It seems plausible, however, that additional titles might be needed; hence, the second alternative seems more robust, and therefore the attribute Title has been added to STUDENT in Figure 4-12.

Again, these changes illustrate the iterative nature of data modeling. Design decisions often need to be rethought and revised again and again. Such iteration does not mean that the design process is faulty; in fact, it is typical and expected.

SPECIFYING OBJECTS

Figure 4-13 shows the completed object diagrams for the Highline University database. A few changes have been made: Both DeanName and Chairperson have been modeled in the format {FirstName, LastName} so that all names are in a similar format. And to improve the precision of the model, the PROFESSOR

> FIGURE 4-13

A Complete Set of Semantic Object Diagrams

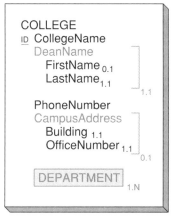

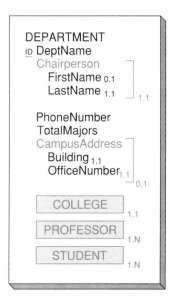

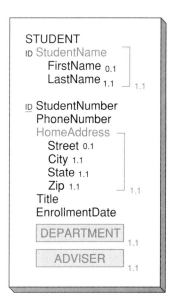

➤ FIGURE 4-14

Object Specifications for the Highline University Database: (a) Semantic Object Specifications and (b) Domain Specifications

Object Name	Property Name	Min Card	Max Card	ID Status	Domain Name
COLLEGE	CollegeName	1	1	ID	CollegeName
	DeanName	1	1		PersonName
	FirstName	0	1		FirstName
	LastName	1	1		LastName
	PhoneNumber	0	1		Phone
	CampusAddress	0	1		CampusAddress
	Building	1	1		Building
	OfficeNumber	1	1		OfficeNumber
	DEPARTMENT	1	N		DEPARTMENT
DEPARTMENT	DeptName	1	1	ID	DeptName
	Chairperson	1	1		PersonName
	FirstName	0	1		FirstName
	LastName	1	1		LastName
	PhoneNumber	0	1		Phone
	TotalMajors	0	1		MajorCount
	CampusAddress	0	1		CampusAddress
	Building	1	1		Building
	OfficeNumber	1	1		OfficeNumber
	COLLEGE	1	1		COLLEGE
	PROFESSOR	1	N		PROFESSOR
	STUDENT	1	N		STUDENT
PROFESSOR	ProfessorName	1	1	ID	PersonName
	FirstName	0	1		FirstName
	LastName	1	1		LastName
	CampusAddress	0	1		CampusAddress
	Building	1	1		Building
	OfficeNumber	1	1		OfficeNumber
	PhoneNumber	0	1		Phone
	DEPARTMENT	1	1		DEPARTMENT
	ADVISER	1	N		STUDENT
STUDENT	StudentName	1	1	ID	PersonName
	FirstName	0	1		FirstName
	LastName	1	1		LastName
	StudentNumber	1	1	ID	StudentNumber
	PhoneNumber	0	1		Phone
	HomeAddress	1	1		Address
	Title	0	1		Title
	EnrollmentDate	0	1		QuarterDate
	DEPARTMENT	1	1		DEPARTMENT
	ADVISER	1	1		PROFESSOR

(a)

attribute in STUDENT has been renamed ADVISER. The PROFESSOR instance that is connected to a STUDENT instance through this attribute is not just any of the STUDENT's professors; it is the particular PROFESSOR who serves as that STUDENT's adviser, and the term *Adviser* is more precise than the term *PROFESSOR*.

The domain of this attribute is unchanged. The domain of ADVISER is PRO-FESSOR, just as the domain of the attribute PROFESSOR was PROFESSOR. This attribute still points to or connects to instances of the PROFESSOR semantic object. The name change is only that: an improvement in specifying the role that the PROFESSOR domain plays in the STUDENT semantic objects. A similar change was made in PROFESSOR. The STUDENT attribute was renamed ADVISEE, but this attribute is still connected to objects from the STUDENT domain.

Figure 4-14 presents a tabular specification of the data model. The semantic objects and attributes are defined in the semantic object specification, and the

➤ FIGURE 4-14

(Continued)

Domain Name	Type[a]	Semantic Description	Physical Description
Address	G	A U.S. address	Street City State Zip
Building	S	A name of a building on campus	Text 20
CampusAddress	G	An address on campus	Building OfficeNumber
City	S	A city name	Text 25
COLLEGE	SO	One of Highline's ten colleges	See semantic object specification table
CollegeName	S	The official name of a college at Highline	Text 25
DEPARTMENT	SO	An academic department on campus	See semantic object specification table
DeptName	S	The official name of an academic department	Text 25
FirstName	S	The first-name portion of PersonName	Text 20
LastName	S	The last-name portion of PersonName	Text 30
MajorCount	F	Count of the students assigned to a given department	Integer; values {0 to 999}; format 999.
OfficeNumber	S	The number of an office on campus	Text 4
PersonName	G	First and last names of an administrator, professor, or student	FirstName LastName
Phone	S	Phone number within local area code	Text 4
PROFESSOR	SO	The name of a full-time member of Highline's faculty	See semantic object specification table
QuarterDate	S	An academic quarter and year	Text 3; values {$q99$, where q = one of {'F', 'W', 'S', 'M'} and 99 is decimal number from 00 to 99.}
State	S	A two-digit state abbreviation	Text 2
Street	S	A street address	Text 30
STUDENT	SO	A person who has been admitted for study at Highline	See semantic object specification table
StudentNumber	S	The ID assigned to a student admitted to Highline	Integer; values {10000 to 99999}; format 99999
Title	S	The title of individuals to be used in addresses	Text 3; values {Mr., Ms.}
Zip	S	A nine-digit zip code	Text 10; format 99999-9999

[a]F = formula
G = Group
S = Simple
SO = semantic object

domains are defined in the domain specification. The first table is an alternative presentation of the information in the semantic object diagrams, and its interpretation is straightforward.

The second table, the domain table, supplies information about domains that is not available from the semantic object diagrams. As we stated earlier, a domain has both a semantic and a physical description. The semantic description of each domain is shown in the Description column, and the physical description is shown in the Specification column. The Description column is self-explanatory.

The specification for domains includes a physical description and, in some cases, a set of values and a format. StudentNumber, for example, is specified as integer with values between 10,000 and 99,999 and with a format of five decimal digits. (In this table, a 9 in a format specification means a decimal digit.) Other domains are documented in a similar way. Title is an example of an enumerated domain whose values for Title are Mr., Ms. The physical description of a group domain consists of a list of the domains included in the group. The physical description of a semantic object domain is just a reference to the semantic object description.

The domain of TotalMajors is an example of a fourth type of domain, the **formula domain.** Formulas represent attributes computed from other values. The MajorCount domain is the count of the STUDENT objects that are connected to a given DEPARTMENT object. We shall not try to document the means by which this computation is to be carried out in the domain definition. At this point, all that is important is documenting the need for and the specification of the formula.

➤ TYPES OF OBJECTS

This section describes and illustrates seven types of objects. For each type, we examine a report or form and show how to model that report or form with an object. Later, in Chapter 7, we transform each of these types of objects into database designs.

Three new terms are used in this section. A **single-value attribute** is an attribute whose maximum cardinality is 1. A **multi-value attribute** is one whose maximum cardinality is greater than 1. And a **nonobject attribute** is a simple or group attribute.

SIMPLE OBJECTS

A **simple object** is a semantic object that contains only single-value, nonobject attributes. An example is shown in Figure 4-15. Part (a) of this figure shows two instances of a report called an *Equipment Tag*. Such tags are applied to items of office equipment in order to help keep track of inventory. These tags can be considered a report.

Figure 4-15(b) shows a simple object, EQUIPMENT, that models Equipment Tag. The attributes of the object include the items shown on the tag: EquipmentNumber, Description, AcquisitionDate, and PurchaseCost. Note that none of these attributes is multi-value, and none is an object attribute. Hence, EQUIPMENT is a simple object.

COMPOSITE OBJECTS

A **composite object** is a semantic object that contains one or more multi-value, nonobject attributes. The Hotel Bill shown in Figure 4-16(a) gives rise to the need for a composite object. The bill includes data that concerns the bill as a whole:

➤ FIGURE 4-15

Example of a Simple Object: (a) Reports Based on a Simple Object and (b) EQUIPMENT Simple Object

(a)

(b)

InvoiceNumber, ArrivalDate, CustomerName, and TotalDue. It also contains a group of attributes that is repeated for services provided to the guest. Each group includes ServiceDate, ServiceDescription, and Price.

Figure 4-16(b) shows an object diagram for the HOTEL-BILL object. The attribute LineItem is a group attribute having a maximum cardinality of N, which means that the group ServiceDate, ServiceDescription, Price can occur many times in an instance of the HOTEL-BILL semantic object.

LineItem is not modeled as an independent semantic object; instead, it is considered to be an attribute within a HOTEL-BILL. This design is appropriate because the hotel does not view one line of a guest's charges as a separate thing, so line items on the guest's bill do not have identifiers of their own. No employee attempts to enter a LineItem except in the context of a bill. The employee enters

➤ FIGURE 4-16

Example of a Composite Object: (a) Report Based on a Composite Object and (b) HOTEL-BILL Composite Object

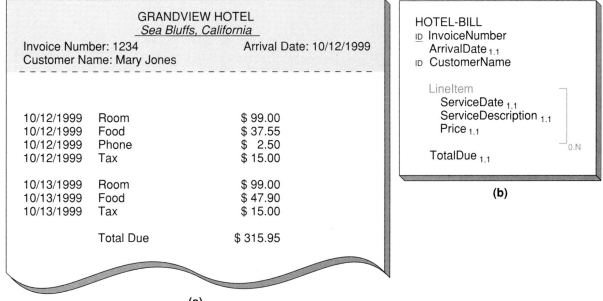

(b)

(a)

the data for bill number 1234 and then, in the context of that bill, enters the charges. Or the employee retrieves an existing bill and enters additional charges in the context of that bill.

The minimum cardinality of LineItem is 0, which means that a HOTEL-BILL object can exist without any LineItem data. This allows a bill to be started when the customer checks in and before there are any charges. If the minimum cardinality were 1, then no HOTEL-BILL could be started until there was at least one charge. This design decision must be made in light of the business rules. It may be that the hotel's policy is not to start the bill until there has been a charge. If so, then the minimum cardinality of LineItem should be 1.

A composite object can have more than one multi-value attribute. Figure 4-17(a) shows a hotel bill that has a multi-value attribute for CustomerName, as well as a multi-value group for service charges. Each of these groups is independent of the other. The second instance of CustomerName, for example, is not logically associated with the second LineItem.

Figure 4-17(b) is an object diagram for the hotel bill in Figure 4-17(a). CustomerName is shown as a multi-value attribute. It is not included in the bracket of service charges because the repetitions of CustomerName have nothing to do with the repetitions of services. The two are independent, as we just noted.

Both simple and group attributes can be multi-value. In Figure 4-17(a), for example, CustomerName is a multi-value, simple attribute. By itself, it is sufficient for the object to be considered a composite object.

Multi-value attributes can also be nested within one another. For example, suppose it is important to keep track of individual expenses within a LineItem. In the form in Figure 4-18(a), the charges are subdivided. Food, for example, is broken down by meal. An object diagram for such nested attributes is presented in Figure 4-18(b) and shows that any service charge can have subitems.

➤ FIGURE 4-17

A Composite Object with Two Groups: (a) HOTEL-BILL with Multivalued Customer Names and (b) HOTEL-BILL with Two Multivalued Groups

GRANDVIEW HOTEL
Sea Bluffs, California

Invoice Number: 1234		Arrival Date: 10/12/1999
Customer Name:	Mary Jones	
	Fred Jones	
	Sally Jones	

10/12/1999	Room	$ 99.00
10/12/1999	Food	$ 37.55
10/12/1999	Phone	$ 2.50
10/12/1999	Tax	$ 15.00
10/13/1999	Room	$ 99.00
10/13/1999	Food	$ 47.90
10/13/1999	Tax	$ 15.00
	Total Due	$ 315.95

(a)

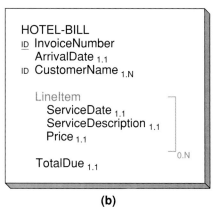

(b)

> ➤ FIGURE 4-18

A Composite Object with Nested Groups: (a) HOTEL-BILL with Service Subdescriptions and (b) HOTEL-BILL with Nested Multivalued Groups

GRANDVIEW HOTEL
Sea Bluffs, California

Invoice Number: 1234   Arrival Date: 10/12/1999
Customer Name: Mary Jones

- -

10/12/1999	Room		$ 99.00
10/12/1999	Food		
	Breakfast	$ 15.25	
	Dinner	$ 22.30	
			$ 37.55
10/12/1999	Phone		$ 2.50
10/12/1999	Tax		$ 15.00
10/13/1999	Room		$ 99.00
10/13/1999	Food		
	Breakfast	$ 15.25	
	Snack	$ 5.50	
	Dinner	$ 27.15	
			$ 47.90
10/13/1999	Tax		$ 15.00
	Total Due		$ 315.95

(a)

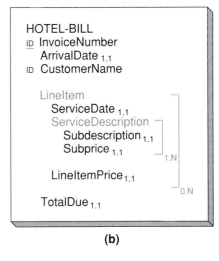

(b)

To repeat, a composite object is an object that contains one or more multi-value simple or group attributes. It has no object attributes.

COMPOUND OBJECTS

A **compound object** contains at least one object attribute. Figure 4-19(a) shows two different data entry forms. One form, used by the company's motor pool, is used to keep track of the vehicles. The second form is used to maintain data about the employees. According to these forms, a vehicle is assigned to at most one employee, and an employee has at most one auto assigned.

We cannot tell from these forms whether an auto must be assigned to an employee or whether every employee must have an auto. To obtain that information, we would have to ask the users in the motor pool or human resources departments. Assume that we find out that an EMPLOYEE need not have a VEHICLE but that a VEHICLE must be assigned to an employee.

Figure 4-19(b) shows object diagrams for EMPLOYEE and VEHICLE. An EMPLOYEE contains VEHICLE as one of its attributes, and VEHICLE, in turn, contains EMPLOYEE as one of its attributes. Since both EMPLOYEE and VEHICLE contain object attributes, they both are compound objects. Furthermore, since neither attribute is multi-value, the relationship from EMPLOYEE to VEHICLE is one to one, or 1:1.

In Figure 4-19(a), the Employee and Vehicle forms contain each other. That is, Vehicle Data has a field Employee assignment, and Employee Work Data has a field Auto assigned. But this is not always the case; sometimes the relationship can appear in only one direction. Consider the report and form in Figure 4-20(a),

➤ FIGURE 4-19

*Compound Objects
with 1:1 Paired
Properties:
(a) Example Vehicle
and Employee Data
Entry Forms and
(b) EMPLOYEE and
VEHICLE Compound
Objects*

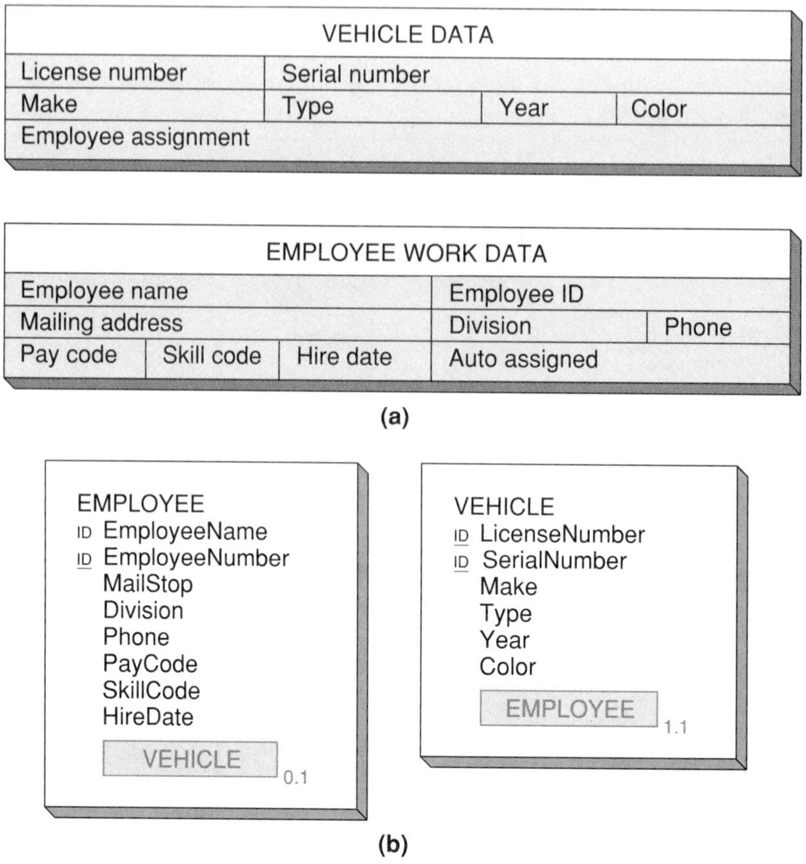

VEHICLE DATA			
License number	Serial number		
Make	Type	Year	Color
Employee assignment			

EMPLOYEE WORK DATA			
Employee name		Employee ID	
Mailing address		Division	Phone
Pay code	Skill code	Hire date	Auto assigned

(a)

EMPLOYEE
ID EmployeeName
ID EmployeeNumber
MailStop
Division
Phone
PayCode
SkillCode
HireDate
VEHICLE 0.1

VEHICLE
ID LicenseNumber
ID SerialNumber
Make
Type
Year
Color
EMPLOYEE 1.1

(b)

which concern two objects: DORMITORY and STUDENT. From the Dormitory Occupancy Report, we can see that users think of a dorm as having attributes regarding the dorm (Name, ResidentAssistant, Phone) and also attributes regarding the students (StudentName, StudentNumber, Class) who live in the dorm.

On the other hand, the Student Data Form shows only student data; it does not include any dormitory data. (The local address might contain a dorm address, but this, if true, is apparently not important enough to document on the form. In a database development project, this possibility should be checked out with the users in an interview. Here we will assume that the Student Data Form does not include dormitory data.)

As we stated earlier, object attributes always occur in pairs. Even if the forms, reports, and queries indicate that only one side of the relationship can be seen, both sides of the relationship always exist. By analogy, a bridge that connects two islands touches both islands and can be used in both directions, even if the bridge is, by custom or law, a one-way bridge.

When no form or report can be found to document one side of a relationship, the development team must ask the users about the cardinality of that relationship. In this case, the team would need to find out how many DORMITORYs a STUDENT could have and whether a STUDENT must be related to a DORMITORY. Here let us suppose the answers to these questions are that a STUDENT is related to just one DORMITORY and may be related to no DORMITORY. Thus in Figure 4-20(b), DORMITORY contains multiple values of STUDENT, and STUDENT contains one value of DORMITORY, so the relationship from DORMITORY to STUDENT is one to many, or 1:N.

A third illustration of compound objects appears in Figure 4-21(a). From these two forms, we can deduce that one book can be written by many authors

➤ FIGURE 4-20

Compound Objects with 1:N Paired Properties: (a) Example Dormitory Report and Student Data Form and (b) DORMITORY and STUDENT Compound Objects

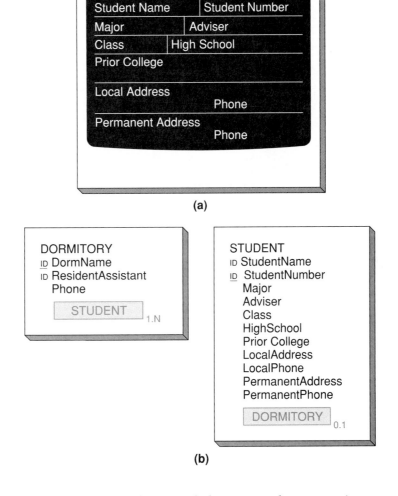

DORMITORY OCCUPANCY REPORT

Dormitory	Resident Assistant	Phone
Ingersoll	Sarah and Allen French	3-5567

Student name	Student Number	Class
Adams, Elizabeth	710	SO
Baker, Rex	104	FR
Baker, Brydie	744	JN
Charles, Stewart	319	SO
Scott, Sally	447	SO
Taylor, Lynne	810	FR

STUDENT DATA FORM

Student Name	Student Number
Major	Adviser
Class	High School
Prior College	
Local Address	
	Phone
Permanent Address	
	Phone

(a)

DORMITORY
ID DormName
ID ResidentAssistant
   Phone

   STUDENT 1.N

STUDENT
ID StudentName
ID StudentNumber
   Major
   Adviser
   Class
   HighSchool
   Prior College
   LocalAddress
   LocalPhone
   PermanentAddress
   PermanentPhone

   DORMITORY 0.1

(b)

(from the Book Stock Data form) and that one author can write many books (from the Books in Stock, by Author form). Thus in Figure 4-21(b), the BOOK object contains many values of AUTHOR, and AUTHOR contains many values of BOOK. Hence the relationship from BOOK to AUTHOR is many to many, or N:M. Furthermore, a BOOK must have an AUTHOR, and an AUTHOR (to be an author) must have written at least one BOOK. Therefore, both of these objects have a minimum cardinality of one.

➤ FIGURE 4-21

Compound Objects with N:M Paired Properties: (a) Bookstore Data Entry Forms and (b) BOOK and AUTHOR Objects

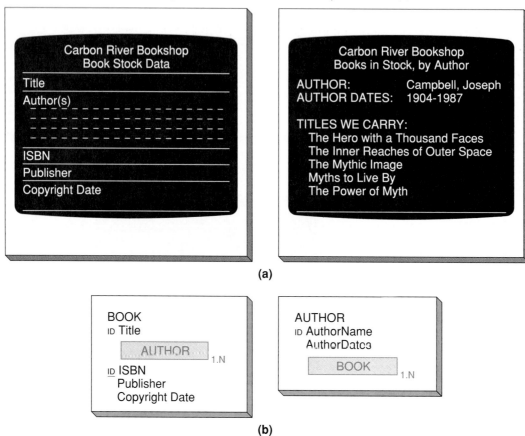

(a)

(b)

Figure 4-22 summarizes the four types of compound objects. In general, OB-JECT-1 can contain a maximum of one or many OBJECT-2s. Similarly, OBJECT-2 can contain one or many OBJECT-1s. We use this table when we discuss database design in Chapter 7.

HYBRID OBJECTS

As the term implies, **hybrid objects** are combinations of objects of two types. In particular, a hybrid object is a semantic object with at least one multi-value group attribute that includes a semantic object attribute.

Figure 4-23(a) is a second version of the report about dormitory occupancy shown in Figure 4-20(a). The difference is that the third column of the student data contains Rent instead of Class. This is an important difference because rent is not an attribute of STUDENT but pertains to the combination of STUDENT and DORMITORY and is an attribute of DORMITORY.

➤ FIGURE 4-22

Four Types of Compound Objects

	Object1 Can Contain		
Object2		One	Many
Can	One	1:1	1:N
Contain	Many	M:1	M:N

DORMITORY Hybrid Object: (a) Dormitory Report with Rent Property, (b) Correct DORMITORY and STUDENT Objects, and (c) Incorrect DORMITORY and STUDENT Objects

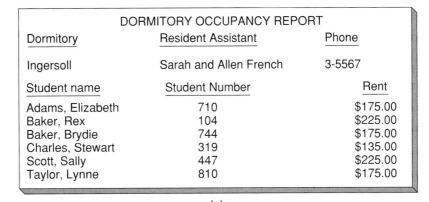

(a)

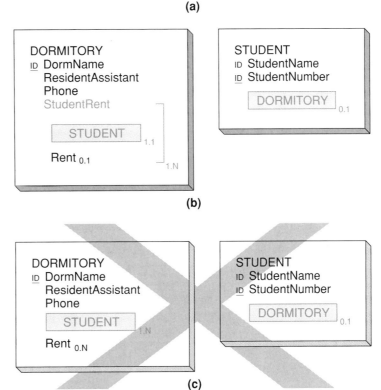

(b)

(c)

Figure 4-23(b) is an object diagram that models this form. DORMITORY contains a multi-value group with both the object attribute STUDENT and the nonobject attribute Rent. This means that Rent is paired with STUDENT in the context of DORMITORY.

Now examine the alternative DORMITORY object in Figure 4-23(c). This is an *incorrect* model of the report in Figure 4-23(a), as it shows that Rent and STUDENT are independently multi-value, which is incorrect because Rent and STUDENT are multi-value as a pair.

Figure 4-24(a) shows a form based on another hybrid object. This Sales Order form contains data about an order (SalesOrderNumber, Date, Subtotal, Tax, and Total), data about a CUSTOMER and a SALESPERSON, and a multi-value group that itself contains data about items on the order. Furthermore, ITEM data (item number, description, and unit price) appear within the multi-value group.

Figure 4-24(b) shows the SALES-ORDER semantic object. It contains the nonobject attributes SalesOrderNumber, Date, Subtotal, Tax, and Total. It also contains the CUSTOMER and SALESPERSON object attributes and a multi-value group that represents each line item on the sales order. The group contains nonobject attributes Quantity and ExtendedPrice and the object attribute ITEM.

The object diagrams in Figure 4-24(b) are ambiguous in one aspect that may or may not be important, depending on the application. According to the ITEM

➤ FIGURE 4-24

Hybrid SALES-ORDER and Related Objects: (a) Sales Order Form and (b) Objects to Model Sales Order Form

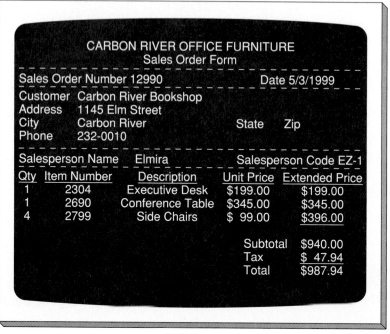

(a)

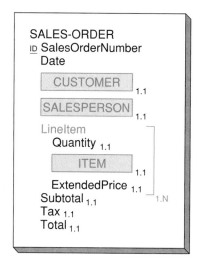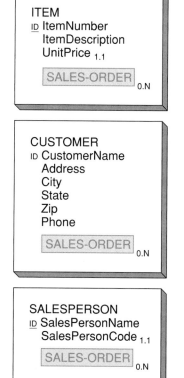

(b)

object diagram, an ITEM can be connected to more than one SALES-ORDER. But since the multi-value group LineItem is encapsulated (hidden within) SALES-ORDER, it is not clear from this diagram whether an ITEM can occur *once or many times* on the same SALES-ORDER.

In general, there are four interpretations of maximum cardinality for the paired attributes in the SALES-ORDER hybrid object:

1. An ITEM can appear on only one SALES-ORDER and in only one of the LineItems within that SALES-ORDER.

2. An ITEM can appear on only one SALES-ORDER but in many different LineItems within that SALES-ORDER.

3. An ITEM can appear on many different SALES-ORDERs but in only one LineItem within each of those SALES-ORDERs.

4. An ITEM can appear on many different SALES-ORDERs and in many different LineItems within those SALES-ORDERs.

When it is important to distinguish among these cases, the following notation should be used: If either Case 1 or 2 is in force, the maximum cardinality of the hybrid object attribute should be set to 1. Thus, for this example, the maximum cardinality of SALES-ORDER in ITEM is set to 1. If an ITEM is to appear in only one LineItem of the SALES-ORDER (Case 1), it should be marked as having a unique ID in that group. Otherwise (Case 2), it need not be marked. These two cases are shown in Figure 4-25 (a) and (b).

If either Case 3 or 4 is in force, the maximum cardinality of the hybrid object attribute is set to N. Thus, for this example, the maximum cardinality of SALES-ORDER in ITEM is set to N. Furthermore, if an ITEM is to appear in only one LineItem of a SALES-ORDER (Case 3), it should be marked as having a unique ID in that group. Otherwise (Case 4), it need not be marked. These two cases are shown in Figure 4-25(c) and (d).

ASSOCIATION OBJECTS

An **association object** is an object that relates two (or more) objects and stores data that are peculiar to that relationship. Figure 4-26(a) on page 99 shows a report and two data entry screens that give rise to the need for an association object. The report contains data about an airline flight and data about the particular airplane and pilot assigned to that flight. The two data entry forms contain data about a pilot and an airplane.

In Figure 4-26(b), the object FLIGHT is an association object that associates the two objects AIRPLANE and PILOT and stores data about their association. FLIGHT contains one each of AIRPLANE and PILOT, but both AIRPLANE and PILOT contain multiple values of FLIGHT. This particular pattern of associating two (or more) objects with data about the association occurs frequently, especially in applications that involve the assignment of two or more things. Other examples are a JOB that assigns an ARCHITECT to a CLIENT, a TASK that assigns an EMPLOYEE to a PROJECT, and a PURCHASE-ORDER that assigns a VENDOR to a SERVICE.

For the example in Figure 4-26, the association object FLIGHT has an identifier of its own, the group {FlightNumber, Date}. Often association objects do not have identifiers of their own, in which case the identifier is the combination of the identifiers of the objects that are associated.

To understand this better, consider Figure 4-27(a) on page 100, which shows a report about the assignment of architects to projects. Although the assignment has no obvious identifier, in fact the identifier is the combination {ProjectName,

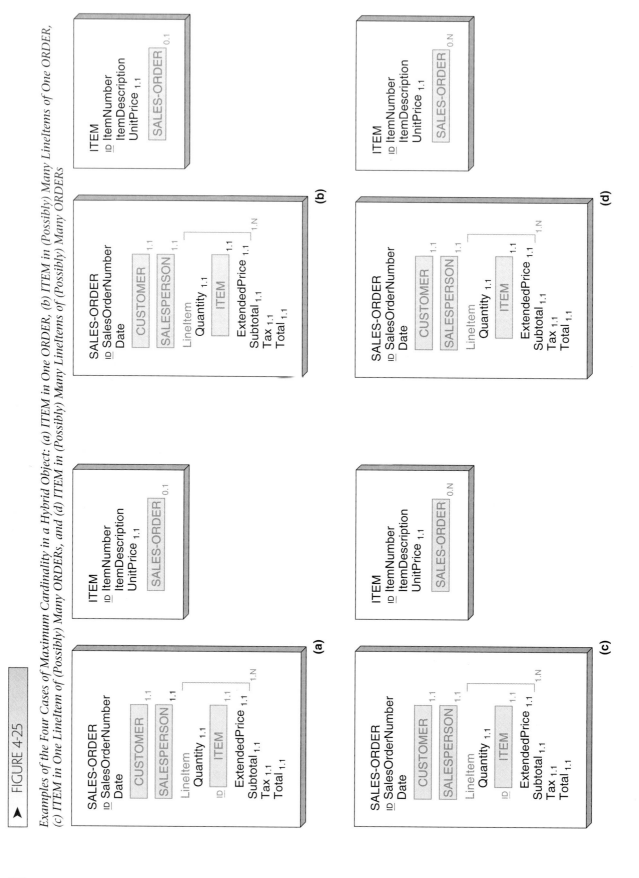

▶ FIGURE 4-25

Examples of the Four Cases of Maximum Cardinality in a Hybrid Object: (a) ITEM in One ORDER, (b) ITEM in (Possibly) Many Lineltems of One ORDER, (c) ITEM in One LineItem of (Possibly) Many ORDERs, and (d) ITEM in (Possibly) Many LineItems of (Possibly) Many ORDERs

➤ FIGURE 4-26

Examples of an Association Object: (a) Example Flight Report and Forms and (b) FLIGHT, PILOT, AIRPLANE Objects

FLY CHEAP INTERNATIONAL
Flight Planning Data Report

FLIGHT NUMBER   *FC-17*   DATE *7/30/2000*
ORIGINATING CITY *Seattle*   DESTINATION *Hong Kong*
FUEL ON TAKEOFF

WEIGHT ON TAKEOFF

AIRPLANE
    Tail Number   *N1234FI*
    Type   *747-SP*
    Capacity   *148*

PILOT
    Name   *Michael Nilson*
    Base   *Los Angeles International*
    FI-ID   *33489-Z*
    Flight Hours   *18,348*

FLY CHEAP INTERNATIONAL
Pilot Summary Data Form

FCI-ID		
Name	Social Security Number	
Address		
City	State	Zip
Phone	Emergency Phone	
Date of Last Checkout	Hours	
Date of Last Physical		

FLY CHEAP INTERNATIONAL
Airplane Data Form

Tail Number: N12324FI
Manufacturer: Boeing
Type: 747-SP
Total Airframe Hours: 112,384
Total Engine Hours: 57,998
Engine Hours Since Overhaul: 3,212
Current Capacity: 148
Range as Configured: 4,200 NM

(a)

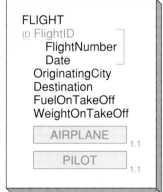

FLIGHT
ID FlightID
    FlightNumber
    Date
OriginatingCity
Destination
FuelOnTakeOff
WeightOnTakeOff

    AIRPLANE   1.1
    PILOT   1.1

AIRPLANE
ID TailNumber
    Manufacturer
    Type
    TotalAirframeHours
    TotalEngineHours
    EngHoursPastOH
    CurrentCapacity
    RangeAsConfig

    FLIGHT   0.N

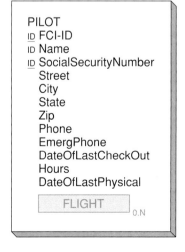

PILOT
ID FCI-ID
ID Name
ID SocialSecurityNumber
    Street
    City
    State
    Zip
    Phone
    EmergPhone
    DateOfLastCheckOut
    Hours
    DateOfLastPhysical

    FLIGHT   0.N

(b)

*ASSIGNMENT
Association Object:
(a) Example
Assignment
Report and
(b) ASSIGNMENT
Object with Semantic
Object ID*

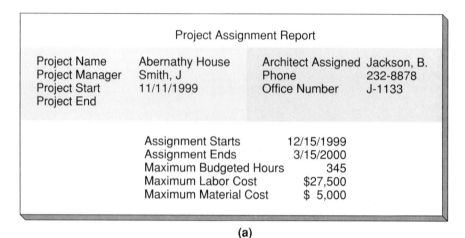

Project Assignment Report

Project Name	Abernathy House	Architect Assigned	Jackson, B.
Project Manager	Smith, J	Phone	232-8878
Project Start	11/11/1999	Office Number	J-1133
Project End			

Assignment Starts   12/15/1999
Assignment Ends   3/15/2000
Maximum Budgeted Hours   345
Maximum Labor Cost $27,500
Maximum Material Cost $ 5,000

(a)

ASSIGNMENT
ID AssignmentID
    PROJECT   1.1
    ARCHITECT   1.1
AssignmentStarts
AssignmentEnds
MaxHours
MaxLaborCost
MaxMaterialCost

PROJECT
ID ProjectName
   ProjectManager
   ProjectStart
   ProjectEnd
   ASSIGNMENT   1.N

ARCHITECT
ID Name
   Phone
   Office
   ASSIGNMENT   1.N

(b)

Name}. These attributes, however, belong to PROJECT and ARCHITECT and not to ASSIGNMENT. The identifier of ASSIGNMENT is thus the combination of those identifiers of the things that are assigned.

Figure 4-27(b) shows the object diagrams for this situation. Both PROJECT and ARCHITECT are object attributes of ASSIGNMENT, and the group {PROJECT, ARCHITECT} is the identifier of ASSIGNMENT. This means that the combination of an instance of PROJECT and an instance of ARCHITECT identifies a particular ASSIGNMENT.

Note that the AssignmentID identifier in Figure 4-27(b) is not unique, thereby indicating that an architect may be assigned to a project more than once. If this is not the case, the identifier should be declared to be unique. Also, if an employee may be assigned to a project more than once and if for some reason it is important to have a unique identifier for an ASSIGNMENT, the attribute Date or some other time-indicating attribute (Week, Quarter, and so forth) should be added to the group.

PARENT/SUBTYPE OBJECTS

To understand parent and subtype objects, consider the object EMPLOYEE in Figure 4-28(a). Some of the attributes in EMPLOYEE pertain to all employees, and others pertain only to employees who are managers. The object in Figure 4-28(a)

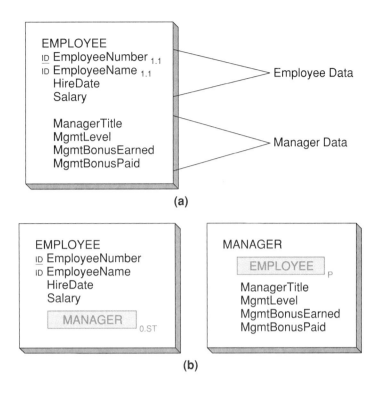

*Need for MANAGER Subtype:
(a) EMPLOYEE Without
Subtype and (b) EMPLOYEE
with MANAGER Subtype*

is not very precise because the manager-oriented attributes are not suitable for nonmanager employees.

A better model is shown in Figure 4-28(b), in which the EMPLOYEE object contains a subtype object, MANAGER. All of the manager-oriented attributes have been moved to the MANAGER object. Employees who are not managers have one EMPLOYEE object instance and no MANAGER object instances. Employees who are managers have both an EMPLOYEE instance and a MANAGER instance. In this example, the EMPLOYEE object is called a **parent object** or **supertype object**, and the MANAGER object is called a **subtype object**.

The first attribute of a subtype is the parent attribute and is denoted by the subscript P. Parent attributes are always required. The identifiers of the subtype are the same as the identifiers of the parent. In Figure 4-28, EmployeeNumber and EmployeeName are identifiers of both EMPLOYEE and MANAGER.

Subtype attributes are shown with the subscript 0.ST or 1.ST. The first digit (0 or 1) is the minimum cardinality of the subtype. If 0, the subtype is optional, and if 1, the subtype is required. (A required subtype does not make sense for this example but will for the more complicated examples to follow.) The *ST* indicates that the attribute is a subtype, or IS-A attribute.

Parent/subtype objects have an important characteristic called inheritance. A subtype acquires, or *inherits*, all of the attributes of its parent, and therefore a MANAGER inherits all of the attributes of an EMPLOYEE. In addition, the parent acquires all of the attributes of its subtypes, and an EMPLOYEE who is a MANAGER acquires all of the attributes of MANAGER.

A semantic object may contain more than one subtype attribute. Figure 4-29 shows a second EMPLOYEE object that has two subtype attributes, MANAGER and PROGRAMMER. Since all of these attributes are optional, an EMPLOYEE can have neither, one, or both of these subtypes. This means that some employees are neither managers nor programmers, some are managers but not programmers, some are programmers but not managers, and some are both programmers and managers.

Sometimes subtypes exclude one another. That is, a VEHICLE can be an AUTO or a TRUCK, but not both. A CLIENT can be an INDIVIDUAL, a PART-

➤ FIGURE 4-29

EMPLOYEE with Two Subtype Properties

NERSHIP, or a CORPORATION, but only one of these three types. When subtypes exclude one another, they are placed into a subtype group, and the group is assigned a subscript of the format *X.Y.Z*. X is the minimum cardinality and is 0 or 1, depending on whether or not the subtype group is required. Y and Z are counts of the number of attributes in the group that are allowed to have a value. Y is the minimum number required, and Z is the maximum number allowed.

Figure 4-30(a) shows three types of CLIENT as a subtype group. The subscript of the group, 0.1.1, means that the subtype is not required, but if it exists, a minimum of one and a maximum of one (or exactly one) of the subtypes in the group must exist. Note that each of the subtypes has the subscript 0.ST, meaning that they all are optional, as they must be. If they all were required, the maximum count would have to be three, not one. This notation is robust enough to allow for situations in which three out of five or seven out of 10 of a list of subtypes must be required.

Even more complex restrictions can be modeled when subtypes are nested. The subtype group in Figure 4-30(b) models a situation in which the subtype CORPORATION must be either a TAXABLE-CORP or a NONTAXABLE-CORP. If it is a NONTAXABLE-CORP, it must be either GOV-AGENCY or a SCHOOL. Only a few nonobject attributes are shown in this example. In reality, if such a complex structure were required, there would likely be more attributes.

ARCHETYPE/VERSION OBJECTS

The final type of object is the **archetype/version object**. An archetype object is a semantic object that produces other semantic objects that represent versions, releases, or editions of the archetype. For example, in Figure 4-31, the archetype object TEXTBOOK produces the version objects EDITIONs. According to this model, the attributes Title, Author, and Publisher belong to the object TEXTBOOK, and the attributes EditionNumber, PublicationDate, and NumberOfPages belong to the EDITION of the TEXTBOOK.

The ID group in EDITION has two portions, TEXTBOOK and EditionNumber; this is the typical pattern for an ID of a version object. One part of the ID contains the archetype object, and the second part is a simple attribute that identifies the version within the archetype. Figure 4-32 shows another instance of archetype/version objects.

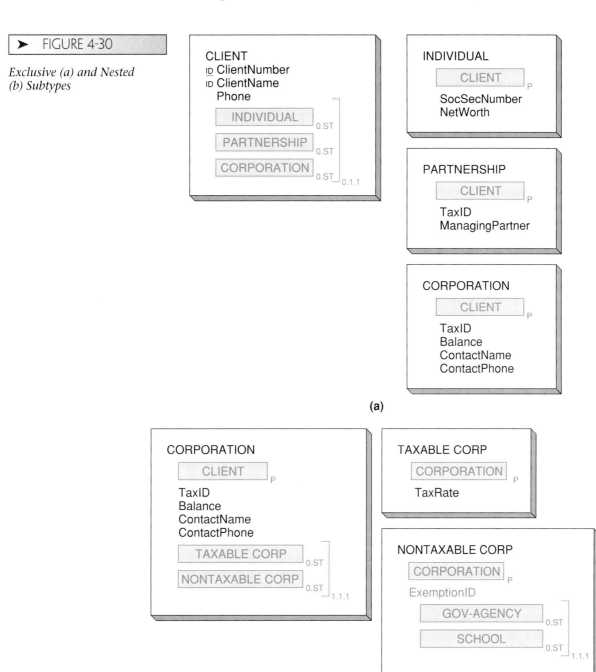

➤ FIGURE 4-30

Exclusive (a) and Nested (b) Subtypes

(a)

(b)

➤ FIGURE 4-31

*Example of an
Archetype/Version Object*

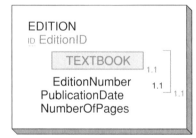

➤ COMPARING THE SEMANTIC OBJECT AND THE E-R MODEL

The E-R model and the semantic object model have both similarities and differences. They are similar in that they both are tools for understanding and documenting the structure of the users' data. They both strive to model the structure of the things in the users' world and the relationships among them.

The principal difference between the two models is one of orientation. The E-R model sees the concept of *entity* as basic. Entities and their relationships are considered the atoms, if you will, of a data model. These atoms can be combined to form what the E-R model calls *user views,* which are combinations of entities whose structure is similar to that of semantic objects.

The semantic object model takes the concept of *semantic object* as basic. The set of semantic objects in a data model is a map of the essential structure of the things that the user considers important. These objects are the atoms of the users' world and are the smallest distinguishable units that the users want to process. They may be decomposed into smaller parts inside the DBMS (or application), but those smaller parts are of no interest or utility to the users.

According to the semantic object perspective, entities, as defined in the E-R model, do not exist. They are only pieces or chunks of the real entities. The only entities that have meaning to users are, in fact, semantic objects. Another way to state this is to say that semantic objects are *semantically self-contained* or *semantically complete.* Consider an example. Figure 4-33 shows four semantic objects, SALES-ORDER, CUSTOMER, SALESPERSON, and ITEM. When a user says, "Show me sales order number 2000," he or she means show SALES-ORDER as modeled in Figure 4-33. That includes, among other attributes, CUSTOMER data. Because CUSTOMER is part of SALES-ORDER, the SALES-ORDER object includes CUSTOMER.

Figure 4-34 is an E-R model of this same data and contains the SALES-ORDER, CUSTOMER, SALESPERSON, LINE-ITEM, and INVENTORY entities. The SALES-ORDER entity includes the attributes OrderNumber, Date, Subtotal, Tax,

➤ FIGURE 4-32

*Another Example of an
Archetype/Version Object*

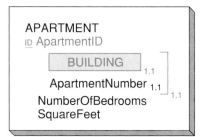

SALES-ORDER and Related Semantic Objects

Entity-Relationship Model of SALES-ORDER and CUSTOMER

and Total. Now if a user were to say, "Show me sales order number 2000" and be given only the attributes Date, Subtotal, Tax, and Total, he or she would be disappointed. Most likely the user's response would be, "Where's the rest of the data?" That is, the entity SALES-ORDER does not represent the user's meaning of the distinct identity SALES-ORDER. The entity is only a part of SALES-ORDER.

At the same time, when a user (perhaps even the same user) says, "Show me customer 12345," he or she means show all of the data modeled for CUSTOMER in Figure 4-33, including CustomerName, all of the attributes of the group Address, and all of the SALES-ORDERs for that CUSTOMER. The entity CUSTOMER in Figure 4-34 has only the attributes CustomerName, Street, City, State, Zip. If the user were to say, "Show me customer ABC" and be given only this data, he or she again would be disappointed: "No, that's only part of what I want."

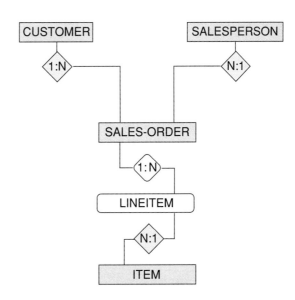

According to the semantic object view, E-R entities are unnecessary. Semantic objects can be readily transformed into database designs without ever considering E-R model entities. They are halfway houses, so to speak, constructed in the process of moving away from the paradigm of computer data structures to the paradigm of the user.

Another difference is that the semantic objects contain more metadata than do the entities. In Figure 4-33, the semantic object model records the fact that CustomerNumber is a unique identifier in the users' minds. It may or may not be used as an identifier for the underlying table, but that fact is not important to the data model. In addition, CustomerName is a nonunique identifier to the users. Furthermore, the semantic objects represent the fact that there is a semantic group of attributes called *Address*. This group contains other attributes that form the address. The fact that this group exists will become important when forms and reports are designed. Finally, the semantic objects indicate that an ITEM may relate to more than one SALES-ORDER but that it can relate to only one LineItem within that SALES-ORDER. This fact cannot be shown on the entity-relationship diagram.

In the final analysis, decide which of Figures 4–33 and 4–34 gives you a better idea of what the database should contain. Many people find that the boundaries drawn around the semantic objects and the brackets around the group attributes help them get a better idea of the overall picture of the data model.

➤ SUMMARY

Both the E-R and the semantic object models are used to interpret requirements and to build models of the users' data. These models are like lenses through which developers look when studying and documenting the users' data. Both ultimately lead to a database design.

A semantic object is a named collection of attributes that sufficiently describes a distinct identity. Semantic objects are grouped into classes, and both classes and instances of semantic objects have names. For example, the name of a class is EMPLOYEE, and the name of an instance is Employee 2000.

Attributes represent characteristics of the identities being represented. The set of attributes is sufficient in that it represents all of the characteristics that the users need to do their work. Objects represent distinct identities, instances that the users view as independent and separate. The distinct identities represented may or may not be physical; indeed, they may themselves be representative, such as a contract.

Object attributes can be simple data items, groups, or other semantic objects. Object diagrams summarize the structure of objects. Object names are spelled in capital letters at the top of the diagram. Nonobject attributes are written with initial capitals, and attribute groups are indicated by brackets.

All attributes have a minimum cardinality that indicates how many instances of the attribute must exist in order for the object to be valid. They also have a maximum cardinality that indicates the maximum number of instances of the attribute allowed. Cardinality is written in the format N.M, where N is the minimum cardinality and M is the maximum. To reduce the clutter in an object diagram, if the cardinality of a simple value attribute is 0.1, it is not shown. But cardinality is always shown for group and object attributes.

Object attributes are always paired. If one object has a relationship with a second, the second must have a relationship with the first. Object identifiers are attributes that serve, in the users' minds, to identify objects. Identifiers can be unique or not unique. Any type of attribute can be an identifier. Identifiers are shown with the letters ID in front of the attribute. If the attribute is unique, then the letters ID are underlined. The cardinalities of an identifier are normally 1.1.

The domain of an attribute is the set of all possible values that the attribute can have. Domains have both a physical and a semantic definition. There are three types of domains: simple, group, and semantic object.

Applications process objects through users' views. A view of an object consists of the name of the object and all of the attributes visible from that view. View and object definition is often an iterative process.

The process of developing a set of object diagrams is iterative. Reports or forms are examined; an initial set of objects is documented; and the new reports and forms are then checked to reveal new objects and changes in existing objects. This process continues until all the forms and reports have been examined.

There are seven types of objects. Simple objects have no multi-value attributes and no object attributes. Composite objects have multi-value attributes but no object attributes. Compound objects have object attributes, and hybrid objects combine composite and compound objects. Association objects relate two or more other objects. Subtype objects are used to represent the specializations of objects. Finally, archetype/version objects are used to model objects that contain base data along with multiple variations, or versions.

The E-R model considers entities as basic, whereas the semantic object model considers semantic objects as basic. The semantic object model also contains more information about the meaning of the data than does the E-R model.

➤ GROUP I QUESTIONS

4.1   Explain why the E-R model and the semantic object model are like lenses.

4.2   Define *semantic object*.

4.3   Explain the difference between an object class name and an object instance name. Give an example of each.

4.4   What is required for a set of attributes to be a sufficient description?

4.5   Explain the words *distinct identity* as they pertain to the definition of a semantic object.

4.6   Explain why a line item of an order is not a semantic object.

4.7   List the three types of attributes.

4.8   Give an example of each of the following:
   a. a simple, single-value attribute
   b. a group, single-value attribute
   c. a simple, multi-value attribute
   d. a group, multi-value attribute
   e. a simple object attribute
   f. a multi-value object attribute

4.9   What is minimum cardinality? How is it used? Which types of attributes have minimum cardinality?

4.10 What is maximum cardinality? How is it used? Which types of attributes have maximum cardinality?

4.11 What are paired attributes? Why are they needed?

4.12 What is an object identifier? Give an example of a simple attribute object identifier and an example of a group attribute object identifier.

4.13 Define *attribute domain*. What are the types of attribute domain? Why is a semantic description necessary?

4.14 What is a semantic object view? Give an example of an object and two views other than those in this text.

4.15 Give an example of a simple object other than the one discussed in this chapter.

4.16 Give three examples of composite objects other than those in this chapter. One of your examples should have just one composite group; one should have two independent composite groups; and the third should have nested composite groups.

4.17 Give an example of four sets of compound objects other than those in this chapter. One set should have a 1:1 relationship; one set should have a 1:N relationship; one set should have an M:1 relationship; and one set should have an M:N relationship.

4.18 Give an example of a hybrid object other than the one in this chapter.

4.19 Give an example of one association and two compound objects other than those in this chapter.

4.20 Give an example of a supertype object with three subtype objects other than those in this chapter.

4.21 Give an example of archetype/version objects other than those in this chapter.

4.22 Explain the similarities between the E-R model and the semantic object model.

4.23 Explain the major differences between the E-R model and the semantic object model.

4.24 Explain the reasoning that entities, as defined in the E-R model, do not truly exist.

4.25 Show how both the E-R model and the semantic object model would represent the data underlying the SALES-ORDER form in Figure 4-24(a), and explain the main differences.

➤ GROUP II QUESTIONS

4.26 Modify the semantic object diagram in Figure 4-13 to include CLASS, CLASS-OFFERING, and ENROLLMENT objects. Assume ENROLLMENT is an association object that relates a STUDENT to a CLASS.

4.27 Modify the semantic object diagram in Figure 4-13 to include a COMMITTEE object. Assume that many PROFESSORs are assigned to a committee and that a COMMITTEE includes many PROFESSORs. Create a MEETING object as an archetype/version object that represents the meetings of a COMMITTEE.

4.28 Modify your answer to Question 4.27 to create MEETING as a multi-value group within COMMITTEE. Is this model a better model than the one in Question 4.27? Justify your answer.

➤ PROJECTS

A. Develop a semantic object model for the MHA case in Project A at the end of Chapter 3.

B. Access the World Wide Web site for a computer manufacturer such as Dell (www.dell.com). Use the Web site to determine which laptop computer you would buy for a power user who has a budget of $10,000. As you use the Web site, think about the structure of a possible database of computer systems and subsystems to support this site.

Develop a semantic object model of computer system and subsystem database for this Web site. Possible objects are BASE-SYSTEM, MEMORY-OPTION, VIDEO-CARD, and PRINTER. Show object relationships and at least two or three attributes per object. Indicate the type of each semantic object. To keep this project from exploding in size, constrain your design to the needs of someone who is making a purchase decision.

 C. Access the Web site for a bookseller such as Amazon (www.amazon.com). Use the Web site to determine the three best books on XML (Extended Markup Language) for someone who is just learning that subject. As you use the Web site, think about the structure of a possible database of books, authors, subjects, and related topics.

Develop a semantic object model of a book database for this Web site. Possible objects are TITLE, AUTHOR, PUBLISHER, and SUBJECT. Show object relationships and at least two or three attributes per object. Indicate the type of each semantic object. To keep this project from exploding in size, assume that only books are to be tracked. Further, constrain your design to the needs of someone who is looking for books to purchase. Do not consider customer ordering, order fulfillment, purchase ordering, and other such business processes.

DATABASE DESIGN

The chapters in Part III discuss database design. Chapter 5 presents the relational model and normalization. The relational model is important because it is the standard in which most database designs are expressed; it is also the foundation of most of today's DBMS products.

Normalization is important because it is a technique for checking the quality of a relational design. Given the groundwork in Chapter 5, we then consider, in Chapter 6, the process of transforming entity-relationship data models into DBMS-independent, relational designs. Next, Chapter 7 describes the process for transforming semantic object data models into such designs.

The Relational Model and Normalization

The relational model is important for two reasons. First, because the constructs of the relational model are broad and general, it can be used to express DBMS-independent database designs. Second, the relational model is the basis for almost all DBMS products. Understanding the concepts of this model is therefore essential.

This chapter presents the basics of the relational model and explains the fundamental concepts of *normalization*. We begin with the fact that not all relations are equal, that some are better than others. Normalization is a process for converting a relation that has certain problems to two or more relations that do not have these problems. Even more important, normalization can be used as a guideline for checking the desirability and correctness of relations. Much theoretical work has been done on the question of what a well-structured relation is. This work is termed *normalization* because one of the pioneers in database technology, E. F. Codd, defined various *normal forms* of relations. In this chapter we survey normalization, including the results of theorems that are useful and significant to database practitioners. The proofs of these theorems and a formal, more rigorous treatment of this subject can be found in the work of C. J. Date and of J. D. Ullman.[1]

➤ THE RELATIONAL MODEL

A **relation** is a two-dimensional table. Each row in the table holds data that pertain to some thing or a portion of some thing. Each column of the table contains data regarding an attribute. Sometimes rows are called **tuples** (rhymes with "couples"), and columns are called **attributes.**

---

[1]C. J. Date, *An Introduction to Database Systems*, Sixth Edition (Reading, MA: Addison-Wesley, 1994); and J. D. Ullman and Jennifer Widom, *A First Course in Database Systems* (Upper Saddle River, NJ: Prentice Hall, 1997).

> ➤ FIGURE 5-1

Equivalent Relational Terminology

Relational Model	Programmer	User
Relation	File	Table
Tuple (Row)	Record	Row
Attribute	Field	Column

The terms *relation, tuple,* and *attribute* arose from relational mathematics, which is the theoretical source of this model. MIS professionals find more comfortable the analogous terms *file, record,* and *field,* and most users find the terms *table, row,* and *column* most sensible. Figure 5-1 summarizes this terminology.

For a table to be a relation, it must meet certain restrictions.[2] First, the cells of the table must be of single value; neither repeating groups nor arrays are allowed as values.[3] All of the entries in any column must be of the same kind. For example, if the third column in the first row of a table contains EmployeeNumbers, then the third column must contain EmployeeNumbers in all other rows of the table as well. Each column has a unique name, and the order of the columns in the table is insignificant. Finally, no two rows in a table may be identical, and the order of the rows is insignificant.

Figure 5-2 is a sample table. Notice that it has seven rows made up of four columns. If we were to rearrange the order of the columns (say, by placing EmployeeNumber at the far left) or to reorder the rows (perhaps in ascending sequence on Age), we would have an equivalent table.

Figure 5-2 shows one occurrence, or instance, of a table. The generalized format, EMPLOYEE (Name, Age, Sex, EmployeeNumber), is called the relation structure, and it is what most people mean when they use the term *relation.*

To understand the relational model and normalization, we need to define two important terms, **functional dependency** and **key.**

FUNCTIONAL DEPENDENCIES

A *functional dependency* is a relationship between or among attributes. Suppose that if we are given the value of one attribute, we can obtain (or look up) the value of another attribute. For example, if we know the value of

> ➤ FIGURE 5-2

EMPLOYEE Relation

	Attribute1 Name	Attribute2 Age	Attribute3 Sex	Attribute4 EmployeeNumber
Tuple 1	Anderson	21	F	010110
Tuple 2	Decker	22	M	010100
.	Glover	22	M	101000
.	Jackson	21	F	201100
.	Moore	19	M	111100
.	Nakata	20	F	111101
Tuple 7	Smith	19	M	111111

---

[2]E. F. Codd, "A Relational Model of Data for Large Shared Databanks," *Communications of the ACM,* June 1970, pp. 377–87.

[3]This does not mean that the values must be a fixed length. A variable-length memo field, for example, is a perfectly legitimate value. Only *one* such value is allowed, however.

CustomerAccountNumber, we can find the value of CustomerBalance. If this is true, we can say that CustomerBalance is *functionally dependent* on Customer AccountNumber.

In more general terms, attribute Y is functionally dependent on attribute X if the value of X determines the value of Y. Stated differently, if we know the value of X, we can obtain the value of Y.

Equations represent functional dependencies. For example, if we know the price of an item and the quantity of items purchased, we can calculate the total price of those items, as follows:

TotalPrice = ItemPrice × Quantity

In this case, we would say that TotalPrice is functionally dependent on ItemPrice and Quantity.

The functional dependencies between attributes in a relation usually do not involve equations. For example, suppose that students have a unique identification number, SID, and that every student has one, and only one, major. Given the value of an SID, we can find out that student's major, so Major is functionally dependent on SID. Or consider microcomputers in a computer lab. Each has one, and only one, size of main memory, so MemorySize is functionally dependent on ComputerSerialNumber.

Unlike an equation, such functional dependencies cannot be solved using arithmetic; instead, they are listed in the database. In fact, one can argue that the storage and retrieval of functional dependencies is the only reason for having a database.

Functional dependencies are written using the following notation:

SID → Major
ComputerSerialNumber → MemorySize

The first expression is read as "SID functionally determines Major," "SID determines Major," or "Major is dependent on SID." The attributes on the left side of the arrow are called **determinants.**

As stated, if SID determines Major, a particular value of SID will be paired with only *one* value of Major. Conversely, however, a value of Major may be paired with *one or more* different values of SID. Suppose the student whose SID is 123 majors in accounting. Whenever SID and Major are found together in a relation, the SID value of 123 will always be paired with the Major value of Accounting. The opposite is not true, however, as the Major Accounting may be paired with many values of SID (many students may major in accounting). Consequently, we can say that the relationship of SID with Major is many to one (N:1). In general, we can say that if A determines B, the relationship of the values of A to B is N:1.

Functional dependencies can involve groups of attributes. Consider the relation GRADES (SID, ClassName, Grade). The combination of a SID and a ClassName determines a grade, a functional dependency that is written

(SID, ClassName) → Grade

Note that both SID and ClassName are needed to determine a Grade. We cannot subdivide the functional dependency because neither SID nor ClassName determines Grade by itself.

Notice the difference in the following two patterns: If X → (Y, Z), then X → Y and X → Z. For example, if SID → (StudentName, Major), then SID → StudentName and SID → Major. But if (X, Y) → Z, then in general, it is not true that X → Y or Y → Z. Hence, if (SID, ClassName) → Grade, then neither SID nor ClassName by itself determines Grade.

Keys

A *key* is a group of one or more attributes that uniquely identifies a row. Consider the relation ACTIVITY in Figure 5-3, whose attributes are SID, Activity, and Fee. The meaning of a row is that a student engages in the named activity for the specified fee. Assume that a student is allowed to participate in only one activity at a time. In this case, a value of SID determines a unique row, and so it is a key.

Keys can also be composed of a group of attributes taken together. For example, if students were allowed to enroll in many activities at the same time, it would be possible for one value of SID to appear in two or more rows of the table, so SID could not uniquely identify the row. Some combination of attributes, perhaps (SID, Activity), would be required.

As an aside, there is a subtle but important point in the preceding paragraph. Whether or not attributes are keys and whether or not they are functional dependencies are determined not by an abstract set of rules but, rather, by the users' mental models and by the business rules of the organization using the database. In this example, whether SID is the key or whether (SID, Activity) is the key or whether some other combination is the key is determined entirely by the underlying semantics of the people in the organization using the database. We must ask the users to resolve these questions. As we continue, keep in mind that all the assumptions we make about functional dependencies, keys, and the like are determined by the users' mental models.

After interviewing the users, suppose we discover that students are, in fact, allowed to participate in several activities at one time. This situation is represented by the relation ACTIVITIES, shown in Figure 5-4. As we stated, SID is *not* a key of this relation. Student 100, for example, has enrolled in both skiing and golf, and the SID value of 100 occurs in two different rows. In fact, for this relation, no single attribute is a key, so the key must be a combination of two or more attributes.

Consider the combinations of two attributes from this table. There are three possibilities: (SID, Activity), (SID, Fee), and (Activity, Fee). Is any one of these combinations a key? To be a key, it must uniquely identify a row. Again, to decide questions like this, we must ask the users. We cannot simply depend on sample data like those in Figure 5-4 or rely on our own assumptions to make the decision.

After talking with the users, suppose we find out that several activities might charge the same fee. Since this is the case, the combination (SID, Fee) cannot determine a unique row. Student 100, for example, could engage in two different activities, both of which cost $200. This would mean that the combination (100, $200) occurs twice in the table, so this combination cannot be a key.

Can the combination (Activity, Fee) be a key? Does the combination (Skiing, $200) determine a unique row? No, it does not, because many students can participate in skiing. What about (SID, Activity)? Given what we know from the

FIGURE 5-3

ACTIVITY Relation

ACTIVITY (SID, Activity, Fee)
Key: SID
Sample Data

SID	Activity	Fee
100	Skiing	200
150	Swimming	50
175	Squash	50
200	Swimming	50

FIGURE 5-4

ACTIVITIES Relation

SID	Activity	Fee
100	Skiing	200
100	Golf	65
150	Swimming	50
175	Squash	50
175	Swimming	50
200	Swimming	50
200	Golf	65

users, can a combination of values for SID and Activity determine a unique row? Yes, it can, so long as we are not required to keep records of the different occasions on which a student enrolled in a given activity. In other words, is this table to be used to record only a student's current activities, or is it supposed to keep records of past activities as well?

Again, we must consult the users to answer this question. Suppose we learn that only records of current activities are to be kept. Then the combination (SID, Activity) can determine a unique row, and consequently, (SID, Activity) is the key for this relation. If the users specified that records of current and past activities were to be kept, the relation in Figure 5-3 would have duplicate rows. Because this is prohibited by the definition of relation, we would need to add other attributes such as Date.

This brings up an important point. Every relation has at least one key. This must be true because no relation can have duplicate rows and hence, at the extreme, the key consists of all of the attributes of the relation.

FUNCTIONAL DEPENDENCIES, KEYS, AND UNIQUENESS

Many students confuse the concepts of functional dependencies, keys, and uniqueness. To avoid that confusion, consider the following: A determinant of a functional dependency may or may not be unique in a relation. If we know that A determines B and that A and B are in the same relation, we still do not know whether A is unique in that relation. We only know that A determines B.

For example, in the ACTIVITIES relation, Activity functionally determines Fee, and yet there can be many instances of a particular Activity in the relation. The functional dependency states only that wherever Activity occurs with Fee, it always occurs with the same value of Fee. That is, skiing always costs $200, regardless of how many times the value skiing occurs in the table.

Unlike determinants, keys are always unique. A key functionally determines the entire row. If the value of the key were duplicated, the entire tuple would be duplicated. But this is not allowed because, by definition, rows in a relation must be unique. Thus, when we say that an attribute (or combination) is a key, we know that it will be unique. If (SID, Activity) is a key, then, for example, the combination (100, skiing) will occur only once in a relation.

To test your understanding of these concepts, try to explain why, in the ACTIVITY relation in Figure 5-3, SID is both a determinant and a key but Activity is a determinant and not a key. (Keep in mind that the relation in Figure 5-3 reflects the policy that a student may participate in, at most, one activity at a time.)

➤ NORMALIZATION

Unfortunately, not all relations are equally desirable. A table that meets the minimum definition of a relation may not have an effective or appropriate structure. For some relations, changing the data can have undesirable consequences, called

modification anomalies. Anomalies can be eliminated by redefining the relation into two or more relations. In most circumstances, the redefined, or **normalized,** relations are preferred.

MODIFICATION ANOMALIES

Again consider Activity in Figure 5-3. If we delete the tuple for Student 100, we will lose not only the fact that Student 100 is a skier but also the fact that skiing costs $200. This is called a **deletion anomaly;** that is, by deleting the facts about one entity (that Student 100 is a skier), we inadvertently delete facts about another entity (that skiing costs $200). With one deletion, we lose facts about two entities.

The same relation can be used to illustrate an **insertion anomaly.** Suppose we want to store the fact that scuba diving costs $175, but we cannot enter this data into the ACTIVITY relation until a student takes up scuba diving. This restriction seems silly. Why should we have to wait until someone takes the activity before we can record its price? This restriction is called an insertion anomaly. We cannot insert a fact about one entity until we have an additional fact about another entity.

The relation in Figure 5-3 can be used for some applications, but it obviously has problems. We can eliminate both the deletion and the insertion anomalies by dividing the ACTIVITY relation into two relations, each one dealing with a different theme. For example, we can put the SID and Activity attributes into one relation (we will call the new relation STU-ACT for student activity), and we can put the Activity and Fee attributes into a relation called ACT-COST (for activity cost). Figure 5-5 shows the same sample data stored in these two new relations.

Now if we delete Student 100 from STU-ACT, we do not lose the fact that skiing costs $200. Furthermore, we can add scuba diving and its fee to the ACT-COST relation even before anyone enrolls. Thus, the deletion and the insertion anomalies have been eliminated.

Separating one relation into two relations has a disadvantage, however. Suppose a student tries to sign up for a nonexistent activity. For instance, Student 250 wants to enroll in racquetball. We can insert this new tuple in STU-ACT (the row would contain 250, RACQUETBALL), but should we? Should a student be allowed to enroll in an activity that is not in the relation ACT-COST? Put another way, should the system somehow prevent student rows from being added if the value of the ACTIVITY is not in the ACT-COST table? The answer to this question lies with the users' requirements. If the action should be prohibited, this constraint must be documented as part of the schema design. Later, in implementation, the constraint will be defined to the DBMS if the product in use provides such constraint checking. If not, the constraint must be enforced by application programs.

Suppose the user specifies that activities can exist before any student enrolls in them but that no student may enroll in an activity that does not have a fee assigned to it (that is, no activities that are not in the ACT-COST table). We can

---

➤ FIGURE 5-5

The Division of ACTIVITY into Two Relations

STU-ACT (SID, Activity)
Key: SID

SID	Activity
100	Skiing
150	Swimming
175	Squash
200	Swimming

ACT-COST (Activity, Fee)
Key: Activity

Activity	Fee
Skiing	200
Swimming	50
Squash	50

document this constraint in any of several ways in the database design: Activity in STU-ACT is a subset of Activity in ACT-COST, or STU-ACT [Activity] is a subset of ACT-COST [Activity], or STU-ACT [Activity] $\subseteq$ ACT-COST [Activity].

According to this notation, the brackets [ ] denote a column of data that is extracted from a relation. These expressions simply mean that the values in the Activity attribute of STU-ACT must exist in the Activity attribute of ACT-COST. It also means that before we allow an Activity to be entered into STU-ACT, we must check to make sure that it is already present in ACT-COST. Constraints like this are called **referential integrity constraints.**

ESSENCE OF NORMALIZATION

The anomalies in the ACTIVITY relation in Figure 5-3 can be stated in the following intuitive way: Problems occur because ACTIVITY contains facts about two different themes:

➤ the students who participate in each activity
➤ how much each activity costs

When we add a new row, we must add data about two themes at once, and when we delete a row, we are forced to delete data about two themes at once.

Remember your eighth-grade English teacher? He or she claimed that a paragraph should have a single theme. If a paragraph had more than one theme, you were taught to break up the paragraph into two or more paragraphs so that each paragraph would have only one theme. Similar statements apply to relations. Every normalized relation has a single theme. Any relation having two or more themes should be broken up into two or more relations, each of which has a single theme. This process is the essence of normalization. When we find a relation with modification anomalies, we eliminate them by splitting the relation into two or more separate ones, each containing a single theme.

Every time we break up a relation, however, we may create a referential integrity constraint. Hence, it is good practice to check for such constraints every time you break a relation into two or more.

In the remainder of this chapter, you will learn a number of rules about normalization. All of these rules are special cases of the process just described.

CLASSES OF RELATIONS

Relations can be classified by the types of modification anomalies to which they are vulnerable. In the 1970s, relational theorists chipped away at these types. Someone would find an anomaly, classify it, and think of a way to prevent it. Each time this happened, the criteria for designing relations improved. These classes of relations and the techniques for preventing anomalies are called **normal forms.** Depending on its structure, a relation may be in first normal form, second normal form, or some other normal form.

In the work that followed his landmark 1970 paper, Codd and others defined first, second, and third normal forms (1NF, 2NF, 3NF). Later, Boyce-Codd normal form (BCNF) was specified, and then fourth and fifth normal forms were defined. As shown in Figure 5-6, these normal forms are nested. That is, a relation in second normal form is also in first normal form, and a relation in 5NF (fifth normal form) is also in 4NF, BCNF, 3NF, 2NF, and 1NF.

These normal forms were helpful, but they had a serious limitation. No theory guaranteed that any of them would eliminate all anomalies; each form could eliminate just certain ones. This changed, however, in 1981 when R. Fagin defined a new normal form called **domain/key normal form (DK/NF).** In an

FIGURE 5-6

Relationship of Normal Forms

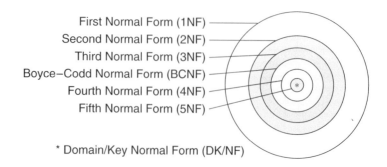

First Normal Form (1NF)
Second Normal Form (2NF)
Third Normal Form (3NF)
Boyce–Codd Normal Form (BCNF)
Fourth Normal Form (4NF)
Fifth Normal Form (5NF)

* Domain/Key Normal Form (DK/NF)

important paper, Fagin showed that a relation in DK/NF is free of all modification anomalies, regardless of their type.[4] He also showed that any relation that is free of modification anomalies must be in DK/NF.

Until DK/NF was defined, it was necessary for relational database theorists to continue looking for more and more anomalies and more and more normal forms. Fagin's proof, however, simplified the situation. If we can put a relation in DK/NF, then we can be sure that it will have no anomalies. The trick is knowing how to put relations in DK/NF.

➤ FIRST THROUGH FIFTH NORMAL FORMS

Any table of data that meets the definition of a relation is said to be in **first normal form.** Remember that for a table to be a relation, the following must hold: The cells of the table must be of single value, and neither repeating groups nor arrays are allowed as values. All entries in any column (attribute) must be of the same kind. Each column must have a unique name, but the order of the columns in the table is insignificant. Finally, no two rows in a table may be identical, and the order of the rows is insignificant.

The relation in Figure 5-3 is in first normal form. As we have seen, however, relations in first normal form may have modification anomalies. To eliminate those anomalies, we split the relation into two or more relations. When we do this, the new relations are in some other normal form—just which one depends on the anomalies we have eliminated, as well as the ones to which the new relations are vulnerable.

SECOND NORMAL FORM

To understand second normal form, consider the ACTIVITIES relation in Figure 5-4. This relation has modification anomalies similar to the ones we examined earlier. If we delete the tuple for Student 175, we will lose the fact that squash costs $50. Also, we cannot enter an activity until a student signs up for it. Thus, the relation suffers from both deletion and insertion anomalies.

The problem with this relation is that it has a dependency involving only part of the key. The key is the combination (SID, Activity), but the relation contains a dependency, Activity → Fee. The determinant of this dependency (Activity) is only part of the key (SID, Activity). In this case, we say that Fee is *partially dependent* on the key of the table. There would be no modification anomalies if Fee were dependent on all of the key. To eliminate the anomalies, we must separate the relation into two relations.

---

[4]R. Fagin, "A Normal Form for Relational Databases That Is Based on Domains and Keys," *ACM Transactions on Database Systems*, September 1981, pp. 387–415.

This example leads to the definition of second normal form: *A relation is in second normal form if all its nonkey attributes are dependent on all of the key.* According to this definition, if a relation has a single attribute as its key, then it is automatically in second normal form. Because the key is only one attribute, by default, every nonkey attribute is dependent on *all* of the key; there can be no partial dependencies. Thus, second normal is of concern only in relations that have composite keys.

ACTIVITIES can be decomposed to form two relations in second normal form. The relations are the same as those in Figure 5-5, namely, STU-ACT and ACT-COST. We know the new relations are in second normal form because they both have single-attribute keys.

THIRD NORMAL FORM

Relations in second normal form can also have anomalies. Consider the HOUS-ING relation in Figure 5-7(a). The key is SID, and the functional dependencies are SID → Building and Building → Fee. These dependencies arise because each student lives in only one building and each building charges only one fee. Everyone living in Randolph Hall, for example, pays $1,200 per quarter.

Since SID determines Building and Building determines Fee, then, indirectly SID → Fee. An arrangement of functional dependencies like this is called a **transitive dependency,** since SID determines Fee through the attribute Building.

The key of HOUSING is SID, which is a single attribute, and hence the relation is in second normal form (both Building and Fee are determined by SID). Despite this, however, HOUSING has anomalies because of the transitive dependency.

What happens if we delete the second tuple shown in Figure 5-7(a)? We lose not only the fact that Student 150 lives in Ingersoll Hall but also the fact that it

> ➤ FIGURE 5-7

Elimination of Transitive Dependency: (a) Relation with Transitive Dependency and (b) Relations Eliminating the Transitive Dependency

HOUSING (SID, Building, Fee)
Key: SID
Functional
dependencies: Building → Fee
                    SID → Building → Fee

SID	Building	Fee
100	Randolph	1200
150	Ingersoll	1100
200	Randolph	1200
250	Pitkin	1100
300	Randolph	1200

(a)

STU-HOUSING (SID, Building)
Key: SID

SID	Building
100	Randolph
150	Ingersoll
200	Randolph
250	Pitkin
300	Randolph

BLDG-FEE (Building, Fee)
Key: Building

Building	Fee
Randolph	1200
Ingersoll	1100
Pitkin	1100

(b)

costs $1100 to live there. This is a deletion anomaly. And how can we record the fact that the Fee for Carrigg Hall is $1,500? We cannot until a student decides to move in. This is an insertion anomaly.

To eliminate the anomalies from a relation in second normal form, the transitive dependency must be removed, which leads to a definition of third normal form: *A relation is in third normal form if it is in second normal form and has no transitive dependencies.*

The HOUSING relation can be divided into two relations in third normal form. This has been done for the relations STU-HOUSING (SID, Building) and BLDG-FEE (Building, Fee) in Figure 5-7(b).

The ACTIVITY relation in Figure 5-3 also has a transitive dependency. In ACTIVITY, SID determines Activity and Activity determines Fee. Therefore, ACTIVITY is not in third normal form. Decomposing ACTIVITY into the relations STU-ACT (SID, Activity) and ACT-COST (Activity, Fee) eliminates the anomalies.

BOYCE-CODD NORMAL FORM

Unfortunately, even relations in third normal form can have anomalies. Consider the ADVISER relation in Figure 5-8(a). Suppose the requirements underlying this relation are that a student (SID) can have one or more majors (Major), a major can have several faculty members (Fname) as advisers, and a faculty member (Fname) advises in only one major area.

Since students can have several majors, SID does not determine Major. Moreover, since students can have several advisers, SID also does not determine Fname. Thus, SID, by itself, cannot be a key

➤ FIGURE 5-8

Boyce-Codd Normal Form:
(a) Relation in Third Normal Form but Not in Boyce-Codd Normal Form and
(b) Relations in Boyce-Codd Normal Form

ADVISER (SID, Major, Fname)

Key (primary): (SID, Major)
Key (candidate): (SID, Fname)

Functional
dependencies: Fname → Major

SID	Major	Fname
100	Math	Cauchy
150	Psychology	Jung
200	Math	Riemann
250	Math	Cauchy
300	Psychology	Perls
300	Math	Riemann

(a)

STU-ADV (SID, Fname)
Key: SID, Fname

SID	Fname
100	Cauchy
150	Jung
200	Riemann
250	Cauchy
300	Perls
300	Riemann

ADV-SUBJ (Fname, Subject)
Key: Fname

Fname	Subject
Cauchy	Math
Jung	Psychology
Riemann	Math
Perls	Psychology

(b)

The combination (SID, Major) determines Fname, and the combination (SID, Fname) determines Major. Hence, either of the combinations can be a key. Two or more attributes or attribute collections that can be a key are called **candidate keys.** Whichever of the candidates is selected to be *the* key is called the **primary key.**

In addition to the candidate keys, there is another functional dependency to consider: Fname determines Major (any faculty member advises in only one major. Therefore, given the Fname, we can determine the Major). Thus, Fname is a determinant.

By definition, ADVISER is in first normal form. It is also in second normal form, since any nonkey attributes are dependent on the entire key (no matter which candidate key we select). And it also is in third normal form because it has no transitive dependencies. Despite all this, however, it has modification anomalies.

Suppose Student 300 drops out of school. If we delete Student 300's tuple, we will lose the fact that Perls advises in psychology. This is a deletion anomaly. Similarly, how can we store the fact that Keynes advises in economics? We cannot until a student majors in economics. This is an insertion anomaly.

Situations like this lead to the definition of Boyce-Codd normal form (BCNF): *A relation is in BCNF if every determinant is a candidate key.* ADVISER is not in BCNF, because the determinant, Fname, is not a candidate key.

As with the other examples, ADVISER can be decomposed into two relations having no anomalies. For example, the relations STU-ADV (SID, Fname) and ADV-SUBJ (Fname, Subject) have no anomalies.

Relations in BCNF have no anomalies in regard to functional dependencies, and this seemed to put the issue of modification anomalies to rest. It was soon discovered, however, that anomalies can arise from situations other than functional dependencies.

FOURTH NORMAL FORM

Consider the STUDENT relation in Figure 5-9, showing the relationship among students, majors, and activities. Suppose that students can enroll in several different majors and participate in several different activities. Because this is so, the only key is the combination of attributes (SID, Major, Activity). Student 100 majors in music and accounting, and she also participates in swimming and tennis. Student 150 majors only in math and participates in jogging.

What is the relationship between SID and Major? It is not a functional dependency because students can have several majors. A single value of SID can have many values of Major. Also, a single value of SID can have many values of Activity.

► FIGURE 5-9

Relation with Multi-value Dependencies

STUDENT (SID, Major, Activity)
Key: (SID, Major, Activity)

Multivalued
dependencies: SID →→ Major
                  SID →→ Activity

SID	Major	Activity
100	Music	Swimming
100	Accounting	Swimming
100	Music	Tennis
100	Accounting	Tennis
150	Math	Jogging

This attribute dependency is called a **multi-value dependency.** Multi-value dependencies lead to modification anomalies. To begin, note the data redundancy in Figure 5-9. Student 100 has four records, each of which shows one of her majors paired with one of her activities. If the data were stored with fewer rows—say there were only two tuples, one for music and swimming and one for accounting and tennis—the implications would be misleading. It would *appear* that Student 100 swam only when she was a music major and played tennis only when she was an accounting major. But this interpretation is not logical. Her majors and her activities are completely independent of each other. So to prevent such a misleading conclusion, we store all the combinations of majors and activities.

Suppose that because Student 100 decides to sign up for skiing, we add the tuple [100, MUSIC, SKIING], as in Figure 5-10(a). The relation at this point implies that Student 100 skis as a music major but not as an accounting major. In order to keep the data consistent, we must add one row for each of her majors paired with skiing. Thus, we must also add the row [100, ACCOUNTING, SKIING], as in Figure 5-10(b). This is an update anomaly—too much updating needs to be done to make a simple change in the data.

In general, a multi-value dependency exists when a relation has at least three attributes, two of them are multi-value, and their values depend on only the third attribute. In other words, in a relation R (A, B, C), a multi-value dependency exists if A determines multiple values of B, A determines multiple values of C, and B and C are independent of each other. As we saw in the previous example, SID determines multiple values of Major and SID determines multiple values of Activity, but Major and Activity are independent of each other.

Refer again to Figure 5-9. Notice how multi-value dependencies are written: SID →→ Major, and SID →→ Activity. This is read "SID multi-determines Major, and SID multi-determines Activity." This relation is in BCNF (2-NF because it is all key; 3NF because it has no transitive dependencies; and BCNF because it has no nonkey determinants). However, as we have seen, it has anomalies: If a stu-

➤ FIGURE 5-10

STUDENT Relations with Insertion Anomalies: (a) Insertion of a Single Tuple and (b) Insertion of Two Tuples

STUDENT (SID, Major, Activity)
Key: (SID, Major, Activity)

SID	Major	Activity
100	Music	Skiing
100	Music	Swimming
100	Accounting	Swimming
100	Music	Tennis
100	Accounting	Tennis
150	Math	Jogging

(a)

SID	Major	Activity
100	Music	Skiing
100	Accounting	Skiing
100	Music	Swimming
100	Accounting	Swimming
100	Music	Tennis
100	Accounting	Tennis
150	Math	Jogging

(b)

Elimination of Multi-value Dependency

STU-MAJOR (SID, Major)
Key: (SID, Major)

STU-ACT (SID, Activity)
Key: (SID, Activity)

SID	Major
100	Music
100	Accounting
150	Math

SID	Activity
100	Skiing
100	Swimming
100	Tennis
150	Jogging

dent adds a major, we must enter a tuple for the new major, paired with each of the student's activities. The same holds true if a student enrolls in a new activity. If a student drops a major, we must delete each of his records containing that major. If he participates in four activities, there will be four tuples containing the major he has dropped, and each of them must be deleted.

To eliminate these anomalies, we must eliminate the multi-value dependency. We do this by creating two relations, each one storing data for only one of the multi-value attributes. The resulting relations do not have anomalies. They are STU-MAJOR (SID, Major) and STU-ACT (SID, Activity), as seen in Figure 5-11.

From these observations, we define fourth normal form in the following way: *A relation is in fourth normal form if it is in BCNF and has no multi-value dependencies.* After we have discussed domain/key normal form later in this chapter, we will return to describe multi-value dependencies in another, more intuitive way.

FIFTH NORMAL FORM

Fifth normal form concerns dependencies that are rather obscure. It has to do with relations that can be divided into subrelations, as we have been doing, but then cannot be reconstructed. The condition under which this situation arises has no clear, intuitive meaning. We do not know what the consequences of such dependencies are or even if they have any practical consequences. For more information about fifth normal form, refer to the work by Date that was cited earlier in this chapter.

➤ DOMAIN/KEY NORMAL FORM

Each of the normal forms we have discussed was identified by researchers who found anomalies with some relations that were in a lower normal form: Noticing modification anomalies with relations in second normal form led to the definition of third normal form, etc. Although each normal form solved some of the problems that had been identified with the previous one, no one could know what problems had not yet been identified. With each step, progress was made toward a well-structured database design, but no one could guarantee that no more anomalies would be found. In this section we study a normal form that guarantees that there will be no anomalies of any type. When we put relations into that form, we know that even the obscure anomalies associated with fifth normal form cannot occur.

In 1981, Fagin published an important paper in which he defined domain/key normal form (DK/NF).[5] He showed that a relation in DK/NF has no modification anomalies and, furthermore, that a relation having no modification

---

[5]*Ibid.*

anomalies must be in DK/NF. This finding establishes a bound on the definition of normal forms, and so no higher normal form is needed, at least in order to eliminate modification anomalies.

Equally important, DK/NF involves only the concepts of key and domain, concepts that are fundamental and close to the heart of database practitioners. They are readily supported by DBMS products (or could be, at least). In a sense, Fagin's work formalized and justified what many practitioners believed intuitively but were unable to express precisely.

DEFINITION

In concept, DK/NF is quite simple: A relation is in DK/NF if every constraint on the relation is a logical consequence of the definition of keys and domains. Consider the important terms in this definition: constraint, key, and domain.

Constraint in this definition is intended to be very broad. Fagin defines a constraint as any rule governing static values of attributes that is precise enough that we can ascertain whether or not it is true. Edit rules, intrarelation and interrelation constraints, functional dependencies, and multi-value dependencies are examples of such constraints. Fagin expressly excludes constraints pertaining to changes in data values, or time-dependent constraints. For example, the rule "Salesperson salary in the current period can never be less than salary in the prior period" is excluded from Fagin's definition of constraint. Except for time-dependent constraints, Fagin's definition is both broad and inclusive.

A **key** is a unique identifier of a tuple, as we have already defined. The third significant term in the definition of DK/NF is **domain.** In Chapter 4, we stated that a domain is a description of an attribute's allowed values. It has two parts: a physical description and a semantic, or logical, description. The physical description is the set of values the attribute can have, and the logical description is the meaning of the attribute. Fagin's proof refers to both parts.

Informally, a relation is in DK/NF if enforcing key and domain restrictions causes all of the constraints to be met. Moreover, because relations in DK/NF cannot have modification anomalies, the DBMS can prohibit them by enforcing key and domain restrictions.

Unfortunately, there is no known algorithm for converting a relation to DK/NF, nor is it even known which relations can be converted to DK/NF. Finding, or designing, DK/NF relations is more of an art than a science.

In spite of this, in the practical world of database design, DK/NF is an exceedingly useful design objective. If we can define relations in a way that constraints on them are logical consequences of domains and keys, then there will be no modification anomalies. For many designs, this objective can be accomplished. When it cannot, the constraints must be built into the logic of application programs that process the database. We will see more of this later in this chapter and in Chapter 8.

The following three examples illustrate DK/NF.

EXAMPLE 1 OF DOMAIN/KEY NORMAL FORM

Consider the STUDENT relation in Figure 5-12, which contains attributes SID, GradeLevel, Building, and Fee. Building is the building in which the student lives, and Fee is the amount the student pays to live in that building.

SID functionally determines the other three attributes, so SID is a key. Assume we also know, from the requirements definition, that Building → Fee and that SIDs must not begin with 1. If we can express these constraints as logical consequences of domain and key definitions, we can be certain, according to Fagin's theorem, that there will be no modification anomalies. For this example, it will be easy.

➤ FIGURE 5-12

Example 1 of DK/NF

STUDENT (SID, GradeLevel, Building, Fee)

Key: SID

Constraints: Building → Fee
             SID must not begin with digit 1

To enforce the constraint that student numbers not begin with 1, we simply define the domain for student numbers to incorporate this constraint (Figure 5-13). Enforcing the domain restriction guarantees that this constraint will be met.

Next we need to make the functional dependency Building → Fee a logical consequence of keys. If Building were a key attribute, Building → Fee would be a logical consequence of a key. Therefore, the question becomes how to make Building a key. It cannot be a key in STUDENT because more than one student lives in the same building, but it can be a key of its own relation. Thus, we define the relation BLDG-FEE with Building and Fee as its attributes. Building is the key of this relation. Having defined this new relation, we can remove Fee from STUDENT. The final domain and relation definitions for this example appear in Figure 5-13.

This is the same result we obtained when converting a relation from 2NF to 3NF to remove transitive dependencies. In this case, however, the process was simpler and the result more robust. It was simpler because we did not need to know that we were eliminating a transitive dependency. We simply needed to find creative ways to make all the constraints logical consequences of domain and key definitions. The result was more robust because when converting the relation to 3NF, we knew only that it had fewer anomalies than when it was in 2NF. By converting the relation to DK/NF, we know that the relations have no modification anomalies whatsoever.

EXAMPLE 2 OF DOMAIN/KEY NORMAL FORM

The next example involves the relation described in Figure 5-14 and is more complicated than the previous one. The PROFESSOR relation contains data about professors, the classes they teach, and the students they advise. FID (for Faculty ID) and Fname uniquely identify a professor. SID uniquely identifies a student,

➤ FIGURE 5-13

Domain/Key Definition of Example 1

Domain Definitions

SID   in   CDDD, where C is decimal digit not = 1; D = decimal digit
GradeLevel in   {'FR', 'SO', 'JR', 'SN', 'GR'}
Building   in   CHAR(4)
Fee   in   DEC(4)

Relation and Key Definitions

STUDENT (SID, GradeLevel, Building)
Key: SID

BLDG-FEE
(Building, Fee)
Key: Building

➤ FIGURE 5-14

Example 2 of DK/NF

PROFESSOR (FID, Fname, Class, SID, Sname)
Key: (FID, Class, SID)
Constraints:
FID → Fname
Fname → FID
FID →→ Class | SID
Fname →→ Class | SID
SID → FID
SID → Fname
SID → Sname
FID must start with 1; SID must not start with 1

but Sname does not necessarily identify a SID. Professors can teach several classes and advise several students, but a student is advised by only one professor. FIDs start with a 1, but SIDs must not start with a 1.

These statements can be expressed more precisely by the functional and multi-value dependencies shown in Figure 5-14. FID and Fname functionally determine each other (in essence, they are equivalent). FID and Fname multidetermine Class and SID. SID functionally determines FID and Fname. SID determines Sname.

In more complex examples such as this one, it is helpful to consider DK/NF from a more intuitive light. Remember that the essence of normalization is that every relation should have a single theme. Considered from this perspective, there are three themes in PROFESSOR. One is the correspondence between FIDs and Fnames. Another concerns the classes that a professor teaches, and the third concerns the identification number, name, and adviser of a given student.

Figure 5-15 shows three relations that reflect these themes. The FACULTY relation represents the equivalence of FID and Fname. FID is the key and Fname is an alternative key, which means that both attributes are unique to the relation. Because both are keys, the functional dependencies FID → Fname and Fname → FID are logical consequences of keys.

The PREPARATION relation contains the correspondence of faculty and classes; it shows the classes that a professor is prepared to teach. The key is the

➤ FIGURE 5-15

Domain/Key Definition of Example 2

Domain Definitions

FID	in	CDDD, C = 1; D = decimal digit
Fname	in	CHAR(30)
Class	in	CHAR(10)
SID	in	CDDD, C is decimal digit, not = 1; D = decimal digit
Sname	in	CHAR(30)

Relation and Key Definitions

FACULTY (FID, Fname)
Key (primary): FID
Key (candidate): Fname

PREPARATION (Fname, Class)
Key: Fname, Class

STUDENT (SID, Sname, Fname)
Key: SID

combination (Fname, Class). Both attributes are required in the key because a professor may teach several classes and a class may be taught by several professors. Finally, STUDENT represents the student and adviser names for a particular SID. Observe that each of these relations has a single theme. These relations express all of the constraints of Figure 5-14 as a logical consequence of domains and key definitions. These relations are, therefore, in DK/NF.

Note that separating the PREPARATION theme from the STUDENT theme has eliminated the multi-value dependencies. When we examined fourth normal form, we found that in order to eliminate multi-value dependencies, we had to separate the multi-value attributes into different relations. Our approach here is to break a relation with several themes into several relations, each with one theme. In doing that, we eliminated a multi-value dependency. In fact, we arrived at the same solution using both approaches.

EXAMPLE 3 OF DOMAIN/KEY NORMAL FORM

The next example concerns a situation that was not addressed by any of the other normal forms but that occurs frequently in practice. This relation has a constraint among data values within a tuple that is neither a functional dependency nor a multi-value dependency.

Consider the constraints in the relation STU-ADVISER in Figure 5-16. This relation contains information about a student and his or her adviser. SID determines Sname, FID, Fname, and GradFacultyStatus and is therefore the key. FID and Fname identify a unique faculty member and are equivalent to each other, as in Example 2. Both FID and Fname determine GradFacultyStatus. Finally, the new type of constraint is that only members of the graduate faculty are allowed to advise graduate students.

The domain restrictions are that SID must not begin with a 1, SID must begin with a 9 for graduate students, FID must begin with a 1, and GradFacultyStatus is 0 for undergraduate faculty and 1 for graduate faculty. With these domain definitions, the constraint that graduate students must be advised by graduate faculty can be expressed as a constraint on row values. Specifically, if the SID starts with 9, the value of GradFacultyStatus must be 1.

To put this relation in DK/NF, we proceed as in Example 2. What are the basic themes of this relation? There is one regarding faculty personnel that relates FID, Fname, and GradFacultyStatus. Since FID and Fname determine GradFacultyStatus, either of these attributes can be the key, and this relation is in DK/NF (see Figure 5-17).

➤ FIGURE 5-16

Example 3 of DK/NF

STU-ADVISER (SID, Sname, FID, Fname, GradFacultyStatus)

Key: SID

Constraints:
　　　　FID → Fname
　　　　Fname → FID
　　　　FID and Fname → GradFacultyStatus
　　　　Only graduate faculty can advise graduate students
　　　　FID begins with 1
　　　　SID must not begin with 1
　　　　SID of graduate student begins with 9
　　　　GradFacultyStatus = { 0 for undergraduate faculty
　　　　　　　　　　　　　　　　{ 1 for graduate faculty

> FIGURE 5-17

Domain/Key Definition of Example 3

Domain Definitions

FID	in	CDDD, where C = 1; D = decimal digit
Fname	in	CHAR (30)
Grad-faculty-status	in	[0, 1]
GSID	in	CDDD, where C = 9; D = decimal digit; graduate student
UGSID	in	CDDD, WHERE C ≠ 1 and C ≠ 9; D = decimal digit; undergraduate student
Sname	in	CHAR (30)

Additional Domain Definitions

Gfname	in	{Fname of FACULTY, where GradFacultyStatus = 1}

Relations and Key Definitions

FACULTY (FID, Fname, GradFacultyStatus)
Key: FID or Fname

G-ADV (GSID, Sname, Gfname)
Key: GSID

UG-ADV (UGSID, Sname, Fname)
Key: UGSID

Now consider the data regarding students and advisers. Although it may first appear that there is only one theme, that of advising, the constraint that only graduate faculty can advise graduate students implies otherwise. Actually, there are two themes: graduate advising and undergraduate advising. Thus, Figure 5-17 contains a G-ADV relation for graduate students and a UG-ADV relation for undergraduates. Look at the domain definitions: GSID starts with a 9; Gfname is the Fname of a FACULTY tuple with GradFacultyStatus equal to 1; and UGSID must not begin with 1 or 9. All the constraints described in Figure 5-16 are implied by the key and domain definitions in Figure 5-17. These relations are therefore in DK/NF and have no modification anomalies.

To summarize, Figure 5-18 lists the normal forms and presents the defining characteristic of each.

> FIGURE 5-18

Summary of Normal Forms

Form	Defining Characteristic
1NF	Any relation
2NF	All nonkey attributes are dependent on all of the keys.
3NF	There are no transitive dependencies.
BCNF	Every determinant is a candidate key.
4NF	There are no multivalued dependencies.
5NF	Not described in this discussion.
DK/NF	All constraints on relations are logical consequences of domains and keys.

➤ THE SYNTHESIS OF RELATIONS

In the previous section, we approached relational design from an analytical perspective. The question we asked was, Given a relation, is it in good form? Does it have modification anomalies? In this section, we look at relational design from a different perspective—a synthetic one. From this perspective, we ask, "Given a set of attributes with certain functional dependencies, what relations should we form?"

First, observe that two attributes, say A and B, can be related in three ways:

1. They determine each other:

$A \rightarrow B$ and $B \rightarrow A$

Hence A and B have a one-to-one attribute relationship.

2. One determines the other.

$A \rightarrow B$, but B not $\rightarrow A$

Hence A and B have a many-to-one relationship.

3. They are functionally unrelated.

A not $\rightarrow B$ and B not $\rightarrow A$

Hence, A and B have a many-to-many attribute relationship.

ONE-TO-ONE ATTRIBUTE RELATIONSHIPS

If A determines B and B determines A, the values of the attributes have a one-to-one relationship. This must be because if A determines B, the relationship between A and B is many to one. It is also true, however, that if B determines A, the relationship between B and A must be many to one. For both statements to be true at the same time, the relationship between A and B must actually be one to one (which is a special case of many to one), and the relationship between B and A is also actually one to one. Therefore, the relationship is one to one.

This case is illustrated by FID and Fname in Examples 2 and 3 in the previous section on domain/key normal form. Each of these attributes uniquely identifies a faculty person. Consequently, one value of FID corresponds to exactly one value of Fname, and vice versa.

Three equivalent statements can be drawn from the example of FID and Fname:

➤ If two attributes functionally determine each other, the relationship of their data values is one to one.

➤ If two attributes uniquely identify the same thing (entity or object), the relationship of their data values is one to one.

➤ If two attributes have a one-to-one relationship, they functionally determine each other.

When creating a database with attributes that have a one-to-one relationship, the two attributes must occur together in at least one relation. Other attributes that are functionally determined by these (an attribute that is functionally determined by one of them is functionally determined by the other as well) may also reside in this same relation.

Consider FACULTY (FID, Fname, GradFacultyStatus) in Example 3 in the previous section. FID and Fname determine each other. GradFacultyStatus can also occur in this relation because it is determined by FID and Fname. Attributes that are not functionally determined by these attributes may not occur in a relation

➤ FIGURE 5-19

Summary of Three Types of Attribute Relationships

Type of Attribute Relationship

	One-to-One	Many-to-One	Many-to-Many
Relation Definition*	R(A,B)	S(C,D)	T(E,F)
Dependencies	A ⟶ B B ⟶ A	C ⟶ D D ⇸ C	E ⇻ F F ⇻ E
Key	Either A or B	C	(E,F)
Rule for Adding Another Attribute	Either A or B ⟶ C	C ⟶ E	(E,F) ⟶ G

* The letters used in these relation definitions match those used in Figure 5-20

with them. Consider the relations FACULTY and PREPARATION in Example 2, in which both FID and Fname occur in FACULTY, but Class (from PREPARATION) may not. Class can have multiple values for a faculty member, so Class is not dependent on FID or Fname. If we added Class to the FACULTY relation, the key of FACULTY would need to be either (FID, Class) or (Fname, Class). In this case, however, FACULTY would not be in DK/NF because the dependencies between FID and Fname would not be logically implied by either of the possible keys.

These statements are summarized in the first column of Figure 5-19, and the record definition rules are listed in Figure 5-20. If A and B have a 1:1 relationship, they can reside in the same relation, say R. A determines B, and B determines A. The key of the relation can be either A or B. A new attribute, C, can be added to R if either A or B functionally determines C.

➤ FIGURE 5-20

Summary of Rules for Constructing Relations

Concerning One-to-One Relationships

- Attributes that have a one-to-one relationship must occur together in at least one relation. Call the relation R and the attributes A and B.
- Either A or B must be the key of R.
- An attribute can be added to R if it is functionally determined by A or B.
- An attribute that is not functionally determined by A or B cannot be added to R.
- A and B must occur together in R, but should not occur togeher in other relations.
- Either A or B should be consistently used to represent the pair in relations other than R.

Concerning Many-to-One Relationships

- Attributes that have a many-to-one relationship can exist in a relation together. Assume C determines D in relation S.
- C must be the key of S.
- An attribute can be added to S if it is determined by C.
- An attribute that is not determined by C cannot be added to S.

Concerning Many-to-Many Relationships

- Attributes that have a many-to-many relationship can exist in a relation together. Assume two such attributes, E and F, reside together in relation T.
- The key of T must be (E,F).
- An attribute can be added to T if it is determined by the combination (E,F).
- An attribute may not be added to T if it is not determined by the combination (E,F).
- If adding a new attribute, G, expands the key to (E,F,G), then the theme of the relation has been changed. Either G does not belong in T or the name of T must be changed to reflect the new theme.

Attributes having a one-to-one relationship must exist together in at least one relation in order to establish their equivalence (FID of 198, for example, refers to Professor Heart). It is generally undesirable to have them occur together in more than one relation, however, because this causes needless data duplication. Often, one or both of the two attributes occur in other relations. In Example 2, Fname occurs in both PREPARATION and STUDENT. Although it would be possible to place Fname in PREPARATION and FID in STUDENT, this generally is bad practice, because when attributes are paired in this way, one of them should be selected to represent the pair in all other relations. Fname was selected in Example 2.

MANY-TO-ONE ATTRIBUTE RELATIONSHIPS

If attribute A determines B but B does not determine A, the relationship among their data values is many to one. In the adviser relationship in Example 2, SID determines FID. Many students (SID) are advised by a faculty member (FID), but each student is advised by only one faculty member. This, then, is a many-to-one relationship.

For a relation to be in DK/NF, all constraints must be implied by keys, and thus every determinant must be a key. If A, B, and C are in the same relation and if A determines B, then A must be the key (meaning it also determines C). If, instead, (A, B) determines C, then (A, B) must be the key. In this latter case, no other functional dependency, such as A determines B, is allowed.

You can apply these statements to database design in the following way: When constructing a relation, if A determines B, the only other attributes you can add to the relation must also be determined by A. For example, suppose you have put SID and Building together in a relation called STUDENT. You may add any other attribute determined by SID, such as Sname, to this relation. But if the attribute Fee is determined by Building, you may not add it to this relation. Fee can be added only if SID → Fee.

These statements are summarized in the center column of Figure 5-19. If C and D have an N:1 relationship, they may reside together in a relation, say S. C will determine D, but D will not determine C. The key of S will be C. Another attribute, E, can be added to S only if C determines E.

MANY-TO-MANY ATTRIBUTE RELATIONSHIPS

If A does not determine B and B does not determine A, the relationship among their data values is many to many. In Example 2, Fname and Class have a many-to-many relationship. A professor teaches many classes, and a class is taught by many professors. In a many-to-many relationship, both attributes must be a key of the relation. For instance, the key of PREPARATION in Example 2 is the combination (Fname, Class).

When constructing relations that have multiple attributes as keys, you can add new attributes that are functionally dependent on all of the key. NumberOfTimesTaught is functionally dependent on both (Fname, Class) and can be added to the relation. FacultyOffice, however, cannot be added because it would be dependent only on Fname, not on Class. If FacultyOffice needs to be stored in the database, it must be added to the relation regarding faculty, not to the relation regarding preparations.

These statements are summarized in the right column of Figure 5-19. If E and F have an M:N relationship, E does not determine F, and F does not determine E. Both E and F can be put into a relation T, and if this is done, the key of T will be the composite (E,F). A new attribute, G, can be added to T if it is determined by all of (E,F). It cannot be added to T if it is determined by only one of E or F.

Consider a similar, but different, example. Suppose we add Classroom Number to PREPARATION. Is ClassroomNumber functionally determined by the key of PREPARATION, (Fname, Class)? Most likely it is not, because a professor could teach a particular class in many different rooms.

The composite (Fname, Class) and ClassroomNumber have an M:N relationship. Since this is so, the rules in Figure 5-19 can be applied, but with E representing (Fname, Class) and F representing ClassroomNumber. Now we can compose a new relation, T, with attributes Fname, Class, and ClassroomNumber. The key becomes (Fname, Class, ClassroomNumber). In this situation, we have created a new relation with a new theme. Consider relation T, which contains faculty names, classes, and classroom numbers. The theme of this relation is therefore no longer PREPARATION but, rather, WHO-WHAT-WHERE-TAUGHT.

Changing the theme may or may not be appropriate. If ClassroomNumber is important, the theme does need to be changed. In that case, PREPARATION is the wrong relation, and WHO-WHAT-WHERE-TAUGHT is a more suitable theme.

On the other hand, depending on user requirements, PREPARATION may be completely suitable as it is. If so, then if ClassroomNumber belongs in the database at all, it should be located in a different relation—perhaps SECTION-NUMBER, CLASS-SECTION, or some similar relation.

➤ MULTI VALUE DEPENDENCIES, ITERATION 2

The discussion about many-to-many attribute value relationships may make the concept of multi-value dependencies easier to understand. The problem with the relation STUDENT (SID, Major, Activity) in Figure 5-9 is that it has *two* different many-to-many relationships, one between SID and Major and the other between SID and Activity. Clearly, a student's various majors have nothing to do with his or her various activities. Putting both of these many-to-many relationships in the same relation, however, makes it appear as if there is some association.

Major and Activity are independent, and there would be no problem if a student had only one of each. SID would functionally determine Major and Activity, and the relation would be in DK/NF. In this case, both the relationships between Major and SID and Activity and SID would be many to one.

Another way of perceiving the difficulty is to examine the key (SID, Major, Activity). Since STUDENT has many-to-many relationships, all of the attributes have to be in the key. Now what theme does this key represent? We might say the combination of a student's studies and activities. But this is not one thing; it is plural. One row of this relation describes only part of the combination, and in order to get the whole picture, we need all of the rows about a particular student. In general, a row should have all of the data about one instance of the relation's theme. A row of Customer, for example, should have all the data we want about a particular customer.

Consider PREPARATION in Example 2 in the section on domain/key normal form. The key is (Fname, Class). The theme this represents is that a particular professor is prepared to teach a particular class. We need only one row of the relation to get all of the information (the relation might include NumberOfTimesTaught, AverageCourseEvaluationScore, and so on) we have about the combination of that professor and that class. Looking at more rows will not generate any more information about it.

As you know, the solution to the multi-value dependency constraint problem is to split the relation into two relations, each with a single theme. STU-MAJOR shows the combination of a student and a major. Everything we know about the combination is in a single row, and we will not gain more information about that combination by examining more rows.

➤ OPTIMIZATION

In this chapter we examined the concepts of normalization and demonstrated how to create tables that are in DK/NF. The process we used is usually suitable, but sometimes the result of normalization is not worth the cost. In this last section we look at two ways in which that can happen.

DE-NORMALIZATION

As stated, normalized relations avoid modification anomalies, and on that ground they are preferred to unnormalized relations. Judged on other grounds, however, normalization is sometimes not worth it.

Consider this relation:

CUSTOMER (CustNumber, CustName, City, State, Zip),

where CustNumber is the key.

This relation is not in DK/NF because it contains the functional dependency Zip → (City, State), which is not implied by the key, CustNumber. Hence, there is a constraint not implied by the definition of keys.

This relation can be transformed into the following two DK/NF relations:

CUSTOMER (CustNumber, CustName, Zip)

where the key is CustNumber

CODES (Zip, City, State)

where the key is Zip

These two tables are in domain/key normal form, but they most likely do not represent a better design. The unnormalized table is probably better because it will be easier to process and the disadvantages of duplicating the City and State data are not very important.

For another example of de-normalization, consider the relation

COLLEGE (CollegeName, Dean, AssistantDean)

and suppose that a college has one dean and from one to three assistant deans. In this case, the key of the table is (CollegeName, AssistantDean). This table is not in domain/key normal form because the constraint, CollegeName → Dean, is not a logical consequence of the table's key.

COLLEGE can be normalized into the relations

DEAN (CollegeName, Dean)

and

ASSISTANT-DEAN(CollegeName, AssistantDean)

But now whenever a database application needs to obtain data about the college, it must read at least two rows and possibly as many as four rows of data. An alternative to this design is to place all three AssistantDeans into the COLLEGE table, each in a separate attribute. The table would then be

COLLEGE1 (CollegeName, Dean, AssistantDean1, AssistantDean2, AssistantDean3)

COLLEGE1 is in DK/NF because all of its attributes are functionally dependent on the key CollegeName. But something has been lost. To see what, suppose that you wanted to determine the names of the COLLEGEs that had an assistant dean named 'Mary Abernathy.' To do this, you would have to look for this value in each of the three AssistantDean columns. Your query would appear something like this:[6]

SELECT	CollegeName
FROM	COLLEGE1
WHERE	AssistantDean1 = 'Mary Abernathy' OR
	AssistantDean2 = 'Mary Abernathy' OR
	AssistantDean3 = 'Mary Abernathy'

Using the normalized design with ASSISTANT-DEAN, you would need only to state

SELECT	CollegeName
FROM	ASSISTANT-DEAN
WHERE	AssistantDean = 'Mary Abernathy'

In this example there are three possible solutions, each with advantages and disadvantages. The choice among them is an artistic one; there is no hard and fast rule stating how to select among them. The best choice depends on the processing characteristics of the applications that use this database.

In summary, relations are sometimes purposely left unnormalized or are normalized and then de-normalized. Often this is done to improve performance. Whenever data must be combined from two separate tables, the DBMS must perform additional work. In most cases, at least two reads are required instead of one.

CONTROLLED REDUNDANCY

One of the advantages of normalized relations is that data duplication is minimized (only key values appear in more than one relation). For performance reasons, however, it is sometimes appropriate to duplicate data intentionally. Consider, for example, an order-processing application that accesses the ITEM table having the following columns:

PartNumber

PartName

PartColor

PartDescription

PartPicture

QuantityOnHand

QuantityOnOrder

StandardPrice

StandardCost

BuyerName

Assume that PartNumber is the key and that the table is in DK/NF. Also assume the attribute PartDescription is a potentially long memo field, and PartPicture is a binary column at least 256K bytes in length.

---

[6]These statements are examples of SQL, a relational language that we will discuss in detail in Chapter 9. For now, just think of them intuitively; you will learn the format of them in that chapter.

The order-processing application will need to access this table to obtain PartName, PartColor, StandardPrice, and QuantityOnHand. Assume it does not need PartDescription nor PartPicture. Depending on the characteristics of the DBMS in use, it is possible that the presence of these two large columns will slow processing considerably. If this is the case, the database designers might decide to duplicate some of the data in a second table that contains only data required for the ordering process. They might define a table like ORDERITEM (PartNumber, PartName, PartColor, StandardPrice, QuantityOnHand) that is used only for the order-processing application.

In this case, the designers are creating a potential for serious data integrity problems. They will need to develop both programmatic and manual controls to ensure that such problems do not occur. They would only create such a design if they judged the increased performance was worth the cost of the controls and the risk of the integrity problems.

Another reason for controlled redundancy is to create tables that are used for reporting and decision support purposes only. We will address this topic further in Chapter 14.

➤ SUMMARY

The relational model is important for two reasons: It can be used to express DBMS-independent database designs, and it is the basis for an important category of DBMS-products. Normalization can be used as a guideline for checking the desirability and correctness of relations.

A relation is a two-dimensional table that has single-value entries. All entries in a given column are of the same kind; columns have a unique name; and the order of the columns is not important. Columns are also called attributes. No two rows of a table are identical, and the order of the rows in the table is not important. Rows are also called tuples. The terms *table, file,* and *relation* are synonymous; the terms *column, field,* and *attribute* are synonymous; and the terms *row, record,* and *tuple* are synonymous.

A functional dependency is a relationship between attributes. Y is functionally dependent on X if the value of X determines the value of Y. A determinant is a group of one or more attributes on the left-hand side of a functional dependency. For example, if X determines Y, then X is the determinant. A key is a group of one or more attributes that uniquely identifies a tuple. Every relation has at least one key; because every row is unique, in the most extreme case, the key is the collection of all of the attributes in the relation. Although a key is always unique, the determinant in a functional dependency need not be. Whether or not attributes are keys and whether or not they are attributes are determined not by an abstract set of rules but by the users' semantics.

When updated, some relations suffer from undesirable consequences called modification anomalies. A deletion anomaly occurs when the deletion of a row loses information about two or more entities. An insertion anomaly occurs when the relational structure forces the addition of facts about two entities at the same time. Anomalies can be removed by splitting the relation into two or more relations.

There are many types of modification anomalies. Relations can be classified by the types of anomaly that they eliminate. Such classifications are called normal forms.

By definition, every relation is in first normal form. A relation is in second normal form if all nonkey attributes are dependent on all of the key. A relation is in third normal form if it is in second normal form and has no transitive dependencies. A relation is in Boyce-Codd normal form if every determinant is a candidate key. A relation is in fourth normal form if it is in Boyce-Codd normal form and has no multi-value dependencies. The definition of fifth normal form is intuitively obscure, and so we did not define it.

A relation is in domain/key normal form if every constraint on the relation is a logical consequence of the definition of domains and keys. A constraint is any constraint on the static values of attributes whose truth can be evaluated. As we defined them, domains have both a physical and a semantic part. In the context of DK/NF, however, domain refers only to the physical description.

An informal way of expressing DK/NF is to say that every relation must have only a single theme. For example, it might concern PROFESSORs or STUDENTs but not both PROFESSORs and STUDENTs at the same time.

Normalization is a process of analyzing relations. It is also possible to construct relations by a process of synthesis by considering the relationships among attributes. If two attributes functionally determine each other, they have a one-to-one relationship. If one attribute functionally determines the other, but not the reverse, the attributes have a one-to-many relationship. If neither attribute determines the other, they have a many-to-many relationship. These facts can be used when constructing relations as summarized in Figure 5-20.

In some cases, normalization is not desirable. Whenever a table is split into two or more tables, referential integrity constraints are created. If the cost of the extra processing of the two tables and their integrity constraint is greater than the benefit of avoiding modification anomalies, then normalization is not recommended. In addition, in some cases, creating repeating columns is preferred to the standard normalization techniques, and in other cases controlled redundancy is used to improve performance.

➤ GROUP I QUESTIONS

5.1 What restrictions must be placed on a table for it to be considered a relation?

5.2 Define the following terms: *relation, tuple, attribute, file, record, field, table, row, column.*

5.3 Define *functional dependency.* Give an example of two attributes that have a functional dependency, and give an example of two attributes that do not have a functional dependency.

5.4 If SID functionally determines Activity, does this mean that only one value of SID can exist in the relation? Why or why not?

5.5 Define *determinant.*

5.6 Give an example of a relation having a functional dependency in which the determinant has two or more attributes.

5.7 Define *key.*

5.8 If SID is a key of a relation, is it a determinant? Can a given value of SID occur more than once in the relation?

5.9 What is a deletion anomaly? Give an example other than one in this text.

5.10 What is an insertion anomaly? Give an example other than one in this text.

5.11 Explain the relationship of first, second, third, Boyce-Codd, fourth, fifth, and domain/key normal forms.

5.12 Define *second normal form.* Give an example of a relation in 1NF but not in 2NF. Transform the relation into relations in 2NF.

5.13 Define *third normal form.* Give an example of a relation in 2NF but not in 3NF. Transform the relation into relations in 3NF.

5.14 Define *BCNF*. Give an example of a relation in 3NF but not in BCNF. Transform the relation into relations in BCNF.

5.15 Define *multi-value dependency*. Give an example.

5.16 Why are multi-value dependencies not a problem in relations with only two attributes?

5.17 Define *fourth normal form*. Give an example of a relation in BCNF but not in 4NF. Transform the relation into relations in 4NF.

5.18 Define *domain/key normal form*. Why is it important?

5.19 Transform the following relation into DK/NF. Make and state the appropriate assumptions about functional dependencies and domains.

   EQUIPMENT (Manufacturer, Model, AcquisitionDate, BuyerName, BuyerPhone, PlantLocation, City, State, ZIP)

5.20 Transform the following relation into DK/NF. Make and state the appropriate assumptions about functional dependencies and domains.

   INVOICE (Number, CustomerName, CustomerNumber, CustomerAddress, ItemNumber, ItemPrice, ItemQuantity, SalespersonNumber, SalespersonName, Subtotal, Tax, TotalDue)

5.21 Answer Question 5.20 again, but this time add attribute CustomerTaxStatus (0 if nonexempt, 1 if exempt). Also add the constraint that there will be no tax if CustomerTaxStatus = 1.

5.22 Give an example, other than one in this text, in which you would judge normalization to be not worthwhile. Show the relations and justify your design.

5.23 Explain two situations in which database designers might intentionally choose to create data duplication. What is the risk of such designs?

➤ GROUP II QUESTIONS

5.24 Consider the following relation definition and sample data:

PROJECT Relation

ProjectID	EmployeeName	EmployeeSalary
100A	Jones	64K
100A	Smith	51K
100B	Smith	51K
200A	Jones	64K
200B	Jones	64K
200C	Parks	28K
200C	Smith	51K
200D	Parks	28K

PROJECT (ProjectID, EmployeeName, EmployeeSalary)

Where ProjectID is the name of a work project

   EmployeeName is the name of an employee who works on that project

   EmployeeSalary is the salary of the employee whose name is EmployeeName

Assuming that all of the functional dependencies and constraints are apparent in this data, which of the following statements is true?

a. ProjectID → EmployeeName

b. ProjectID → EmployeeSalary

c. (ProjectID, EmployeeName) → EmployeeSalary

d. EmployeeName → EmployeeSalary

e. EmployeeSalary → ProjectID

f. EmployeeSalary → (ProjectID, EmployeeName)

Answer these questions:

g. What is the key of PROJECT?

h. Are all nonkey attributes (if any) dependent on all of the key?

i. In what normal form is PROJECT?

j. Describe two modification anomalies from which PROJECT suffers.

k. Is ProjectID a determinant?

l. Is EmployeeName a determinant?

m. Is (ProjectID, EmployeeName) a determinant?

n. Is EmployeeSalary a determinant?

o. Does this relation contain a transitive dependency? If so, what is it?

p. Redesign this relation to eliminate the modification anomalies.

5.25 Consider the following relation definition and sample data:

PROJECT-HOURS Relation

EmployeeName	ProjectID	TaskID	Phone	TotalHours
Don	100A	B-1	12345	12
Don	100A	P-1	12345	12
Don	200B	B-1	12345	12
Don	200B	P-1	12345	12
Pam	100A	C-1	67890	26
Pam	200A	C-1	67890	26
Pam	200D	C-1	67890	26

PROJECT-HOURS (EmployeeName, ProjectID, TaskID, Phone, TotalHours)

Where EmployeeName is the name of an employee

ProjectID is the name of a project

TaskID is the name standard work task

Phone is the employee's telephone number

TotalHours is the hours worked by the employee on this project

Assuming that all of the functional dependencies and constraints are apparent in this data, which of the following statements is true?

a. EmployeeName → ProjectID

b. EmployeeName →→ ProjectID

c. EmployeeName → TaskID

d. EmployeeName →→ TaskID

e. EmployeeName → Phone

f. EmployeeName → TotalHours

g. (EmployeeName, ProjectID) → TotalHours

> h. (EmployeeName, Phone) → TaskID
>
> i. ProjectID → TaskID
>
> j. TaskID → ProjectID

Answer these questions:

> k. List all of the determinants.
>
> l. Does this relation contain a transitive dependency? If so, what is it?
>
> m. Does this relation contain a multi-value dependency? If so, what are the unrelated attributes?
>
> n. Describe the deletion anomaly that this relation contains.
>
> o. How many themes does this relation have?
>
> p. Redesign this relation to eliminate the modification anomalies. How many relations did you use? How many themes does each of your new relations contain?

5.26 Consider the following domain, relation, and key definitions:

Domain Definitions

EmployeeName	in	CHAR(20)
PhoneNumber	in	DEC(5)
EquipmentName	in	CHAR(10)
Location	in	CHAR(7)
Cost	in	CURRENCY
Date	in	YYMMDD
Time	in	HHMM where HH between 00 and 23 and MM between 00 and 59

Definitions of Relation, Key, and Constraint

EMPLOYEE (EmployeeName, PhoneNumber)

> Key: EmployeeName
>
> Constraints: EmployeeName → PhoneNumber

EQUIPMENT (EquipmentName, Location, Cost)

> Key: EquipmentName
>
> Constraints: EquipmentName → Location
>
>   EquipmentName → Cost

APPOINTMENT (Date, Time, EquipmentName, EmployeeName)

> Key: (Date, Time, EquipmentName)
>
> Constraints: (Date, Time, EquipmentName) → EmployeeName

> a. Modify the definitions to add this constraint: An employee may not sign up for more than one equipment appointment.
>
> b. Define nighttime to refer to the hours between 2100 and 0500. Add an attribute Employee Type whose value is 1 if the employee works during nighttime. Change this design to enforce the constraint that only employees who work at night can schedule nighttime appointments.

CHAPTER 6

Database Design Using Entity-Relationship Models

In Chapter 3 we discussed the specification of data models using the entity-relationship model, and in Chapter 5 we studied the relational model and normalization. In this chapter, we bring these subjects together to illustrate the transformation of users' requirements expressed in entity-relationship models into relational database designs. These designs are independent of any particular DBMS. In Chapter 7 we show how to transform semantic object data models into similar designs.

This chapter has two main sections. In the first, we show how to transform entity-relationship data models into relational designs. Normalization is important to this process because entities can contain more than one semantic theme. After demonstrating how to represent entities, we examine the representation of relationships using the relational model.

The second section applies the concepts described in the first section, illustrating the transformation of entity-relationship models into the representation of four common data structures. These structures are special cases of E-R constructs, and the techniques shown in the first section are applied to represent them with relations. We give these structures special attention because they occur so frequently as common patterns of entities and relationships.

➤ TRANSFORMATION OF ENTITY-RELATIONSHIP MODELS INTO RELATIONAL DATABASE DESIGNS

Chapter 3 demonstrated how to express user data requirements in an entity-relationship model. With this model, those things that users want to track are represented by **entities,** and the relationships among those entities are represented by explicitly defined **relationships.** This section describes how to transform entities and relationships into the terms of the relational model.

REPRESENTING ENTITIES WITH THE RELATIONAL MODEL

In general, the representation of entities by means of a relational model is straightforward. We begin by defining a relation for each entity. The name of the relation is the name of the entity, and the attributes of the relation are the attributes of the entity. Then we examine each relation according to the normalization criteria discussed in Chapter 5. It may or may not be necessary to change this initial design.

The example in Figure 6-1(a) is the entity shown in Figure 3-1. The CUSTOMER entity contains the following attributes: CustNumber, CustName, Address, City, State, Zip, ContactName, and PhoneNumber. To represent this entity with a relation, we define a relation for the entity and place the attributes in it as columns in the relation. If we know from the data model which attribute identifies this entity, that attribute will become the key of the relation. Otherwise, we must ask the users or otherwise investigate the requirements to determine what attribute or attributes can identify an entity. In this case, we assume that CustNumber is the key. In this figure, as in others to follow, the keys of the relations are underlined.

THE ROLE OF NORMALIZATION During the requirements phase, the only stipulation placed on an entity is that it be important to the user. No attempt is made to determine whether the entity fits any of the criteria for normalization discussed in Chapter 5. Therefore, once a relation has been defined for an entity, it should be examined according to the normalization criteria.

Consider, for example, the CUSTOMER relation in Figure 6-1(b). Is it in DK/NF? To find out, we need to know the constraints on this relation. Without a full description of the underlying requirements, we do not know all of the con-

---

➤ FIGURE 6-1

Representation of an Entity with a Relation: (a) CUSTOMER Entity and (b) Relation Representing CUSTOMER Entity

CUSTOMER entity contains

CustNumber
CustName
Address
City
State
Zip
ContactName
PhoneNumber

(a)

CUSTOMER (CustNumber, CustName, Address, City, State, Zip, ContactName, PhoneNumber)

(b)

straints, such as all of the domain constraints. But we can discover some of the requirements just from the names of the attributes and knowledge about the nature of the business.

First, CustNumber determines all of the other attributes, because the unique values of CustName, Address, City, State, Zip, ContactName, and PhoneNumber can be determined from a given value of CustNumber. There are other constraints, however, that arise from other functional dependencies. Zip determines City and State, and ContactName determines PhoneNumber. As we stated in Chapter 5, to create a set of relations in DK/NF, we need to make these additional functional dependencies a logical consequence of domains and keys, and we can do that by defining the three relations shown in Figure 6-2. Observe that the key of CUSTOMER is CustNumber, the key of ZIP-TABLE is Zip, and the key of CONTACT is ContactName.

The design in Figure 6-2 is in DK/NF, and there will be no modification anomalies. That is, we can add new zip codes and new contacts without having to add a customer with the new zip code or contact. Furthermore, when we delete the last customer in a given zip code, we do not lose the city and state for that zip code. But as we pointed out at the end of Chapter 5, most practitioners would consider this design too pure; breaking out Zip, City, and State will make the design hard to use. Hence, a better design would probably result by leaving Zip, City, and State in the CUSTOMER relation.

In other examples it is clearer that a pure DK/NF design is preferable. Consider the SALES-COMMISSION entity in Figure 6-3(a). If we attempt to represent this entity with one relation, as shown in Figure 6-3(b), the result is a confused mess of attributes with many potential modification anomalies.

This relation obviously contains more than one theme. On examination, it contains a theme about salespeople, a theme about sales during some period, and a theme about sales commission checks. The relations in DK/NF that represent this entity are shown in Figure 6-3(c). Intuitively, this design seems superior to that in Figure 6-3(b); it is more straightforward and better fitting.

To summarize the discussion so far, when representing an entity with the relational model, the first step is to construct a relation that has all of the entity's attributes as columns. Then the relation is examined against the normalization criteria. In many cases the design can be improved by developing sets of relations in DK/NF.

DK/NF relations are not always preferred, however. If the relations are contrived and difficult to work with, a non-DK/NF design may be better. Performance can also be a factor. Having to access two or three relations to obtain the data needed about a customer may be prohibitively time-consuming.

Regardless of our decision about whether to normalize, we should examine every entity's relation(s) against the normalization criteria. That is, if we are

➤ FIGURE 6-2

Representing the Customer Entity with Relations in Domain/Key Normal Form

CUSTOMER (<u>CustomerNumber</u>, Address, Zip, ContactName)

ZIP-TABLE (<u>Zip</u>, City, State)

CONTACT (<u>ContactName</u>, PhoneNumber)

Interrelation constraints:

    Zip in CUSTOMER must exist in Zip in ZIP-TABLE
    ContactName in CUSTOMER must = a ContactName in CONTACT

Entity with Appropriate Normalization: (a) SALES-COMMISSION Entity, (b) Representing SALES-COMMISSION with a Single Relation, and (c) Representing SALES-COMMISSION with Domain/Key Normal Form Relations

SALES-COMMISSION entity contains

SalespersonNumber
SalespersonName
Phone
CheckNumber
CheckDate
CommissionPeriod
TotalCommissionSales
CommissionAmount
BudgetCategory

(a)

SALES-COMMISSION (SalespersonNumber, SalespersonName, Phone, CheckNumber, CheckDate, CommissionPeriod, TotalCommissionSales, CommissionAmount, BudgetCategory)

Functional dependencies:
CheckNumber is key
SalespersonNumber determines SalespersonName, Phone, BudgetCategory
(SalespersonNumber, CommissionPeriod) determines TotalCommissionSales, CommissionAmount

(b)

SALESPERSON(SalespersonNumber, SalespersonName, Phone, BudgetCategory)
SALES (SalespersonNumber, CommissionPeriod, TotalCommissionSales, CommissionAmount)
COMMISSION-CHECK (CheckNumber, CheckDate, SalespersonNumber, CommissionPeriod)

(c)

going to sin, we should make an informed and conscious decision to do so. In the process, we also learn the types of modification anomalies to which the relations are vulnerable.

REPRESENTATION OF WEAK ENTITIES   Weak entities require special treatment when creating the relational design. Recall that a weak entity depends for its existence on another entity. If the weak entity is existence dependent but not ID dependent, it can be represented using the techniques described in the last section. The existence dependency needs to be recorded in the relational design so that no application will create a weak entity without its proper parent (the entity on which the weak entity depends). Moreover, a processing constraint needs to be implemented so that when the parent is deleted, the weak entity is also deleted. These rules should be described in the relational design.

This situation is slightly different if the weak entity also is ID dependent. In Figure 6-4(a), LINE-ITEM is an ID-dependent weak entity. It is weak because its logical existence depends on INVOICE, and it is ID dependent because its identifier contains the identifier of INVOICE.

When creating a relation for an ID-dependent entity, we must ensure that both the key of the parent and the key of the entity itself appear in the relation. For example, consider what would happen if we merely established a relation for LINE-ITEM and did not include the key of INVOICE. Such a relation is shown in Figure 6-4(b). What is the key of this relation? Because LINE-ITEM is ID depen-

► FIGURE 6-4

Relational Representation of a Weak Entity: (a) Example Weak Entity, (b) Relation Representing LINE-ITEM with No Key, and (c) LINE-ITEM Relation with Proper Key (Partly from INVOICE)

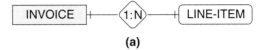

(a)

LINE-ITEM (<u>LineNumber</u>, Qty, ItemNumber, Description, Price, ExtPrice)

(b)

LINE-ITEM (<u>InvoiceNumber</u>, <u>LineNumber</u>, Qty, ItemNumber, Description, Price, ExtPrice)

(c)

dent, it does not have a complete key, and, in fact, this relation could very well have duplicate rows. (This would happen if two invoices had the same quantity of the same item on the same line.) The problem is that the relation in Figure 6-4(b) has no unique identifier.

Thus, for an ID-dependent weak entity, it is necessary to add the key of the parent entity to the weak entity's relation, and this added attribute becomes part of the weak entity's key. In Figure 6-4(c), we have added InvoiceNumber, the key of INVOICE, to the attributes in LINE-ITEM. The key of LINE-ITEM is the composite {InvoiceNumber, LineNumber}.

REPRESENTING HAS-A RELATIONSHIPS

There are two types of relationships in the E-R model: HAS-A relationships among entities of different logical types and IS-A relationships among entities that are subtypes of a common logical type. In this section we consider HAS-A relationships; later we discuss IS-A relationships.

REPRESENTING ONE-TO-ONE RELATIONSHIPS The simplest form of binary relationship is a one-to-one (1:1) relationship, in which an entity of one type is related to no more than one entity of another type. In the example of EMPLOYEE and AUTO, suppose that an employee is assigned exactly one automobile and an auto is assigned to exactly one employee. An E-R diagram for this relationship is shown in Figure 6-5.

Representing a 1:1 relationship with the relational model is straightforward. First each entity is represented with a relation, and then the key of one of the relations is placed in the other. In Figure 6-6(a), the key of EMPLOYEE is stored in AUTO, and in Figure 6-6(b), the key of AUTO is stored in EMPLOYEE.

When the key of one relation is stored in a second relation, it is called a **foreign key.** In Figure 6-6(a), EmployeeNumber is a foreign key in AUTO, and in Figure 6-6(b), LicenseNumber is a foreign key in EMPLOYEE. In this figure, foreign keys are shown in italics, but sometimes you may see foreign keys depicted by a dashed underline. In still other cases, foreign keys are not denoted in any special way. In this text, when there is a danger of confusion, we show foreign keys in italics, but most of the time, they do not receive any special notation.

For a 1:1 relationship, the key of either table can be placed as a foreign key in the other table. In Figure 6-6(a) the foreign key EmployeeNumber is placed in

► FIGURE 6-5

EMPLOYEE —————⟨1:1⟩————— AUTO

Example of a 1:1 Relationship

Alternatives for Representing 1:1 Relationships: (a) Placing the Key of EMPLOYEE in AUTO and (b) Placing the Key of AUTO in EMPLOYEE

EMPLOYEE (<u>EmployeeNumber</u>, EmployeeName, Phone, . . .)

AUTO (<u>LicenseNumber</u>, SerialNumber, Color, Make, Model, . . .*EmployeeNumber*)

(a)

EMPLOYEE (<u>EmployeeNumber</u>, EmployeeName, Phone, . . .*LicenseNumber*)

AUTO (<u>LicenseNumber</u>, SerialNumber, Color, Make, Model, . . .)

(b)

AUTO. With this design, we can navigate from EMPLOYEE to AUTO or from AUTO to EMPLOYEE. In the first case, we have an employee and want the auto assigned to that employee. To get the employee data, we use EmployeeNumber to obtain the employee's row in EMPLOYEE. From this row, we obtain the LicenseNumber of the auto assigned to that employee. We then use this number to look up the auto data in AUTO.

Now consider the other direction. Assume that we have an auto and want the employee assigned to that auto. Using the design in Figure 6-6(a), we access the EMPLOYEE table and look up the row that has the given license number. The data about the employee who has been assigned that auto appear in that row.

We take similar actions to travel in either direction for the alternative design, in which the foreign key of LicenseNumber is placed in EMPLOYEE. Using this design, to go from EMPLOYEE to AUTO, we go directly to the AUTO relation and look up the row in AUTO that has the given employee's number as its value of EmployeeNumber. To travel from AUTO to EMPLOYEE, we look up the row in AUTO having a given LicenseNumber. From this row, we extract the EmployeeNumber and use it to access the employee data in EMPLOYEE. Here we are using the term *look up* to mean "find a row given a value of one of its columns." Later, when we discuss particular DBMS models, we demonstrate how this is done.

Although the two designs in Figure 6-6 are equivalent in concept, they may be different in performance. For instance, if a query in one direction is more common than a query in the other, we may prefer one design to the other. Also, if the DBMS product is much faster in lookups on primary keys versus lookups on foreign keys, we might also prefer one design to another.

QUESTIONABLE 1:1 RELATIONSHIPS   Figure 6-7 shows another 1:1 relationship, in which each EMPLOYEE has a JOB-EVALUATION and each JOB-EVALUATION corresponds to a particular employee. Observe from the hash marks that the relationship is mandatory in both directions. When the relationship is 1:1 and is mandatory in both directions, it is likely that the records are describing different aspects of the same entity, especially if, as is the case in Figure 6-7, both entities have the same key. When this occurs, the records should generally be combined into one relation. Learn to regard such 1:1 mandatory relationships with suspicion.

The separation of an entity into two relations can, however, sometimes be justified. One justification concerns performance. For example, suppose that the JOB-EVALUATION data are lengthy and are used far less frequently than are the other employee data. In these circumstances it may be appropriate to store JOB-EVALUATIONs in a separate table so that the more common requests for nonevaluation employee data can be processed faster.

➤ FIGURE 6-7

EMPLOYEE ——<1:1>—— JOB-EVALUATION

Suspect 1:1 Relationship

Better security is the second justification for separating a single logical entity into two. If the DBMS does not support security at the data-item level, the JOB-EVALUATION data may need to be separated in order to prevent unauthorized users from accessing them. Or it may be desirable to place JOB-EVALUATION in a separate table so that the table can be placed on disk media that are accessible by certain users.

Do not conclude from this discussion that all 1:1 relationships are questionable; only those that appear to describe different aspects of the same entity are suspect. For example, the 1:1 mandatory relationship between EMPLOYEE and AUTO is quite suitable because each relation describes a logically different thing.

REPRESENTING ONE-TO-MANY RELATIONSHIPS   The second type of binary relationship is one to many (1:N), in which an entity of one type can be related to many entities of another type. Figure 6-8 is an E-R diagram of a one-to-many relationship between professors and students. In this relationship, PROFESSOR is related to the many STUDENTs that he or she advises. As stated in Chapter 3, the oval means that the relationship between PROFESSOR and STUDENT is optional; that is, a professor need not have any advisees. The bar across the line at the other end means that a STUDENT row must correspond to a PROFESSOR row.

The terms **parent** and **child** are sometimes applied to relations in 1:N relationships. The parent relation is on the *one* side of the relationship, and the child relation is on the *many* side. In Figure 6-8(a), PROFESSOR is the parent entity, and STUDENT is the child entity.

Figure 6-8 shows two other one-to-many relationships. In Figure 6-8(b), a DORMITORY entity corresponds to many STUDENT entities, but a STUDENT entity corresponds to one DORMITORY. Furthermore, a dormitory does not have to have any students assigned to it, nor is a student required to live in a dormitory.

In Figure 6-8(c), a CUSTOMER is related to many APPOINTMENT entities, and a particular APPOINTMENT corresponds to only one CUSTOMER. Moreover, a CUSTOMER may or may not have an APPOINTMENT, but every APPOINTMENT must correspond to a CUSTOMER.

Representing 1:N relationships is simple and straightforward. First each entity is represented by a relation, and then the key of the relation representing the parent entity is placed in the relation representing the child entity. Thus, to represent the ADVISES relationship of Figure 6-8(a), we place the key of PROFESSOR, ProfessorName, in the STUDENT relation as shown in Figure 6-9.

Figure 6-9 is an example of what is sometimes called a **data structure diagram,** in which relations are shown in rectangles with lines representing relationships and the key attributes are underlined. A fork, or crow's foot, on a relationship line indicates a many relationship.

In Figure 6-9, the fork at the STUDENT end of the relationship line means that there can be many STUDENT rows for each PROFESSOR. No fork at the other end means that each STUDENT can be advised by, at most, one PROFESSOR. As

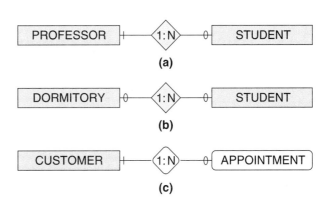

➤ FIGURE 6-8

Examples of One-to-Many Relationships: (a) Optional-to-Mandatory 1:N Relationship, (b) Optional-to-Optional 1:N Relationship, and (c) 1:N Relationship with Weak Entity

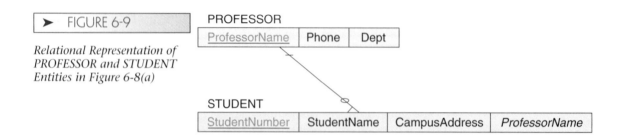

Relational Representation of PROFESSOR and STUDENT Entities in Figure 6-8(a)

with E-R diagrams, hash lines are used to denote mandatory relationships, and ovals denote optional ones.

Notice that with ProfessorName stored as a foreign key in STUDENT, we can process the relationship in both directions. Given a StudentNumber, we can look up the appropriate row in STUDENT and get the name of his or her adviser from the row data. To obtain the rest of the PROFESSOR data, we use the professor name obtained from STUDENT to look up the appropriate row in PROFESSOR. To determine all of the students advised by a particular faculty member, we look up all rows in STUDENT having the professor's name as a value for ProfessorName. Student data is then taken from those rows.

Contrast this situation with one representing 1:1 relationships. In both cases, we store the key of one relation as a foreign key in the second relation. In a 1:1 relationship, however, it does not matter which key is moved to the second relation. But in a 1:N relationship, it does matter. *The key of the parent relation must be placed in the child relation.*

To understand this better, notice what would happen if we tried to put the key of the child into the parent relation (placing StudentNumber in PROFESSOR). Because attributes in a relation can have only a single value, each PROFESSOR record has room for only one student. Consequently, such a structure cannot be used to represent the "many" side of the 1:N relationship. Hence, to represent a 1:N relationship, we must place the key of the parent relation in the child relation.

Figure 6-10 shows the representation of the CUSTOMER and APPOINTMENT entities. We represent each entity with a relation. APPOINTMENT is an ID-dependent weak entity, so it has a composite key consisting of the key of the entity on which its key depends plus an attribute from itself. Here the key is (CustomerNumber, Date, Time). To represent the 1:N relationship, we would normally add the key of the parent to the child. In this case, however, the key of the parent (CustomerNumber) is already part of the child, so we do not need to add it.

REPRESENTING MANY-TO-MANY RELATIONSHIPS The third and final type of binary relationship is many to many (M:N), in which an entity of one type corresponds to many entities of the second type, and an entity of the second type corresponds to many entities of the first type.

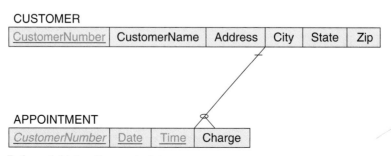

Relational Representation of the Weak Entity in Figure 6-8(c)

Referential integrity constraint:
CustomerName in APPOINTMENT must exist in CustomerNumber in CUSTOMER

FIGURE 6-11

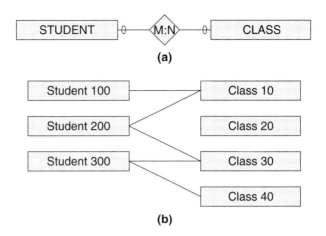

(a)

(b)

Example of an M:N Relationship: (a) E-R Diagram of STUDENT to CLASS Relationship and (b) Sample Data for STUDENT to CLASS Relationship

Figure 6-11(a) presents an E-R diagram of the many-to-many relationship between students and classes. A STUDENT entity can correspond to many CLASS entities, and a CLASS entity can correspond to many STUDENT entities. Notice that both participants in the relationship are optional: A student does not need to be enrolled in a class, and a class does not need to have any students. Figure 6-11(b) gives sample data.

Many-to-many relationships cannot be directly represented by relations in the same way that one-to-one and one-to-many relationships are. To understand why this is so, try using the same strategy we did for 1:1 and 1:N relationships—placing the key of one relation as a foreign key in the other relation. First, define a relation for each of the entities; call them STUDENT and CLASS. Now try to put the key of STUDENT (say StudentNumber) in CLASS. Because multiple values are not allowed in the cells of a relation, we have room for only one StudentNumber, so we have no place to record the StudentNumber of the second and subsequent students.

The same problem will occur if we try to put the key of CLASS (say ClassNumber) in STUDENT. We can readily store the identifier of the first class in which a student is enrolled, but we have no place to store the identifier of additional classes.

Figure 6-12 shows another (*but incorrect*) strategy. In this case, we have stored a row in the CLASS relation for each STUDENT enrolled in one class, so there are two records for Class 10 and two for Class 30. The problem with this scheme is that we duplicate the class data and thus create modification anomalies. Many rows will need to be changed if, say, Class 10's schedule is modified. Also con-

FIGURE 6-12

Incorrect *Representation of an M:N Relationship*

SID	Other STUDENT Data
100	. . .
200	. . .
300	. . .

STUDENT

ClassNumber	ClassTime	Other CLASS Data	SID
10	10:00 MWF	. . .	100
10	10:00 MWF	. . .	200
30	3:00 TH	. . .	200
30	3:00 TH	. . .	300
40	8:00 MWF	. . .	300

CLASS

Representing an M:N
Relationship:
(a) Relations Needed
to Represent
STUDENT
to CLASS
Relationship and
(b) Example Data for
STUDENT to CLASS
Relationship

STUDENT (<u>StudentNumber</u>, StudentName)

CLASS (<u>ClassNumber</u>, ClassName)

STU-CLASS (<u>*ClassNumber*</u>, <u>*StudentNumber*</u>)

(a)

100	Jones, Mary
200	Parker, Fred
300	Wu, Jason

100	10
200	10
200	30
300	30
300	40

10	Accounting
20	Finance
30	Marketing
40	Database

(b)

sider the insertion and deletion anomalies: How can we schedule a new class until a student has enrolled? And what will happen if Student 300 drops out of Class 40? Obviously, this strategy is unworkable.

The solution to this problem is to create a third relation that represents the relationship itself. Relation STU-CLASS has been defined in Figure 6-13(a). An instance of this relation is shown in Figure 6-13(b). Such relations are called **intersection relations** because each row documents the intersection of a particular student with a particular class. Notice in Figure 6-13(b) that there is one row in the intersection relation for each line between STUDENT and CLASS in Figure 6-11(b).

The data structure diagrams for the STUDENT-CLASS relationship appear in Figure 6-14. The relationship from CLASS to STU-CLASS is 1:N, and the relationship from STUDENT to STU-CLASS is also 1:N. In essence, we have decomposed the M:N relationship into two 1:N relationships. The key of STU-CLASS is the combination of the keys of both of its parents, (SID, ClassNumber). The key for an intersection relation is always the combination of parent keys. Also, note the parent relations are both required. A parent now must exist for each key value in the intersection relation.

REPRESENTING RECURSIVE RELATIONSHIPS

A **recursive relationship** is a relationship among entities of the same class. Recursive relationships are not fundamentally different from other HAS-A relationships and can be represented using the same techniques. As with nonrecursive HAS-A relationships, there are three types of recursive relationships: 1:1, 1:N, and N:M; Figure 6-15 shows an example of each.

Consider first the SPONSOR relationship in Figure 6-15(a). As with a 1:1 relationship, one person can sponsor another person, and each person is sponsored by no more than one person. Figure 6-16(a) shows sample data for this relationship.

To represent 1:1 recursive relationships, we take an approach nearly identical to that for regular 1:1 relationships: We can place the key of the person being

Data Structure Diagram for
STUDENT to CLASS
Relationship

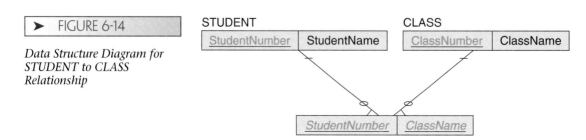

FIGURE 6-15

Examples of Recursive
Relationships: (a) 1:1
Recursive Relationship, (b) 1:N
Recursive Relationship, and
(c) N:M Recursive Relationship

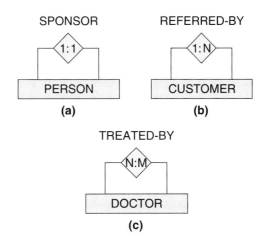

sponsored in the row of the sponsor, or we can place the key of the sponsor in the row of the person being sponsored. Figure 6-16(b) shows the first alternative, and Figure 6-16(c) shows the second. Both work, and so the choice depends on performance issues.

This technique is identical to that for nonrecursive 1:1 relationships, except that both the child and parent rows reside in the same relation. You can think of the process as follows: Pretend that the relationship is between two different relations. Determine where the key goes, and then combine the two relations into a single one.

To illustrate, consider the REFERRED-BY relationship in Figure 6-15(b). This is a 1:N relationship, as shown in the sample data in Figure 6-17(a). When this data is placed in a relation, one row represents the referrer, and the other rows represent those who have been referred. The referrer row takes the role of the par-

FIGURE 6-16

Example of a 1:1 Recursive
Relationship: (a) Sample Data
for 1:1 Recursive Relationship,
(b) First Alternative for
Representing a 1:1 Recursive
Relationship, and (c) Second
Alternative for Representing a
1:1 Recursive Relationship

Person

Jones
Smith
Parks
Myrtle
Pines

(a)

Person	PersonSponsored
Jones	Smith
Smith	Parks
Parks	null
Myrtle	Pines
Pines	null

(b)

Person	PersonSponsoredBy
Jones	null
Smith	Jones
Parks	Smith
Myrtle	null
Pines	Myrtle

(c)

Example of a 1:N Recursive Relationship: (a) Sample Data for the REFERRED-BY Relationship and (b) Representing a 1:N Recursive Relationship by Means of a Relation

Customer Number	Referred These Customers
100	200, 400
300	500
400	600, 700

(a)

CUSTOMER Relation

CustomerNumber	CustomerData	ReferredBy
100	. . .	null
200	. . .	100
300	. . .	null
400	. . .	100
500	. . .	300
600	. . .	400
700	. . .	400

(b)

ent, and the referred rows take the role of the child. As with all 1:N relationships, we place the key of the parent in the child. In Figure 6-17(b), we place the number of the referrer in all the rows that have been referred.

Now consider M:N recursive relationships. The TREATED-BY relationship in Figure 6-15(c) represents the situation in which doctors give treatments to each other. Sample data is shown in Figure 6-18(a). As with other M:N relationships,

Example of an M:N Recursive Relationship: (a) Sample Data for the TREATED-BY Relationship and (b) Representing an M:N Recursive Relationship by Means of Relations

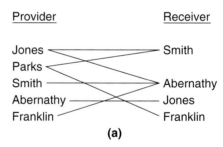

Provider	Receiver
Jones	Smith
Parks	Abernathy
Smith	Jones
Abernathy	Franklin
Franklin	

(a)

DOCTOR relation

Name	Other Attributes
Jones	. . .
Parks	. . .
Smith	. . .
Abernathy	. . .
O'Leary	. . .
Franklin	. . .

TREATMENT-INTERSECTION relation

Physician	Patient
Jones	Smith
Parks	Smith
Smith	Abernathy
Abernathy	Jones
Parks	Franklin
Franklin	Abernathy
Jones	Abernathy

(b)

we must create an intersection table that shows pairs of related rows. The name of the doctor in the first column is the one who provided the treatment, and the name of the doctor in the second column is the one who received the treatment. This structure is shown in Figure 6-18(b).

Recursive relationships are thus represented in the same way as are other relationships. The rows of the tables can take two different roles, however. Some are parent rows, and others are child rows. If a key is supposed to be a parent key and if the row has no parent, its value will be null. If a key is supposed to be a child key and the row has no child, its value will be null.

REPRESENTING TERNARY AND HIGHER-ORDER RELATIONSHIPS

Ternary relationships are represented using the techniques just described, but there is often a special consideration that needs to be documented as a business rule. Consider, for example, the entities ORDER, CUSTOMER, and SALESPERSON. In most cases, we can treat this ternary relationship as two separate binary relationships.

For example, assume an ORDER has a single CUSTOMER, but a CUSTOMER can have many ORDERs. Hence that relationship is binary N:1. Similarly, suppose the ORDER has just one SALESPERSON, and a SALESPERSON has many ORDERs. That relationship is also binary N:1.

Both of these relationships can be represented using the techniques just described. We represent the first by placing the key of CUSTOMER in ORDER and the second by placing the key of SALESPERSON in ORDER. Thus, we have treated the ternary relationship among ORDER:CUSTOMER:SALESPERSON as two separate binary relationships.

Suppose, however, that the business has a rule that states that each CUSTOMER can place orders only with a particular SALESPERSON. In this case, the ternary relationship ORDER:CUSTOMER:SALESPERSON is constrained by an ad-

FIGURE 6-19

Examples of Binary Constraints on Ternary Relationships (a) Example of MUST Binary Constraint on a Ternary Relationship

SALESPERSON Table

SalespersonNumber	Other nonkey data
10	
20	
30	

CUSTOMER Table

CustomerNumber	Other nonkey data	SalespersonNumber
1000		10
2000		20
3000		30

Binary MUST Constraint

ORDER Table

OrderNumber	Other nonkey data	SalespersonNumber	CustomerNumber
100		10	1000
200		20	2000
300		10	1000
400		30	3000
500			2000

Only 20 is allowed here

(a)

(Continued)

(b) Example of Binary MUST NOT Constraint on a Ternary Relationship

DRUG Table

DrugNumber	Other nonkey data
10	
20	
30	
45	
70	
90	

ALLERGY Table

CustomerNumber	DrugNumber	Other nonkey data
1000	10	
1000	20	
2000	20	
2000	45	
3000	30	
3000	45	
3000	70	

⎰ Binary MUST NOT Constraint ⎱

PRESCRIPTION Table

PrescriptionNumber	Other nonkey data	DrugNumber	CustomerNumber
100		45	1000
200		10	2000
300		70	1000
400		20	3000
500			2000

Neither 20 nor 45 can appear here ⎱

(b)

ditional binary N:1 relationship between CUSTOMER and SALESPERSON. To represent the constraint, we need to add the key of SALESPERSON to CUSTOMER. The three relations will be as follows:

ORDER (<u>OrderNumber</u>, nonkey data attributes, *CustomerNumber*, *SalespersonNumber*)

CUSTOMER (<u>CustomerNumber</u>, nonkey data attributes, *SalespersonNumber*)

SALESPERSON (<u>SalespersonNumber</u>, nonkey data attributes)

The constraint that a particular CUSTOMER is called only by a particular SALESPERSON means that only certain values of CustomerNumber and SalespersonNumber can exist together in ORDER. Unfortunately, there is no way to express this constraint using the relational model. It must be documented in the design, however, and enforced either by the DBMS (if it has such capability) or by application programs.

Other types of such binary constraints are MUST NOT and MUST COVER constraints. In a MUST NOT constraint, the binary relationship indicates combinations that are not allowed to occur in the ternary relationship. For example, the ternary relationship PRESCRIPTION:DRUG:PERSON can be constrained by a binary relationship DRUG:PERSON that indicates drugs that a person is not allowed to take.

In a MUST COVER constraint, the binary relationship indicates all combinations that must appear in the ternary relationship. For example, consider the re-

(Continued)

(c) Example of Binary MUST COVER Constraint on a Ternary Relationship

REPAIR Table

RepairNumber	Other nonkey data
10	
20	
30	
40	

TASK Table

TaskNumber	Other nonkey data	*RepairNumber*
1001		10
1002		10
1003		10
2001		20
2002		20
3001		30
4001		40

⟵ Binary MUST COVER Constraint ⟶

AUTO-REPAIR Table

InvoiceNumber	RepairNumber	TaskNumber	Other nonkey data
100	10	1001	
200	10	1002	
300	10	1003	
400	20	2001	
500	20		

2002 must appear here ⟶

(c)

lationship AUTO:REPAIR:TASK. Suppose that a given repair consists of a number of TASKs, all of which must be performed for the REPAIR to be successful. In this case, in the relation AUTO-REPAIR, when a given auto has a given REPAIR, then all of the TASKs for that repair must appear as rows in that relation.

None of the three types of binary constraints discussed here can be represented in the relational design. Instead, all of the relationships must be treated as a combination of binary relationships. The constraints, however, must be documented as part of the design.

REPRESENTING IS-A RELATIONSHIPS (SUBTYPES)

The strategy for representing subtypes, or IS-A relationships, is somewhat different from the strategy used for HAS-A relationships. Consider the example of CLIENT with attributes ClientNumber, ClientName, and AmountDue. Suppose that there are three subtypes of CLIENT, namely, INDIVIDUAL-CLIENT, PARTNERSHIP-CLIENT, and CORPORATE-CLIENT, with the following attributes:

INDIVIDUAL-CLIENT: Address, SocialSecurityNumber

PARTNERSHIP-CLIENT: ManagingPartnerName, Address, TaxIdentificationNumber

CORPORATE-CLIENT: ContactPerson, Phone, TaxIdentificationNumber

To represent this structure by means of relations, we define one relation for the supertype (CLIENT) and one relation for each subtype. Then we place each of the attributes of the supertype into the relation that represents it and each of the attributes of the subtypes into the relations that represent them. At this point, the subtype relations do not have a key. To create a key, we add the key of the supertype, or ClientNumber, to each of the subtypes. The final list of relations is

CLIENT (<u>ClientNumber,</u> ClientName, AmountDue)

INDIVIDUAL-CLIENT (<u>ClientNumber,</u> Address, SocialSecurityNumber)

PARTNERSHIP-CLIENT (<u>ClientNumber,</u> ManagingPartnerName, Address, TaxIdentificationNumber)

CORPORATE-CLIENT (<u>ClientNumber,</u> ContactPerson, Phone, TaxIdentificationNumber)

Note that with this structure, the relationship between a row in CLIENT and a row in one of the subtypes is 1:1. No client has more than one row in a subtype relation, and each subtype corresponds uniquely to one row of the supertype. Depending on the restrictions of the application, it might be possible for a row in CLIENT to correspond to multiple rows, each in a different subtype. But no row of CLIENT can correspond to more than one row in the *same* subtype relation.

It is possible for one or more of the subtypes to have a key of its own. For example, the application may call for a CorporateClientNumber that is distinct from ClientNumber. In that case, the key of CORPORATE-CLIENT is CorporateClientNumber. Since the relationship between CLIENT and CORPORATE-CLIENT is 1:1, it can be established by placing the key of one in the other. Most often, it is considered better design to place the key of the supertype relation in the key of the subtype relation. For this case, the structure of CORPORATE-CLIENT is

CORPORATE-CLIENT (<u>CorporateClientNumber,</u> ClientNumber, ContactPerson, Phone, TaxIdentificationNumber)

➤ EXAMPLE DESIGN

Figure 6-20(a) is a copy of the E-R diagram introduced in Chapter 3 as Figure 3-9. It contains all of the basic elements used in E-R diagrams. To represent this diagram by means of relations, we begin by establishing one relation for each entity. We assume the keys as follows:

RELATION	KEY
EMPLOYEE	EmployeeNumber
ENGINEER	EmployeeNumber
TRUCK	LicenseNumber
SERVICE	InvoiceNumber
CLIENT	ClientNumber
ENGINEER-CERTIFICATION	(EmployeeNumber, CertificationName)
CERTIFICATION	CertificationName

The next step is to examine each of these relations against the normalization criteria. The example does not tell us what attributes must be represented, so we cannot determine the constraints. We will assume that these relations are in DK/NF, although in practice we would need to check out that assumption against the attribute lists and constraints. For now, we will focus on the representation of relationships. The relations and their key attributes (including foreign keys) are listed in Figure 6-20(b).

The relationship between EMPLOYEE and ENGINEER is already represented because the relations have the same key, EmployeeNumber. ENGINEER and

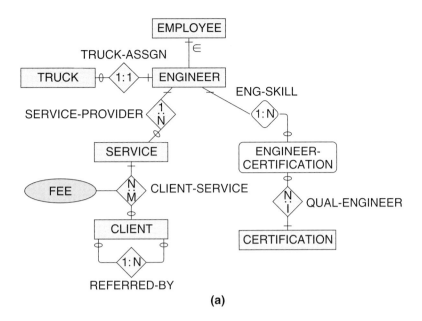

➤ FIGURE 6-20

*Relational
Representation of an
Example E-R
Diagram: (a) E-R
Diagram from
Chapter 3 and
(b) Relations Needed
to Represent This E-R
Diagram*

(a)

EMPLOYEE (<u>EmployeeNumber</u>, other nonkey EMPLOYEE attributes . . .)

ENGINEER (<u>EmployeeNumber</u>, other nonkey ENGINEER attributes . . .)

TRUCK (<u>LicenseNumber</u>, other nonkey TRUCK attributes, *EmployeeNumber*)

SERVICE (<u>InvoiceNumber</u>, other nonkey SERVICE attributes, *EmployeeNumber*)

CLIENT (<u>ClientNumber</u>, other nonkey CLIENT attributes, *ReferredBy*)

SERVICE-CLIENT (<u>InvoiceNumber</u>, <u>ClientNumber</u>, Fee)

ENGINEER-CERTIFICATION (<u>EmployeeNumber</u>, <u>CertificationName</u>, other nonkey
    ENGINEER-CERTIFICATION attributes)

CERTIFICATION (<u>CertificationName</u>, other nonkey CERTIFICATION attributes)

(b)

TRUCK have a 1:1 relationship and so can be related by placing the key of one in the other. Because a truck must be assigned to an employee, there will be no null values if we place EmployeeNumber in TRUCK, and so we will do that.

For the 1:N relationship between ENGINEER and SERVICE, we place the key of ENGINEER (the parent) in SERVICE (the child). The relationship between SERVICE and CLIENT is M:N, so we must create an intersection relation. Because this relationship has an attribute, Fee, we add that attribute to the intersection relation. For the 1:N recursive relationship, REFERRED-BY, we add the attribute ReferredBy to CLIENT. The name *ReferredBy* implies, correctly, that the key of the parent—the one client doing the referring—is being placed in the relation.

Because ENGINEER-CERTIFICATION is ID-dependent on ENGINEER, we know that EmployeeNumber must be part of its key; thus the key is a composite (EmployeeNumber, CertificationName). The dependency relationship is 1:N and so will be carried by EmployeeNumber. Finally, the relationship between CERTIFICATION and ENGINEER-CERTIFICATION is 1:N, so we would normally add the key of CERTIFICATION (the parent) to ENGINEER-CERTIFICATION. But that key is already part of the relation, so we need not do this.

Study this example to make sure that you understand the various types of relationships and how they are expressed in terms of the relations. All of the elements of the E-R model are present in this diagram.

➤ TREES, NETWORKS, AND BILLS OF MATERIALS

Although neither the E-R model nor the semantic-object model makes any assumptions about patterns of relationships among entities, some patterns do occur often enough that they have been given special names. These patterns are trees, simple networks, complex networks, and bills of materials. We introduce the concept of these patterns here, in the context of the E-R model.

TREES

A **tree,** or **hierarchy,** as it is sometimes called, is a data structure in which the elements of the structure have only one-to-many relationships with one another. Each element has at most one parent. Figure 6-21 is an example of a tree. According to standard terminology, each element is called a **node,** and the relationships among the elements are called **branches.** The node at the top of the tree is called the **root** (what a metaphor—the roots of real trees are normally at the bottom!). In Figure 6-21, Node 1 is the root of the tree.

Every node of a tree, except the root, has a **parent,** which is the node immediately above it. Thus, Node 2 is the parent of Node 5; Node 4 is the parent of Node 8; and so on. As we stated earlier, trees are distinguished from other data structures in that every node has at most one parent. We say at most one parent because the root node has no parent.

The descendants of a node are called **children.** In general, there is no limitation on the number of children that a node may have. Node 2 has two children, Nodes 5 and 6; Node 3 has no children; and Node 4 has three children, Nodes 7, 8, and 9. Nodes having the same parent are called **twins,** or **siblings.** For example, Nodes 5 and 6 are twins or siblings.

Figure 6-22(a) illustrates a tree of entities in which you can see several one-to-many relationships among entities in a university system. Colleges consist of many departments, which in turn have many professors and many administrative employees. Finally, professors advise many students who have received many grades. There are six different entity types in this structure, but all of the relationships are 1:N.

To represent a tree of entities using the relational model, we simply apply the concepts described in earlier sections of this chapter. First we transform each entity into a relation. Then we examine the relations generated against the normalization criteria and subdivide the relations if necessary. We represent the 1:N relationships by storing the key of the parent in the child. Figure 6-22(b) is a data structure diagram corresponding to the tree in Figure 6-22(a).

In summary, a hierarchy, or tree, is a collection of records organized in such a way that all relationships are 1:N. All records have exactly one parent, except

➤ FIGURE 6-21

Example of a Tree

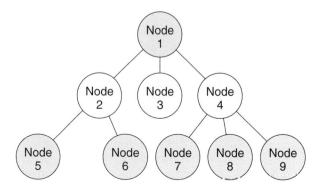

➤   FIGURE 6-22

Representation of a Tree by
Means of Relations: (a) Tree
Composed of Entities and
(b) Representation of This
Tree by Means of Relations

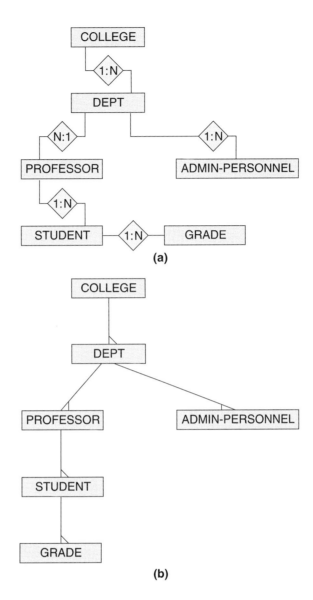

(a)

(b)

the root, which has no parent. A hierarchy can be represented by a set of relations using the methods defined earlier. Hierarchies are common in businesses,
especially in manufacturing applications.

Simple Networks

A **simple network** is also a data structure of elements having only one-to-many
relationships. In a simple network, however, the elements may have more than
one parent as long as the parents are of different types. For example, in the simple network shown in Figure 6-23, each STUDENT entity has two parents, an AD-
VISER entity and a MAJOR entity. The data structure in Figure 6-23 is not a tree
because STUDENT entities have more than one parent.

Figure 6-24(a) shows the general structure of this simple network. Notice that
all relationships are one to many but that STUDENT has two parents. In this figure, the parent records are on top, and the children records are beneath them.
This arrangement is convenient but not essential. You may see simple networks
depicted with parents beside or below the children. You can identify simple networks in such arrangements by the fact that a single record type participates as a
child in two (or more) one-to-many relationships.

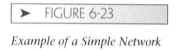

Example of a Simple Network

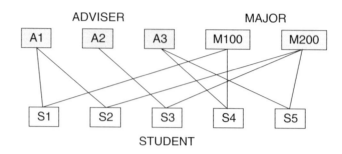

To represent a simple network of entities with the relational model, we follow the procedures described earlier. First we transform each entity into a relation and normalize the relations if necessary. Then we represent each 1:N relationship by storing the key of the parent relation in the child relation. The result of this process for the network in Figure 6-24(a) is shown in Figure 6-24(b).

COMPLEX NETWORKS

A **complex network** is a data structure of elements in which at least one of the relationships is many-to-many. The complex network in Figure 6-25(a) illustrates the relationships among invoices, line items, parts, and suppliers. Two of the three relationships are 1:N, and the third is M:N. Because there is at least one many-to-many relationship, this structure is called a complex network.

As discussed, M:N relationships have no direct representation in the relational model. Consequently, before this structure can be stored in relational form, we must define an intersection relation. In Figure 6-25(b), the intersection relation is part-supplier.

BILLS OF MATERIALS

A **bill of materials** is a special data structure that occurs frequently in manufacturing applications. In fact, such structures provided a major impetus for the development of database technology in the 1960s.

Figure 6-26 is an example of a bill of materials, which shows the parts that constitute products. When viewed from the standpoint of a given product, say Product A, this data structure is a hierarchy. But because a part can be used in more than one product, this structure is actually a network. For example, the part ABC100 has two parents, Product A and Product B.

Representation of a Simple Network by Means of Relations: (a) Simple Network Composed of Entities and (b) Its Representation by Means of Relations

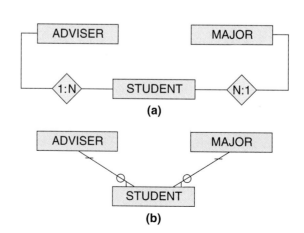

➤ FIGURE 6-25

Representation of a Complex Network by Means of Relations: (a) Complex Network Composed of Entities and (b) Its Representation by Means of Relations

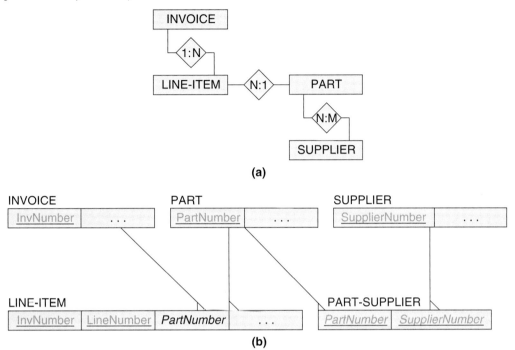

A bill of materials can be represented by means of relations in several ways. The most common is to consider it as an M:N recursive relationship. A part (or product or assembly or subassembly or whatever) contains many elements. At the same time, there may be many elements that contain it. Figure 6-27(a) shows the general data structure of the M:N recursive relationship, and Figure 6-27(b) shows an instance of the intersection relation created to represent this bill of materials.

➤ FIGURE 6-26

Example of a Bill of Materials

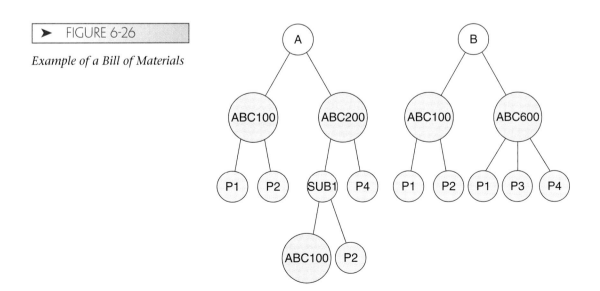

Representation of a Bill of Materials with Relations: (a) Relations Representing a Bill of Materials and (b) Data for
the ELEMENT RELATIONSHIP Intersection Relation

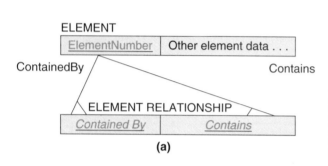

Contained By	Contains
A	ABC100
A	ABC200
B	ABC100
B	ABC600
ABC100	P1
ABC100	P2
ABC200	SUB1
ABC200	P4
ABC600	P1
ABC600	P3
ABC600	P4
SUB1	ABC100
SUB1	P2

Observe element A
contains an ABC100
and element ABC100
is contained by an A

(b)

ELEMENT

ElementNumber	Other element data . . .

ContainedBy   Contains

ELEMENT RELATIONSHIP

Contained By	Contains

(a)

➤ SUMMARY

To transform entity-relationship data models, each entity is represented by a relation. The attributes of the entity become the attributes of the relation. Once the relation has been created, it must be examined against normalization criteria and divided into two or more relations if necessary.

There are three types of binary HAS-A relationships in the E-R model: 1:1, 1:N, and N:M. To represent a 1:1 relationship, we place the key of one relation into the other relation. One-to-one relationships sometimes indicate that two relations have been defined on the same entity and so should be combined into one relation.

To represent a 1:N relationship, we place the key of the parent in the child. Finally, to represent an M:N relationship, we create an intersection relation that contains the keys of the other two relations.

Recursive relationships are relationships in which the participants in the relationship arise from the same entity class. There are three types: 1:1, 1:N, and N:M. The types are represented in the same way as are nonrecursive relationships. For 1:1 and 1:N relationships, we add a foreign key to the relation that represents the entity. For an N:M recursion, we create an intersection table that represents the M:N relationship.

Ternary and higher-order relationships can be treated as combinations of binary relationships. If this is done, however, any binary constraints on the ternary relationship must also be represented in the design. Because it is not possible to enforce the constraint by the relational design, it must be documented as a business rule. Three types of such constraints occur: MUST, MUST NOT, and MUST COVER.

Supertype and subtype entities (IS-A relationships) are also represented by relations. One relation is defined for the supertype entity, and other relations are defined for each subtype. Usually the keys of the relations are the same, and the relationship among the rows is defined through those keys. If they are not the same, the key of the subtype relation can be placed in the supertype relation or the key of the supertype relation can be placed in the subtype. Most often, the key of the supertype relation is placed in the subtype relation.

Binary relationships can be combined to form three types of more complicated structures. A tree is a collection of record types in which each record has exactly one parent, except the root, which has no parent. In a simple network, records may have multiple parents, but the parents must be of different types. In a complex network, records have multiple parents of the same type. Another way of saying this is that in a complex network, at least one of the binary relationships is M:N.

A bill of materials is a data structure frequently seen in manufacturing applications. Such structures can be represented by M:N recursive relationships.

➤ GROUP I QUESTIONS

6.1   Explain how E-R entities are transformed into relations.

6.2   Why is it necessary to examine relations transformed from entities against normalization criteria? Under what conditions should the relations be altered if they are not in DK/NF? Under what conditions should they not be altered?

6.3   Explain how the representation of weak entities differs from the representation of strong entities.

6.4   List the three types of binary relationships and give an example of each. Do not use the examples in this text.

6.5   Define *foreign key* and give an example.

6.6   Show two different ways to represent the 1:1 relationship in your answer to Question 6.4. Use data structure diagrams.

6.7   For your answers to Question 6.6, describe a method for obtaining data about one of the entities, given the key of the other. Describe a method for obtaining data about the second entity, given the key of the first. Describe answers for both of your alternatives in Question 6.6.

6.8   Why are some 1:1 relationships considered suspicious? Under what conditions should relations in a 1:1 relationship be combined into one relation?

6.9   Define the terms *parent* and *child* and give an example of each.

6.10 Show how to represent the 1:N relationship in your answer to Question 6.4. Use a data structure diagram.

6.11 For your answer to Question 6.10, describe a method for obtaining data for all of the children, given the key of the parent. Describe a method for obtaining data for the parent, given a key of the child.

6.12 For a 1:N relationship, explain why you must place the key of the parent in the child, rather than placing the key of the child in the parent.

6.13 Give examples of binary 1:N relationships, other than those in this text, for

a. An optional-to-optional relationship.

b. An optional-to-mandatory relationship.

c. A mandatory-to-optional relationship.

d. A mandatory-to-mandatory relationship.

Illustrate your answer using data structure diagrams.

6.14 Show how to represent the N:M relationship in your answer to Question 6.4. Use a data structure diagram.

6.15 For your answer to Question 6.14, describe a method for obtaining the children for one entity, given the key of the other. Also describe a method for obtaining the children for the second entity, given the key of the first.

6.16 Why is it not possible to represent N:M relationships with the same strategy used to represent 1:N relationships?

6.17 Explain the meaning of the term *intersection relation*.

6.18 Define three types of recursive binary relationships and give an example of each.

6.19 Show how to represent the 1:1 recursive relationship in your answer to Question 6.18. How does this differ from the representation of 1:1 nonrecursive relationships?

6.20 Show how to represent the 1:N recursive relationship in your answer to Question 6.18. How does this differ from the representation of 1:N nonrecursive relationships?

6.21 Show how to represent the M:N recursive relationship in your answer to Question 6.18. How does this differ from the representation of M:N nonrecursive relationships?

6.22 Explain how to use binary relationships to represent a ternary relationship. Give an example other than the ones in this text.

6.23 In your answer to question 6.22, define a binary constraint on the ternary relationship. Explain how to represent the constraint. Since the constraint cannot be enforced in the relational model, what should be done?

6.24 Give examples of MUST NOT and MUST COVER binary constraints other than the ones in this text.

6.25 Give an example of a supertype and subtypes, and show how to represent it using relations.

6.26 Define tree, simple network, and complex network.

6.27 Give an example of a tree structure other than one in this text, and show how to represent it by means of relations.

6.28 Give an example of a simple network other than one in this text, and show how to represent it by means of relations.

6.29 Give an example of a complex network other than one in this text, and show how to represent it by means of relations.

6.30 What is a bill of materials? Give an example other than the one in this text, and show how to represent your example by means of relations.

➤ GROUP II QUESTIONS

6.31 Transform the entity-relationship diagram for the Jefferson Dance Club (Figure 3-12) into relations. Express your answer with a data structure diagram, and show the interrelation constraints.

6.32 Transform the entity-relationship diagram for San Juan Charters (Figure 3-14) into relations. Express your answer with a data structure diagram, and show the interrelation constraints.

6.33 Some of the relations in Figure 6-19 are not in DK/NF. Identify them and explain why not. What normal form do they have? How can this design be justified? How else could the database application enforce the binary constraints?

➤ PROJECTS

A. Complete project A at the end of Chapter 3 if you have not already done so. Transform your E-R diagram into a set of relations. If any of your relations are not in DK/NF, justify your decision to create un-normalized relations.

B. Complete project B at the end of Chapter 3 if you have not already done so. Transform your E-R diagram into a set of relations. If any of your relations are not in DK/NF, justify your decision to create un-normalized relations.

C. Complete project C at the end of Chapter 3 if you have not already done so. Transform your E-R diagram into a set of relations. If any of your relations are not in DK/NF, justify your decision to create un-normalized relations.

CHAPTER 7

Database Design with Semantic Object Models

This chapter discusses the transformation of semantic object models into relational database designs. First we describe the transformation of each of seven common types of semantic objects. Then we illustrate these concepts by showing the semantic object modeling and relational representation of several real-world objects. Since the best way to learn this subject is to work examples yourself, you are strongly encouraged to do the projects at the end of this chapter.

➤ TRANSFORMATION OF SEMANTIC OBJECTS INTO RELATIONAL DATABASE DESIGNS

Chapter 4 introduced the semantic object data model and defined seven types of semantic objects. In this section, we present methods for transforming each of those seven types into relations. When working with semantic objects, normalization problems are less likely than they are when working with the E-R models because the definition of semantic objects usually separates semantic themes into group attributes or objects. Thus, when transforming an object into relations, the relations are generally either already in DK/NF or are in very close to domain/key normal form.

*Relational Representation of
Example Simple Object:
(a) EQUIPMENT Object
Diagram and (b) Relation
Representing EQUIPMENT*

EQUIPMENT
ID EquipmentNumber
Description
AcquisitionDate
PurchaseCost

(a)

EQUIPMENT (EquipmentNumber, Description, AcquisitionDate, PurchaseCost)
(b)

SIMPLE OBJECTS

Figure 7-1 illustrates the transformation of a simple object into a relation. Recall that a simple object has no multi-value attributes and no object attributes. Consequently, simple objects can be represented by a single relation in the database.

Figure 7-1(a) is an example of a simple object, EQUIPMENT, which can be represented by a single relation, as shown in Figure 7-1(b). Each attribute of the object is defined as an attribute of the relation, and the identifying attribute, EquipmentNumber, becomes the key attribute of the relation, denoted by underlining EquipmentNumber in Figure 7-1(b).

The general transformation of simple objects is illustrated in Figure 7-2. Object OBJECT1 is transformed into relation R1. The attribute that identifies OBJECT1 instances is O1; it becomes the key of relation R1. Nonkey data is represented in this and subsequent figures with ellipses (. . .).

Because a key is an attribute that uniquely identifies a row of a table, only unique identifiers—those with the ID underlined—can be transformed into keys. If there is no unique identifier in the object, then one must be created, by either creating a new attribute that is a unique identifier or combining the existing attributes to form a unique identifier.[1]

COMPOSITE OBJECTS

A composite object is an object that has one or more multi-value simple or group attributes but no object attributes. Figure 7-3(a) shows an example composite object, HOTEL-BILL. To represent this object, one relation is created for the base ob-

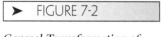

➤ FIGURE 7-2

*General Transformation of
Simple Object into a Relation*

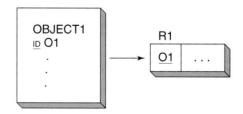

---

[1]In some situations, database developers (or the DBMS) create a unique key, called a *surrogate key*, that identifies each row of a relation. Because it has no meaning, this key is hidden from the users by the application. When a user creates a new row, the application creates, behind the scenes, a new value for the surrogate key, but the user never sees the key or is even aware of its existence. Such keys are used to give a unique identity to objects that do not have a unique identifier useful to the user. See the discussion of SQL3 in Chapter 17.

➤ FIGURE 7-3

Relational Representation of
Example Composite Object:
(a) HOTEL-BILL Object
Diagram and (b) Relations
Representing HOTEL-BILL

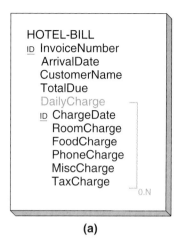

(a)

HOTEL-BILL (InvoiceNumber, ArrivalDate, CustomerName, TotalDue)

DAILY-CHARGE (*InvoiceNumber*, ChargeDate, RoomCharge, FoodCharge, PhoneCharge, MiscCharge, TaxCharge)

(b)

ject, HOTEL-BILL, and an additional relation is created for the repeating group attribute, DailyCharge. This relational design is shown in Figure 7-3(b).

In the key of DAILY-CHARGE, InvoiceNumber is underlined because it is part of the key of DAILY-CHARGE, and it is italicized because it is also a foreign key. (It is a key of HOTEL-BILL.) ChargeDate is underlined because it is part of the key of DAILY-CHARGE, but it is not italicized because it is not a foreign key.

In general, composite objects are transformed by defining one relation for the object itself and another relation for each multi-value attribute. In Figure 7-4(a), object OBJECT1 contains two groups of multi-value attributes, each of which is represented by a relation in the database design. The key of each of these tables is the composite of the identifier of the object plus the identifier of the group. Thus, the representation of OBJECT1 is a relation R1 with key O1, a relation R2 with key (O1, G1), and a relation R3 with key (O1, G2).

The minimum cardinality from the object to the group is specified by the minimum cardinality of group attribute. In Figure 7-4(a), the minimum cardinality of Group1 is 1 and that of Group2 is 0. These cardinalities are shown as a hash mark (on R2) and an oval (on R3) in the data structure diagram. The minimum cardinality from the group to the object is, by default, always 1, because a group cannot exist if the object that contains that group does not exist. These minimum cardinalities are shown by hash marks on the relationship lines into R1.

As noted in Chapter 4, groups can be nested. Figure 7-4(b) shows an object in which Group2 is nested within Group1. When this occurs, the relation representing the nested group is made subordinate to the relation that represents its containing group. In Figure 7-4(b), relation R3 is subordinate to relation R2. The key of R3 is the key of R2, which is (O1, G1) plus the identifier of Group2, which is G2; thus the key of R3 is (O1, G1, G2).

Make sure that you understand why the keys in Figure 7-4(b) are constructed as they are. Also note that some attributes are underlined and italicized and some are simply underlined, because some attributes are both local and foreign keys and some are just local keys.

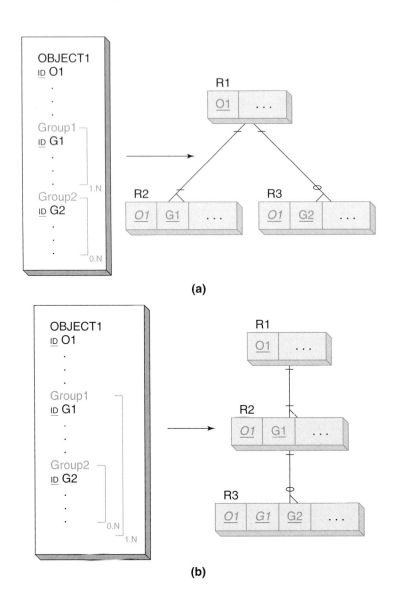

➤ FIGURE 7-4

General Transformation of Composite Objects:
(a) Composite Object with Separate Groups and
(b) Composite Object with Nested Groups

COMPOUND OBJECTS

The relational representation of compound objects is similar to the representation of entities. In fact, compound objects and entities are in many ways quite similar.

As we stated in Chapter 4, an object, OBJECT1, can contain one or many instances of a second object, OBJECT2, and OBJECT2 can contain one or many instances of the first object, OBJECT1. This leads to the object types shown in Figure 7-5.

All of these relationships involve some variation of one-to-one, one-to-many, or many-to-many relationships. Specifically, the relationship from OBJECT1 to OBJECT2 can be 1:1, 1:N, or N:M, whereas the relationship from OBJECT2 to OBJECT1 can be 1:1, 1:M, or M:N. To represent any of these, we need only address these three types of relationships.

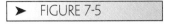

➤ FIGURE 7-5

Four Types of Compound Objects

Object2	Object1 Can Contain	
	One	Many
Can One	1:1	1:N
Contain Many	M:1	M:N

FIGURE 7-6

Example Relational Representation of 1:1 Compound Objects: (a) Example 1:1 Compound Objects and (b) Their Representation

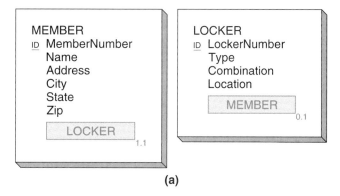

MEMBER
ID MemberNumber
Name
Address
City
State
Zip

LOCKER
1.1

LOCKER
ID LockerNumber
Type
Combination
Location

MEMBER
0.1

(a)

MEMBER (MemberNumber, Name, Address, City, State, Zip, *LockerNumber*)

LOCKER (LockerNumber, Type, Combination, Location)

(b)

REPRESENTING ONE-TO-ONE COMPOUND OBJECTS

Consider the assignment of a LOCKER to a health club MEMBER. A LOCKER is assigned to one MEMBER, and each MEMBER has one, and only one, LOCKER. Figure 7-6(a) shows the object diagrams. To represent these objects with relations, we define a relation for each object, and, as with 1:1 entity relationships, we place the key of either relation in the other relation. That is, we can place the key of MEMBER in LOCKER or the key of LOCKER in MEMBER. Figure 7-6(b) shows the placement of the key of LOCKER in MEMBER. Note that LockerNumber is underlined in LOCKER because it is the key of LOCKER and is italicized in MEMBER because it is a foreign key in MEMBER.

In general, for a 1:1 relationship between OBJECT1 and OBJECT2, we define one relation for each object, R1 and R2. Then we place the key of either relation (O1 or O2) as a foreign key in the other relation, as in Figure 7-7.

FIGURE 7-7

General Transformation of 1:1 Compound Objects

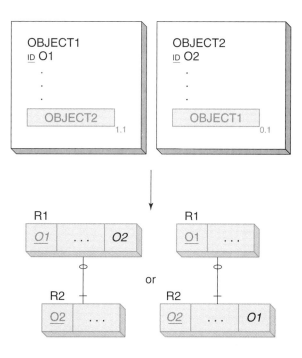

Example Relational Representation of 1:N Compound Objects: (a) Example 1:N Compound Objects and (b) Their Representation

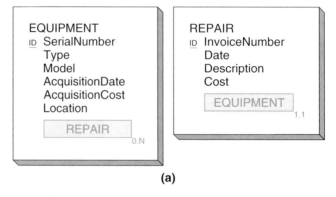

(a)

EQUIPMENT (<u>SerialNumber</u>, Type, Model, AcquisitionDate, AcquisitionCost, Location)

REPAIR (<u>InvoiceNumber</u>, Date, Description, Cost, *SerialNumber*)

(b)

REPRESENTING ONE-TO-MANY AND MANY-TO-ONE RELATIONSHIPS

Now consider 1:N relationships and N:1 relationships. Figure 7-8(a) shows an example of a 1:N object relationship between EQUIPMENT and REPAIR. An item of EQUIPMENT can have many REPAIRs, but a REPAIR can be related to only one item of EQUIPMENT.

The objects in Figure 7-8(a) are represented by the relations in Figure 7-8(b). Observe that the key of the parent (the object on the one side of the relationship) is placed in the child (the object on the many side of the relationship).

Figure 7-9 shows the general transformation of 1:N compound objects. Object OBJECT1 contains many objects OBJECT2, and object OBJECT2 contains just one OBJECT1. To represent this structure by means of relations, we represent each object with a relation and place the key of the parent in the child. Thus, in Figure 7-9 the attribute O1 is placed in R2.

General Transformation of 1:N Compound Objects

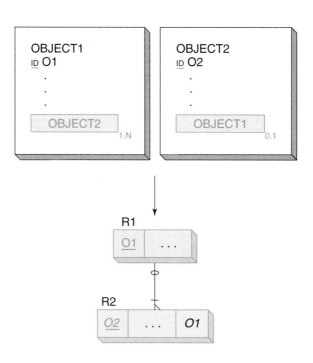

If OBJECT2 were to contain many OBJECT1s and OBJECT1 were to contain just one OBJECT2, we would use the same strategy but reverse the role of R1 and R2. That is, we would place O2 in R1.

The minimum cardinalities in either case are determined by the minimum cardinalities of the object attributes. In Figure 7-9, OBJECT1 requires at least one OBJECT2, but OBJECT2 does not necessarily require an OBJECT1. These cardinalities are shown in the data structure diagram as an oval on the R1 side of the relationship and as a hash mark on the R2 side of the relationship. These minimum cardinality values are simply examples; either or both objects could have a cardinality of 0, 1, or some other number.

REPRESENTING MANY-TO-MANY RELATIONSHIPS

Finally, consider M:N relationships. As with M:N entity relationships, we define three relations, one for each of the objects and a third intersection relation. The intersection relation represents the relationship of the two objects and consists of the keys of both of its parents. Figure 7-10(a) shows the M:N relationship between BOOK and AUTHOR. Figure 7-10(b) depicts the three relations that represent these objects: BOOK, AUTHOR, and BOOK-AUTHOR-INT, the intersection relation. Notice that BOOK-AUTHOR-INT has no nonkey data. Both the attributes ISBN and SocialSecurityNumber are underlined and in italics because they both are local and foreign keys.

In general, for two objects that have an M:N relationship, we define a relation R1 for object OBJECT1, a relation R2 for object OBJECT2, and a relation R3 for the intersection relation. The general scheme is shown in Figure 7-11. Note that the attributes of R3 are only O1 and O2. For M:N compound objects, R3 never contains nonkey data. The importance of this statement will become clear when we contrast M:N compound relationships with association relationships.

Considering minimum cardinality, the parents of the intersection relation are always required. The minimum cardinalities of the relationships into the intersection relation are determined by the minimum cardinalities of the object links. In Figure 7-11, for example, a row in R1 requires a row in R3 because the minimum cardinality of OBJECT2 in OBJECT1 is 1. Similarly, a row in R2 does not require a row in R3 because the minimum cardinality of OBJECT1 in OBJECT2 is 0.

> FIGURE 7-10

Relational Representation of Example N:M Compound Objects: (a) BOOK and AUTHOR Objects and (b) Their Relational Representation

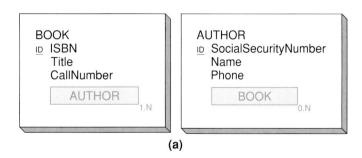

BOOK
ID ISBN
Title
CallNumber

AUTHOR
1.N

AUTHOR
ID SocialSecurityNumber
Name
Phone

BOOK
0.N

(a)

BOOK (ISBN, Title, CallNumber)

AUTHOR (SocialSecurityNumber, Name, Phone)

BOOK-AUTHOR-INT (*ISBN, SocialSecurityNumber*)

(b)

FIGURE 7-11

General Transformation of M:N Compound Objects into Relations

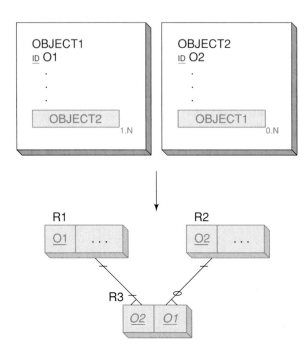

HYBRID OBJECTS

Hybrid objects can be transformed into relational designs using a combination of the techniques for composite and compound objects. Figure 7-12(a) shows SALES-ORDER, a hybrid object, and related objects. To represent this object by means of relations, we establish one relation for the object itself and another relation for each of the contained objects CUSTOMER and SALESPERSON. Then, as with a composite object, we establish a relation for the multi-value group, which is LineItem. Since this group contains another object, ITEM, we also establish a relation for ITEM. All of the one-to-many relationships are represented by placing the key of the parent relation in the child relation, as shown in Figure 7-12(b).

The example in Figure 7-12 is deceptively simple. As we mentioned in Chapter 4, there are actually four cases of hybrid objects, which are summarized in Figure 7-13.

Cases 3 and 4 are more common than Cases 1 and 2, so we consider them first. OBJECT1 in Figure 7-14 shows two groups; Group1 illustrates Case 3 and Group2 illustrates Case 4.

Group1 has a maximum cardinality of N, which means that there can be many instances of Group1 within an OBJECT1. Furthermore, since OBJECT2 is marked as ID unique, this means that a particular OBJECT2 can appear in only one of the Group1 instances within an OBJECT1. Thus OBJECT2 acts as an identifier for Group1 within OBJECT1.

(The SALES-ORDER in Figure 7-12 illustrates this case. ITEM is an identifier of LineItem, so a given ITEM can appear on only one LineItem in a particular ORDER. But an ITEM can appear on many ORDERs.)

Consider the relational representation of Group1 in Figure 7-14. A relation, R1, is created for OBJECT1, and a relation, R2, is created for OBJECT2. In addition, a third relation, R-G1, is created for Group1. The relationship between R1 and R-G1 is 1:N, so we place the key of R1 (which is O1) into R-G1; the relationship between R2 and R-G1 is also 1:N, so we place the key of R2 (which is O2) in R-G1. Because an OBJECT2 can appear with a particular value of OBJECT1 only once, the composite (O1, O2) is unique to R-G1 and can be made the key of that relation.

➤ FIGURE 7-12

Relational Representation of Example Hybrid Object: (a) Example Hybrid Object and (b) Relational Representation of SALES-ORDER and Related Objects

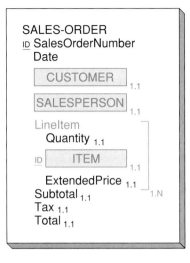

(a)

SALES-ORDER (SalesOrderNumber, Date, Subtotal, Tax, Total, *Phone*, *SalespersonName*)

CUSTOMER (CustomerName, Address, City, State, Zip, Phone)

SALESPERSON (SalesPersonName, SalesPersonCode)

LINE-ITEM (*SalesOrderNumber, ItemNumber*, Quantity, ExtendedPrice)

ITEM (ItemNumber, ItemDescription, UnitPrice)

(b)

Now consider Group2. OBJECT3 does not identify Group2, so OBJECT3 can appear in many Group2 instances in the same OBJECT1. (The SALES-ORDER in Figure 7-12 would be like this if ITEM were not ID unique in LineItem. This means that an ITEM could appear many times on the same ORDER.) Since OBJECT3 is not the identifier of Group2, we assume that some other attribute, G2, is the identifier.

In Figure 7-14, we create a relation R3 for OBJECT3 and another relation R-G2 for Group2. The relationship between R1 and R-G2 is 1:N, so place the key of R1 (which is O1) into R-G2. The relationship between R3 and R-G2 is also 1:N, so place the key of R3 (which is O3) into R-G2.

Now, however, unlike Group1, (O1, O3) cannot be the key of R-G2 because an O3 can be paired with a given O1 many times. That is, the composite (O1,O3) is not unique to R-G2, so the key of R-G2 must be (O1, G2).

Case 1 is similar to Case 3 except for the restriction that an OBJECT2 can be related to only one OBJECT1. The relations in Figure 7-14 will still work, but we must add the key of R1 (which is O1) to R2 and establish the restriction that (O1, O2) of R-G1 must equal (O1,O2) of R2.

➤ FIGURE 7-13

Four Cases of Hybrid Object Cardinality

Case	Description	Example
1	OBJECT2 relates to one instance of OBJECT1 and appears in only one group instance within that object.	ITEM relates to one ORDER and can appear on only one LineItem of that ORDER.
2	OBJECT2 relates to one instance of OBJECT1 and appears in possibly many group instances within that object.	ITEM relates to one ORDER and can appear on many LineItems of that ORDER.
3	OBJECT2 relates to possibly many instances of OBJECT1 and appears in only one group instance within each object.	ITEM relates to many ORDERs and can appear on only one LineItem of that ORDER.
4	OBJECT2 relates to possibly many instances of OBJECT1 and appears in possibly many group instances within those objects.	ITEM relates to many ORDERs and can appear on many LineItems of that ORDER.

Case 2 is similar to Case 4 except for the restriction that an OBJECT3 can be related to only one OBJECT1. Again, the relations in Figure 7-14 will work, but we must add the key of R1 (which is O1) to R3 and establish the restriction that (O1,O3) of R-G2 is a subset of (O1,O3) in R3 (see Questions 7.7 and 7.8).

➤ FIGURE 7-14

General Transformation of Hybrid Object into Relations

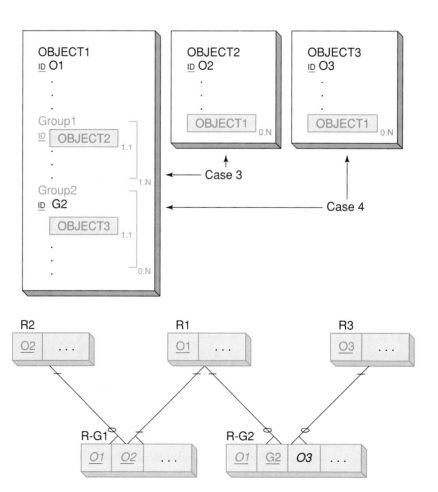

ASSOCIATION OBJECTS

An association object is an object that associates two other objects. It is a special case of compound objects that most often occurs in assignment situations. Figure 7-15(a) shows a FLIGHT object that associates an AIRPLANE with a PILOT.

To represent association objects, we define a relationship for each of the three objects, and then we represent the relationships among the objects using one of the strategies used with compound objects. In Figure 7-15(b), for example, one relation is defined for AIRPLANE, one for PILOT, and one for FLIGHT. The relationships between FLIGHT and AIRPLANE and between FLIGHT and PILOT are 1:N, so we place the keys of the parent in the children. In this case, we place the key of AIRPLANE and the key of PILOT in FLIGHT.

FLIGHT contains a key of its own. Although it contains foreign keys, these keys are only attributes and are not part of FLIGHT's key. But this is not always the case. If FLIGHT had no key of its own, its key would be the combination of the foreign keys of the objects that it associates. Here that combination would be {TailNumber, PilotNumber, Date}.

In general, when transforming association object structures into relations, we define one relation for each of the objects participating in the relationship. In Figure 7-16, OBJECT3 associates OBJECT1 and OBJECT2. In this case, we define R1, R2, and R3, as shown. The key of each of the parent relations, O1 and O2, appears as foreign key attributes in R3, the relation representing the association object. If the association object has no unique identifying attribute, the combination of the attributes of R1 and R2 will be used to create a unique identifier.

Note the difference between the association relation in Figure 7-16 and the intersection relation in Figure 7-11. The principal distinction is that the associa-

Relational Representation of Example Association Object: (a) FLIGHT Association Object and Related Objects and (b) Relational Representation of AIRPLANE, PILOT, and FLIGHT Objects

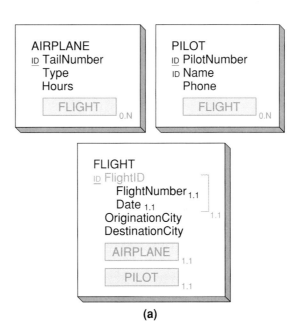

(a)

AIRPLANE (<u>TailNumber</u>, TypeHours)

PILOT (<u>PilotNumber</u>, Name, Phone)

FLIGHT (<u>FlightNumber</u>, <u>Date</u>, OriginationCity, DestinationCity, *TailNumber*, *PilotNumber*)

(b)

FIGURE 7-16

General Transformation of Association Objects into Relations

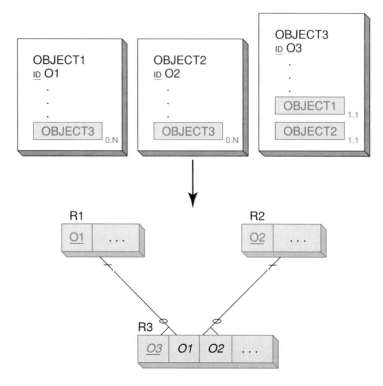

tion table carries data that represent some aspect of the combination of the objects. The intersection relation carries no data; its only reason for existence is to specify which objects have a relationship with one another.

PARENT/SUBTYPE OBJECTS

Parent (also called *supertype*) and subtype objects are represented in a way similar to that for parent and subtype entities. We define a relation for the parent object and one for each of the subtype objects. The key of each of these relations is the key of the parent.

Figure 7-17(a) shows a parent object, PERSON, that includes two mutually exclusive subtypes, STUDENT and PROFESSOR. Figure 7-17(b) shows a relational representation of these three objects. Each object is represented by a table, and the key of all of the tables is the same.

The relations in Figure 7-17(b) pose a problem, however. The application program still needs to look in both the STUDENT and PROFESSOR tables to determine the type of PERSON. If an entry is found in STUDENT, the person is a student; if an entry is found in PROFESSOR, the person is a professor. This is an indirect and possibly slow way to determine the type of a person, and if, as may happen, the PERSON is of neither type, both tables will have been searched for no reason. Because of this problem, a type indicator attribute is sometimes placed in the parent table.

Figure 7-17(c) shows two variations of a type indicator. In the first variation, relation PERSON1, the type of object is stored in the attribute PersonType. Possible values of this attribute are 'Neither', 'STUDENT', or 'PROFESSOR'. The application would obtain the value of this attribute and thereby determine whether a subtype exists and, if so, which type it is.

A second possibility is shown in the relation PERSON2, to which two attributes have been added, one for StudentType and another for ProfessorType. Each of the attributes is a Boolean variable; the allowed values are true or false. Note that if, as is the case here, a person can be of only one type, then if one of these values is true, the other one must be false.

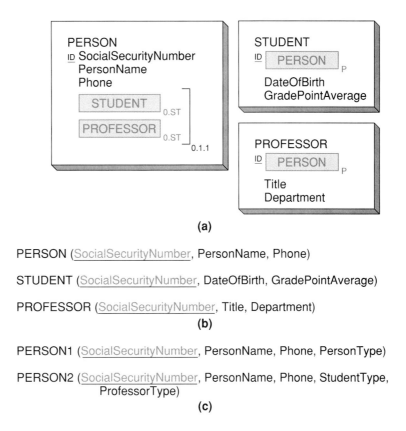

► FIGURE 7-17

*Representation of Example
Parent and Subtypes:
(a) PERSON Parent and
STUDENT and PROFESSOR
Subtypes, (b) Relational
Representation of Parent and
Subtypes, and (c) Alternative
Representations of the Parent
Relation*

(a)

PERSON (<u>SocialSecurityNumber</u>, PersonName, Phone)

STUDENT (<u>SocialSecurityNumber</u>, DateOfBirth, GradePointAverage)

PROFESSOR (<u>SocialSecurityNumber</u>, Title, Department)
(b)

PERSON1 (<u>SocialSecurityNumber</u>, PersonName, Phone, PersonType)

PERSON2 (<u>SocialSecurityNumber</u>, PersonName, Phone, StudentType,
    ProfessorType)
(c)

In general, designs of type PERSON1 are better when the subtypes are mutually exclusive. Designs of type PERSON2 are better when the subtypes are not exclusive.

A general scheme for representing subtypes is shown in Figure 7-18. One relation is created for the parent and one each for the subtypes. The key of all of the relations is the identifier of the parent. All relationships between the parent and the subtype are 1:1. Note the bar across the relationship lines and the presence of the subtype group's cardinality. The value shown, 0.1.1, means that no subtype is required but, if present, at most one of the subtypes is allowed.

(Recall that in general, the format of group cardinality is **r.m.n.**, where **r** is a Boolean true or false depending on whether or not the subtype group is required, **m** is the minimum number of subtypes that must have a value within the group, and **n** is the maximum number of subtypes that may have a value within the group. In a group of five subtypes, therefore, the cardinality of 1.2.4 indicates that the subtype group is required, that at least two subtypes must have a value, and that a maximum of four subtypes may have a value.)

ARCHETYPE/VERSION OBJECTS

Archetype/version objects are compound objects that model various iterations, releases, or instances of a basic object. The objects in Figure 7-19(a) model software products for which there are various releases. Examples of such products are Microsoft Internet Explorer or Netscape Navigator. Examples of releases are Netscape 4.0 or 5.0.

The relational representation of PRODUCT and RELEASE is shown in Figure 7-19(b). One relation is created for PRODUCT, and another is created for RELEASE. The key of RELEASE is the combination of the key of PRODUCT and the local key (ReleaseNumber) of RELEASE.

➤   FIGURE 7-18

*General Transformation of
Parent/Subtype Objects into
Relations*

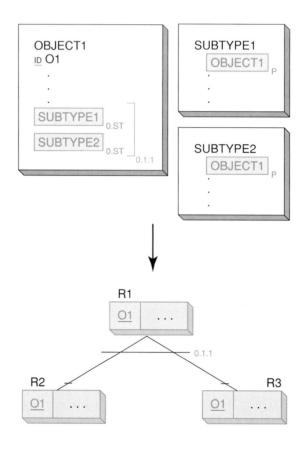

Figure 7-20 shows the general transformation of archetype/version objects. Attribute O1 of R2 is both a local and a foreign key, but O2 is only a local key.

➤ SAMPLE OBJECTS

To reinforce the concepts presented so far, we now consider several example objects taken from actual businesses, presented in increasing order of complexity. We model the underlying object and represent it in relations using the methods described in this chapter.

➤   FIGURE 7-19

*Relational Representation of
Example Archetype/Version
Objects: (a) PRODUCT
Archetype and RELEASE
Version Objects and
(b) Relational Representation
of PRODUCT and RELEASE*

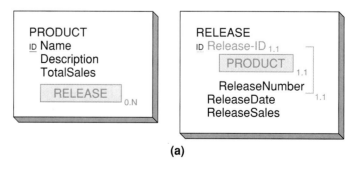

(a)

PRODUCT (<u>Name</u>, Description, TotalSales)

RELEASE (*<u>Name</u>*, <u>ReleaseNumber</u>, ReleaseDate, ReleaseSales)

(b)

FIGURE 7-20

*General Transformation of
Archetype/Version Objects
and RELEASE Version Objects
and (b)*

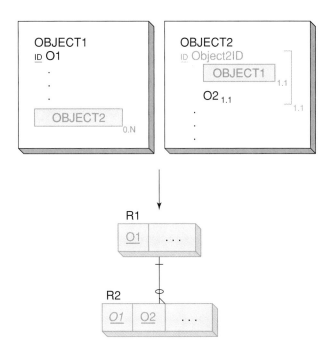

SUBSCRIPTION FORM

Figure 7-21(a) shows a magazine subscription form. At least two object structures could represent this form. If the publishers of *Fine Woodworking* consider a subscriber to be an attribute of a subscription, a subscription could be a simple object represented as a single relation, as in Figure 7-21(b).

If this company has only a single publication and no plans to produce additional publications, the design in Figure 7-21(b) will work. If, however, this company has several publications and if a customer may subscribe to more than one of them, this design will duplicate the customer data for each publication. This will not only waste file space for the publisher but will also exasperate the customer because, for example, he or she will be required to submit address changes for each publication of the same publisher.

If the publisher has several publications or plans to have several publications, a better design would be to model subscriber as a separate object, as shown in Figure 7-21(c). CUSTOMER is a 1:N compound object and is represented by the relations in this figure.

PRODUCT DESCRIPTION

Figure 7-22(a) shows the description of a popular packaged-goods product. Whereas Figure 7-21(a) shows a generic form with no data, Figure 7-22(a) shows an instance of a specific report with data about a cereal product. The reports for all of Kellogg's cereal products use this format.

Figure 7-22(b) shows a composite object that could underlie this report. We say *could* because there are many different ways that this object might be represented. Also, further investigation may reveal other objects that are not apparent in this one report. For example, USDA Recommendation may be a semantic object in its own right.

For illustration purposes, we make different assumptions about the Nutrient and USDARecDailyAllow groups. The CEREAL-PRODUCT object assumes that every element of the Nutrient group—namely, calories, protein, carbohydrate,

➤ FIGURE 7-21

Alternative
Representations of
Subscription:
(a) Subscription
Order Form,
(b) Subscription
Modeled as One
Object, and (c)
Subscription Modeled
as Two Objects

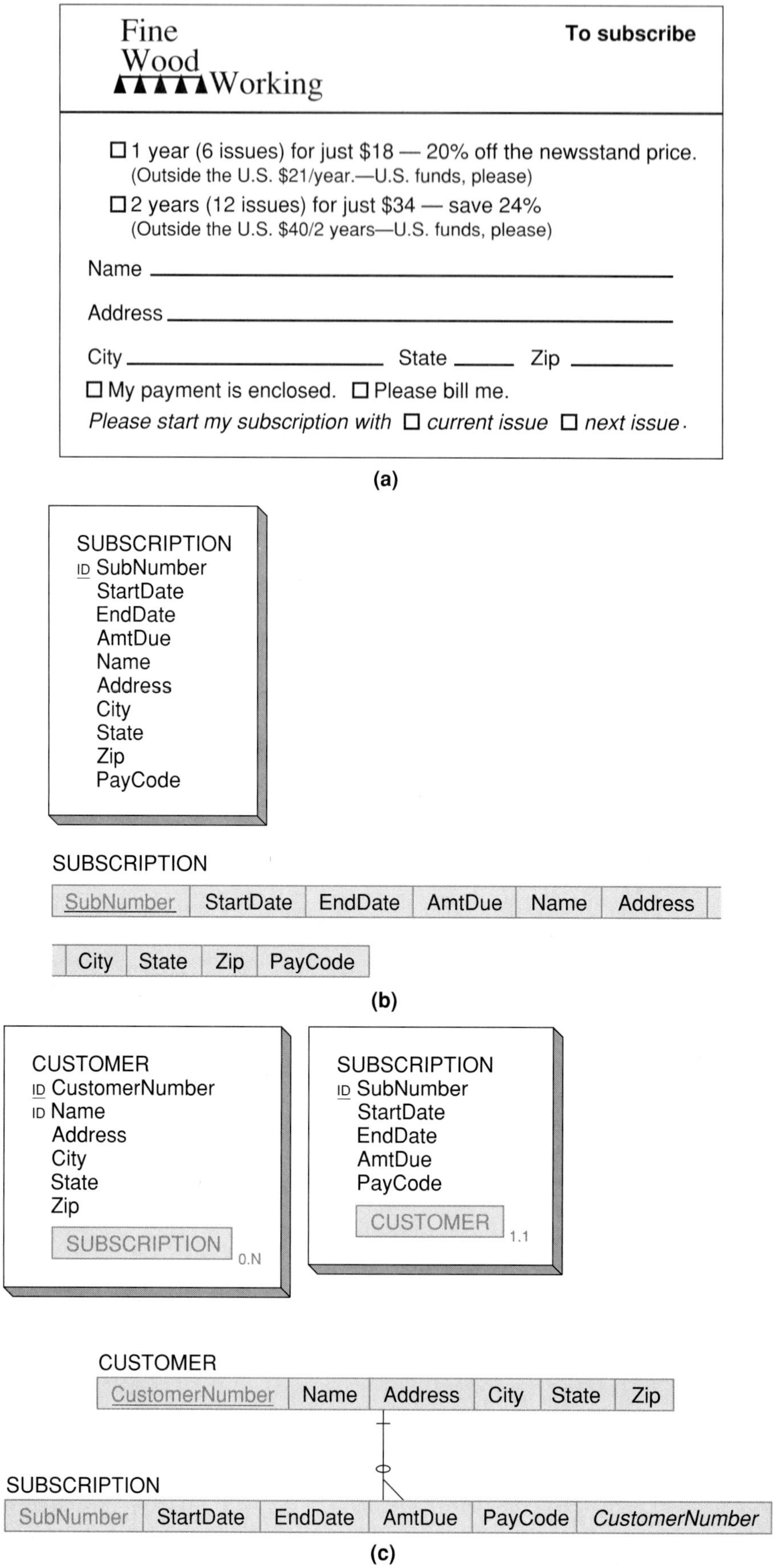

Fine
Wood
▲▲▲▲▲Working

To subscribe

☐ 1 year (6 issues) for just $18 — 20% off the newsstand price.
   (Outside the U.S. $21/year.—U.S. funds, please)

☐ 2 years (12 issues) for just $34 — save 24%
   (Outside the U.S. $40/2 years—U.S. funds, please)

Name _____

Address _____

City _____ State _____ Zip _____

☐ My payment is enclosed. ☐ Please bill me.

Please start my subscription with ☐ *current issue* ☐ *next issue*.

(a)

SUBSCRIPTION
ID SubNumber
   StartDate
   EndDate
   AmtDue
   Name
   Address
   City
   State
   Zip
   PayCode

SUBSCRIPTION

SubNumber	StartDate	EndDate	AmtDue	Name	Address

City	State	Zip	PayCode

(b)

CUSTOMER
ID CustomerNumber
ID Name
   Address
   City
   State
   Zip
   [SUBSCRIPTION] 0.N

SUBSCRIPTION
ID SubNumber
   StartDate
   EndDate
   AmtDue
   PayCode
   [CUSTOMER] 1.1

CUSTOMER

CustomerNumber	Name	Address	City	State	Zip

SUBSCRIPTION

SubNumber	StartDate	EndDate	AmtDue	PayCode	*CustomerNumber*

(c)

Cereal Product Representation:
(a) Cereal Product Report,
(b) CEREAL-PRODUCT Object
Diagram, and (c) Relational
Representation of CEREAL-
PRODUCT

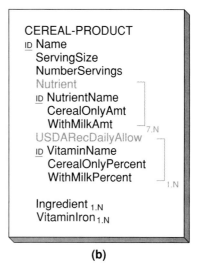

(b)

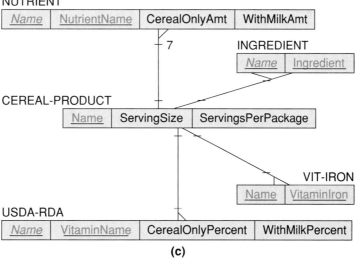

fat, cholesterol, sodium, and potassium—is required in every instance of this object. We do not assume this for the USDARecDailyAllow group, because only one instance of this group must exist.

The report in Figure 7-22(a) has many interpretations and could be modeled in several different ways. In an actual development project, it would be impor-

➤ FIGURE 7-23

Representation of a Correction Notice: (a) Example Form, (b) CORRECTION-NOTICE Object Diagram, and (c) Relational Representation of CORRECTION-NOTICE

WASHINGTON STATE PATROL CORRECTION NOTICE

(a)

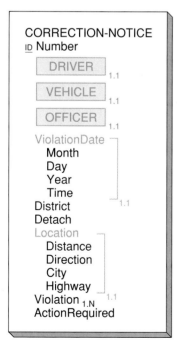
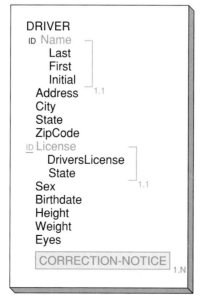

(b)

➤ FIGURE 7-23

(Continued)

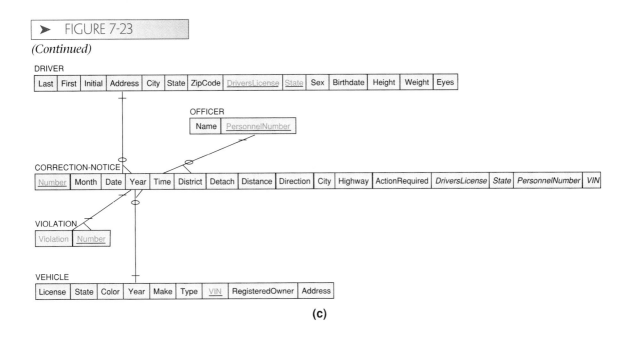

(c)

tant to obtain as many other reports about other cereal products and about the ingredients and nutritional information in this report. These other documents would most likely give additional structure to this semantic object.

Figure 7-22(c) shows the relational representation for the CEREAL-PRODUCT object. The minimum cardinality of *7* is shown by placing the numeral *7* next to the required hash mark on the relationship line. Foreign keys have been placed as described previously for composite objects.

TRAFFIC-WARNING CITATION

Figure 7-23(a) shows an instance of the traffic-warning citation form used in the state of Washington. The designer of this form has given us important clues to the underlying objects of this form. Notice that portions of the form are distinguished by rounded corners, indicating that different sections pertain to different objects. Also, some groups of attributes have names, indicating the need for group attributes.

Figure 7-23(b) is one way to illustrate the underlying objects of the traffic-warning citation. Although we cannot be certain from just this one form, there are certain clues that lead us to believe that the driver, vehicle, and officer are independent objects. First, the data concerning each of these subjects are in a separate section on the form. But more important, each section has fields that are undoubtedly identifying attributes of something apart from CORRECTION-NOTICE. For example, {DriversLicense, State} uniquely identifies a driver; VehicleLicense, State and VIN (Vehicle Identification Number) identify registered vehicles; and PersonnelNumber identifies an officer. These key fields obviously are determinants, so objects were defined for each. The relation representation of these diagrams appears in Figure 7-23(c).

➤ SUMMARY

The transformation of semantic objects into relations depends on the type of object. Simple objects are represented by a single relation. The nonobject attributes are carried as attributes of the relation.

Composite objects require two or more relations for their representation. One relation contains the single-value attributes of the object. Another relation is constructed for each multi-value simple or group attribute. The key of the relations representing the multi-value attributes is always a composite key that contains the key of the object plus an identifier of the composite group within that object.

At least two relations are required to represent a compound object. Each relation has its own distinct key. There are four different types of compound objects— one to one, one to many, many to one, and many to many—which are represented by inserting foreign keys. For one-to-one relationships, the key of either table is placed in the other table, and for one-to-many and many-to-one relationships, the key of the parent is placed in the child relation. Finally, for many-to-many relationships, an intersection table is created that carries the keys of both relations.

Hybrid objects are represented by creating a table for the multi-value group attribute of the composite object and placing the key of the relation representing the noncomposite object into that table. The four cases of hybrid are listed in Figure 7-13.

Association objects require at least three relations for their representation, one for each of the objects involved. Each relation has its own key, and the relation representing the association object contains, as foreign keys, the keys of the other two objects.

Parent and subtype objects are represented by creating a relation for the parent and one for each subtype. The key of all relations is normally the same. An identifier attribute is sometimes placed in the parent to indicate the object's type.

For archetype/version objects, one relation is created for the archetype object and a second is created for the version. The key of the version's relation always contains the key of the archetype.

➤ GROUP I QUESTIONS

7.1   Give an example of a simple object other than one in this text. Show how to represent this object by means of a relation.

7.2   Give an example of a composite object other than one in this text. Show how to represent this object by means of relations.

7.3   Give an example of a 1:1 compound object other than one in this text. Show two ways to represent it by means of relations.

7.4   Give an example of a 1:N compound object other than one in this text. Show how to represent it by means of relations.

7.5   Give an example of an M:1 compound object other than one in this text. Show how to represent it by means of relations.

7.6   Give an example of an M:N compound object other than one in this text. Show how to represent it by means of relations.

7.7   Give an example of a Case 1 (see Figure 7-13) hybrid object. Show how to represent it by means of relations.

7.8   Give an example of a Case 2 (see Figure 7-13) hybrid object. Show how to represent it by means of relations.

7.9   Give an example of an association and related objects other than one in this text. Show how to represent these objects by means of relations. Assume that the association object has an identifier of its own.

7.10 Do the same as for Question 7.9, but assume that the association object does not have an identifier of its own.

7.11 Give an example of a parent object with at least two exclusive subtypes. Show how to represent these objects by means of relations. Use a type indicator attribute.

7.12 Give an example of a parent object with at least two nonexclusive subtypes. Show how to represent these objects by means of relations. Use a type indicator attribute.

7.13 Find an example of a form on your campus that would be appropriately modeled with a simple object. Show how to represent this object by means of a relation.

7.14 Find an example of a form on your campus that would be appropriately modeled with a composite object. Show how to represent this object by means of relations.

7.15 Find an example of a form on your campus that would be appropriately modeled with one of the types of a compound object. Show how to represent these objects by means of relations.

7.16 Find an example of a form on your campus that would be appropriately modeled with a hybrid object. Classify the object according to Figure 7-13, and show how to represent these objects by means of relations.

7.17 Find an example of a form on your campus that would be appropriately modeled with an association and related objects. Show how to represent these objects by means of relations.

7.18 Find an example of a form on your campus that would be appropriately modeled with parent/subtypes objects. Show how to represent these objects by means of relations.

7.19 Find an example of a form on your campus that would be appropriately modeled with archetype/version objects. Show how to represent these objects by means of relations.

➤ GROUP II QUESTIONS

7.20 In Figure 7-13, give a different example for each of the four cases in the right column. Show how each of your examples would be represented with relations.

7.21 Modify Figures 7-22(b) and (c) to add the reports shown in Figure 7-24.

➤ FIGURE 7-24

Reports for Question 7.21

FDA REPORT #6272
Date: 06/30/1999
Issuer: Kellogg's Corporation
Report Title: Product Summary by Ingredient

Corn	Corn Flakes
	Krispix
	Nutrigrain (Corn)
Corn syrup	Rice Krispies
	Frosted Flakes
	Sugar Pops
Malt	Rice Krispies
	Sugar Smacks
Wheat	Sugar Smacks
	Nutrigrain (Wheat)

(a)

SUPPLIERS LIST
Date: 06/30/1999

Ingredient	Supplier	Price
Corn	Wilson	2.80
	J. Perkins	2.72
	Pollack	2.83
	McKay	2.80
Wheat	Adams	1.19
	Kroner	1.19
	Schmidt	1.22
Barley	Wilson	0.85
	Pollack	0.84

(b)

➤ FIGURE 7-25

Reports for Question 7.22

West Side Story
Based on a conception of Jerome Robbins

Book by ARTHUR LAURENTS
Music by LEONARD BERNSTEIN
Lyrics by STEPHEN SONDHEIM

Entire Original Production Directed
and Choreographed by JEROME ROBBINS

Originally produced on Broadway by Robert E. Griffith and Harold S. Prince
by arrangement with Roger L. Stevens
Orchestration by Leonard Bernstein with Sid Ramin and Irwin Kostal

HIGHLIGHTS FROM THE COMPLETE RECORDING

Maria . . . . .KIRI TE KANAWA
Tony . . . . JOSE CARRERAS
Anita . . . . TATIANA TROYANOS
Riff . . . . KURT OLLMAN
and MARILYN HORNE singing "Somewhere"

Rosalia . . . . Louise Edeiken	Diesel . . . . Marty Nelson
Consuela . . . . Stella Zambalis	Baby John . . . . . Stephen Bogardus
Fancisca . . . . Angelina Reaux	A-rab . . . . Peter Thom
Action . . . . David Livingston	Snowboy . . . . .Todd Lester

Bernardo—Richard Harrell

1	**Jet Song** (Riff, Action, Baby John, A-rab, Chorus)	[3'13]
2	**Something's Coming** (Tony)	[2'33]
3	**Maria** (Tony)	[2'56]
4	**Tonight** (Maria, Tony)	[5'27]
5	**America** (Anita, Rosalia, Chorus)	[4'47]
6	**Cool** (Riff, Chorus)	[4'37]
7	**One Hand, One Heart** (Tony, Maria)	[5'38]
8	**Tonight** (Ensemble) (Entire Cast)	[3'40]
9	**I Feel Pretty** (Maria, Chorus)	[3'22]
10	**Somewhere** (A Girl)	[2'34]
11	**Gee OFicer Krupke** (Action, Snowboy, Diesel, A-rab, Baby John, Chorus)	[4'18]
12	**A Boy Like That** (Anita, Maria)	[2'05]
13	**I Have a Love** (Maria, Anita)	[3'30]
14	**Taunting Scene** (Orchestra)	[1'21]
15	**Finale** (Maria, Tony)	[2'40]

7.22 Using the album cover shown in Figure 7-25 as a guide, perform the following tasks:

a. Draw the object diagrams for the underlying objects ARTIST, ROLE, and SONG.

b. Identify the relationships among those objects. What types of objects are they (simple, composite, and so on)?

c. Indicate for each participant in a relationship whether it is optional or mandatory.

d. Transform the object diagrams into relation diagrams.

What is the key of each relation? What foreign keys appear in each relation?

➤ PROJECTS

A. Complete project A at the end of Chapter 4 if you have not already done so. Transform your semantic object model into a set of relations. If any of your relations are not in DK/NF, justify your decision to create un-normalized relations.

B. Complete project B at the end of Chapter 4 if you have not already done so. Transform your semantic object model into a set of relations. If any of your relations are not in DK/NF, justify your decision to create un-normalized relations.

C. Complete project C at the end of Chapter 4 if you have not already done so. Transform your semantic object model into a set of relations. If any of your relations are not in DK/NF, justify your decision to create un-normalized relations.

DATABASE IMPLEMENTATION WITH THE RELATIONAL MODEL

Part IV considers database implementation using the relational model. Chapter 8 begins with a discussion of relational data manipulation. First we look at the types of relational data manipulation languages, and then we explain the basic operators of relational algebra and illustrate their use.

Chapter 9 describes Structured Query Language, or SQL. This language has been endorsed by the American National Standards Institute as a standard for manipulating relational databases, and it also is the primary data manipulation language for commercial relational DBMS products. Chapter 10 concludes this part with a discussion of the design and functions of database applications.

Foundations of Relational Implementation

This and the next two chapters discuss the implementation of relational databases. We begin in this chapter by describing relational data definition, reviewing relational terminology, and explaining how a design is defined to the DBMS. Next we turn to space allocation and database data creation. The remainder of the chapter addresses relational data manipulation: first, a survey of four types of relational data manipulation language (DML), then the three common modes of DML interfaces to the DBMS, and finally, the basic operators of relational algebra and example queries expressed in terms of relational algebra.

➤ DEFINING RELATIONAL DATA

Several tasks must be performed when implementing a relational database. First, the structure of the database must be defined to the DBMS. To do this, the developer uses a data definition language (DDL) or some equivalent means (such as a graphical display) to describe the structure. Then the database is allocated to physical storage media and filled with data. In this section we discuss each of these tasks, but first we review the relational terminology.

REVIEW OF TERMINOLOGY

As stated in Chapter 5, a **relation** is a table that has several properties:

1. The entries in the relation are single value; multiple values are not allowed. Hence, the intersection of a row and a column contains only one value.

2. All the entries in any column are of the same kind. For example, one column may contain customer names and another, birthdates. Each column has a unique name, and the order of the columns is not important to the relation. The columns of a relation are called **attributes.** Each attribute has a **domain,** which is a physical and logical description of allowed values.

3. No two rows in the relation are identical, and the order of the rows is not important (see Figure 8-1). Each row of the relation is known as a tuple.

*Occurrence of
PATIENT Relation
Structure*

	Col 1 (or Attribute 1)	Col 2	Col 3	Col 4	Col 5
	Name	DateOfBirth	Gender	Account Number	Physician
Row 1 (or Tuple 1)	Riley	01/19/1946	F	147	Lee
Row 2	Murphy	12/28/1981	M	289	Singh
Row 3	Krajewski	10/21/1973	F	533	Levy
Row 4	Ting	05/23/1938	F	681	Spock
Row 5	Dixon	04/15/1987	M	704	Levy
Row 6	Abel	06/19/1957	M	193	Singh

Figure 8-1 is an example, or occurrence. The generalized format, PATIENT (Name, DateOfBirth, Gender, AccountNumber, Physician), is the relation structure and is what most people mean when they use the term *relation*. (Recall from Chapter 5 that an underlined attribute is a key.) If we add constraints on allowable data values to the relation structure, we then have a **relational schema.** These terms are summarized in Figure 8-2.

CONFUSION REGARDING THE TERM *KEY*   The term **key** is a common source of confusion because it has different meanings in the design and the implementation stages. During the design, the term *key* refers to one or more columns that uniquely identify a row in a relation. As we explained in Chapter 5, we know every relation has a key because every row is unique; at the limit, the composite of every column in the relation is the key. Usually the key is composed of one or two columns, however.

During implementation, the term *key* is used differently. For most relational products, a key is a column on which the DBMS builds an index or other data structure. This is done to access rows quickly by means of that column's value. Such keys need not be unique, and often, in fact, they are not. They are constructed only to improve performance. (See the Appendix A for information about such data structures.)

For example, consider the relation ORDER (OrderNumber, OrderDate, CustNumber, Amount). From the standpoint of relational *design,* the key of this relation is OrderNumber, since the underline means OrderNumber uniquely identifies rows of the relation. From the standpoint of relational *implementation,* however, any of the four columns could be a key. OrderDate, for example, could be defined as a key. If it is, the DBMS will create a data structure so that ORDER rows can be quickly accessed by the value of OrderDate. Most likely, there will be many rows for a given value of OrderDate. Defining it as this type of key says nothing about its uniqueness.

Sometimes the terms **logical key** and **physical key** are used to distinguish between these two meanings of key. A logical key is a unique identifier, whereas a physical key is a column that has a special data structure defined for it in order to improve performance. A logical key need not be a physical key, and a physical key need not be a logical key.

INDEXES   Since a physical key is usually an index, some people reserve the term key for a logical key and use the term *index* for a physical key. In this text, we will do exactly that—use the term *key* to mean a logical key, and use the term *index* to mean a physical key.

► FIGURE 8-2

Summary of Relational
Terminology

Term	Meaning
Relation (or Table) (or File)	Two-dimensional table
Attribute (or Column) (or Field) (or Data Item)	Column of a relation
Tuple (or Row) (or Record)	Row in a relation
Domain	Physical and logical description of allowed values
Relation structure	Format of relation
Occurrence	Relation structure with data
Relational schema	Relation structure plus constraints
Key	Group of one or more attributes that uniquely identifies a tuple in a relation
Logical key	Same as key
Physical key (or Index)	A group of one or more attributes that is supported by a data structure that facilitates fast retrieval or rapid sequential access

There are three reasons for defining indexes. One is to allow rows to be quickly accessed by means of the indexed attribute's value. The second is to facilitate sorting rows by that attribute. For instance, in ORDER, OrderDate might be defined as a key so that a report showing orders by dates can be more quickly generated.

A third reason for building an index concerns uniqueness. Although indexes do not have to be unique, when the developer wants a column to be unique, an index is created by the DBMS. This index is used to ensure that no duplicated values are accepted by the DBMS. With most relational DBMS products, a column or group of columns can be forced to be unique by using the keyword UNIQUE when defining the appearance of a column in a table.

IMPLEMENTING A RELATIONAL DATABASE

In this text, we use the relational model to express database designs. Since we have done so, we can proceed directly from designing the database to implementing it. There is no need to transform the design during the implementation stage; we simply define the existing relational design to the DBMS.

The situation is different when we implement databases using DBMS products based on data models other than the relational model. For example, when implementing a database for a CODASYL DBTG DBMS, we must convert the relational design to a CODASYL DBTG design and then define the converted design to the DBMS product. You will see examples of such design transformations in Chapter 16.

DEFINING THE DATABASE STRUCTURE TO THE DBMS   There are a number of different means by which the structure of the database is described to the DBMS, depending on the DBMS product being used. With some products, a text file is constructed that describes the database structure. The language used to describe such a structure is sometimes called the **data definition language,** or DDL. The DDL text file names the tables in the database, names and describes the columns of those tables, defines indexes, and describes other structures such as constraints and security restrictions. Figure 8-3 shows the typical data definition language used for defining a simple relational database for a hypothetical DBMS. A more realistic example of such a language for the DBMS product DB2 is shown in Chapter 15.

Some DBMS products do not require that the database be defined by DDL in text file format. One common alternative is to provide a graphical means for defining the structure of the database. With Access 2000, for example, the developer is shown a graphical list structure and asked to fill in the table and column names in the appropriate places. We saw an example of this in Chapter 2 (Figure 2-4).

In general, graphical definition facilities are common for DBMS products on personal computers and textual DDL is common for DBMS products on servers and mainframes. ORACLE and DB2, for example, both employ text files for database structure definition. Figure 8-4 summarizes the database definition process.

Regardless of the means by which the database structure is defined, the developer must name each table, define the columns in that table, and describe the physical format (for example, TEXT 10) of each column. Also, depending on the facilities of the DBMS, the developer may specify constraints that the DBMS is to enforce. Column values can be defined to be NOT NULL or UNIQUE, for example. Some products also allow the definition of range and value constraints (Part less than 10000 or Color equal to one of ['Red', 'Green',

---

> FIGURE 8-3

Example DDL Text File for Database Definition

```
CREATE SCHEMA PHYSICIAN

CREATE TABLE PATIENT

    ( Name                  CHARACTER VARYING (35) NOT NULL,
      DateOfBirth           DATE/TIME,
      Gender                CHARACTER VARYING (10),
      AccountNumber         INTEGER NOT NULL,
      PhysicianName_FK1     CHARACTER VARYING (35) NOT NULL,

      PRIMARY KEY ( AccountNumber ),
      FOREIGN KEY ( PhysicianName_FK1 )
          REFERENCES PHYSICIAN
    )

CREATE TABLE PHYSICIAN

    ( PhysicianName         CHARACTER VARYING (35) NOT NULL,
      AreaCode              CHARACTER VARYING (3),
      LocalNumber           CHARACTER VARYING (8) NOT NULL,

      PRIMARY KEY (PhysicianName)
    )
```

Database Definition Process

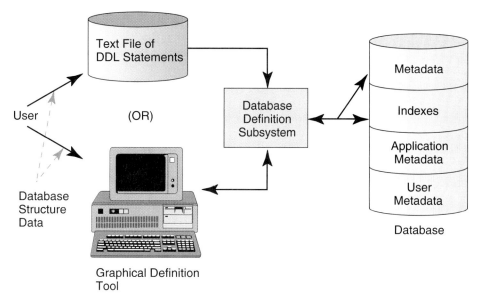

'Blue'], for example). Finally, interrelation constraints can be defined. An example is that DeptNumber in EMPLOYEE must match a value of DeptNumber in DEPARTMENT.

With many products, the developer can also define passwords and other control and security facilities. As shown in Chapter 12, a number of different strategies can be used. Some strategies place controls on data constructs (passwords on tables, for example), and others place controls on people (the user of password X can read and update tables T1 and T2).

ALLOCATING MEDIA SPACE   In addition to defining the structure of the database, the developer must allocate database structures to physical media. Again, the specific tasks depend on the particular DBMS product used. For a personal database, all that needs to be done is to assign the database to a directory and give the database a name. The DBMS then allocates storage space automatically.

Other DBMS products, especially those used for servers and mainframes, require more work. To improve performance and control, the distribution of the database data across disks and channels must be carefully planned. For example, depending on the nature of application processing, it may be advantageous to locate certain tables on the same disk, or it may be important to ensure that certain tables are not located on the same disk.

Consider, for example, an order object that is composed of data from ORDER, LINE-ITEM, and ITEM tables. Suppose that when processing an order, the application retrieves one row from ORDER, several rows from LINE-ITEM, and one row from ITEM for each LINE-ITEM row. Furthermore, the LINE-ITEM rows for a given order tend to be clustered together, but the ITEM rows are not at all clustered. Figure 8-5 illustrates this situation.

Now suppose that an organization concurrently processes many orders and has one large, fast disk and one smaller, slower disk. The developer must determine the best place to locate the data. One possibility is that the performance will be better if the ITEM table is stored on the larger, faster disk and the ORDER and LINE-ITEM data on the smaller, slower disk. Or perhaps the performance will be better if the ORDER and LINE-ITEM data for prior months' orders are placed on the slower disk and all the data for this month's orders are placed on the faster disk.

We cannot answer this question here, as the answer depends on the amount of data, the processing characteristics of the DBMS and the operating system, the

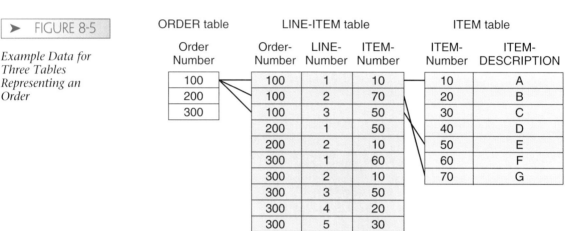

ORDER table   LINE-ITEM table   ITEM table

Order Number
100
200
300

Order-Number	LINE-Number	ITEM-Number
100	1	10
100	2	70
100	3	50
200	1	50
200	2	10
300	1	60
300	2	10
300	3	50
300	4	20
300	5	30

ITEM-Number	ITEM-DESCRIPTION
10	A
20	B
30	C
40	D
50	E
60	F
70	G

Note: For a given order, LINE-ITEM rows are clustered, but ITEM rows are not.

size and speed of the disks and channels, and the application-processing requirements of all applications that use the database. The point is that factors such as
these must be considered when allocating media space to the database.

CREATING THE DATABASE DATA   Once the database has been defined and
allocated to physical storage, it can be filled with data. The means by which this
is done depends on the application requirements and the features of the DBMS
product. In the best case, all of the data are already in a computer-sensible format, and the DBMS has features and tools to facilitate importing the data from
magnetic media. In the worst case, all of the data must be entered via manual key
entry using application programs created from scratch by the developers. Most
data conversions lie between these two extremes.

Once the data are input, they must be verified for accuracy. Verification is a
labor-intensive and tedious but important task. Often, especially for large databases, it is well worth the time and expense for the development team to write
verification programs. Such programs count the number of records of various categories, compute control totals, perform reasonableness checks on data item values, and provide other kinds of verification.

➤ RELATIONAL DATA MANIPULATION

So far in this text, we have discussed the design of relational databases and the
means by which such designs are defined to the DBMS. Whenever we have referred to processing relations, we have done so in a general and intuitive manner.
Although this is fine for discussing designs, to implement applications we need
clear, unambiguous languages for expressing processing logic.

CATEGORIES OF RELATIONAL DATA
MANIPULATION LANGUAGE

To date, four different strategies for relational data manipulation have been proposed. **Relational algebra,** the first of the strategies, defines operators that
work on relations (akin to the operators +, −, and so forth of high school algebra). Relations can be manipulated using these operators to achieve a desired result. But relational algebra is hard to use, partly because it is procedural. That is,
when using relational algebra we must know not only *what* we want but also *how*
to get it.

Relational algebra is infrequently used in commercial database processing. Although a few commercially successful DBMS products do provide relational algebra facilities, these facilities are seldom used because of their complexity. Even so, we will discuss relational algebra here, as it helps clarify relational manipulation and establishes a foundation on which to learn SQL.

Relational calculus is a second type of relational data manipulation. Relational calculus is nonprocedural; it is a language for expressing what we want without expressing how to get it. Recall the variable of integration in calculus, which ranges over an interval to be integrated. Relational calculus has a similar variable. For tuple relational calculus, the variable ranges over the tuples of a relation, and for domain relational calculus, the variable ranges over the values of a domain. Relational calculus is derived from a branch of mathematics called predicate calculus.

Unless you are going to become a theoretician of relational technology, you will probably not need to learn relational calculus. It is never used in commercial database processing, and therefore, we do not discuss it in this text.

Although relational calculus is hard to understand and use, its nonprocedural property is highly desirable. Therefore, DBMS designers looked for other nonprocedural techniques, which led to the third and fourth categories of relational DML.

Transform-oriented languages are a class of nonprocedural languages that transform input data expressed as relations into results expressed as a single relation. These languages provide easy-to-use structures for expressing what is desired regarding the data supplied. SQUARE, SEQUEL, and SQL, all are transform-oriented languages. We study SQL in depth in the next chapter.

The fourth category of relational DML is graphical. **Query-by-Example** and **Query-by-Form** fall into this category. Products that support this category include Approach (from Lotus), Access, and Cyberprise DBApp (from Wall Data). With a graphical interface, the user is presented a materialization of one or more relations. The materialization might be a data entry form, it might be a spreadsheet, or it might be some other structure. The DBMS maps the materialization to the underlying relation and constructs queries (most likely in SQL) on behalf of the user. The users are then causing the execution of DML statements, but they are unaware of that fact. The four categories of relational DML are listed in Figure 8-6.

DML INTERFACES TO THE DBMS

As we pointed out in Chapter 2, there are several different ways that users can interface to a database: They can use the form and report capabilities supplied by the DBMS; they can access the database via a query/update language; or they can process the database through application programs that access the database by means of DBMS commands.

DATA MANIPULATION BY MEANS OF FORMS   Most relational DBMS products include tools for building forms. Some of these are created automatically when a table is defined, but others must be created by the developer, per-

➤ FIGURE 8-6

Four Categories of Relational DML

• Relational algebra
• Relational calculus
• Transform-oriented languages (such as SQL)
• Query-by-example/Query-by-form

➤ FIGURE 8-7

Example of a Tabular Default Screen Form

Name	DateOfBirth	Gender	AccountNumber	Physician
Riley	1/19/46	F	147	Lee
Abel	6/19/57	M	193	Singh
Murphy	12/28/81	M	289	Singh
Krajewski	10/21/73	F	533	Levy
Ting	5/23/38	F	661	Spock
Dixon	4/15/87	M	704	Levy

haps with intelligent assistance like that provided by Access's Wizards. A form may be tabular, like a spreadsheet, in which case it shows multiple rows at a time, or the form may show each row as an independent entity. Figures 8-7 and 8-8 show an example of each for the PATIENT table in Figure 8-1. With most products, some flexibility is provided in the processing of the forms and reports. For example, rows can be selected for processing based on column values, and they can also be sorted. The table in Figure 8-7 is sorted by AccountNumber.

Many of the default forms present data from only a single relation at a time. If data are required from two or more relations, then customized forms must be created using DBMS tools. It is possible for both multi-table and multi-row forms to be created using such tools. The use of such tools is very specific to the product, however, and so we do not discuss them further here.

QUERY/UPDATE LANGUAGE INTERFACE   The second type of interface to a database is via a **query/update language,** or simply a **query language.** (Although most such languages perform both query and update, they are generally referred to as query languages.) With this type, the user enters query commands that specify actions on the database. The DBMS decodes the commands and carries out the appropriate actions. Figure 8-9 shows the programs involved in query processing.

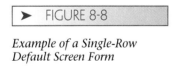

➤ FIGURE 8-8

Example of a Single-Row Default Screen Form

*Programs Involved in
Query Processing*

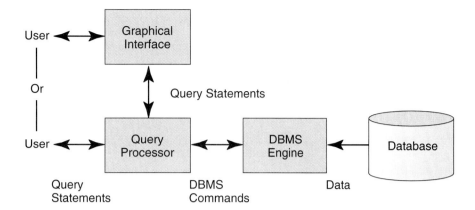

The single most important query language is SQL. To give you an idea of query languages, consider the following SQL statement that processes the relation PATIENT (Name, Age, Gender, AccountNumber, Physician) shown in Figure 8-1:

SELECT   Name, Age
FROM   PATIENT
WHERE   Physician = 'Levy'

This SQL query statement extracts all the rows from the relation PATIENT for which the physician is 'Levy.' It then displays the Name and Age for the qualifying rows in a second table.

Query languages were developed to provide a robust interface to the database that does not require writing traditional computer programs in a procedural language. This was especially important before the advent of the microcomputer. At that time, when most databases resided on mainframes, there was not enough processing power at the users' terminals to create and process the sophisticated forms and reports that are so common today. Query languages were thus a way of giving the nonprogramming user access to a database.

STORED PROCEDURE INTERFACE   Although query languages are simpler than computer-programming languages, they have generally proved to be too complicated for the average end user. Consequently, many end users have specialists write the query procedures, which are stored as files. Such procedures can be written to be parameter driven, thereby enabling the users to execute them when they change the data. As an example, the following command invokes a query procedure called BILLING and gives it a date value:

DO BILLING FOR BDATE = '9/15/1999'

When query procedures are stored and processed in this way, there is, in fact, little difference in concept between them and the stored programs that are written in a traditional programming language. The primary justification for their use is productivity, as stored query procedures are often quicker to write.

APPLICATION PROGRAM INTERFACE   The third type of data access interface is through application programs written in programming languages such as COBOL, BASIC, Perl, Pascal, and C++. In addition, some application programs are written in languages provided by the DBMS vendors, of which the dBASE programming language is the best known.

There are two styles of application program interface to the DBMS. In one, the application program makes function calls to routines in a function library provided with the DBMS. For example, to read a particular row of a table, the application program calls the DBMS read function and passes parameters that indicate the table to be accessed, the data to be retrieved, the criteria for row selection, and the like.

In some cases, object-oriented syntax is used rather than function calls. In the following Access 2000 code, the object reference *db* is set to the currently opened database and a second object reference *rs* is set to point to the rows in the PATIENT table.

```
set db = currentdb( )
set rs = db.OpenRecordset("PATIENT")
```

Properties of the open record set can then be accessed and methods executed using the reference variable. For example, the property *rs.AllowDeletions* can be referenced to determine whether records in the PATIENT record set can be deleted. The method *rs.MoveFirst* can be used to position a cursor to the first row.

A second, older style of interface is sometimes used with mainframe and server DBMS products. Here, a set of high-level data access commands is defined by the DBMS vendor. These commands—which are peculiar to database processing and not part of any standard language—are embedded in the application program code.

The application program, with embedded commands, is then submitted to a precompiler provided by the DBMS vendor. This precompiler translates the data access statements into valid function calls and data structure definitions. In this process, the precompiler sets up parameter sequences for the calls and defines data areas that will be shared between the application program and the DBMS. The precompiler also inserts program logic to maintain the data areas. Then the precompiled routine is submitted to the language compiler. Figure 8-10 shows the relationships of the programs involved in this process.

In addition to its role in query processing, SQL is also used as a data access language in application programs. In this mode, SQL statements are embedded in the programs and translated into function calls by a precompiler. Training costs and learning time are reduced, because the same language can be used for access to both query and application programs. There is one problem to be overcome, however. SQL is a transform-oriented language that accepts relations, manipulates them, and outputs a result relation. Thus, it deals with relations one at a time. Almost all appli-

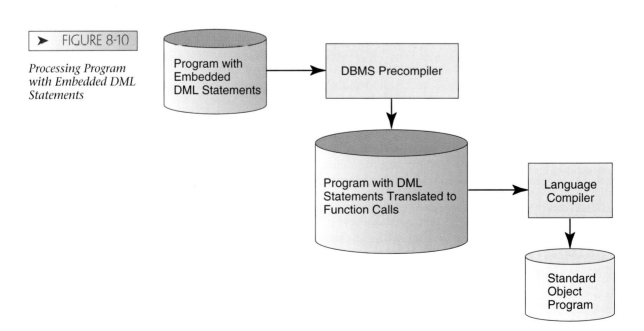

➤ FIGURE 8-10

Processing Program with Embedded DML Statements

cation programs are row (record) oriented; that is, they read one row, process it, read the next row, and so forth. Such programs deal with a row at a time.

Thus, there is a mismatch in the basic orientation of SQL and application program languages. To correct for this mismatch, the results of SQL statements are assumed, in the application program, to be files. To illustrate, assume that the following SQL statement (the same as that earlier) is embedded in an application program:

SELECT   Name, Age
FROM   PATIENT
WHERE   Physician = 'Levy'

The result of these statements is a table with two columns and *N* rows. In order to accept the results of this query, the application program is written to assume that these statements have produced a file with *N* records. The application opens the query, processes the first row, processes the next row, and so forth, until the last row has been processed. This logic is the same as that for processing a sequential file. You will see examples of such application programs in Chapter 15. For now, just be aware that there is a mismatch in the basic orientation of SQL (relation oriented) and programming languages (row, or record, oriented) and that this mismatch must be corrected when programs access a relational database via SQL.

➤ RELATIONAL ALGEBRA

Relational algebra is similar to the algebra you learned in high school, but with an important difference. In high school algebra, variables represented numbers, and operators like +, −, ×, and / operated on numeric quantities. In relational algebra, however, the variables are relations, and the operators manipulate relations to form new relations. For example, the union operation combines the tuples of one relation with the tuples of another relation, thereby producing a third relation. In fact, relational algebra is *closed,* which means that the results of one or more relational operations are *always* a relation.

Relations are sets. The tuples of a relation can be considered elements of a set, and so operations that can be performed on sets can also be performed on relations. We first show four such set operators and then discuss other operators that are peculiar to relational algebra. Before proceeding, however, consider the following sample relations that we will use in this and the next chapter.

RELATIONAL OPERATORS

Figure 8-11 shows six relations and their attribute and domain definitions. Note that the attribute Name is used in several relations. When we refer to a specific attribute, we qualify it with its relation name. Accordingly, Name in CLASS is sometimes denoted as CLASS.Name.

Also, observe that the physical description of the Ages and the ClassSizes domains is the same, yet the domains are different. This is because their logical description is different; they are not the same semantically, because they do not represent the same attributes. The integer 21 in Ages represents 21 years, but the same integer 21 in ClassSizes refers to the number of people in a class. Thus the value 21 represents two entirely different characteristics.

(As an aside, a better design would be to use DateOfBirth instead of Age. DateOfBirth never changes whereas Age must be updated every birthday. Our goal here, however, is to teach you relational algebra and SQL and cluttering up the examples with date arithmetic will not add to this goal. To make ourselves feel better about this situation, however, assume that Age is computed behind the scenes from a DateOfBirth attribute. Depending on college policy, a similar

➤ FIGURE 8-11

Examples of Relations and Domains: (a) Relation Definitions, (b) Attribute Domains, and (c) Domain Definitions

1. JUNIOR (Snum, Name, Major)
2. HONOR-STUDENT (Number, Name, Interest)
3. STUDENT (SID, Name, Major, GradeLevel, Age)
4. CLASS (Name, Time, Room)
5. ENROLLMENT (StudentNumber, ClassName, PositionNumber)
6. FACULTY (FID, Name, Department)

(a)

	Attribute	Domain
1.	Snum	PeopleIdentifiers
	JUNIOR.Name	PeopleNames
	Major	SubjectNames
2.	Number	PeopleIdentifiers
	HONOR-STUDENT.Name	PeopleNames
	Interest	SubjectNames
3.	SID	PeopleIdentifiers
	STUDENT.Name	PeopleNames
	Major	SubjectNames
	GradeLevel	Classes
	Age	Ages
4.	CLASS.Name	ClassNames
	Time	ClassTimes
	Room	Rooms
5.	StudentNumber	PeopleIdentifiers
	ClassName	ClassNames
	PositionNumber	ClassSizes
6.	FID	PeopleIdentifiers
	FACULTY.Name	PeopleNames
	Department	SubjectNames

(b)

Domain Name	Format
PeopleIdentifiers	Decimal (3)
PeopleNames	Char (8) (unrealistic, but handy for these examples)
SubjectNames	Char (10)
Classes	One of [FR, SO, JR, SN, GR]
Ages	Decimal from 0 to 100
ClassNames	Char (5)
ClassTimes	Char (5) format: DDDHH, where D is one of [M, T, W, R, F, or blank], and HH is decimal between 1 and 12
Rooms	Char (5) format: BBRRR, where BB is a building code, and RRR, is a room number
ClassSizes	Decimal from 0 to 100

(c)

comment could be made about GradeLevel. DateEntered might be a better attribute, or GradeLevel might be computed from HoursEarned [not shown], or it could be set by administration personnel with the concurrence of an advisor.)

In the following discussion, character values are shown in single quotes, and those characters not in quotes represent names. Thus 'ROOM' differs from Room because 'ROOM' is a value, whereas Room is, say, a domain name. In regard to numeric data, those numbers not in quotes refer to numeric quantities, and those numbers in quotes refer to character strings. Thus, 123 is a number, and '123' is a string of the characters '1,' '2,' and '3.'

UNION   The **union** of two relations is formed by adding the tuples from one relation to those of a second relation to produce a third relation. The order in which the tuples appear in the third relation is not important, but duplicate tuples must be eliminated. The union of relations A and B is denoted A + B.

For this operation to make sense, the relations must be **union compatible;** that is, each relation must have the same number of attributes, and the attributes in corresponding columns must come from the same domain. If, for example, the third attribute of one relation comes from the Ages domain, the third attribute of the second relation must also come from the Ages domain.

In Figure 8-11, the JUNIOR and the HONOR-STUDENT relations are union compatible because they both have three attributes, and the corresponding attributes come from the same domain. JUNIOR.Snum and HONOR-STUDENT.Number come from the domain PeopleIdentifiers; JUNIOR.Name and HONOR-STUDENT.Name have the domain PeopleNames; and JUNIOR.Major and HONOR-STUDENT.Interest have the domain SubjectNames. The relations JUNIOR and CLASS both have three attributes, but they are **union incompatible** because the three attributes do not have the same domain.

Figure 8-12 shows the union of the JUNIOR and HONOR-STUDENT relations. Note that the tuple [123, JONES, HISTORY], which occurs in both relations, is not duplicated in the union.

DIFFERENCE   The **difference** of two relations is a third relation containing tuples that occur in the first relation but not in the second. The relations must be union compatible. The difference of JUNIOR and HONOR-STUDENT is shown in

➤ FIGURE 8-12

JUNIOR and HONOR-STUDENT Relations and Their Union: (a) Example JUNIOR Relation, (b) Example HONOR-STUDENT Relation, and (c) Union of JUNIOR and HONOR-STUDENT Relations

Snum	Name	Major
123	JONES	HISTORY
158	PARKS	MATH
271	SMITH	HISTORY

(a)

Number	Name	Interest
105	ANDERSON	MANAGEMENT
123	JONES	HISTORY

(b)

Snum or Number	Name	Major or Interest
123	JONES	HISTORY
158	PARKS	MATH
271	SMITH	HISTORY
105	ANDERSON	MANAGEMENT

(c)

Snum	Name	Major
158	PARKS	MATH
271	SMITH	HISTORY

*JUNIOR Minus HONOR-
STUDENT Relation*

Figure 8-13. As in arithmetic, the order of the subtraction matters, and so A − B *is not* the same as B − A.

INTERSECTION   The **intersection** of two relations is a third relation containing the tuples that appear in both the first and second relations. Again, the relations must be union compatible. In Figure 8-14 the intersection of JUNIOR and HONOR-STUDENT is the single tuple [123, JONES, HISTORY], which is the only tuple that occurs in both JUNIOR and HONOR-STUDENT.

PRODUCT   The **product** of two relations (sometimes called the **Cartesian product**) is the concatenation of every tuple of one relation with every tuple of a second relation. The product of relation A (having *m* tuples) and relation B (having *n* tuples) has *m* times *n* tuples. The product is denoted A × B or A TIMES B. In Figure 8-15, the relation STUDENT has four tuples, and the relation ENROLLMENT has three. STUDENT TIMES ENROLLMENT therefore has twelve tuples, which are shown in Figure 8-16. (The resulting relation in Figure 8-16 contains some meaningless tuples. Other operations, shown later, would need to be performed in order to extract any meaningful information from this relation. This is simply an illustration of the product operator.)

PROJECTION   **Projection** is an operation that selects specified attributes from a relation. The result of the projection is a new relation with the selected attributes; in other words, a projection chooses columns from a relation. For example, consider the STUDENT relation data in Figure 8-15(a), from which the projection of STUDENT on Name and Major attributes, denoted with brackets as STUDENT [Name, Major], is shown in Figure 8-17(a). The projection of STUDENT on Major and GradeLevel, denoted as STUDENT [Major, GradeLevel], appears in Figure 8-17(b).

Note that although STUDENT has four tuples to begin with, the projection STUDENT [Major, GradeLevel] has only three. A tuple was eliminated because after the projection was completed, the tuple [HISTORY, JR] occurred twice. Because the result of projection is a relation and because relations cannot contain duplicate tuples, the redundant tuple is eliminated.

Projection can also be used to change the order of attributes in a relation. For example, the projection STUDENT [Age, GradeLevel, Major, Name, SID] reverses the order of STUDENT attributes (see Figure 8-11 for the original order). This feature can sometimes be used to make two relations union compatible.

SELECTION   Whereas the projection operator takes a vertical subset (columns) of a relation, the **selection** operator takes a horizontal subset (rows). Projection identifies those *attributes* to be included in the new relation, and selection identifies those *tuples* to be included in the new relation. Selection is denoted by specifying the relation name, followed by the keyword WHERE, followed by a condition involving attributes. Figure 8-18(a) shows the selection of the relation STUDENT WHERE Major = 'MATH,' and Figure 8-18(b) shows the selection of STUDENT WHERE Age < 25.

Snum or Number	Name	Major or Interest
123	JONES	HISTORY

*Intersection of JUNIOR and
HONOR-STUDENT Relations*

➤ FIGURE 8-15

Examples of (a) STUDENT and (b) ENROLLMENT Relations

SID	Name	Major	GradeLevel	Age
123	JONES	HISTORY	JR	21
158	PARKS	MATH	GR	26
105	ANDERSON	MANAGEMENT	SN	27
271	SMITH	HISTORY	JR	19

(a)

StudentNumber	ClassName	PositionNumber
123	H350	1
105	BA490	3
123	BA490	7

(b)

JOIN   The **join** operation is a combination of the product, selection, and (possibly) projection operations. The join of two relations, say A and B, operates as follows: First, form the product of A times B. Then do a selection to eliminate some tuples (the criteria for the selection are specified as part of the join). Then (optionally) remove some attributes by means of projection.

Consider the STUDENT and ENROLLMENT relations shown in Figure 8-15. Suppose we want to know the Name and Position Number of each student. To find this out, we need to join STUDENT tuples by matching ENROLLMENT tuples based on the SID. We denote such a join as STUDENT JOIN (SID = StudentNumber) ENROLLMENT. The meaning of this expression is "Join a STUDENT tuple to an ENROLLMENT tuple if SID of STUDENT equals StudentNumber of ENROLLMENT."

To form this join, we first find the product of STUDENT and ENROLLMENT, an operation that was shown in Figure 8-16. Next we SELECT those tuples from the product where SID of STUDENT equals StudentNumber of ENROLLMENT (there are only three). This operation leads to the relation in Figure 8-19(a). Note that two attributes are identical: SID and StudentNumber. One of these is redundant, so we eliminate it (in this case, we choose StudentNumber) with projection. The result is the join in Figure 8-19(b). The join in Figure 8-19(a) is called the **equijoin,** and the one in Figure 8-19(b) is called the **natural join.** Unless otherwise specified, when people say join, they mean the natural join.

➤ FIGURE 8-16

Product of the STUDENT and ENROLLMENT Relations in Figure 8-15

SID	Name	Major	GradeLevel	Age	Student-Number	Class-Name	Position-Number
123	JONES	HISTORY	JR	21	123	H350	1
123	JONES	HISTORY	JR	21	105	BA490	3
123	JONES	HISTORY	JR	21	123	BA490	7
158	PARKS	MATH	GR	26	123	H350	1
158	PARKS	MATH	GR	26	105	BA490	3
158	PARKS	MATH	GR	26	123	BA490	7
105	ANDERSON	MANAGEMENT	SN	27	123	H350	1
105	ANDERSON	MANAGEMENT	SN	27	105	BA490	3
105	ANDERSON	MANAGEMENT	SN	27	123	BA490	7
271	SMITH	HISTORY	JR	19	123	H350	1
271	SMITH	HISTORY	JR	19	105	BA490	3
271	SMITH	HISTORY	JR	19	123	BA490	7

*Projections of
STUDENT Relations:
(a) STUDENT
[Name, Major] and
(b) STUDENT
[Major, GradeLevel]*

Name	Major
JONES	HISTORY
PARKS	MATH
ANDERSON	MANAGEMENT
SMITH	HISTORY

(a)

Major	GradeLevel
HISTORY	JR
MATH	GR
MANAGEMENT	SN

(b)

Because forming the product of two large relations is time-consuming, the algorithm used by a DBMS to join two relations will be different from that described here. The result will be identical, however.

Joining on conditions other than equality also is possible. For example, STUDENT JOIN (SID not = StudentNumber) ENROLLMENT, or STUDENT JOIN (SID < FID) FACULTY. The latter join would result in tuples in which the student numbers are lower than the faculty numbers. Such a join may have meaning if, say, PeopleIdentifiers were assigned in chronological order. Such a join would portray pairs of students and teachers in such a way that the student would appear to have been at the institution longer than the teacher had.

There is one important limit on the conditions of a join: The attributes in the condition must arise from a common domain, so STUDENT JOIN (Age = ClassSize) ENROLLMENT is *illogical*. Even though the values of Age and ClassSize are compatible, they do not arise from the same domain. Semantically, this type of a join makes no sense. (Unfortunately, many relational DBMS products permit such a join.)

OUTER JOIN The join operation will produce a relation of students and the classes that they are taking. Students who are not taking any class will, however, be omitted from the result. If we want to include all students, an **outer join** can be used. Thus, STUDENT LEFT OUTER JOIN (SID = StudentNumber) ENROLLMENT will include every student row. The result is shown in Figure 8-19(c). Student Smith is included even though he or she enrolled in no class. The keyword LEFT specifies that all rows in the table on the left-hand side of the expression (STUDENT) will appear in the result. The STUDENT RIGHT OUTER JOIN (SID = StudentNumber) ENROLLMENT specifies that all rows in ENROLLMENT are to be included in the result. Outer joins are useful when working with relationships in which the minimum cardinality is zero on one or both sides. When ambiguity can arise between the two types of join, the term INNER JOIN is sometimes used instead of JOIN.

EXPRESSING QUERIES IN RELATIONAL ALGEBRA

Figure 8-20 summarizes the basic relational operations just discussed. Standard set operations include +, −, intersection, and product. Selection chooses specific tuples (rows) from a relation in accordance with the conditions for attribute val-

*Examples of Relational
Selection: (a) STUDENT
WHERE Major = 'Math'
and (b) STUDENT WHERE
Age < 25*

SID	Name	Major	GradeLevel	Age
158	PARKS	MATH	GR	26

(a)

SID	Name	Major	GradeLevel	Age
123	JONES	HISTORY	JR	21
271	SMITH	HISTORY	JR	19

(b)

➤ FIGURE 8-19

Examples of Joining STUDENT and ENROLLMENT Relations: (a) Equijoin and (b) Natural Join (c) Left Outer Join

SID	Name	Major	Grade-Level	Age	Student-Number	Class-Name	Position-Number
123	JONES	HISTORY	JR	21	123	H350	1
123	JONES	HISTORY	JR	21	123	BA490	7
105	ANDERSON	MANAGEMENT	SN	27	105	BA490	3

(a)

SID	Name	Major	GradeLevel	Age	ClassName	PositionNumber
123	JONES	HISTORY	JR	21	H350	1
123	JONES	HISTORY	JR	21	BA490	7
105	ANDERSON	MANAGEMENT	SN	27	BA490	3

(b)

SID	Name	Major	Grade-Level	Age	Student-Number	Class-Name	Position-Number
123	JONES	HISTORY	JR	21	123	H350	1
123	JONES	HISTORY	JR	21	123	BA490	7
105	ANDERSON	MANAGEMENT	SN	27	105	BA490	3
271	SMITH	HISTORY	JR	19	null	null	null

(c)

ues. Projection chooses specific attributes (columns) from a relation by means of the attribute name. Finally, join concatenates the tuples of two relations in accordance with a condition on the values of attributes.

We now turn to how relational operators can be used to express queries, using the relations STUDENT, CLASS, and ENROLLMENT from Figure 8-11; sample data

➤ FIGURE 8-20

Summary of Relational Algebra Operations

Type	Format	Example
Set operations	+, −, intersection, product	STUDENT [Name] − JUNIOR [Name]
Selection	Relation WHERE condition	CLASS WHERE Name = 'A'
Projection	relation [list of attributes]	STUDENT [Name, Major, Age]
Join	relation 1 JOIN (condition) relation 2	STUDENT JOIN (SID = StudentNumber) ENROLLMENT
Inner Join	Synonymous with join	
Outer Join	relation 1 LEFT OUTER JOIN (condition) relation 2	STUDENT LEFT OUTER JOIN (SID = StudentNumber) ENROLLMENT
	or	
	relation 1 RIGHT OUTER JOIN (condition) relation 2	STUDENT RIGHT OUTER JOIN (SID = StudentNumber) ENROLLMENT

► FIGURE 8-21

Example Data for Relations
Defined in Figure 8-11:
(a) STUDENT Relation,
(b) ENROLLMENT Relation,
and (c) CLASS Relation

SID	Name	Major	GradeLevel	Age
100	JONES	HISTORY	GR	21
150	PARKS	ACCOUNTING	SO	19
200	BAKER	MATH	GR	50
250	GLASS	HISTORY	SN	50
300	BAKER	ACCOUNTING	SN	41
350	RUSSELL	MATH	JR	20
400	RYE	ACCOUNTING	FR	18
450	JONES	HISTORY	SN	24

(a)

StudentNumber	ClassName	PositionNumber
100	BD445	1
150	BA200	1
200	BD445	2
200	CS250	1
300	CS150	1
400	BA200	2
400	BF410	1
400	CS250	2
450	BA200	3

(b)

Name	Time	Room
BA200	M-F9	SC110
BD445	MWF3	SC213
BF410	MWF8	SC213
CS150	MWF3	EA304
CS250	MWF12	EB210

(c)

are shown in Figure 8-21. Our purpose is to demonstrate the use of relations. Although you will probably never use relational algebra in a commercial environment, these examples will help you understand how relations can be manipulated.

1. What are the names of all students?

    STUDENT [Name]

    This is simply the projection of the Name attribute of the STUDENT relation, and the result is

JONES
PARKS
BAKER
GLASS
RUSSELL
RYE

    Duplicate names have been omitted. Although the names JONES and BAKER actually occur twice in the relation STUDENT, repetitions have been omitted because the result of a projection is a relation, and relations may not have duplicate tuples.

2. What are the student numbers of all students enrolled in a class?

ENROLLMENT [StudentNumber]

This is similar to the first query, but the projection occurs on the relation ENROLLMENT. The result is

100
150
200
300
400
450

Again, duplicate tuples have been omitted.

3. What are the student numbers of all students not enrolled in a class?

STUDENT [SID] − ENROLLMENT [StudentNumber]

This expression finds the difference of the projection of two relations: STUDENT [SID] has the student numbers of all students, and ENROLLMENT [StudentNumber] has the student numbers of all students enrolled in a class. The difference is the number of students not enrolled in a class. The result is

250

4. What are the numbers of students enrolled in the class 'BD445'?

ENROLLMENT WHERE ClassName = 'BD445' [StudentNumber]

This expression selects the appropriate tuples and then projects them onto the attribute StudentNumber. The result is

100
200

5. What are the names of the students enrolled in class 'BD445'?

STUDENT JOIN (SID = StudentNumber) ENROLLMENT WHERE
ClassName = 'BD445' [STUDENT.Name]

To answer this query, data from both STUDENT and ENROLLMENT are needed. Specifically, student names must come from STUDENT, whereas the condition "enrolled in BD445" must be checked in ENROLLMENT. Since both relations are needed, they must be joined. After STUDENT and ENROLLMENT have been joined, the selection is applied, followed by a projection on student names. The result is

JONES
BAKER

As we stated earlier, when two or more relations are considered, attribute names can be duplicated. Therefore, for clarity, the relation name may be prefixed to the attribute name. Thus, in our example, the projection is on [STUDENT.Name]. In this example, this prefix was added only for clarity, since the attribute names are different. But when attribute names are identical (a join involving STUDENT and CLASS yields two attributes, both called Name), the prefix is required. Consider the following query:

6. What are the names and meeting times of 'PARKS' classes?

To answer this, we must bring together data in all three relations. We need STUDENT data to find PARKS's student number; we need ENROLLMENT data to learn which classes PARKS is in; and we need CLASS data to determine the class meeting times.

STUDENT WHERE Name = 'PARKS' JOIN (SID = StudentNumber)

ENROLLMENT JOIN (ClassName = Name) CLASS [CLASS.Name, Time]

This expression first selects PARKS's tuple and joins it to matching ENROLLMENT tuples. Then the result is joined to matching CLASS tuples. Finally, the projection is taken to print classes and times. The result is

| BA200 | M-F9 |

We must specify CLASS.Name; simply specifying Name is ambiguous because both STUDENT and CLASS have an attribute called Name.

There are other, equivalent ways of responding to this query. One is

STUDENT JOIN (SID = StudentNumber) ENROLLMENT JOIN (ClassName = Name) CLASS WHERE STUDENT.Name = 'PARKS' [CLASS.Name, Time]

This expression differs from the first one because the selection on PARKS is not done until after all of the joins have been performed. Assuming that the computer performs the operations as stated, this expression will be slower than the earlier one because many more tuples will be joined.

Such differences are a major disadvantage of relational algebra. To the user, two equivalent queries should take the same amount of time (and hence cost the same). Imagine the frustration if one form of a query costs $1.17 and another costs $4,356. To the unwary and unsophisticated user, the cost difference appears capricious.

7. What are the grade levels and meeting rooms of all students, including students not enrolled in a class?

Since all students are to be included, this query requires the use of an outer join. The syntax is straightforward:

STUDENT LEFT OUTER JOIN (SID = StudentNumber) ENROLLMENT JOIN (ClassName = Name) CLASS [GradeLevel, Room].

The result includes the GradeLevels of Glass and Russell, who are not enrolled in any class.

GR	SC213
SO	SC110
GR	EB210
SN	Null
SN	EA304
JR	Null
FR	SC110
FR	SC213
FR	EB210
SN	SC110

➤ SUMMARY

Several tasks must be carried out when implementing a relational database. First, the structure of the database must be defined to the DBMS. Then file space needs to be allocated, and finally the database is filled with data.

The relational model represents and processes data in the form of tables called relations. The columns of the tables are called attributes, and the rows are called tuples. The values of the attributes arise from domains. The terms *table, column,* and *row* and *file, field,* and *record* are used synonymously with the terms *relation, attribute,* and *tuple,* respectively.

The use of the term *key* can be confusing because it is used differently in the design and implementation stages. During design, the term means a logical key, which is one or more attributes that uniquely define a row. During implementation, the term means a physical key, which is a data structure used to improve performance. A logical key may or may not be a physical key, and a physical key may or may not be a logical key. In this text we use key to mean logical key and index to mean physical key.

Because we are using the relational model to express database designs, there is no need to transform the design during the implementation stage. We simply define the relational design to the DBMS. Two ways of defining the design are to express it in a DDL text file and to use a graphical data definition tool. In either case, the tables, columns, indexes, constraints, passwords, and other controls are defined to the DBMS.

In addition to defining the database structure, the developers must allocate media space for the database. With multiuser systems, such allocation can be important to the DBMS's effective performance. Finally, the database is filled with data using tools provided by the DBMS vendor, programs developed by the vendor, or both.

The four categories of relational data manipulation language are relational algebra, relational calculus, transform-oriented languages, and query-by-example. Relational algebra consists of a group of relational operators that can be used to manipulate relations to obtain a desired result. Relational algebra is procedural. The transform-oriented languages offer a nonprocedural means to transform a set of relations into a desired result. SQL is the most common example.

There are three means of accessing a relational database. One is to use the form and report facilities provided by the DBMS. A second is to use a query/update language, of which SQL is the most common. A third is through application programs.

Application program interfaces can be either by function call, object methods, or special-purpose database commands that are translated by a precompiler. The processing orientation of the relational model is relation at a time, but the orientation of most programming languages is row at a time. Some means must be devised to correct for this mismatch.

Relational algebra is used to manipulate relations to obtain a desired result. The operators are union, difference, intersection, product, projection, selection, (inner) join, and outer join.

➤ GROUP I QUESTIONS

8.1 Name and describe the three tasks necessary to implement a relational database.

8.2 Define *relation, attribute, tuple,* and *domain.*

8.3   Explain the use of the terms *table, column, row, file, field,* and *record.*

8.4   Explain the difference between a relational schema and a relation.

8.5   Define *key, index, logical key,* and *physical key.*

8.6   Describe three reasons for using indexes.

8.7   Under what conditions is it necessary to transform the database design during the implementation stage?

8.8   Explain the term *data definition language.* What purpose does it serve?

8.9   How can a database structure be defined other than through a text file?

8.10 What aspects of a database design need to be defined to the DBMS?

8.11 Give an example, other than the one in this text, in which the allocation of the database to physical media is important.

8.12 Describe the best and worst extremes for loading the database with data.

8.13 Name and briefly explain four categories of relational DML.

8.14 Describe how relational data can be manipulated by means of forms.

8.15 Explain the role of query languages in relational data manipulation. How do stored queries differ from application programs? Why are they used?

8.16 Describe the two styles of application program interface to the database. In your answer, explain the role of a precompiler.

8.17 Describe the mismatch between the orientation of the SQL and the orientation of most programming languages. How is this mismatch corrected?

8.18 How does relational algebra differ from high school algebra?

8.19 Why is relational algebra *closed?*

8.20 Define *union compatible.* Give an example of two relations that are union compatible and two that are union incompatible.

Questions 8.21 through 8.23 refer to the following two relations:

COMPANY (Name, NumberEmployees, Sales)

MANUFACTURERS (Name, PeopleCount, Revenue)

8.21 Give an example of a union of these two relations.

8.22 Give an example of a difference of these two relations.

8.23 Give an example of an intersection of these two relations.

Questions 8.24 through 8.28 refer to the following three relations:

SALESPERSON (Name, Age, Salary)

ORDER (Number, CustName, SalespersonName, Amount)

CUSTOMER (Name, City, IndustryType)

An instance of these relations is shown in Figure 8-22. Use the data in those tables for the following problems:

8.24 Give an example of the product of SALESPERSON and ORDER.

8.25 Show an example of

SALESPERSON [Name, Salary]

SALESPERSON [Age, Salary]

Under what conditions will SALESPERSON [Age, Salary] have fewer rows than SALESPERSON does?

8.26 Show an example of a select on SALESPERSON Name, on SALESPERSON Age, and on both SALESPERSON Name and Age.

➤ FIGURE 8-22

Sample Data for Questions 8.24 Through 8.28

Name	Age	Salary
Abel	63	120,000
Baker	38	42,000
Jones	26	36,000
Murphy	42	50,000
Zenith	59	118,000
Kobad	27	34,000

SALESPERSON

Number	CustName	SalespersonName	Amount
100	Abernathy Construction	Zenith	560
200	Abernathy Construction	Jones	1800
300	Manchester Lumber	Abel	480
400	Amalgamated Housing	Abel	2500
500	Abernathy Construction	Murphy	6000
600	Tri-City Builders	Abel	700
700	Manchester Lumber	Jones	150

ORDER

Name	City	IndustryType
Abernathy Construction	Willow	B
Manchester Lumber	Manchester	F
Tri-City Builders	Memphis	B
Amalgamated Housing	Memphis	B

CUSTOMER

8.27 Show an example of an equijoin and a natural join of SALESPERSON and ORDER in which the Name of SALESPERSON equals the SalespersonName of ORDER.

8.28 Show relational algebra expressions for

a. The names of all salespeople

b. The names of all salespeople having an ORDER row

c. The names of salespeople not having an ORDER row

d. The names of salespeople having an order with Abernathy Construction

e. The ages of salespeople having an order with Abernathy Construction

f. The city of all CUSTOMERS having an order with salesperson Jones

g. The names of all salespeople with the names of customers who have ordered from them. Include salespeople who have no orders.

CHAPTER 9

Structured Query Language

Structured Query Language, or SQL, is the most important relational data manipulation language in use today. It has been endorsed by the American National Standards Institute (ANSI) as the language of choice for manipulating relational databases, and it is the data access language used by many commercial DBMS products, including DB2, SQL/DS, ORACLE, INGRES, SYBASE, SQL Server, dBASE for Windows, Paradox, Microsoft Access, and many others. Because of its popularity, SQL has become the standard language for information interchange among computers. Since there is a version of SQL that can run on almost any computer and operating system, computer systems are able to exchange data by passing SQL requests and responses to one another.

The development of SQL began at IBM's San Jose research facilities in the mid-1970s under the name SEQUEL. Several versions of SEQUEL were released, and in 1980 the product was renamed SQL. Since then, IBM has been joined by many other vendors in developing products for SQL. The American National Standards Institute has taken over the role of maintaining SQL and periodically publishes updated versions of the SQL standard. This chapter discusses the core of SQL as described in the 1992 ANSI standard, which is often referred to as SQL92.[1] The most recent version, SQL3, concerns extensions to the language for object-oriented programming. That version is discussed in Chapter 17.

The constructs and expressions in a particular implementation of SQL (for example, in ORACLE or SQL Server) may differ in minor ways from the ANSI standard, in part because many of the DBMS products were developed before there was agreement on the standard and also because vendors added capabilities to their products to gain a competitive advantage. From a marketing perspective, simply supporting the ANSI standard was at times judged as not having enough sizzle.

SQL commands can be used interactively as a query language, or they can be embedded in application programs. Thus SQL is not a programming language (like COBOL); rather, it is a *data sublanguage,* or *data access language,* that is embedded in other languages.

---

[1]International Standards Organization Publication ISO/IEC 9075: 1992, *Database Language SQL*.

In this chapter, we present interactive SQL statements, which need to be adjusted and modified when they are embedded in programs, as illustrated in Chapter 13. This chapter is concerned only with data manipulation statements, although there also are SQL commands for data definition and control, examples of which are also given in Chapter 15.

SQL is a transform-oriented language that accepts one or more relations as input and produces a single relation as output. The result of every SQL query is a relation; even if the result is a single number, that number is considered to be a relation with a single row and a single column. Thus SQL, like relational algebra, is *closed*.

➤ QUERYING A SINGLE TABLE

In this section, we consider SQL facilities for querying a single table. We will discuss multitable and update statements later in this chapter. By custom, SQL reserved words such as SELECT and FROM are written in capital letters. Also, SQL statements are normally written in multiple lines as illustrated in this chapter. SQL language compilers do not require either capitals or multiple lines, however. These conventions are used only to provide better clarity to humans who read the SQL statements.

➤ FIGURE 9-1

Relations Used for SQL Examples

1. JUNIOR (<u>Snum</u>, Name, Major)
2. HONOR-STUDENT (<u>Number</u>, Name, Interest)
3. STUDENT (<u>SID</u>, Name, Major, GradeLevel, Age)
4. CLASS (<u>Name</u>, Time, Room)
5. ENROLLMENT (<u>StudentNumber</u>, <u>ClassName</u>, PositionNumber)
6. FACULTY (<u>FID</u>, Name, Department)

	Attribute	Domain
1.	Snum	PeopleIdentifiers
	JUNIOR.Name	PeopleNames
	Major	SubjectNames
2.	Number	PeopleIdentifiers
	HONOR-STUDENT.Name	PeopleNames
	Interest	SubjectNames
3.	SID	PeopleIdentifiers
	STUDENT.Name	PeopleNames
	Major	SubjectNames
	GradeLevel	Classes
	Age	Ages
4.	CLASS.Name	ClassNames
	Time	ClassTimes
	Room	Rooms
5.	StudentNumber	PeopleIdentifiers
	ClassName	ClassNames
	PositionNumber	ClassSizes
6.	FID	PeopleIdentifiers
	FACULTY.Name	PeopleNames
	Department	SubjectNames

➤ FIGURE 9-2

Sample Data Used for SQL Examples: (a) STUDENT Relation, (b) ENROLLMENT Relation, and (c) CLASS Relation

SID	Name	Major	GradeLevel	Age
100	JONES	HISTORY	GR	21
150	PARKS	ACCOUNTING	SO	19
200	BAKER	MATH	GR	50
250	GLASS	HISTORY	SN	50
300	BAKER	ACCOUNTING	SN	41
350	RUSSELL	MATH	JR	20
400	RYE	ACCOUNTING	FR	18
450	JONES	HISTORY	SN	24

(a)

StudentNumber	ClassName	PositionNumber
100	BD445	1
150	BA200	1
200	BD445	2
200	CS250	1
300	CS150	1
400	BA200	2
400	BF410	1
400	CS250	2
450	BA200	3

(b)

Name	Time	Room
BA200	M-F9	SC110
BD445	MWF3	SC213
BF410	MWF8	SC213
CS150	MWF3	EA304
CS250	MWF12	EB210

(c)

We use the same set of six relations with which we illustrated relational algebra in Chapter 8. The structure of those relations is shown in Figure 9-1, and sample data for three of them appears in Figure 9-2.

PROJECTIONS USING SQL

To form a projection with SQL, we name the relation to be projected and list the columns to be shown. Using standard SQL syntax, the projection STUDENT [SID, Name, Major] is specified as:

SELECT   SID, Name, Major
FROM   STUDENT

The keywords SELECT and FROM are always required; the columns to be obtained are listed after the keyword SELECT; and the table to be used is listed after the keyword FROM. The result of this projection for the data in Figure 9-2 is

100	JONES	HISTORY
150	PARKS	ACCOUNTING
200	BAKER	MATH
250	GLASS	HISTORY
300	BAKER	ACCOUNTING
350	RUSSELL	MATH
400	RYE	ACCOUNTING
450	JONES	HISTORY

Do not confuse the keyword SELECT with the relational algebra operator selection. SELECT is an SQL verb that can be used to perform a relational algebra projection, selection, and to specify other actions. Selection, on the other hand, differs from SELECT because it is the relational algebra operation of obtaining a subset of rows from a table.

Consider another example:

SELECT   Major
FROM   STUDENT

The result of this operation is the following:

| HISTORY |
| ACCOUNTING |
| MATH |
| HISTORY |
| ACCOUNTING |
| MATH |
| ACCOUNTING |
| HISTORY |

As you can see, this table contains duplicate rows, and consequently, in a strict sense, this table is not a relation. In fact, SQL does not automatically eliminate duplicates because such removal can be very time-consuming and, in many cases, is not desirable or necessary.

If duplicate rows must be removed, the qualifier DISTINCT must be specified, as follows:

SELECT   DISTINCT Major
FROM   STUDENT

The result of this operation is the relation

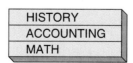

| HISTORY |
| ACCOUNTING |
| MATH |

SELECTIONS USING SQL

The relational algebra selection operator is also performed with the SQL SELECT command. An example is the following:

SELECT   SID, Name, Major, GradeLevel, Age
FROM   STUDENT
WHERE   Major = 'MATH'

This SELECT expression specifies the names of all the table's columns. FROM specifies the table to be used, and the new phrase, WHERE, provides the condition(s) for the selection. The format SELECT—FROM—WHERE is the fundamental structure of SQL statements. The following is an equivalent form of the preceding query:

```
SELECT    *
FROM      STUDENT
WHERE     Major = 'MATH'
```

The asterisk (*) means that all columns of the table are to be obtained. The result of both of these queries is

200	BAKER	MATH	GR	50
350	RUSSELL	MATH	JR	20

We can combine the selection and projection as follows:

```
SELECT    Name, Age
FROM      STUDENT
WHERE     Major = 'MATH'
```

The result is

BAKER	50
RUSSELL	20

Several conditions can be expressed in the WHERE clause. For example, the expression

```
SELECT    Name, Age
FROM      STUDENT
WHERE     Major = 'MATH' AND Age > 21
```

obtains the following:

BAKER	50

The conditions in WHERE clauses can refer to a set of values. To do this, the keywords IN or NOT IN may be used. Consider

```
SELECT    Name
FROM      STUDENT
WHERE     Major IN ['MATH', 'ACCOUNTING']
```

Notice that multiple values can be placed inside the brackets. This expression means "Display the names of students who have either a math or an accounting major." The result is

PARKS
BAKER
BAKER
RUSSELL
RYE

The expression

```
SELECT    Name
FROM      STUDENT
WHERE     Major NOT IN ['MATH', 'ACCOUNTING']
```

causes the names of students other than math or accounting majors to be presented. The result is

| JONES |
| GLASS |
| JONES |

The expression MAJOR IN means the value of the Major column can equal *any* of the listed majors. This is equivalent to the logical OR operator. The expression MAJOR NOT IN means the value must be different from *all* the listed majors.

WHERE clauses can also refer to ranges and to partial values. The keyword BETWEEN is used for ranges. For example, the statement

SELECT   Name, Major
FROM   STUDENT
WHERE   Age BETWEEN 19 AND 30

will obtain the names and majors of all students in their twenties. The result is

JONES	HISTORY
RUSSELL	MATH
JONES	HISTORY

This expression is equivalent to

SELECT   Name, Major
FROM   STUDENT
WHERE   Age > 19 AND Age < 30

Thus, the end values of BETWEEN (here 19 and 30) are excluded from the selected range.

The LIKE keyword is used in SQL expressions to select on partial values. The symbol _ (underscore) represents a single unspecified character. The symbol % represents a series of one or more unspecified characters. Thus the result of the expression

SELECT   Name, GradeLevel
FROM   STUDENT
WHERE   GradeLevel LIKE '_R'

is a relation having Name and GradeLevel columns and where GradeLevel consists of two characters, the second of which is the character R:

JONES	GR
BAKER	GR
RUSSELL	JR
RYE	FR

Similarly, the following expression will find students whose last names end with S:

SELECT   Name
FROM   STUDENT
WHERE   Name LIKE '%S'

the result is

| JONES |
| PARKS |
| GLASS |
| JONES |

(Microsoft Access uses a different set of wildcard symbols than the ANSI standard. A "?" is used in place of the underscore, and an "*" is used in place of "%".)

Finally, the keywords IS NULL are used to search for null (or missing) values. The expression

SELECT	Name
FROM	STUDENT
WHERE	GradeLevel IS NULL

will obtain the names of students who do not have a recorded value of GradeLevel. For the data in Figure 9-2, all students have a GradeLevel and this expression will return a relation with no rows.

SORTING

The rows of the result relation can be sorted by the values in one or more columns. Consider the following example:

SELECT	Name, Major, Age
FROM	STUDENT
WHERE	Major = 'ACCOUNTING'
ORDER BY	Name

This query will list the accounting majors in ascending sequence by value of name. The result is

BAKER	ACCOUNTING	41
PARKS	ACCOUNTING	19
RYE	ACCOUNTING	18

More than one column can be chosen for sorting. If so, the first column listed will be the major sort field, the next column the next major sort field, and so on. Columns can also be declared to be ascending (ASC) or descending (DESC), as shown in the next statement:

SELECT	Name, Major, Age
FROM	STUDENT
WHERE	GradeLevel IN ['FR', 'SO', 'SN']
ORDER BY	Major ASC, Age DESC

The result is

BAKER	ACCOUNTING	41
PARKS	ACCOUNTING	19
RYE	ACCOUNTING	18
GLASS	HISTORY	50
JONES	HISTORY	24

ORDER BY can be combined with any of the SELECT statements.

SQL BUILT-IN FUNCTIONS

SQL provides five built-in functions: COUNT, SUM, AVG, MAX, and MIN.[2] Although COUNT and SUM sound similar, they actually are different. COUNT computes the number of rows in a table, whereas SUM totals numeric columns.

---

[2]Sometimes built-in functions are referred to as *aggregate functions* to distinguish them from program languages' built-in functions such as SUBSTRING.

AVG, MAX, and MIN also operate on numeric columns: AVG computes the average value, and MAX and MIN obtain the maximum and minimum values of a column in a table.

The query expression

SELECT   COUNT(*)
FROM   STUDENT

counts the number of STUDENT rows and displays this total in a table with a single row and single column:

8

Consider the expressions

SELECT   COUNT (Major)
FROM   STUDENT

and

SELECT   COUNT (DISTINCT Major)
FROM   STUDENT

The first expression counts all majors, including duplicates, and the second counts only unique majors. The results are

8

and

3

respectively.

With the exception of GROUP BY (considered below), built-in functions cannot be mixed with column names in the SELECT statement. Thus

SELECT   Name, COUNT (*)

is not allowed.

The built-in functions can be used to request a result, as in the preceding examples. In most implementations of SQL, and in the ANSI standard SQL, the built-in functions *cannot* be used as part of a WHERE clause.

BUILT-IN FUNCTIONS AND GROUPING

To increase their utility, built-in functions can be applied to groups of rows within a table. Such groups are formed by collecting those rows (logically, not physically) that have the same value of a specified column. For example, students can be grouped by major, which means that one group will be formed for each value of MAJOR. For the data in Figure 9-2, there is a group of HISTORY majors, a group of ACCOUNTING majors, and a group of MATH majors.

The SQL keyword GROUP BY instructs the DBMS to group together those rows that have the same value of a column. Consider

SELECT   Major, COUNT (*)
FROM   STUDENT
GROUP BY   Major

The result of this expression is

HISTORY	3
ACCOUNTING	3
MATH	2

The rows of the STUDENT table have been logically grouped by the value of MAJOR, and the COUNT function sums the number of rows in each group. The result is a table with two columns, the major name and the sum. For subgroups, both columns and built-in functions can be specified in the SELECT statement.

In some cases, we do not want to consider all of the groups. For example, we might form groups of students having the same major and then wish to consider only those groups that have more than two students. In this case, we use the SQL HAVING clause to identify the subset of groups we want to consider.

The following SQL statements can list the majors that have more than two students and also the count of students in each of those majors.

SELECT   Major, COUNT (*)
FROM   STUDENT
GROUP BY   Major
HAVING   COUNT (*) > 2

Here, groups of students having the same major are formed, and then groups having more than two students are selected. (Other groups are ignored.) The major and the count of students in these selected groups are produced. The result is

| HISTORY | 3 |
| ACCOUNTING | 3 |

For even greater generality, WHERE clauses can be added as well. Doing so, however, can create ambiguity. For example:

SELECT   Major, AVG (Age)
FROM   STUDENT
WHERE   GradeLevel = 'SN'
GROUP BY   Major
HAVING   COUNT (*) > 1

The result of this expression will differ depending on whether the WHERE condition is applied before or after the HAVING condition. To eliminate this uncertainty, the SQL standard specifies that WHERE clauses are to be applied first. Accordingly, in the preceding statement, the operations are: select the senior students; form the groups; select the groups that meet the HAVING condition; display the results. In this case, the result is

| HISTORY | 37 |

(This query is not valid for all implementations of SQL. For some implementations, the only attributes that can appear in the SELECT phrase of a query with GROUP BY are attributes that appear in the GROUP BY phrase and built-in functions of those attributes. Thus in this query, only MAJOR and built-in functions of MAJOR would be allowed.)

➤ QUERYING MULTIPLE TABLES

In this section we extend our discussion of SQL to include operations on two or more tables. The STUDENT, CLASS, and ENROLLMENT data in Figure 9-2 are used to illustrate these SQL commands.

RETRIEVAL USING SUBQUERY

Suppose we need to know the names of those students enrolled in the class BD445. If we know that students with SIDs of 100 and 200 are enrolled in this class, the following will produce the correct names:

```
SELECT   Name
FROM     STUDENT
WHERE    SID IN [100, 200]
```

Usually we do not know the SIDs of students in a class, but we do have a facility for finding those out. Examine the expression

```
SELECT   StudentNumber
FROM     ENROLLMENT
WHERE    ClassName = 'BD445'
```

The result of this operation is

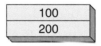

These are the student numbers we need. Combining the last two queries, we obtain the following:

```
SELECT   Name
FROM     STUDENT
WHERE    SID IN
             (SELECT   StudentNumber
              FROM     ENROLLMENT
              WHERE    ClassName = 'BD445' )
```

The second SELECT, which is called a **subquery**, is enclosed in parentheses.

It may be easier to understand these statements if you work from the bottom and read up. The last three statements obtain the student numbers for people enrolled in BD445, and the first three statements produce the names for the two students selected. The result of this query is

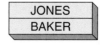

For this operation to be semantically correct, SID and StudentNumber must come from the same domain.

Subqueries can consist of three or even more tables. For example, suppose we want to know the names of the students enrolled in classes on Monday, Wednesday, and Friday at 3 o'clock (denoted as MWF3 in our data). First, we need the names of those classes that meet at that time:

```
SELECT   CLASS.Name
FROM     CLASS
WHERE    Time = 'MWF3'
```

(Since we are dealing with three different tables, we qualify the column names with table names to avoid confusion and ambiguity. Thus, CLASS.Name refers to the column Name in the relation CLASS.)

Now we get the identifying numbers of students in these classes with the following expression:

```
SELECT      ENROLLMENT.StudentNumber
FROM        ENROLLMENT
WHERE       ENROLLMENT.ClassName IN
                (SELECT     CLASS.Name
                 FROM       CLASS
                 WHERE      Time = 'MWF3')
```

This yields

which are the numbers of the students in the class MWF3. To get the names of those students, we specify

```
SELECT      STUDENT.Name
FROM        STUDENT
WHERE       STUDENT.SID IN
                (SELECT ENROLLMENT.StudentNumber
                 FROM ENROLLMENT
                 WHERE ENROLLMENT.ClassName IN
                     (SELECT   CLASS.Name
                      FROM     CLASS
                      WHERE    CLASS.Time = 'MWF3'))
```

The result is

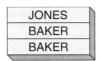

This strategy works well as long as the attributes in the answer come from a single table. If, however, the result comes from two or more tables, we have a problem. For example, suppose we want to know the names of students and the names of their classes. Say we need SID, StudentName, and ClassName. In this case, the results come from two different tables (STUDENT and ENROLLMENT), and so the subquery strategy will not work.

JOINING WITH SQL

To produce the SID, StudentName, and ClassName for every student, we must join the STUDENT table with the ENROLLMENT table. The following statements will do this:

```
SELECT      STUDENT.SID, STUDENT.Name, ENROLLMENT.ClassName
FROM        STUDENT, ENROLLMENT
WHERE       STUDENT.SID = ENROLLMENT.StudentNumber
```

Recall that a join is the combination of a product operation, followed by a selection, followed (usually) by a projection. In this expression, the FROM statement expresses the product of STUDENT and ENROLLMENT, and then the WHERE statement expresses the selection. The meaning is "Select from the product of STUDENT and ENROLLMENT those rows in which SID of STUDENT equals StudentNumber of ENROLLMENT." Finally, after the selection, the projection of the student number, name, and class name is taken. The result is

100	JONES	BD445
150	PARKS	BA200
200	BAKER	BD445
200	BAKER	CS250
300	BAKER	CS125
400	RYE	BA200
400	RYE	BF410
400	RYE	CS250
450	JONES	BA200

The WHERE clause can contain qualifiers in addition to those needed for the join. For example,

```
SELECT    STUDENT.SID, ENROLLMENT.ClassName
FROM      STUDENT, ENROLLMENT
WHERE     STUDENT.SID = ENROLLMENT.StudentNumber
AND       STUDENT.Name = 'RYE'
AND       ENROLLMENT.PositionNumber = 1
```

The additional qualifiers here are STUDENT.Name = 'RYE' and ENROLLMENT.PositionNumber = 1. This operation will list the student number and class name of all students named RYE who were first to enroll in a class. The result is

| 400 | BF410 |

When data are needed from more than two tables, we can use a similar strategy. In the next example, three tables are joined:

```
SELECT    STUDENT.SID, CLASS.Name, CLASS.Time,
          ENROLLMENT.PositionNumber
FROM      STUDENT, ENROLLMENT, CLASS
WHERE     STUDENT.SID = ENROLLMENT.StudentNumber
AND       ENROLLMENT.ClassName = CLASS.Name
AND       STUDENT.Name = 'BAKER'
```

The result of this operation is

200	BD445	MWF3	2
200	CS250	MWF12	1
300	CS150	MWF3	1

COMPARISON OF SQL SUBQUERY AND JOIN

A join can be used as an alternative way of expressing many subqueries. For example, we used a subquery to find the students enrolled in the class BD445. We can also use a join to express this query:

```
SELECT    STUDENT.Name
FROM      STUDENT, ENROLLMENT
WHERE     STUDENT.SID = ENROLLMENT.StudentNumber
AND       ENROLLMENT.ClassName = 'BD445'
```

Similarly, the query "What are the names of the students in class MWF at 3?" can be expressed as

```
SELECT    STUDENT.NAME
FROM      STUDENT, ENROLLMENT, CLASS
WHERE     STUDENT.SID = ENROLLMENT.StudentNumber
AND       ENROLLMENT.ClassName = CLASS.Name
AND       CLASS.Time = 'MWF3'
```

Although join expressions can substitute for many subquery expressions, they cannot substitute for all of them. For instance, subqueries that involve EXISTS and NOT EXISTS (discussed in the next section) cannot be represented by joins.

Similarly, subqueries cannot be substituted for all joins. When using a join, the displayed columns may come from any of the joined tables, but when using a subquery, the displayed columns may come from only the table named in the FROM expression in the first SELECT. For example, suppose we want to know the names of classes taken by undergraduates. We can express this as a subquery:

```
SELECT    DISTINCT ClassName
FROM      ENROLLMENT
WHERE     StudentNumber IN
              (SELECT SID
              FROM STUDENT
              WHERE GradeLevel NOT = 'GR')
```

or as a join:

```
SELECT    DISTINCT ENROLLMENT.ClassName
FROM      ENROLLMENT, STUDENT
WHERE     ENROLLMENT.StudentNumber = STUDENT.SID
AND       STUDENT.GradeLevel NOT = 'GR'
```

But if we want to know both the names of the classes and the grade levels of the undergraduate students, we must use a join. A subquery will not suffice because the desired results come from two different tables. That is, the names of the classes are stored in ENROLLMENT, and the names of the students are stored in STUDENT. The following obtains the correct answer:

```
SELECT    DISTINCT ENROLLMENT.ClassName, STUDENT.GradeLevel
FROM      ENROLLMENT, STUDENT
WHERE     ENROLLMENT.StudentNumber = STUDENT.SID
AND       STUDENT.GradeLevel NOT = 'GR'
```

The result is

BA200	SO
CS150	SN
BA200	FR
BF410	FR
CS250	FR
BA200	SN

OUTER JOIN

ANSI standard SQL does not support outer joins. They are, however, supported by many DBMS products. Here we will illustrate the use of one of them.

Suppose we want a list of all students and the names of the classes that they are taking. Further, suppose that we want to include all students, even those who are taking no class. The following SQL expression will obtain this result using Microsoft Access

```
SELECT    Name, ClassName
FROM      STUDENT LEFT JOIN ENROLLMENT
          ON SID = StudentNumber;
```

The result is

JONES	BD445
PARKS	BA200
BAKER	BD445
BAKER	CS250
GLASS	null
BAKER	CS150
RUSSELL	Null
RYE	BA200
RYE	BF410
RYE	CS250
JONES	BA200

Observe the differences in Access SQL and ANSI standard notation. The join conditions are specified using the keyword ON. Also, all SQL expressions are terminated with a semicolon.

➤ EXISTS AND NOT EXISTS

EXISTS and NOT EXISTS are logical operators whose value is either true or false depending on the presence or absence of rows that fit the qualifying conditions. For example, suppose we want to know the student numbers of students enrolled in more than one class.

```
SELECT    DISTINCT StudentNumber
FROM      ENROLLMENT A
WHERE     EXISTS
             (SELECT      *
              FROM        ENROLLMENT B
              WHERE       A.StudentNumber = B.StudentNumber
              AND         A.ClassName NOT = B.ClassName)
```

In this example, both the query and the subquery refer to the ENROLLMENT table. To prevent ambiguity, these two uses of ENROLLMENT have been assigned a different name. In the first FROM statement, ENROLLMENT is assigned the temporary and arbitrary name A, and in the second FROM statement, it is assigned another temporary and arbitrary name, B.

The meaning of the subquery expression is this: Find two rows in ENROLL-MENT having the same student number but different class names. (This means that the student is taking more than one class.) If two such rows exist, then the logical value of EXISTS is true. In this case, we present the student number in the answer. Otherwise, the logical value of the EXISTS is false, so we do not present that SID in the answer.

Another way of viewing this query is to imagine two separate and identical copies of the ENROLLMENT table. Call one copy Table A and the other copy Table B. We compare each row in A with each row in B. First we look at the first row in A and the first row in B. In this case, since the two rows are identical, both the StudentNumbers and the ClassNames are the same, so we do not display the SID.

Now look at the first row in A and the second row in B. If the StudentNumbers are the same and the ClassNames are different, we display the StudentNumber. Essentially, we are comparing the first row of ENROLLMENT with the second row of ENROLLMENT. For the data in Figure 9-2, neither the StudentNumbers nor the ClassNames are the same.

We continue comparing the first row of A with each row of B. If the conditions are ever met, we print the StudentNumber. When all of the rows in B have been examined, we move to the second row of A and compare it with all the rows in B (actually, if we are considering the *n*th rows in A, only those rows greater than *n* need to be considered in B).

The result of this query is

To illustrate the application of NOT EXISTS, suppose we want to know the names of students taking all classes. Another way of stating this is that we want the names of students such that there are no classes that the student did not take. The following expresses this:

```
SELECT    STUDENT.Name
FROM      STUDENT
WHERE     NOT EXISTS
              (SELECT *
              FROM    ENROLLMENT
              WHERE  NOT EXISTS
                  (SELECT      *
                  FROM         CLASS
                  WHERE        CLASS.Name = ENROLLMENT.ClassName
                  AND          ENROLLMENT.StudentNumber = STUDENT.SID))
```

This query has three parts. In the bottom part, it finds classes the student did take. The middle part determines whether any classes were found that the student did not take. If not, then the student is taking all classes, and his or her name is displayed.

This query may be difficult to understand. If you have trouble with it, use the data in Figure 9-2 and follow the instructions. For that data, the answer is that no student is taking all classes. You might try to change the data so that a student does take all classes. Another way to look at this query is to try to solve it in a way other than with NOT EXISTS. The problems you encounter will help you understand why NOT EXISTS is necessary.

➤ CHANGING DATA

SQL has provisions for changing data in tables by inserting new rows, deleting rows, and modifying values in existing rows. SQL also can change the data structure, although we will not explore this until we study DB2 in Chapter 15.

INSERTING DATA

Rows can be inserted into a table one at a time or in groups. To insert a single row, we state

```
INSERT    INTO ENROLLMENT
          VALUES (400, 'BD445', 44)
```

If we do not know all of this data—for instance, if we do not know PositionNumber—we could say

```
INSERT    INTO ENROLLMENT
          (StudentNumber, ClassName)
          VALUES (400, 'BD445')
```

PositionNumber could then be added later. Note that this causes the value of PositionNumber to have a null value in the new row.

We can also copy rows in mass from one table to another. For example, suppose we want to fill the JUNIOR table defined in Figure 9.1.

```
INSERT    INTO JUNIOR
          VALUES
          (SELECT SID, Name, Major
          FROM      STUDENT
          WHERE     GradeLevel = 'JR')
```

The contained SELECT, and all of the SQL SELECT expressions developed in the previous two sections, can be used to identify the rows to be copied. This feature offers quite powerful capabilities.

DELETING DATA

As with insertion, rows can be deleted one at a time or in groups. The following example deletes the row for Student 100:

```
DELETE    STUDENT
WHERE     STUDENT.SID = 100
```

Note that if Student 100 is enrolled in classes, this delete will cause an integrity problem, as the ENROLLMENT rows having StudentNumber = 100 will have no corresponding STUDENT row.

Groups of rows can be deleted as shown in the next two examples, which delete all enrollments for accounting majors as well as all accounting majors.

```
DELETE    ENROLLMENT
WHERE     ENROLLMENT.StudentNumber IN
          (SELECT    STUDENT.SID
          FROM       STUDENT
          WHERE      STUDENT.Major = 'Accounting')
DELETE    STUDENT
WHERE     STUDENT.Major = 'Accounting'
```

The order of these two operations is important, for if it were reversed, none of the ENROLLMENT rows would be deleted because the matching STUDENT rows would already have been deleted.

MODIFYING DATA

Rows can also be modified one at a time or in groups. The keyword SET is used to change a column value. After SET, the name of the column to be changed and then the new value or way of computing the new value is specified. Consider two examples:

```
UPDATE    ENROLLMENT
SET       PositionNumber = 44
WHERE     SID = 400
```

and

```
UPDATE    ENROLLMENT
SET       PositionNumber = MAX(PositionNumber) + 1
WHERE     SID = 400
```

In the second UPDATE statement, the value of the column is calculated using the MAX built-in function. Some implementations of SQL, however, may not allow the built-in function to be used as an argument in the SET command.

To illustrate mass updates, suppose the name of a course has been changed from BD445 to BD564. In this case, to prevent integrity problems, both the EN-ROLLMENT and the CLASS tables must be changed.

```
UPDATE    ENROLLMENT
SET       ClassName = 'BD564'
WHERE     ClassName = 'BD445'
UPDATE    CLASS
SET       ClassName = 'BD564'
WHERE     ClassName = 'BD445'
```

Remember that mass updates can be quite dangerous. The user is given great power—power that when used correctly can rapidly perform the task at hand but when used incorrectly can cause serious problems.

➤ SUMMARY

SQL is today's most important relational data manipulation language. It has become the standard for information exchange among computers, and its popularity continues to grow. SQL statements that operate on a single table include SELECT, SELECT with WHERE, SELECT with GROUP BY, and SELECT with GROUP BY and HAVING. SQL also contains the built-in functions of COUNT, SUM, AVG, MAX, and MIN.

Operations on two or more tables can be done using subquery, joins, EXISTS, and NOT EXISTS. Subqueries and joins perform many of the same operations, but they do not completely substitute for each other. Subqueries require that the attributes retrieved arise from a single relation, but joins do not. On the other hand, some queries are possible with subqueries and EXISTS and NOT EXISTS that are impossible with joins.

The SQL statements for data modification include INSERT, DELETE, and UP-DATE commands, which are used to add, remove, and change data values.

In this chapter we presented the basic SQL commands in generic form, and in Chapters 13 and 15 we use these commands to process a database using commercial DBMS products.

➤ GROUP I QUESTIONS

The questions in this group refer to the following three relations:

SALESPERSON (<u>Name</u>, Age, Salary)

ORDER (<u>Number</u>, CustName, SalespersonName, Amount)

CUSTOMER (<u>Name</u>, City, IndustryType)

An instance of these relations is shown in Figure 9-3. Use the data in those tables and show the SQL statements to display or modify data as indicated in the following questions:

9.1 Show the ages and salaries of all salespeople.

9.2 Show the ages and salaries of all salespeople but omit duplicates.

9.3 Show the names of all salespeople under 30 years old.

9.4 Show the names of all salespeople who have an order with Abernathy Construction.

9.5 Show the names of all salespeople who earn more than $49,999 and less than $100,000.

➤ FIGURE 9-3

Sample Data for Group I Questions

Name	Age	Salary
Abel	63	120,000
Baker	38	42,000
Jones	26	36,000
Murphy	42	50,000
Zenith	59	118,000
Kobad	27	34,000

SALESPERSON

Number	CustName	SalespersonName	Amount
100	Abernathy Construction	Zenith	560
200	Abernathy Construction	Jones	1800
300	Manchester Lumber	Abel	480
400	Amalgamated Housing	Abel	2500
500	Abernathy Construction	Murphy	6000
600	Tri-City Builders	Abel	700
700	Manchester Lumber	Jones	150

ORDER

Name	City	IndustryType
Abernathy Construction	Willow	B
Manchester Lumber	Manchester	F
Tri-City Builders	Memphis	B
Amalgamated Housing	Memphis	B

CUSTOMER

9.6   Show the names of all salespeople in their fifties. Use the BETWEEN keyword.

9.7   Show the names of all salespeople in their fifties. Use the LIKE keyword.

9.8   Show the names of customers which are located in a City ending with S.

9.9   Show the names and salary of all salespeople who do not have an order with Abernathy Construction, in ascending order of salary.

9.10   Compute the number of orders.

9.11   Compute the number of different customers who have an order.

9.12   Compute the average age of a salesperson.

9.13   Show the name of the oldest salesperson.

9.14   Compute the number of orders for each salesperson.

9.15   Compute the number of orders for each salesperson, considering only orders for an amount exceeding 500.

9.16   Show the names and ages of salespeople who have an order with ABERNATHY CONSTRUCTION, in descending order of age (use a subquery).

9.17   Show the names and ages of salespeople who have an order with ABERNATHY CONSTRUCTION, in descending order of age (use a join).

9.18   Show the age of salespeople who have an order with a customer in MEMPHIS (use a subquery).

9.19   Show the age of salespeople who have an order with a customer in MEMPHIS (use a join).

9.20   Show the industry type and ages of the salespeople of all orders for companies in MEMPHIS.

9.21   Show the names of salespeople along with the names of the customers which have ordered from them. Include salespeople who have had no orders. Use Microsoft Access notation.

9.22   Show the names of salespeople who have two or more orders.

9.23   Show the names and ages of salespeople who have two or more orders.

9.24   Show the names and ages of salespeople who have an order with all customers.

9.25   Show an SQL statement to insert a new row into CUSTOMER.

9.26   Show an SQL statement to insert a new name and age into SALESPERSON; assume that salary is not determined.

9.27   Show an SQL statement to insert rows into a new table, HIGH-ACHIEVER (Name, Age), in which, to be included, a salesperson must have a salary of at least 100,000.

9.28   Show an SQL statement to delete customer ABERNATHY CONSTRUCTION.

9.29   Show an SQL statement to delete all orders for ABERNATHY CONSTRUCTION.

9.30   Show an SQL statement to change the salary of salesperson JONES to 45,000.

9.31   Show an SQL statement to give all salespeople a 10 percent pay increase.

9.32   Assume that salesperson JONES changes his name to PARKS. Show the SQL statements that make the appropriate changes.

➤ GROUP II QUESTIONS

9.33 Install SQL Server, open the Query Analyzer, and select the Northwind database. Write SQL statements for the following queries and print them.

   a. List all columns of suppliers.

   b. List CompanyName from suppliers with CompanyName starting with "New."

   c. List all columns from products supplied by suppliers with CompanyName starting with "New." Show answers using both a join and a subquery.

   d. List the ReorderLevel and count for all products.

   e. List the ReorderLevel and count for all ReorderLevels having more than one element.

   f. List the RecorderLevel and count for all ReorderLevels having more than one element for products from suppliers whose names start with "New."

➤ PROJECTS

A. Install SQL Server as explained in Appendix B and complete Project A in Chapter 6 or 7 if you have not already done so. Using the Open Table function (see Appendix B), fill sample data into the OWNER, BUILDING, and UNIT (or APARTMENT) tables, including the associated intersection table. Ensure your data includes an owner who is related to at least two buildings and a building that has at least two owners. Using Query Analyzer, create SQL statements to show the names of owners and buildings that they own. Create SQL to list all buildings and any apartments they contain that are unoccupied. Give an example of a subquery on any two related tables.

B. Install SQL Server as explained in Appendix B and complete Project B in Chapter 6 or 7 if you have not already done so. Using the Open Table function (see Appendix B), fill sample data into the BASE-SYSTEM, OPERATING-SYSTEM, and MEMORY-OPTION tables, including the associated intersection table. Ensure your data includes a base-system that has at least two different operating systems, and an operating system that is used on at least two base systems. Also create at least one base system that has no memory options and at least one that has two or more memory options. Using Query Analyzer, create SQL statements to show the names of base systems and operating systems that they have. Create SQL to list all base systems and memory options that they have. Give an example of a subquery on any two related tables.

C. Install SQL Server as explained in Appendix B and complete Project C in Chapter 6 or 7 if you have not already done so. Using the Open Table function (see Appendix B), fill sample data into the SUBJECT, TITLE, and TITLE-KEY-WORDS tables, including the associated intersection table. Ensure your data includes a subject having at least two titles, and a title having at least two subjects. Also create at least one title that has no keywords and at least one that has two or more keywords. Using Query Analyzer, create SQL statements to show the names of subjects and titles that they have. Create SQL to list all titles and keywords that they have. Give an example of a subquery on any two related tables.

CHAPTER 10

Database Application Design

This chapter introduces the fundamental concepts in database application design. We begin by listing and describing the functions of a database application. Then each of these functions is described in further detail using an example application of an art gallery. The ideas presented in this chapter pertain best to database applications that are developed for use in traditional environments such as Windows. The next chapter will extend these concepts for the design of applications that use Internet technology.

Before we begin, a note on terminology is necessary. In the early days of database processing, it was easy to find a line between the DBMS and the application—applications were separate programs that invoked the DBMS. Today, especially with desktop DBMS products like Microsoft Access, the line has become blurred. To avoid confusion in this chapter, we will assume that all forms, reports, menus, and any program code that is contained in any of those are part of the database application. Additionally, stand-alone programs that call the DBMS are also part of the application. Any structures, rules, or constraints that are part of the table and relationship definitions are managed by the DBMS and are part of the database. Thus, a rule placed on a column of a table in table definition is considered a rule that is enforced by the DBMS. The same rule, placed on a form control, is considered a rule that is enforced by the database application. You will see the importance of this distinction as we proceed.

➤ FUNCTIONS OF A DATABASE APPLICATION

Figure 10-1 lists the functions of a database application. The first is to process views of data. There are four basic processing functions: create, read, update, and delete. These functions are sometimes referred to by the (unfortunate) acronym **CRUD**. Thus the first function of a database application is to CRUD views.

An application view is more than a row of a table and more than the result of a SQL statement. Often the construction of an application view requires two or more SQL statements, as you will see in the next section.

 FIGURE 10-1

Functions of a Database Application

- Create, Read, Update and Delete Views
- Format (or Materialize) Views
  - Forms
  - Reports
  - Inter-process
  - OLAP cubes
  - Other
- Enforce Constraints
  - Domains
  - Uniqueness
  - Relationship Cardinality
  - Business rules
- Provide Security and Control
- Execute Application Logic

A second application function is to **format** or **materialize** the views that are being processed. Note that there is a difference between the data content (the view) and the appearance of that content (the format or materialization). A given view usually has many different formats. The distinction between content and form is especially important for database applications that use Internet technology.

There are several types of view materialization. Forms and reports are the two most common types. Other types are also important, however. An inter-process materialization is used to send a view from one server to another or from one application to another. The format of such materializations is determined by a standard interface like Microsoft COM or a protocol like XML, which will be introduced in Chapter 11. Electronic data interchange is a good example of the use of this type. Other types of materialization are more specialized. You will see the role of OLAP cubes in Chapter 14. Natural language is an example of yet another type.

Enforcing constraints is a third application function. Such constraints can be structural, such as requiring data values to fit domain specifications, ensuring uniqueness, and enforcing relationship cardinalities. Other constraints involve business rules, such as "No salesperson can sell to a customer whose billing address is outside of his or her region."

The fourth function of a database application is to provide mechanisms for security and control. The application will work in conjunction with the operating system and the DBMS to augment security provided by user names and passwords. Menus and similar constructs limit what and when users can take particular actions.

The last function of a database application is to execute business logic. For example, in an order entry application, when a customer orders five copies of a book, the application needs to reduce the quantity of that book on hand by five. If insufficient copies are in inventory, or if the quantity on hand is less than the reorder quantity, other action needs to be taken as well.

The last two functions are addressed in detail in systems development classes, and, consequently, we will have the least to say about them in this text. The first three functions, however, are particular to database applications, and we will focus the bulk of our attention on them.

Before learning about these functions in more detail, consider the needs for a database and application at View Ridge Gallery.

➤ CASE APPLICATION: VIEW RIDGE GALLERY

View Ridge Gallery is a small art gallery that sells contemporary fine art, including lithographs, original paintings, and photographs. All of the lithographs and photos are signed and numbered, and most of the art is priced between $1,000 and $25,000. View Ridge has been in business for 27 years, has one full-time owner, three salespeople, and two workers who make frames, hang art in the gallery, and prepare art works for shipment.

View Ridge holds openings and other gallery events to attract customers to the gallery. Art is also placed on display in local companies and restaurants and in other public places. View Ridge owns all of the art that it sells; it holds no items on a consignment basis.

APPLICATION REQUIREMENTS

View Ridge wants to build database applications to satisfy the requirements shown in Figure 10-2. First, both the owner and the salespeople want to keep track of their customers and their art-purchasing interests. The salespeople need to know whom to contact when new art arrives, and they also need this information so that they can create personal written and verbal communications with their customers.

In addition, the database should record the customers' art purchases so that the salespeople can devote more time to the most active buyers. They also sometimes use the purchase records to identify the location of the art, because the gallery occasionally repurchases hard-to-find art for resale. The database application also should have a form for adding new works that the gallery purchases.

View Ridge wants its database application to provide a list of artists and works that have appeared in the gallery. The owner would also like to be able to determine how fast an artist's work sells and at what sales margins, and the database application should display current inventory on a Web page that customers can access via the Internet. Finally, View Ridge would like the database to produce reports that would reduce the work of the gallery's part-time bookkeeper/accountant.

DATABASE DESIGN

Figure 10-3(a) shows the structure of the objects required to support the gallery's database. CUSTOMER and ARTIST are compound objects, and WORK is a hybrid object whose unique identifier is the group {ARTIST, Title, and Copy}. The multi-value group Transaction represents the gallery's purchase and sale of the work. Because a given work can pass through the gallery several times (because of re-

---

➤ FIGURE 10-2

Summary of Requirements for the View Ridge Gallery Database Applications

Track customers and their purchasing interests.

Record customers' art purchases.

Record gallery's purchases.

List the artists and works that have appeared in the gallery.

Report how fast an artist's works have sold and at what margin.

Show current inventory in a Web page.

List product reports to be used by the gallery's bookkeeper/accountant.

➤ FIGURE 10-3

Database Design for View Ridge Gallery: (a) Semantic Objects, (b) E-R Diagram, (c) Relational Design, (d) Relational Design with Surrogate Keys, (e) Relationship Diagram from Access 2000

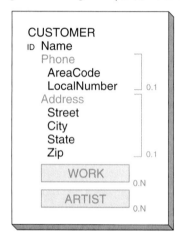

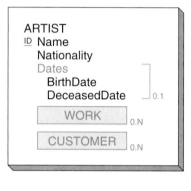

(a)

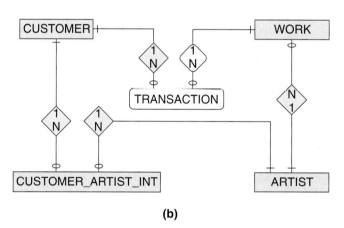

(b)

CUSTOMER (<u>CustNumber</u>, Name, AreaCode, LocalNumber, Street, City, State, Zip)

WORK (<u>ArtistName</u>, <u>Title</u>, <u>Copy</u>, Description)

TRANSACTION (*<u>ArtistName</u>*, *<u>Title</u>*, *<u>Copy</u>*, <u>DateAcquired</u>, AcquisitionPrice, PurchaseDate, *CustNumber*, SalesPrice)

ARTIST (<u>ArtistName</u>, Nationality, Birthdate, DeceasedDate)

CUSTOMER-ARTIST-INT (<u>CustNumber</u>, <u>ArtistName</u>)

(c)

CUSTOMER (<u>CustomerID</u>, Name, AreaCode, LocalNumber, Street, City, State, Zip)

WORK (<u>WorkID</u>, ArtistName, Title, Copy, Description)

TRANSACTION (<u>TransactionID</u>, *WorkID*, DateAcquired, AcquisitionPrice, PurchaseDate, *CustomerID*, SalesPrice)

ARTIST (<u>ArtistID</u>, ArtistName, Nationality, Birthdate, DeceasedDate)

CUSTOMER-ARTIST-INT (*<u>CustomerID</u>*, *<u>ArtistID</u>*)

(d)

➤ FIGURE 10-3

(Continued)

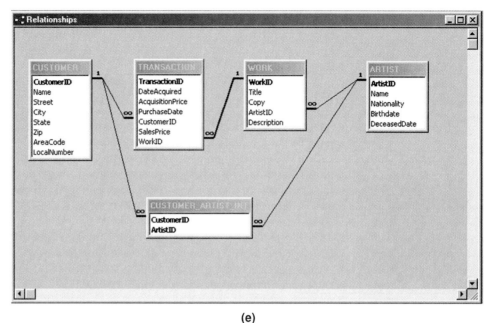

(e)

purchases and trade-ins), Transaction is multi-value. WORK is a hybrid object because it contains the object attribute CUSTOMER in the multi-value Transaction group.

View Ridge wants to be able to track its customers' interests. In particular, it wants to know the artists in which a particular customer is interested and the customers who have an interest in a particular artist. These requirements are supported by placing the multi-value attribute ARTIST in CUSTOMER and the multi-value attribute CUSTOMER in ARTIST. An E-R diagram appears in Figure 10-3(b).

The relational representation of the View Ridge objects is shown in Figure 10-3(c). Since the CUSTOMER object does not have a unique identifier, one must be created to use as a key. Here we have added an identifying number, CustNumber. The maximum cardinality of the Phone and Address groups is 1, so the attributes in those groups can be placed in the CUSTOMER table. These groups, in fact, do not appear in the table as groups; instead, the group information is used later to construct forms.

The key of WORK consists of the key of ARTIST plus Title and Copy. The only nonkey attribute of WORK is Description. Since the Transaction attribute is multi-value, a table must be created for it. Its key is the key of the object in which it is contained plus the key of the group, which is DateAcquired. Note that CustNumber is carried as a foreign key in TRANSACTION.

The ARTIST object is represented by a single table, and ArtistName can be used as the table key, because artists' names are modeled as being unique. The intersection table CUSTOMER-ARTIST-INT must be created to carry the M:N relationship between CUSTOMER and ARTIST.

The design in Figure 10-3(c) could be improved by replacing the data keys with surrogate keys. Recall that such keys are supplied by the DBMS or the application program as hidden identifiers that are maintained, behind the scenes, for the user. Such a design is shown in Figure 10-3(d), in which the names of the surrogate keys are constructed by appending the letters ID to the name of the table.

The design in Figure 10-3(d) is better because less data are duplicated. The columns ArtistName, Title, and Copy need not be copied into the Transaction table. Because there may be many transactions for a given work, this savings may be appreciable. The cost is that if the DBMS does not support such keys, application programs must be developed to create and maintain the surrogate key values.

➤ CREATING, READING, UPDATING, AND DELETING VIEW INSTANCES

A **view** is a structured list of data items from the entities or semantic objects defined in the data model. A view instance is a view that is populated with data for one entity or semantic object. Figure 10-4(a) shows a sample view for the gallery database in Figure 10-3. This view shows data about a customer, about that customer's transactions, and about that customer's artist interests. In this view, there are potentially many TRANSACTIONs for each CUSTOMER, and each TRANSACTION has one WORK. Also, there can be many ARTIST Names for each CUSTOMER (the artists in which the customer is interested).

Notice that ARTIST.Name occurs twice in this view. The first time it is the name of an artist of a work that the CUSTOMER has purchased. The second time it is the name of an artist in which the CUSTOMER is interested. For the example in Figure 10-4(b) a customer has purchased one painting, by Juan Miro, but is interested in paintings not just by Miro, but also by Mark Tobey and Dennis Frings. In this case, Juan Miro occurs once as a value of WORK.ARTIST.Name and again as one of the values of ARTIST.Name.

Again, a view is a structured list of attributes. Because it is structured, attributes can occur more than once in a view. Also notice that a view is a list of data values only. It can be formatted or materialized in many different ways—as a form, as a report, or in some other type of materialization.

➤ FIGURE 10-4

Customer View: (a) Structured List of Attributes, (b) Sample Data

CUSTOMER.Name
CUSTOMER.AreaCode
CUSTOMER.LocalNumber
　　TRANSACTION.PurchaseDate
　　TRANSACTION.SalesPrice . . .
　　WORK.ARTIST.Name
　　WORK.Title
　　WORK.Copy
　　ARTIST.Name . . .

a. Structured List of Attributes

Jackson, Elizabeth		
206		
989-4344		
	12/10/1999	
	$4,300	
		Juan Miro
		Poster
		14/85
	Juan Miro	
	Mark Tobey	
	Dennis Frings	

b. Sample Data

Now consider the CRUD actions that can be performed on a view. We begin with Read.

READING VIEWS INSTANCES

To read an existing view, the application must execute one or more SQL statements to obtain data values and then place the resulting values into the view structure. The Customer View in Figure 10-4 contains data on two paths: one through the TRANSACTION table and another through the CUSTOMER_ARTIST_INT table. The structure of SQL statements is such that only one path through the schema can be followed with a single SQL statement. Thus, this view will require a separate SQL statement for each path. For the first path, the following SQL will obtain the necessary data for the customer named "Jackson, Mary":

```
SELECT    CUSTOMER.CustomerID, CUSTOMER.Name,
          CUSTOMER.AreaCode, CUSTOMER.LocalNumber,
          ARTIST.Name, WORK.Title, WORK.Copy,
          TRANSACTION.PurchaseDate, TRANSACTION.SalesPrice
FROM      CUSTOMER, TRANSACTION, WORK, ARTIST
WHERE     CUSTOMER.CustomerID = TRANSACTION.CustomerID
   AND    WORK.WorkID = TRANSACTION.WorkID
   AND    ARTIST.ArtistID = WORK.ArtistID
   AND    CUSTOMER.Name = "Jackson, Mary"
```

Review this SQL statement while looking at the relationship diagram in Figure 10-3(e). The three joins are necessary to obtain data across the three relationships at the top of the diagram.

In the context of application development, the result of a SQL statement is sometimes termed a **recordset**. To Microsoft, this term means a relation with an object programming wrapper. A recordset has both methods and properties. *Open* is an example recordset method, *CursorType* is an example recordset property. You will learn more about this in Chapter 13.

To obtain the customer's artist interests, a second SQL statement is required to follow the path through CUSTOMER_ARTIST_INT. The SQL statement for this path is:

```
SELECT    CUSTOMER.CustomerID, ARTIST.Name
FROM      CUSTOMER, CUSTOMER_ARTIST_INT, ARTIST
WHERE     CUSTOMER.CustomerID = CUSTOMER_ARTIST_INT.CustomerID
   AND    CUSTOMER_ARTIST_INT.ArtistID = ARTIST.ArtistID
   AND    CUSTOMER.Name = "Jackson, Mary"
```

Because CUSTOMER.Name is not unique, it is possible that the two recordsets from these statements will retrieve data about more than one customer. Hence the application will need to have logic to examine the CustomerID values in the recordsets and to associate the correct rows together.

After executing these two statements, the application has all of the data necessary to construct one or more instances of the view in Figure 10-3. How that is done depends on the language in use. In COBOL, data would be placed in structures defined in the Data Division. In Visual Basic, the data could be placed in a data structure or a series of arrays. In C++ the data would be placed into a data structure. We are not concerned with those issues here. Rather, you should gain a sense of how the application must execute one or more SQL statements to fill the view data structure.

CREATING VIEW INSTANCES

To create a new view instance, the application must first obtain the new data values and relationships. This is most likely done via a data entry form, but applications also receive data from other programs and in other ways. In any case, once the application has data values, it then executes SQL statements to store the data in the database.

Consider the New Customer view in Figure 10-5. This view is used when a new customer purchases a painting. It contains data about the customer, about the purchase transaction, and about multiple customer interests. This view differs from that in Figure 10-4 because it has more customer data and it also only allows a single transaction. There can, however, be multiple ARTIST.Name values that record the new customer's interests.

Assume that data values for this view are located in a program structure called NewCust; further suppose that we can access the values in the structure by appending the characters NewCust to the names in the structure. Thus NewCust.CUSTOMER.Name accesses the Name of the CUSTOMER in the NewCust structure.

To create this view in the database, we must store the new customer data in CUSTOMER, store the new transaction data in TRANSACTION, and create a row in the intersection table CUSTOMER_ARTIST_INT for each of the artists in whom the customer is interested.

The following SQL statement will store the new customer data:

```
INSERT    INTO CUSTOMER
                (CUSTOMER.Name,
                CUSTOMER.AreaCode,
                CUSTOMER.LocalNumber,
                CUSTOMER.Address,
                CUSTOMER.City,
                CUSTOMER.State,
                CUSTOMER.Zip)
VALUES    (NewCust.CUSTOMER.Name,
                NewCust.CUSTOMER.AreaCode,
                NewCust.CUSTOMER.LocalNumber,
                NewCust.CUSTOMER.Address,
                NewCust.CUSTOMER.City,
                NewCust.CUSTOMER.State,
                NewCust.CUSTOMER.Zip)
```

Assume that when the new row is created, the DBMS assigns the value of the surrogate key CUSTOMER.CustomerID. We will need the value of this key to finish the creation of the new view instance, so the application will need to obtain it. One way to do so is to execute the following SQL SELECT:

```
SELECT    CUSTOMER.CustomerID, CUSTOMER.AreaCode,
                CUSTOMER.LocalNumber
FROM      CUSTOMER
WHERE     CUSTOMER.Name = NewCust.CUSTOMER.Name
```

Because CUSTOMER.Name is not unique, more than one row can appear in the recordset. In this case, the correct one would be identified by examining the

➤ FIGURE 10-5

New Customer View

CUSTOMER.Name
CUSTOMER.AreaCode
CUSTOMER.LocalNumber
CUSTOMER.Address
CUSTOMER.City
CUSTOMER.State
CUSTOMER.Zip
  TRANSACTION.DateAcquired
  TRANSACTION.AcquisitionPrice
  TRANSACTION.PurchaseDate
  TRANSACTION.SalesPrice
    WORK.ARTIST.Name
    WORK.Title
    WORK.Copy
  ARTIST.Name . . .

phone data. Assume that this has been done if necessary and the correct value is placed in the program structure as NewCust.CUSTOMER.CustomerID.

An INSERT statement will also be used to store the new TRANSACTION record. However, in this case values for the foreign keys TRANSACTION.WorkID and TRANSACTION.CustomerID will have to be supplied. We already have shown how to obtain the value of CustomerID, so all that remains is to obtain the value of WorkID. The following SQL will do that:

```
SELECT   WORK.WorkID
FROM     WORK, ARTIST
WHERE    WORK.ArtistID = ARTIST.ArtistID
  AND    ARTIST.Name = NewCust.WORK.ARTIST.Name
  AND    WORK.Title = NewCust.WORK.Title
  AND    WORK.Copy = NewCust.WORK.Copy
```

Assume that the returned surrogate key value is stored as NewCust.WORK.WorkID.

The following SQL can be executed to add the new TRANSACTION row:

```
INSERT   INTO TRANSACTION
             (TRANSACTION.WorkID,
             TRANSACTION.DateAcquired,
             TRANSACTION.AcquisitionPrice,
             TRANSACTION.PurchaseDate,
             TRANSACTION.CustomerID,
             TRANSACTION.SalesPrice)
         VALUES
             (NewCust.WORK.WorkID,
             NewCust.TRANSACTION.DateAcquired,
             NewCust.TRANSACTION.AcquisitionPrice,
             NewCust.TRANSACTION.PurchaseDate,
             NewCust.CUSTOMER.CustomerID,
             NewCust.TRANSACTION.SalesPrice)
```

Now all that remains is to create rows for the intersection table CUSTOMER_ARTIST_INT. To do that, we need to obtain the ArtistID for each artist in whom the customer is interested, and then create a new row in the intersection table. The following pseudocode illustrates the logic:

For each NewCust.ARTIST.Name

```
            SELECT    ARTIST.ArtistID
            FROM      ARTIST
            WHERE     ARTIST.Name = NewCust.ARTIST.Name

            INSERT    INTO        CUSTOMER_ARTIST_INT
                      (CustomerID, ArtistID)
                      VALUES      (NewCust.CUSTOMER.CustomerID,
                      ARTIST.ArtistID)
```

Next NewCust.ARTIST.Name

At this point, the New Customer view has been stored in the database. Of course, a complete application would include logic to catch errors returned from the DBMS and process them.

UPDATING VIEW INSTANCES

The third fundamental action to be performed on a view is update. When updating a view, three types of change are possible. One is a simple value change such as a customer changing his or her phone number. Another is a change to a relationship. An example is when a customer no longer maintains an interest in a particular artist. A third type of update requires the addition of one or more new rows; that would occur in our example when a customer makes a new purchase.

The first type of update can be accomplished with SQL UPDATE statements. For example, assume that a program has a structure named UpdateCust and that this structure has the CustomerID, AreaCode, and LocalNumber. The following SQL will update the new values:

```
UPDATE    CUSTOMER
SET       CUSTOMER.AreaCode = UpdateCust.AreaCode
          CUSTOMER.LocalNumber = UpdateCust.LocalNumber
WHERE     CUSTOMER.CustomerID = UpdateCust.CustomerID
```

Changes to relationships are also straightforward. If the relationship is one-to-many, then the foreign key value just needs to be updated to the new value. For example, assume the relationship from DEPT to EMPLOYEE is 1:N. Then Dept# (or other key) will be stored as a foreign key in EMPLOYEE. To move an EMPLOYEE to a new DEPT, the application need only change the value of Dept# to the new value.

If the relationship is many to many, then the foreign key in the intersection table needs to be modified. For example, at the gallery, if a customer changes his or her interest from Mark Tobey to an interest in Dennis Frings, then the intersection row that represents the connection to Mark Tobey needs to be changed to point to Dennis Frings.

Assume UpdateCust.CustomerID has the ID of the customer, UpdateCust.OldArtistID has the ID of the Mark Tobey row in ARTIST, and UpdateCust.NewArtistID has the ID of the Dennis Frings row in ARTIST. The following SQL will make the necessary change:

```
UPDATE    CUSTOMER_ARTIST_INT
SET       CUSTOMER_ARTIST_INT.ArtistID = UpdateCust.NewArtistID
WHERE     CUSTOMER_ARTIST_INT.CustomerID = UpdateCust.CustomerID
  AND     CUSTOMER_ARTIST_INT.ArtistID = UpdateCust.OldArtistID
```

In a many-to-many relationship, it is also possible to delete a connection without replacing it and to create a new connection without deleting an old one. To delete a connection, we would just delete the appropriate row in the intersection table. To create one, we would add a new row in the intersection table.

The third type of update requires the addition of a new row in one or more tables. If, for example, an existing customer makes a new purchase, then a new row in the TRANSACTION table will need to be created. This can be done in the same way that a new TRANSACTION row was added when creating a new view instance.

DELETING VIEW INSTANCES

Deleting view instances involves removing rows from the tables that make up the view. The trick is to know how much to delete. For example, suppose that the gallery wants to delete data for a Customer whose name is "Jones, Mary." Clearly, the "Jones, Mary" row in CUSTOMER needs to be deleted. Also, all of the intersection rows in CUSTOMER_ARTIST_INT that pertain to her need to be deleted as well. But what about rows in the TRANSACTION table? This table contains CustomerID and if her row is deleted, all rows in TRANSACTION that have her value of CustomerID will have invalid data.

The answers to questions like this are determined from the data model. In the case of the E-R model, all weak entities are deleted if the entity upon which they depend is also deleted. Otherwise, no additional table rows are deleted. In the case of the semantic object model, all data within an object is deleted (there may be many tables in an object if it has multi-value attributes), but no data in a different object is deleted. In addition to these rules, no deletion can be allowed if it will cause a violation of relationship cardinalities. We will touch on that topic here and consider it in more depth later in this chapter.

Consider the model in Figure 10-3. When a customer is deleted, the row in CUSTOMER will be deleted along with all rows in CUSTOMER_ARTIST_INT that pertain to that customer. TRANSACTION data will not be deleted because it resides in a different object—namely, WORK. Note, however, that the minimum cardinality of CUSTOMER in TRANSACTION is 1. Hence, if a given CUSTOMER is bound to a TRANSACTION, then that CUSTOMER is required and its deletion cannot be allowed.

We can also conclude from Figure 10-3, that if a WORK view is deleted, then the WORK row and all TRANSACTION rows relating to that row will be deleted.

Finally, if an ARTIST view is deleted, then only ARTIST and CUSTOMER_ARTIST_INT rows will be deleted. Further, if there are any WORK objects that are bound to that ARTIST, then the deletion cannot be allowed.

Some DBMS products support deletion of dependent rows, usually under the term **cascading deletions**. Figure 10-6 shows the relationship dialog box for Access 2000. Notice that the box Cascade Delete Related Records has been checked. This means that when a WORK row is deleted, Access will automatically delete any connected TRANSACTION rows as well.

As stated, relationship cardinality plays an important role in determining whether or not rows in views can be deleted. We will turn to this subject later in this chapter under the topic of enforcing constraints.

This section surveyed the actions that need to be taken when creating, reading, updating, and deleting view instances. Some of the actions described here can be done automatically by DBMS products. For example, Access 2000 has wizards that will generate a form containing Customer and a single path—either to Transactions or to Artist interests. Users of this form can create, read, update, and delete instances of a Customer and data on one of the paths. The Access 2000 wizards will not generate a form that will support both paths in the Customer view in Figure 10-3, however. To do that, a developer will need to write program code.

► FIGURE 10-6

Specifying Cascading Deletions

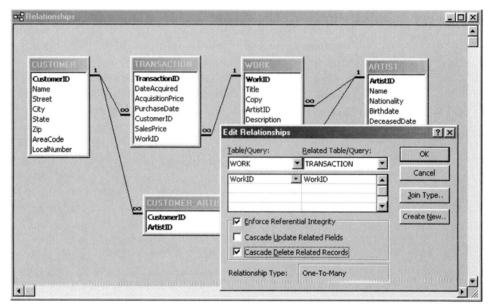

► FORM DESIGN

As shown in Figure 10-1, the second major function of a database application is to generate materializations of views. In this chapter we will consider form and report materializations. In the next chapter we will consider interprocess materializations using XML, and in Chapter 14 we will consider OLAP cube materializations.

A **form** is a screen display used for data entry and edit. Read-only forms can also be used to report data, but in most cases, when developers speak of forms, they mean those used for data entry and edit.

Some forms are easy to use and result in few data entry errors. Others seem awkward and contrived and are difficult to use without creating errors. In this section, we discuss and illustrate several principles of good form design.

THE FORM STRUCTURE SHOULD REFLECT THE VIEW STRUCTURE

First, to seem natural and be easy to use, *the structure of a form must reflect the structure of the view that it materializes.* Look at the form in Figure 10-7, which is a materialization of the Customer view in Figure 10-4(a).

The structure of this form reflects the structure of the Customer view. One section of the form has the basic customer data such as Name, Phone, and Address. The second section shows the customer's Artist interests. Finally, the third section lists the customer's purchase transactions. Users find this form easy to use because the attributes are grouped in a way that reflects their understanding of the structure of the customer data.

In general, when designing a form, all of the data from a single relation should be placed in one contiguous section of the form. Assuming that the database is in DK/NF, each relation should pertain to a specific theme, and the user should expect to have in one location all of the data for that theme. Thus, there are customer, artist interest, and transaction sections on the form.

There is one exception to this rule: Attributes in the base relation of the view (here, the relation CUSTOMER) are sometimes not placed contiguously. Suppose,

FIGURE 10-7

Form Materialization of Customer View in Figure 10-4a

for example, that CUSTOMER had a simple attribute named TotalPurchases. If we followed this rule, we would place TotalPurchases in the first section of the form. But it would be more sensible to the users to place that attribute at the end of the form, after all of the purchases have been listed.

The form in Figure 10-7 is not the only acceptable form of this view. Transactions could be placed before Artist Interests, for example. The base CUSTOMER data could be rearranged to be more horizontal in appearance. CustomerName, AreaCode, and LocalNumber could be placed in one column, and Street, City, State, and Zip could be placed in another. All of these alternatives enable the structure of the form to reflect the structure of the underlying objects.

THE SEMANTICS OF THE DATA SHOULD BE GRAPHICALLY EVIDENT

Another characteristic of a well-designed form is that the semantics of the data are graphically evident. Consider the base customer data section of the CUSTOMER form in Figure 10-7. Observe there are rectangles around AreaCode and LocalNumber and around Street, City, State, and Zip.

To understand why this is done, refer again to Figure 10-3(a). The CUSTOMER semantic object has a group attribute named Phone and another group attribute named Address. Since both of these attributes have a maximum cardinality of 1, they are—from the standpoint of the relational design—not really required. In fact, they do not appear in the relations in Figure 10-3(c) or (d). The only purpose of these group attributes is to semantically associate AreaCode with LocalNumber and Street and City, State, and Zip with one another.

The purpose of the rectangles in the Customer Purchase Form is to make these associations graphically clear. Most users are comforted by this arrangement. Knowing that phone number consists of AreaCode and LocalNumber, they find the graphically close association of those two to be very sensible.

THE FORM STRUCTURE SHOULD ENCOURAGE APPROPRIATE ACTION

The structure of forms should make it easy to perform appropriate actions and difficult to perform inappropriate or erroneous actions. For example, the field for entering State in the form in Figure 10-7 is small. Clearly, the user is supposed to enter only a two-digit state abbreviation. But a better design would allow only two digits to be entered, and the best design would present the states in a drop-down list and allow the user to choose from only that list.

In Figure 10-7, some fields are white and some are gray. The forms in this application have been designed so that users can enter data only in the white spaces; the gray data items cannot be changed in the form. Thus, the user cannot type into the Title or Copy fields in the Transaction section. Instead, to select or change a work, the user clicks on the combo box under Artist. When the user clicks on the arrow, a drop-down list of works is displayed, as shown in Figure 10-8. If the user wants to update work or artist data, or add or delete work or artist data, he or she must use a different form.

The reason for this design is that when users are entering new transactions for customers, they should only be adding transaction data, namely, the PurchaseDate and SalesPrice. Allowing them to change ARTIST or WORK data would open the door for accidental and erroneous changes, and such changes need not be made in order to sell a work.

A similar design is used for Artist Interests. Users can only pick from a list. Here, the case is not as strong, however. Salespeople might want to be able to record that a customer has an interest in an artist even if that artist is not in the gallery's database. If so, the form would be changed to allow users to add to the list. In justification of the design in Figure 10-7, the gallery owner may only want to record interests in artists that the gallery has or will represent. He or she may want control over what names can appear.

Use of Drop-Down List Box

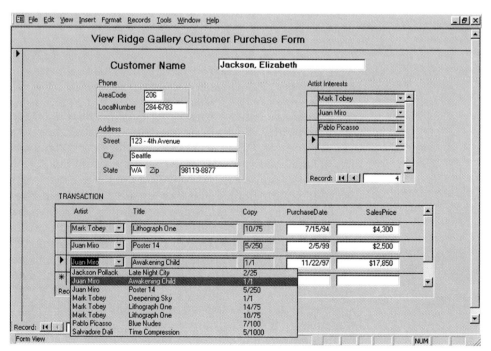

Forms in a GUI Environment

A number of form features peculiar to GUI systems can dramatically facilitate the use of database applications.

DROP-DOWN LIST BOXES   A **drop-down list box** is a GUI control that presents a list of items from which the user can choose. A property of the control determines whether the list is fixed or whether users can add to it. Figure 10-9 shows a different version of the Customer Purchase Form in which users can add Artist Names that are not present in the list. Behind the scenes, the application is storing a new ARTIST row in the database. For this to work, of course, only ArtistName can be a required attribute. If there were other required fields, the DBMS would reject the insert of the new row. (Note: For this to work in Access 2000, the primary key of ARTIST needs to be set to ArtistName. This means the foreign keys in both CUSTOMER_ARTIST_INT and WORK must also be changed.)

List boxes have a number of advantages over data entry boxes. First, people find it easier to *recognize* than to *recollect*. For example, in the Form in Figure 10-8, it is easier to choose an artist's name from the list than it is to remember all of the artists in the database. It is also easier to recognize a name than it is to spell it correctly. Finally, if the list box is set up to display only those values present in the database, the user cannot enter keystroke mistakes. Unfortunately, Juan Miro (one space between the *n* and the *M*) and Juan Miro (two spaces between the *n* and the *M*) will be considered different artists by the DBMS. Fixed-list drop-down list boxes prevent these mistakes.

OPTION BUTTONS AND GROUPS   An **option button**, or **radio button**, is a display device that enables users to select one alternative condition or state from a list of possibilities. For example, suppose the gallery decides that it needs to track the tax status of its customers. Assume that tax status has two possibilities, Taxable and Nontaxable, and that these possibilities are mutually exclusive. An option group like the one shown in Figure 10-10 could be used to gather this

> FIGURE 10-9

List Box That Allows New Values

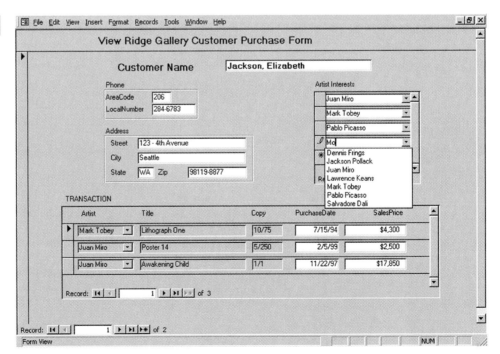

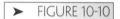

FIGURE 10-10

*Use of Group and
Option Buttons*

data. Because of the way that the option group works, if the user selects Taxable, then Nontaxable is automatically de-selected. If the user selects Nontaxable, then Taxable is automatically de-selected.

Behind the form, the application program must store data in a table column that represents the radio button selected. For this example, the column is named TaxStatus. One of two possible ways for storing the option button data is used. One is to store an integer number from 1 to the number of buttons. In this example, one of the values 1 or 2 would be stored. The second option is to store a text value that describes the option chosen. The possibilities are Yes or No.

FIGURE 10-11

Use of Check Boxes

CHECK BOXES   **Check boxes** are similar to option buttons except that the alternatives in a group of check boxes are not mutually exclusive—more than one alternative may be chosen. Suppose, for example, that the gallery wants to record the type or types of art in which its customers are interested. The possible types are Lithographs, Oils, Pastels, and Photographs, shown in a series of check boxes in the version of the CUSTOMER form in Figure 10-11. The user selects or checks the appropriate boxes.

There are a number of ways of representing check boxes in relations. One common and simple way is to define a Boolean-valued column for each item in the check box group. The value of each of such columns is binary; that is, it can be 1 or 0, representing yes or no. There are other possibilities, such as encoding bits in a byte, although they are not important to our discussion.

CURSOR MOVEMENT AND PERVASIVE KEYS

Another consideration in forms design is the action of the cursor. The cursor should move through the form easily and naturally. This usually means that the cursor follows the end user's processing pattern as he or she reads the source data entry documents. If forms are used to enter data over the telephone, the cursor should control the flow of the conversation. In this case, its movement should progress in a manner that the customer finds natural and appropriate.

Cursor movement is especially important during and after an exception condition. Suppose that in using the form in Figure 10-7, an error is made—perhaps an invalid state code is entered. The form should be processed so that the cursor moves to a logical location. For example, the application might display a list box of available state values and place the cursor on a logical position in the list—perhaps on the first state that starts with the first letter the user entered. When the state is selected, the cursor should move back to Zip, the next appropriate space on the form.

The actions of special-purpose keys such as ESC and function keys should be *consistent* and *pervasive*. If ESC is used to exit forms, use it consistently for this purpose and none other (except for actions that are logically equivalent to exiting from forms). The actions of the keys should be consistent throughout the application. That is, if ESC is used to exit from one form, it should be used to exit from all forms. If Cntrl-D is used to delete data in one form, it should be used to delete data in all forms. Otherwise, habits formed in one portion of the application must be disregarded or relearned in other portions of the application. This is wasteful, frustrating, and aggravating, and it causes errors. Although these comments may seem obvious, attention to such details is what makes a form easy and convenient to use.

➤ REPORT DESIGN

The subject of report design, even more so than form design, has been discussed extensively in texts on application development. We will not duplicate or even attempt to summarize those discussions here but, rather, look at several concepts directly related to the notion of a report as a materialization of a database view.

REPORT STRUCTURE

The principles of effective report design are similar to those for form design. Just as with forms, *the structure of a report should reflect the structure of the underlying view*. This means that data from one table should generally be located in one contiguous group on the report. As with forms, one exception to this rule is that the base relation of the view (for example, the CUSTOMER relation for the Customer view) may be separated on the report. Attribute groups, like Phone, should also be located together and distinguished in some way.

Figure 10-12 shows a sample report for the View Ridge Gallery that lists the data for each work of art and the transactions for each work of art, computes the gross margin by work and artist, as well as a grand total.

The structure of the report in Figure 10-12 reflects the structure of the WORK object. The section for each work begins with the name of the work, which includes artist, title, and copy. Next is a section of repeating lines that shows the transactions for the work. Within each section, the name of the customer has been found from the CUSTOMER table.

Be aware that with most report writers, it is difficult to construct a report that follows more than one multi-value path through the database schema. The report in Figure 10-12 is a materialization of an ARTIST view that follows the path from ARTIST to WORK to TRANSACTION. The relationship diagram in Figure 10-4(e) shows another path—one through the CUSTOMER-ARTIST_INT table to the CUSTOMERs who are interested in a given artist. With most report writers, it will be difficult to construct a report that shows both of these paths.

➤   FIGURE 10-12

Sales Listing Report

Sales Listing
15-Nov-99

ArtistName	Title		Copy		
Dennis Frings	**South Toward Emerald Sea**		**106/195**		
DateAcquired	**AcquisitionPrice**	**DateSold**	**Sold To**	**SalesPrice**	**GrossMargin**
4/17/1986	$750.00	5/3/1986	Heller, Max	$1,000.00	$250.00
3/15/1998	$1,200.00	5/11/1998	Jackson, Elizabeth	$1,800.00	$600.00
	Total margin for South Toward Emerald Seas, Copy 106/195				**$850.00**
	Total margin for Dennis Frings				**$850.00**
Mark Tobey	**Patterns III**		**27/95**		
DateAcquired	**AcquisitionPrice**	**DateSold**	**Sold To**	**SalesPrice**	**GrossMargin**
7/3/1971	$7,500.00	9/11/1971	Cooper, Tom	$10,000.00	$2,500.00
1/4/1986	$11,500.00	3/18/1986	Jackson, Elizabeth	$15,000.00	$3,500.00
9/11/1999	$17,000.00	10/17/1999	Cooper, Tom	$21,000.00	$4,000.00
	Total margin for Patterns III, Copy 27/95				**$10,000.00**
Mark Tobey	**Rhythm**		**2/75**		
DateAcquired	**AcquisitionPrice**	**DateSold**	**Sold To**	**SalesPrice**	**GrossMargin**
4/8/1998	$17,000.00	7/14/1998	Heller, Max	$27,000.00	$10,000.00
	Total margin for Rhythm, Copy 2/75				**$10,000.00**
	Total margin for Mark Tobey				**$20,000.00**
	Grand Total:				**$20,850.00**

Reports often have calculated data attributes that are not part of the underlying view and are not stored in the database. The report in Figure 10-12 has calculations for GrossMargin, Total Gross Margin by Work, Total Gross Margin by Artist, and a Grand Total of Gross Margin. All of these values are computed on the fly as the report is produced.

While these computed values could be stored in the database, doing so is seldom a good idea because the values used to compute them can change. If for example, a user altered the SalesPrice for a particular transaction and did not recompute GrossMargin and the totals based on it, the stored values would be in error. However, making all of the necessary computations while processing update transactions will probably result in unacceptably slow processing. Hence, totals like this are usually best computed on the fly. Formulae for computing such totals are thus considered part of the materialization of the report and not part of the underlying view.

IMPLIED OBJECTS

Consider the request "Print all ARTISTs Sorted by Total Margin." At first glance, this appears to be a request to print a report about the object ARTIST. The words *sorted by,* however, indicate that more than one ARTIST is to be considered. In fact, this request is not based on the object ARTIST but, rather, is based on the object SET OF ALL ARTISTs. The report in Figure 10-12 shows data for multiple ARTISTs and is, in fact, based on the object SET OF ALL ARTISTs, not on the object ARTIST.

The human mind is so quick to shift from the object *OBJECT-A* to the object *SET OF ALL OBJECTS-A* that we normally do not even know there has been a change. When developing database applications, however, it is important to notice this shift because the application needs to behave differently when it occurs. Consider three ways in which sorting can change the nature of the base object: (1) sorting by object identifier; (2) sorting by nonidentifier, nonobject columns; and (3) sorting by attributes contained in object attributes.

SORTED BY OBJECT IDENTIFIER   If the report is to be sorted by an attribute that is an identifier of object, the true object is the collection of those objects. Thus, an ARTIST report sorted by ArtistName is a report about the object SET OF ALL ARTISTS. For most DBMS report-writing products, a report about the object SET OF ALL X is no more difficult to produce than a report about object X. It is important to know, however, that there has been a shift in object type.

SORTED BY NONIDENTIFIER, NONOBJECT COLUMNS   When a user needs a report sorted by an attribute that is a nonidentifier of the object, the true object in the user's mind is most likely a totally different type of object. For example, the user wants to produce a report about ARTIST sorted by Nationality. Such a report is actually a materialization of a NATIONALITY object, not a materialization of the ARTIST object. Similarly, if the user asks for a report about CUSTOMER sorted by AreaCode, the report is actually based on an object called PHONE-REGION, or some similar object. Figure 10-13 shows an example PHONE-REGION object.

➤ FIGURE 10-13

PHONE-REGION Object

Objects such as NATIONALITY and PHONE-REGION are **implied objects;** that is, their existence can be inferred by the fact that the user asked for such a report. If it makes sense to the user to ask for something as a sort value, then that something must be an object in the user's mind, regardless of whether it is modeled in the database or not.

SORTED BY ATTRIBUTES CONTAINED IN OBJECT ATTRIBUTES The third way in which reports can be sorted is by attributes contained in object attributes. For example, the user might ask for a report about WORKs sorted by Birthdate of ARTIST. ARTIST is an object attribute of WORK, and Birthdate is an attribute contained in ARTIST. In this case, the user is actually asking for a report about an implied object (say, TIME or ARTISTIC PERIOD) that contains many ARTISTs, each of which includes many WORKs in the gallery.

Understanding this switch in objects may ease the task of developing the report. Proceeding as if WORK were the base object of the report will make the report logic contrived. If WORK is considered the base, the materializations of WORK objects that include ARTIST and Birthdate must be created for all WORK objects, stored on disk, and then sorted by Birthdate. On the other hand, if this report is about an implied object that contains ARTIST, which in turn contains WORK, then ARTIST objects can be created and sorted by Birthdate and WORK objects treated as multi-value rows in each ARTIST object.

➤ ENFORCING CONSTRAINTS

As listed in Figure 10-1, the third major function of a database application is to enforce constraints. In many cases, the DBMS is better able to enforce constraints than the application, and so this is not strictly an application program function. Our concern, here, however, is to describe types of constraints and how they can be enforced, regardless of whether application code or the DBMS enforces them.

First, the reason that the DBMS is often the better place to enforce constraints is that it is a central point through which all data changes must pass. Regardless of the source of a data change (form, another program, bulk data import) the DBMS will have a chance to examine and reject the change, if necessary. Further, certain rules (uniqueness is one) may require the examination of all the rows in a table; the DBMS is better able to perform such a function than an application. Additionally, if the DBMS enforces a rule, then that rule need be coded just once. If the applications enforce a rule, then it will need to be coded for each new application. This is wasteful and generates the possibility that application programs will enforce rules inconsistently.

Having said that, not all DBMS products have the features and functions necessary to enforce constraints. Sometimes, too, it is far more difficult to write and install constraint enforcement code in DBMS facilities than in application code. Further, in some architectures (Microsoft Transaction Server is one), processing is more efficient if constraint checking is removed from the data server. Also, there are some constraints that are application dependent. A user of a particular form, for example, may not be allowed to take certain actions or enter certain data. In that case, the application is better able to enforce the constraint.

Your goal should be to understand the types of constraints and the means by which they are enforced. When possible, enforce them at the DBMS; if not, enforce them in application. We will now consider four types of constraint: domain, uniqueness, relationship cardinality, and business rules.

DOMAIN CONSTRAINTS

Recall from Chapter 4 that a domain is the set of values that an attribute may have. Domain definitions have a semantic component (the Name of an Artist) and a physical component (Text 25, alphabetic). In general, it is not possible to enforce the semantic component by an automated process. We are not yet at the stage of development in the computer industry that automated processes can determine that 3M is the name of a company and not the name of an artist. Therefore, today we are primarily concerned with enforcing the physical part of a domain definition.

Domain constraints arise from the data model as described in Chapter 4. The specificity of domain constraints varies widely. In the View Ridge Gallery database, ARTIST.Name can be any set of 25 or less text characters. A domain such as that for Copy, however, is more specific. The format used by the gallery is nn/mm where nn is a particular copy number and mm is the total number of copies made. Thus 5/100 means the fifth copy out of a run of 100. Clearly, a value like 105/100 makes no sense. Therefore, validation code should be developed to ensure that this format is followed.

Figure 10-14 shows an example domain constraint in Access 2000. The constraint is that PurchaseDate must be less than or equal to the computer's clock date at the time the purchase is entered. Notice the line labeled Validation Rule. The expression <= Now( ) defines the rule. If the user attempts to enter data that violates this rule, a message box is generated using the text that is entered in the next line (Validation Rule). Figure 10-15 shows what happens when the user attempts to enter a date of 10/15/99 when the computer's date was less than 10/15/99. The submitted data is then rejected by Access.

Another type of constraint is whether or not values are required. Strictly speaking, the requirement that a value be provided is a table constraint rather than a domain constraint. A domain is a set of values; whether or not a value is required is a question that arises when the domain appears in a table.

➤ FIGURE 10-14

Creating a Domain Constraint with Access 2000

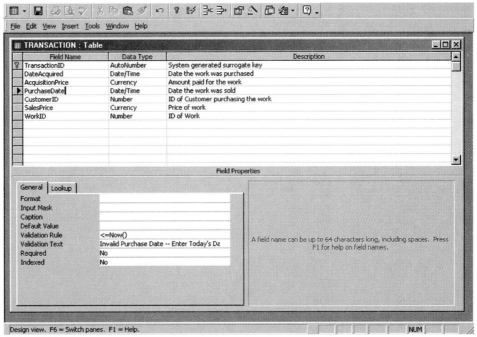

➤ FIGURE 10-15

Result of Violating Validation Rule

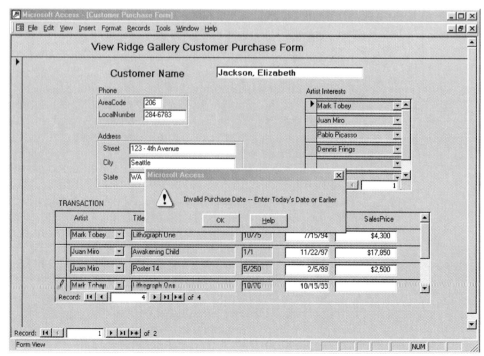

The data model should indicate if attribute values are required. In the semantic object model, if the minimum cardinality of an attribute is 1, then that attribute is required. To enforce this constraint with Access 2000, all that is needed is to set the Required property of a column to Yes. This was done for Name in the ARTIST table definition in Figure 10-16. Other means are used with other DBMS products as you will see.

Required value constraints are important because ambiguity arises when values are not provided. A value that has never been entered is called a **null value**.

➤ FIGURE 10-16

Defining Uniqueness for Name in ARTIST

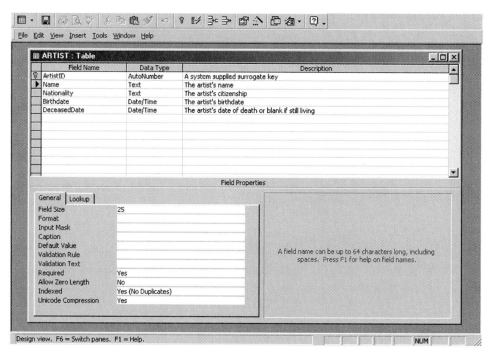

Such a value can mean that the value is unknown, that it is inappropriate, or something else. Consider DeceasedDate in ARTIST. A null value for this attribute could mean either that the date of death is unknown or that the artist is still living. If the artist is a company or co-op or other non-human entity, a null value of DeceasedDate would mean that a value is inappropriate.

To eliminate such ambiguity, several actions can be taken. One is to make the value required. Another is to eliminate value-inappropriate nulls by defining subtypes. In this case, the schema could be defined with LIVING_ARTIST and DEAD_ARTIST subtypes of ARTIST. LIVING_ARTIST would not have a DeceasedDate attribute.

For this example, the ambiguity is most likely not a problem and the cost in complexity of eliminating it is probably not worth it. Be aware, however, that ambiguity does occur whenever attributes are not required.

UNIQUENESS CONSTRAINTS

Uniqueness is a second type of constraint. As stated, constraints of this type are best enforced by the DBMS because it can create data structures to make uniqueness checking very fast. See Appendix A for a description of the way that indexes can be used for this purpose.

Figure 10-16 shows how Name in ARTIST can be defined as unique in Access 2000. Observe that Indexed has been set to Yes (No Duplicates). With this setting Access will ensure that no duplicate artist names are entered from any source.

RELATIONSHIP CARDINALITY CONSTRAINTS

Relationship cardinality constraints arise from the cardinality settings on object link attributes. For example, in Figure 10-3(a), the CUSTOMER link in WORK.Transaction has cardinality of 1.1; hence a Transaction must have a CUSTOMER link.

In general, such constraints arise from two sources: non-zero settings of minimum cardinality, or settings of maximum cardinality that are neither 1 nor N. Thus, cardinalities of 1.1, 1.N, 2.N will cause cardinality constraints to arise, as will cardinalities of 0.3, 1.4, and 2.4. With one exception, these constraints must be enforced by application code.

The exception is 1.1 cardinalities on the child side of 1:N relationships. In that case, the constraint can be enforced by making the foreign key mandatory. Thus, the 1.1 constraint on CUSTOMER in WORK.Transaction can be enforced by making CustomerID mandatory in the TRANSACTION table.

Other than this exception, the database developer must write code to enforce cardinality constraints. That code can be stored with the database to be invoked by the DBMS when relationship changes are made, or it can be placed in application programs, or it can be called during certain form events such as BeforeUpdate (discussed next).

1.1 AND 1.N CONSTRAINTS

To simplify the discussion, we will only consider 1.1 and 1.N constraints. The logic for the other constraints is a straightforward extension of that presented here.

Figure 10-17 depicts the relationship between MAJOR and STUDENT relations. As shown in Figure 10-17(a), a MAJOR must have at least one STUDENT, and a STUDENT must have exactly one MAJOR. When users update either of these relations, constraint enforcement code must be invoked. In Figure 10-17(b), for example, if a user attempted to delete the row for Student 400, the code

Example of a Mandatory-to-Mandatory Constraint: (a) Sample Mandatory-to-Mandatory Relationship and (b) Sample Data for It

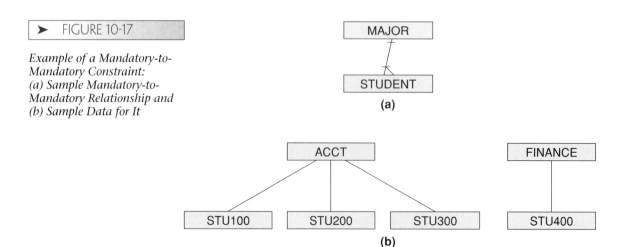

should deny this request. If the request were allowed, the row for FINANCE would not have a child row, and the mandatory constraint would be violated. Similarly, a new MAJOR, say BIOLOGY, cannot be added until there is a student who is majoring in that subject.

A row that exists inappropriately without a required parent or child is sometimes called a **fragment,** and child rows that exist without a mandatory parent are sometimes called **orphans.** One of the functions of an application program is to prevent the creation of fragments and orphans.

The means of preventing fragments depends on the type of constraint. Figure 10-18 shows examples of the four possible constraints in 1:N relationships: mandatory to mandatory (M–M), mandatory to optional (M–O), optional to mandatory (O–M), and optional to optional (O–O). These constraints are shown on one-to-many relationships, but the same four types also apply to other relationships.

Constraints can be violated whenever there are changes in the key attributes. For example, in Figure 10-17(b), changing the major of Student 300 from ACCT to FINANCE reassigns that student to the finance department. Although this results in a change of parent, it does not cause a constraint violation.

Such a violation will be committed, however, if the major of Student 400 is changed to ACCT. When this is done, FINANCE no longer has any majors, and so the M-M constraint between MAJOR and STUDENT is violated.

Figure 10-19 presents rules for preventing fragments for each of these types of constraints. Figure 10-19(a) concerns actions on the parent row, and Figure 10-

Examples of the Four Types of Relationship Constraints: (a) Mandatory-to-Mandatory (M–M) Constraint, (b) Mandatory-to-Optional (M–O) Constraint, (c) Optional-to-Mandatory (O–M) Constraint, and (d) Optional-to-Optional (O–O) Constraint

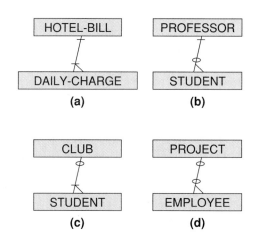

FIGURE 10-19

Rules for Preventing Fragments:
(a) Conditions for Allowing Changes in Parent Records and
(b) Conditions for Allowing Changes in Child Records

Proposed Action on Parent

Type of Rela-tionship		*Insert*	*Modify (key)*	*Delete*
	M-M	Create at least one child	Change matching keys of all children	Delete all children OR Reassign all children
	M-O	OK	Change matching keys of all children	Delete all children OR Reassign all children
	O-M	Insert new child OR Appropriate child exists	Change key of at least one child OR Appropriate child exists	OK
	O-O	OK	OK	OK

(a)

Proposed Action on Child

Type of Rela-tionship		*Insert*	*Modify (key)*	*Delete*
	M-M	Parent exists OR Create parent	Parent with new value exists (or create one) AND Sibling exists	Sibling exists
	M-O	Parent exists OR Create parent	Parent with new value exists OR Create parent	OK
	O-M	OK	Sibling exists	Sibling exists
	O-O	OK	OK	OK

(b)

19(b) concerns actions on the child rows. As these figures indicate, the possible actions are to insert new rows, modify key data, and delete rows. Figure 10-19 lists the rules for one-to-many relationships; the rules for one-to-one relationships are similar.

RESTRICTIONS ON UPDATES TO PARENT ROWS   The first row of Figure 10-19(a) concerns M–M constraints. A new parent row can be inserted only if at least one child row is being created at the same time, which can be done by inserting a new child row or by reassigning a child from a different parent (however, this latter action may itself cause a constraint violation).

A change in the key of a parent is permitted in an M–M relationship only if the values in the corresponding foreign key in the child rows also are changed in the new value. (It is possible to reassign all of the children to another parent and then create at least one new child for the parent, but this seldom is done.) Thus, changing the Invoice in HOTEL-BILL is allowed as long as the Invoice is changed in all the appropriate DAY-CHARGE rows as well. Note that if surrogate keys are used, this action will never occur.

Finally, a parent of an M–M relationship can be deleted as long as all of the children also are deleted or are reassigned.

In regard to M–O constraints, a new parent can be added without restriction, since parents need not have children. For the relationship in Figure 10-18(b), a new PROFESSOR row can be added without restriction. A change in the parent's key value, however, is permitted only if the corresponding values in the child rows are changed as well. If a PROFESSOR in the relationship in Figure 10-18(b) changes his or her key, the value of Adviser in all of that professor's advisees' rows also must be changed.

Finally, in a relationship with an M–O constraint, the parent row can be deleted only if all the children are deleted or reassigned. For the PROFESSOR-STUDENT relationship, all of the student rows would probably be reassigned.

For O–M constraints, a parent can be inserted only if at least one child is added at the same time or if an appropriate child already exists. For the O–M relationship between CLUB and STUDENT in Figure 10-18(c), for example, a new club can be added only if an appropriate STUDENT row can be created (by either adding a new student or changing the value of CLUB in an existing STUDENT). Alternatively, an appropriate student row may already exist.

Similarly, the key of the parent of an O–M relationship may be changed only if a child is created or if a suitable child row already exists. That is, the Ski Club can change its name to Scuba only if at least one skier is willing to join Scuba or if a student has already enrolled in Scuba. There are no restrictions on the deletion of a parent row in an O–M relationship.

The last type of relationship constraint, O–O, is shown in Figure 10-18(d). There are no restrictions on any type of update on rows in an O–O relationship. Both PROJECT and EMPLOYEE rows can be updated as necessary.

RESTRICTIONS ON UPDATING CHILD ROWS   The rules for preventing fragments when updating child rows are shown in Figure 10-19(b) and are similar to those in Figure 10-19(a). The one notable difference is that in several cases, child rows can be modified or deleted as long as sibling rows exist. For example, in an M–M constraint, a child row can be deleted as long as there are siblings in existence. (The last child never leaves home!) For the M–M constraint in Figure 10-18(a), a particular DAILY-CHARGE row can be deleted as long as at least one remains.

With the exception of the considerations regarding siblings, the rules for avoiding fragments when processing child rows are similar to those for parents. Make certain you understand each statement in Figure 10-19(b).

USING THE DBMS TO ENFORCE CARDINALITY CONSTRAINTS   Given the preceding discussion, it is useful to consider the constraints in Figure 10-19 in the context of the relationship definition facilities in Access 2000. Suppose a database has an EMPLOYEE object with multiple phone numbers. To show the relevance of the middle columns of Figure 10-19, suppose that the key of EMPLOYEE is not a surrogate but is EMPLOYEE.Name instead.

Figure 10-20 shows the relationship definition window for this example. The check in the Enforce Referential Integrity box indicates that Access will not allow a new row of EMPLOYEE_PhoneNumber to be created unless the value of EmployeeName is already present in a row in EMPLOYEE. This is the meaning of referential integrity as discussed in Chapter 5. The second check, in Cascade Update Related Fields, means that if the name of an employee is changed in the EMPLOYEE table, then that change will be propagated to all related rows in EMPLOYEE_ PhoneNumber. This enforces the rules in the middle columns of Figure 10-19. (Again, this would be unnecessary if surrogate keys were used instead.)

Relationship Properties in Access 2000

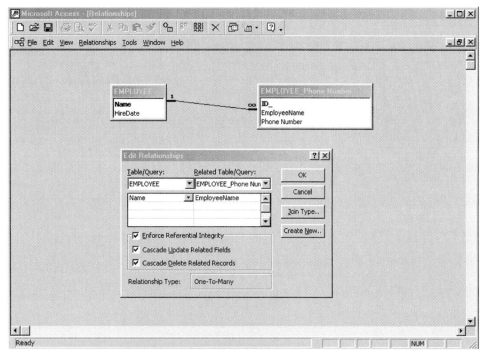

The last check, in Cascade Delete Related Records means that when an EMPLOYEE row is deleted, all of the connected EMPLOYEE_PhoneNumber rows will be deleted as well. This is similar to that discussed earlier in the section on deleting view instances.

This feature of Access addresses the rules in the second and third columns of Figure 10-19(a), and those in the first and second columns of Figure 10-19(b). It does not address the rules in the first column of Figure 10-19(a), nor those in the third column of Figure 10-19(b). Those rules will need to be coded in the application.

BUSINESS RULE CONSTRAINTS

Business rule constraints are particular to the logic and requirements of a given application. They arise from procedures and policies that exist in the organization that will use the database application. Examples of business rules in a sales application are:

➤ No commission check can exceed 50 percent of the total commission pool.

➤ No backorder will be generated if the total value of the ordered items is less than $200.

➤ Shipping costs are waived for preferred customers.

➤ Salespeople cannot create orders for themselves.

➤ To be a sales manager, an employee must first be a salesperson.

Because business rules are application dependent, there are no generic features of DBMS products for enforcing them. Rather, DBMS products provide means for inserting code before or after most important events. Figure 10-21 shows a list of the events that can be trapped on Access 2000 forms. In this figure, the developer is in the process of adding logic to the Before Insert event. The logic can take one of several forms: an event procedure in Access's expression language or in a Visual Basic (or other language program), or an Access macro. All of the data in the form and in the database is accessible by the event

> FIGURE 10-21

Events for Access 2000 Forms

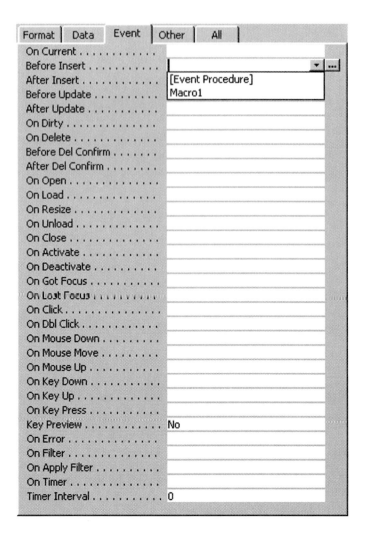

procedure or macro. Thus, any of the rules above could be enforced by trapping events.

With server DBMS products such as ORACLE or SQL Server, a similar means is used. Logic can be encoded in **triggers**, which are program segments that are invoked when events occur in the database. The events that can be trapped are similar to those shown in Figure 10-21.

> SECURITY AND CONTROL

The fourth major function of a database application listed in Figure 10-1 is to provide security and control mechanisms. The goal is to create applications in which only authorized users can perform appropriate activities at the proper time.

SECURITY

Most DBMS products provide user name and password level of security. Once a user signs in, access can be limited to certain forms, reports, tables, and even columns of tables. This is appropriate and useful as far as it goes. It does not help, however, in limiting the instances of data that users can view.

For example, in a human resources database application, every employee should be able only to see his or her own employee records. Certain human resource employees should be able to see some data about all employees, and senior human resource managers should be able to see all data about all employees.

Limiting access to certain forms and reports does not help. Every employee needs to see the Employee Form; the restriction needs to be that the employee can only see data in that form that pertains to him or her (with the exceptions noted). Sometimes you will hear the terms **horizontal security** and **vertical security**. To understand them, think about a table. Vertical security would limit access to certain columns, but all rows could be seen. Horizontal security would limit access to certain rows, but all columns could be seen.

Applications that limit users to certain forms, reports, tables, or columns provide vertical security. Those that limit users to certain data in forms, reports, tables, or columns provide horizontal security. User name and passwords can be readily used to provide vertical security. Horizontal security generally requires developers to write application code.

To provide horizontal security in the employee application, for example, application code would obtain the user's name from the DBMS security system and limit access to rows that contain that name or are linked to rows that contain that name via joins. One way to do this is to append the user's name as a WHERE clause in SQL statements.

Because every situation is different, we cannot say more. Just be aware that when DBMS products say they support security, most often that only means vertical security via user name and passwords.

CONTROL

Most database applications provide control via menus. Figure 10-22(a) shows a system of menus for a pre-GUI application and Figure 10-22(b) shows the same menus for a GUI application.

The menus in Figure 10-22 are static. More effective control can be provided by dynamically changing menu content as the user changes context. You see menus of that type in Access 2000 when the toolbar changes depending on whether you are in the table definition, form definition, or report definition tools. Database application developers can use a similar strategy to change menu choices depending on the form or report that a user is viewing, and even depending on the action that the user is taking in the form. Using Access 2000, a developer could change menu choices by trapping events like those shown in Figure 10-21 and dynamically restructuring the menu choices.

A different type of control concerns transactions. In Chapter 12, you will learn means of controlling multi-user processing so that one user's actions do not have inappropriate side consequences on a second user's actions. A key part multi-user control is to identify boundaries of work that must be completed as a unit, sometimes called **transaction boundaries**. For example, the series of SQL statements for creating a view shown at the start of this chapter need to be completed as a unit, as a single transaction.

We will not anticipate the discussion in that chapter except to say that it is the job of the application to specify transaction boundaries. It typically does so by executing a statement like BEGIN TRANSACTION at the start of a unit of work and END TRANSACTION when the work is completed.

Setting boundaries is easy if the user views are well designed. The application issues the BEGIN TRANSACTION at the start of the view and the END TRANSACTION at the end of the view. We will hold the rest of this discussion for Chapter 12.

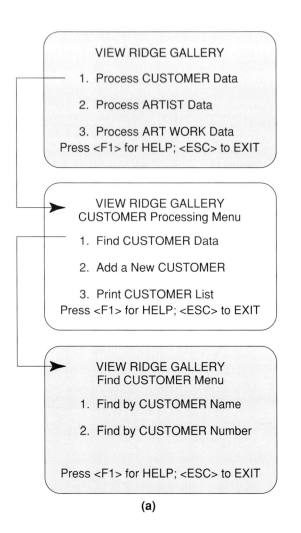

Hierarchy of Menus for View Ridge Gallery: (a) Not Using a Graphical User Interface (b) Using a Graphical User Interface

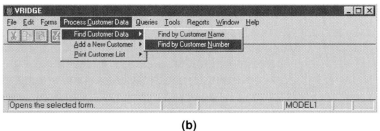

➤ APPLICATION LOGIC

The last function of a database application listed in Figure 10-1 is to execute application logic. This topic is generally discussed in systems development classes and texts, thus we will say little about it here.

The needs for application logic arise from the systems requirements. In an order-entry system, application logic concerns how to take inventory from stock, how to deal with insufficient stock in inventory, how to schedule a backorder, and the like. In a form-based database application like the one for the gallery, code to support this logic is attached to events like those in Figure 10-21.

For other database applications, where forms are materialized by the application instead of by the DBMS (common in mainframe applications), the application processes the data in a way similar to that for file processing. Logic is encoded in-line inside the application as it gets data from and puts data to the DBMS. Some application programs receive data from other programs; in that case, the application logic is contained in-line as well.

Thus, the means by which application logic is embedded in database applications depend both on the logic and the environment. Different means are used for desktop, client-server, mainframe, and Internet technology applications. You have seen how to trap events for desktop applications. We will consider the other means in subsequent chapters.

➤ SUMMARY

The five major functions of a database application are (1) to create, read, update, and delete (CRUD) views, (2) to materialize or format views, (3) to enforce constraints, (4) to provide security and control mechanisms, and (5) to execute business logic.

A view is a structured list of data items from the entities or semantic objects in the data model. A view instance is a view populated with data. Because views are structured, a given data item may appear more than once in a view. To read a view, one or more SQL statements are issued to obtain data values. More than one SQL statement will be required if the view includes two or more relationship paths through the schema. A recordset is a relation with an object programming wrapper.

Creating a view requires storing one or more new rows in tables and possibly creating or changing foreign key values so as to establish relationships. Three types of update are possible: changing existing data, changing relationships, and creating new rows for multi-value attributes. Deleting a view involves removing one or more rows and adjusting foreign keys. The issue when deleting is knowing how much to delete. Weak entities should be deleted if the entity upon which they depend is deleted. Multi-value attributes inside a semantic object should also be deleted. With some DBMS products, relationships can be marked for cascading deletions so that the DBMS will remove appropriate dependent rows.

A form is a screen display used for data entry and edit. Principles of form design are that the form structure should reflect the view structure, the semantics of the data should be graphically evident, and the form structure should encourage appropriate action. Drop-down list boxes, option buttons, and check boxes can be used to increase the usability of forms.

Reports should also be designed so that their structure reflects the structure of the view they materialize. Report sorting often implies the existence of other objects. With most report writers it is difficult to construct reports that follow more than one multi-value path through the schema. Reports often have calculated data attributes; usually it is best not to store those attributes in the database.

Constraints can be enforced by either the DBMS or by application program. In most cases, it is better for the DBMS to enforce them when possible, primarily because the DBMS is a central point through which all data changes must pass. In some cases, the DBMS does not have the features to enforce constraints, however, and they must be enforced by the application. Domain constraints enforce the physical part of domain definitions. Required values are another type of constraint. Making a value required avoids the ambiguity of null values. Uniqueness constraints are best enforced by the DBMS; this is usually done by building indexes.

Relationship cardinality constraints arise from cardinality settings on object links; either non-zero settings of minimum cardinality or maximum cardinality values that are neither 1 nor N. Except for 1.1 cardinality on the child side of 1:N relationships, such constraints must be enforced by application code. Rules for constraint enforcement on 1:N relationships are summarized in Figure 10-19.

Business rule constraints by application code that is invoked by trapping events, by triggers, or in-line in application programs.

Most DBMS products provide user name and password security. This can be used to provide horizontal security; vertical security must be provided by application code. Most applications provide control via menus. The best control occurs when menus change as the user's context changes. Application programs have the important role of defining transaction boundaries. Application logic is encoded in code and invoked by trapping events and by other means that will be explained in later chapters.

➤ GROUP I QUESTIONS

10.1 List the five major functions of a database application.

10.2 Explain the meaning of the acronym CRUD.

10.3 Define the term *view* as used in this chapter.

10.4 What is a view instance?

10.5 Explain how a view is different from a materialization.

10.6 Can an attribute appear more than once in a view? Why?

10.7 Under what conditions can a view be read with one SQL statement?

10.8 Under what conditions does reading a view require more than one SQL statement?

10.9 Explain the two paths that exist in the Customer view in Figure 10-4.

10.10 Define the term *recordset*.

10.11 Describe in general terms the work that is required when creating a view instance.

10.12 How are new relationships created when creating a view instance?

10.13 What technique can be used to obtain the value of a surrogate key when inserting new rows into a table?

10.14 List the three types of change that can occur when updating a view instance.

10.15 Explain how to change 1:N relationships. Explain how to change N:M relationships.

10.16 What is the major difficulty when writing code to delete a view instance?

10.17 How can an E-R model help determine how much to delete?

10.18 How can a semantic object model help determine how much to delete?

10.19 What are cascading deletions, and why are they important?

10.20 Explain the statement "Form structure should reflect view structure."

10.21 How can forms be designed to make the semantics of the data graphically evident?

10.22 How can forms be designed to encourage appropriate action?

10.23 Explain the role of drop-down list boxes, option groups, and check boxes in form design.

10.24 What limitation exists for report materialization of views?

10.25 Explain why the calculated values on reports should normally not be stored in the database.

10.26 Explain how the request to report objects sorted by a value changes the underlying object of the report.

10.27 Why should constraints normally be enforced by the DBMS and not by a particular form, report, or application program?

10.28 Why are constraints sometimes enforced in application programs?

10.29 Give an example of a domain constraint and explain how it might be enforced by Access 2000.

10.30 Describe the ambiguity that arises when values are null. Describe two ways such values can be eliminated.

10.31 Why should the DBMS normally enforce uniqueness constraints?

10.32 Describe the two sources of cardinality constraints.

10.33 How can a 1.1 cardinality constraint on the child side of a 1:N relationship be enforced?

10.34 Define *fragment* and *orphan*.

10.35 Explain the entries in the first column of Figure 10-19(a).

10.36 Explain why the center column of Figure 10-19(a) is unnecessary when surrogate keys are used.

10.37 Explain the entries in the third column of Figure 10-19(a).

10.38 Explain the entries in the first column of Figure 10-19(b).

10.39 Explain the entries in the third column of Figure 10-19(b).

10.40 Explain why the first column of Figure 10-19(a) and the third column of Figure 10-19(b) are not enforced by the Access 2000 relationship properties shown in Figure 10-20.

10.41 Give an example of a business rule constraint that could apply to the data model in Figure 10-3. Explain how this constraint could be enforced by trapping an event.

10.42 Define *horizontal* and *vertical* security.

10.43 Which type of security is supported by user name and password?

10.44 Which type of security must be supported by application code?

10.45 Explain why dynamic menus are better than static ones.

10.46 How is business logic connected to a database when using Access 2000?

➤ GROUP II QUESTIONS

Questions 10.47 through 10.50 pertain to the following Artist View which is based on the data model in Figure 10-3.

```
ARTIST.Name
ARTIST.Nationality
    TRANSACTION.PurchaseDate
    TRANSACTION.SalesPrice. . .
        CUSTOMER.Name
        CUSTOMER.Phone.AreaCode
        CUSTOMER.Phone.LocalNumber
    CUSTOMER.Name. . .
```

The ellipses (. . .) refer to structures that can repeat.

10.47 Code SQL statements for reading the "Mark Tobey" instance of this view.

10.48 Code SQL statements to create a new instance of this view. Assume that you have data for ARTIST, one TRANSACTION, and many CUSTOMER.Name(s) for the second instance of CUSTOMER.Name. Assume this data is located in a structure named NewArtist. Use syntax similar to that in the text.

10.49 Code SQL statements to update this view as follows:

A. Change the spelling of Mark Tobey to Mark Toby.

B. Create a new Transaction for Mark Toby. Assume you have the necessary transaction, work, and customer data in a structure named NewTrans.

C. Add new interested customers for Mark Toby. Assume they are stored in a collection that you can access with the command "For Each NewCust.Name."

10.50 Code SQL statements to delete the row for Mark Toby and all related WORK and TRANSACTION rows.

➤ PROJECTS

A. Using Access 2000, create the database shown in Figure 10-3. Create a form for the Artist View shown above Question 10.47. Justify the design of your form using the principles in this chapter. Hint: You can use a wizard to create one of the subforms, but you will need to add the second one manually. Also, add the combo boxes manually, after you have created the forms for the subform.

B. Complete one of the projects A at the end of Chapter 3 or 4 if you have not already done so.

1. List and describe the purpose of three views, three forms, and three reports that you think would be necessary for this application.

2. Show the structure of a GUI drop-down menu for this application. Using your model, design one of the forms for entering new housing properties. Explain which type of control (text box, drop-down list) is used for each field. Justify the structure of your form using the concepts presented in this chapter.

PART V

USING INTERNET TECHNOLOGY

This part considers database applications that utilize Internet technology. The reason we do not say that it concerns "Internet database applications" is because some of these applications reside on private intranets rather than on the Internet. We are concerned here, however, with any database application that uses the technology first developed for the Internet. Thus, the knowledge you gain from this part will help you create database applications for either the Internet or private intranets.

Chapter 11 introduces basic Web concepts and describes the three-tier processing architecture. It then focuses on the client and Web server tiers. Web-oriented programming languages are described and the features and functions of DHTML and XML are discussed. The chapter concludes with an explanation of the role and purpose of Active Server Pages.

All database applications that use Internet technology are multi-user applications, and so Chapter 12 discusses the management of multi-user databases. Concurrency control, transaction management, backup and recovery, and security are all addressed. Finally, Chapter 13 describes standards for accessing Web databases including ODBC, OLE DB, and ADO. These standard interfaces are used to execute SQL statements and receive results. An example Internet-technology database application concludes this chapter.

Database Applications Using Internet Technology

The Internet has given rise to technologies that are used today to publish database applications on the Internet and private intranets. We begin with a short history of the development of this technology. From there, we will describe the three-tier architecture, functions, and processing. Next, Web-oriented languages such as JavaScript, VBScript, Perl, and Java are introduced. Then, we consider two very important Web standards: DHTML and XML. Finally, the use and role of ASP (active server pages) is described.

➤ NETWORK ENVIRONMENTS

A **network** is a collection of computers that communicate with one another using a standardized protocol. Some networks āre **public;** anyone can utilize the network by paying a fee to a vendor who will provide access (or, like students, by joining an organization that has already paid to have access). Other networks are **private.** With these, only users who are preauthorized to connect to the network can gain access.

The most widely used public network is the Internet, and we begin with it.

THE INTERNET

The Internet is a public network of computers that communicate using a communications protocol called **Terminal Control Program/Internet Protocol (TCP/IP).** This network was created by the Advanced Research Projects Agency

(ARPA) of the U.S. armed services in the 1960s. Initially, it was called ARPANET, and it connected major computing centers at military, university, and research institutions. Over time, more and more organizations joined the network, and it became desirable for nonresearch, commercially oriented organizations to join as well. In 1984, the military split its organizations off from ARPANET to form MILNET. ARPANET continued to grow in popularity with universities, research, and commercial organizations. Today it is referred to as the Internet. MILNET and the Internet are still connected, however.

A number of standard services are provided on the Internet. Any Internet user has access to **Internet mail services** for E-mail. Services for public **newsgroups** are provided by NetNews, an Internet facility that allows users with common interests to conduct public discussions with one another. Other services include **TelNet,** which allows an Internet user to sign on to a remote computer, and **FTP,** which allows users to send or retrieve files from remote computers.

In the beginning, almost all Internet servers ran some version of the UNIX operating system. Hence, the format and syntax of commands for accessing Internet services were UNIX-like. While this was acceptable, even an advantage, to technical users and computer programmers, it was off-putting to most people in business or at home. E-mail was popular because the complexity of UNIX was hidden by most mail applications, but TelNet, FTP, and other more sophisticated Internet services were not very popular among noncomputer experts. This situation changed with the advent of the World Wide Web.

THE WORLD WIDE WEB   In 1989, Tim Berners-Lee of the European Particle Physics Laboratory (CERN) began work on a project that would enable researchers to share their work over the Internet. This project led to the development of the **hypertext transfer protocol (HTTP),** which is a TCP/IP-based protocol that enables the sharing of documents with embedded links to other documents over a TCP/IP network.

Berners-Lee and others proposed using a standard set of codes to mark text in documents both to indicate headings, emphasis, italics, and the like and also to indicate links to other documents. This language, called **hypertext markup language (HTML),** was a subset of an already accepted publishing industry markup language called the **standard generalized markup language (SGML).** Figure 11-1 shows an example of an HTML document, and Figure 11-2 shows the way in which that document would appear to the client user.

In 1993, the National Center for Supercomputing Applications (NCSA) developed Mosaic, which was a client application for reading HTML (and other) documents. Later that year, Marc Andresen of NCSA proposed extending HTML to add the capability to add images and other types of media to HTML documents. Later Andresen and others left NCSA to form Netscape Communications, where they developed the Netscape Navigator. Today Mosaic, Netscape Navigator, and Microsoft's Internet Explorer are the most widely used Internet browsers.

Internet servers are programs that provide services in response to HTML commands. While many Internet server programs exist, the most popular are Apache, Netscape Server, and Microsoft's IIS.

The result of these products and technologies was the creation of a dynamic network of hypertext documents distributed across thousands of computers. This network of documents is called the **World Wide Web.**

INTERNET STANDARDS AND CHARACTERISTICS Three standards emerged from all of this activity that are important to network database applications. The first is HTML and related markup languages. While some database applications use HTML, today it is more common for them to use DHTML and XML, as you will see.

➤ FIGURE 11-1

Example HTML

```
<html>

<head>
<title>HTML Example</title>
</head>

<body>

<p><b><font face="Arial Black">Document Markup Languages Are:</font></b></p>
<ul>
    <li>Hypertext Markup Language  (HTML)</li>
    <li>Dynamic Hypertext Markup Language  (DHTML)</li>
    <li>Extensible Markup Language  (XML)</li>
</ul>

<p><font face="Arial Black"><b>Scripting Languages Are:</b></font></p>
<ul>
    <li>JavaScript, JScript, ECMAScript-262</li>
    <li>VBScript</li>
    <li>Perl</li>
</ul>

</body>

</html>
```

➤ FIGURE 11-2

Browser Rendering of HTML in Figure 11-1

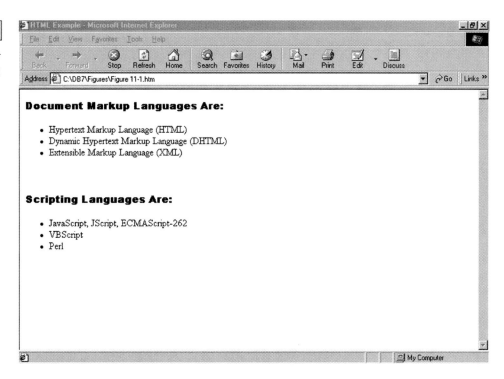

Another important standard for database applications is the syntax by which documents are referenced on the Internet. The **universal resource locator (URL)** provides a standardized means to locate any document. A URL consists of three parts: a service name, a domain name, and a path name with an optional file name. Thus, in the URL

http://www.companyx.com/dir1/myfile.abc

http:// is the name of the service (in this case hypertext transfer protocol), www.companyx.com is the name of a domain, and dir1/myfile.abc is the name of the path and file.

A third important standard that emerged from the Internet concerns the means by which URL files are to be processed. Not all files are HTML; some are graphics, or sound, or movie, or animation. When a server sends a file to a client, it also sends a code indicating the file's type. The client interprets the code to determine which program can process the file. The system of codes used is called **multipurpose Internet mail code (MIME).** The code was initially developed for mail, but today it is used more frequently in the processing of HTML documents. Figure 11-3 lists several types of files, their normal file extensions, and their MIME types. Three-letter file extensions are used on Windows and Macintosh systems, and four-letter extensions are used on Unix.

MIME typing is important in database applications, not only for the obvious reason of generating standardized HTML, but also because MIME types can be extended. (In Figure 11-3, types preceded by x- are extended types.) Each server has a file that lists MIME types. An application-defined type can be added to this list, as well as to a similar list that is used by client browsers.

Thus, it is possible to create a database application that has a specific MIME type code. That code can be placed in the MIME lists on both the clients and the servers and associated with a given graphic image. When the user clicks on that image, the browser will check the MIME code and determine that it should invoke the database application. (It may need to call the server to download the application and then invoke it.) Thus, organizations can extend the MIME type system to include their own specific codes.

Two characteristics of WWW applications are especially noteworthy for database applications. First, WWW applications are request-oriented. WWW servers wait to be accessed and provide services when asked to do so. Unlike some traditional MIS applications, they do not poll or otherwise solicit application activity.

Second, WWW applications are stateless. The server receives a request, processes it, and then forgets about the client who made the request. No attempt is made to conduct a continuing session or conversation with a given client. This stateless characteristic poses no problems for Web applications like those that dis-

➤ FIGURE 11-3

Sample MIME Types

MIME Type	Name	File Extension
text/HTML	HyperText Markup	.htm, html
text/plain	Text	.txt
application/postscript	Postscript	.pdf, .ps, .ai
image/gif	Graphics Interchange Format	.gif
image/jpeg	Joint Photographic Experts Group	.jpg, .jpeg
audio/basic	mu-law	.au
audio/x-wav	Microsoft Wave File	.wav
audio/basic	Macintosh Sound File	.snd
video/quicktime	Macintosh Quick Time	.qt, .mov
video/x-msvideo	Microsoft Video	.avi

play pages of promotional material. It is a problem for most database applications, however, because database applications usually involve the processing of a transaction, which may require several or many exchanges between the client and the server. We will return to this topic later in this chapter.

INTRANETS

The term *intranet* has several different interpretations. Most commonly, the term means a private, local or wide-area network (LAN or WAN) that uses TCP/IP, HTML, and related browser technology on client computers and Web server technology on servers. Less commonly, the term is used to mean any private LAN or WAN that involves clients and servers.

Two characteristics of intranets differentiate them from the Internet. First, intranets are private. Either they are not connected to a public network at all, or they are connected to a public network via a **firewall,** which is a computer that serves as a security gateway. Firewall computers monitor the source and destination of traffic between the intranet and the Internet and filter it. Some firewalls operate so as to allow only certain traffic through; others operate so as to prohibit certain traffic; still others operate in both modes.

Because intranets are private, security is less of a concern. This does not mean that security is not a concern at all but rather that less elaborate security measures need to be taken. In most cases, computers on an intranet are known and supported by the organization that owns and maintains the intranet. Unauthorized activity and security problems are more easily identified and managed than on a public network.

The second major differentiating characteristic of an intranet is speed. Most users connect to the Internet via a modem. Since today's modems operate in the range of 56 kbs (thousands of bits per second), anyone planning an Internet application needs to size the application's transmission requirements accordingly. Large files cannot be transferred in a reasonable amount of time.

On the other hand, the transmission speed of a LAN can be in the range of 100,000 kbs. Hence, files downloaded on an intranet can be more than 1,000 to 10,000 times larger than those downloaded from the Internet.

Because of the speed difference, large bitmaps, sound files, and animations can be included in intranet applications. More important in the database world, large query responses can be transmitted to client computers. In addition, because of the increased speed, it is possible to download large program files to the client computer. This means, as you will see, that more of the application processing can be conducted on the client in an intranet than can be conducted on a client using the Internet.

NETWORK DATABASE APPLICATIONS

Several types of database applications are emerging on the Internet and intranets. The term *publishing* is often used for these applications because of the request-oriented nature of Internet and intranet processing. That is, a server is available to be accessed by the client, when and if the client chooses to access it. The server does not solicit activity from the clients.

STATIC REPORT PUBLISHING   Some network database applications provide static report publishing. This means that the DBMS (or application program) generates a report, static form, or query response in HTML format and posts it to a Web site. (A static form is a display-only data entry form. It is a picture of a data entry form that displays data but that cannot be used for data entry.)

*Example Static
Report*

Figure 11-4 shows an HTML report that was prepared from the database application in Chapter 10. This report was generated in Access 2000 and exported to HTML.

A report like the one in Figure 11-4 can be generated and a URL to that report file placed in a Web page. If the DBMS supports triggers or related functionality, the file containing the report can automatically be generated by the DBMS either after the passage of a certain amount of time or when a particular event occurs. For example, an application could post a daily sales summary report every hour onto a Web page. Or the application could generate a new report every time daily sales increase by $100,000 or some similar figure.

Notice that the transmission traffic in static report publishing is one-way. The user provides no data; all of the data flow from the server to the user at the user's request. Because of this, no data about the state of the interaction between the client and the network server need be maintained by either.

DB QUERY PUBLISHING   A second type of network database application is query publishing. In this application, an HTML form is generated that has text boxes in which the user enters query criteria. For example, in the form in Figure 11-5, the user enters an order number and presses the submit query button. At that point the application sends a request to initiate a query for that order on the server. The server responds with order data or an error message.

From a database standpoint, there is nothing particularly unique about this query; such queries have been processed by DBMS products for many years. What is different about it, however, is that it is embedded in an HTML file that can be processed by any computer having a browser and access to the network. Hence, the query can be readily distributed. If a company wants its customers to be able to query orders, it need only distribute the URL of the Web site having a link to this query page. In doing so, the company will most likely want to add a restriction to the query response so that it sends responses only to orders that originated at the client's company.

➤ FIGURE 11-5

Example of Query Publishing Form

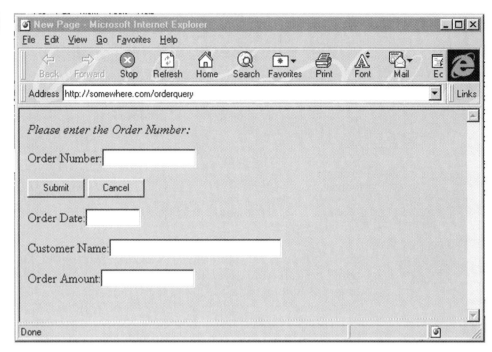

Unlike static report publishing, the data transmission for query publishing is two-way. In the example, the client provides an order number, and the server responds with query results. More realistically, the client would probably need to send identifying data as well.

If each query is considered to be an independent unit, then neither the client nor the server need maintain any data about the state of their interaction. It might be, however, that in order to reduce transmission traffic, queries should be remembered so that if the user enters the number of an order that has already been queried, the results can be obtained locally. In this case, the client computer would need to keep track of the queries that have been made and the responses to each.

APPLICATION PUBLISHING   Application publishing is a type of network database application that is closest to what we called database applications in Chapter 10. Such applications have potentially many data entry forms and reports. They support transaction logic, provide concurrency control over database changes, and have all of the other database application characteristics. The remainder of this chapter will address this type of network database application.

➤ THREE-TIER ARCHITECTURE

Figure 11-6 shows the three tier architecture that is used for Internet-technology database applications. We will use many acronyms in this and the three following figures. Do not worry if these terms are strange to you. We will explain the languages (like Java) and the markup languages (like DHTML) after we describe the general architecture. The database standards (like ODBC) will be explained in Chapter 13.

Three types of processor, or tiers, are shown in Figure 11-6. From right to left, they are: the database server, the Web server, and the browser or client computers. As shown, each of these tiers can run a different operating system. In this example, the database server runs UNIX, the Web server runs Windows 2000 (for-

*Three-Tier
Architecture*

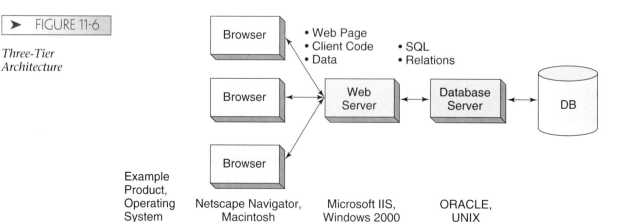

merly Windows NT), and the browsers are running the Macintosh operating system. These are only examples. More likely, the browsers would be running a mixture of Windows 98, UNIX, Macintosh, and Windows 2000. The Web server and the database server could be either UNIX or Windows 2000.

Example products shown in Figure 11-6 are the ORACLE DBMS on the database server, Microsoft Internet Information Server (IIS) on the Web server, and Netscape Navigator on the clients. Again, these are only examples. The data server could be running any DBMS from Access to DB2. Common Web servers are IIS, Netscape Server, and Apache. Common browsers are Netscape Navigator and Microsoft Internet Explorer.

As shown, the interface between the Web server and the database server transmits SQL statements and relational data. The interface between the Web server and the browser transmits Web pages, client code, and data. We will say much more about each of these interfaces in this and the next two chapters.

The functions of the three tiers are summarized in Figure 11-7. The purpose of the database server is to run the DBMS to process SQL statements and perform database management tasks. Here, the DBMS is operating in its traditional role of serving up data; the application tools capabilities that you have seen with Access 2000 are not in use. The DBMS on the data server in Figure 11-7 is not creating forms or reports or menus. Instead, it is a pure data engine; receiving SQL requests and processing rows in tables. As you will see in the next chapter, it also has many important functions concerning transaction management.

Functions of Tiers

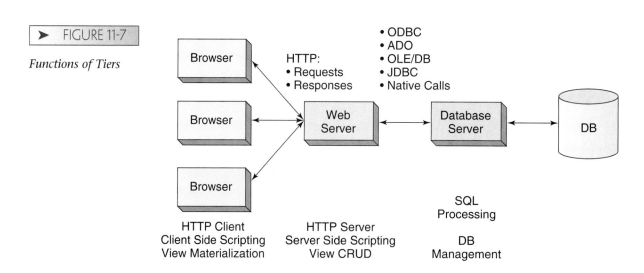

Figure 11-7 shows the standards and application program interfaces that are used between the data server and the Web server. We will discuss ODBC, OLE DB, and ADO in Chapter 13. For now, just think of those standards as means of transmitting SQL and relations between the Web server and the database server.

The Web server performs three major functions. First, it is an HTTP server meaning that it processes the HTTP protocol, receiving requests and generating responses in HTTP format. The Web server also hosts scripting environments so that developers can write code in languages like VBScript and JavaScript and execute that code on the Web server. Finally, in database applications, the third function of the Web server is to create, read, update, and delete view instances as discussed in Chapter 10. Again, keep in mind the difference between a relation and a view; views are constructions of relations.

In database applications, the browser has three functions that are analogous to those on the Web server. First, the browser is an HTTP client, generating requests for pages and for other activity. It also hosts a scripting environment for executing scripts on the client machine. Finally, the browser materializes views, transforming HTML or other markup language into a display in the client's browser window.

This architecture allows for scripting on both the Web server and client computers. One of the important tasks when developing an Internet-technology database application is to decide what work is to be done on which machine. Because there are many browsers and only one server, it is desirable to place as much code on the client as possible. However, if the client needs to keep going back to the Web server to obtain data for its calculations, this advantage can be off-set by the time required for the data request and response round trips. Also, the client code needs to be sent down to the browser in the HTTP message. Large chunks of code will require a long time for download. A good rule of thumb is shown in Figure 11-7: Use client code for scripting tasks that support view materialization. Use server code for scripting tasks that support view CRUD. Also, code for immediate calculations (ExtendedPrice = Quantity * Price) is usually done on the browser.

Figures 11-8 and 11-9 show products and languages that are common when using a Windows Web server and a UNIX Web server, respectively. With

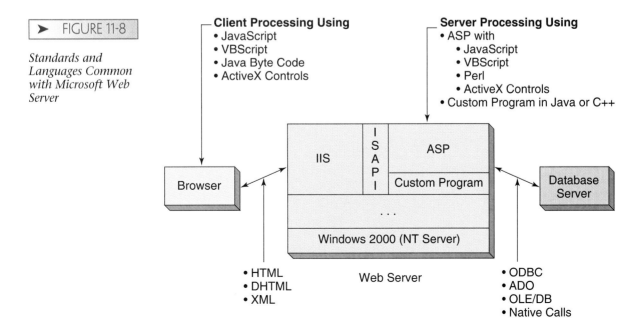

➤ FIGURE 11-8

Standards and Languages Common with Microsoft Web Server

Client Processing Using
• JavaScript
• VBScript
• Java Byte Code
• ActiveX Controls

Server Processing Using
• ASP with
  • JavaScript
  • VBScript
  • Perl
  • ActiveX Controls
• Custom Program in Java or C++

Browser

IIS   ISAPI   ASP   Custom Program

. . .

Windows 2000 (NT Server)

Database Server

Web Server

• HTML
• DHTML
• XML

• ODBC
• ADO
• OLE/DB
• Native Calls

FIGURE 11-9

Standards and Languages Common with UNIX Server

the Windows server, the HTTP server will almost always be IIS since it is part of the Windows operating system. IIS provides an interface called Internet Server Application Program Interface (ISAPI) by which other programs can trap and process HTTP messages. The Active Server Processor (ASP) is one such program. It processes all Web pages with the suffix *.asp*. When IIS receives such a page, it sends it to Active Server Processor over the ISAPI interface. ASP then processes the page and sends a response back to the client via the ISAPI interface to IIS.

ASP hosts scripting languages; therefore, ASP pages can contain JavaScript, VBScript, Perl, and other scripting language statements. These statements will be executed when ASP processes the page. In addition, ActiveX controls can be embedded in the page and they will be invoked as well.

ASP is not the only program that can use the ISAPI interface. C++ and Java developers can create custom programs for processing HTTP messages instead of using the ASP facility.

When using a Microsoft Web server, the data access standard used will most likely be ODBC, ADO, or OLE DB since these standards are supported and promulgated by Microsoft.

When using a UNIX Web server (Figure 11-9), IIS is not used as the HTTP server. Instead, products like Apache or the Netscape Web Server are used. Apache supports the ISAPI interface, and there are versions of ASP that can run with it. It is possible, therefore, to process .asp pages on UNIX (unless, of course, those pages invoke ActiveX controls that can only run on Windows). The Netscape server provides its own interface, NSAPI, that serves a role similar to that for ISAPI.

On UNIX Web servers, however, the Common Gateway Interface (CGI) is used more frequently than either ISAPI or NSAPI. Because of its superior string processing capabilities, the language Perl is often used with CGI. Unfortunately, when writing Web server programs using CGI, there is no processor equivalent to ASP. This means that more work needs to be done by the application developer. Of course, it is possible to write custom programs in Java or C++ and utilize the ISAPI, NSAPI, or CGI interfaces.

ODBC, JDBC, and native DBMS calls are generally used by applications that run on a UNIX Web server. Neither OLE DB nor ADO is implemented on UNIX. JavaScript and Java byte code are most commonly used for processing on the client browsers.

➤ LANGUAGES USED FOR INTERNET-TECHNOLOGY APPLICATIONS

There are a number of different languages used for processing database applications using Internet technology. You will not need to learn how to program in all of them; knowledge of one scripting language will likely be sufficient to create database applications. Nevertheless, you should understand the nature of some of the major languages and how they relate to one another.

SCRIPTING LANGUAGES: JAVASCRIPT, JSCRIPT, ECMASCRIPT-262, AND VBSCRIPT

Scripting languages are easily learned, interpreted languages that execute procedural logic. They can be used on the server to construct and communicate SQL requests to the DBMS, to process resulting recordsets, to enforce constraints, and for other work related to managing view instances. Scripting languages can also be used on the client for tasks like data validation, dynamic materialization (changing a font, for example, when the cursor moves over it) and layout, and for simple calculations. They can also be used on either the server or the client to invoke ActiveX or other COM objects (discussed in the next section).

JavaScript (sometimes spelled Java Script) is a proprietary scripting language owned by Netscape (now AOL). JavaScript has little in common with the Java language, so do not be misled by the common word. Microsoft developed its own version of the same language and called it JScript. In 1997, scripting experts from Microsoft, Netscape, IBM, Sun, and other companies met and developed a specification for a standard Web scripting language, which is known as ECMAScript-262. (ECMA stands for European Computer Manufacturer's Association—none of the members of which participated. That's another story.) Microsoft upgraded JScript to conform to the ECMAScript-262 standard in Internet Explorer version 4.0 and in IIS version 4.0. Netscape has not yet done so, but JavaScript is not substantially different from ECMAScript-262.

VBScript is a subset of Visual Basic that has essentially the same functionality as JScript. If you know VB, it will be very easy for you to learn VBScript. Also, since there are legions of VB programmers, it will also be easier for you to find other developers who know VBScript. At time of publication, VBScript will run only on Microsoft browsers, however, so if you are developing script for client processing, then your users will be restricted to using Microsoft browsers.

Figure 11-10 shows HTML with embedded VBScript. This code will generate the form shown in Figure 11-11; here the user has just entered the value 10 and clicked the Compute button. For comparison purposes, the equivalent procedure using JScript is shown in Figure 11-12. Both of these scripts are simple, but from them you can get an idea of how code is blended with HTML for client-side scripting.

The bottom line of this discussion is that there is a Web standard scripting language and JScript conforms to it. Thus, if you want to learn just one scripting language, learn JScript. Also, if you are coding scripts to be run on the client, and if there is a chance that some of your users will have a browser other than Internet Explorer, then you should use JScript.

PERL   Perl (Practical Extraction and Report Language) is an interpreted language invented by Larry Wall. It is frequently used to create server-side script on Web servers because it has very strong string-manipulation capabilities. This is impor-

➤ FIGURE 11-10

Example Web Page with VBScript

```
<HTML>
<HEAD>
<TITLE>Labor Estimation Calculator</TITLE>
<SCRIPT LANGUAGE="VBScript">
        <!--
        Sub CalcButton_OnClick()
        Dim LHours, LTotal, Tax, Total
        If LaborHours. Value = "" Then
                MsgBox "Please enter a value for labor hours"
        End if
        LHours = LaborHours. Value
        LTotal = LHours* 65.0
        Tax = LTotal * .0891
        Total = LTotal + Tax
        LaborTotal.Value = LTotal
        TaxAmount.Value =Tax
        TotalBid. Value = Total
        End Sub
        -->
</SCRIPT>
</HEAD>
<BODY>
<HR>
<CENTER>
Enter the number of labor hours:
<BR>
(Standard labor rate is $65.00; tax is 8.91 percent)
<P>
<INPUT NAME="LaborHours">
<INPUT TYPE=BUTTON NAME ="CalcButton" VALUE ="Compute">
<BR>
Labor Total:
<INPUT NAME="Labor Total">
<BR>
Tax Amount:
<INPUT NAME="TAX AMOUNT">
<BR>
Total Bid:
<INPUT NAME="TotalBid">

</BODY>
</HTML>
```

➤ FIGURE 11-11

Form Resulting from HTML in Figure 11-10

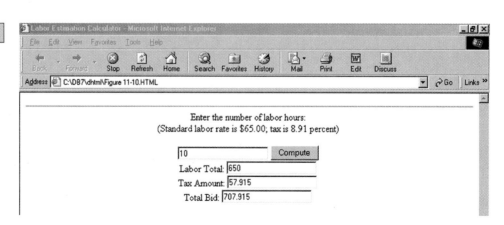

➤ FIGURE 11-12

*Example Web Page
with JScript*

```
<HTML>
<HEAD>
<TITLE>Labor Estimation Calculator</TITLE>
<SCRIPT LANGUAGE="JScript">
        <!--
        function CalcButton_OnClick() {
        //Dim LHours, LTotal, Tax, Total
        If (LaborHours. Value = "")
        {
                MsgBox "Please enter a value for labor hours";
        }
        LHours = LaborHours. Value;
        LTotal = LHours * 65.0;
        Tax = LTotal * .0891;
        Total = LTotal + Tax;
        LaborTotal.Value = LTotal;
        TaxAmount. Value = Tax;
        TotalBid. Value = Total;
        }
        -->
</SCRIPT>
</HEAD>
<BODY>
<HR>
<CENTER>
Enter the number of labor hours:
<BR>
(Standard labor rate is $65.00; tax is 8.91 percent)
<P>
<INPUT NAME="LaborHours">
<INPUT TYPE=BUTTON NAME ="CalcButton" VALUE ="Compute">
<BR>
Labor Total:
<INPUT NAME="LaborTotal">
<BR>
Tax Amount:
<INPUT NAME="TaxAmount">
<BR>
Total Bid:
<INPUT NAME="TotalBid">

</BODY>
</HTML>
```

tant when decoding parameter strings that accompany forms when using the CGI forms interface. In addition, Perl is free and portable. There are Perl interpreters for UNIX, Windows, and Macintosh. Databases can be accessed using ODBC from Perl.

Hackers love Perl like they love their family dog. It has a strange syntax that can be used to create odd programs that accomplish almost any string-manipulation task. Because its syntax does not appeal to everyone, it is unlikely to have the prominence for Web applications that JScript and VBScript will have.

Still, Perl is an exceedingly useful and powerful language, and if you have the hope of achieving even junior hacker status, you must learn it. Because we have so much else to do, we must pass it by. One last note: Perl—which, according to Larry Wall, can also be interpreted as the Pathologically Eclectic Rubbish Lister—is the only software product on the market to have a copyleft notice.

JAVA

Java is a programming language developed by Sun Microsystems, Inc. Some people believe that Java is the language that C++ should have been, while others refer to Java as a subset of C++. In any case, Java is an object programming language (see Chapter 17) that has better memory management and bounds-checking capabilities than C++.

When Java is compiled, the result of the compilation is a file of Java bytecode. This bytecode resides on the server, and when the user accesses an HTML page (or other resources) that has a Java program, the bytecode is transmitted to the client. This bytecode is then input to an interpreter, called a Java virtual machine, that resides on the client.

Java was designed to be portable. Java bytecode is machine-independent; for it to run on a particular operating system, only the bytecode interpreter need be converted to the new operating system. There are Java bytecode interpreters for UNIX, Windows, and Macintosh operating systems.

Unlike VBScript and JavaScript, Java is a full and complete object-oriented programming language. This means that it can be used to write code for processing on the client side, code for processing on the server side, or both. Clearly, the more of the application that is written for processing on the client side, the larger the Java application will be, and the more bytecode will need to be downloaded. This means that startup times will be slower. On the other hand, once the code has been downloaded, the client computer will be able to process a larger share of the application, and the network server is less likely to be a bottleneck.

There are libraries for binding Java to ODBC, called JDBC, as well as for binding it directly to the native libraries of DBMS products.

The major advantages of Java are machine portability and the fact that it is a modern, fully featured object-oriented programming language. The major disadvantage is that Java is less common than C++; hence, there are fewer Java programmers and fewer prebuilt Java components. Also, as an object-oriented programming language, Java requires considerable skill and training.

VISUAL BASIC, C++, AND ACTIVEX

Visual Basic and C++ can both be used to create ActiveX controls that provide services on both the server and client tiers. An ActiveX control is a specialized implementation of Microsoft's Component Object Model (**COM**).

COM is a specification for the development of object-oriented programs that enables such programs to work together. The COM specification defines a set of interfaces; an object that supports those interfaces is called a **COM object**. Any COM object can communicate and work with any other COM object even though the two were created by different programmers at different times and for different purposes.

For example, suppose company A creates a COM object that obtains schedule data from a mainframe and company B creates a COM object for displaying a calendar on a Web page. A developer could place these two objects together on a ASP page so that company A's object would feed schedule data to company B's object for display, even though the two companies never planned for their objects to work together. (The developer might have to provide some JScript to integrate the two.)

The only required COM interface, and the base of all the others, is **IUnknown**. Using IUknown, one object can establish a connection with another object. Given that connection, it can then use the **QueryInterface** method of the IUknown object to determine what other interfaces the second object supports. In this way one object can establish communication with a second object and then dynamically determine what that object can do.

Microsoft defined two other specifications based on the COM specification. **OLE objects** (for Object Linking and Embedding) are COM objects that support additional interfaces for embedding objects into other objects. You use an OLE object when you embed an Excel spreadsheet into a Word document. **ActiveX** objects support a slimmed down version of the OLE specification. An **ActiveX Control** is an ActiveX object that supports additional interfaces that allow the control's properties and methods to be accessed in many different development environments.

All of this brings us to the important part for developing database applications using Internet technology. There are many ActiveX objects and controls available for constructing database applications. These objects allow you to use functionality that someone else programmed. Some ActiveX objects are used to display data (you will see two of them in this chapter in the discussion of DHTML). Others, such as ADO—to be discussed in Chapter 13—are used for processing databases with SQL. Still other ActiveX controls are used for obtaining services from IIS or Internet Explorer.

The HTML tag ⟨OBJECT⟩ is used to place ActiveX objects into Web pages. As you will see, attributes of that tag are used to provide data to the control and to specify its appearance and behavior. Figure 11-13 shows the relationship of these objects.

Developers can create their own ActiveX controls in Visual Basic or C++ and blend those controls with existing controls developed by Microsoft, other vendors, or other developers. For example, you might develop an ActiveX control to access the Web to obtain data about particular companies' financial performance. You could then develop a Web page that invokes your control and then uses other existing controls to display the data that your control obtains.

➤ FIGURE 11-13

Relationship of Microsoft Component Objects

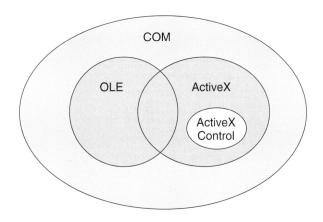

➤ MARKUP LANGUAGES: DHTML AND XML

Markup languages are used to specify the appearance and behavior of a Web page. As noted, the first such language to obtain prominence on the Web was HTML, which is a subset of a more powerful and sophisticated language called SGML. In this section we will consider the markup languages dynamic HTML (DHTML) and XML. In complexity, these languages lie between HTML and SGML. Before delving into them, however, we need to establish an historical context regarding Web standards.

Markup Language Standards

HTML was a tremendous success in that it fostered the development of hundreds of thousands of Web sites and made Web communication a reality for the general computing public. Over time, it became clear, however, that the original version of HTML had significant disadvantages, especially for the development of database applications on the Web. As people worked to overcome these disadvantages, it became apparent that standards were needed. Otherwise, every vendor would make improvements on its own, and soon, only certain browsers would be able to process certain pages, which would take away one of the most important advantages of the Web.

Consequently, starting in 1994, the World Wide Web Consortium (W3C) began to promulgate standards for HTML and other markup languages. These standards have become very important. Visit the consortium's Web site at www.w3.org. There you will find helpful information, tutorials, the endorsed (or recommended) standards, and standards that are in process of development.

The role and importance of standards will be clearer if you understand that vendors of software products have a love/hate relationship with them. On one hand, they love standards because they provide order in the marketplace and establish a base set of capabilities that products need to have. On the other hand, they hate them because they can invalidate features, functions, and technologies in which vendors have made a significant investment.

Also, standards put vendors in a double bind. If they only develop to the standard, then there is no reason for customers to buy their product over their competitors' products. But if they add features and functions to the standard, then they will be criticized for not adhering to the standard. Thus, when Microsoft developed DHTML, it supported the W3C standard called HTML 4.0. It also, however, added features and functions that go beyond that standard. Depending on which hat you wear, those features are wonderful because of their added functionality, or they are terrible because pages that use them may not behave properly in all browsers.

For this reason, when non-standard features are added to a product, it is done in such a way that products not supporting those additional features will degrade gracefully. For example, an outline will dynamically open and close on browsers that support that feature; it will appear always open on browsers that do not support that feature.

Problems with HTML

The original version of HTML suffered from a number of problems. For one, the content, layout, and format of pages were confounded; there is no way to separate the definition of content from layout from format. This means that if you want the same content delivered in different ways, you need to create two complete copies of that content, layout, and format. For database applications, it also meant that view data and view materialization were inextricably mixed.

Another disadvantage was the lack of style definitions. It was not possible to say, for example, that all headings would have a particular font face, size, and emphasis. Hence, if a Web developer wanted to change the format of all level one headings, he or she would have to find all of the level one headings in the page (or on the Web site) and then change their format one-by-one. What was needed was a facility to define the style of a given format element.

A third disadvantage of the original HTML was that Web page elements could not be accessed from scripts or other programs. For example, there was no way to refer to the title element of a page in a script to dynamically alter its appearance or layout. Also, code could not be written to respond to Windows events like mouse movements and clicks. Hence, to change the structure or appearance of a page, the browser needed to return to the server to obtain a complete new page. Such round trips were unnecessary, slow, and wasteful.

Finally, and most important to us, there were no constructs to facilitate the caching and data manipulation on the client. Whenever a browser needed to display more data, a round trip had to be made to the server. W3C developed a new standard for HTML called HTML 4.0 to define features and functions to overcome these, and other, disadvantages.

DHTML

DHTML is a Microsoft implementation of HTML 4.0. It includes all of that standard plus additional features and functions. DHTML is supported by Microsoft Internet Explorer 4.0 (and later versions) and by IIS 4.0 (and later versions). Netscape Navigator supports only the HTML 4.0 portion of DHTML; it does not support all of the features that were added to DHTML beyond that standard. Hence, when using DHTML, developers need to be careful to stay within the HTML 4.0 feature set if their users will view the application through non-Microsoft browsers.

There are a number of key features of DHTML that overcome the disadvantages of earlier versions of HTML. First, DHTML provides an object model called the Document Object Model (DOM). This model exposes all page elements as objects. These objects can be manipulated from script to change element attributes and invoke element methods. Thus, an outline can be first shown in compacted form, then fully opened when the user clicks on it.

Because of DOM, page content, layout, and format can be altered through a program without refreshing the page from the server. Not only does this save time, but also the user is not confronted with flashing, changing pages whenever a headline changes. Instead, only the changing text portion is altered.

Another key feature of DHTML is supported for Cascading Style Sheets (CSS). This facility enables formats to be defined for the types of elements in a page. Thus, the following DHTML code will set background and color of level one and two headings:

⟨STYLE TYPE=“text/class”⟩

⟨!—

H1 { font-family:Lucida; font-style:normal; color:black}

H2 { font-family:Lucida; font-style:normal; color:green}

—⟩

⟨/STYLE⟩

In the document, when a level one or two head is encountered, it will appear as defined by the style element. Thus, in the following

⟨H2⟩

This is an example:

⟨/H2⟩

the level two heading "This is an example:" will appear in green, normal Lucida type. In this case, both styles referred to standard HTML tags (H1 and H2). It is also possible to define styles for developer-defined tags and then insert those tags into the document where needed.

With DHTML, it is possible for an element to have two conflicting styles. For example, a style sheet may specify a particular format for all paragraphs, but within a particular page, a given paragraph may be marked as having a different style. In this case, the style on the paragraph will override the style in the style sheet. As a general rule, the style markings closest to the content will be used. This characteristic is what causes such style sheets to be called *cascading* style sheets.

Style sheets can be contained within the page, or they can be obtained externally, from other documents that contain the style definitions. Thus, with DHTML, content and materialization can be separated.

The combination of style sheets and DOM mean that Web pages can be changed without page refreshes from the server. For example, style can be changed for level two headings as the mouse moves over level one headings; even more dramatic changes are possible.

All of these improvements to HTML are important, but none is as important to us as the changes that were made to facilitate data binding. A set of ActiveX controls and features called **Remote Data Services (RDS)** were developed to allow data to be cached (meaning copied and stored) locally on the client machine. That data can then be formatted, sorted, and filtered without a round trip back to the Web server. Also, display controls were made to be more interactive so that column widths and order could be changed by the user on the client machine—much as is done in Access 2000 table displays for non-Internet technology applications.

Two RDS controls are illustrated in Figure 11-14. Do not panic at this notation; you only need to gain the essence of the ideas presented here. You can find current examples by searching for the term *Remote Data Service* on www.microsoft.com.

This code first is executed on the Web server by ASP. Any script contained within percent signs will be executed on the server. For example, in the middle of the SCRIPT section, there is a statement

"http://⟨%=Request.ServerVariables("SERVER_NAME")%⟩"

when the ASP processor on the web server encounters this expression, it executes the code inside the %. In this case, it inserts a URL to itself, thus causing the Web page to refer back to the server. Of course, any valid script code can be inserted between %s for execution on the server. We will discuss other uses of this facility in the last section of this chapter and in Chapter 13.

Once the code inside the % has been processed, the resulting text stream is transmitted to the browser. There, the first two sections of this code create instances of two ActiveX objects; the first, named ADS1, is a remote data server data space and is used to create and manage a data cache on the browser. The result of a recordset will be placed in this cache. The second object is a data control used to display the cached data in the browser.

The VBScript shown in Figure 11-14 uses a method of the data space object called "DataFactory". This method sets up a data connection object on the Web server (at http:// . . .). Next, a query is executed against that data connection. The database is identified by the value of a DSN (data source name), which in this case is ViewRidge. This DSN value is the name of an ODBC data source, which you will learn about in Chapter 13. For now, just think of it as a special name that allows the Web server computer to establish a connection to a particular database on the database server computer.

Dynamic HTML
Example for
Presenting Query
Data in a Browser

```
<HTML>
<HEAD></HEAD>
<BODY>

<!-- RDS.DataSpace -->
<OBJECT ID="ADS1" WIDTH=1 HEIGHT=1
  CLASSID="CLSID:BD96C556-65A3-11D0-983A-00C04FC29E36">
</OBJECT>

<!-- RDS.DataControl -->
<OBJECT classid="clsid:BD96C556-65A3-11D0-983A-00C04FC29E33" ID=ADC1>
</OBJECT>
.

.

.
<SCRIPT LANGUAGE="VBScript">
Option Explicit
Sub Window_OnLoad()
  Dim ADF1, myRS
  Set ADF1 = ADS1.CreateObject("RDSServer.DataFactory", _
  "http://<%=Request.ServerVariables("SERVER_NAME")%>")
  Set myRS = _ ADF1.Query("DSN=ViewRidge;UID=sa;PWD=permission;", _
  "Select * From ARTIST")
  ' Assign the returned recordset to SourceRecordset.
  ADC1.SourceRecordset = myRS
End Sub
</SCRIPT>
</BODY>
</HTML>

<BR>
<Center>
<OBJECT ID="GRID" WIDTH=600 HEIGHT=200Datasrc="#ADC1"
  CODEBASE="http://<%=Request.ServerVariables("SERVER_NAME")%>
  /ViewRidge.cab" CLASSID="CLSID:AC
  05DC80-7DF1-11d0-839E-00A024A94B3A">
<PARAM NAME="_Version"        VALUE="131072">
<PARAM NAME="BackColor"       VALUE="-2147483643">
<PARAM NAME="BackColorOdd" VALUE="-2147483643">
<PARAM NAME="ForeColorEven" VALUE="0">
<PARAM NAME="AllowAddNew" VALUE="TRUE">
<PARAM NAME="AllowDelete" VALUE="TRUE">
<PARAM NAME="AllowUpdate" VALUE="TRUE">
</OBJECT>
<BR>
```

The SQL to be executed is passed as a parameter in the Query method. Here, we are obtaining all rows of the ARTIST table (using the database discussed in Chapter 10). Finally, a pointer to the resulting recordset is assigned to the SourceRecordset property of the data control object, ADC1. The result of these actions is to store the rows of the ARTIST table in the cache on the client computer.

The last section of code in this figure sets up the grid to display the cached data. The Datasrc parameter is set to ADC1, which is the name of the control that manages the cached data. The rest of the code sets some of the grid's properties and allowable actions. The result of all of this is the display of the artist data in a grid on the browser. Note that much formatting of the grid is automatic; the grid determines the number of columns and their names, for example, by examining properties of the ADC1 object.

To recap the discussion so far, DHTML provides three facilities that are important for Internet-technology database applications. The first is DOM, or the document object model. DOM allows code in Web pages to have full access to the elements on the page and to respond to user interface events like keystrokes and mouse moves. Thus, Web pages can be programmed like Visual Basic forms can be programmed. Second, DHTML supports cascading style sheets, which means that page formatting can be readily controlled and altered; it also allows formatting to be separated from content. Finally, DHTML provides a set of ActiveX objects that can be used to obtain (or send) data from the Web server (which in turn interfaces with the database server), and to dynamically display that data on the browser.

DHTML and HTML 4.0 correct many of the deficiencies in the original HTML. Fundamentally, however, they maintain the same structure and character of HTML. We will now turn to a page markup language having a fundamentally different nature.

ENTENSIBLE MARKUP LANGUAGE (XML)

XML, or the Extensible Markup Language, is a significantly better alternative to HTML and DHTML. There are a number of reasons for XML's superiority. For one, the designers of XML created a clear separation between document structure, content, and materialization. XML has facilities for dealing with each, and the nature of those facilities is such that they cannot be confounded as they can with HTML.

Additionally, XML is standardized, but as its name implies, the standards allow for extension by developers. With XML, you are not limited to a fixed set of elements like ⟨TITLE⟩, ⟨H1⟩, ⟨P⟩, but can create your own.

One of the problems with HTML and DHTML is that there is too much freedom. Consider the following HTML:

⟨h2⟩Hello World ⟨/h2⟩

This ⟨h2⟩ tag can be used to mark a level two heading in an outline. But, it can also be used simply to cause "Hello World" to be displayed with a particular style. Because of this characteristic, we cannot rely on tags to indicate the true structure of an HTML page. Tag use is too arbitrary; ⟨h2⟩ may mean a heading, or it may mean nothing at all.

As you will see, with XML, the structure of the document is formally defined. If we find the tag ⟨street⟩, we know exactly where that tag belongs and how it relates in the document structure to other tags. Thus, XML documents are said to accurately represent the semantics of their data.

XML is a broad topic that deserves a text of its own, but we just have this section to explore it. We must distill our discussion to the essential fundamentals. Supplement this section with the excellent material you can find on www.W3.org.

XML DOCUMENT STRUCTURE

Figure 11-15 shows a sample XML document. Notice that the document has two sections. The first section defines the structure of the document; it is referred to as the document type declaration or **DTD**. The second part is the document data.

The DTD begins with the word DOCTYPE and specifies the name of this type of document, which is customer. Then, it calls out the content of the customer document. It consists of two groups: name and address. The name group consists of two elements firstname and lastname. Firstname and lastname are defined as #PCDATA, which means they are strings of character data. Next, the address ele-

➤ FIGURE 11-15

Example XML Document

```
<!DOCTYPE customer [
        <!ELEMENT name (firstname, lastname)>
        <!ELEMENT firstname (#PCDATA)>
        <!ELEMENT lastname (#PCDATA)>
        <!ELEMENT address (street+, city, state, zip)>
        <!ELEMENT street (#PCDATA)>
        <!ELEMENT city (#PCDATA)>
        <!ELEMENT state (#PCDATA)>
        <!ELEMENT zip (#PCDATA)>
]>
<customer>
<name>
<firstname>Michelle</firstname>
<lastname>Correlli</lastname>
</name>
<address>
<street>1824 East 7th Avenue</street>
<street>Suite 700</street>
<city>Memphis</city>
<state>TN</state>
<zip>32123-7788</zip>
</address>
</customer>
```

ment is defined to consist of four elements: street, city, state, and zip. Each of these is also defined as character data. The plus sign after street indicates that one value is required and that multiple values are possible.

The data instance of customer shown in Figure 11-15 conforms to the DTD, hence this document is said to be a **type-valid XML document**. If it did not conform to the DTD it would be a **not-type-valid** document. Documents that are not-type-valid can still be perfectly good XML, they are just not valid instances of their type. For example, if the document in Figure 11-15 had two city elements, it would still be valid XML, but it would be not-type-valid.

While DTDs are almost always desirable, they are not required in XML documents. Documents that have no DTD are by definition not-type-valid, since there is no type to validate them against.

The DTD does not need to be contained inside the document. Figure 11-16 shows a customer document in which the DTD is obtained from the URL

➤ FIGURE 11-16

XML Document with External DTD

```
<!DOCTYPE customer SYSTEM "http://www.somewhere.com/dtds/customer.dtd>
<customer>
<name>
<firstname>Michelle</firstname>
<lastname>Correlli</lastname>
</name>
<address>
<street>1824 East 7th Avenue</street>
<street>Suite 700</street>
<city>Memphis</city>
<state>TN</state>
<zip>32123-7788</zip>
</address>
</customer>
```

⟨http://www.somewhere.com/dtds/customer.dtd⟩. The advantage of storing the DTD externally is that many documents can be validated against the same DTD.

The creator of a DTD is free to choose any elements he or she wants. Hence, XML documents can be extended, but in a standardized and controlled way. As you will see, DTDs can readily be used to represent database views.

The XML document in Figure 11-15 shows both the document's structure and content. Nothing in the document, however, indicates how it is to be materialized. As stated, the designers of XML created a clear separation among structure, content, and format.

MATERIALIZING XML DOCUMENTS

Two facilities are provided for materializing XML documents: CSS and XSL. We discussed CSS (cascading style sheets) in the section on DHTML; its use for XML documents is similar. That is, styles are defined for tags and applied in a cascading manner. Consider the following style definition for the document in Figure 11-15:

⟨STYLE TYPE=“text/class”⟩

⟨!—

customer	{ font-family:Lucida; font-style:normal; color:black}
name	{ font-family:Lucida; font-style:normal; color:green}
lastname	{ font-family:Lucida; font-style:normal; color:red}

—⟩

⟨/STYLE⟩

According to this style specification, the default color for the customer document is black. However, the color for name elements is overridden from black to green, and that for lastname elements is overridden from green to red. Hence the styles cascade over one another.

Currently, there is no standard agreement on where such style definitions are to be placed. They could be placed in the document or in an external file and a reference to them placed in the document. Different products implement them in different ways.

The second means of materializing XML documents is to use XSL, or the Extensible Style Language. XSL is more powerful and robust than CSS and will likely become the preferred way for materializing XML. Unfortunately, there is currently no agreed-upon XSL standard, and browsers are just now being announced with support for XSL. (Internet Explorer 5.0 is an example.) This situation is dynamic. Look for recent developments on the Web sites for W3C, Microsoft, Netscape, and other companies that have emerged since this was written.

XSL is a declarative, transformation language. It is declarative because instead of specifying a procedure for materializing document elements, you create a set of rules that govern how the document is to be materialized. It is transformational because it transforms the input document into another document. In the simplest case, XSL transforms an XML document into an equivalent HTML document. But, XSL can also be used to change the document into a different structure. For example, XSL could be used to transform an XML document in one form into another XML document with a different form, for example, transform a document into an index on that document.

Figure 11-17 shows a customerlist XML document with data for two customers. It has a DTD and is a type-valid document. The statement after the DTD invokes the XSL stylesheet named CustomerList.xsl, which is shown in Figure 11-18. The result of the processing of this XML document is shown in Figure 11-19.

➤ FIGURE 11-17

Customer List XML Document

```
<?xml version='1.0'?>
<!DOCTYPE customerlist [
        <!ELEMENT  customer (name, address) >
        <!ELEMENT  name (firstname, lastname)>
        <!ELEMENT  firstname (#PCDATA)>
        <!ELEMENT  lastname (#PCDATA)>
        <!ELEMENT  address (street+, city, state, zip)>
        <!ELEMENT  street (#PCDATA)>
        <!ELEMENT  city (#PCDATA)>
        <!ELEMENT  state (#PCDATA)>
        <!ELEMENT  zip (#PCDATA)>
]>

<?xml:stylesheet type="text/xsl" href="CustomerList.xsl" ?>

<customerlist>
<customer>
<name>
<firstname>Michelle</firstname>
<lastname>Correlli</lastname>
</name>
<address>
<street>1824 East 7th Avenue</street>
<street>Suite 700</street>
<city>Memphis</city>
<state>TN</state>
<zip>32123-7788</zip>
</address>
<customer>

<customer>
<name>
<firstname>Lynda</firstname>
<lastname>Jaynes</lastname>
</name>
<address>
<street>2 Elm Street</street>
<city>New York City</city>
<state>NY</state>
<zip>02123-7445</zip>
</address>
</customer>
</customerlist>
```

This style sheet uses the XSL facilities in Microsoft's Internet Explorer 5.0, which has an XSL processor that can be accessed from the stylesheet. In Figure 11-18, for example, any of the elements that begin ⟨xsl: are invoking the Internet Explorer 5.0 XSL processor.

The logic of XSL stylesheets is of the form *{match, action}*. The idea is that the XSL processor will look for a match for an element in the document, and when one is found, take the indicated action. Thus, the first xsl statement

⟨xsl:for-each select="customerlist/customer"/⟩

starts a search in the document for an element labeled customerlist. When one is found, a second search is started for an element labeled customer (it must be

► FIGURE 11-18

*Sample XSL
Document Using
Internet Explorer XSL
COM Facility*

```
<?xml version="1.0"?>
<HTML xmlns:xsl="http://www.w3.org/TR/WD-xsl">
  <BODY STYLE="font-family:Arial, helvetica, sans-serif; font-size:14pt;
                              background-color:teal">

  <xsl:for-each select="customerlist/customer">
      <DIV STYLE="background-color:purple; color:white; padding:4px">
          <SPAN STYLE="font-weight:bold; color:white">
              <xsl:value-of select="name/lastname"/></SPAN>
              - <xsl:value-of select="name/firstname"/>
      </DIV>

      <xsl:for-each select="address/street">
        <DIV STYLE="margin-left:20px; margin-bottom:1em; font-size:10pt;
                              font-style:bold; color:blue">
              <xsl:value-of select="node()"/>
      <DIV>
      <xsl:for-each>

      <DIV STYLE="margin-left:20px; margin-bottom:1em; font-size:12pt;
                  font-style:bold"><xsl:value-of select="address/city"/>,
              <xsl:value-of select="address/zip"/>
      </DIV>

      <DIV STYLE="margin-left:20px; margin-bottom:1em; font-size:14pt; color:red">
              <xsl:value-of select="address/zip"/>
      </DIV>
  <xsl:for-each>

  </body>
</HTML>
```

within customerlist). If a match is found, the actions indicated in the loop that ends with ⟨/xsl:for-each⟩ (third from the bottom in the style sheet) are taken.

Within the loop, styles are set for each element in customer within customerlist. Notice the inner for-each loop that handles the possibility of more than one street element.

XSL processors are context oriented; each statement is evaluated in the context of the match that has been made. Thus, the statement

⟨xsl:value-of select="name/lastname"⟩

operates in the context of the customerlist/customer match that has been made. There is no need to code

⟨xsl:select="customerlist/customer/name/lastname"/⟩

because the context has already been set to customerlist/customer. In fact, if the select were coded in this second way, nothing would be found. Similarly, ⟨xsl:select "lastname"/⟩ results in no match because lastname occurs only in the context customerlist/customer/name and not in the context customerlist/customer.

This context orientation explains the need for the statement

⟨xsl:value-of select="node()"/⟩

(in the center of the style sheet). The context at the location of this statement has been set to customerlist/customer/address/street. Hence, the current node is a street element, and this expression indicates that the value of that node is to be produced.

► FIGURE 11-19

Materialization Using XSL in Figure 11-18

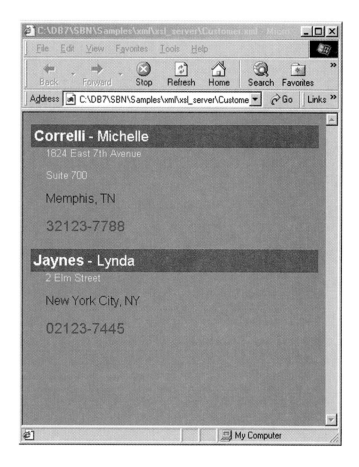

Observe, too, that a small transformation has been made by the stylesheet. The original document has firstname followed by lastname, but the output stream (shown in Figure 11-19) has lastname followed by firstname.

This example uses the Microsoft version of XSL that was current with the shipment of Internet Explorer 5.0. At the time, there was no agreed on W3C standard for XSL. As one becomes available, Microsoft will likely change this product. Further, other vendors will develop their own XSL engines. Hence, treat this example as just that: a simple, easily understood use of XSL. Better versions will be along, so keep watching!

THE IMPORTANCE OF XML TO DATABASE APPLICATIONS

XML may be the most important development for database applications since the relational model. Figure 11-20 lists the reasons why. For one, XML provides a standard means for expressing the structure of database views. Because of the standard, any application that can interpret a DTD can process any arbitrary type-valid XML document that contains a database view. That means that database applications can transmit and process arbitrary views.

Figure 11-21 shows a DTD for the View Ridge Artist View from Figure 10-4. Prior to the XML standard, for two programs to exchange this view, they would need to develop a private protocol for specifying its structure. With XML, they need only interpret the DTD Figure 11-21; there need not be any prior agreement on a protocol.

In the past, developers used SQL as a stand-in for a standard way for describing database view data. As you learned in Chapter 10, however, SQL cannot be used for any view that involves more than one multi-value path through the

FIGURE 11-20

*XML Characteristics
Important to Database
Applications*

Standard means for expressing database views

Clean separation of structure, content, and materialization

Document validity checking

Standards for XML document types

schema. The view in Figure 11-21 has two multi-value paths; one through Transaction and one through Artist. Hence, multiple SQL statements are required, and there is no standard way to express how they should be connected. XML overcomes this deficiency.

The second major benefit of XML is the clean breaks between structure, content, and materialization. The structure of a document can be stored in one place as a DTD and all documents based on that structure can include references to it. Boeing, for example, can place a DTD for airplane part orders on one of its Web sites, and all airplane part purchasers can use that DTD when creating order documents.

Companies that order from Boeing can develop their own database applications to construct XML order documents that conform to the DTD structure. The means they use to create such documents is completely hidden from Boeing and everyone else. They might use a database application or they might use a word processor; how the data is created is unknown and unimportant.

Furthermore, Boeing can develop many different XSL stylesheets for materializing this document. They can have one for their order entry department, one for their production department, one for their accounting department, and one for their marketing department. They can also provide one for use by their customers. Boeing's customers can also create their own stylesheets for documents based on this DTD. Thus, everyone can materialize the content of the standard order document in whatever way is appropriate for them.

Document validity checking is a third important characteristic of XML. Using the Boeing example, when a customer creates an order document, they can

FIGURE 11-21

*DTD for the View
Ridge Customer View
(Figure 10-4)*

```
<!DOCTYPE customerview [
    <!ELEMENT customer (name, phone, transaction*, interestedartist*) >
    <!ELEMENT name (#PCDATA)>
    <!ELEMENT phone (areacode, localnumber)>
    <!ELEMENT areacode (#PCDATA)>
    <!ELEMENT localnumber (#PCDATA)>
    <!ELEMENT transaction (purchasedate, salesprice, work)>
    <!ELEMENT purchasedate (#PCDATA)>
    <!ELEMENT salesprice (#PCDATA)>
    <!ELEMENT work (workartistname, title, copy)>
    <!ELEMENT workartistname (#PCDATA)>
    <!ELEMENT title (#PCDATA)>
    <!ELEMENT copy (#PCDATA)>
    <!ELEMENT interestedartist (#PCDATA)>

]>
```

* denotes zero to many instances are allowed

verify the validity of that document against the DTD. In this way they can ensure that they are transmitting only type-valid orders. Similarly, when Boeing Web sites receive order documents, they can automatically check them against the DTD to ensure that they are accepting only type-valid documents.

Such validity checking can be performed without XML, but it is much more difficult. Boeing would need to develop a specialized program to validate order documents and then send that specialized program to all customers or departments who need it. They would need to create a different specialized program for a second document type, and a third for a third document type, and so forth. With the XML standard, they need only place DTDs in a public location and all interested parties can validate their own documents of the varying types.

The last important advantage is that with XML, industry groups can develop industry-wide DTDs and other XML standards. Figure 11-22 lists some of the standards that exist or are in process of creation. For example, the financial community is in the process of developing standards for documents involving funds transfer, payments, statements, and the like. With these standards, organizations or individuals can create XML documents from whatever sources they have and validate those documents against the DTD. Further, industry groups can develop XSL stylesheets to materialize them in specific ways. Undoubtedly governments will be large users of the XML standard. Tax forms are obvious candidates for conversion to XML documents.

➤ FIGURE 11-22

Example of Evolving Industry XML Standards

Name	Purpose
XML/EDI	DTDs for use in electronic data interchange. Allows organizations to exchange documents without concern for how the data is stored. Heterogeneous systems can exchange data.
Open Financial Exchange	DTD specifications for financial services. Supports transfers of funds, payments, statements, and related documents in the financial industry.
HL7 Kona Proposal	Standards for documents used in the medical community. Allows for hybrid documents of standard and application-specific content.
Channel Definition Format (CDF)	Specification of document exchange for channels use for push publishing. A channel is a set of documents that is treated as a unit.
Resource Description Format	Standard for describing the contents of a web site. Can be used by search engines or intelligent agents.

Source: www.texcel.no/sgm197.htm

➤ THE ROLE OF WEB SERVERS: IIS AND ASP

We conclude this chapter with a discussion of the role of Web servers using Microsoft IIS and ASP as examples. The functionality described here can be found with other products. We are just using these products to illustrate capabilities.

The Web server is the middle tier in the three-tier architecture, so it comes as no surprise that it operates as a middle-man between the data source and the browser. Functions that it serves for database applications are listed in Figure 11-23.

MAINTAINING STATE

The first function is the maintenance of session state. As stated at the beginning of this chapter, HTTP is a stateless protocol. When the browser makes a request of the server, the server responds to that request and then forgets about the client.

This stateless behavior is fine for serving graphics, brochures, and other display-only documents, but it will not do for database transactions. In an order processing application, for example, the client may request five units of some product. The request is sent to the Web server, which, in turn, accesses the database server to determine if five units are available. When the database server responds, the Web server needs to send the result back to the same client that issued the request. Consequently, it needs to maintain the identity of that client.

One of the functions of the ASP processor is to maintain such state. When the first request is made for an application (for example, some user types *http://someserver/anapplication/default.asp* or the equivalent), ASP retrieves the indicated asp page from storage and creates two objects: an application object and session object. The application object references the application in use and the session object references the client that issued the request for that application. When a second user makes a request for that same application, a second session object is created. ASP will maintain the application object as long as there is at least one session object using it. Each session object will exist until either the client exits the application or until the session is inactive for 20 minutes (an interval that can be changed in the IIS administration settings).

➤ FIGURE 11-23

Functions Provided by the Web Server for Database Applications

Maintain session state

Provide server side scripting environment for

      Communication with db server

      Data caching

      Constraint enforcement

      View construction (XML or other)

      Security and control

      Application logic

      View materialization (for materialization-impaired browsers)

DTD and Stylesheet publishing

The properties of both the application and the session objects can be referenced by script in the ASP page. In addition, the application can create new properties for them as well. In an order entry application, a developer could record a quantity requested, say 5, with the statement

SESSION("NumberRequested") = 5

In response, the ASP processor would create a property named NumberRequested and save the value of 5 in it for this particular user. Later, the ASP script could obtain the property's value with a statement like

N = SESSION("NumberRequested").

In this way, session identity and data can be maintained in the server. This is a relatively expensive way to store data, however, and if a lot of session data needs to be maintained, it should be written to a database. A session property could then be used to point to the relevant rows in the database for that session.

SERVER SIDE SCRIPTING ENVIRONMENT

The second function of the Web server is to maintain a server-side scripting environment. Chapter 10 discussed five functions for a database application: process (CRUD) views, materialize views, enforce constraints, provide security and control, and execute application logic. With newer browsers that support CSS and XSL, the materialization function can be handed off to the browser. As discussed in Chapter 10, some of the constraint enforcement and security functions can be handed off to the DBMS on the database server. Otherwise, all of the application functions must be performed in ASP pages. This fact caused one industry pundit to refer to ASP pages as the COBOL programs of the 21st century.

Not all of this work need be done in JScript or VBScript. Some of the logic can be contained in pre-built COM objects or in Java servlets (Java programs that are executed by a Java virtual machine on the Web server). Common functions for database applications on the server are listed in Figure 11-23. Chapter 13 will illustrate these functions for example ASP pages for a sample database application.

STYLESHEET AND DTD PUBLISHING

One last important function for a Web server in a database application is to publish both stylesheets and DTDs. As indicated, DHTML and XML pages can reference external CSS styles. XML pages can also reference XSL style sheets and DTDs. These documents need to be stored and served from a Web server.

This chapter has focused on the first two tiers of the three-tier architecture. The next chapter will focus on functions that are performed on the database server. We will then bring all three tiers together for an example application in Chapter 13.

➤ SUMMARY

A computer network is a collection of computers that communicate using a standardized protocol. Public networks can be used by anyone who pays the required fee; users of private networks must be preauthorized to connect to the network. The Internet is a public computer network based on the TCP/IP protocol. The Internet began as a military research project known as ARPANET. In 1984, MILNET split off from ARPANET, and over time ARPANET has come to be known as the Internet.

Services available on the Internet include mail, newsgroups, TelNet, FTP, and the World Wide Web. Initially, almost all Internet users ran a version of UNIX, and base-level Internet commands have a UNIX flavor to them. In 1989, the hypertext transfer protocol or HTTP was proposed at CERN. The hypertext markup language (HTML), a subset of the standard generalized markup language (SGML), was proposed at the same time. In 1993, NCSA invented a graphical HTML display program known as Mosaic. Today Mosaic, Netscape Navigator, and Microsoft Internet Explorer are the most popular Web browsers. HTML, URL, and MIME type codes are three standards that emerged from the early days of the Web that are important to network database applications. Web applications are request-oriented and stateless.

An intranet is a private LAN or WAN that uses TCP/IP, HTML, and browsers. Intranets are either not connected to the Internet or are connected via a firewall. Intranets have performance that is orders of magnitude faster than that of the Internet. Three common types of network database applications are static report publishing, query publishing, and application publishing.

Most database applications that use Internet technology have a three-tier architecture: a database server, a Web server, and client computers. Each of these tiers can use a different operating system and products from different vendors. The purpose of the database server is to run the DBMS to process SQL and to provide multi-user database services. The Web server is an HTTP server that hosts scripting languages and enables the database application to process database views (CRUD). The client machine operates as an HTTP client that hosts a second scripting environment and materializes database views. Common Web servers are Microsoft's IIS, Netscape Web Server, and Apache. Active Server Pages are commonly used with IIS on Windows servers and the Common Gateway Interface (CGI) is commonly used with UNIX servers.

The standard for Internet scripting languages is ECMAScript-262. JScript is an implementation of this standard and JavaScript is nearly an implementation of it. VBScript is also used for scripting Internet-technology applications, but it does not operate on all browsers. Perl is a unique, interpreted language that is commonly used with CGI. Java is a fully featured object-oriented language that generates byte code that can run on any operating system that has a Java byte code interpreter. Visual Basic and C++ can be used to create ActiveX objects. The relationship of COM, OLE, ActiveX objects, and ActiveX controls is summarized in Figure 11-13.

Standards are important for markup languages so that Web pages can be processed on any browser. The W3C publishes standards and administers the process of developing them. Commercial products can extend standards, but when they do, they create problems for users of products that do not support the extensions. HTML 4.0 was developed as a standard to overcome problems in earlier versions of HTML. Microsoft's dynamic HTML (DHTML) implements and extends HTML 4.0. Three features of DHTML are important to database applications: the Document Object Model (DOM), Cascading Style Sheets (CSS), and Remote Data Services (RD)—a set of ActiveX controls that allow for caching and materialization of data on the client without round trips to and from the server.

The Extensible Markup Language (XML) is a markup language that was designed to provide a clear separation among document structure, content, and materialization. It is extendable, but in a standardized way. Document structure is defined by document-type descriptions (DTDs); XML documents that conform to their DTDs are type-valid documents. XML documents can be materialized using either CSS or the Extensible Style Language (XSL). XSL is a declarative, transform facility for manipulating XML documents. XSL can be used to transform an XML document into HTML or into another XML document having different structure.

XML is most important to database applications because it provides a standard means for expressing the structure of database views; it cleanly breaks document structure, content, and materialization; it allows for standardized document validly checking; and it enables industry groups to define useful standards for the structure of industry-standard database views.

Web servers operate in the middle tier between data sources and client browsers. The Active Server Processor in IIS is important to database applications because it provides a means to maintain state over the otherwise stateless HTTP protocol, it hosts a server scripting environment that can be used to perform all of the functions of a database application as defined in Chapter 10, and it publishes style sheets and XSL documents.

➤ GROUP I QUESTIONS

11.1   Define the terms *network*, *public network*, and *private network*.

11.2   Define *Internet*.

11.3   What is TCP/IP, and how it is used?

11.4   List and explain four Internet services besides the World Wide Web.

11.5   Define HTTP and explain its role.

11.6   Define HTML and explain its role.

11.7   What does SGML stand for?

11.8   What is a browser? Name two important browser products.

11.9   What is a URL? Give two examples.

11.10 What is MIME and how is it used?

11.11 Explain why HTTP is both request-oriented and stateless. Why does this matter to database applications?

11.12 What is the difference between an intranet and the Internet?

11.13 What is the purpose of a firewall?

11.14 List and briefly describe three types of database publishing on the Web.

11.15 Name the three tiers in an Internet-technology database application. Describe the role of each.

11.16 Explain how the three-tier architecture allows for interoperability of operating systems and Web products.

11.17 Explain the function of each of the components of the Web server in Figure 11-8.

11.18 Explain the function of each of the components of the Web server in Figure 11-9.

11.19 Explain the relationship of JavaScript, JScript, and ECMAScript-262.

11.20 Compare and contrast the advantages and disadvantages of JScript and VBScript.

11.21 What is Perl, and why is it often used with CGI?

11.22 Define COM, OLE, ActiveX objects, and ActiveX controls.

11.23 Explain how ActiveX controls can be used for Internet-technology database applications.

11.24 Why are standards important for markup languages?

11.25 What is W3C, and why is it important?

11.26 Why do vendors have a love/hate relationship with standards?

11.27 Summarize the disadvantages of early versions of HTML.

11.28 What is the difference between DHTML and HTML 4.0?

11.29 Define DOM and explain its importance.

11.30 Define CSS and explain its importance.

11.31 Define RDS and explain its importance.

11.32 Describe, in general terms, the purpose of the two controls in Figure 11-14.

11.33 Is a knowledge of SQL important when using RDS? Explain why or why not.

11.34 Define XML and explain why it is superior to HTML and DHTML.

11.35 Explain why there is too much freedom with HTML.

11.36 What is a DTD, and why is it important?

11.37 Define *type-valid* and *not-type-valid* XML documents.

11.38 Explain how CSS is used with XML documents.

11.39 Define XSL and explain its importance.

11.40 Why is XSL declarative? Why is it transformational?

11.41 Explain the importance of context when working with XSL.

11.42 Why is XML important to database applications?

11.43 Why is SQL not an effective way for defining the structure of database views?

11.44 Explain the three important functions served by ASP for Internet-technology database applications.

➤ GROUP II QUESTIONS

11.45 Visit www.w3.org and determine what is the current recommended standard for HTML. How does it differ from that described in this chapter? Is there a new standard for HTML underway? If so, what is it and what new features will it have?

11.46 Visit www.w3.org and determine what is the current recommended standard for XSL. How does it differ from the implementation of XSL as described in this chapter for Internet Explorer 5.0? What XSL standards are in process?

11.47 Search the Web for products besides Internet Explorer 5.0 that support XSL. Explain the purpose, features, and functions of two of them.

11.48 Visit www.microsoft.com and search for Remote Data Services. How have the features, functions, and facilities of RDS changed since this chapter was written?

➤ PROJECT

A. Suppose that the Metropolitan Housing Authority (Project A at the end of Chapter 3) wants to use an Internet database application to maintain its inventory of low income housing units. Assume that the users of the application reside in a number of different government and non-profit organizations.

   1. Sketch a possible three-tier system for supporting this application. Assume the data resides in an Access database. Describe the functions of each of the tiers and of the major components on each of the tiers. Assume Windows 2000 is used on the Web server.

2. Repeat Question A.1, but assume UNIX is used on the Web server.

3. Describe the advantage of using DHTML over HTML for this application. What are the risks of using it?

4. Assuming Windows 2000 is used for the Web server, compare and contrast the advantages and disadvantages of JScript and VBScript. Which would you recommend?

5. Design a database view of the Apartments in a Building. Using Figure 11-15 as a guide, develop a DTD of an XML document that defines your view. Show two sample Apartment XML documents.

6. Using the XSL in Figure 11-18 as a guide, develop an XSL document for materializing your view.

7. If you can gain access to Internet Explorer 5.0, materialize your Apartment XML views using your XSL document.

CHAPTER 12

Managing Multi-user Databases

Database applications on the Internet or on organizational intranets can have dozens, hundreds, or even thousands of users. The databases in such systems become immeasurably valuable assets. Consider, for example, the value of the inventory database to Amazon.com or the production database to Dell Computer. Because these databases are so valuable, they need to be managed and protected with great care.

In this chapter we consider four important topics regarding multi-user database management. First, we discuss concurrency control, which concerns the management of data activity so that one user's work does not inappropriately influence another's. Second, we address database reliability, or what happens when failure occurs. Failures can be modest, like a single user connection failure, or they can be serious, like the loss of disk media that contains the database metadata.

The third management issue is database security. Internet-technology applications involve several layers of security: operating system security, network/communications security, and database security. In this chapter, we are concerned just with DBMS security. Internet and intranet databases are shared, and from time immemorial, humans have difficulty sharing. We conclude this chapter by discussing database administration—a function that must exist to protect the database and ensure that it is used to benefit all of the user community.

The ideas presented in this chapter have evolved over the past 30 years. They were learned in the early days of mainframe database processing, and applied (in some cases relearned) in the early days of client–server database processing. Today they are being applied again to Internet and intranet database processing. Unfortunately, not everyone who is building an Internet-technology database understands the necessity of multi-user database management. The goal of this chapter is to give you the benefit of these ideas so that you do not need to learn them from your own mistakes and hard experience.

As you learned in Chapter 11, the database server can run any multi-user operating system with any multi-user DBMS. Common product sets include Windows 2000 with Access 2000, SQL Server, or ORACLE. Another popular set is UNIX with ORACLE, Sybase, or Informix. Each of these products implements concurrency control, reliability, and security in different ways and you may work with a variety of them in your career. Consequently, we do not want to consider how a particular product achieves these ends. Instead, we focus on the concepts that are applicable to all of these products. You will then be able to apply these concepts to the features, functions, and terminology of the products that you encounter.

➤ CONCURRENCY CONTROL

Concurrency control measures are taken to ensure that one user's work does not inappropriately influence another user's work. In some cases, these measures ensure that a user gets the same result when processing with other users as he or she would have received if processing alone. In other cases, it means that the user's work is influenced by other users, but in an anticipated way.

For example, in an order-entry system, a user should be able to enter an order and get the same result regardless of whether there are no other users or hundreds of other users. On the other hand, a user who is printing a report of the most current inventory status, may want to obtain in-process data changes from other users, even if there is a danger that those changes may later be aborted.

Unfortunately, no concurrency control technique or mechanism is ideal for all circumstances. They all involve trade-offs. For example, a user can obtain very strict concurrency control by locking the entire database, but while he or she is processing, no other user will be able to do anything. This is strict protection, but at a high cost. As you will see, other measures are available that are more difficult to program or enforce but that allow more throughput. Still other measures are available that maximize throughput, but for a low level of concurrency control. When designing Internet-technology database applications, you will need to choose among these trade-offs.

THE NEED FOR ATOMIC TRANSACTIONS

In most database applications, users submit work in the form of **transactions**, which are also known as **logical units of work** (LUWs). A transaction (or LUW) is a series of actions to be taken on the database such that either all of them are performed successfully or none of them is performed at all, in which case the database remains unchanged. Such a transaction is sometimes called **atomic**, since it is performed as a unit.

Consider the following sequence of database actions that could occur when recording a new order:

1. Change the customer record, increasing Amount Owed.
2. Change the salesperson record, increasing Commission Due.
3. Insert the new order record into the database.

Suppose the last step failed, perhaps because of insufficient file space. Imagine the confusion that would ensue if the first two changes were made but not the third one. The customer would be billed for an order never received, and a salesperson would receive a commission on an order that was never sent to the customer. Clearly, these three actions need to be taken as a unit—either all of them should be done or none of them should be done.

Figure 12-1 compares the results of performing these activities as a series of independent steps [Figure 12-1(a)] and as an atomic transaction [Figure 12-1(b)]. Notice that when the steps are carried out atomically and one fails, no changes are made in the database. Also note that the commands Start Transaction,

Comparison of the Results of Applying Serial Actions Versus a Multiple-Step Transaction: (a) Two out of Three Activities Successfully Completed, Resulting in Database Anomalies, and (b) No Change Made Because Entire Transaction Not Successful

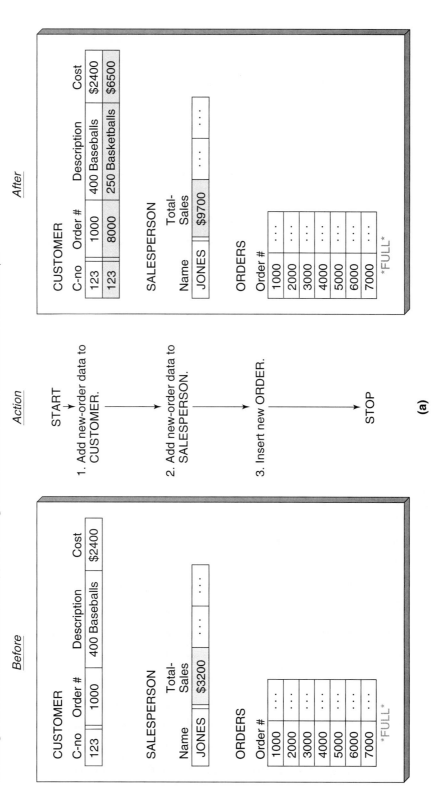

▲ FIGURE 12-1

(Continued)

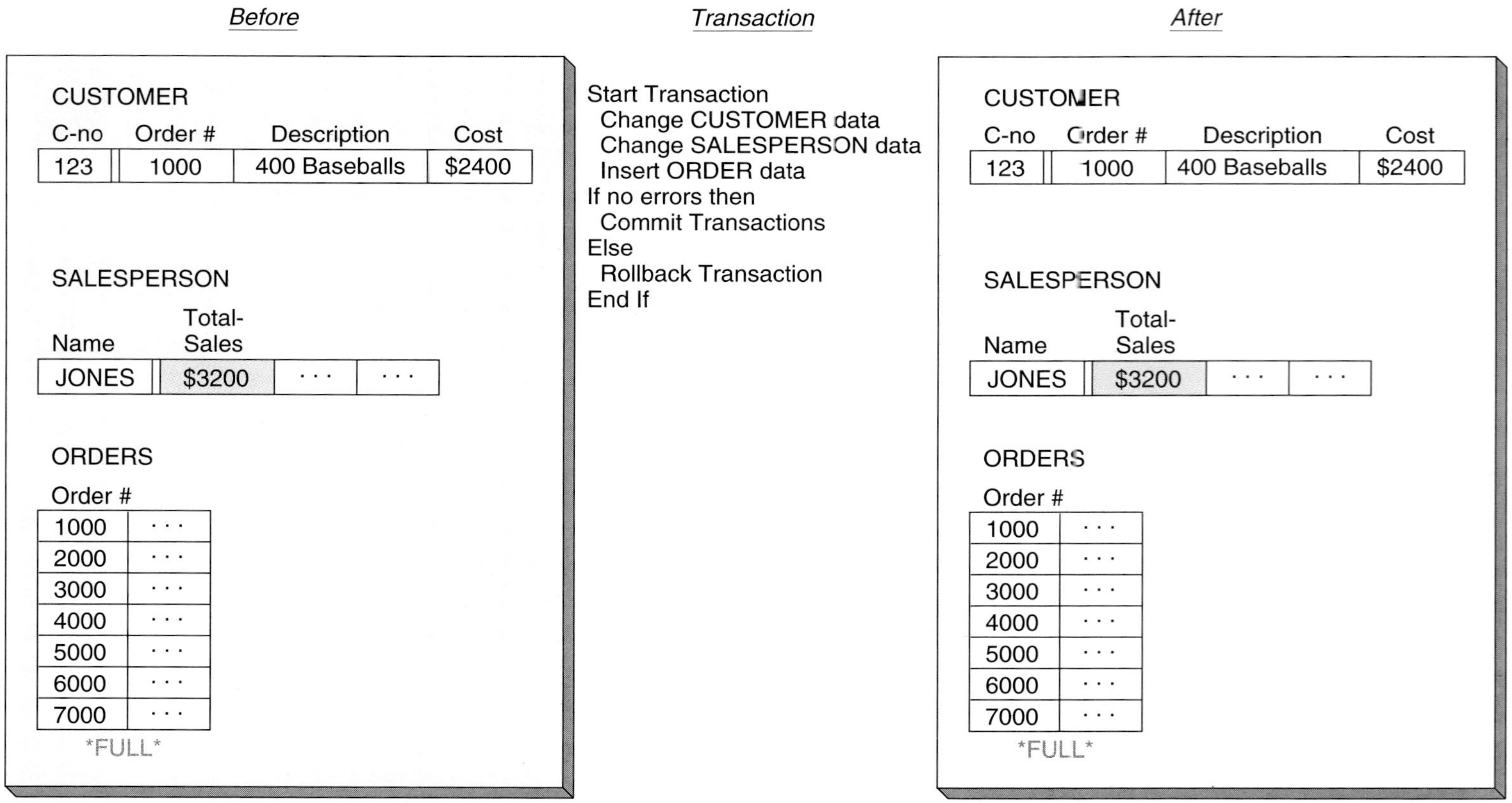

Before

CUSTOMER

C-no	Order #	Description	Cost
123	1000	400 Baseballs	$2400

SALESPERSON

Name	Total-Sales		
JONES	$3200	...	...

ORDERS

Order #
1000 ...
2000 ...
3000 ...
4000 ...
5000 ...
6000 ...
7000 ...

FULL

Transaction

Start Transaction
  Change CUSTOMER data
  Change SALESPERSON data
  Insert ORDER data
  If no errors then
    Commit Transactions
  Else
    Rollback Transaction
  End If

After

CUSTOMER

C-no	Order #	Description	Cost
123	1000	400 Baseballs	$2400

SALESPERSON

Name	Total-Sales		
JONES	$3200	...	...

ORDERS

Order #
1000 ...
2000 ...
3000 ...
4000 ...
5000 ...
6000 ...
7000 ...

FULL

(b)

Commit Transaction, or Rollback Transaction must be issued by the application program to mark the boundaries of the transaction logic. The particular form of these commands varies from one DBMS product to another.

CONCURRENT TRANSACTION PROCESSING When two transactions are being processed against a database at the same time, they are termed *concurrent transactions*. While it may appear to the users that concurrent transactions are being processed simultaneously, this cannot be true, since the CPU of the machine processing the database can execute only one instruction at a time. Usually transactions are interleaved, which means that the operating system switches CPU services among tasks so that some portion of each of them is carried out in a given interval. This switching among tasks is done so quickly that two people seated at browsers side by side, processing the same database, may believe that their two transactions are completed simultaneously, but, in reality, the two transactions are interleaved.

Figure 12-2 shows two concurrent transactions. User A's transaction reads Item 100, changes it, and rewrites it in the database. User B's transaction takes the same actions, but on Item 200. The CPU processes User A until it encounters an I/O interrupt or some other delay for User A. The operating system shifts control to User B. The CPU now processes User B until an interrupt, at which point the operating system passes control back to User A. To the users, the processing appears to be simultaneous, but actually it is interleaved, or concurrent.

LOST UPDATE PROBLEM The concurrent processing illustrated in Figure 12-2 poses no problems because the users are processing different data. But suppose that both users want to process Item 100. For example, User A wants to order five units of Item 100, and User B wants to order three units of the same item.

Figure 12-3 illustrates the problem. User A reads Item 100's record into a user work area. According to the record, there are 10 items in inventory. Then User B reads Item 100's record into another user work area. Again, according to the record there are 10 in inventory. Now User A takes five, decrements the count of items in its user work area to five, and rewrites the record for Item 100. Then User B takes three, decrements the count in its user work area to seven, and rewrites the record for Item 100. The database now shows, incorrectly, that there are seven Item 100s in inventory. To review: We started with 10 in inventory, User A took five, User B took three, and the database shows that seven are in inventory. Clearly, this is a problem.

➤ FIGURE 12-2

Example of Concurrent Processing of Two Users' Tasks

User A
1. Read item 100.
2. Change item 100.
3. Write item 100.

User B
1. Read item 200.
2. Change item 200.
3. Write item 200.

Order of processing at database server
1. Read item 100 for A.
2. Read item 200 for B.
3. Change item 100 for A.
4. Write item 100 for A.
5. Change item 200 for B.
6. Write item 200 for B.

➤ FIGURE 12-3

Lost Update Problem

User A

1. Read item 100
   (assume item count is 10).
2. Reduce count of items by 5.
3. Write item 100.

User B

1. Read item 100
   (assume item count is 10).
2. Reduce count of items by 3.
3. Write item 100.

Order of processing at database server

1. Read item 100 (for A).
2. Read item 100 (for B).
3. Set item count to 5 (for A).
4. Write item 100 for A.
5. Set item count to 7 (for B).
6. Write item 100 for B.

Note: The change and write in Steps 3 and 4 are lost.

Both users obtained data that were correct at the time they obtained them. But when User B read the record, User A already had a copy that it was about to update. This situation is called the **lost update problem** or the **concurrent update problem**. There is another, similar problem, called the **inconsistent read problem**. With it, User A reads data that have been processed by a portion of a transaction from User B. As a result, User A reads incorrect data.

One remedy for the inconsistencies caused by concurrent processing is to prevent multiple applications from obtaining copies of the same record when the record is about to be changed. This remedy is called **resource locking**.

RESOURCE LOCKING

One way to prevent concurrent processing problems is to disallow sharing by locking data that are retrieved for update. Figure 12-4 shows the order of processing using a **lock** command. Because of the lock User B's transaction must wait until User A is finished with the Item 100 data. Using this strategy, User B can read Item 100's record only after User A has completed the modification. In this case, the final item count stored in the database is two, as it should be. (We started with 10, A took five, and B took three, leaving two.)

LOCK TERMINOLOGY Locks can be placed either automatically by the DBMS or by a command issued to the DBMS from the application program or query user. Locks placed by the DBMS are called **implicit locks**; those placed by command are called **explicit locks**.

In the preceding example, the locks were applied to rows of data. Not all locks are applied at this level, however. Some DBMS products lock at the page level, some at the table level, and some at the database level. The size of a lock is referred to as the **lock granularity**. Locks with large granularity are easy for the DBMS to administer but frequently cause conflicts. Locks with small granularity are difficult to administer (there are many more details for the DBMS to keep track of and check), but conflicts are less common.

Locks also vary by type. An **exclusive lock** locks the item from access of any type. No other transaction can read or change the data. A **shared lock** locks the item from change but not from read. That is, other transactions can read the item as long as they do not attempt to alter it.

Concurrent Processing with Explicit Locks

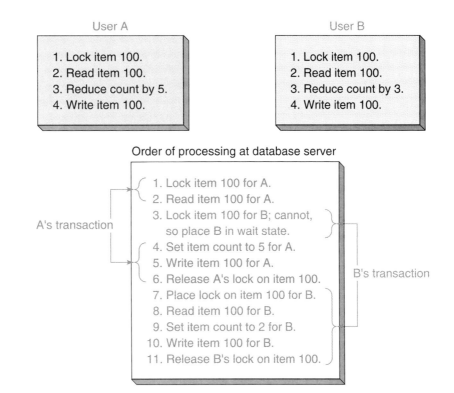

SERIALIZABLE TRANSACTIONS When two or more transactions are processed concurrently, the results in the database should be logically consistent with the results that would have been achieved had the transactions been processed in an arbitrary serial fashion. A scheme for processing concurrent transactions in this way is said to be **serializable**.

Serializability can be achieved by a number of different means. One way is to process the transaction using **two-phased locking**. With this strategy, transactions are allowed to obtain locks as necessary, but once the first lock is released, no other lock can be obtained. Transactions thus have a **growing phase**, in which the locks are obtained, and a **shrinking phase**, in which the locks are released.

A special case of two-phased locking is used with a number of DBMS products. With it, locks are obtained throughout the transaction, but no lock is released until the COMMIT or ROLLBACK command is issued. This strategy is more restrictive than two-phase locking requires, but it is easier to implement.

In general, the boundaries of a transaction should correspond to the definition of the database view it is processing. Following the two-phase strategy, the rows of each relation in the view are locked as needed. Changes are made, but the data are not committed to the database until all of the view has been processed. At this point, changes are made in the actual database, and all locks are released.

Consider an order-entry transaction that involves an object CUSTOMER-ORDER that is constructed from data in the CUSTOMER table, the SALESPERSON table, and the ORDER table. To make sure that the database will suffer no anomalies due to concurrency, the order-entry transaction issues locks on CUSTOMER, SALESPERSON, and ORDER as needed and concludes by making all the database changes and then releasing all its locks.

DEADLOCK Although locking solves one problem, it introduces another. Consider what might happen when two users want to order two items from inventory. Suppose User A wants to order some paper, and if she can get the paper,

► FIGURE 12-5

Deadlock

User A

1. Lock paper.
2. Take paper.
3. Lock pencils.

User B

1. Lock pencils.
2. Take pencils.
3. Lock paper.

Order of processing at database server

1. Lock paper for user A.
2. Lock pencils for user B.
3. Process A's requests; write paper record.
4. Process B's requests; write pencil record.
5. Put A in wait state for pencils.
6. Put B in wait state for paper.
            ** Locked **

she wants to order some pencils. Then suppose User B wants to order some pencils, and if he can get the pencils, he wants to order some paper. The order of processing could be that shown in Figure 12-5.

In this figure, users A and B are locked in a condition known as **deadlock**, or sometimes the **deadly embrace**. Each is waiting for a resource that the other person has locked. There are two common ways of solving this problem: preventing the deadlock from occurring or allowing the deadlock to occur and then breaking it.

Deadlock can be prevented in several ways. One way is to allow users to issue only one lock request at a time. In essence, users must lock all the resources they want at once. If User A in the illustration had locked both the paper and the pencil records at the beginning, the embrace would never have taken place.

The other strategy is to allow the deadlock to occur, detect it, and then break it. Unfortunately, there is only one way to break deadlock—kill one of the transactions. In the situation in Figure 12-5, one of the two transactions must be aborted. When that happens, the lock is released, and the other transaction can process the database unhindered. Obviously, any changes the killed transaction has made in the database must be undone; we discuss the techniques for this in the next section.

OPTIMISTIC VS. PESSIMISTIC LOCKING

Locks can be invoked in two basic styles. With **optimistic locking**, the assumption is made that no conflict will occur. Data is read, the transaction is processed, updates are issued, and then a check is made to see if conflict occurred. If not, the transaction is finished. If so, the transaction is repeated until it processes with no conflict. With **pessimistic locking**, the assumption is made that conflict will occur. First, locks are issued, then the transaction is processed, and then locks are freed.

Figure 12-6 shows an example of each style for a transaction that is reducing the quantity of the pencil row in PRODUCT by five. Figure 12-6(a) shows optimistic locking. First the data is read and the current value of Quantity of pencils is saved in the variable OldQuantity. The transaction is then processed, and assuming that all is OK, a lock is obtained on PRODUCT. The lock might be only for the pencil row, or it might be at a larger level of granularity. In any case, a SQL statement is then issued to update the pencil row with a WHERE condition

➤ FIGURE 12-6

*Optimistic vs. Pessimistic
Locking (a) Optimistic Locking
(b) Pessimistic Locking*

```
SELECT      PRODUCT.Name, PRODUCT.Quantity
FROM        PRODUCT
WHERE       PRODUCT.Name = 'Pencil'

OldQuantity = PRODUCT.Quantity

Set NewQuantity = PRODUCT.Quantity – 5

{process transaction – take exception action if NewQuantity < 0, etc.

Assuming all is OK: }

LOCK PRODUCT {at some level of granularity}

UPDATE      PRODUCT
SET         PRODUCT.Quantity = NewQuantity
WHERE       PRODUCT.Name = 'Pencil'
        AND PRODUCT.Quantity = OldQuantity

UNLOCK    PRODUCT

{check to see if update was successful;
if not, repeat transaction}
```

(a)

```
LOCK        PRODUCT {at some level of granularity}

SELECT      PRODUCT.Name, PRODUCT.Quantity
FROM        PRODUCT
WHERE       PRODUCT.Name = 'Pencil'

Set NewQuantity = PRODUCT.Quantity – 5

{process transaction – take exception action if NewQuantity < 0, etc.

Assuming all is OK: }

UPDATE      PRODUCT
SET         PRODUCT.Quantity = NewQuantity
WHERE       PRODUCT.Name = 'Pencil'

UNLOCK    PRODUCT

{no need to check if update was successful}
```

(b)

that the current value of Quantity equal OldQuantity. If no other transaction has changed the Quantity of the pencil row, then this UPDATE will be successful. If another transaction has changed the Quantity of the pencil row, the UPDATE will fail and the transaction will need to be repeated.

Figure 12-6(b) shows the logic for the same transaction using pessimistic locking. Here, a lock is obtained on PRODUCT (at some level of granularity) before any work is begun. Then values are read, the transaction is processed, the UPDATE occurs, and PRODUCT is unlocked.

The advantage of optimistic locking is that the lock is obtained only after the transaction has processed. Thus, the lock is held for less time than with pessimistic locking. If the transaction is complicated or if the client is slow (due to transmission delays, or the client doing other work, or the user getting a cup of coffee or shutting down without exiting the browser), the lock will be held considerably less time. This advantage will be even more important if the lock granularity lock is large—say the entire PRODUCT table.

The disadvantage of optimistic locking is that if there is a lot of activity on the pencil row, the transaction may have to be repeated many times. Thus, transactions that involve a lot of activity on a given row (purchasing a popular stock, for example) are poorly suited for optimistic locking.

In general, the Internet is a wild and wooly place, and users are likely to take unexpected actions like abandoning transactions in the middle. So unless Internet users have been prequalified (by enrolling in an online brokerage stock purchase plan, for example), optimistic locking is the better choice. On intranets, however, the decision is more difficult. Probably optimistic locking is still preferred unless there is some characteristic of the application that causes substantial activity on particular rows, or if application requirements make reprocessing transactions particularly undesirable.

DECLARING LOCK CHARACTERISTICS

As you can see, concurrency control is a complicated subject; some of the decisions about lock types and strategy have to be made on the basis of trial and error. For this and other reasons, database application programs do not generally explicitly issue locks. Instead, they mark transaction boundaries, and then declare the type of locking behavior they want to the DBMS. In this way, if the locking behavior needs to be changed, the application need not be rewritten to place locks in different locations in the transaction. Instead, the lock declaration is changed.

Figure 12-7 shows the pencil transaction with transaction boundaries marked with BEGIN TRANSACTION, COMMIT TRANSACTION, and ABORT TRANSAC-

---

> FIGURE 12-7

Marking Transaction Boundaries

```
BEGIN TRANSACTION:

SELECT       PRODUCT.Name, PRODUCT.Quantity
FROM         PRODUCT
WHERE        PRODUCT.Name = 'Pencil'

Old Quantity = PRODUCT.Quantity

Set NewQuantity = PRODUCT.Quantity – 5

{process part of transaction – take exception action if NewQuantity < 0, etc.}

UPDATE       PRODUCT
SET          PRODUCT.Quantity = NewQuantity
WHERE        PRODUCT.Name = 'Pencil'

{continue processing transaction} . . .


IF transaction has completed normally       THEN

        COMMIT TRANSACTION

ELSE

        ABORT TRANSACTION

END IF

Continue processing other actions not part of this transaction . . .
```

TION statements. These boundaries are the essential information that the DBMS needs in order to enforce different locking strategies. If the developer now declares (via a system parameter or similar means) that he or she wants optimistic locking, the DBMS will implicitly set the locks in the correct place for that locking style. If he or she later changes tactics and requests pessimistic locking, the DBMS will implicitly set the locks in a different place.

TRANSACTION ISOLATION LEVEL

In addition to pessimistic and optimistic locking, most DBMS products also support a variety of transaction isolation levels. Figure 12-8 shows four basic types of isolation level. These levels were first defined by IBM for DB2, but they have been adopted under one name or another by almost all DBMS products. OLE DB and ADO, for example, provide similar levels using slightly different terminology.

The isolation levels are shown in decreasing level of exclusivity. A transaction operating with exclusive use locks the entire database. This level is used by database administrators who are making changes to the structure of the database or taking some other wide-ranging action. Throughput for other users is nil. Repeatable reads are used by transactions that read multiple rows and depend on the values of those rows not changing during the life of the transaction. A transaction that constructs a stock portfolio is a possible example. The transaction reads the amount held of various stocks and then issues a purchase order for an amount of a different stock. The amount purchased depends on the amount of the other stocks held, and these amounts cannot be changed during the life of the transaction. The term arises because at any point, the transaction could reread rows and would obtain the same values as first read.

➤ FIGURE 12-8

Transaction Isolation Levels

Isolation Level	Meaning	Possible Use
Exclusive Use	The transaction has exclusive use of the database. No other transaction can access the database in any way.	Add a new table or relationship or otherwise change the structure of the database; reorganize database files.
Repeatable Read	Shared locks are issued on all rows that have been read by the transaction. Exclusive locks are issued on all rows that have been updated by the transaction.	Constructing a portfolio in which updates depend on values previously read, *e.g.*, the amount of Company A stock purchased depends on the amount Companies' B, C, and D stock already held.
Cursor Stability	Shared locks are issued on rows that are currently read. Exclusive locks are issued on all rows that have been updated by the transaction.	Order entry in which a shared lock is held on customer to ensure the customer row is not deleted while the order is in process.
Dirty Read	No locks are issued; other transaction locks are ignored.	Producing a report in which the very latest data is required. OK if data changes are later aborted by other transactions.

A **cursor** is a pointer into a relation, or more specifically, into a recordset. When an application opens a recordset and reads the first row, the cursor points to that row. Subsequent reads move the cursor through the rows of the relation. Cursor stability isolation means that a shared lock is obtained on the row currently pointed to by the cursor. When the application moves the cursor to a new row (say by executing the MoveNext method on the recordset), the lock is released on the row just left and obtained on the next row. The word *stability* is used because this form of isolation means, among other things, that no other transaction can delete the current row from underneath the cursor.

A dirty read is the least exclusive level of isolation. Here, the transaction is neither issuing nor obeying locks. This is primarily used for producing up-to-the-minute reports in which the possibility of reading a subsequently aborted update is unimportant.

Again, the locking required to enforce these isolation levels is done implicitly by the DBMS. The developer need only mark the transaction boundaries and declare the type of isolation to be enforced. The DBMS will issue appropriate locks at appropriate times.

CURSOR TYPE

Generally, the boundaries of a transaction are determined by the database view to be processed. As you have seen, a view may be composed of many different relations. Further, a relation can appear more than once in a given view. In the View Ridge Gallery Customer view in Figure 10-4, for example, the ARTIST table appears twice. To process the rows in a relation, the database application must open the relation and establish a cursor for it. All of this means that a single transaction may have several or even many cursors open at once, and that two or more cursors may be open on the same relation.

Maintaining cursors requires considerable overhead in main memory and processing cycles. In some cases, the server load can be reduced by moving the cursor to the client, but there is overhead in doing that as well. Therefore, it is desirable to reduce the amount of overhead required for cursors. One way to do this is to define reduced-capability cursors and to use them when the full capability of a cursor is not needed.

Figure 12-9 lists four cursor types used in the Windows NT and 2000 environment. (Cursor types for other systems are similar.) The simplest cursor is forward only. With it, the application can only move forward through the recordset. Changes made by other cursors in this transaction and by other transactions will be visible only if they occur in rows ahead of the cursor.

The next three types of cursor are called **scrollable cursors** since the application can scroll forward and backward through the recordset. A static cursor processes a snapshot of the relation that was taken when the cursor was opened. Changes made using this cursor are visible to it; changes from any other source are not visible.

Keyset cursors combine some features of static cursors with some features of dynamic cursors. When the cursor is opened, a primary key value is saved for each row in the recordset. When the application positions the cursor on a row, the DBMS uses the key value to read the current value of the row. If the application issues an update on a row that has been deleted either by a different cursor in this transaction or by a different transaction, the DBMS creates a new row with the old key value and places the updated values in the new row (assuming that all required fields are present). Inserts of new rows by other cursors in this transaction or by other transactions are not visible to a keyset cursor. Unless the isolation level of the transaction is a dirty read, only committed updates and deletions are visible to the cursor.

Summary of Cursor Types

CursorType	Description	Comments
Forward only	Application can only move forward through the record set.	Changes made by other cursors in this transaction or in other transactions will be visible only if they occur on rows ahead of the cursor.
Static	Application sees the data as it was at the time the cursor was opened.	Changes made by this cursor are visible. Changes from other sources are not visible. Backward and forward scrolling allowed.
Keyset	When the cursor is opened, a primary key value is saved for each row in the recordset. When the application accesses a row, the key is used to fetch the current values for the row.	Updates form any source are visible. Inserts from sources outside this cursor are not visible (there is no key for them in the keyset). Inserts from this cursor appear at the bottom of the rec-ordset. Deletions from any source are visible. Changes in row order are not visible. If the isolation level is dirty read, then uncommitted updates and deletions are visible; otherwise only commited updates and deletions are visible.
Dynamic	Changes of any type and from any source are visible.	All inserts, updates, deletions, and changes in recordset order are visible. If the isolation level is dirty read, then uncomitted changes are visible. Otherwise, only committed changes are visible.

A dynamic cursor is a fully featured cursor. All inserts, updates, deletions, changes in row order are visible to a dynamic cursor. As with keyset cursors, unless the isolation level of the transaction is a dirty read, only committed changes are visible.

The amount of overhead and processing required to support a cursor is different for each type. In general, the cost goes up as we move down the cursor types in Figure 12-9. In order to improve DBMS performance, therefore, the application developer should create cursors that are just powerful enough to do the job. It is also very important to understand how a particular DBMS implements cursors and whether cursors are located on the server or on the client. In some cases, it might be better to place a dynamic cursor on the client than to have a static cursor on the server. No general rule can be stated because performance depends on the implementation used by DBMS product and the application requirements.

A word of caution: If you do not specify the isolation level of a transaction or do not specify the type of cursors you open, the DBMS will use a default level and types. These defaults may be perfect for your application, but they also may be terrible. Thus, even though these issues can be ignored, the consequences of them cannot be avoided. Learn the capabilities of your DBMS product and use them wisely.

➤ DATABASE RECOVERY

Computer systems can fail. Hardware breaks. Programs have bugs. Human procedures contain errors, and people make mistakes. All of these failures can and do occur in database applications. Since a database is shared by many people and since it often is a key element of an organization's operations, it is important to recover it as soon as possible.

Several problems must be addressed. First, from a business standpoint, business functions must continue. For example, customer orders, financial transactions, and packing lists must be completed manually. Later, when the database application is operational again, the new data can be entered. Second, computer operations personnel must restore the system to a usable state as quickly as possible and as close as possible to what it was when the system crashed. Third, users must know what to do when the system becomes available again. Some work may need to be reentered, and users must know how far back they need to go.

When failures occur, it is impossible simply to fix the problem and resume processing. Even if no data are lost during a failure (which assumes that all types of memory are nonvolatile—an unrealistic assumption), the timing and scheduling of computer processing are too complex to be accurately recreated. Enormous amounts of overhead data and processing would be required for the operating system to be able to restart processing precisely where it was interrupted. It is simply not possible to roll back the clock and put all the electrons in the same configuration they were in at the time of the failure. Two other approaches are possible: recovery via reprocessing, and recovery via rollback/rollforward.

RECOVERY VIA REPROCESSING   Since processing cannot be resumed at a precise point, the next best alternative is to go back to a known point and reprocess the workload from there. The simplest form of this type of recovery is to make a copy periodically of the database (called a **database save**) and to keep a record of all transactions that have been processed since the save. Then, when there is a failure, the operations staff can restore the database from the save and reprocess all the transactions.

Unfortunately, this simple strategy is normally unfeasible. First, reprocessing transactions takes the same amount of time as did processing them in the first place. If the computer is heavily scheduled, the system may never catch up.

Second, when transactions are processed concurrently, events are asynchronous. Slight variations in human activity, such as a user inserting a floppy disk more slowly or a user reading an electronic mail message before responding to an application prompt, may change the order of the execution of concurrent transactions. Therefore, whereas Customer A got the last seat on a flight during the original processing, Customer B may get the last seat during reprocessing. For these reasons, reprocessing is normally not a viable form of recovery from failure in concurrent processing systems.

RECOVERY VIA ROLLBACK/ROLLFORWARD   A second approach is periodically to make a copy of the database (the database save) and to keep a log of the changes made by transactions against the database since the save. Then, when there is a failure, one of two methods can be used. Using the first method, called **rollforward**, the database is restored using the saved data, and all valid transactions since the save are reapplied. (We are not reprocessing the transactions, as the application programs are not involved in the rollforward. Instead, the processed changes, as recorded in the log, are reapplied.)

The second method is **rollback**, in which we undo changes made by erroneous or partially processed transactions by undoing the changes they have made in the database. Then the valid transactions that were in process at the time of the failure are restarted.

Both of these methods require that a **log** of the transaction results be kept. This log contains records of the data changes in chronological order. Transactions must be written to the log before they are applied to the database. That way, if the system crashes between the time a transaction is logged and the time it is applied, then at worst there is a record of an unapplied transaction. If, on the other hand, the transactions were to be applied before they were logged, it would be possible (as well as undesirable) to change the database but have no record of the change. If this happened, an unwary user might reenter an already completed transaction.

In the event of a failure, the log is used both to undo and to redo transactions, as shown in Figure 12-10. To undo a transaction, the log must contain a copy of every database record (or page) before it was changed. Such records are called **before-images**. A transaction is undone by applying before-images of all its changes to the database.

To redo a transaction, the log must contain a copy of every database record (or page) after it was changed. These records are called **after-images**. A transaction is redone by applying after-images of all its changes to the database. Possible data items of a transaction log are shown in Figure 12-11(a).

For this example log, each transaction has a unique name for identification purposes. Furthermore, all images for a given transaction are linked together with pointers. One pointer points to the previous change made by this transaction (the reverse pointer), and the other points to the next change made by this transaction (the forward pointer). A zero in the pointer field means that this is the end

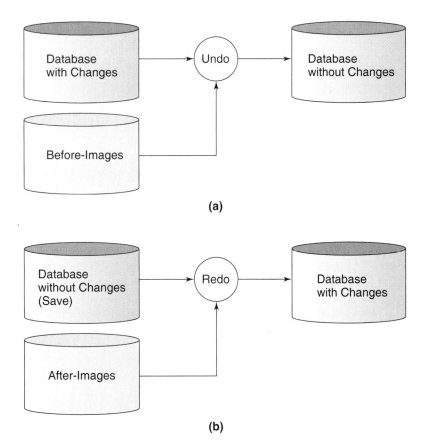

➤ FIGURE 12-10

Undo and Redo Transactions: (a) Removing Changes in the Database (Rollback) and (b) Reapplying Changes in the Database (Rollforward)

➤   FIGURE 12-11

Transaction Log:
(a) Data Items in a
Log Record and
(b) Log Instance for
Three Transactions

Transaction ID	Type of Operation
Reverse Pointer	Object
Forward Pointer	Before-Image
Time	After-Image

(a)

Relative
Record
Number

1	OT1	0	2	11:42	START			
2	OT1	1	4	11:43	MODIFY	CUST 100	(old value)	(new value)
3	OT2	0	8	11:46	START			
4	OT1	2	5	11:47	MODIFY	SP AA	(old value)	(new value)
5	OT1	4	7	11:47	INSERT	ORDER 11		(value)
6	CT1	0	9	11:48	START			
7	OT1	5	0	11:49	COMMIT			
8	OT2	3	0	11:50	COMMIT			
9	CT1	6	10	11:51	MODIFY	SP BB	(old value)	(new value)
10	CT1	9	0	11:51	COMMIT			

(b)

of the list. The DBMS recovery subsystem uses these pointers to locate all records for a particular transaction. Figure 12-11(b) shows an example of the linking of log records.

Other data items in the log are: the time of the action; the type of operation (START marks the beginning of a transaction, and COMMIT terminates a transaction, releasing all locks that were in place); the object acted on, such as record type and identifier; and finally, the before-images and after-images.

Given a log with both before-images and after-images, the undo and redo actions are straightforward (to describe, anyway). To undo the transaction in Figure 12-12, the recovery processor simply replaces each changed record with its before-image. When all before-images have been restored, the transaction is undone. To redo a transaction, the recovery processor starts with the version of the database at the time the transaction started and applies all after-images. As stated, this action assumes that an earlier version of the database is available from a database save.

Restoring a database to its most recent save and reapplying all transactions may require considerable processing. To reduce the delay, DBMS products sometimes use checkpoints. A **checkpoint** is a point of synchronization between the database and the transaction log. To perform a checkpoint, the DBMS refuses new requests, finishes processing outstanding requests, and writes its buffers to disk. The DBMS then waits until the operating system notifies it that all outstanding write requests to the database and to the log have been successfully completed. At this point, the log and the database are synchronized. A checkpoint record is then written to the log. Later, the database can be recovered from the checkpoint and only after-images for transactions that started after the checkpoint need to be applied.

Checkpoints are inexpensive operations, and it is feasible to take three or four (or more) per hour. In this way, no more than 15 or 20 minutes of processing need to be recovered. Some DBMS products automatically checkpoint themselves, making human intervention unnecessary.

► FIGURE 12-12

*Example of a
Recovery Strategy:
(a) ORDER
Transaction and
(b) Recovery
Processing to Undo
an ORDER Record*

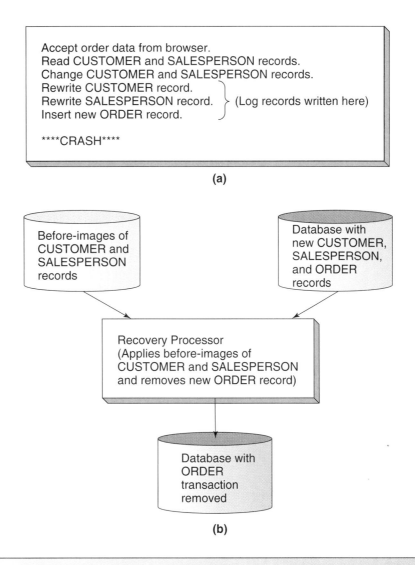

Accept order data from browser.
Read CUSTOMER and SALESPERSON records.
Change CUSTOMER and SALESPERSON records.
Rewrite CUSTOMER record.
Rewrite SALESPERSON record.   } (Log records written here)
Insert new ORDER record.

****CRASH****

(a)

Before-images of
CUSTOMER and
SALESPERSON
records

Database with
new CUSTOMER,
SALESPERSON,
and ORDER
records

Recovery Processor
(Applies before-images of
CUSTOMER and SALESPERSON
and removes new ORDER record)

Database with
ORDER
transaction
removed

(b)

► DATABASE SECURITY

Internet-technology databases and their applications are valuable assets that are
exposed to a large and frequently unknown user community. As such, access to
them needs to be carefully controlled. There are a number of different security
systems involved in Internet or intranet processing: network security between
the client and the Web server; operating system security on both the Web server
and the database server; database security provided by the DBMS; and application security provided by the application. In this text we will only be concerned
with the latter two. Network and operating system security are important, but
they are beyond the scope of this text.

DBMS SECURITY

The terminology, features, and functions of DBMS security depend on the DBMS
product in use. Basically, however, all such products provide facilities that limit
certain actions on certain objects to certain users. A general model of DBMS security is shown in Figure 12-13. A group consists of one or more users and a user
can belong to one or more groups. Groups and users have many permissions.
Objects (here used in a generic sense and not as a semantic object nor COM object) have many permissions defined for them.

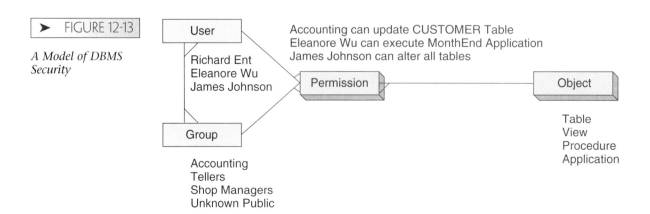

A Model of DBMS Security

When a user signs on to the database, the DBMS limits his or her actions to the defined permissions for that user and to the permissions for groups to which that user has been assigned. Determining whether someone actually is who they claim to be is, in general, a difficult task. All commercial DBMS products use some version of user name and password, even though such security is readily circumvented if users are careless with their identities.

Users can enter their name and password, or, in some applications, the name and password is entered on behalf of the user. For example, the Windows 2000 user name and password can be directly passed to SQL Server. In other cases, an application program provides the name and password.

Internet applications usually define a group like "Unknown Public," and assign anonymous users to that group when they sign on. In this way, companies like Dell Computer need not enter every customer into their security system by name and password.

Models of the security systems used by ORACLE and SQL Server are illustrated in Figures 12-14 and 12-15. As you can see, both of these are variants of the general model in Figure 12-13. Considering the ORACLE model in Figure 12-14(a), users have a profile, which is a specification of systems resources that they can use. An example profile definition is shown in Figure 12-14(b). Users can be assigned many roles, and a role is assigned to many users. Each user or role has many privileges. There are two subtypes of privilege: Object privileges concern actions that can be taken on database objects like tables, views, and indexes; system privileges concern the actions using ORACLE commands.

An example of this security system is shown in Figure 12-14(c). Observe that the user DK has been granted roles for CONNECT and RESOURCE. Looking further down the list, the CONNECT role has been granted system privileges like ALTER SESSION, CREATE CLUSTER, and others, including CREATE TABLE. Looking even further down the list, the user DK has been assigned to the DEFAULT profile.

The security system for SQL Server is shown in Figure 12-15. Users have a login, which is different from an ORACLE profile. A login is the name and password that the user employs when signing on to the database. (ORACLE also has facilities for specifying name and password, but they are different.) As shown in Figure 12-15(a), a user can have multiple logins (which are called aliases), and a login can be used by more than one user.

The admin login in Figure 12-15(b) permits the admin user to access the CyberDB database under the user name admin, to access the dk database under the user name CStanford, and to access the master database under the name MGardner. Also, when someone signs on as admin, he or she is signed into the master database by default.

Users can be assigned to many groups, and a group may contain many users. Further, both users and groups have permissions on database objects. Figure 12-15(c) shows the permissions that have been granted for accessing the table DC_Channels (cm). The user group *demo* can issue selected statements against this table; the user *Fred* can both select and update data in it; the user *Mary* can select, insert, and update data in it.

If the developer were to click the By User tab in this window, they could then show the permissions allowed for a given user. This dialog box is materializing the many-to-many relationship between Group/User and Object. One tab works from Group/User to Object and the other works from Object to Group/User.

<table>
<tr>
<td>➤ FIGURE 12-14</td>
</tr>
</table>

ORACLE Security (a) Model of ORACLE Security (b) Defining an ORACLE Profile (c) ORACLE User, Roles, and Profiles

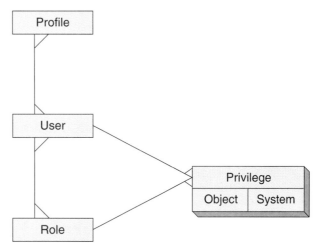

(a) Model of ORACLE Security

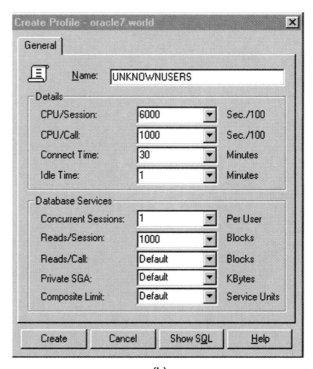

(b)

(Continued)

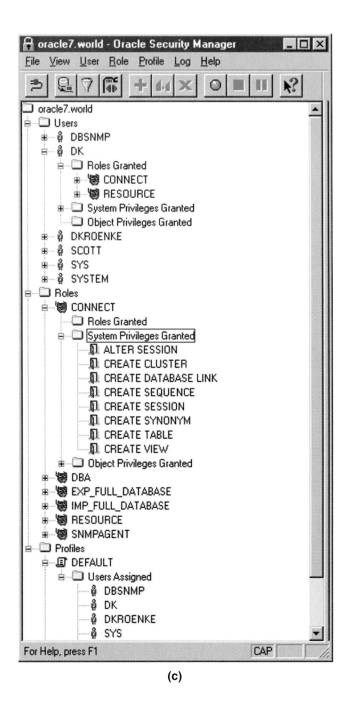

(c)

APPLICATION SECURITY

While DBMS products like ORACLE and SQL Server do provide substantial database security capabilities, by their very nature, they are generic. If the application requires specific security measures such as "No user can view a row of a table or of a join of a table that has an employee name other than his or her own," the DBMS facilities will not be adequate. In these cases, the security system must be augmented by features in the database application.

In the three-tier architecture, the best place to process application security is on the Web server. Executing application security on this server means that sen-

➤ FIGURE 12-15

SQL Server Security
(a) A Model of SQL
Server Security
(b) SQL Server Login
(c) Defining
Permissions on a
Table

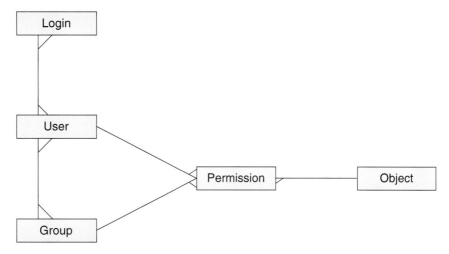

(a) A Model of SQL Server Security

(b)

sitive security data need never be sent over the network. You saw in Chapter 11, for example, any script contained within ⟨% %⟩, will be executed on the ASP server. The script itself is never sent over the network to the client.

To see how this is useful, suppose an application is written such that when users click a particular button on a browser page, the following query is sent to the Web server for subsequent transmission to the database server:

SELECT *
FROM EMPLOYEE

➤ FIGURE 12-15

(Continued)

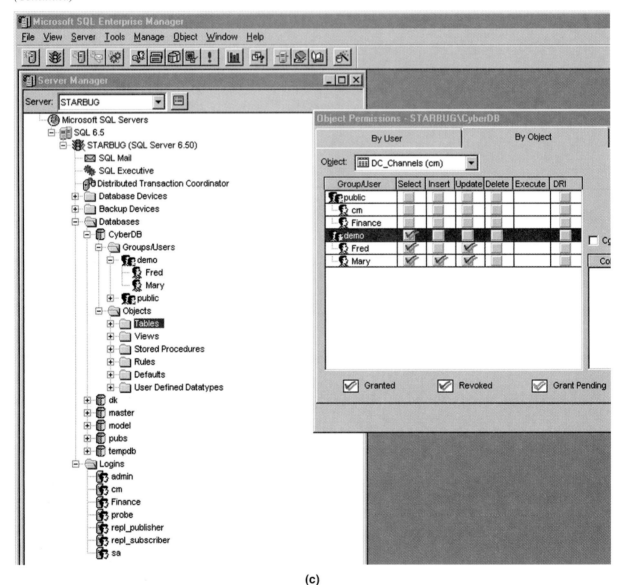

(c)

This statement will, of course, return all EMPLOYEE rows. If the application security is such that employees are only allowed to see their own data, then ASP script could add the following:

SELECT *
FROM EMPLOYEE
⟨%WHERE EMPLOYEE.Name "=SESSION("EmployeeName")"%⟩

where the SESSION variable EmployeeName has been set equal to the name the user employed when signing on to the application. Because this is done on the Web server, the browser user does not know that it is occurring and cannot interfere with it even if he or she did.

This idea can be extended by storing additional data in a security database that is accessed only by Web server programs. That database could contain, for example, the identities of users paired with additional values for WHERE clauses. For example, suppose that some users (those in the personnel department) can access more than just their own data. The predicates for appropriate WHERE clauses could be stored in the security database, read during the processing of the ASP page, and appended to SQL SELECT statements as necessary.

Many other possibilities exist for using the Web server to augment DBMS security. In general, however, you should use the DBMS security features first. Only if they are inadequate for the requirements, should you add to them with application code. The closer the security enforcement is to the data, the less chance there is for infiltration. Also, using the DBMS security features is faster, cheaper, and probably results in higher quality results than developing your own.

➤ DATABASE ADMINISTRATION

Both the terms **data administration** and **database administration** are used in industry. In some cases the terms are considered synonymous; in other cases, they have different meanings. In this text, we use the term *data administration* to refer to a function that applies to all of the organization. Sometimes the term *global database administration* is used instead of *data administration*. The term *database administration* refers to a function that is specific to a particular database, including the applications that process that database. This chapter addresses database administration. Data administration is discussed in Chapter 14.

Databases vary considerably in size and scope, from single-user personal database to large interorganizational databases like airline reservations systems. All of these databases have a need for database administration, although the tasks to be accomplished vary in complexity. For example, for a personal database individuals follow simple procedures for backing up their data, and they keep minimal records for documentation. In this case, the person who uses the database also performs the DBA functions, even though he or she is probably unaware of it.

For multi-user database applications, database administration becomes both more important and more difficult. Consequently, it generally has formal recognition. For some applications, one or two people are given this function on a part-time basis. For large Internet or intranet databases, database administration responsibilities are often too time-consuming and too varied to be handled even by a single full-time person. Supporting a database with dozens or hundreds of users requires considerable time as well as both technical knowledge and diplomatic skills and usually is handled by an office of database administration. The manager of the office is often known as the **database administrator**; in this case, the acronym **DBA** refers to either the office or the manager.

The overall responsibility of the DBA is to facilitate the development and use of the database. Usually, this means balancing the conflicting goals of protecting the database and maximizing its availability and benefit to users. The DBA is responsible for the development, operation, and maintenance of the database and its applications, specifically

➤ Managing the database structure

➤ Managing data activity

➤ Managing the DBMS

➤ Maintaining the data repository

MANAGING THE DATABASE STRUCTURE

Managing the database structure includes participating in the initial database design and implementation as well as controlling and managing changes to it. Ideally, the DBA is involved early in the development of the database and its applications, participates in the requirements study, helps evaluate alternatives, including the DBMS to be used, and helps design the database structure. For large, organizational applications, the DBA usually is a manager who supervises the work of technically oriented database design personnel.

Once the database has been designed, it is implemented using the DBMS product, and the database data are created. The DBA participates in the development of procedures and controls to ensure high integrity and quality of the database data.

CONFIGURATION CONTROL   After a database and its applications have been implemented, changes in requirements are inevitable. Such changes can arise from new needs, from changes in the business environment, from changes in policy, and so forth. When changes to requirements necessitate changes to the database structure, great care must be used because database structure changes seldom involve just one application.

Hence, effective database administration must include procedures and policies by which users can register their needs for changes, the entire database community can discuss the impacts of the changes, and a global decision can be made whether or not to implement proposed changes.

Because of the size and complexity of a database and its applications, changes sometimes have unexpected results. The DBA thus must be prepared to repair the database and to gather sufficient information to diagnose and correct the problem that caused the damage. The database is most vulnerable to failure after a change in its structure.

DOCUMENTATION   The DBA's final responsibility in managing the database structure is documentation. It is extremely important to know what changes have been made, how they were made, and when they were made. A change in the database structure may cause an error that is not revealed for six months; without proper documentation of the change, diagnosing the problem is next to impossible. Dozens of job reruns may be required to identify the point at which certain symptoms first appeared, and for this reason, it also is important to maintain a record of the test procedures and test runs made to verify a change. If standardized test procedures, test forms, and record-keeping methods are used, recording the test results does not have to be time-consuming.

Although maintaining documentation is tedious and unfulfilling, the effort pays off when disaster strikes and the documentation is the difference between solving and not solving a major (and costly) problem. Today, a number of products are emerging that ease the burden of documentation. Many CASE tools, for example, can be used to document logical database designs. Version control software can be used to track changes. Data dictionaries provide reports and other products read and interpret the database data structures.

Another reason for carefully documenting changes in the database structure is to use historical data properly. If, for example, marketing wants to analyze three-year-old sales data that have been in the archives for two years, it will be necessary to know what structure was current at the time the data were last active. Records that show the changes in the structure can be used to answer that question. A similar situation arises when a six-month-old backup copy of data must be used to repair a damaged database (although this should not happen, sometimes it does). The backup copy can be used to reconstruct the database to the state it was in at the time of the backup. Then transactions and structural

➤ FIGURE 12-16

Summary of the DBA's Responsibilities for Managing the Database Structure

Participate in Database and Application Development
- Assist in requirements stage and evaluation of alternatives.
- Play an active role in database design and creation.
- Develop procedures for integrity and quality of database data.

Facilitate Changes to Database Structure
- Seek communitywide solutions.
- Assess impact on all users.
- Provide configuration control forum.
- Be prepared for problems after changes are made.
- Maintain documentation.

changes can be made in chronological order to restore the database to its current state. Figure 12-16 summarizes the DBA's responsibilities for managing the database structure.

MANAGEMENT OF DATA ACTIVITY

Although the DBA protects the data, he or she does not process it. The DBA is not a user of the system, and, consequently, does not manage *data values*. Rather, the DBA manages *data activity*. The database is a shared resource, and the DBA provides standards, guidelines, control procedures, and documentation to ensure that the users work in a cooperative and complementary fashion when processing database data.

Because of the abundance of interrelated activity, database processing must be standardized. Providing database standards is one aspect of managing data activity: Every database field must have a standard name and format; every database record must have a standard name, format, and access strategies; and every database file must have a standard name and relationships with other files. The DBA establishes these standards in a manner that satisfies most of the needs of all the database users. Those organizations with an effective data administration will already have many of these standards, in which case the DBA may broaden them and ensure that they are enforced. Once established, the details of standardization are recorded in the DBMS **data dictionary**, which both the systems developers and the users can query to determine exactly what data are being maintained, the names and formats of the data items, and their relationships.

Another aspect of managing data activity is identifying key database users, sometimes called **data proponents**. The DBA works with the data proponents to establish access and modification rights. Because the data are a shared resource, there may be problems regarding processing rights. The DBA and the relevant data proponents should consider each shared data item and determine the access and modification rights of particular applications and users. This should be done with regard for the greater community's benefit rather than that of one particular application, group, or user. Once processing rights have been determined, they can be implemented by the DBMS, by applications that process the database via the DBMS, or by both.

Another important function of database administration concerns database reliability. The DBA needs to ensure that proper programs and procedures have

➤ FIGURE 12-17

Summary of the DBA's Responsibilities for Managing Data Activity

- Establish database standards consistent with data administration standards.
- Establish and maintain data dictionary.
- Establish data proponents.
- Work with data proponents to develop data access and modification rights.
- Develop, document, and train staff on backup and recovery procedures.
- Publish and maintain data activity standards documentation.

been established to control concurrent processing and to provide for database recovery. He or she must ensure that the techniques discussed earlier in this chapter are implemented and used.

Finally, the DBA is responsible for publishing and maintaining documentation regarding the data activity, including database standards, data retrieval and access rights, recovery procedures, and policy enforcement. Good documentation is especially important because it is needed by users throughout the organization. As with all documentation, keeping the documentation current is a major and unpopular task.

Many DBMS products provide utility services to assist in managing data activity. Some systems record the names of users and application programs that access (or are authorized to access) objects in the database. In this case, the DBMS data dictionary can be queried to determine which programs can access a particular record and what actions each can take. Figure 12-17 summarizes the DBA's responsibilities for managing data activity.

MANAGING THE DBMS

In addition to managing data activity and the database structure, the DBA must manage the DBMS itself. He or she should compile and analyze statistics concerning the system's performance and identify potential problem areas. Keep in mind that the database is serving many user groups. The DBA needs to investigate all complaints about the system's response time, accuracy of data, ease of use, and so forth. If changes are needed, the DBA must plan and implement them.

The DBA must periodically monitor the users' activity on the database. DBMS products include features that collect and report statistics. Some of these reports may indicate, for example, which users have been active, which files and perhaps which data items have been used, and which access methods have been employed. Error rates and types can also be captured and reported. The DBA analyzes these data to determine whether a change to the database design is needed to improve performance or to ease the users' tasks. If change is necessary, the DBA will ensure that it is accomplished.

The DBA should analyze run-time statistics on database activity and performance. When a performance problem is identified (by either a report or a user's complaint), the DBA must determine whether a modification of the database structure or system is appropriate. Examples of possible structure modifications are establishing new keys, purging data, deleting keys, and establishing new relationships among objects.

When the vendor of the DBMS being used announces new product features, the DBA must consider them in light of the overall needs of the user community.

Summary of the DBA's Responsibilities for Managing the DBMS

- Generate database application performance reports.
- Investigate user performance complaints.
- Assess need for changes in database structure or application design.
- Modify database structure.
- Evaluate and implement new DBMS features.
- Tune the DBMS.

If she decides to incorporate the new DBMS features, the developers must be notified and trained in their use. Accordingly, the DBA must manage and control changes in the DBMS, as well as in the database structure.

Other changes in the system for which the DBA is responsible vary widely, depending on the DBMS product as well as on other software and hardware in use. For example, changes in other software (such as the operating system or the Web server) may mean that some DBMS features, functions, or parameters must be changed. The DBA must therefore also tune the DBMS product to other software in use.

The DBMS options (such as transaction isolation levels) are initially chosen when little is known about how the system will perform in the particular user environment. Consequently, operational experience and performance analysis over a period of time may reveal that changes are necessary. Even if the performance seems acceptable, the DBA may want to alter the options and observe the effect on performance. This process is referred to as *tuning,* or *optimizing,* the system. Figure 12-18 summarizes the DBA's responsibilities for managing the DBMS product.

MAINTAINING THE DATA REPOSITORY

Consider a large and active Internet database application like those used by e-commerce companies, for instance, an application that is used by a company that sells music over the Internet. Such a system may involve data from several different databases, dozens of different Web pages, and hundreds, or even thousands, of users.

Suppose the company using this application decides to expand its product line to include the sale of sporting goods. Senior management of this company might ask the DBA to develop an estimate of the time and other resources required to modify the database application to support this new product line.

For the DBA to respond to this request, he or she needs accurate metadata about the database, about the database applications and application components, about the users and their rights and privileges, and about other system elements. The database does carry some of this metadata in system tables, but this metadata is inadequate to answer the questions senior management poses. The DBA needs additional metadata about COM and ActiveX objects, script procedures and functions, ASP pages, stylesheets, document type definitions, and the like. Furthermore, while DBMS security mechanisms do document users, groups, and privileges, they do so in a highly structured and often inconvenient form.

For all of these reasons, many organizations develop and maintain **data repositories**, which are collections of metadata about databases, database applications, Web pages, users, and other application components. The repository may be virtual in that it is composed of metadata from many different sources: the DBMS, version control software, code libraries, Web page generation and editing tools, and so forth. Or, the data repository may be an integrated product from a CASE tool vendor or from other companies such as Microsoft or ORACLE.

Either way, the time for the DBA to think about constructing such a facility is long before senior management asks questions. In fact, the repository should be constructed as the system is developed and should be considered an important part of the system deliverables. If not, the DBA will always be playing catchup, trying to maintain the existing applications, adapt them to new needs, and somehow gather together the metadata to form a repository.

The best repositories are **active**; they are part of the system development process in such a way that metadata is created automatically as the system components are created. Less desirable, but still effective, are **passive repositories** that are filled only when someone takes the time to generate the needed metadata and place it in the repository.

The Internet has created enormous opportunities for businesses to expand their customer base and increase their sales and profitability. The databases and database applications that support these companies are an essential element of that success. Unfortunately, there will be organizations whose growth is stymied for lack of ability to grow their applications or adapt them to changing needs. Often, building a new system is easier than adapting an existing one; certainly building a new system that integrates with an old one while it replaces that old one can be very difficult.

➤ SUMMARY

Databases and database applications on the Internet or intranets can be immeasurably valuable. Consequently, they need to be carefully managed. This chapter considers four categories of database management: concurrency control, failure recovery, security, and database administration.

The goal of concurrency control is to ensure that one user's work does not inappropriately influence another user's work. No single concurrency control technique is ideal for all circumstances. Trade-offs need to be made between level of protection and throughput. A transaction or logical unit of work is a series of actions taken against the database that occur as an atomic unit; either all of them occur or none of them do. The activity of concurrent transactions is interleaved on the database server. In some cases, updates can be lost if concurrent transactions are not controlled. Another concurrency problem concerns inconsistent reads.

To avoid concurrency problems, database elements are locked. Implicit locks are placed by the DBMS; explicit locks are issued by the application program. The size of the locked resource is called lock granularity. An exclusive lock prohibits other users from reading the locked resource; a shared lock allows other users to read the locked resource, but they cannot update it.

Two transactions that run concurrently and generate results that are consistent with the results that would have occurred if they had run separately are referred to as serializable transactions. Two-phased locking, in which locks are acquired in a growing phase and released in a shrinking phase, is one scheme for serializability. A special case of two-phase locking is to acquire locks throughout the transaction, but not to free any lock until the transaction is finished.

Deadlock, or the deadly embrace, occurs when two transactions are each waiting on a resource that the other transaction holds. Deadlock can be prevented by requiring transactions to acquire all locks at the same time; once it occurs, the only way to cure it is to abort one of the transactions (and back out partially completed work). Optimistic locking assumes no transaction conflict will occur and deals with the consequences if it does. Pessimistic locking assumes that conflict will occur and so prevents it ahead of time with locks. In general, optimistic locking is preferred for the Internet and for many intranet applications.

Most application programs today do not explicitly declare locks. Instead they mark transaction boundaries with BEGIN, COMMIT, and ABORT TRANSACTION statements, and then declare the locking scheme that the DBMS is to enforce. The DBMS places locks accordingly.

Four types of transaction isolation level are: exclusive use, repeatable read, cursor stability, and dirty read. The characteristics of each are summarized in Figure 12-8. A cursor is a pointer into a recordset. Four cursor types are: forward only, static, keyset, and dynamic. The characteristics of each are summarized in Figure 12-9. Developers should select isolation levels and cursor types that are appropriate for their application and for the DBMS product in use.

In the event of system failure, that database must be restored to a usable state as soon as possible. Transactions in process at the time of the failure must be reapplied or restarted. While in some cases, recovery can be done by reprocessing, the use of logs and rollback and rollforward is almost always preferred. Checkpoints can be taken to reduce the amount of work that needs to be done after a failure.

DBMS products provide security facilities. Most involve the declaration of users, groups, objects to be protected, and permissions or privileges on those objects. Almost all DBMS products use some form of user name and password security. DBMS security can be augmented by application security processed on the Web server.

Important functions for database administration are managing the database structure, managing data activity, managing the DBMS, and maintaining the data repository. Internet and intranet database applications are an important part of many company's success; unfortunately, if the needs for changing such systems are not anticipated, they will probably also be limiting factors in the growth of some organizations.

➤ GROUP I QUESTIONS

12.1 Justify the statement "The databases used in Internet or intranet applications can become immeasurable valuable assets." Use Amazon.com or Dell Computer as examples.

12.2 List the four major areas of database management discussed in this chapter.

12.3 Are the ideas in this chapter new? If not, why are they important to you now?

12.4 Explain the meaning of the word *inappropriately* in the phrase "one user's work does not inappropriately influence another user's work."

12.5 Explain the trade-off that exists in concurrency control.

12.6 Define an atomic transaction and explain why atomicity is important.

12.7 Explain the difference between concurrent transactions and simultaneous transactions. How many CPUs are required for simultaneous transactions?

12.8 Give an example, other than the one in this text, of the lost update problem.

12.9 Explain the difference between an explicit and an implicit lock.

12.10 What is lock granularity?

12.11 Explain the difference between an exclusive lock and a shared lock.

12.12 Explain two-phased locking.

12.13 How does releasing all locks at the end of the transaction relate to two-phase locking?

12.14 In general, how should the boundaries of a transaction be defined?

12.15 What is deadlock? How can it be avoided? How can it be resolved once it occurs?

12.16 Explain the difference between optimistic and pessimistic locking.

12.17 In general, is optimistic or pessimistic locking preferred for Internet applications? Justify your answer.

12.18 Explain the benefits of marking transaction boundaries, declaring lock characteristics, and letting the DBMS place locks.

12.19 Explain the use of BEGIN, COMMIT, and ABORT TRANSACTION statements.

12.20 What is transaction isolation level? What is its purpose?

12.21 Explain exclusive use isolation level. Give an example of its use.

12.22 Explain repeatable read isolation level. Give an example of its use.

12.23 Define *cursor.*

12.24 Explain cursor stability isolation level. Give an example of its use.

12.25 Explain dirty read isolation level. Give an example of its use.

12.26 Explain why a transaction may have many cursors. Also, how is it possible that a transaction may have more than one cursor on a given table?

12.27 What is the advantage of using different types of cursors?

12.28 Explain forward only cursors. Give an example of their use.

12.29 Explain static cursors. Give an example of their use.

12.30 Explain keyset cursors. Give an example of their use.

12.31 Explain dynamic cursors. Give an example of their use.

12.32 What happens if you do not declare transaction isolation level and cursor type to the DBMS? Is this good or bad?

12.33 Explain how a database could be recovered via reprocessing. Why is this generally not feasible?

12.34 Define *rollback* and *rollforward.*

12.35 Why is it important to write to the log before changing the database values?

12.36 Describe the rollback process. Under what conditions should it be used?

12.37 Describe the rollforward process. Under what conditions should it be used?

12.38 What is the advantage of taking frequent checkpoints of a database?

12.39 Explain the relationship of USERS, GROUPS, PERMISSIONS, and OBJECTS in a generic DBMS security system.

12.40 Describe the differences between ORACLE and SQL server security as described in this chapter.

12.41 Describe the need for database administration. What would happen in an Internet database application if there were no DBA?

12.42 Summarize the DBA's responsibilities for managing database structure.

12.43 What is configuration control? Why is it necessary?

12.44 Summarize the DBA's responsibilities for managing data activity.

12.45 Who is a data proponent and how does one work with the DBA?

12.46 Summarize the DBA's responsibilities for managing the DBMS.

12.47 What is a data repository? A passive data repository? An active data repository?

12.48 Explain why a data repository is important. What is likely to happen if one is not available?

➤ GROUP II QUESTIONS

12.49 Visit www.microsoft.com and search for information about transaction isolation levels and cursor types. For now, ignore information about RDS, ADO, ODBC, and OLE/DB and focus instead on the features and functions of SQL server. Compare and contrast its capabilities with those described in this text.

12.50 Visit www.oracle.com and search for information about transactions isolation levels and cursor types. Ignore information about ODBC, and focus instead of the features and functions of ORACLE. Compare and contrast its capabilities with those described in this text.

12.51 Describe the advantages and disadvantages of user name and password security. In what ways might users be careless with their identities? How can such carelessness compromise the security of the database? What steps could be taken to reduce the risk of such problems?

12.52 Search the Web for CASE tools that provide repositories and for repository products. Find what you think is the best one and list its major functions and features. Explain how those functions and features could be used to help the DBA of an e-commerce company that is adding new product lines to its business.

➤ PROJECT

A. Consider the Customer view in Figure 10-4.

1. Suppose that you are developing an application to create new instances of this view. What transaction isolation level would you use? Name the cursors involved and recommend a cursor type for each.

2. Suppose that you are developing an application to modify the values (only values, not relationships) in this view. What transaction isolation level would you use? Name the cursors involved and recommend a cursor type for each.

3. Suppose that you are developing an application to modify both data values and relationships in this view. How does your answer to Question A.2 change?

4. Suppose that you are developing an application to delete instances of inactive customers (defined as customers who have never purchased art). What transaction isolation level would you use? Name the cursors involved and recommend a cursor type for each.

CHAPTER 13

Accessing the Database Server: ODBC, OLE DB, and ADO

This chapter discusses standard interfaces for accessing database servers. ODBC or the Open Database Connectivity standard, was developed in the early 1990s to provide a DBMS-independent means for processing relational database data. In the mid 1990s Microsoft announced OLE DB, which is an object-oriented interface that encapsulates data-server functionality. As you will learn, OLE DB was designed not just for relational databases but for many other types of data as well. As a COM interface, OLE DB is readily accessible to C++ and Java programmers, but is not as accessible to VisualBasic and scripting developers. Therefore, Microsoft developed Active Data Objects (ADO), which is a set of objects for utilizing OLE DB that is designed for use by any language, including VB, VBScript, and JScript.

Before considering these standards, we need to gain a perspective on the data environment that surrounds the Web server in Internet technology database applications.

➤ THE WEB SERVER DATA ENVIRONMENT

The environment in which today's Internet technology database applications reside is rich and complicated. As shown in Figure 13-1, a typical Web server needs to publish applications that involve data of dozens of different data types. So far in this text we have considered only relational databases, but as you can see from this figure, there are many other data types as well.

Consider the problems that the developer of Web server applications has when integrating this data. He or she may need to connect to an ORACLE data-

Internet Application
Data Needs

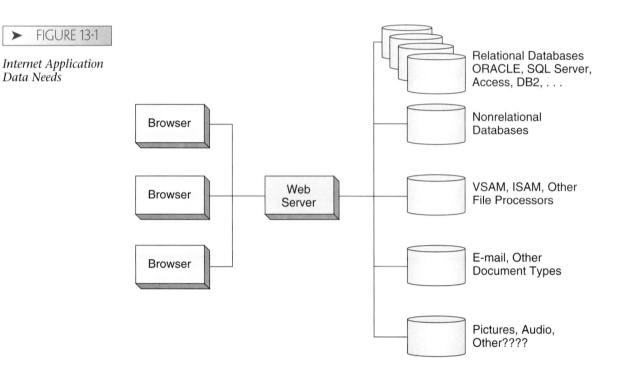

base, a DB2 mainframe database, a non-relational database like IMS (see Chapter 16), file processing data like VSAM and ISAM, E-mail directories, and so forth. Each one of these products has a different programming interface that the developer must learn. Further, each of these products evolves, so over time new features and functions will be added that will increase the developer's challenge.

ODBC was created to address the part of this problem that concerns relational databases and data sources that are very table-like such as spreadsheets. As shown in Figure 13-2, ODBC is an interface between the Web server (or other

Role of ODBC
Standard

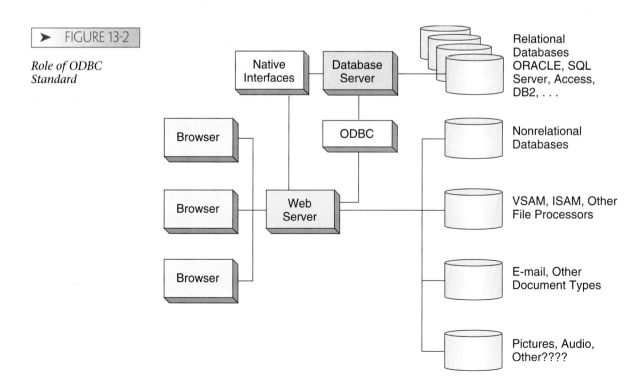

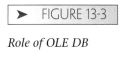

Role of OLE DB

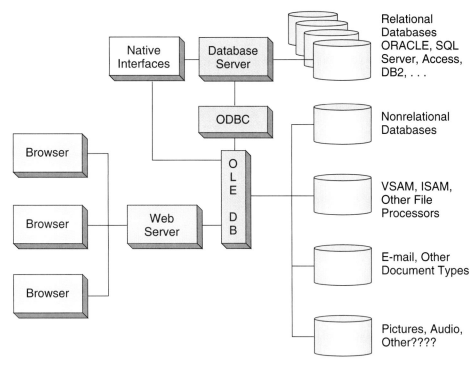

database user) and the database server. It consists of a set of standards by which SQL statements also can be issued and results and error messages returned. As shown, developers can call data servers using native DBMS calls if they want to (sometimes done to increase performance), but the beleaguered developer who does not have the time or desire to learn many different DBMS native libraries can use ODBC instead.

ODBC has been a tremendous success and greatly simplified some database development tasks. As you will learn, it has a substantial disadvantage that was addressed by Microsoft when they developed OLE DB. Figure 13-3 shows the relationship of OLE DB, ODBC, and other data types. OLE DB provides an object-oriented interface to data of almost any type. DBMS vendors can wrap portions of their native libraries in OLE DB objects to expose their product's functionality through this interface. OLE DB can also be used as an interface to ODBC data sources. Finally, OLE DB was developed to support the processing of non-relational data as well.

Because OLE DB is an object-oriented interface, it is particularly suited to object-oriented languages like C++. Most database application developers, however, program in Visual Basic, or scripting languages such as VBScript and JScript. Consequently, Microsoft defined ADO as a cover over OLE DB objects (see Figure 13-4) ADO enables programmers in almost any language to be able to access OLE DB functionality. Additionally, the ADO interface is designed to work in conjunction with Remote Data Services objects. As discussed in Chapter 11, these objects can be used to cache and process data on client computers. The objects shown in Figure 11-14 are interfacing with ADO objects on the Web server.

You may feel uncomfortable with the strong Microsoft presence in this discussion. Both OLE DB and ADO were developed and promulgated by Microsoft, and even ODBC received prominence in large measure because of support from Microsoft. In fact, other vendors and standards committees did propose alternatives to OLE DB and ADO, but because Microsoft Windows resides on nearly 90

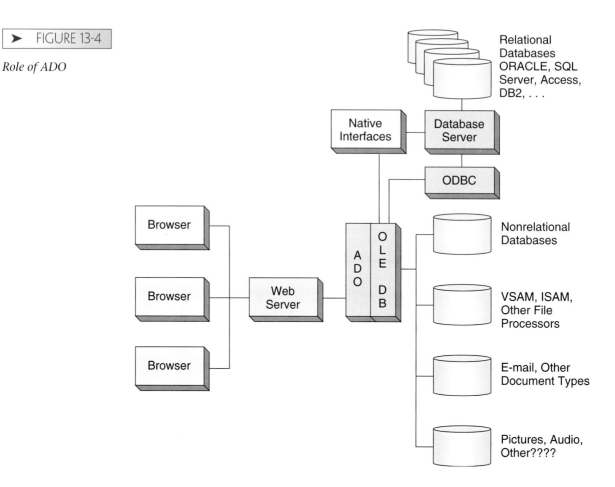

Role of ADO

percent of the world's desktops, it is difficult for others to promulgate opposing standards. Furthermore, in defense of Microsoft, both OLE DB and ADO are excellent. They simplify the job of the database developer and they probably would have won out even on a level playing field.

Our aims, here, however, are more pedestrian. You need to learn ADO so that you can build better Internet-technology database applications. To that end, we will now address each of these standards in more detail.

► OPEN DATABASE CONNECTIVITY (ODBC) STANDARD

The **open database connectivity (ODBC)** standard is an interface by which application programs can access and process SQL databases in a DBMS-independent manner. This means, for example, that an application that uses the ODBC interface could process an ORACLE database, a SYBASE database, an INFORMIX database, and any other database that is ODBC-compliant without any program coding changes. The goal is to allow a developer to create a single application that can access databases supported by different DBMS products without needing to be changed or even recompiled.

ODBC was developed by a committee of industry experts from the X/Open and SQL Access Group committees. A number of such standards were proposed, but ODBC emerged as the winner, primarily because it has been implemented by Microsoft and is an important part of Windows. Microsoft's initial interest in support of such a standard was to allow products like Microsoft Excel to access database data from a variety of DBMS products without having to be recompiled. Of course, Microsoft's interests have changed since the introduction of OLE DB.

ODBC is important to Internet-technology database systems because, in theory, it is possible to develop an application that can process databases that are supported by different DBMS products. We say "in theory" because products vary in the way in which they comply with the standard. Fortunately, variance in conformance levels was anticipated by the ODBC committee, as you will learn.

ODBC ARCHITECTURE

Figure 13-5 shows the components of the ODBC standard. The application program, driver manager, and DBMS drivers all reside on the Web server computer. The drivers send requests to data sources, which reside on the database server. According to the standard, a **data source** is the database, its associated DBMS, operating system, and network platform. An ODBC data source can be a relational database; it can also be a file server such as BTrieve, and it can even be a spreadsheet.

The application issues requests to create a connection with a data source, to issue SQL statements and receive results, to process errors, and to start, commit, and rollback transactions. ODBC provides a standard means for each of these requests, and it defines a standard set of error codes and messages.

The **driver manager** serves as an intermediary between the application and the DBMS drivers. When the application requests a connection, the driver determines the type of DBMS that processes a given ODBC data source and loads that driver in memory (if it is not already loaded). The driver manager also processes certain initialization requests and validates the format and order of ODBC requests that it receives from the application. The driver manager is provided by Microsoft and is included with Windows.

A **driver** processes ODBC requests and submits specific SQL statements to a given type of data source. There is a different driver for each data source type. For example, there are drivers for DB2, for ORACLE, for Access, and for all of the other products whose vendors have chosen to participate in the ODBC standard. Drivers are supplied by DBMS vendors and by independent software companies.

It is the responsibility of the driver to ensure that standard ODBC commands execute correctly. In some cases, if the data source is itself not SQL-compliant, the driver may need to perform considerable processing to fill in for a lack of capability at the data source. In other cases, where the data source supports full

ODBC Architecture

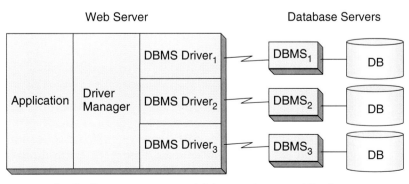

Application can process a database using any of the three DBMS products.

*ODBC Driver Types:
(a) ODBC Single-Tier
Driver (b) ODBC
Multiple-Tier Driver*

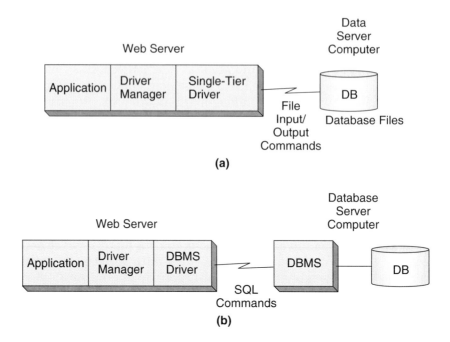

SQL, the driver need only pass the request through for processing by the data source. The driver also converts data source error codes and messages into the ODBC standard codes and messages.

ODBC identifies two types of drivers: single-tier and multiple-tier. A **single-tier** driver processes both ODBC calls and SQL statements. An example of a single-tier driver is shown in Figure 13-6(a). In this example, the data is stored in Xbase files (the format used by FoxPro, dBase, and others). Since Xbase file managers do not process SQL, it is the job of the driver to translate the SQL request into Xbase file manipulation commands and to transform the results back into SQL form.

A **multiple-tier** driver processes ODBC calls but passes the SQL requests directly to the database server. While it may reformat an SQL request to conform to the dialect of a particular data source, it does not process the SQL. An example of the use of a multiple-tier driver is shown in Figure 13-6(b).

CONFORMANCE LEVELS

The creators of the ODBC standard faced a dilemma. If they chose to describe a standard for a minimal level of capability, many vendors would be able to comply. But if they did so, the standard would represent only a small portion of the complete power and expressiveness of ODBC and SQL. On the other hand, if the standard addressed a very high level of capability, then only a few vendors would be able to comply with the standard, and it would become unimportant. To deal with this dilemma, the committee wisely chose to define levels of conformance to the standard. There are two types: ODBC conformance and SQL conformance.

ODBC CONFORMANCE LEVEL **ODBC conformance levels** concern the features and functions that are made available through the driver's application program interface (**API**). A driver API is a set of functions that the application can call to receive services. Figure 13-7 summarizes the three levels of ODBC conformance that are addressed in the standard. In practice, almost all drivers provide at least Level 1 API conformance, so the core API level is not too important.

Summary of ODBC Conformance Levels

Core API
- • Connect to data sources
- • Prepare and execute SQL statements
- • Retrieve data from a result set
- • Commit or rollback transactions
- • Retrieve error information

Level 1 API
- • Core API
- • Connect to data sources with driver-specific information
- • Send and receive partial results
- • Retrieve catalog information
- • Retrieve information about driver options, capabilities, and functions

Level 2 API
- • Core and Level 1 API
- • Browse possible connections and data sources
- • Retrieve native form of SQL
- • Retrieve catalog information
- • Call a translation library
- • Process a scrollable cursor

An application can call a driver to determine which level of ODBC conformance it provides. If the application requires a level of conformance that is not present, it can terminate the session in an orderly fashion and generate appropriate messages to the user. Or the application can be written to use higher-level conformance features if they are available and to work around the missing functions if a higher level is not available.

For example, drivers at the Level 2 API must provide a scrollable cursor. Using conformance levels, an application could be written to use cursors if they are available, but, if they are not, to work around the missing feature, selecting needed data using very restrictive WHERE clauses. Doing this would ensure that only a few rows were returned at a time to the application, and it would process those rows using a cursor that it maintained itself. Performance would likely be slower in the second case, but at least the application would be able to successfully execute.

SQL CONFORMANCE LEVEL **SQL conformance levels** specify which SQL statements, expressions, and data types a driver can process. Three levels are defined as summarized in Figure 13-8. The capability of the minimum SQL grammar is very limited, and most drivers support at least the core SQL grammar.

As with ODBC conformance levels, an application can call the driver to determine what level of SQL conformance it supports. With that information, the application can then determine which SQL statements can be issued. If necessary, the application can then terminate the session or use alternative, less powerful means of obtaining the data.

➤ FIGURE 13-8

Summary of SQL Conformance Levels

Minimum SQL Grammar
- CREATE TABLE, DROP TABLE
- simple SELECT (does not include subqueries)
- INSERT, UPDATE, DELETE
- Simple expressions (A > B + C)
- CHAR, VARCHAR, LONGVARCHAR data types

Core SQL Grammar
- Minimum SQL Grammar
- ALTER TABLE, CREATE INDEX, DROP INDEX
- CREATE VIEW, DROP VIEW
- GRANT, REVOKE
- Full SELECT (includes subqueries)
- Aggregate functions such as SUM, COUNT, MAX, MIN, AVG
- DECIMAL, NUMERIC, SMALLINT, INTEGER, REAL, FLOAT, DOUBLE PRECISION data types

Extended SQL Grammar
- Core SQL Grammar
- Outer joins
- UPDATE and DELETE using cursor positions
- Scalar functions such as SUBSTRING, ABS
- Literals for date, time, and timestamp
- Batch SQL statements
- Procedure Calls

ESTABLISHING AN ODBC DATA SOURCE NAME

A **data source** is an ODBC data structure that identifies a database and the DBMS that processes it. Data sources identify other types of data such as spreadsheets and other non-database data stores, but we are not concerned with that use here.

There are three types of sources: file, system, and user. A **file data source** is a file that can be shared among database users. The only requirement is that the users have the same DBMS driver and privilege to access the database. The data source file can be E-mailed or otherwise distributed to possible users. A **system data source** is one that is local to a single computer. The operating system and any user on that system (with proper privileges) can use a system data source. A **user data source** is only available to the user who created it.

In general, the best choice for Web applications is to create a system data source on the Web server. Browser users then access the Web server, which in turn uses a system data source to set up a connection with the DBMS and the database.

Figure 13-9 shows the process of creating a system data source using the ODBC Data Source Administrator Service that can be found in the Windows Control Panel. In Figure 13-9(a), the user is selecting a driver to an Access database. This particular user also has drivers to dBase, FoxPro, Paradox, ORACLE, AS/400, and SQL Server as well as drivers for Excel and text files. In Figure 13-9(b), the user is selecting the database (here VIEWRIDGE.MDB). The name of this DSN is ViewRidgeDSN, and this is the name that will be used subsequently in the ADO examples.

➤ FIGURE 13-9

*Creating a System
Data Source
a. Selecting the
Driver b. Selecting
the Database*

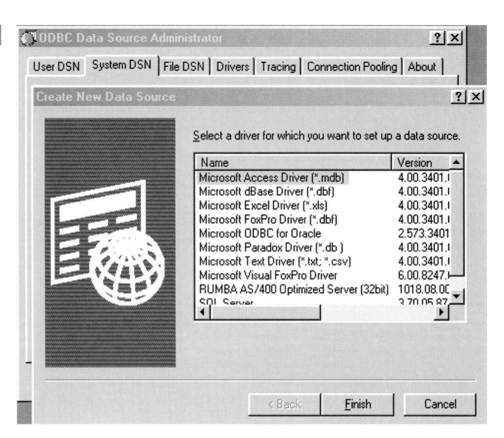

(a)

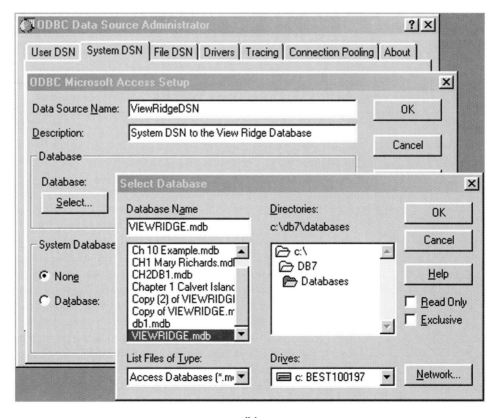

(b)

➤ OLE DB

OLE DB is the foundation of data access in the Microsoft world. Its characteristics determine the characteristics of Access 2000, SQL Server, ADO, RDS, etc. As such, it is important to understand the fundamental ideas of OLE DB, even if you will only work with the ADO interfaces that lie on top of it. In this section we present essential OLE DB concepts.

OLE DB is an implementation of the Microsoft OLE object standard. As such, OLE DB objects are COM objects and support all required interfaces for such objects. This means that they support both IUknown and IQuery (with COM, interface names always start with *I*).

Fundamentally, OLE DB breaks the features and functions of a DBMS up into objects. There can be objects that support query operations, others that perform updates, others that support the creation of database schema constructs such as tables, indexes, and views, and still others that perform transaction management such as optimistic locking.

This characteristic overcomes a major disadvantage of ODBC. With ODBC, a vendor must create an ODBC driver for almost all DBMS features and functions in order to participate in ODBC at all. This is a large task and requires a substantial initial investment. With OLE DB, however, a DBMS vendor can implement portions of their product. One could, for example, implement only the query processor, participate in OLE DB, and hence be accessible to customers using ADO and RDS. Later the vendor could add more objects and interfaces to increase their OLE DB functionality.

This text does not assume that you are an object-oriented programmer, so we need to develop a few concepts. In particular, you need to understand abstractions, methods, properties, and collections. An **abstraction** is a generalization of something. ODBC interfaces are abstractions of native DBMS access methods. When we abstract something, we lose detail, but we gain the ability to work with a broader range of types.

For example, a recordset is an abstraction of a relation. In this abstraction, a recordset is defined to have certain characteristics that will be common to all recordsets. Every recordset, for instance, has a set of columns, which in this abstraction are called Fields. Now, the goal of abstraction is to capture everything important but omit details that are not needed by users of the abstraction. Thus, Access relations may have some characteristic that is not represented in a recordset; the same might be true for relations in SQL Server, AS/400, DB2, and in other DBMS products. These unique characteristics will be lost in the abstraction, but if the abstraction is a good one, no one will care.

Moving up a level, a **rowset** is the OLE DB abstraction of a recordset. Now, why does OLE DB need to define another abstraction? Because OLE DB addresses data sources that are not tables, but have *some of* the characteristics of tables. Consider all E-mail addresses in your personal E-mail file. Are those addresses the same as a relation? No, but they do share some of the characteristics that relations have. Each address is a semantically related group of data items. Like rows of a table, it is sensible to go to the first one, move to the next one, and so forth. But, unlike relations, they are not all of the same type. Some addresses are for individuals and some are for mailing lists. Thus, any action on a recordset that depends on everything in the recordset being the same kind of thing cannot be used on a rowset.

Working from the top, down, OLE DB defines a set of data properties and behaviors for rowsets. Every rowset has those properties and behaviors. Furthermore, OLE DB defines a recordset as a subtype of a rowset. Recordsets have all of the properties and behaviors that rowsets have, plus they have some that are uniquely characteristic of recordsets.

Abstraction is both common and useful. You will hear of abstractions of transaction management or abstractions of querying or abstractions of interfaces. This simply means that certain characteristics of a set of things are formally defined as a type.

An object (an object-oriented programming object, not a semantic object) is an abstraction that is defined by its properties and methods. For example, a recordset object has an AllowEdits property and a RecordsetType property and an EOF property. These **properties** represent characteristics of the recordset abstraction. An object also has actions that it can perform that are called **methods.** A recordset has methods such as Open, MoveFirst, MoveNext, and Close.

Strictly speaking, the definition of an object abstraction is called an **object class,** or just class. An instance of an object class, such as a particular recordset, is called an object. All objects of a class have the same methods and the same properties, but the values of those properties vary from object to object.

The last term we need to address is collection. A **collection** is an object that contains a group of other objects. A recordset has a collection of other objects called Fields. The collection has properties and methods. One of the properties of all collections is Count, which is the number of objects in the collection. Thus, recordset.Fields.Count is the number of fields in the collection. In ADO and OLE DB, collections are named as the plural of the objects they collect. Thus, there is a Fields collection of Field objects, an Errors collection of Error objects, a Parameters collection of Parameters, and so forth. An important method of a collection is an iterator, which is a method that can be used to pass through or otherwise identify the items in the collection.

If you're getting frustrated with all these definitions, don't give up. You will see a practical use of these concepts before the end of this chapter!

Goals of OLE DB

The major goals for OLE DB are listed in Figure 13-10. First, as mentioned, OLE DB breaks DBMS functionality and services into object pieces. This partitioning means great flexibility for both **data consumers** (users of OLE DB functional-

➤ FIGURE 13-10

OLE DB Goals

- Create object interfaces for DBMS functionality pieces
    ◦ Query
    ◦ Update
    ◦ Transaction management
    ◦ Etc
- Increase flexibility
  Allow data consumers to use only the objects they need
  Allow data providers to expose pieces of DBMS functionality
  Providers can deliver functionality in multiple interfaces
  Interfaces are standardized and extensible
- Object interface over any type of data
  Relational database
  ODBC or native
  Non-relational database
  VSAM and other files
  E-mail
  Other
- Do not force data to be converted or moved from where it is

ity) and **data providers** (vendors of products that deliver OLE DB functionality). Data consumers take only the objects and functionality they need; a pocket device for reading a database can have a very slim footprint. Unlike with ODBC, data providers need only implement a portion of DBMS functionality. This partitioning also means that data providers can deliver capabilities in multiple interfaces.

This last point needs expansion. An object interface is a packaging of objects. An **interface** is specified by a set of objects and the properties and methods that they expose. An object need not expose all of its properties and methods in a given interface. Thus, a recordset object would expose only read methods in a query interface, but create, update, and delete methods in a modification interface.

How the object supports the interface, or the **implementation,** is completely hidden from the user. In fact, the developers of an object are free to change the implementation whenever they want. Who will know? But they may not ever change the interface without incurring the justifiable disdain of their users!

OLE DB defines standardized interfaces. Data providers, however, are free to add interfaces on top of the basic standards. Such extensibility is essential for the next goal, which is to provide an object interface to any type of data. Relational databases can be processed through OLE DB objects that use ODBC or that use the native DBMS drivers. OLE DB includes support for the other types as indicated.

The net result of these design goals is that data need not be converted from one form to another, nor need it be moved from one data source to another. The Web server in Figure 13-1 can utilize OLE DB to process data in any of the formats, right where the data resides. This means that transactions may span multiple data sources and may be distributed on different computers. The OLE DB provision for this is the **Microsoft Transaction Manager** (MTS), but discussion of it is beyond the scope of this chapter.

OLE DB Basic Constructs

As shown in Figure 13-11, OLE DB has two types of data providers. **Tabular data providers** present their data via rowsets. Examples are DBMS products, spreadsheets, and ISAM file processors like dbase and FoxPro. Additionally, other types of data like E-mail can also be presented in rowsets. Tabular data providers bring data of some type into the OLE DB world.

A **service provider,** on the other hand, is a transformer of data. Service providers accept OLE DB data from an OLE DB tabular data provider and transform it some way. Service providers are both consumers and providers of transformed data. An example of a service provider is one that obtains data from a relational DBMS and transforms it into XML documents.

➤ FIGURE 13-11

*Two Types of OLE DB
Data Providers*

- Tabular data provider
  - Exposes data via rowsets
  - Examples: DBMS, spreadsheets, ISAMs, E-mail
- Service provider
  - Does not own data
  - Transforms data through OLE DB interfaces
  - Both a consumer and a provider of data
  - Examples: query processors, XML document creator

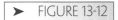

Rowset Interfaces

- IRowSet
  Methods for sequential iteration through a rowset
- IAccessor
  Methods for setting and determining bindings between rowset and client program variables
- IColumnsInfo
  Methods for determining Information about the columns in the rowset
- Other interfaces
  Scrollable cursors
  Create, update, delete rows
  Directly access particular rows (bookmarks)
  Explicitly set locks
  Etc.

The **rowset** object is fundamental to OLE DB; rowsets are equivalent to what we called **cursors** in Chapter 12, and in fact the two terms are used synonymously. Figure 13-12 lists the basic rowset interfaces that are supported. IRowSet provides object methods for forward only sequential movement through a rowset. When you declare a forward only cursor in OLE DB, you are invoking the IRowSet interface. The IAccessor interface is used to bind program variables to rowset fields. When using ADO, this interface is largely hidden because it is used behind the scenes in the scripting engine. If you work with type libraries in VB, however, you may use methods from this interface.

The IColumnsInfo interface has methods for obtaining information about the columns in a rowset. We will use this interface to advantage in two of the ADO examples at the end of this chapter. IRowSet, IAccessor, and IColumnsInfo are the basic rowset interfaces. Other interfaces are defined for more advanced operations like scrollable cursors, update, direct access to particular rows, explicit locks and so forth.

Consider these interfaces in the context of two rowsets—one a traditional relation and another that is a collection of E-mail addresses. The first three interfaces readily pertain to either type of rowset. The last set of interfaces will likely be different in the features and functions between the two rowsets if they pertain at all. One final note, rowsets can contain pointers to objects so quite complicated structures can be created with them.

➤ ADO (ACTIVE DATA OBJECTS)

ADO is a simple object model that can be used by data consumers to process any OLE DB data. It can be called from scripting languages like JScript and VBScript, from VisualBasic, Java, and C++. Microsoft has stated that it will replace all other data access methods, so that learning it is important not just for Internet-technology database applications, but for any data applications that use Microsoft products.

ADO is closely integrated with RDS. This means that you can develop scripts that create ADO objects for accessing OLE DB data providers and those ADO objects work directly with RDS objects on the browser for data caching and remote processing. Finally, because of OLE DB abstractions and object structure, the ADO object model and interfaces are the same regardless of the type of data

Characteristics of ADO

> • Simple object model for OLE DB data consumers
> • Can be used from VBScript, JScript, Visual Basic, Java, C++
> • Single Microsoft data access standard
> • Integration with RDS for remote data caching
> • Data access objects are the same for all types of OLE DB data

processed. Thus, a developer who learns ADO for processing a relational database can use that knowledge for processing an E-mail directory as well. Characteristics of ADO are listed in Figure 13-13.

ADO OBJECT MODEL

The ADO object model shown in Figure 13-14 is built on top of the OLE DB object model. The Connection object is the first ADO object to be created and the basis for the others. From a connection, a developer can create one or more RecordSet objects (cursors) and one or more Command objects. In the process of creating or working with any of these objects, ADO will place any errors that are generated in the Errors collection.

Each RecordSet object has a Fields collection; each Field element corresponds to a column in the record set. In addition, each Command object has a Parameters Collection that contains objects for the parameters of the command.

CONNECTION OBJECT

The following VBScript code will work in an ASP page. It creates a connection object, sets a pointer to it in the variable objConn, and then opens the View Ridge DSN created in Figure 13-9:

```
Dim objConn
Set objConn = Server.CreateObject ("ADODB.connection")
objConn.IsolationLevel = 4096 ' means repeatable read
objConn.open "ViewRidgeDSN"
```

ADO Object Model

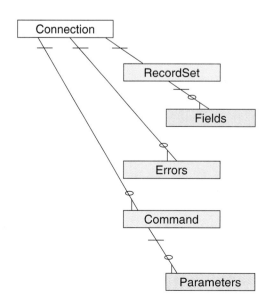

Constant Values for
ADO Processing

Isolation Level	Const Name	Value
Dirty reads	adXactChaos	16
Cursor stability	adXactCursorStability	4096
Repeatable read	adXactRepeatableRead	65536
Exclusive use	adXactSerializable	1048576

(a) Isolation Levels

Cursor Type	Const Name	Value
Forward only	adOpenForwardOnly	0
Keyset	adOpenKeyset	1
Dynamic	adOpenDynamic	2
Static	adOpenStatic	3

(b) Cursor Types

Cursor Type	Const Name	Value
Read only	adLockReadOnly	1
Pessimistic locking	adLockPessimistic	2
Optimistic locking	adLockOptimistic	3
Optimistic with batch updates	adBatchOptimistic	4

(c) Lock Types

In this code, the statement Server.CreateObject is invoking the CreateObject method of the ASP Server object. The type of object to create is passed as a parameter; here we are creating an ADO connection object. At this point, the variable objConn contains a pointer to the new connection. This pointer is then used to set the value of the isolation level property for the connection. Here it is set to the value 4096, which according to Figure 13-15, means the connection is to have cursor stability isolation.

The Microsoft development libraries contain a constant file ADOVBS.inc that can be included into the ASP pages with the include statement

⟨!—#include virtual="/relative folder(s)/ADOVBS.inc"—⟩

(The relative folders would be set to indicate the relative position of this file.) If this were done, then the constant adXactCursorStability would have been used instead of the value 4096. Use of such constants results in better documented code.

The third statement invokes the open method of a connection to open the ViewRidgeDSN. Other parameters could be passed such as username and password, and in fact, if the data source were managed by ORACLE or SQL Server, they would be required.

At this point, a connection has been established and the database is open. Now, the pointer in objConn can be used to refer to any other methods for a connection, including the creation or use of RecordSet, or Command objects, and the processing of the Errors collection (See Figure 13-14).

RECORDSET OBJECT

Given a connection with an open database, we can now create a RecordSet object with the following code:

```
Dim objRecordSet, varSql
Const adoCursorType = 3 ' static cursor
Const adoLockType = 3 ' optimistic locking
varSql = "SELECT * FROM [ARTIST]"
Set objRecordSet = Server.CreateObject("ADODB.Recordset")
objRecordSet.CursorType = adoCursorType
objRecordSet.LockType = adoLockType
objRecordSet.Open varSql, objConn
```

The first section of code defines objRecordSet and varSql (the prefix *obj* is used for object pointers and the prefix *var* is used for program variables) and then sets two constants (assuming we did not include ADOVBS.inc). The first declares cursor type and the second sets locking style. Figure 13-15 shows other possibilities (and you thought you'd never use any of what you learned in Chapter 12!).

The SQL statement encoded in varSql is pure SQL. Of course, any other SQL statement could be used, but note that the columns selected determine the contents of the Fields collection. Here, since we select with *, we will obtain all five of them [See Figure 10-3(d)]. A select on Name and Nationality only would result in a RecordSet with just those two columns.

To create the recordset object, the Create method of the server is called again with the parameter "ADODB.Recordset," the CursorType and LockType properties are set, and then the recordset is opened using the recordset object method Open. The SQL statement and the connection object pointer are passed as parameters.

Alternatively, the cursor type and lock type properties would not need to be set prior to the open, they could be added to the parameter list as:

```
objRecordSet.Open varSql, objConn, adoCursorType, adoLockType
```

You will see examples of this format in the ASP pages to follow.

FIELDS COLLECTION

Once the recordset has been created, its fields collection is instantiated. We can process that collection with the following:

```
Dim varI, varNumCols, objField
varNumCols = objRecordSet.Fields.Count
For varI = 0 to varNumCols − 1
   Set objField = objRecordSet.Fields(varI)
   ' objField.Name now has the name of the field
   ' objField.Value now has the value of the field
   ' can do something with them here
Next
```

In the second statement, varNumCols is set to the number of columns in the recordset by accessing the Count property of the Fields collection. Then a loop is executed to iterate over this collection. The property Fields(0) refers to the first column of the record set, so the loop needs to run from 0 to Count − 1.

Nothing is done with the fields objects in this example, but in an actual application, the developer could reference objField.Name to get the name of a column and objField.Value to obtain its value. You will see uses like this in the following examples.

ERRORS COLLECTION

Whenever an error occurs, ADO instantiates an errors collection. It must be a collection since more than one error can be generated by a single ADO statement. This collection can be processed in a manner similar to that for the Fields collection:

```
Dim varErrorCount, varI, objError
On Error Resume Next
varErrorCount = objConn.Errors.Count
If varErrorCount > 0 Then
   For varI = 0 to varErrorCount − 1
      Set objError = objConn.Errors(varI)
      ' objError.Description contains
      ' a description of the error
   Next
End If
```

In the loop, objError is set to objConn.Errors(varI). Note that this collection belongs to objConn and not to objRecordSet. Also the Description property of objError can be used to display the error to the user.

Unfortunately, VBScript has quite limited error processing. The code for checking errors (starting with On Error Resume Next) must be placed after every ADO object statement that might cause an error. Because this can bulk up the code undesirably, it would be better to write an error handling function and call it after every ADO object invocation.

COMMAND OBJECT

The ADO command object is used to execute queries and stored procedures that are stored with the database. The parameters collection of Command is used to pass parameters. For example, suppose that there is a SQL query stored in the

View Ridge database that deletes an ARTIST row and all of the intersection table rows for that artist. Suppose this query is named "ArtistDelete" and that it expects to receive the name of the artist as a parameter into the query. (See Access 2000 help on parameterized queries if you are unfamiliar with this.) The following code will cause this query to be executed:

```
Dim objCommand
Set objCommand = Server.CreateObject("AdoCommand")
' assume objConn has the current connection as above
Set objCommand.ActiveConnection = objConn
objCommand.CommandText = "ArtistDelete"
objCommand.CommandType = adCmdStoredProcedure ' from ADOVBS.inc
cmd.Parameters(0) = "Juan Miro"
cmd.Execute
```

This code works similarly to that for the other examples. objCommand is set to point to a Command object; the CommandText and CommandType properties are set and the query is executed.

These code snippets give you some examples of how ADO can be invoked from VBScript in ASP pages. Now we will examine several actual ASP examples.

EXAMPLE 1—READING A TABLE

Figure 13-16 shows an ASP page that will display the contents of the ARTIST table. You can run this page by placing it in a directory that is managed by IIS. Make sure that the directory is marked for script execution if you do this.

As mentioned earlier, all statements inside ⟨% . . . %⟩ are statements to be executed on the Web server by the ASP processor. Statements outside of the percent signs will be sent down to the client for execution on the browser. In the next several figures, all ASP code is shown in red ink and all browser code is shown in blue.

The top of the page is standard HTML. The first section of server code establishes a connection object and a recordset object that is the result of the SQL statement

```
SELECT  Name, Nationality
FROM    ARTIST
```

Because the process of obtaining these objects is relatively expensive, this code preserves them in session variables. In that way, if the user returns to view the table again, these objects need not be recreated. The session variable _conn stores the pointer to the connection object, and the session variable _rs stores a pointer to the recordset object.

The first time a client invokes this page, neither the connection nor the recordset object will have been created. In this case, the function IsObject(Session("_Conn")) will return false because _Conn has not yet been set. Thus, the code after the Else will be executed. It starts with Set objConn.

Next, a similar strategy is used for the recordset. If the recordset object does not exist, it will be created. Note that code that begins

```
If objRecordSet.eof
```

is checking to determine if the recordset is empty (*eof* means end of file). If so, the statement objRecordSet.AddNew invokes the AddNew method to set up one empty row. Without this statement, the MoveFirst method below it will fail.

Artist.asp

```
<HTML>
<HEAD>
<META HTTP-EQUIV ="Content-Type" CONTENT ="text/html;charset=windows-1252">
<TITLE>Artist</TITLE>
</HEAD>
<BODY>
<%
Const adoCursorType = 3 ' static cursor
Const adoLockType = 3 ' optimistic locking
Const adoIsolationLevel = 4096 ' means cursor stability

Dim objConn, objRecordSet, varSql

If IsObject (Session("_conn")) Then
    Set objConn = Session ("_conn")
Else
    Set objConn = Server.CreateObject ("ADODB.connection")
    objConn.IsolationLevel = adoIsolationLevel
    objConn.open "ViewRidgeDSN" ' could also pass user name and password here
    Set Session ("_conn") = objConn
End If
%>
<%
If IsObject (Session ("_rs")) Then
    Set objRecordSet = Session ("_rs")
    objRecordSet.Requery
Else
    varSql = "SELECT Name, Nationality FROM [ARTIST]"
    Set objRecordSet = Server.CreateObject ("ADODB.Recordset")
    ' in the next statement, note use of cursor and lock types
    objRecordSet.Open varSql, objConn, adoCursorType , adoLockType
    If objRecordSet.eof Then
        objRecordSet.AddNew
    End If
    Set Session ("_rs") = objRecordSet
End If
%>

<TABLE BORDER =1 BGCOLOR=#ffffff CELLSPACING =0><FONT FACE ="Arial" COLOR=#000000><CAPTION><B>ARTIST
</B></CAPTION></FONT>
<THEAD>
<TR>
<TH BGCOLOR=#c0c0c0 BORDERCOLOR=#000000 ><FONT SIZE=2 FACE ="Arial" COLOR=#000000>Name</FONT></TH>
<TH BGCOLOR=#c0c0c0 BORDERCOLOR=#000000 ><FONT SIZE=2 FACE ="Arial" COLOR=#000000>Nationality</FONT>
</TH>

</TR>
</THEAD>
<TBODY>
<%
On Error Resume Next
objRecordSet.MoveFirst
do while Not objRecordSet.eof
    %>

<TR VALIGN =TOP>
<TD BORDERCOLOR=#c0c0c0 ><FONT SIZE=2 FACE ="Arial" COLOR=#000000><%=Server.HTMLEncode (objRecordSet
("Name"))%><BR></FONT></TD>
<TD BORDERCOLOR=#c0c0c0 ><FONT SIZE=2 FACE ="Arial" COLOR=#000000><%=Server.HTMLEncode (objRecordSet
("Nationality")) %><BR></FONT></TD>

</TR>
<%
objRecordSet.MoveNext
loop%>
</TBODY>
</TFOOT></TFOOT>
</TABLE>
</BODY>
</HTML>
```

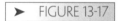

Result of ASP Page in Figure 13-16

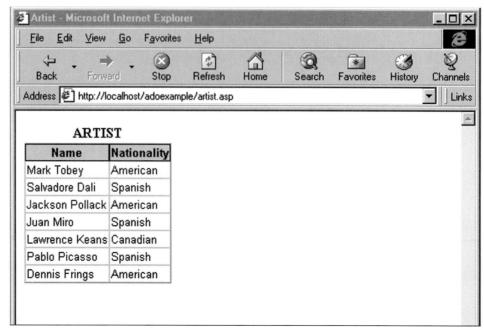

If a recordset has been created in this session before, then the statements

Set objRecordSet = Session (_rs)

objRecordSet.Requery

will reestablish the recordset pointer. The Requery method is invoked because this is a static recordset and changes made by other concurrent users will not be visible without a requery.

The next section of the ASP page contains HTML for the browser. It is followed by several snippets of server script code intermixed with HTML. The statement On Error Resume Next overrides the ASP script engine's error processing to continue the script. A better page would process the errors instead.

The last part of the page simply produces the HTML and fills in read values. The objRecordSet.MoveFirst. . . . MoveNext loop is the logic for standard sequential processing of a file.

The result of this ASP page is shown in Figure 13-17. There is nothing spectacular about this page nor about this ASP file except the following: If this is on the Internet, any of over 150 million people worldwide would be able to view it! They would need no software other than what is already on their computer.

EXAMPLE 2—READING A TABLE IN A GENERALIZED FASHION

The first example made minimal use of the ADO objects in the object model. We can extend this example by using the Fields collection. Suppose we want to take the name of a table as input and display all of the columns in it except the surrogate key, which we assume has the format tablenameID, for example, ArtistID or CustomerID.

The ASP page in Figure 13-18 will accomplish this task, except that the name of the table is set in the variable varTableName. The next example will show how to obtain a value for the desired table name using HTML form processing.

The first part of the server script has the same function as that in Figure 13-6 with three exceptions. The first difference is the code used to set a value for varKeyName. The name of the table is CUSTOMER, but the name of the surro-

Customer.asp

```
<HTML>
<HEAD>
<META HTTP–EQUIV ="Content–Type" CONTENT ="text/html;charset=windows–1252">
<TITLE>Table Display Page</TITLE>
</HEAD>
<BODY>
<%
Const adoCursorType = 3 ' static cursor
Const adoLockType = 3 ' optimistic locking
Const adoIsolationLevel = 4096 ' means cursor stability

Dim objConn, objRecordSet, objField
Dim varNumCols, varI, varSql, varTableNameRest
Dim varTableName, varRecordSetName, varKeyName

varTablename = "CUSTOMER"
' set key name to upper first initial lower rest w/ ID, e.g., CustomerID
varTableNameFirst = UCase(Left(varTableName, 1))
varTableNameRest = LCase(Right(varTableName, Len(varTableName) −1))
varKeyName = varTableNameFirst & varTableNameRest &"ID"

varRecordSetName = "_rs" & varTableName

If IsObject (Session("_conn")) Then
    Set objConn = Session("_conn")
Else
    Set objConn = Server.CreateObject ("ADODB.connection")
    objConn.IsolationLevel = adoIsolationLevel
    objConn.open "ViewRidgeDSN" ' could also pass user name and password here
    Set Session("_conn") = objConn
End If

If IsObject (Session(varRecordSetName)) Then
    Set objRecordSet = Session(varRecordSetName)
    objRecordSet.Requery
Else
    varSQL = "SELECT * FROM [" & varTableName & "]"
    Set objRecordSet = Server.CreateObject("ADODB.Recordset")
    ' in the next statement, note use of cursor and lock types
    objRecordSet.Open varSQL, objConn, adoCursorType,  adoLockType
    If objRecordSet.eof Then
         objRecordSet.AddNew
    End If
    Set Session (varRecordSetName) = objRecordSet
End If
%>

<TABLE BORDER =1 BGCOLOR=#ffffff CELLSPACING =0><FONT FACE ="Arial" COLOR=#000000><CAPTION><B><%
 =varTableName%></B></CAPTION></FONT>
<THEAD>
<TR>
<%
varNumCols = objRecordSet.Fields.Count
For varI = 0 to varNumCols – 1
Set objField = objRecordSet.Fields(varI)
If objField.Name <> varKeyName Then ' omit surrogate key %>
<TH BGCOLOR=#c0c0c0 BORDERCOLOR=#000000 ><FONT SIZE=2 FACE ="Arial" COLOR=#000000><%=objField.Name%>
</FONT></TH>
<%
End If
Next%>
</TR>
</THEAD>
<TBODY>
<%
On Error Resume Next
objRecordSet.MoveFirst
do while Not objRecordSet.eof
%>
<TR VALIGN= TOP>
```

► FIGURE 13-18

(Continued)

```
<%
varNumCols = objRecordSet.Fields.Count
For varI = 0 to varNumCols − 1
Set objField = objRecordSet.Fields (varI)
If objField.Name <> varKeyName Then ' omit surrogate key%>
<TD BORDERCOLOR=#c0c0c0 ><FONT SIZE=2 FACE="Arial" COLOR=#000000><%=Server.HTMLEncode
(objField.Value)%><BR></FONT></TD>
<%
End If
NEXT%>
</TR>
<%
objRecordSet.MoveNext
loop%>
</TBODY>
<TFOOT></TFOOT>
</TABLE>
</BODY>
</HTML>
```

gate key is CustomerID. Because VBScript comparison is case sensitive, the string "CUSTOMERID" will not equal the string "CustomerID." The purpose of the statements starting with varTableNameFirst is to set the capitalization correctly using the string functions UCase (for upper case) and LCase (for lower case).

The second difference is that a different session variable is saved for each recordset that is to be created. A query of the CUSTOMER table will cause a session variable _rsCUSTOMER to be saved with a pointer to the CUSTOMER recordset. Later, when we generalize this code, a query of a different table, for instance, ARTIST, will cause a session variable _rsARTIST to be saved with a pointer to the ARTIST recordset.

The third change is that the varSql variable is set using the varTableName variable. The & is an operator that concatenates two strings together. The result of this expression is the string:

SELECT * FROM [CUSTOMER]

The brackets are not really necessary as long as there are no spaces in the table name. If we had a table named CUSTOMER WORK, then the brackets would be required. We place them here because we will generalize this code for any table name.

Note, too, the table name is included in the HTML table caption with the code ⟨CAPTION⟩⟨B⟩⟨%=varTableName%⟩⟨/B⟩⟨/CAPTION⟩. The code inside the % will cause the value of varTableName to be placed in HTML for the caption.

The next set of server script statements process the Fields collection. The variable varNumCols is set to the count property of the Fields collection and then the collection is enumerated in the loop. Observe how HTML is interspersed in the server code (or server code is interspersed in the HTML, depending on your point of view). Previously varKeyName has been set to the name of the surrogate key, so this loop checks to determine that the name of the current field object is not the name of the surrogate key. If not, HTML is generated to create the table header. A similar enumeration loop is used on the next page to populate the table with values from the recordset.

The advantage of this page is that it can process any table, not just a particular one. In fact, using terminology developed earlier, we can say the page

FIGURE 13-19

Result of ASP Page in Figure 13-18

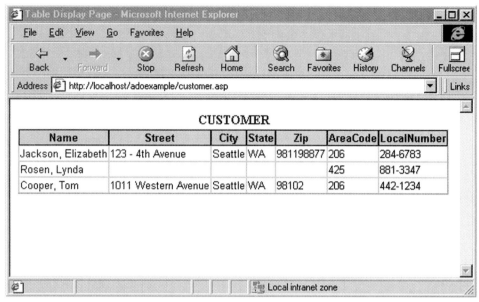

in Figure 13-18 is an abstraction of that in Figure 13-16. The results of this page are shown in Figure 13-19. The CustomerID column is not displayed, as we expected.

EXAMPLE 3—READING ANY TABLE

Figure 13-20(a) shows a data entry form in which a customer can type the name of the table to be displayed. (A better design would be to use a drop-down list to display valid choices, but that discussion would take us away from the discussion of ADO.) The user of this form has typed *artist*. Assume now that when he or she clicks the Show Table button, the form is to cause script to be executed on the server that will display the ARTIST table in this same browser session. Also, assume the surrogate key is not to be displayed. The desired results are shown in Figure 13-20(b). (None of the dates are set in this instance of the ViewRidge database.)

This processing necessitates two ASP pages. The first, shown in Figure 13-21(a), is an HTML page that contains the FORM tag

⟨FORM METHOD=“post” ACTION=“GeneralTable.asp”⟩

This tag defines a form section on the page; the section will contain data entry values. In this form, there is only one: the table name. The post method refers to an HTML process that causes the data in form (here the table name *artist*) to be delivered to the ASP server in an object called Form. An alternative method is *get,* which would cause the data values to be delivered via parameters. This distinction is not too important to us; check HTML documentation if you want to know more. The second parameter of the FORM tag is ACTION, which is set to GeneralTable.asp. This parameter tells IIS that when it receives the response from this form, it should pass the ASP file GeneralTable.asp to the ASP processor. The values from the form will be passed in an object called Form.

The rest of the page is standard HTML. Note that the name of the text input box is text1.

➤ FIGURE 13-20

Use of Data Input Form: (a) Data Input Form (b) Listing of Requested Table

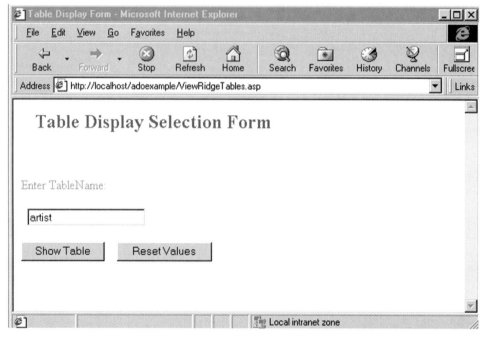

(a)

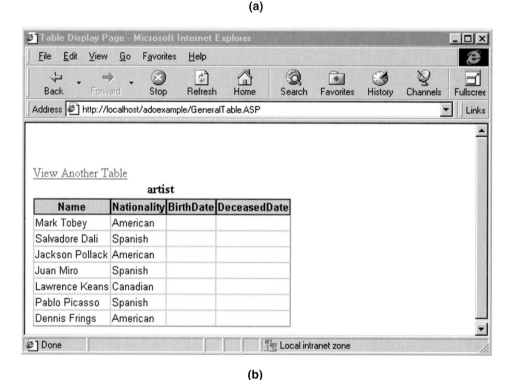

(b)

Figure 13-21(b) shows GeneralTable.asp, the page that will be invoked when the response is received from the form page in Figure 13-21(a). The first executable script statement is

varTableName = Request.Form("text1")

Request.Form is the name of the object that contains the values sent back from the browser. In this case, text1 will be set to *artist*.

The remainder of this page is the same as the Customer.asp page shown in Figure 13-19(b). Note again that varKeyName will be set to ArtistID, which is the name of the surrogate key column that we do not wish to display.

EXAMPLE 4—UPDATING A TABLE

The three previous examples all concern reading data. This last example shows how to update table data by adding a row with ADO. Figure 13-22(a) shows a data entry form that will capture artist name and nationality and create a new row. This form is similar to ViewRidgeTables.asp; it has two data entry fields rather than one. When the user clicks Save New Artist, the artist is added to the database, and if the results are successful, the form in Figure 13-22(b) is produced. The See New List URL will invoke Artist.asp which will display the ARTIST table with the new row as shown in Figure 13-22(c).

➤   FIGURE 13-21

ASP Pages for Generalized Table Listing (a) ViewRidgeTables.asp (b) GeneralTable.asp

```
<HTML>
<HEAD>
<META HTTP–EQUIV ="Content–Type" CONTENT ="text/html;charset=windows–1252">
<TITLE>Table Display Form</TITLE>
</HEAD>
</BODY>

<FORM METHOD ="post" ACTION ="GeneralTable.ASP">

 <P><STRONG><FONT color=purple face="" size=5> nbsp; Table Display Selection Form</FONT>
</STRONG>
<P></P>
<P> </P>

<P><FONT style="BACKGROUND–COLOR: #ffffff"><FONT color=forestgreen face=""
style="BACKGROUND–COLOR: #ffffff">Enter
TableName:</FONT>     </FONT></P>

<P></P>

<P><FONT style="BACKGROUND–COLOR: #ffffff"></FONT> 
<INPUT id=text1 name=text1></P>

<P><FONT style="BACKGROUND–COLOR: #ffffff">
<INPUT id=submit1 name=submit1 type=submit value="Show Table" >   
<INPUT id=reset1 name=reset1 type=reset value="Reset Values"></FONT></P>
<FORM>
</BODY>
</HTML>
```

a. View Ridge Tables.asp

(Continued)

```
<HTML>
<HEAD>
<META HTTP–EQUIV ="Content–Type" CONTENT ="text/html;charset=windows–1252">
<TITLE>Table Display Page</TITLE>
</HEAD>
<BODY>
<%
Const adoCursorType = 3 ' static cursor
Const adoLockType = 3 ' optimistic locking

Dim objConn, objRecordSet, objField
Dim varNumCols, varI, varSql, varTableNameRest
Dim varTableName, varRecordSetName, varKeyName

varTablename = Request.Form ("text1")
' set key name to upper first initial lower rest w/ ID, e.g., CustomerID
varTableNameFirst = UCase(Left(varTableName, 1))
varTableNameRest = LCase(Right(varTableName, Len(varTableName) −1))
varKeyName = varTableNameFirst & varTableNameRest &"ID"
varRecordSetName = "_rs" & varTableName

If IsObject (Session("_conn")) Then
    Set objConn = Session("_conn")
Else
    Set objConn = Server.CreateObject ("ADODB.connection")
    objConn.IsolationLevel = 4096    ' cursor stability
    objConn.open "ViewRidgeDSN"    ' could also pass user name and password here
    Set Session ("_conn") = objConn
End If

If IsObject (Session(varRecordSetName)) Then
    Set objRecordSet = Session(varRecordSetName)
    objRecordSet.Requery
Else
    varSql = "SELECT * FROM [" & varTableName & "]"
    Set objRecordSet = Server.CreateObject ("ADODB.Recordset")
    ' in the next statement, note use of cursor and lock types
   objRecordSet.Open varSql, objConn , adoCursorType , adLockBatchOptimistic
     If objRecordSet.eof Then
      objRecordSet.AddNew
     End If
    Set Session (varRecordSetName) = objRecordSet
End If
%>

<TABLE BORDER =1 BGCOLOR=#ffffff CELLSPACING =0><FONT FACE ="Arial" COLOR=#000000><CAPTION><B><%
=varTableName%></B></CAPTION></FONT>
<THEAD>
<TR>
<%
varNumCols = objRecordSet.Fields.Count
For varI = 0 to varNumCols − 1
Set objField = objRecordSet.Fields(varI)
If objField.Name <> varKeyName Then %>
<TH BGCOLOR=#c0c0c0 BORDERCOLOR=#000000 ><FONT SIZE=2 FACE ="Arial" COLOR=#000000><%=objField.Name%>
</FONT></TH>

<%
End If
Next%>
</TR>
</THEAD>
<TBODY>
<%
On Error Resume Next
objRecordSet.MoveFirst
do while Not objRecordSet.eof
%>
```

(b)

 FIGURE 13-21

(Continued)

```
<TR VALIGN=TOP>
<%
varNumCols = objRecordSet.Fields.Count
For varI = 0 to varNumCols - 1
Set objField = objRecordSet.Fields (varI)
If objField.Name <> varKeyName Then %>
<TD BORDERCOLOR=#c0c0c0 ><FONT SIZE=2 FACE="Arial" COLOR=#000000><%=Server.HTMLEncode
(objField.Value)%><BR></FONT></TD>
<%
End If
NEXT%>
</TR>

<%
objRecordSet.MoveNext
loop%>
<BR><BR><A HREF="ViewRidgeTables.asp">View Another Table</A>
</TBODY>
<TFOOT></TFOOT>
</TABLE>
</BODY>
</HTML>
```

(b) Continued

➤ FIGURE 13-22

*(a) Adding New Data
(b) Add Artist
Response (c) ARTIST
Listing with New
Data*

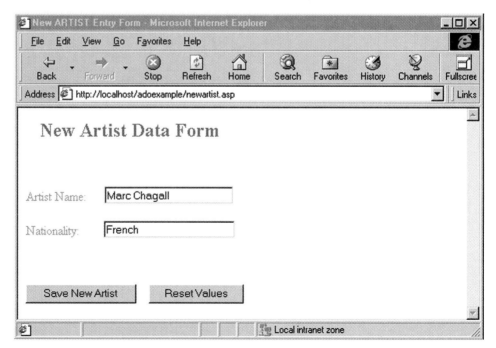

(a)

➤   FIGURE 13-22

(Continued)

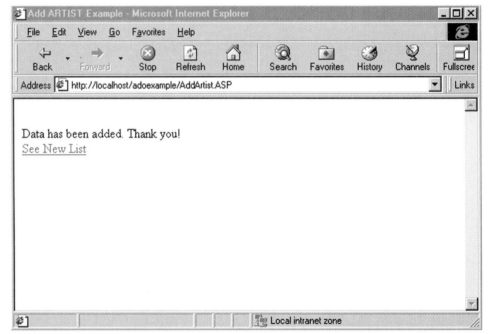

(b)

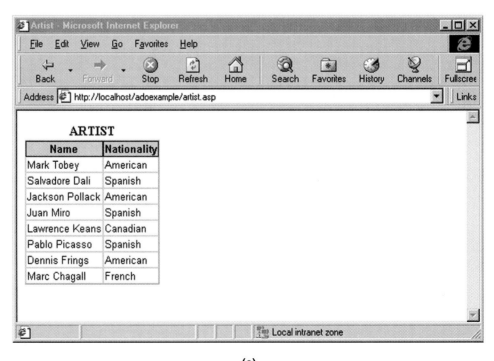

(c)

The ASP pages are shown in Figure 13-23. The first page is a data entry form with two fields, one for artist name (named *name*) and a second for artist nationality (named *nation*). When the user clicks the submit button, this data is to be sent back to IIS which in turn is to send it along with the page AddArtist.asp to the ASP processor.

AddArtist.asp [shown in Figure 13-23(b)] obtains connection and recordset objects. No attempt here is made to save connection and recordset object pointers in session variables. (The assumption is that only one artist will be added per session and saving these would be unnecessary.) If desired, code to save them could certainly be added as shown in the previous examples.

The key difference of this page is shown in the statements

objRecordSet.AddNew

objRecordSet("Name")= Request.Form("Name")

objRecordSet("Nationality")= Request.Form("Nation")

objRecordSet.Update

➤   FIGURE 13-23

(a) ASP Pages for Adding Data with ASP (b) AddArtist.asp

```
<HTML>
<HEAD>
<META HTTP–EQUIV ="Content–Type" CONTENT ="text/html;charset=windows–1252">
<TITLE>New ARTIST Entry Form</TITLE>
</HEAD>
<BODY>

<FORM METHOD="post" ACTION="AddArtist.ASP">

 <P><STRONG><FONT color=purple face="" size=5> nbsp; New Artist Data Form</FONT></STRONG>
<P></P>
<P> </P>

<P><FONT style="BACKGROUND–COLOR: #ffffff"><FONT color=forestgreen face=""
style="BACKGROUND–COLOR: #ffffff">Artist Name:</FONT>     
<INPUT id=text1 name=Name style="HEIGHT: 22px; WIDTH: 164px"></FONT></P>

<P><FONT color=forestgreen face=""
style="BACKGROUND–COLOR: #ffffff">Nationality:       
<INPUT id=text2 name=Nation style="HEIGHT: 22px; WIDTH: 167px"></FONT></P>

<P> </P>

<P><FONT style="BACKGROUND–COLOR: #ffffff">
<INPUT id=submit1 name=submit1 type=submit value="Save New Artist">   
<INPUT id=reset1 name=reset1 type=reset value="Reset Values"></FONT></P>
</FORM>
</BODY>
</HTML>
```

(a)

► FIGURE 13-23

(Continued)

```
<HTML>
<HEAD>
<META HTTP-EQUIV ="Content-Type" CONTENT ="text/html;charset=windows-1252">
<TITLE>Add ARTIST Example</TITLE>
</HEAD>
<BODY>
<%
Const adoCursorType = 2 ' dynamic cursor
Const adoLockType = 3 ' optimistic locking
Const adoIsolationLevel = 4096 ' means cursor stability

Dim objConn, objRecordSet, objField
Dim varNumCols, varI, varSql
Set objConn = Server.CreateObject("ADODB.connection")
objConn.IsolationLevel = adoIsolationLevel
objConn.open "ViewRidgeDSN"   ' could also pass user name and password here
varSql = "SELECT * FROM [ARTIST]"
Set objRecordSet = Server.CreateObject("ADODB.Recordset")
' in the next statement, note use of cursor and lock types
objRecordSet.Open varSql, objConn, adoCursorType , adoLockType

objRecordSet.AddNew
objRecordSet("Name")= Request.Form("Name")
objRecordSet("Nationality")= Request.Form("Nation")

objRecordSet.Update

On Error Resume Next
varErrorCount = objConn.Errors.Count
If varErrorCount > 0 Then
     For varI = 0 to varErrorCount - 1
          Response.Write "<BR><I>" & objConn.Errors(varI).Description & "</I><BR>"
     Next
End If

objRecordSet.Close
objConn.Close

Response.Write "<BR>Data has been added. Thank you!<BR>"
Response.Write "<A HREF="& """" &"artist.asp" & """"& ">See New List</A>"

%>
<BR><BR>
</BODY>
</HTML>
```

(b)

The first statement obtains a new row in the objRecordSet object and then values are obtained for the Name and Nationality columns from the Request.Form object. Note there is no need for the column names and Request.Form names to be the same. Here the second column name is Nationality, but the second value from the form is Nation. The objRecordSet.Update call causes the database update. Note the error processing code which will cause error messages to be displayed via the Response.Write statement (this is a method available in the Response object of

ASP). The page ends with two calls to send a confirmation message back to the user and to create an URL to Artist.asp if the user wants to see the new table.

These examples give you an idea of the use of ADO. In order to run them, you will need Windows NT 4.0 or higher and IIS 4.0 or higher on the Web server. Because the pages generated are pure HTML, any browser should work. Search www.microsoft.com for ADO examples if you want to see more examples of the use of ADO, and in particular, more examples that integrate ADO with RDS.

➤ SUMMARY

Internet-technology database applications reside in a rich and complicated environment. In addition to relational databases, there are nonrelational databases, VSAM and other file processing data, E-mail, and other types of data like pictures, audio, and so forth. To ease the job of the application programmer, various standards have been developed. The ODBC standard is for relational databases; the OLE DB standard is for relational and other databases. ADO was developed to provide easier access to OLE DB data for the non–object-oriented programmer.

ODBC, or the open database connectivity standard, provides an interface by which Web server programs can access and process relational data sources in a DBMS-independent manner. ODBC was developed by an industry committee and has been implemented by Microsoft and many other vendors. ODBC involves applications program, driver manager, DBMS driver, and data source components. Single-tier and multiple-tier drivers are defined. There are three types of data source names: file, system, and user. System data sources are recommended for Web servers. The process of defining a system data source name involves specifying the type of driver and the identity of the database to be processed.

OLE DB is the foundation of the Microsoft data access world. It implements the Microsoft OLE and COM standards and is accessible to object-oriented programs through those interfaces. OLE DB breaks the features and functions of a DBMS into objects, thus making it easier for vendors to implement portions of functionality. Key object terms are abstraction, methods, properties, and collections. A rowset is an abstraction of a recordset, which in turn is an abstraction of a relation. Objects are defined by properties which specify their characteristics and methods which are actions they can perform. A collection is an object that contains a group of other objects. The goals of OLE DB are listed in Figure 13-10. An interface is a set of objects and the properties and methods they expose in that interface. Objects may expose different properties and methods in different interfaces. An implementation is how an object accomplishes its tasks. Implementations are hidden from the outside world and may be changed without impacting the users of the objects. An interface ought not to be changed, ever.

Tabular data providers present data in the form of rowsets. Service providers transform data into another form; such providers are both consumers and providers of data. A rowset is equivalent to a cursor. Basic rowset interfaces are IRowSet, IAccessor, and IColumnsInfo. Other interfaces are defined for more advanced capability.

ADO is a simple object model used by OLE DB data consumers. It can be used from any language supported by Microsoft. ADO works closely with RDS for remote data caching. The ADO object model has Connection, RecordSet, Command, and Errors collection objects. Recordsets have a Fields collection and Commands have a Parameters collection.

A connection object establishes a connection to a data provider and data source. Connections have an isolation mode. Once a connection is created, it can be used to create RecordSet and Command objects. RecordSet objects represent cursors, they have both CursorType and LockType properties. RecordSets can be created with SQL statements. The Fields collection of a RecordSet can be processed to individually manipulate fields.

The Errors collection contains one or more error messages that result from an ADO operation. The command object is used to execute stored parameterized queries or stored procedures. Input data can be sent to the correct ASP page using the HTML FORM tag. Table updates are made using the RecordSet Update method.

➤ GROUP I QUESTIONS

13.1   Describe why the data environment for Web servers is complicated.

13.2   Explain the relationship of ODBC, OLE DB, and ADO.

13.3   Explain the author's justification for describing Microsoft standards. Do you agree?

13.4   Name the components of the ODBC standard.

13.5   What role does the driver manager serve? Who supplies it?

13.6   What role does the DBMS driver serve? Who supplies it?

13.7   What is a single-tier driver?

13.8   What is a multiple-tier driver?

13.9   Do the uses of the term *tier* in the three-tier architecture and its use in ODBC have anything to do with each other?

13.10 Why are conformance levels important?

13.11 Summarize the three ODBC API conformance levels.

13.12 Summarize the three SQL grammar conformance levels.

13.13 Explain the difference among the three types of data sources.

13.14 Which data source type is recommended for Web servers?

13.15 What are the two tasks to be accomplished when setting up an ODBC data source name?

13.16 Why is OLE DB important?

13.17 What disadvantage of ODBC does OLE DB overcome?

13.18 Define *abstraction* and explain how it relates to OLE DB.

13.19 Give an example of abstraction involving rowset.

13.20 Define object *properties* and *methods*.

13.21 What is the difference between an object class and an object?

13.22 Explain the role of data consumers and data providers.

13.23 What is an interface?

13.24 What is the difference between an interface and an implementation?

13.25 Explain why an implementation can be changed but an interface should not be changed.

13.26 Summarize the goals of OLE DB.

13.27 What is MTS, and what does it do?

13.28 Explain the difference between a tabular data provider and a service provider. Which type is a product that transforms OLE DB data into XML documents?

13.29 In the context of OLE DB, what is the difference between a rowset and a cursor?

13.30 What languages can use ADO?

13.31 List the objects in the ADO object model and explain their relationships.

13.32 What is the function of the Connection object?

13.33 Show a snippet of VBScript for creating a Connection object.

13.34 What is the function of the RecordSet object?

13.35 Show a snippet of VBScript for creating a RecordSet object.

13.36 What does the Fields collection contain? Explain a situation in which you would use it.

13.37 Show a snippet of VBScript for processing the Fields collection.

13.38 What does the Errors collection contain? Explain a situation in which you would use it.

13.39 Show a snippet of VBScript for processing the Errors collection.

13.40 What is the purpose of the Command object?

13.41 Show a snippet of VBScript for executing a stored parameterized query that has two parameters, A and B.

13.42 Explain the purpose of the ⟨% and %⟩ tags in ASP pages.

13.43 Explain the purpose of the _conn and _rs session variables in Figure 13-16.

13.44 What is the reason for the code that creates varKeyName in Figure 13-18?

13.45 Explain the purpose of the ACTION parameter of the FORM tag in Figure 13-21(a).

13.46 Explain what happens when the following statement is executed in the ASP page in Figure 13-21(a):

varTableName = Request.Form("text1")

13.47 Show a VBScript snippet for adding a new record to a recordset name objMyRecordSet. Assume the fields are A and B and their values are to be "Avalue" and "Bvalue" respectively.

13.48 What role is served by the Response.Write statement?

➤ GROUP II QUESTIONS

13.49 Microsoft expends much effort to promulgate the OLE DB and ADO standards. It does not directly receive revenue from these standards. IIS is free with Windows NT and Windows 2000. Its Web site has numerous examples of articles to help developers learn more, and all of it is free. Why do you think Microsoft does this? What goal is served?

13.50 In the code in Figure 13-23(b), the cursor type is set to dynamic. What effect will this have on the processing of this and the Customer.asp and Artist.asp pages? Explain how you think the isolation level, cursor type, and lock type parameters should be set for an application that involves all three of these pages.

13.51 Use Access 2000 to create the CUSTOMER and ARTIST tables for View Ridge. Use a standard form wizard to create a table display form for these two tables. Export this form to ASP. Explain the purpose of the major features of this ASP page.

➤ PROJECTS

A. Modify the code in Figure 13-23 to add data to the CUSTOMER table.

B. Modify your code in your answer to Project A to add data to any table.

C. Modify the code in Figure 13-23 to delete a CUSTOMER row. Assume the user picks the row to be deleted from a listing of CUSTOMER data.

PART VI

ENTERPRISE DATABASES

This part addresses database processing in the context of the enterprise. We begin, in Chapter 14, with discussions of the architecture of enterprise database systems, On Line Analytical Processing (OLAP), data warehousing, and data administration. Chapter 15 presents a case application that illustrates IBM DBMS product DB2. We describe the major features and functions of DB2 and illustrate it with a COBOL program. Finally, Chapter 16 discusses Data Language/I and the CODASYL DBTG models; these models are old, but there are still some very large databases using them, and even today you may well encounter them.

CHAPTER 14

Sharing Enterprise Data

Data is an important organizational asset, an asset that can be used not only to facilitate the operations of a company but also for management, planning, forecasting, strategic analysis, and the like. Unfortunately, while many organizations have found that their databases effectively support organizational operations, they know that their databases are ineffectively used for analysis, planning, and other management purposes. In this chapter we address topics that are important in increasing the return of the investment on enterprise data in databases: downloading of centralized data, OLAP, data warehousing, and data administration. We begin, however, with a survey of enterprise database processing architectures.

➤ ENTERPRISE DATABASE PROCESSING ARCHITECTURES

A number of different system architectures are used for enterprise database processing. In the past, teleprocessing systems were the most common. But as microcomputers have become common on the desktop and more powerful as data servers, new multi-user database architectures have arisen. In this section, we introduce teleprocessing, client–server, file-sharing, distributed, and network database alternatives.

TELEPROCESSING SYSTEMS

The classic method of supporting a multi-user database system is teleprocessing, which uses one computer and one CPU. All processing is done by this single computer.

Figure 14-1 shows a typical teleprocessing system. Users operate dumb terminals (or microcomputers that emulate dumb terminals) that transmit transaction messages and data to the centralized computer. The communications control portion of the operating system receives the messages and data and sends them to the appropriate application program. The program then calls on the DBMS for services, and the DBMS uses the data management portion of the operating sys-

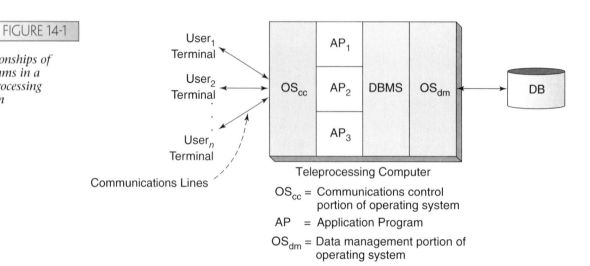

Relationships of Programs in a Teleprocessing System

OS_{cc} = Communications control portion of operating system

AP = Application Program

OS_{dm} = Data management portion of operating system

tem to process the database. When a transaction is completed, the results are returned to the users at the dumb terminals via the communications control portion of the operating system.

Figure 14-1 shows *n* users submitting transactions processed by three different application programs. Because there is little intelligence at the users' end (that is, the *terminals* are dumb), all commands for formatting the screen must be generated by the CPU and transmitted over the communication lines. This means that the users' interface is generally character oriented and primitive. Systems like this are called teleprocessing systems, because all inputs and outputs are communicated over a distance (*tele-* means "distance") to the centralized computer for processing.

Historically, teleprocessing systems have been the most common alternative for multi-user database systems. But as the price-performance ratio of computers has fallen and, in particular, with the advent of the personal computer, other alternatives that require multiple computers have begun to be used.

CLIENT–SERVER SYSTEMS

Figure 14-2 is a schematic of one of these alternatives, called a **client–server system.** Unlike teleprocessing, which involves a single computer, client–server computing involves multiple computers connected in a network. Some of the computers process application programs and are designated as *clients.* Another computer processes the database and is designated as the *server.*

Figure 14-2 shows an example in which each of *n* users has his or her own client (application processing) computer: User$_1$ processes AP$_1$ and AP$_2$ on Computer 1. User$_2$ processes AP$_2$ on Computer 2, and User$_n$ processes AP$_2$ and AP$_3$ on Computer *N*. Another computer is the database server.

There are many options regarding computer type. Theoretically, the client computers can be mainframes or microcomputers. Because of cost, however, in almost all cases the client computers are microcomputers. Similarly, any type of computer can be the server, but again, because of cost, the server is most often a microcomputer. The clients and server are connected using either a local area network (LAN) or wide area network (WAN).

Although it is rare for client computers to be anything other than micros, sometimes the server is a mainframe, especially when considerable power is required from the server or, for reasons of security and control, it is inappropriate to locate the database on a microcomputer.

Client–Server Architecture

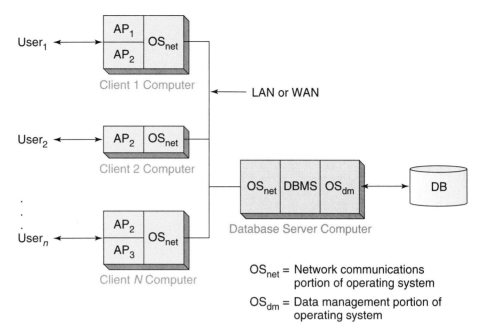

The system in Figure 14-2 has a single server, although this need not always be the case. Multiple servers may process different databases or provide other services on behalf of the clients. For example, in an engineering consulting firm, one server might process the database while a second server supports computer-assisted design applications.

If there are multiple database processing servers, each one must process a different database in order for the system to be considered a client–server system. When two servers process the same database, the system is no longer called a client–server system; rather, it is termed a distributed database system.

FILE-SHARING SYSTEMS

A second multi-user architecture is shown in Figure 14-3. This architecture, called **file-sharing,** distributes to the users' computers not only the application programs but also the DBMS. In this case, the *server* is a file server and not a database server. Almost all file-sharing systems employ LANs of microcomputers.

The file-sharing architecture was developed before the client–server architecture, and in many ways it is more primitive. With file sharing, the DBMS on each user's computer sends requests to the data management portion of the operating system on the file server for file-level processing. This means that considerably more traffic crosses the LAN than with the client–server architecture.

For example, consider the processing of a query to obtain the Name and Address of all rows in the CUSTOMER table where Zip equals 98033. In a client–server system, the application program would send the following SQL command:

```
SELECT    NAME, ADDRESS
FROM      CUSTOMER
WHERE     ZIP = 98033
```

The server would respond with all qualifying Names and Addresses.

In a file-sharing system, the DBMS is on the local computer, and therefore no program on the file server is capable of processing the SQL statement. All such processing must be done on the user computer, so the DBMS must ask the file

File-Sharing
Architecture

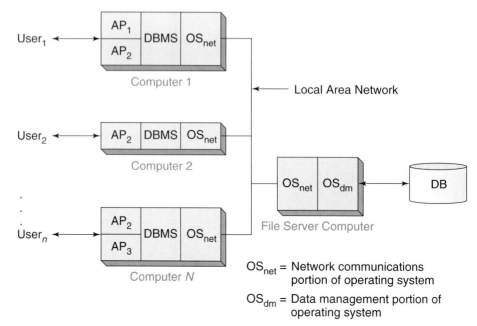

server to transmit the entire CUSTOMER table. If that table has indexes or other overhead associated with it, the overhead structures must be transmitted as well. Clearly, with file sharing, much more data need be transmitted across the LAN.

Because of these problems, file-sharing systems are seldom used for high-volume transaction-oriented processing. Too much data need be locked and transmitted for each transaction, and this architecture would result in very slow performance. There is, however, one database application for which this architecture makes sense: the query processing of downloaded, extracted data. If one or more users need access to large portions of the database in order to produce reports or answer queries, it can make sense to have a server that downloads large sections of data. In this case, the downloaded data are not updated and not returned to the database. We show examples of processing extracted data later in this chapter.

File-sharing systems are also used for nondatabase applications, such as those that require large, fast disks to store large files such as large graphics, audio, and animations. They also are used to share expensive printers, plotters, and other peripheral equipment.

DISTRIBUTED DATABASE SYSTEMS

A fourth alternative, shown in Figure 14-4, is a distributed database system, in which the database itself is distributed. In Figure 14-4, the database (or a portion of it) is stored on all *N* computers. As shown, Computers 1, 2, and *N* process both the applications and the database, and Computer 3 processes only the database.

In Figure 14-4, the dashed line around the files indicates that the database is composed of all the segments of the database on all *N* computers. These computers may be physically located in the same facility, on different sides of the world, or somewhere in between.

DISTRIBUTED PROCESSING VERSUS DISTRIBUTED DATABASE PROCESSING   Consider Figures 14-1, 14-2, 14-3, and 14-4 again. The file-sharing, client–server, and distributed database alternatives all differ from teleprocessing in an important way: They all use multiple computers for applications or DBMS processing. Accordingly, most people would say that all three of these architectures are examples of **distributed systems,** because applications processing has been distributed among several computers.

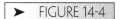

Distributed Database Architecture

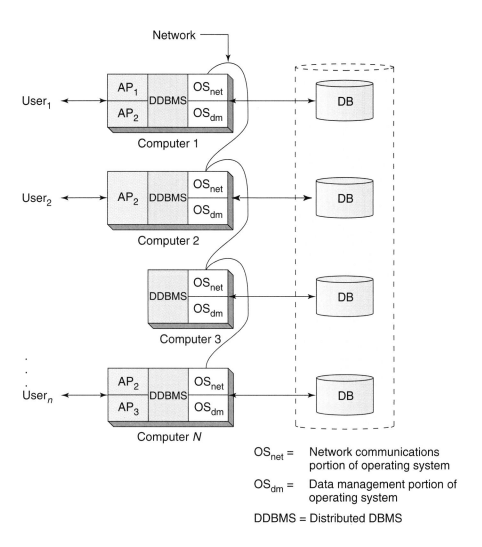

OS_{net} =   Network communications portion of operating system

OS_{dm} =   Data management portion of operating system

DDBMS = Distributed DBMS

Observe, however, that the database itself is distributed only in the architecture shown in Figure 14-4. Neither the client–server nor the file-sharing architectures distribute the database to multiple computers. Consequently, most people would *not* refer to the file-sharing or client–server architectures as **distributed database systems.**

TYPES OF DISTRIBUTED DATABASES   There are a number of types of distributed database systems. First look at Figure 14-5(a), which shows a nondistributed database with four pieces, W, X, Y, and Z. All four pieces of these segments are located on a single database, and there is no data duplication.

Now consider the distributed alternatives in Figures 14-5(b) through (d). Figure 14-5(b) shows the first distributed alternative, in which the database has been distributed to two computers; pieces W and X are stored on Computer 1, and pieces Y and Z are stored on Computer 2. In Figure 14-5(c), the entire database has been replicated on two computers. Finally, in Figure 14-5(d), the database has been partitioned, and a portion (Y) has been replicated.

Two terms are sometimes used with regard to partitioning of databases. A vertical partition or **vertical fragment** refers to a table that is broken into two or more sets of columns. Thus, a table R(C1, C2, C3, C4) could be broken into two vertical partitions of P1(C1, C2) and P2(C3, C4). Depending on the application and the reason for creating the partitions, the key of R would most likely also be placed into P2 to form P2(C1, C3, C4). A horizontal partition or

➤ FIGURE 14-5

Types of Distributed Databases: (a) Nonpartitioned, Nonreplicated Alternative; (b) Partitioned, Nonreplicated Alternative; (c) Nonpartitioned, Replicated Alternative; (d) Partitioned, Replicated Alternative

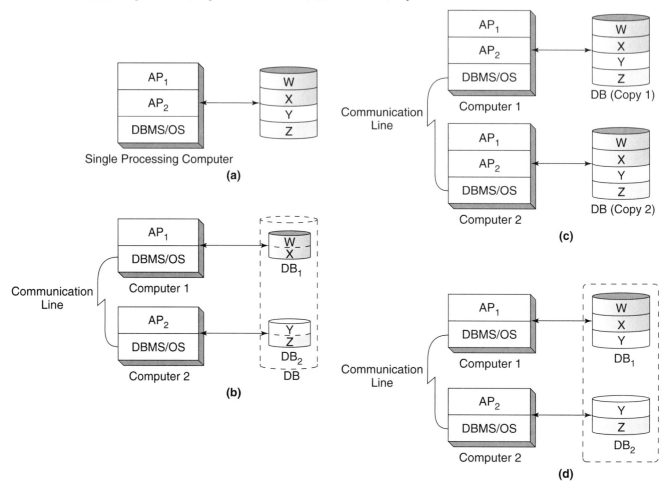

horizontal fragment refers to the rows of a table when they are divided into pieces. Thus, in the relation R, if the first 1000 rows are placed into R1(C1, C2, C3, C4) and the remaining rows are placed into R2(C1, C2, C3, C4), two horizontal partitions will result. Sometimes a database is broken into both horizontal and vertical partitions, and the result is sometimes called a mixed partition.

COMPARISON OF DISTRIBUTED DATABASE ALTERNATIVES   These alternatives are summarized on a continuum in Figure 14-6, arranged in increasing degree of distribution, from left to right. The nondistributed database is on the leftmost point of the continuum, and the partitioned, replicated database is on the rightmost point. In between these extremes is a partitioned database. The partitions are allocated to two or more computers and a database that is not partitioned, but each entire database is replicated on two or more computers.

The characteristics of the alternatives on this continuum are listed in Figure 14-6. The alternatives toward the right increase parallelism, independence, flexibility, and availability, but they also mean greater expense, complexity, difficulty of control, and risk to security.

One of these advantages is particularly significant to business organizations. The alternatives on the right of Figure 14-6 provide greater flexibility and hence

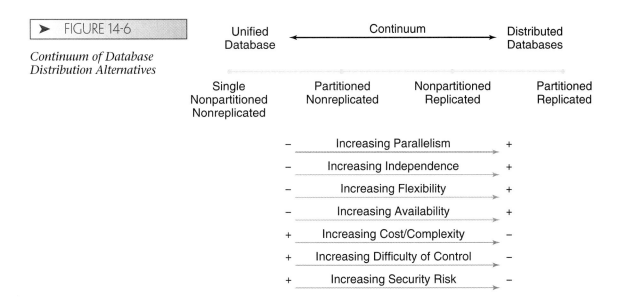

Continuum of Database Distribution Alternatives

can be better tailored to the organizational structure and the organizational process. A highly decentralized manufacturing company, for example, in which plant managers have wide latitude in their planning, will never be satisfied with an organizational information system with the structure of Figure 14-5(a) because the structure of the information system architecture and the structure of the company fight with each other. Thus, the alternatives on the right side provide a better and more appropriate fit to that organization than do those on the left.

The greatest disadvantage is the difficulty of control and the resulting potential loss of data integrity. Consider the database architecture in Figure 14-5(d). A user connected to Computer 1 can read and update a data item in Partition Y on Computer 1 at the very same time that a different user connected to Computer 2 can read and update that data item in Partition Y on Computer 2.

Because of the difficulty of control and possible integrity problems, distributed databases have been infrequently used for business information systems. This may change with the advent of the Microsoft Transaction Server OLE DB service mentioned in Chapter 13.

INTRANET AND INTERNET DATABASE PROCESSING

Of course the newest and most promising processing architecture involves the use of Internet-technology as discussed in Chapters 11–13. Such applications can be used both for transaction management (as they are for e-commerce), and also for decision support as you will see later in this chapter. Because we discussed these systems extensively in the prior three chapters, we will omit further discussion of them here.

➤ DOWNLOADING DATA

With advent of powerful personal computers, it has become feasible to download large quantities of enterprise data to departmental and user computers for local processing. Users can query these data using local DBMS products, and they can also import the data into spreadsheets, financial analysis programs, graphics programs, and other tools with which they are familiar.

In general, downloaded data can be used for query and reporting purposes only. They cannot be updated because once the data are removed from the operational database, they are no longer subject to concurrency control. Several users could update the same data and, if they were allowed to move them back, cause the lost update problem. In some applications, local data are merged with downloaded data. In these cases, users sometimes make unofficial changes to the data for the purposes of their analyses. Such changes, however, can cause consistency problems, as described later.

In some very rare situations, the applications processing the downloaded data are allowed to update and return the data to the source database. But, when this is done, elaborate manual procedures must be developed to ensure that data integrity problems do not occur when the data are returned. Since manual procedures are easily misunderstood, circumvented, or forgotten, they are not reliable. Hence, allowing users to update downloaded data is always risky and consequently is seldom done.

To understand more about the processing of downloaded data, consider a typical scenario.

UNIVERSAL EQUIPMENT

The Universal Equipment Company manufactures and sells heavy equipment for the construction industry. Its products include bulldozers, graders, loaders, and drilling rigs. Every product is assigned to a product manager in the marketing department who is responsible for product planning, advertising, marketing support, development of sales support material, and so forth. Each product manager is assigned a group of two or three related products.

Advertising is the product managers' largest budget item, so managers want to be able to measure the effectiveness of the ads they run. Universal's ads always contain a mail-in card to request information. The cards have a preprinted number unique to each ad appearance so that this number can be used to identify the ad that generated a particular lead. To facilitate lead tracking, the marketing department has developed a microcomputer database application that the product managers can use.

Figure 14-7(a) shows the semantic objects processed by this application. AD represents an advertisement; AD-APPEARANCE is the occurrence of a particular ad in a particular publication; PRODUCT represents a particular product such as a bulldozer; and PRODUCT contains two repeating groups, one on quotas and one on sales. The groups are multi-value because sales quotas are assigned for each quarter and product sales are recorded on a weekly basis.

This view of PRODUCT is quite simple. The complete PRODUCT object actually contains more attributes. But because the other data are not needed for the product managers' application, we have omitted them. The database structure that supports these objects is shown in Figure 14-7(b).

DOWNLOAD PROCESS

The product managers are assigned a microcomputer connected to other micros through a LAN in Universal's marketing department. To obtain sales and product-lead data, the micros call on a file server that serves as a gateway to Universal's mainframe (transaction-processing computer). The architecture is similar to that shown in Figure 14-8.

Every Monday, a key user in the marketing department runs a program developed by Universal's MIS department that updates the SALES, QUOTA, and PRODUCT-LEAD tables on the file server's database with data from the corporation's mainframe database. This program adds to the database the data from the previous week and also makes corrections. Product and sales data are imported for all related products to enable product managers to do comparative studies.

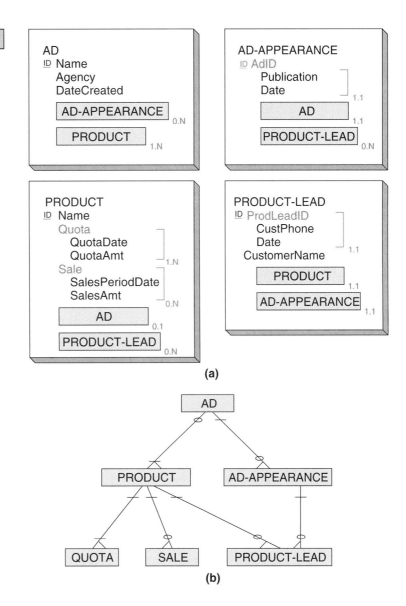

> ➤ FIGURE 14-7

Objects and Relations Supporting Universal's Product-Marketing Database: (a) Objects Processed by the Universal Product Managers and (b) Relational Structure Supporting These Objects

Once the data have been downloaded to the file server, each product manager can obtain the data of interest to him or her from that server. Controls ensure that the product managers do not obtain data for which access has not been authorized.

POTENTIAL PROBLEMS IN PROCESSING DOWNLOADED DATABASES

Downloading data moves the data closer to the user and increases the data's utility. Unfortunately, it may cause problems, including coordination, consistency, access control, and computer crime.

COORDINATION   First consider coordination, using the PRODUCT-LEAD and AD-APPEARANCE tables for illustration. The PRODUCT-LEAD table is updated from data on the mainframe (leads are handled by sales personnel and are recorded on the mainframe). But the AD-APPEARANCE table is updated "locally" by the key user in the marketing department, who gets the data from reports prepared by the advertising manager and the advertising agency.

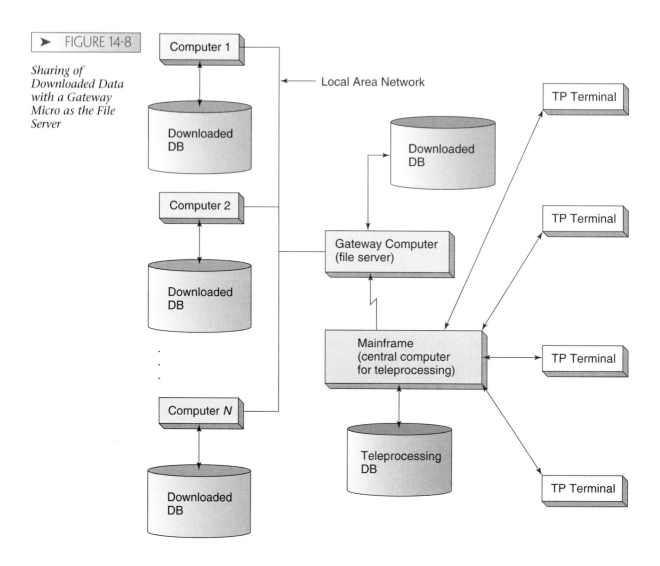

Sharing of Downloaded Data with a Gateway Micro as the File Server

This situation could cause problems when an ad is run for the first time in a new issue or publication. For example, the ad could generate leads that are recorded on the mainframe database before the AD-APPEARANCE data is stored on the file server. Then, when those leads are downloaded, the program importing the data will have to reject the lead data, because such data violate the constraint that a PRODUCT-LEAD must have an AD-APPEARANCE parent. Thus, the activities of local updating and downloading must be carefully coordinated: The key user needs to insert AD-APPEARANCE data before importing data from the mainframe. Similar coordination problems can occur when updating SALES and QUOTA data.

CONSISTENCY   The second problem with downloaded data concerns **consistency.** Each of the product managers receives downloaded SALES and QUOTA data that they are not supposed to change. But what would happen if a product manager did change the data? In this case, the data in that product manager's database might not match the data in the corporate database, the data in the file server, and possibly the data in other product managers' databases. The reports produced by that product manager could therefore disagree with other reports. And if several product managers update data, many inconsistent data could be generated.

Clearly this situation calls for strict control. The database should be designed so that data cannot be updated. If this is not possible—say, the microcomputer database product will not enforce such a restriction, and the costs of writing programs to enforce it are prohibitively high—the solution to this problem is education. Product managers should be aware of the problems that will ensue if they change data, and they should be directed not to do so.

ACCESS CONTROL   A third problem is access control. When data are transferred to several computer systems, access control becomes more difficult. At Universal, for example, SALES and QUOTA data may be sensitive. For example, the vice president of sales may not want the sales personnel to learn about upcoming sales quotas until the annual sales meeting. But if 15 product managers have copies of these data in their databases, it can be difficult to ensure that the data will be kept confidential until the appropriate time.

Furthermore, the file server receives all SALES and QUOTA data, which are supposed to be downloaded in such a way that a product manager receives only the SALES and QUOTA data for the products that he or she manages. Product managers can be quite competitive, however, and they may want to find the data for one another's products. Making this data accessible on the file server in the marketing department may thus create management problems.

COMPUTER CRIME   The fourth problem, a greater possibility of computer crime, is closely allied to access control. Whereas access control concerns inappropriate but legal activity, crime concerns illegal actions. Data on the corporate mainframe can be very valuable. Universal Equipment's sales and quota data, for example, are of great interest to its competitors.

When data are downloaded in bulk to the file server and then to one or many microcomputers, illegal copying becomes difficult to prevent. A diskette is easily concealed, and employees sometimes have modems with which they access work computers from off-site locations. In these situations, copying data over the telephone is nearly impossible to detect or prevent. The greater risk of computer crime is an important problem of downloaded databases. In fact, it alone might prohibit such a system from being developed, even though it would otherwise be an excellent solution. The potential problems of downloaded databases are summarized in Figure 14-9.

➤ FIGURE 14-9

*Issues and Potential Problems
Regarding Downloaded Data
Applications*

Coordination
• Downloaded data must conform to database constraints.
• Local updates must be coordinated with downloads.
Consistency
• In general, downloaded data should not be updated.
• Applications need features to prevent updating.
• Users should be made aware of possible problems.
Access Control
• Data may be replicated on many computers.
• Procedures to control data access are more complicated.
Potential for Computer Crime
• Illegal copying is difficult to prevent.
• Diskettes and access via modem are easy to conceal.
• Risk may prevent the development of downloaded data
  applications.

Processing Downloaded Data with a Web Server

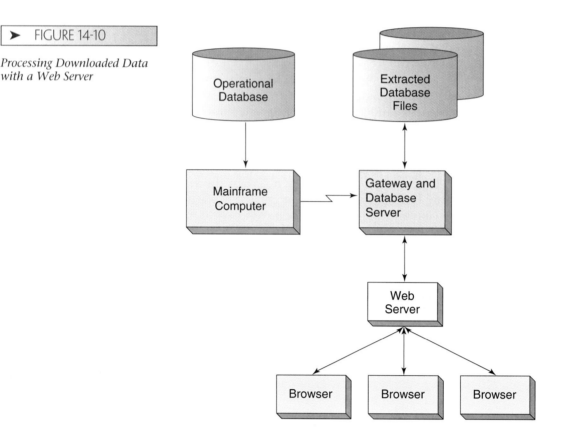

USING A WEB SERVER TO PUBLISH DOWNLOADED DATA

Figure 14-10 shows one way to use a Web server to publish downloaded data. The gateway and database servers are shown here on one computer, but they could reside on two—one computer for the gateway and a second for the server. The Web server communicates with the database server to obtain downloaded data. This data is then published to browser users.

➤ ON LINE ANALYTIC PROCESSING (OLAP)

In recent years a new way of presenting information has emerged that is called **On Line Analytical Processing,** or more frequently, **OLAP.** With OLAP, data is viewed in the frame of a table, or with three axes, in that of a **cube.** OLAP makes no limit on the number of axes, hence you will sometimes hear the term **OLAP hypercube.** This term means a display with an unlimited number of axes. The term *OLAP cube* is used most frequently.

Consider the example relation shown in Figure 14-11. This data concerns the sales of single family and condo housing properties in California and Nevada. As you can see from the data, the Sales Price and Asking Price for both new construction and existing properties are included.

OLAP TERMINOLOGY   An OLAP cube for this data is shown in Figure 14-12. This data has two **axes,** which are columns and rows. The row axis displays the Date **dimension,** and the columns axis displays both the Category and the Location dimensions. When two or more dimensions are shown on an axis, every combination of one is shown with every combination of the other. Thus, Existing Structures is shown for all locations, and New Construction is shown for

➤ FIGURE 14-11

Relational Source Data for OLAP Cube

Category	Type	City	State	Date	Sales Price	Asking Price
New	Single Family	San Francisco	California	1/1/1998	679,000	685,000
Existing	Condo	Los Angeles	California	3/5/1999	327,989	350,000
Existing	Single Family	Elko	Nevada	7/17/1999	105,675	125,000
New	Condo	San Diego	California	12/22/1998	375,000	375,000
Existing	Single Family	Paradise	California	11/19/1999	425,000	449,000
Existing	Single Family	Las Vegas	Nevada	1/19/1999	317,000	325,000
New	Single Family	San Francisco	California	1/1/1998	679,000	685,000
Existing	Condo	Los Angeles	California	3/5/1999	327,989	350,000
Existing	Condo	Las Vegas	Nevada	6/19/1999	297,000	305,000
Existing	Single Family	Los Angeles	California	4/1/1998	579,000	625,000
New	Condo	Los Angeles	California	8/5/1999	321,000	320,000
Etc.						

all locations. The cells of the cube represent the **measures** of the cube, or the data that is to be displayed. In this cube, the measure is average Sales Price. Other measures concern Asking Price or even the difference between Sales Price and Asking Price.

Notice that all of the data in Figure 14-12 concern single-family dwellings. There is no condo data in this cube. In fact, there are two such cubes—one for single family and a second for condos. You could think of the two cubes as one behind the other, as sketched in Figure 14-13. When viewed this way, these two cubes appear to be slices of data, and, in fact, the dimension(s) that are held constant in a cube are called **slices.** Thus, in this example, the cube is sliced on Type.

The values of a dimension are called **members.** The members of the Type dimension are {Single Family, Condo}, and the members of the Category dimension are {New, Existing}. For this cube, the members of the State dimension are {California, Nevada}, but in general, there could be 50 such members for United States properties. Sometimes there are a very large number of members in a dimension; consider all of the members for the combination {State, City}. Finally, in some cases, members are computed. Date and time are good examples. Given a date, we can compute the month, quarter, year, or century members for that date.

One last important OLAP term is **level.** The level of a dimension is its position in a hierarchy. For example, consider the Date dimension. Its levels are Year, Quarter, Month. The levels in the location dimension are State, City. OLAP terminology is summarized in Figure 14-14.

Example OLAP Cube

Average Sales Price of Single Family Dwellings ($thousands)										
			Existing Structures				New Construction			
			California			Nevada	California			Nevada
			San Francisco	Los Angeles	San Diego		San Francisco	Los Angeles	San Diego	
1998	Q1	Jan	408	465	375	179	418	468	371	190
		Feb	419	438	382	180	429	437	382	185
		Mar	427	477	380	195	426	471	387	198
	Q2		433	431	382	188	437	437	380	193
	Q3		437	437	380	190	438	439	382	190
	Q4		435	439	377	193	432	434	370	198
1999	Q1	Jan	452	454	368	198	450	457	367	197
		Feb	450	467	381	187	457	464	388	191
		Mar	432	444	373	188	436	446	371	201
	Q2		437	437	368	190	444	432	363	196
	Q3		436	452	388	196	447	455	385	199
	Q4		441	455	355	198	449	455	355	202

OLAP Cube Slice Dimensions

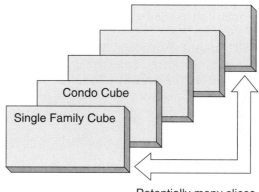

Potentially many slices

➤ FIGURE 14-14

OLAP Terminology

Term	Description	Example in Figure 14-12
Axis	A coordinate of the hypercube	Rows, columns
Dimension	A feature of the data to be placed on an axis	Time, Housing Type, Location
Level	A (hierarchical) subset of a dimension	{California, Nevada} {San Francisco, Los Angeles, Other} {Q1, Q2, Q3, Q4}
Member	A data value in a dimension	{New, Existing}, {Jan, Feb, Mar}
Measure	The source data for the hypercube	Sales Price, Asking Price
Slice	A dimension or measure held constant for the display	Housing Type—all shown are for Single Family—another cube exists for Condo

CUBE AND VIEW DEFINITIONS   OLAP terminology is evolving and is currently ambiguous in an important way. The term *cube* is used both to describe a semantic structure and also to describe materializations of that underlying structure. The cube shown in Figure 14-12 is one possible view or materialization of a semantic structure that has certain dimensions, levels, and measures. We could create a second cube on this data by exchanging the rows and columns; we could create a third cube on this data by showing Location at the top and then placing a New and Existing column for each Location member. So as you read OLAP documents, be careful to understand which meaning of *cube* is being used.

To illustrate this point further, consider the cube definition in Figure 14-15. The syntax used here is based on Microsoft's OLE DB for OLAP documentation, but it is similar to that used by other vendors as well. This Create Cube statement defines four dimensions and two levels in the logical structure. The Time and Location dimensions have levels, and the HousingCategory and HousingType dimensions do not. Although we do not show it here, it is possible for a dimension to have more than one set of Levels. In that case, two or more hierarchies are defined for that dimension.

The structure shown in Figure 14-15 is a definition of a way to interpret or comprehend housing data. It is not a presentation of data. To define a data presentation or materialization, the OLAP world has extended the syntax of SQL. Figure 14-16 shows the OLAP SQL to create the cube materialization shown in Figure 14-11. The only thing confusing about this statement is the CROSSJOIN term. A CROSSJOIN ({A, B}, {1, 2}) results in the following display:

A		B	
1	2	1	2

A CROSSJOIN ({1, 2}, {A, B}) results in this display:

1		2	
A	B	A	B

➤ FIGURE 14-15

Example Create Cube Data Definition Statement

```
CREATE CUBE HousingSalesCube (

    DIMENSION Time TYPE TIME,

        LEVEL Year TYPE YEAR,

        LEVEL Quarter TYPE QUARTER,

        LEVEL Month TYPE MONTH,

    DIMENSION Location,

        LEVEL USA TYPE ALL,

        LEVEL State,

        LEVEL City,

    DIMENSION HousingCategory,

    DIMENSION HousingType,

    MEASURE SalesPrice,

        FUNCTION AVG

    MEASURE AskingPrice,

        FUNCTION AVG

    )
```

Extending this idea a bit, the CROSSJOIN ({Existing Structure, New Construction}, {California.Children, Nevada}) results in:

Existing Structures				New Construction			
California			Nevada	California			Nevada
San Francisco	Los Angeles	San Diego		San Francisco	Los Angeles	San Diego	

The only addition to this last statement was the expression California.Children. This term simply means to breakout all of the children for California for all of the levels defined in the cube.

➤ FIGURE 14-16

Example Multidimensional SELECT Statement

```
SELECT      CROSSJOIN ({Existing Structure, New Construction}, {California.Children,

            Nevada})

            ON COLUMNS,

            {1998.Q1.Children, 1998.Q2, 1998.Q3, 1998.Q4,

            1999.Q1.Children, 1999.Q2, 1999.Q3, 1999.Q4}

            ON ROWS

FROM        HousingSalesCube

WHERE       (SalesPrice, HousingType = 'SingleFamily')
```

The SQL in Figure 14-16 includes the expression ON COLUMNS and ON ROWS. This declares the axes on which the dimensions are to be placed. Note too that the WHERE clause is used to specify the slicers for the presentation. Only Sales Price and a HousingType of Single Family are to be shown. Note that both a measure and a dimension can serve as a slicer.

One of the key ideas of OLAP is that users be able to dynamically reformat a cube with ease while at their desks (hence the words **on line**). To do this, programs that process cube materializations need to be able dynamically to construct OLAP SQL like that in Figure 14-16.

OLAP STORAGE ALTERNATIVES (ROLAP, MOLAP, AND HOLAP)   No, we are not talking about a high-tech version of the seven dwarves. ROLAP, MOLAP, and HOLAP refer to different means for storing OLAP data. Basically, the question is, in order to gain the best performance, should relational DBMS products be extended to include special facilities for OLAP, or should a special-purpose processing engine be used, or should both be used?

ROLAP storage (relational OLAP) proponents claim that with preprocessing of certain queries and with other extensions, relational DBMS products are more than adequate. Proponents of MOLAP (multidimensional OLAP) storage believe that, while relational DBMS are fine for transaction processing and query and reporting, the processing requirements for OLAP are so specialized that no DBMS can produce acceptable OLAP performance. The third group, HOLAP (hybrid OLAP) believes that both DBMS products and specialized OLAP engines have a role and can be used to advantage.

Figure 14-17 shows the OLAP architecture that Microsoft announced with SQL Server 7.0 and Office 2000. This HOLAP architecture involves OLAP processing on central data servers, on the Web server, and on client computers. Enterprise databases are processed by central data servers shown on the right-hand side of this diagram. The results of such processing are then made available to the Pivot Table Service on either a Web server or a client computer. Additionally, either the Web server or the client computer may have local versions of OLAP data.

There are several key elements of this architecture. First, the pivot table service is an OLAP processor that is available as an NT and Windows 2000 service. It is also available on other versions of windows that are running Office 2000. In fact, the pivot table service is invoked whenever creating data access pages in Access 2000. This service is even more frequently used by Excel.

The Pivot Table Service is exposed through an extension to OLE DB called OLE DB for OLAP. This extension builds on the OLE DB that you learned in Chapter 13; basically, it extends the rowset abstraction to include not just record-sets but also to include datasets, which are abstractions of cubes. The ADO extension for processing OLE DB for OLAP is called ADO MD (multidimensional). With ADO MD, Connection and Command objects can open datasets and process them dynamically similarly to the way shown for recordsets in Chapter 13. Data can be both read and written. RDS will also be extended to include support for ADO MD.

This architecture moves as much OLAP processing as possible to the client because the processing requirements of OLAP can be great. There is no disadvantage to this when processing data that is stored locally, but when creating cubes that require data from a central enterprise server, considerable data transmission may occur. This may not be acceptable; certainly, such systems will need to be tuned as experience is gained.

As indicated in Figure 14-17, OLAP processing can be done on centralized, downloaded, or local data. As organizations disburse more of their data to the users, data management problems increase. Data warehousing is a possible solution to this problem, and we consider it next.

➤ FIGURE 14-17

Microsoft OLAP Architecture

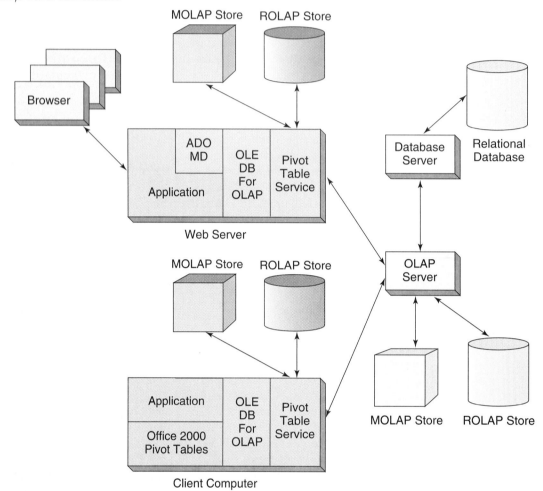

➤ DATA WAREHOUSES

Downloading does move the data closer to the user and thereby increase its potential utility. Unfortunately, while one or two download sites can be managed without problem, if every department wants to have its own source of downloaded data, the management problems become immense. Accordingly, organizations began to look for some means of providing a standardized service for moving data to the user and making them more useful. That service is called data warehousing.

A **data warehouse** is a store of enterprise data that is designed to facilitate management decision making. A data warehouse includes not only data but also tools, procedures, training, personnel, and other resources that make access to the data easier and more relevant to decision makers. The goal of the data warehouse is to increase the value of the organization's data asset.

As shown in Figure 14-18, the role of the data warehouse is to store extracts from operational data and make those extracts available to users in a useful format. The data can be extracts from databases and files, but it can also be document im-

FIGURE 14-18

Data Warehouse

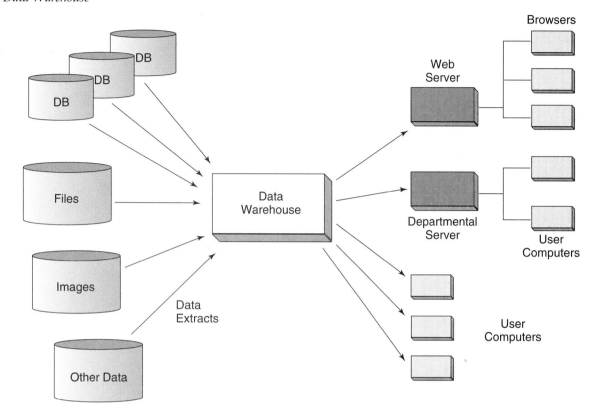

ages, recordings, photos, and other nonscalar data. The source data could also be purchased from other organizations. The data warehouse stores the extracted data and also combines it, aggregates it, transforms it, and makes it available to users via tools that are designed for analysis and decision making, such as OLAP.

COMPONENTS OF A DATA WAREHOUSE

The components of a data warehouse are listed in Figure 14-19. As stated, the source of the warehouse is operational data. Hence, the data warehouse needs tools for extracting the data and storing them. These data, however, are not useful without metadata that describe the nature of the data, their origins, their format, limits on their use, and other characteristics of the data that influence the way they can and should be used.

Potentially, the data warehouse contains billions of bytes of data in many different formats. Accordingly, it needs DBMS and OLAP servers of its own to store and process the data. In fact, several DBMS and OLAP products may be used, and the features and functions of these may be augmented by additional in-house developed software that reformats, aggregates, integrates, and transfers data from one processor to another within the data warehouse. Programs may be needed to store and process nonscalar data like graphics and animations, also.

Because the purpose of the data warehouse is to make organizational data more available, the warehouse must include tools not only to deliver the data to the users but also to transform the data for analysis, query, and reporting, and OLAP for user-specified aggregation and disaggregation.

Components of a Data
Warehouse

- Data extraction tools
- Extracted data
- Metadata of warehouse contents
- Warehouse DBMS(s) and OLAP servers
- Warehouse data management tools
- Data delivery programs
- End-user analysis tools
- User training courses and materials
- Warehouse consultants

The data warehouse provides an important, but complicated, set of resources and services. Hence, the warehouse needs to include training courses, training materials, on-line help utilities, and other similar training products to make it easy for users to take advantage of the warehouse resources. Finally, the data warehouse includes knowledgeable personnel who can serve as consultants.

REQUIREMENTS FOR A DATA WAREHOUSE

The requirements for a data warehouse are different from the requirements for a traditional database application. For one, in a typical database application, the structure of reports and queries is standardized. While the data in a report or query vary from month to month, for instance, the structure of the report or query stays the same. Data warehouse users, on the other hand, often need to change the structure of queries and reports.

Consider an example. Suppose a company defines sales territories geographically—for simplicity, say one salesperson is assigned to each state or province in North America. Now, say a user of a data warehouse wants to investigate the impact on sales commissions if, instead of allocating salespeople geographically, staff are allocated to specific, named accounts. To compare these alternatives, sales must be grouped by company on the one hand and by state on another. Queries and reports with different structures will need to be created for this purpose.

Another difference is that users want to do their own data aggregation. For example, a user who wants to investigate the impact of different marketing campaigns may want to aggregate product sales according to package color at one time; according to marketing program at another; according to package color within marketing program at a third; and according to marketing program with package color on a fourth. The analyst wants the same data in each report; she simply wants to *slice and dice it differently*.

Not only do data warehouse users want to aggregate data in their own terms; they may also want to disaggregate them in their own terms, or, as it is commonly called, such users want to **drill down** their data. For example, a user may be presented a screen that shows total product sales for a given year. The user may then want to be able to click on the data and have them explode into sales by month; to click again and have the data explode into sales by product by month or sales by region by product by month. While database applications can be written to meet this need for a specific set of drill-down requirements, more often, the requirements vary by user and task. In fact, sometimes the users do not know how they want to drill down until they see the data and start drilling down; hence, drill-down tools need to be flexible.

Categories of Requirements for a Data Warehouse

- Queries and reports with variable structure
- User-specified data aggregation
- User-specified drill down
- Graphical outputs
- Integration with domain-specific programs

Graphical output is another common requirement. Users want to see the results of geographic data in geographic form. Sales by state and province should be shown on a map of North America. A reshuffling of employees and offices should be shown on a diagram of office space. Again, these requirements are more difficult because they vary from user to user and from task to task.

Finally, many users of data warehouse facilities want to import warehouse data into domain-specific programs. For example, financial analysts want to import data into their spreadsheet models and into more sophisticated financial analysis programs. Portfolio managers want to import data into portfolio management programs, and oil drilling engineers want to import data into seismic analysis programs. All of this importing usually means that the warehouse data needs to be formatted in specific ways. These requirements are summarized in Figure 14-20.

CHALLENGES FOR DATA WAREHOUSES

So far, we've described data warehouses in an idealized way that makes them appear to be a panacea for management decision making. In point of fact, delivering the capabilities we have described is very difficult. There are a number of important challenges that must be met and problems that must be solved.

INCONSISTENT DATA   Obviously, the data warehouse is useless, if not downright harmful, if the data that it provides are inaccurate. The issue goes beyond the quality of the data that the warehouse extracts from its sources. The source data can be accurate as extracted, but inaccuracies can be introduced by unwittingly integrating data that are inconsistent in timing or domain.

Consider the example of extracted data in Figure 14-21. One table is an extract of order data, and a second is an extract of checks that were written as bonuses to salespeople. Suppose that a data warehouse user wants to investigate the relationship of sales performance to sales bonuses. At first glance, it would seem that all that need be done is to sum the order amounts for each salesperson and compare the total to the bonus. The following SQL code will accomplish that task:

```
SELECT     SPName, Sum(OrderAmount), BonusAmount
FROM       ORDER, BONUS
WHERE      ORDER.SPNum = BONUS.SP#
GROUP BY   SpNum
```

(As an aside, the typical data warehouse user probably does not know sufficient SQL to write this code, so it would need to be written for him or her or provided indirectly through some type of graphical query interface.)

Now suppose that these data were correct when extracted, and further suppose that they were obtained from two different information systems—order pro-

> FIGURE 14-21

Example Extracts of Order and Bonus Data

ORDER Table

SPNum	OrderNumber	OrderAmount
100	1000	$12,000
200	1200	$17,000
100	1400	$13,500
300	1600	$11,335

BONUS Table

SP#	SPName	BonusAmount
100	Mary Smith	$3,000
200	Fred Johnson	$2,500
300	Laura Jackson	$3,250

cessing and accounts payable. Since they were obtained from two different systems, it is unknown whether the timing of the data is consistent. It might be that the order data were correct as of the last Friday of the month but that the bonus check data were correct as of the last day of the month. There is nothing in the data to indicate that difference, and, in fact, no one may note that such a difference exists. It may have a substantial impact on the results of the analysis, however.

In addition to timing differences, there can also be differences in the underlying domains. Consider the SALESPERSON and REGION tables in Figure 14-22, and suppose that someone wants to produce a report of total sales for each region. To do that, the following SQL needs to be executed:

```
SELECT      SalesRegion, Sum(TotalSales)
FROM        REGION, SALESPERSON
WHERE       REGION.SalesRegion = SALESPERSON.Region
GROUP BY    Region
```

For the data shown, the result of this query will be a table having three rows, one each for the NW, NE, and SO sales regions. Because neither SE nor SW regions

> FIGURE 14-22

Salesperson and Region Data for Two Years

SALESPERSON Table

SPName	Region	Year	TotalSales
Johnson	SO	1998	$175,998
Wu	NW	1998	$223,445
O'Connor	NE	1998	$337,665
Abernathy	SE	1998	$276,889
Lopez	SW	1998	$334,557
Johnson	SO	1999	$225,998
Wu	NW	1999	$276,445
O'Connor	NE	1999	$389,737
Abernathy	SO	1999	$362,768
Lopez	SO	1999	$419,334

REGION Table

SalesRegion	Manager
NW	Allen
NE	Brendlmann
SO	Currid

had a match in REGION, they were omitted from the join, and the sales from those regions will not appear in the result. This is most likely not what the user intended.

In actuality, between 1998 and 1999, this business changed its sales territories by merging the SE and SW sales regions into the SO region. Hence, all of the sales for salespeople in the SE and SW regions should have been added to the SO row in the query result. Put in database terms, the underlying domain of SalesRegion and Region are different. The domain of SalesRegion is the set of current regions; the domain of Region is the name of the region in which the sale occurred, at the time of the sale.

For the small amounts of data in Figures 14-21 and 14-22, these problems are obvious. If, however, there were thousands of rows of data, such problems could slip past the analyst, and incorrect information would be provided to the decision-making process.

To solve this problem, metadata must be created that describe both the timing and the domains of the source data. These metadata must be made easily accessible to the users of the data warehouse, and those users need to be trained on the importance of considering such issues.

TOOL INTEGRATION   Another serious problem for data warehouses concerns the integration of various tools that the users need. The paradigms of different products, in different product categories, are usually different. DBMS products are table oriented; OLAP products are cube oriented; spreadsheets are spreadsheet oriented; financial planning packages are plan oriented, and so on. As a result, the user interfaces in the products are dissimilar. Users may need substantial training to learn how to use several products from several categories, and they often have neither the time nor the inclination to learn them.

Even more serious, the process for exporting and importing data across products from different categories may be difficult. Consider the spreadsheet in Figure 14-23(a). This spreadsheet contains data about three themes: Departments, Managers, and Employees. To import this spreadsheet into a normalized database, each of the themes will need to be allocated to separate tables like those in Figure 14-23(b). If the normalization is not done, considerable duplicated data

➤ FIGURE 14-23

Example of Conceptual Difference Between Spreadsheet and Database Products

EmpNumber	EmpName	DeptNum	Manager	ManagerPhone	DeptCode
1000	Wu	10	Murphy	232-1000	A47
2000	O'Connor	20	Joplin	244-7788	D87
3000	Abernathy	10	Murphy	232-1000	A47
4000	Lopez	20	Joplin	244-7788	D87

(a)

EMPLOYEE(EmpNumber, EmpName, *DeptNum*)

DEPARTMENT(DeptNum, DeptCode, *Manager*)

MANAGER(Manager, ManagerPhone)

(b)

will result as described in Chapter 5. The typical data warehouse user, however, will not understand the need for normalization nor have any idea about how to do it.

Finally, when products are acquired from different vendors, it is often difficult to get to the source of problems when they occur. For example, the vendor of the product that is exporting data may believe that a problem in the export/import process is due to the product that is importing the data, and the vendor of the product that is importing the data may claim the opposite. Since vendors are not experienced in using one another's products, nor are they motivated to encourage the use of other companies' offerings, technical support can be a nightmare.

MISSING WAREHOUSE DATA MANAGEMENT TOOLS   While there are many products and tools for extracting data from data sources and many tools for end-user query/reporting and data analysis, there is, at present, a lack of tools for managing the data warehouse itself. If the data warehouse consisted only of extracts from relational databases, and if the problems of timing and domain differences could be solved with training and procedures, then an off-the-shelf DBMS could be used to manage the data warehouse resources. In most cases, however, this is not the case.

Most data warehouses contain extracts from databases, files, spreadsheets, images, and external data sources. Since this is the case, these resources cannot be readily managed by a commercial DBMS, so the organization creating the data warehouse must write its own software. Usually this software has a commercial DBMS at its core, and the in-house data warehouse staff develops the additional features and functions necessary to manage the data warehouse resources.

The management of metadata presents another, similar problem. Few DBMS data dictionaries have sufficient capability to meet the metadata needs of the data warehouse. As stated, users need to know not only what's in the data warehouse but also where it came from, what its timing was, what the underlying domains of the data were, what assumptions were made when the data was extracted, and so forth. Data warehouse personnel will need to write their own metadata management software to augment the capabilities of the DBMS and other data dictionary products that they have.

Writing data management software is difficult and expensive. Once it is written, it must be supported. The vendors of the extraction programs and the data analysis programs will change their products, and any in-house developed software that uses them will need to be altered to conform to new interfaces. Further, the users' requirements will change, and this will necessitate adding new programs that will then need to be integrated with the data warehouse management software.

AD HOC NATURE OF REQUIREMENTS   Data warehouses exist to support management decision making. While a good portion of management decisions are regular and recurring, many other decisions are of an ad hoc nature. Questions like, Should we combine sales territories? Sell a product line? Consolidate warehouses? Adopt new Internet-based sales and marketing strategies? are not regular and recurring.

Computer systems, like bureaucracies, are slow and expensive to set up, are relatively inflexible, and work best with needs that follow a pattern. For that reason, such systems excel at tasks like order entry and reservations processing. It is most difficult, however, to design systems that readily respond to changing needs and requirements on an ad hoc basis. Thus, data warehouses have the most success in applications in which the variance in requirements follows a pattern. If a new requirement is similar in structure to an earlier one, that is, "consolidating the northern sales region will be like the process we followed when consolidating the southern region," then the data warehouse will likely be able to respond in a timely fashion. If not, then considerable time, expense, and anguish will probably need to be expended to meet the requirements.

DATA MARTS

Because of the challenges just described, some organizations have decided to limit the scope of the warehouse to more manageable chunks. A **data mart** is a facility akin to a data warehouse but for a much smaller domain. Data marts can be restricted to a particular type of input data, to a particular business function, or to a particular business unit or geographic area.

Restricting a data mart to a particular type of data (e.g., database and spreadsheets) makes the management of the data warehouse simpler and probably means that an off-the-shelf DBMS product can be used to manage the data warehouse. Metadata are also simpler and easier to maintain.

A data mart that is restricted to a particular business function, such as marketing analysis, may have many types of data and metadata to maintain, but all of those data serve the same type of user. Tools for managing the data warehouse and for providing data to the users can be written with an eye toward the requirements that marketing analysts are likely to have.

Finally, a data mart that is restricted to a particular business unit or geographic area may have many types of input and many types of users, but the amount of data to be managed is less than for the entire company. There will also be fewer requests for service, so the data warehouse resources can be allocated to fewer users.

Figure 14-24 summarizes the scope of the alternatives for sharing data that we have addressed in this chapter. Data downloading is the smallest and easiest alternative. Data are extracted from operational systems and delivered to particular users for specific purposes. The downloaded data are provided on a regular and recurring basis, so the structure of the application is fixed, the users are well trained, and problems such as timing and domain inconsistencies are unlikely to occur because users gain experience working with the same data. At the other extreme, a data warehouse provides extensive types of data and services for both recurring and ad hoc requests. Data marts fall in the middle. As we move from left to right in this figure, the alternatives become more powerful but also more expensive and difficult to create.

➤ FIGURE 14-24

Continuum of Enterprise Data Sharing

Data Marts			
Data Downloading	Particular Data Inputs	Particular Business Function	Particular Business Unit or Geographic Region	Data Warehouse

Easier ———————————————————————— More Difficult

➤ DATA ADMINISTRATION

An organization's data are as much a resource as are its plant, equipment, and financial assets. Data are time-consuming and expensive to acquire, and they have utility beyond operations. Information derived from data can be used to assess the effectiveness of personnel, products, marketing programs and to determine trends in customers' preferences, buying behavior, and so forth. It can be used to simulate the effect of changes in products, sales strategies, and territories. The list of potential applications is so long that, in fact, data often serve to establish and maintain the organization's competitive advantage. Unfortunately, however, as long as the data are locked in operational databases, their utility is limited.

Because of the potential value of the organizational data resource, many organizations have established offices of data administration. The purpose of these offices is not just to guard and protect the data but also to ensure that they are used effectively.

In some ways, data administration is to data what the controller is to money. The responsibility of a controller is to ensure not only that financial assets are protected and accounted for but also that they are effectively used. Storing an organization's money in a vault can protect it, but it will not be effectively used. Instead, it must be invested in ways that advance the organization's goals and objectives. Similarly, with data administration, simply protecting the data is not enough. Data administration must also try to increase the utility of the organization's data.

NEED FOR DATA ADMINISTRATION

To understand the need for data administration, consider the analogy of a university library. The typical university library contains hundreds of thousands of books, journals, magazines, government reports, and so forth, but they offer no utility while they are on the bookshelves. To be useful, they must be made available to people who have an interest in and need for them.

Clearly, the library must have some means of describing its collection so that potential users can determine what is available. At first glance, this might seem like a trivial problem. You might say, "Well, build a card catalog." But much work must be done to be able to do that. How should the library's works be identified? How should they be described? Even more basic, what constitutes a work? How can we accommodate different ways of identifying works (ISBN, Dewey decimal system, government report number)? How do we help people find things that they may not know exist?

Other complications arise. Suppose the university is so large that it has several libraries. In this case, how are the collections to be managed as one resource? Furthermore, some departments may maintain their own libraries. Are these to be made part of the university system? Many professors have extensive personal libraries. Should these be part of the system?

CHALLENGES OF DATA ADMINISTRATION

The library analogy does not go far enough, however, as organizational data administration is considerably more difficult than library administration. First, it is not at all clear what constitutes a "work." Libraries contain books, periodicals, and so forth, but organizational data come in myriads of formats. Organizations have traditional data records, but they also have documents, spreadsheets, graphics and illustrations, technical drawings, and audio and video files. How should all of these be described? What are the basic categories of organizational data? These questions are important because their answers determine how the data will be organized, cataloged, managed, protected, and accessed.

Most organizations have many names for the same thing. For instance, a telephone number can be described as a PhoneNumber, Phone, TelephoneNumber, EmployeePhone, or DeptPhone. Which of these names is preferable? When a graphic designer places a telephone number on a new form, what label should he or she use? When a programmer writes a new program, what name should he or she use for the program variable that holds the telephone number? When a user wants to query for a customer area code while developing a buying trend analysis, which name should she use in her query?

There also are many ways of representing the data element. A phone number can be represented as a 10-digit integer, a 10-digit text field, a 13-digit text field in the form *(nnn)nnn-nnnn,* a 12-digit text field in the form *nnn-nnn-nnnn,* or in still other formats. Which of these should be allowed? Which, if any, should be the standard?

Such differences between organizational data and library materials are minuscule, however, when compared with the next difference: People must be able to change organizational data.

Consider what would happen at the library if people checked out books, wrote in them, tore out pages, added pages, and then put the books back on the shelves. Or, even worse, suppose someone checked out three books, made changes in all three, checked them back in, and told the librarian: "Either change all of these or none of them."

Since data are a shared asset, limits must be placed on processing rights and responsibilities. For example, when an employee leaves the company, his or her records cannot be immediately deleted; they need to be maintained for several years for management reporting and tax purposes. Hence, one department cannot delete data from the database just because that department is finished with them. The office of data administration needs to help define users' processing rights and responsibilities. This role is similar to that described for database administration in Chapter 12; there, however, the scope was a particular database. Here, the scope is the entire organization.

In addition to all of these operationally oriented challenges, there are organizational issues. For example, data and processing rights can mean organizational power; hence, changes in data control can mean changes in power. Thus, behind the tasks of data administration lie all sorts of political issues. A discussion of these is beyond the scope of this text, but they are important nonetheless. The challenges for data administration are summarized in Figure 14-25.

➤ FIGURE 14-25

Challenges of Data Administration

- Many types of data exist.
- Basic categories of data are not obvious.
- The same data can have many names.
- The same data can have many descriptions and formats.
- Data are changed — often concurrently.
- Political – organizational issues complicate operational issues.

FUNCTIONS OF DATA ADMINISTRATION

Because of the challenges just described, data administration is complex. To protect the data asset while at the same time increasing its utility to the organization, a number of different functions or tasks must be performed. As shown in Figure 14-26, these activities can be grouped into several different categories.

MARKETING   First and foremost, data administration is responsible for declaring its existence and selling its services to the rest of the organization. Employees need to know that data administration exists and that there are policies, standards, and guidelines that pertain to organizational data and the reasons for them, and they need to be given reasons for respecting and following data administration rules, guidelines, and restrictions.

Data administration must be a service function, and the users must perceive it in that way. Thus, data administration activities must be communicated to the organization in a positive, service-providing light. Employees must believe that they have something to gain from data administration. Otherwise, the function becomes all cost and no benefit to the users, and it will be ignored.

DATA STANDARDS   For organizational data to be managed effectively, they must be organized coherently. If each department, function, or employee were to choose a different definition for a data item or for the means by which data items are to be named or described, the result would be chaos. It would be impossible even to compile an inventory of data, let alone manage it. Consequently, many organizations decide that important data items will be described in a standard way. For example, data administration may decide that every data item of importance to the organization will be described by a standard name, definition, description, set of processing restrictions, and the like. Once this structure is deter-

➤   FIGURE 14-26

Functions of Data Administration

Marketing
• Communicate existence of data administration to organization.
• Explain reason for existence of standards, policies, and guidelines.
• Describe in a positive light the services provided.

Data Standards
• Establish standard means for describing data items. Standards include name, definition, description, processing restrictions, and so forth.
• Establish data proponents.

Data Policies
• Establish organizationwide data policy. Examples are security, data proponency, and distribution.

Forum for Data Conflict Resolution
• Establish procedures for reporting conflicts.
• Provide means for hearing all perspectives and views.
• Have authority to make decision to resolve conflict.

Return on Organization's Data Investment
• Focus attention on value of data investment.
• Investigate new methodologies and technologies.
• Take proactive attitude toward information management.

mined, the next question is, who will set the values of these standard descriptions? For example, who will decide the standard name or standard-processing restrictions?

In many organizations, the data administration group does not determine the standard descriptions. Instead, each item is assigned a **data proponent,** a department or other organizational unit in charge of managing that data item. The proponent is given the responsibility for establishing and maintaining the official organizational definitions for the data items assigned to it. Even though the data administration group may be the proponent of some data items, most proponents come from other departments.

You may encounter the term *data owner,* which is generally used in the same way that the term *data proponent* is used in this text. We avoid the term here because it implies a degree of propriety that does not exist. Both legally and practically, the organization is the one and only owner of the data. Although some group or groups have a legitimate claim to a greater degree of authority over particular data than others do, these groups do not own those data. Hence, we use the term *data proponent,* instead.

To summarize, the foundation of data administration is a system of data standards. The data administration group is responsible for working with users and management to develop a workable system of standards, which must be documented and communicated to the organization by some effective means. Procedures for assessing the employees' compliance with the standards also must be established.

DATA POLICIES   Another group of data administration functions concerns data policies. To illustrate the need for such policies, first consider data security. Every organization has data that are proprietary or sensitive, and data administration is responsible for developing a security system to protect them. Questions like the following need to be addressed: What security schemes should be put in place? Does the organization need a multilevel security system similar to that of the military? Or would a simpler system suffice? The security policy must also decide what is required for people to have access to sensitive data and what agreements they must sign to do so. What about employees of other organizations? Should sensitive data be copied? How should employees be trained with regard to security? What should be done when security procedures are violated?

A second type of data policy concerns data proponents and processing rights. What does being a data proponent mean? What rights does the proponent have that other groups do not? Who decides who will become a data proponent, and how can this be changed?

A third example of the need for data policy concerns the distribution of data, such as whether official data should be distributed on more than one computer and, if so, which, if any, should be the official copy. What processing should be allowed on distributed data? Should data that have been distributed be returned to the official data store? If so, what checks must there be to validate them before accepting them?

FORUM FOR DATA CONFLICT RESOLUTION   To be effective, organizational data must be shared, but humans have difficulty sharing. Consequently, the organization must be prepared to address disputes regarding data proponents, processing restrictions, and other matters.

The first responsibility of data administration in this regard is to establish procedures for reporting conflicts. When one user's or group's needs conflict with another's, the groups need a way to make their conflict known in an orderly manner. Once the conflict has been acknowledged, established procedures should allow all involved parties to present their case. Data administration staff, perhaps in conjunction with the data proponents involved, then must resolve the conflict. This scenario assumes that the organization has granted to data administration the authority to make and enforce the resulting decision.

Data administration provides a forum for resolving conflicts that apply to the entire organization. Database administration also provides a forum for resolving conflicts, but those that pertain to a particular database.

INCREASING THE RETURN ON THE ORGANIZATION'S DATA INVESTMENT   A final function for data administration is the need to increase the organization's return on its data investment. Data administration is the department that asks such questions as Are we getting what we should be getting from our data resource? If so, can we get more? If not, why not? Is it all worthwhile? This function involves all of the others: It includes marketing, the establishment of standards or policies, conflict resolution, and so forth. Sometimes this function also means investigating new techniques for storing, processing, or presenting data; new methodologies and technology; and the like.

The successful fulfillment of this role requires a *proactive* attitude toward information management. Relevant questions are whether we can use information to increase our market position, our economic competitiveness, and our overall net worth. Data administration must work closely with the organization's planning and development departments to anticipate rather than just react to the need for new information requirements.

Finally, data must be made available to their potential users. Availability means not only making it technically feasible for a highly motivated and skilled person to access data; it means that data must be provided to the users via means that are easy for them to use and in formats that are directly applicable to the work that must be done.

➤ SUMMARY

Teleprocessing is the classic architecture for multi-user database processing. With it, users operate dumb terminals or micros that emulate dumb terminals. The communications control program, application programs, DBMS, and operating system all are processed by a single, centralized computer. Because all processing is done by a single computer, the user interface of a teleprocessing system is usually simple and primitive.

A client–server system consists of a network of computers, most often connected via a LAN. In nearly all cases, the user computers, called clients, are microcomputers, and in most cases, the server computer is also a micro, although mainframes can be used. Application programs are processed on the client computer; the DBMS and the data management portion of the operating system reside on a server.

File-sharing systems also involve networks of computers, and like client–server architectures, they usually consist of micros connected via LANs. The chief difference between file-sharing systems and client–server systems is that the server computer provides fewer services for the user computers. The server, which is called a *file* server and not a *database* server, provides access to files and other resources. Consequently, both the DBMS and the application programs must be distributed to the users' computers.

With a distributed database system, multiple computers process the same database. There are several types of distributed databases: partitioned, nonreplicated; nonpartitioned, replicated; and partitioned, replicated. In general, the greater the degree of partitioning and replication, the greater the flexibility, independence, and reliability will be. At the same time, expense, control difficulty, and security problems increase. Because of these problems, distributed database processing has been rarely used for business information systems. This may change in the next several years.

With the advent of powerful microcomputers, it became possible to download substantial amounts of enterprise data to users for local processing. Users can query and report on downloaded data using DBMS products on their own machines. In most cases, users are not allowed to update and return data because doing so could create data integrity problems. Even when downloaded data are not updated and returned, problems of coordination, consistency, access control, and possible computer crime can occur. A Web server can be used to publish downloaded data.

On Line Analytical Processing (OLAP) is a new way of presenting information. With it, data is viewed in cubes that have axes, dimensions, measures, slices, and levels. Axes refer to the physical structure of the presentation like rows and columns. Dimensions are characteristics of the data that are placed on the axes. Measures are the data values to be displayed. Slices are the attributes of the cube (either dimensions or measures) that are to be held constant in the presentation. Level is an attribute of a dimension that describes its position in a hierarchy.

The term *cube* is used both to refer to the underlying semantic structure that is used to interpret data and to a particular materialization of data in such a semantic structure. Figure 14-15 shows one way to define the underlying structure, and Figure 14-16 shows one way to define a materialization of a cube structure.

ROLAP, MOLAP, and HOLAP are three of the seven dwarves in OLAP land. Proponents of ROLAP say a relational DBMS with extensions is sufficient to meet OLAP requirements; proponents of MOLAP say a specialized multidimensional processor is necessary; and proponents of HOLAP want to use both.

Microsoft has extended OLE DB and ADO for OLAP. OLE DB for OLAP includes a dataset object; ADO MD has new objects for processing dataset objects in ways similar to recordset objects. The new Pivot Table Service has been added to Office 2000 and Windows 2000. Microsoft's architecture move much OLAP processing to client computers; whether this will be acceptable for the processing of data on enterprise servers is as yet unknown.

A data warehouse is a store of enterprise data that is designed to facilitate management decision making. A data warehouse stores extracts of operational databases, files, images, recordings, photos, external data, and other data and makes these data available to users in a format that is useful to them.

The components of a data warehouse are data extraction tools, data extracts, metadata, one or more DBMS products, in-house developed warehouse data management tools, data delivery programs, user analysis tools, user training, and warehouse consultants. Typical requirements for a data warehouse include variable-structure queries and reports, user-specified data aggregation, drill-down, graphical outputs, and integration with domain-specific programs.

Data warehouses must overcome a number of important challenges. For one, when data are integrated, inconsistencies can develop due to timing and domain differences. Also, because of the many tools required in a data warehouse, tools will have different user interfaces and inconsistent means of importing and exporting data, and it may be difficult to obtain technical support.

Another challenge is that there is a lack of tools for managing the data warehouse itself. The organization may have to develop its own tools for managing nonrelational data and for maintaining appropriate metadata. Such development is difficult and expensive. Finally, the nature of many requests on the data warehouse is ad hoc; such requests are difficult to satisfy. As a result, some organizations have developed limited-scope warehouses called data marts.

Data are an important organizational asset, one that can support both operations and management decision making. The purpose of the office data administration is not just to guard and protect the data asset but also to ensure that it is effectively used. One of the most important functions of data administration is to document the contents of the organization's data asset. This is a complicated task because data occur in many different formats in many different places in the organization. Data administration needs to help set organizational standards for names and formats of data items and also to define organizational processing rights and responsibilities. Finally, data are an asset, and their use can mean power; because of this, data administration must deal with organizational and political issues.

The specific functions of data administration include marketing its services, facilitating data standards and identifying data proponents, ensuring that appropriate data policies are established, and providing a forum for conflict resolution. All of these functions are aimed at the goal of increasing the return on the organization's data investment.

➤ GROUP I QUESTIONS

14.1   List the architectures that are used to support multi-user databases.

14.2   Sketch the architecture of a teleprocessing system. Name and identify the computer(s) and programs involved, and explain which computer processes which programs.

14.3   Why is the users' interface on teleprocessing applications generally character oriented and primitive?

14.4   Sketch the architecture of a client–server system. Name and identify the computer(s) and programs involved, and explain which computer processes which programs.

14.5   What types of processing hardware are used with client–server systems?

14.6   How many servers can a client–server system have? What restrictions apply to the servers?

14.7   Sketch the architecture of a file-sharing system. Name and identify the computer(s) and programs involved, and explain which computer processes which programs.

14.8   Explain how the processing of the following SQL query would differ in a client–server system and in a file-sharing system:

```
SELECT    StudentName, ClassName
FROM      STUDENT, GRADE
WHERE     STUDENT.StudentNumber = GRADE.StudentNumber
AND       GRADE.Grade = 'A'
```

Assume that the database contains two tables:

STUDENT (StudentNumber, StudentName, StudentPhone)
GRADE (ClassNumber, StudentNumber, Grade)

Also assume that the primary and foreign keys have indexes.

14.9   Explain why file-sharing systems are seldom used for high-volume transaction processing applications.

14.10 Define the terms *partitioned* and *replicated* as they pertain to distributed database applications.

14.11 Explain the difference between a vertical fragment and a horizontal fragment.

14.12 Explain the differences in the four types of distributed databases in Figure 14-5.

14.13 Explain the rationale for downloading data.

14.14 What limitations are normally placed on the processing of downloaded data?

14.15 At Universal Equipment, how do users obtain data extracts?

14.16 Summarize the coordination problem in processing downloaded databases.

14.17 Summarize the consistency problem in processing downloaded databases.

14.18 Summarize the access control problem in processing downloaded databases.

14.19 Why is computer crime a risk when processing downloaded databases?

14.20 Sketch the components of a system that uses a Web server to publish downloaded data.

14.21 What is an OLAP cube? Give an example other than the one in Figure 14-12.

14.22 Explain the difference between an OLAP axis and an OLAP dimension.

14.23 What is the measure of an OLAP cube?

14.24 What does the term *slice* mean in reference to OLAP cubes?

14.25 What is a member of a dimension? Give examples for Time and Location dimensions.

14.26 Explain the use of levels in Figure 14-12.

14.27 Explain the ambiguity in the term *cube*.

14.28 What is the result of the expression CROSSJOIN ({Mary, Lynda}, {Sailing, Skiing})? Of CROSSJOIN ({Sailing, Skiing}, {Mary, Lynda})?

14.29 Give a SQL SELECT statement to produce a cube similar to that in Figure 14-12 except that the rows and columns are reversed and Location is presented before Category (when reading left to right).

14.30 Define ROLAP, MOLAP, and HOLAP.

14.31 What is the function of the Pivot Table Service?

14.32 Considering the discussion in this text only, how has OLE been extended for OLAP?

14.33 What does ADO MD stand for and what is its function?

14.34 Define data warehouse.

14.35 How does having a data warehouse compare to processing downloaded data?

14.36 List and describe the components of a data warehouse.

14.37 Explain what it means to change the structure of a query or report rather than change the data in a query or report.

14.38 Give an example, other than one in this book, of a user's need to aggregate data.

14.39 Give an example, other than one in this book, of a user's need to drill down data.

14.40 Explain two sources of data inconsistencies, and give an example, other than one in this book, of each.

14.41 Summarize the problems of having tools that use different paradigms and are licensed by different vendors.

14.42 Explain which data warehouse tools must be written in-house.

14.43 Why does the ad hoc nature of data warehouse requests pose a problem?

14.44 What is a data mart, and why would a company develop one?

14.45 List and briefly explain three types of data marts.

14.46 Explain why data are an important organizational asset.

14.47 Describe several example uses of data besides operational systems.

14.48 How is data administration similar to the job of a controller?

14.49 Briefly summarize the necessity for data administration.

14.50 List and briefly explain the challenges of data administration.

14.51 Describe data administration's marketing function.

14.52 What role does data administration take with regard to data standards?

14.53 Define data proponent.

14.54 What is the difference between data proponent and data owner?

14.55 Summarize data administration's role in regard to data policy.

14.56 Explain what is involved in establishing a forum for conflict resolution.

14.57 How can data administration help increase the return on an organization's data asset?

➤ GROUP II QUESTIONS

14.58 Consider a company that has a national sales manager and 15 regional salespeople. Each week, the salespeople download sales data from the mainframe and use it to update their sales projections for the next month. When they have done this, they connect via a modem to a server database and store their sales projections into that database. The manager then accumulates the sales data into a companywide forecast. What problems, issues, and difficulties might exist in this situation in terms of coordination, consistency, access control, and computer crime?

14.59 Consider the enterprise data that exists at your college or university. Does it seem to you that your institution makes good use of its data asset? What ways can you identify that the data asset is used for more than operational processing? In what ways do you think your college or university could take advantage of its data asset in the areas of:

➤ Student recruitment

➤ Fund-raising

➤ Program planning

➤ Student affairs

➤ Alumni affairs

➤ Other areas

CHAPTER 15

Relational Implementation with DB2

The size and processing requirements for enterprise-wide databases greatly exceed the capacities of personal DBMS products. Accordingly, the DBMS products that are used for such databases are different in character from Access or other personal DBMS. To illustrate this difference, this chapter presents and discusses DB2, a DBMS product licensed by IBM. DB2 is intended primarily for large IBM mainframes, although versions of it are also used on the AS/400 family of smaller computers.

The chapter begins with a case that concerns information problems faced by the marketing department of a manufacturing company and then outlines the features and functions of an information system that can solve those problems. This information system has a relational database, and we define both the objects and the relations that should be stored in it. Next we turn to Database2 or, as it is more frequently called, DB2. We examine not only its data definition and data manipulation features but also those features that support concurrent processing, backup and recovery, and database security. Finally, we explore those portions of the relational application developed for the manufacturing company, including interactive DB2 queries and a COBOL program that contains embedded DB2 commands.

DB2 is typical of mainframe DBMS products designed to provide fast, highly reliable performance while processing hundreds of concurrent transactions per minute. Such products are complicated and thus require considerable expertise and knowledge on the part of systems and database administrators. Unlike microcomputer DBMS products, mainframe DBMS products are not designed to be easy to use and install but instead are intended to offer high performance and reliability. This chapter omits some important and useful features of DB2; see *DB2 System and Database Administration Guide* and *DB2 Application Programming Guide*, both published by IBM, for more information.

➤ CASE STUDY: KDK APPLIANCES

KDK Appliances manufactures major kitchen appliances, such as refrigerators, ranges, microwave ovens, and dishwashers. The company markets its products to independent dealers that then sell them to the public. Currently, its market is

FIGURE 15-1

*Relationship Among
KDK's Computers*

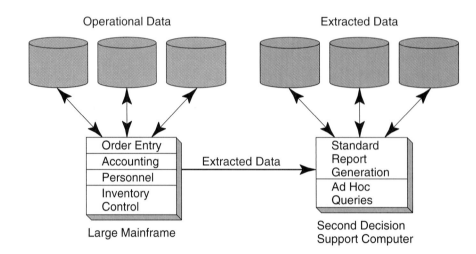

mainly the northeastern United States, but KDK plans to open soon new sales regions in the Midwest and in Canada. Each sales region is serviced by several salespeople who call on dealers and explain KDK's product line, dealer-training program, incentives, and local advertising programs. It is possible for one dealer to work with more than one KDK salesperson.

KDK has a large mainframe computer that handles all order processing, inventory control, personnel, and accounting functions. Stored in this mainframe are files and databases that track sales and other data to meet various reporting requirements. The database structure and processing on this mainframe computer are far too complicated to present in a single chapter. Therefore, we will consider the work that would need to be done to create and process an extract of the operational database like those described in Chapter 14. (See Figure 15-1.)

PROBLEMS

The marketing department plays a key role in the success of the company's plans to expand. It now employs eight product managers (PMs), each responsible for a particular line of products (one for refrigerators, one for ranges, and so forth). As part of their duties, the PMs develop an annual product plan for each major product (for example, a major product is a particular refrigerator model or a specific type of microwave oven). The product plan establishes, among other things, the sales goals for the product and the budget for its marketing. These marketing expenses include advertising, dealer training, salesperson training, and dealer promotions.

In order to spend the marketing dollars wisely, the PMs want to access data stored in the computer. They need to know, for example, product sales by region and by salesperson and the effect of some aspect of marketing (advertising, for example) on product sales.

Instant response time is not vital, because the PMs usually need quarterly, monthly, or weekly summaries of data. For example, immediate access to a particular order is not important. (In contrast, consider how important response time is when performing the order entry function on KDK's operational mainframe.)

KDK Appliances sponsors a co-op advertising program and employs several agencies to create advertising campaigns for various media, including newspapers (daily and weekly), periodicals (weekly and monthly), television, and radio. Much of KDK's advertising is shared with its dealers, which means that in addition to the advertising copy promoting a specific KDK product, a dealer's name, address, and logo appear in the ad (see Figure 15-2). Thus, although KDK prod-

➤ FIGURE 15-2

Advertisement for a KDK Product

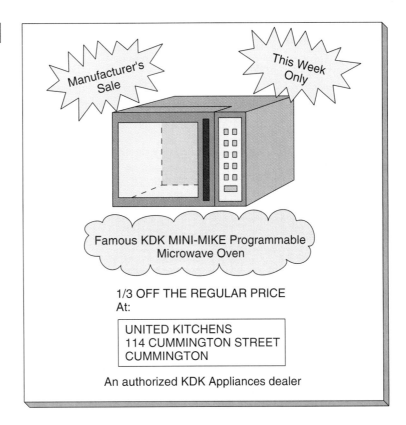

ucts are the central focus of the ad, a local dealer can share in the benefits by sharing the cost of the ad.

Some, though not all, dealers take advantage of this arrangement. The shared costs (percentages of the cost borne by KDK and by the dealer) vary from one ad to another and from one dealer to another, so the sales and marketing personnel must establish the shared costs of each ad.

None of the PMs is familiar with SQL or is willing to learn it, none is a programmer, and none has the time or interest to learn COBOL. Nonetheless, the PMs want the following questions answered: Which dealers participated in our shared advertising program this month? What was the total sales figure for product 45678 in March? How does that compare with its sales in April?

The goal of this chapter is to illustrate what would need to be done to create a database that would produce reports and answer queries that provide the information needed by PMs.

DEFINING OBJECTS

To develop the proposed system, the analyst first had to identify the semantic objects in which the PMs were interested. To start, the analyst and the PMs examined reports, transactions, and other entities. Let us first consider the reports and identify the underlying objects needed to construct them.

PRODUCT SALES SUMMARY REPORTS   Figure 15-3 shows three examples of the product sales summaries that the PMs need each month. Figure 15-3(a) is a sample PRODUCT SALES SUMMARY BY SALESPERSON report that contains data about products (product number, name, description, price), salespeople (name), and sales (total units sold by each salesperson). This suggests the existence of PRODUCT, SALESPERSON, and SALE objects, but we will not be sure until all reports, transactions, and so forth have been examined.

FIGURE 15-3

PRODUCT SALES SUMMARY Reports: (a) SALES SUMMARY BY SALESPERSON Report, (b) SALES SUMMARY BY DEALER Report, and (c) SALES SUMMARY BY REGION Report

PRODUCT SALES SUMMARY BY SALESPERSON

Product Number: 87224

Name/Description: Mini-Mike Programmable compact microwave oven

Price: $194.99

SALESPERSON	UNITS SOLD
John Eberle	280
Margaret Gosselin	200
Hans Jensen	50
TOTAL	530

(a)

PRODUCT SALES SUMMARY BY DEALER

Product Number: 87224

Name/Description: Mini-Mike Programmable compact microwave oven

Price: $194.99

DEALER	UNITS SOLD
Lisbon Furniture and Appliances	30
Parks Department Store	200
United Kitchens	50
Gem Appliances	100
Rich Appliance Co.	100
Sounds Terrific	50
TOTAL	530

(b)

PRODUCT SALES SUMMARY BY REGION

Product Number: 87224

Name/Description: Mini-Mike Programmable compact microwave oven

Price: $194.99

REGION	UNITS SOLD
2	200
5	330
TOTAL	530

(c)

The PRODUCT SALES SUMMARY BY DEALER report (Figure 15-3(b)) contains data about products (product number, name, description, price), dealers (name), and sales (total units sold to each dealer). Thus, in addition to the objects mentioned, it is likely that a DEALER object will exist as well.

The third summary report, PRODUCT SALES SUMMARY BY REGION (Figure 15-3(c)), contains data about products (product number, name, description,

➤ FIGURE 15-4

DEALER ACTIVITY SUMMARY Report

```
                    DEALER ACTIVITY SUMMARY

        #6644              (617) 479-5555
        J&S Department Store
        75 Rock Road
        Plymouth, MA 02787
        - - - - - - - - - - - - - - - - - - - - - - - - - - - - - -
                        Purchases to Date

          Invoice #           Date              Total
          1013              01/02/1999         15349.81
          1071              02/01/1999         22467.00
          1296              03/02/1999         18949.37
          1380              04/01/1999         36755.29
                                    TOTAL  93620.47
        - - - - - - - - - - - - - - - - - - - - - - - - - - - - - -
                        Advertising to Date

        Ad Name            Date      Ad Cost   Dealer's Share (%)
        Ultra            02/10/99    250.00          67
        Free Time        02/15/99    400.00          67
        St. Paddy's Sale 03/14/99    600.00          67
        Ultra            03/15/99    250.00          60
```

price), regions (region number), and sales (total units sold in each region). In addition to the potential objects already identified—PRODUCT, SALESPERSON, SALE, and DEALER—another possible object is found: REGION.

DEALER ACTIVITY SUMMARY REPORT Figure 15-4 shows an example of the DEALER ACTIVITY SUMMARY report, which contains data about dealers (number, name, address, telephone number), sales (invoice number, data, invoice total), and advertisements (advertisement name, date, cost, and dealer's share). We have already identified DEALER and SALE (an invoice is the record of sale) as potential objects, and the DEALER ACTIVITY SUMMARY report suggests a few more attributes of these objects, such as the dealers' addresses, telephone numbers, and invoice numbers. This report also indicates that advertisements are possible objects.

Figure 15-5 illustrates our findings so far. The potential objects are PRODUCT, SALESPERSON, SALE (or INVOICE), REGION, DEALER, and ADVERTISEMENT. But this is by no means a complete and final list, as these objects show only the beginning of our investigation. Study the object diagrams in Figure 15-5, making sure you understand them before continuing.

SALES INVOICE DOCUMENT Product managers derive much information about product sales from one important document: the sales invoice. An invoice for each sale is completed by a salesperson. An *actual* invoice captures many details about the dealer; the product(s) sold; and the dollar amounts of the transaction, discounts, credits, balance due, and shipping charges. All invoice details are entered into KDK's large operational mainframe computer. Keep in mind that the PMs need only a subset of the data on an actual invoice. An invoice as viewed by a product manager is illustrated in Figure 15-6. It contains data about the invoice (Number, Sale Date, Total), salesperson (Number, Name), dealer (Name, Address), and items sold (Line Item Number, Product Number, Name, Price, Quantity Sold, Extended-price).

It is easy to see that what we have just described as an *invoice* is really an embellishment of what we have been calling a *sale*. Because the PMs are more likely

➤ FIGURE 15-5

Preliminary Objects for KDK Appliances

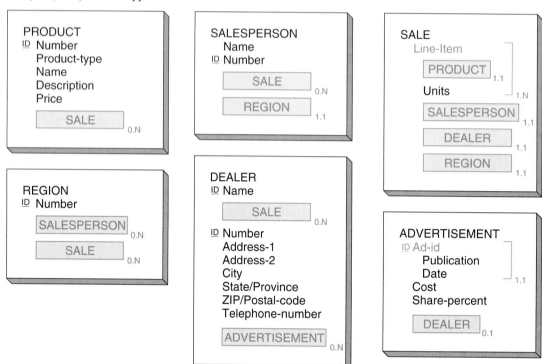

to use the term *invoice* than *sale* (this was discovered by talking to the PMs), we modify the object diagrams from Figure 15-5, replacing the SALE object with the updated INVOICE object. The results are shown in Figure 15-7.

ADVERTISING ACTIVITY   We noted earlier that KDK advertises its products to consumers in various media, such as print and television. An ad that can be run in, for example, a newspaper is referred to as an *ad-copy*. Each ad-copy is given a title by the advertising agency that developed it. When a particular ad-copy is actually run in a newspaper on a certain date at a certain cost, it is re-

➤ FIGURE 15-6

Product Manager's View of an Invoice

		Invoice 1001				02/01/1999
		Sold to:		Sale Date:		#5762
		Lisbon Furniture and Appliances				Paula Jasinski
		692 S. Ellington Rd.				
		South Windsor, CT 06114				

	Number	Name	Price	Qty	Extended-price
1	80911	Kitchen Valet	$1,699.99	2	$ 3,399.98
2	87755	Mini-Mike	344.99	20	6,899.80
3	93861	E. Range-white	679.99	15	10,199.85
4					
5					
6					
				TOTAL	$20,499.63

FIGURE 15-7

Modified Objects for KDK Appliances

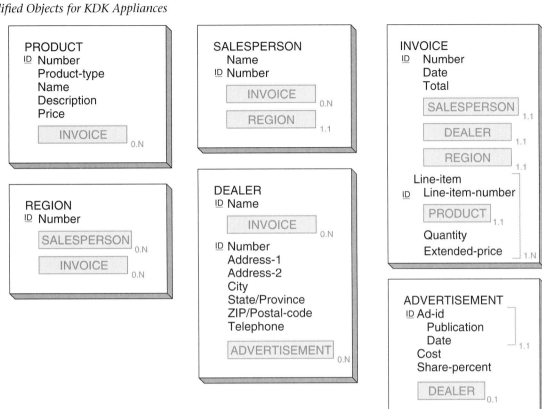

ferred to as an *advertisement.* Thus, an ad-copy called "Free Time" emphasizing the time-saving features of various KDK appliances might be run in several newspapers over a period of three or four months. Each time it is run, it is termed an advertisement.

As we already noted, each advertisement may be shared with a local appliance dealer, as long as the dealer agrees to share the cost of the ad. Because each ad-copy can target several products and because each advertisement can be shared with a dealer, the PMs need to track various aspects of advertising. After all, a large portion of each PM's budget is spent on advertising.

The underlying objects in the system's advertising are AD-COPY and ADVERTISEMENT, and object diagrams for them are shown in Figure 15-8. This more complete definition of the ADVERTISEMENT object replaces the one in Figure 15-7.

FINAL VERSION   Using object diagrams like the ones in Figures 15-7 and 15-8, the analyst reviewed with the PMs his understanding of the problems, thereby giving each of them an opportunity to correct or confirm what the analyst had done. One point that the analyst raised during this review concerned the REGION object. He wanted to be sure that the PMs did not need any data about a region. When the product managers agreed that they did not need any more data, the analyst decided to drop the REGION object. Thus modified, the object diagrams seemed acceptable, and the analyst went to the next step, translating the object definitions into relation definitions.

FIGURE 15-8

*KDK Objects After
Modification for AD-COPY
Object*

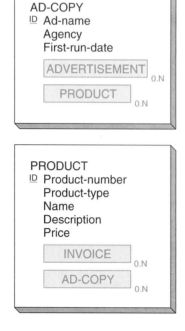

DEFINING RELATIONS

To create a database to store this data, the object model needs to be transformed into a relational design. Consider the INVOICE object first.

INVOICE   INVOICE is a hybrid object because the line-item composite group contains an object attribute. Thus the INVOICE object is represented by several relations. One contains general information about an invoice, and another contains the line items associated with the invoice. The relations have a one-to-many relationship, and both relations are mandatory (see Figure 15-9). The formats of the two relations are

INVOICE (<u>Number</u>, Date, Total, *Salesperson.Number, Dealer.Number*)

LINE-ITEM (*<u>Invoice.Number</u>*, <u>Line-item-number</u>, *Product.Number,* Quantity, Extended-price)

Observe that the keys are underlined and the foreign keys are shown in italics. Those columns that are both local and foreign keys are shown in underlined italics. An example of the INVOICE and LINE-ITEM relation is given in Figure 15-10. Notice that since several attributes are named *Number*, it is necessary to qualify

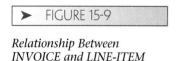

FIGURE 15-9

*Relationship Between
INVOICE and LINE-ITEM*

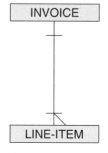

Sample Data in INVOICE and LINE-ITEM Relations

Number	Date	Salesperson.Number	Dealer.Number	Total
10982	03/12/1999	8555	2425	38549.05
75214	03/12/1999	1755	4528	60472.95
63911	03/15/1999	5762	6178	12249.92
41200	03/18/1999	5762	6644	147997.70

INVOICE relation

Invoice. Number	Line-item-number	Product. Number	Quantity	Extended-price
10982	001	14365	50	14999.50
10982	002	74961	30	17999.70
10982	003	87033	15	5549.85
75214	001	87214	25	4874.75
75214	002	87224	100	25999.00
75214	003	87033	80	29599.20
63911	001	56271	3	3749.97
63911	002	80911	5	8499.95
41200	001	15965	200	129998.00
41200	002	74961	30	17999.70

LINE-ITEM relation

the name of these attributes with their relation name. Hence, Invoice.Number is the Number attribute in Invoice. Product.Number is the Number attribute in Product. Also notice that the key for INVOICE (Invoice.Number) is part of the key for LINE-ITEM.

Three foreign keys appear in the INVOICE and LINE-ITEM relations, namely, Salesperson.Number, Dealer.Number, and Product.Number. These keys are needed to establish the one-to-many relationships between DEALER and IN-VOICE, between SALESPERSON and INVOICE, and between PRODUCT and IN-VOICE.

DEALER AND SALESPERSON   The DEALER object in Figure 15-7 is a compound object because it contains multi-value object attributes, INVOICE and AD-VERTISEMENT. There is a 1:N relationship in both cases.

Similarly, the SALESPERSON object in Figure 15-7 is a compound object, and it has a 1:N relationship with INVOICE. In Figure 15-11 we have added the DEALER and SALESPERSON relations to the diagram from Figure 15-9. The rela-

➤ FIGURE 15-11

Result of Adding DEALER and SALESPERSON Relations to Figure 15-9

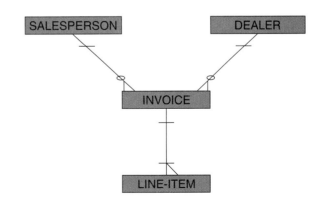

▶ FIGURE 15-12

Sample Data for SALESPERSON and DEALER Relations

Number	Name	Region
1043	Ronald Hunt	1
2711	John Eberle	5
8555	Margaret Gosselin	2
5762	Paula Jasinski	4
1755	Hans Jensen	5
6042	Lawrence Smithers	1
2814	Maxine Whittier	3

SALESPERSON relation

Number	Name	Address-1	Address-2	City	State/Province	ZIP/Postal-code	Telephone
6178	Gem Appliances	1005 Farmington Ave.	-0-	W. Hartford	CT	06754	(203) 555-4312
2425	S. K. Lafferty	Prestige Park	Building 43	E. Hartford	CT	06832	(203) 555-6789
6624	Rich Appliance Co.	17 Whiting Street	Suite 4143	New Britain	CT	06588	(203) 555-6609
0212	Lisbon Furniture & Appliances	692 Ellington Road	-0-	South Windsor	CT	06551	(203) 677-4582
9356	Gallo's Appliance Outlet	P.O. Box 344	264 Park Road	W. Hartford	CT	06431	(203) 549-6772
4516	United Kitchens	114 Cummington Street	-0-	Cummington	MA	07231	(617) 438-0065
9101	Parks Department Store	21 Main Street	-0-	Worcester	MA	07488	(617) 756-2295
6644	J&S Department Store	75 Rock Road	-0-	Plymouth	MA	02787	(617) 479-5555
4528	Sounds Terrific	1433 W. Northeast Highway	Suite 5678	Boston	MA	07665	(617) 885-4000

DEALER relation

➤ FIGURE 15-13

*PRODUCT Relation Added to
Diagram in Figure 15-11*

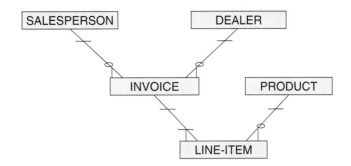

tionships between SALESPERSON and INVOICE and between DEALER and IN-VOICE are mandatory to optional, which means that an invoice must be associated with a salesperson and a dealer but that a salesperson or a dealer does not have to have any invoices. The relation formats are

DEALER (<u>Number</u>, Name, Address-1, Address-2, City, State/Province, ZIP/Postal-code, Telephone)

SALESPERSON (<u>Number</u>, Name, Region)

Sample data for the SALESPERSON and DEALER relations are shown in Figure 15-12.

PRODUCT   Another object in Figure 15-7 is PRODUCT. According to the object diagram, there is an N:1 relationship between a product and an invoice. More specifically, there is an N:1 relationship between a line item and a product. A certain product—for instance, a dishwasher—can be found on line items from the various invoices issued to many different dealers, and this can be represented in relations as shown in Figure 15-13.

The relational format for the PRODUCT relation is

PRODUCT (<u>Number</u>, Name, Description, Price)

Sample data for the PRODUCT relation can be found in Figure 15-14.

ADVERTISEMENT AND AD-COPY   Two more objects, ADVERTISEMENT and AD-COPY (see Figure 15-8), need to be transformed into relations. A dealer can share the cost of several advertisements, but any advertisement features at most one dealer. Thus, there is a 1:N relationship between a dealer and an advertisement.

Similarly, one ad-copy can be run several times in many newspapers, so there is a 1:N relationship between an ad-copy and an advertisement. Adding these relations to the ones in Figure 15-13, we arrive at the result in Figure 15-15.

The next relationship to be incorporated is that between PRODUCT and AD-COPY. Each product can be featured in several ads, and each ad can specify several products. Thus, we have an N:M relationship between PRODUCT and AD-COPY.

Recall from Chapter 7 that many-to-many relationships are represented by creating an intersection relation containing only those keys from the two other relations. In this case, an intersection relation called PRODUCT-AD is defined, in which each row contains a product number and an ad-name. Here the PRODUCT-AD relation is added to the ones from Figure 15-15, and the result is Figure 15-16.

The formats for these three new relations are

AD-COPY (<u>Ad-name</u>, Agency, First-run-date)

ADVERTISEMENT (<u>Publication</u>, <u>Date</u>, Ad-name, Cost, Share-percent, *Dealer.Number*)

PRODUCT-AD (*<u>Ad-name</u>, <u>Product.Number</u>*)

Sample Data for PRODUCT Relation

Number	Name	Description	Price
392761	Electric range–white	Electric range	$299.99
393861	Electric range–white	Electric range; self-clean; window	$679.99
393863	Electric range–toast	Electric range; self-clean; window	$689.99
393867	Electric range–avocado	Electric range; self-clean; window	$689.99
370351	Gas range–white	Gas range; 21-inch	$279.99
370353	Gas range–toast	Gas range; 21-inch	$289.99
374961	Gas range–white	Gas range; 36-inch; continuous clean	$599.99
374963	Gas range–toast	Gas range; 36-inch; continuous clean	$599.99
374976	Gas range–avocado	Gas range; 36-inch; continuous clean	$599.99
380551	Fifth-burner kit	Gas range 5th burner to replace griddle	$19.99
787214	Mini-mike	Compact microwave oven	$194.99
787224	Mini-mike	Programmable compact microwave oven	$259.99
787755	Mity-mike	Programmable solid-state full-size microwave oven	$344.99
787033	Mity-mike	#87755 with carousel	$369.99
415965	Ultra wash	Electronic dishwasher	$649.99
414365	Dishwasher	18-inch; 2-level dishwasher	$299.99
417375	Dishwasher–P	Dishwasher-portable	$409.99
416037	Dishwasher–sp	Space saver dishwasher	$249.99
556681	Porcelain-plus	Refrigerator; porcelain-on-steel; 25.8 cu ft	$1,599.99
556271	Quiet Cold	Frost-free refrigerator; ice maker	$1,249.99
580911	Kitchen Valet	Refrigerator; all-electronic; customized panels	$1,699.99
580922	KDK Limited Edition	Refrigerator; frost-free; special use compartments	$2,549.99
593252	Mini-fridge	Compact refrigerator	$99.00
593286	Mini-fridge	Compact refrigerator/freezer	$174.99
594605	Compact-fridge	3.6 cu ft compact refrigerator	$219.99
594911	Compact-fridge	#94605 with push-button defrost	$299.99

Sample data for the AD-COPY and ADVERTISEMENT relations appear in Figure
15-17 and for PRODUCT-AD in Figure 15-18.

KDK Case Summary

All the objects identified earlier can be constructed from data stored in the relations we defined. Reports summarizing product sales based on various criteria
(such as salesperson, region, and dealer), reports that analyze advertising, and
much more can be readily extracted from the database.

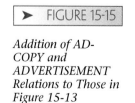

➤ FIGURE 15-15

*Addition of AD-
COPY and
ADVERTISEMENT
Relations to Those in
Figure 15-13*

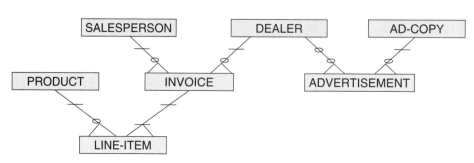

Addition of PRODUCT-AD Relation to Those in Figure 15-15

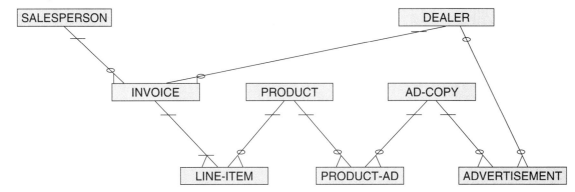

The next step is to implement the database structure: that is, to define tables, fields, and constraints; to assign passwords; to establish security procedures; and to allocate file space. After doing that, application programs can be written to produce the required reports. Before turning to those tasks, consider the features and functions of DB2.

➤ FIGURE 15-17

Sample Data for AD-COPY and ADVERTISEMENT Relations

Ad-name	Agency	First-run-date
Dishwashers	On-Target Ads	03/10/1999
Free Time	Haskins	02/15/1999
Microwaves	On-Target Ads	03/12/1999
Presidents	Haskins	02/03/1999
Ranges	On-Target Ads	02/01/1999
St. Paddy's Sale	J&J Marketing	03/12/1999
The Bachelor	J&J Marketing	01/04/1999
The Fridge	Haskins	02/01/1999
Ultra	J&J Marketing	03/10/1999
Working Woman	Haskins	03/01/1999

AD-COPY relation

Publication	Date	Ad-name	Cost	Share%	Dealer.Num
Herald	02/01/1999	Ranges	300.00	25.	6644
Free Press	02/01/1999	Ranges	320.00	33.	6178
Free Press	02/03/1999	Presidents	450.00	50.	4528
Sentinel	02/15/1999	Free Time	400.00	33.	6178
Herald	02/17/1999	Free Time	350.00	50.	6178
Herald	02/19/1999	Ranges	300.00	40.	4516
Sentinel	03/10/1999	Dishwashers	400.00	50.	9101
Times	03/10/1999	Ultra	250.00	33.	6644
Courier	03/11/1999	Ultra	280.00	40.	0212
Sentinel	03/12/1999	Working Woman	500.00	40.	9356
Times	03/14/1999	St. Paddy's Sale	600.00	33.	6644
Times	03/14/1999	The Bachelor	550.00	25.	4516
Herald	03/15/1999	Ultra	250.00	40.	6644

ADVERTISEMENT relation

➤ FIGURE 15-18

*Sample Data for
PRODUCT-AD
Relation*

Ad-name	Product.Number
Dishwashers	17375
Dishwashers	16037
Dishwashers	14365
Free Time	70351
Free Time	16037
Free Time	92761
Microwaves	87033
Microwaves	87224
Microwaves	87755
Microwaves	87214
Presidents	93286
Presidents	80551
Presidents	93861
Presidents	74961
Presidents	80922
Presidents	14365
Presidents	93252
Ranges	92761
Ranges	74961

Ad-name	Product.Number
Ranges	93861
Ranges	93863
Ranges	93867
Ranges	74967
Ranges	74963
Ranges	80551
St. Paddy's Sale	15965
St. Paddy's Sale	93867
St. Paddy's Sale	94605
St. Paddy's Sale	74967
The Bachelor	15965
The Bachelor	87755
The Bachelor	93867
The Fridge	56681
The Fridge	80922
Ultra	15965
Working Woman	93867
Working Woman	87033
Working Woman	87755

➤ DB2: THE PRODUCT

Database2 (DB2) is IBM's relational database management system for large mainframe computers that run IBM's MVS operating system. Another earlier IBM DBMS is called IMS and is based on the hierarchical (DL/I), rather than the relational, model. DL/I is described in Chapter 16. You are far more likely to encounter databases using DB2 than those using IMS in your career, and we address it in some detail in the next sections.

KEY FEATURES

DB2 uses SQL to perform all database operations: data definition, data access, data manipulation, and authorization functions. The user enters the SQL statements at a computer terminal. This mode employs an interactive terminal interface program called DB2I, but SQL statements can also be embedded in application programs written in assembler language, COBOL, PL/I, FORTRAN, or C++. Later in this chapter we present examples of both interactive commands and COBOL programs containing SQL instructions.

DB2 is well suited to a multi-user environment, as it allows users to create and modify tables, views, and other database structures; to define and modify database security parameters; and to execute various database utilities on-line. Most functions can be performed—within certain limits—even while others are using the database.

DB2's mechanisms for recovery in the event of a system failure are especially important in a multi-user environment. DB2 includes features for activity logging and transaction reprocessing, thus increasing system reliability. Because DB2 is just one of several subsystems that may be operating at the time of a system failure, its recovery processing is coordinated with that of other subsystems that may be present, such as CICS or other communications control programs.

DB2 enables a person—database designer, database administrator, or end user—to define and manipulate various constructs. Constructs include databases, tables, views, and indexes, to name a few. In the next section, we examine DB2 constructs and some SQL data definition (DDL) statements.

DB2 DATA DEFINITION LANGUAGE

This section briefly describes each DB2 construct, including the resources that application programmers (and sometimes end users) need to understand, such as tables and views, as well as the resources that database designers and database administrators (DBAs)[1] need to understand, such as storage groups and table spaces. We also present SQL statements to define several objects for the KDK application. The DB2 constructs we study are tables, views, table spaces, indexes, index spaces, data bases, and storage groups. Although a few other DB2 constructs exist, they are not important to our discussion.

TABLES   Like all products based on the relational model, DB2 stores data as tables with rows and columns. DB2 can retrieve and change data in a table, insert and delete rows, and add new columns to an existing table.

VIEWS[2]   A DB2 **view** is a virtual table derived from one or several base tables and not physically stored in the database (although the table data are). Views can be accessed and manipulated much as tables are, using many of the same SQL data manipulation statements used for tables. Indeed, a user often cannot tell whether he or she is processing a table or a view. Examples of a base table and a view of it are illustrated in Figure 15-19.

Database users, including application programmers and end users, need to know only about tables and views. But database designers and DBAs need to understand not only tables and views but also physical database storage, including table spaces, indexes, index spaces, data bases, and storage groups.

TABLE SPACES   A **table space** is a collection of one or more VSAM data sets (this is the name of standard nondatabase IBM mainframe files) used to store database data on magnetic disk. Both user and system tables are stored in table

FIGURE 15-19

Example of (a) EMPLOYEES (base table) and (b) EMPLOYEE-DIRECTORY (view of EMPLOYEES)

Name	Salary	Hire-date	Office	Extension
Walker	21800	12/88	321	246
Berg	36500	10/85	411	647
Dean	42900	02/91	308	795
Hsiu	36500	09/88	307	581
Cameratta	40000	03/83	419	669

(a)

Name	Office	Extension
Walker	321	246
Berg	411	647
Dean	308	795
Hsiu	307	581
Cameratta	419	669

(b)

[1]DB2 allows separate passwords for *system administrators* and *database administrators*. A system administrator can access and change constructs for all databases on the DB2 system, whereas a database administrator is restricted to a particular database.

[2]DB2 views are different from views as defined in Chapter 10. DB2 views are a subset of a SQL statement. They can have only one multi-value path through the schema.

➤ FIGURE 15-20

Table Spaces and Tables

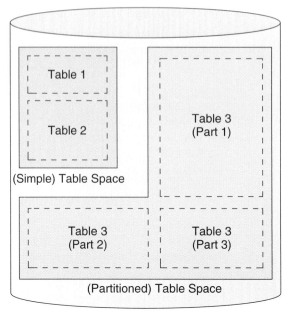

spaces (see Figure 15-20). A table space can hold approximately 64 billion bytes of data, although that size is not practical.

Table spaces are DB2's recoverable units. If the database system crashes, the table spaces will be recovered, not the databases or the individual tables. Perhaps you can see why huge table spaces (such as 64 billion bytes of data), though theoretically possible, are in reality seldom defined, as recovering a table space that large would be very difficult and time-consuming.

A table space can be either a **simple table space** or a **partitioned table space.** A simple table space can hold one or more tables, whereas a partitioned table space holds exactly one table. The DBA would probably define a partitioned table space for a very large table. Each partition would contain a part of the table based on the range of values in one or more columns. For example, each partition might contain taxpayer data based on Social Security Number. Partitions are independent of one another and can be reorganized and recovered individually.

Simple table spaces might contain several small, related tables. For example, the DBA might establish one table space for each user department and use each table space to store all the tables pertinent to a particular department. If an application requires exclusive use of a table, it issues a LOCK TABLE statement. This statement locks an entire table space and prevents other tables in it from being accessed. If separate table spaces "belong" to individual user departments, it is less likely that users from different departments will interfere with one another.

INDEXES   A DB2 **index** is an index as defined in earlier chapters. Indexes are used to reduce table access time and to place the table data in a logical sequence, regardless of its physical sequence. Multiple indexes can be defined for a single table. Consider the table in Figure 15-21(a). (In this example, the rows are numbered to represent relative locations within the table, but in practice, record addressing is far more complex, as discussed in the appendix.) The rows might be stored in the sequence in which they appear in the figure. Now suppose that a user frequently needs to access the data by means of customer name. The index illustrated in Figure 15-21(b) can be used to find a specific name and the location of a row in the CUSTOMER table that has that name. Using the index will be much faster than sequentially searching the table.

FIGURE 15-21

Indexes on CUSTOMER Table:
(a) CUSTOMER Table,
(b) INDEX for Name, and
(c) Index for CustomerNumber

RowNumber	CustNumber	Name	CreditLimit	ZIPcode
1	10	Smith	3000	06413
2	20	Jones	3000	95060
3	30	Whittaker	2000	07814
4	40	Murphy	3000	62200
5	50	Wang	3000	08142
6	60	Youngblood	2000	62200
7	70	Jones	2000	95060

(a)

Name	RowNumber
Jones	2
Jones	7
Murphy	4
Smith	1
Wang	5
Whittaker	3
Youngblood	6

(b)

CustNumber	RowNumber
10	1
20	2
30	3
40	4
50	5
60	6
70	7

(c)

Similarly, suppose another user often accesses the table by means of customer number. The index in Figure 15-21(c) would be useful in that case. Of course, the table in Figure 15-21 is very small, as it is only an example. KDK's real CUSTOMER table has thousands of rows. In fact, using indexes on such a small table would probably downgrade performance. Not only does index searching require time, but every addition or deletion to the CUSTOMER table also requires updating the indexes.

Subject to concurrent processing restrictions, indexes can be defined at any time. An index is a physical construct, completely separate from the table to which it is related. As we mentioned, DB2 automatically maintains an index once it is created. In fact, after an index is defined for a table, DB2 decides without any direction from a user or a programmer when, if ever, to use it. In other words, once an index has been defined, neither a user nor an application programmer actually references it.

INDEX SPACES   An **index space** is an area of disk storage in which DB2 stores an index (see Figure 15-22). When an index is created, DB2 automatically allocates an index space for it.

DATA BASES   IBM uses the term **data base** (two words) to define a collection of DB2 tables and indexes and the storage areas that hold them. Several DB2 data bases can exist on the same computer system. DB2 is designed to use a data base as an operational unit, meaning that it can *start* a data base (make it available), *stop* a data base (make it unavailable), and assign *authorization* to use a data base (allow users to access the data).

Users and application programmers do not deal directly with data bases any more than they deal with table spaces or indexes. Rather, they refer only to tables and views and are shielded from needing to know anything about the underlying database structures.

STORAGE GROUPS   A **storage group** is a group of disk volumes on which DB2 allocates space for user data bases (see Figure 15-23). DB2 manages its own data set (file) allocation unless the system administrator overrides this feature,

DB2 Indexes Stored in Index Spaces

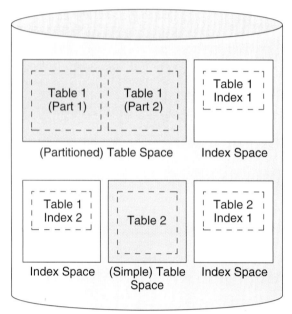

thereby enabling DB2 to keep track of available disk space and locates tables, indexes, and other database constructs in that space. It also releases disk space for use when it becomes available, such as when an index or a table is dropped. The system administrator can also define, locate, and delete data sets. Sometimes this is done when tuning, or optimizing, data base performance.

USING DB2 TO CREATE TABLES, VIEWS, AND INDEXES

DB2 uses its version of the SQL data definition language (DDL) to define the DB2 constructs. In this section and in the sections that follow, we will illustrate SQL DDL by defining several constructs—tables, views, and indexes—for the KDK application.

DEFINING A TABLE   DB2 uses the SQL CREATE statement to define its constructs. In Chapter 10 we examined only the data manipulation functions of SQL, and in this chapter we add data definition statements. Before defining a table, we must decide on the names of all the columns and their data types and lengths and whether we wish to allow null values.

The allowable DB2 data types for field values are summarized in Figure 15-24. As we stated earlier, a **null value** is a field value that is unknown or not applicable. A null value is different from a zero or a blank value. For example, a cus-

DB2 Storage Groups

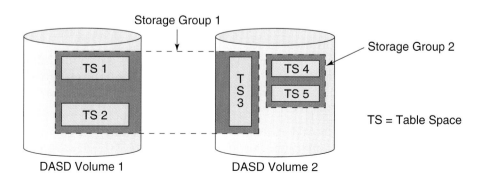

Some Allowable DB2
Data Types

INTEGER	31-bit signed binary values
SMALLINT	15-bit signed binary values
FLOAT	Floating-point values
DECIMAL(p,q)	Packed decimal values of p (1 to 15) digits; a number of decimal places (q) to the right of the decimal point may be specified
CHAR(n)	Fixed-length text data n (1 to 254) characters long
VARCHAR(n)	Variable-length text data up to n (1 to 32674) characters

tomer balance of zero is different from an unknown customer balance. You can prohibit null values from specific columns when you create a table by coding the phrase NOTNULL. If the column does not have this phrase, nulls will be allowed.

Consider the SALESPERSON relation for which sample data appear in Figure 15-12. The following CREATE statement defines it:

```
CREATE TABLE SALESPERSON
    (NUMBER          CHAR (4)           NOT NULL,
    NAME            CHAR (20)          NOT NULL,
    REGION          DECIMAL (1))
```

The next SQL statement creates the PRODUCT relation for the sample data shown in Figure 15-14:

```
CREATE TABLE PRODUCT
    (TYPE           CHAR (1)           NOT NULL,
    NUMBER          CHAR (5)           NOT NULL,
    NAME            CHAR (25)          NOT NULL,
    DESCRIPTION     CHAR (50),
    PRICE           DECIMAL (7,2)      NOT NULL)
```

DEFINING A VIEW   The CREATE statement can also be used to define a view. To do this, you include a SELECT statement that describes the view. The following CREATE statement defines a view of PRODUCT that includes only product numbers and prices:

```
CREATE VIEW PRICELIST
    AS      SELECT   NUMBER, PRICE
            FROM     PRODUCT
```

The view PRICELIST can be manipulated in exactly the same way as a table is. Data is retrieved from a view using the same SQL statements used for a table. If the view is a subset of rows or columns of a single table, it can be used to update base table data. Views that are the result of a join operation cannot be used to update table data.

The next statement creates a view that contains only those rows in the PRODUCT relation for refrigerators (the Type field contains a 5):

```
CREATE VIEW REFRIGERATORS
    AS      SELECT   *
            FROM     PRODUCT
            WHERE    TYPE = '5'
```

By specifying SELECT * we include all of the columns, and by specifying WHERE TYPE = '5' we include only those rows for refrigerators. This view can be used to update base table data.

Consider a third view. Assume that KDK wants a particular user to have only restricted access to the DEALER and ADVERTISEMENT relations, that is, only those dealers who have participated in the advertising (see Figures 15-12 and 15-17). We might define an appropriate joined view in this way:

```
CREATE VIEW ACTIVEDEALER
    AS     SELECT    DEALER.NUMBER, DEALER.NAME, TELEPHONE,
                     ADVERTISEMENT.DATE, COST, SHARE-PERCENT
           FROM      DEALER, ADVERTISEMENT
           WHERE     DEALER.NUMBER = ADVERTISEMENT.DEALER-NUMBER
```

Because this view is based on a join, it cannot be used to update base table data.

DEFINING AN INDEX   Indexes are usually defined and dropped by the DBA or system administrator. As we mentioned earlier, neither users nor application programmers ever reference an index; rather, DB2 decides when to use it and which one to use.

One reason to use an index, as described in the previous section, is to increase processing performance. Several indexes can be defined for one table, thereby allowing rapid access on many different fields. Another reason for defining an index on a table is that an index can force the uniqueness of the values of a column (or multiple columns). For example, the dealer number in KDK's DEALER relation must be unique (although the dealer's name, address, Zip, and so forth do not need to be unique). The way to establish the uniqueness of the dealer number field is to issue this CREATE statement:

```
CREATE    UNIQUE INDEX XDEALER
          ON DEALER (NUMBER)
```

In the next example, since UNIQUE is not specified, the resulting index might include duplicate telephone numbers. Incidentally, the index value is assumed to be ascending (ASC) unless otherwise specified (DESC):

```
CREATE    INDEX XDLRPHONE
          ON DEALER (PHONE DESC)
```

USING DB2 TO CHANGE A TABLE   Often when we design a database, we are unable to anticipate all of the user's needs. Even if we could, the needs change over time, and consequently we sometimes need to modify our database design. Notice that we are not talking about changing the data stored in the tables (that happens all the time, of course) but, rather, the structure of tables themselves.

DB2 offers two ways to modify table specifications: by dropping and then recreating the table and by using the ALTER statement. The ALTER statement can be used only for adding a column to an existing table.

To remove a column or to change a column's data type or length or to change whether null values are allowed, we must drop the table and recreate it. We illustrate how to drop a table in the next section. For now, just be aware that when you drop a table, you lose the table data as well as all the views and indexes based on that table.

To make structure changes other than adding a new column, follow these steps:

1. Define a new table with all the changes and a different name.
2. Copy the table data from the old table to the new one.
3. Define all indexes on the new table.
4. Drop the old table (this loses all the views of it, too).
5. Restore the original table name as a view of the new table. This allows applications that once referenced the old table to remain unchanged, because the new view is processed in exactly the same way as the old table.

6. Define views like the ones defined for the old table. These can be exact duplicates of the old views because you can base a view on another view, just as you can base a view on a table. (Of course, if a view contains a column that has just been dropped, that view is no longer valid.)

7. Authorize users to use the new table and views.

Clearly, this type of database modification is done only by a DBA or someone who is authorized by the DBA.

The second option for changing a table design uses the ALTER statement, with which we can add a column to an existing table. For instance, to add a salary column to the SALESPERSON relation, we would use the following statement:

ALTER   TABLE SALESPERSON
        (ADD SALARY DECIMAL (7,2))

USING DB2 TO DELETE TABLES AND VIEWS

The DBA periodically needs to eliminate tables from the data base. Users are rarely authorized to do this, because they could inadvertently delete data they do not realize that another user needs. In the previous section, we saw how the DBA might need to delete a table in order to change its structure.

Deleting a table erases not only the table but also all its dependent views and indexes. Thus, a table should not be dropped without careful thought. To delete the ADVERTISEMENT table from its database, KDK's DBA would issue the following DROP statement:

DROP   TABLE ADVERTISEMENT

The table and all its data would be deleted from the table space, as well as all the indexes and views associated with it.

The DROP statement can also be used to delete views. For instance, the DBA might authorize a user to create views and then to delete them when they are no longer useful. It is unlikely, however, that a user would be authorized to drop views that might be used by anyone else. That responsibility (and control) should remain with the DBA. This notwithstanding, however, we could delete the AC-TIVEDEALER view by issuing the following statement:

DROP   VIEW ACTIVEDEALER

Any applications that used that view (or views based on that view) would no longer work.

SUMMARY OF DB2 CREATION FACILITIES   DB2 allows the DBA or user to define, modify, and delete various database constructs—tables, views, table spaces, indexes, index spaces, data bases, and storage groups. Users and application programmers are concerned only with tables and views. In addition to tables and views, the DBA and database designers need to understand the underlying physical structures and database storage.

USING DB2 SQL TO MANIPULATE DATA

There are some differences between the DB2 statements used by interactive users and those used by application programmers that occur because of differences in the users' and the programmers' environments. Interactive users want results to be displayed immediately on a screen, whereas application programmers want the DBMS to place the values of columns and rows into program variables.

INTERACTIVE DATA MANIPULATION   Interactive DB2, or DB2I, supports all of the SQL statements described in Chapter 9. Because the format is the same as shown in that chapter, we will not go over it again. The user simply types the commands, as shown in Chapter 9, at the DB2I prompt.

ACCESSING DB2 FROM COBOL   DB2 application programs can be written in COBOL, PL/I, FORTRAN, C, and assembler language, and SQL statements can be embedded in programs written in any of these languages. The examples used in this text are embedded in COBOL programs.

As shown in Figure 15-25, all application programs that access DB2 must first be processed by the DB2 **precompiler.** The precompiler analyzes program source statements and processes those that are flagged as SQL statements (you will see how later). The precompiler inserts into the program the required table formats, which are already written in the host language and stored on disk. It also builds for each SQL statement a **data base request module,** or DBRM, which it stores for later use. Finally, the precompiler replaces the SQL statements with host-language call statements to access the DBRMs. As illustrated in Figure 15-25, the modified source code is then input to a standard language compiler for normal compilation.

The Bind process uses the DBRMs, database table definitions, available indexes, and other database data to determine the access paths for each SQL request. It stores these in the database data as an **application plan,** which is loaded when the first SQL call is executed.

➤ FIGURE 15-25

Steps in Developing an Application Program with DB2

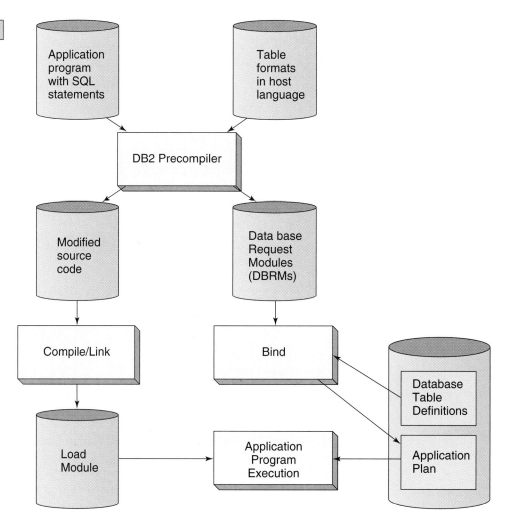

To enable the DB2 precompiler to recognize the statements intended for it, all SQL statements are embedded in keywords. Specifically, every SQL statement is preceded by the keyword EXEC SQL and followed by the keyword END-EXEC. In COBOL, the keyword END-EXEC is followed by a period unless the SQL statement is located in an IF statement. The general format of a DB2 SQL statement in a COBOL program is

EXEC SQL statement END-EXEC.

Only one statement can be included between the keywords. Multiple SQL statements require multiple EXEC SQL . . . END-EXEC statements. DB2 SQL statements are embedded in the DATA DIVISION and the PROCEDURE DIVISION.

SQL STATEMENTS IN THE DATA DIVISION   Two types of statements are embedded in the DATA DIVISION. The first describes data items that are used to pass database data between the application program and DB2. The second type describes the system data shared by the application program and DB2.

Figure 15-26 shows part of a COBOL program that processes the SALESPERSON table defined earlier. The DATA DIVISION includes data item definitions for all three columns of SALESPERSON. These columns have been renamed: NUMBER is SALESPERSON-NUM, NAME is SALESPERSON-NAME, and REGION is SALES-REGION. The correct correspondence of names is established in the PROCEDURE DIVISION.

The data types and lengths of data items do match, although COBOL uses a different vocabulary than SQL does. For example, when we created the table using SQL, we defined SPNUM as CHAR(4), whereas the equivalent COBOL definition for SALESPERSON-NUM is PICTURE X(4).

All the data items that DB2 and the application program share are grouped together, thereby enabling the precompiler to identify them. (We show these statements in the WORKING-STORAGE SECTION, but they could be located elsewhere in the DATA DIVISION.) The DECLARE SECTION is used to define those data items that will be used to transfer database data between the application program and DB2. That group of data item definitions is preceded by the DB2 keywords BEGIN DECLARE SECTION and is terminated with the message END DECLARE SECTION. In Figure 15-26, the definition of SALESPERSON is found in the DECLARE SECTION.

In addition to database data, the application program and the DBMS also need to share system data. For example, after each SQL statement is executed,

➤ FIGURE 15-26

SQL Statements Embedded in COBOL Program

```
DATA DIVISION.
WORKING-STORAGE SECTION.
EXEC  SQL   BEGIN DECLARE SECTION           END-EXEC.
01        SALESPERSON.
          05     SALESPERSON-NUM            PICTURE X(4).
          05     SALESPERSON-NAME           PICTURE X(20).
          05     SALES-REGION               PICTURE 9  COMP-3.
EXEC  SQL   END DECLARE SECTION             END-EXEC.
EXEC  SQL   INCLUDE SQLCA   END-EXEC.
PROCEDURE DIVISION.
          MOVE '5762' TO SALESPERSON-NUM.
          EXEC SQL
               SELECT NAME, REGION
               INTO :SALESPERSON-NAME, :SALES-REGION
               FROM SALESPERSON
               WHERE NUMBER = :SALESPERSON-NUM
          END-EXEC.
```

➤   FIGURE 15-27

DB2 Communications Area: (a) COBOL Description of SQLCA and (b) Content of Selected SQLCA Data Items

```
01    SQLCA.
      05    SQLCAID        PICTURE X(8).
      05    SQLCABC        PICTURE S9(9)  COMPUTATIONAL.
      05    SQLCODE        PICTURE S9(9)  COMPUTATIONAL.
      05    SQLERRM
            49    SQLERRML    PICTURE S9(4)  COMPUTATIONAL.
            49    SQLERRMC    PICTURE X(70).
      05    SQLERRP        PICTURE X(8).
      05    SQLERRD        OCCURS 6 TIMES
                           PICTURE S9(9)  COMPUTATIONAL.
      05    SQLWARN.
            10    SQLWARN0    PICTURE X(1).
            10    SQLWARN1    PICTURE X(1).
            10    SQLWARN2    PICTURE X(1).
            10    SQLWARN3    PICTURE X(1).
            10    SQLWARN4    PICTURE X(1).
            10    SQLWARN5    PICTURE X(1).
            10    SQLWARN6    PICTURE X(1).
            10    SQLWARN7    PICTURE X(1).
      05    SQLEXT         PICTURE X(8).
```

(a)

Data-item	Content
SQLCODE	Return code. Set by DB2 after each command. Zero indicates successful operation. Positive value indicates normal condition (such as end-of-data). Negative value indicates abnormal error.
SQLERRM	Error message. Set when SQLCODE is less than 0.
SQLERRP	Name of DB2 routine detecting error. Set when SQLCODE is less than 0.
SQLERRD	DB2 system status.
SQLWARN	Warning flags. Set for conditions such as data-item truncation (receiving data-item too small); null values encountered when processing SUM, AVG, MIN, or MAX; recovery from deadlock; and so forth.

(b)

DB2 sets a return code that indicates whether an error occurred. Both DB2 and the application program need access to this return code.

System data are defined in the program with the DB2 SQL message INCLUDE SQLCA (which stands for SQL Communications Area). When the precompiler processes this INCLUDE message, it inserts the data definitions in Figure 15-27(a) into the application program.

For brevity, Figure 15-27(b) describes only a few of the data items in SQLCA. Knowing all of them would contribute little to your understanding of DB2, but the one data item you must know is SQLCODE. SQLCODE is set by DB2 after each SQL command is executed. If the command is executed normally, SQLCODE is set to zero. If an unusual but normal condition occurs, SQLCODE is set to a positive value. For example, end-of-data is indicated by the value 100. If an abnormal, unexpected condition occurs, SQLCODE is set to a negative value. Insufficient VSAM file space is an example of an abnormal unexpected event.

SQL STATEMENTS IN THE PROCEDURE DIVISION

SQL statements in the PROCEDURE DIVISION instruct DB2 to perform some action. For example, the SELECT statement in Figure 15-26 causes DB2 to extract from the database the name and region of Salesperson 5762 and to place those values in the data items called SALESPERSON-NAME and SALES-REGION. This SQL statement is almost identical to the format followed when writing interactive SQL commands. The exception is the INTO clause that tells DB2 the name of the **host variable** (or variables) into which DB2 will place the value(s) it obtains from the database.

One problem for the DB2 precompiler is distinguishing between the data names defined in the database and those defined locally within the application program. If all names are unique, it can process the statements correctly. But it is impossible to guarantee that the application programmer will always choose data names not already used in the database. Consequently, a colon (:) precedes the names of program variables used within any embedded SQL statement.

As we stated in Chapter 8, COBOL (as well as many other programming languages) is designed to process data one record at a time. That is, a typical COBOL program retrieves one record, processes it, retrieves the next one, processes it, and so forth, until all the records have been handled. DB2, however, processes tables. That is, a DB2 SELECT statement always returns a table of data. (The example in Figure 15-26 is unusual in that it only returns one row; most SELECT statements return many rows.) This distinction between COBOL file processing and DB2 relation processing is important to the application programmer who might be tempted to think that SQL statements correspond to simple READ and WRITE statements. They do not.

The application programmer would be better served by thinking of DB2 as a vehicle for retrieving an entire input data set, or pseudofile, from the database. Then the data is processed one row at a time. To do this, the programmer defines a cursor within the application program.

A **DB2 cursor** (different but similar to cursors defined in Chapters 12 and 13) is a pointer that operates on a SELECT statement, indicating the row to be processed within the pseudo-file generated by the SELECT statement. In Figure 15-28, for example, the cursor CURRENT is defined to operate on the SELECT statement that will retrieve the names of all the salespeople in Region 5. In subsequent statements the program uses CURRENT to process sequentially the retrieved rows. As you can see in Figure 15-28, the logic is similar to that of sequential file processing. The cursor is opened (similar to opening a file); the first row is fetched (similar to a read); and a loop is executed to process the rest of the data (similar to processing an entire file). The processing stops when SQLCODE is returned with a value of 100, indicating the end-of-data. For now we will ignore other types of error processing.

The format of the FETCH statement is

FETCH cursor-name INTO dataname(s)

The dataname(s) in the FETCH statement must match the column names identified in the SELECT statement in which the cursor is defined. More details about the programming techniques used with DB2 appear in the example at the end of this chapter.

DB2 CONCURRENT PROCESSING

Because DB2 allows concurrent processing, it must provide facilities to control and limit users' interference. This is done by means of locks. Two types of locks employed by DB2 are shared locks and exclusive locks. When an application

> FIGURE 15-28

Using the Cursor to Process Sequentially a Set of Database Records

```
PROCEDURE DIVISION.
    .
    .
    .
        MOVE 5 TO SALES-REGION.
        EXEC SQL DECLARE CURRENT CURSOR FOR
            SELECT NAME FROM SALESPERSON
            WHERE REGION = :SALES-REGION
        END EXEC.
    .
    .
    .
        EXEC SQL OPEN CURRENT END-EXEC.
        EXEC SQL FETCH CURRENT INTO :SALESPERSON-NAME END-EXEC.
        PERFORM PROCESS-FETCH UNTIL SQLCODE NOT = 0.
        EXEC SQL CLOSE CURRENT END-EXEC.
    .
    .
    .
PROCESS-FETCH.
        (Instructions to process SALESPERSON-NAME go here.)
        EXEC SQL FETCH CURRENT INTO :SALESPERSON-NAME END-EXEC.
```

reads database data, DB2 acquires a **shared lock** on the data, which allows other applications to read the same data. Applications that wish to modify those data must wait, however, until the lock has been released, to ensure that everyone has access to the most current data.

When an application needs to modify data (DB2 knows this by analyzing the SQL statements in the application), DB2 acquires an **exclusive lock** on the data, which prevents all other applications from accessing the data. When the application is finished with the data, the lock is released, thereby giving other applications access to the updated data. If DB2 did not acquire exclusive locks, a second application could possibly use the old version of the data while they were being updated by the first application, and this would compromise the integrity of the stored data.

In addition to choices regarding the type of lock, DB2 offers options regarding the level, or locksize. The two locking units in DB2 are table spaces and pages. (Recall that a table space is an area of disk storage in which one or several base tables are stored. Table spaces are made up of **pages,** 4k-byte blocks of disk space. Pages generally contain parts of tables.) Although you might expect DB2 to apply locks to tables or even to rows within tables, this is not the case. When an exclusive lock is acquired for a table space, no application can access the data in *any* table stored in that table space.

When establishing a new database, the DBA can specify the lock level within a table space, through the LOCKSIZE option of the CREATE TABLESPACE command. The format is

LOCKSIZE = ANY | PAGE | TABLESPACE

If the DBA specifies TABLESPACE, then locks (either shared or exclusive) will be applied to the entire table space in which a referenced table resides. This option improves the performance of the application, but in doing so it can seriously delay other applications needing access to something in that table space.

If the DBA selects PAGE, the locks initially are applied at the page level (DB2 may escalate the lock to the table level if it detects poor performance). Although locking at the page level results in fewer conflicts than does locking at the table space level, more resources are required to administer it.

Finally, if the DBA specifies ANY, then DB2 selects the appropriate level, depending on the number of pages that may be required to fulfill an application's needs. If only a few pages are referenced, page-level locks will be applied. On the other hand, if many pages are required, table space-level locks will be applied. ANY is the default value for the LOCKSIZE option, and so the DBA does not need to specify the LOCKSIZE option when creating a table space. By default, DB2 can be allowed to select the proper level of locking based on the type of SQL request and the number of pages involved.

As we mentioned, locks are completely transparent to end users and application programmers. DB2 automatically does all the necessary locking and unlocking.

COMMIT AND ROLLBACK   All DB2 table data modifications must be either committed or discarded. When a change is committed, it is final and becomes part of the actual database data. When a commitment is made, all the page locks placed on that data are released, and the updated data are made available to other applications. A commitment is automatically executed when an application terminates normally, but it can also be explicitly invoked with the SQL COMMIT statement.

Sometimes DB2 table modifications need to be discarded, for example, when an end user wants to terminate a transaction while it is being carried out. To discard the changes, the application program issues an SQL ROLLBACK statement, which returns the tables to their original state (the state after the most recent COMMIT), thus eliminating any pending updates to the table. At that point, all page locks are released, and other applications have access to the unchanged data.

DB2 AND DEADLOCK   When two or more applications are deadlocked, DB2 resolves the problem by examining the number of records that each application has written and terminates the application(s) with the fewest changes since the last commitment. The more active application is selected to continue processing.

DB2 Backup and Recovery

DB2 stores the before-images and after-images of all database changes on a transaction log. Changes are written to the log before they are written to the database, and DB2 periodically checks itself. At the checkpoints, all changes residing in system buffers are written to the database, and a checkpoint record is written to the log. At the time of a checkpoint, therefore, the log and DB2 databases are synchronized.

DB2 can recover from a system failure by first applying all the before-images created since the most recent checkpoint and then applying all the after-images of committed transactions. As a result, all committed changes can endure the crash, although those transactions in progress at the time of the crash must be restarted.

Databases are stored on disks and are therefore vulnerable to physical damage. Should the disk be damaged, the database must be recreated from backup copies, which means that the users' organization must periodically save the database. In DB2, this is done by means of utility programs that copy table spaces (that is, the physical storage areas that contain table data). DB2 includes an option that allows the users' organization to make backup copies of only those pages in a table space that have been modified since the latest backup. This option can save much time because unchanged pages are not copied unnecessarily.

DB2 Security

DB2 provides two types of security mechanisms to protect the database: restricting access via views and limiting processing capabilities to particular users.

VIEWS   Views provide data security at the field level. Remember that a view is a subset of columns, rows, or both derived from one or more base tables. To prevent a user from accessing any data in a base table except the fields that he or she needs to access, the DBA simply defines a view of the table and authorizes the user to access it but not the base table. We explained how to use SQL to create a view earlier in this chapter, so the following two examples are presented without further explanation.

The following SQL creates a view of KDK's DEALER table that allows access only to the dealers' names and telephone numbers:

```
CREATE VIEW DLRPHONES
   AS SELECT NAME, TELEPHONE
   FROM DEALER
```

The user of the next view is given access to only those dealers' records in the state of Massachusetts:

```
CREATE VIEW MASSDLRS
   AS SELECT *
   FROM   DEALER
   WHERE STATE/PROVINCE = 'MA'
```

LIMITING ACCESS TO DB2 RESOURCES   DB2 is able to control access to various database resources, including tables, views, databases, utility programs, the DB2 catalog, and table spaces. Because DB2 users (both end users and application programmers) access only tables and views, we will discuss only them. Though not shown here, system administrators and database administrators have access to all other database resources as well.

DB2 can control access to data in tables and views, so that users can be authorized to issue SELECT, INSERT, DELETE, and UPDATE statements against a table or view. The columns that may be updated can be specified, and the use of the ALTER command to change a table definition can be restricted.

IDENTIFYING USERS   Because DB2 is used in the MVS environment, many users can access it concurrently from a variety of other subsystems, such as IMS and CICS transaction managers, TSO, and batch jobs. Although you need not understand all these subsystems, it is important to know that each has a means of identifying authorized users. For instance, TSO terminal users have a log-on ID that identifies them; a batch job has a special parameter on the job card; and IMS users have a sign-on ID or a logical terminal name (thus, the equipment, not the person, is authorized to access the system). Other systems have similar authorization IDs.

DB2 uses the connecting subsystem's ID to identify the DB2 user and assigns capabilities to access resources according to permissions granted to those IDs. Permissions are given via the SQL GRANT statement:

```
GRANT capability resource-list
   TO authorization-ID-list
   (WITH GRANT OPTION)
```

The capabilities that can be granted to users are the following:

> ➤ ALTER   The definition of the specified tables may be altered.
> ➤ DELETE   Rows may be deleted from the specified tables or views.

➤ INSERT   Rows may be inserted into the specified tables or views.

➤ SELECT   Rows may be selected from the specified tables or views.

➤ UPDATE   The values for the specified list of columns in the specified tables may be updated.

The resource list for most users is simply the names of tables or views for which they will have the specified capabilities. The authorization-ID list is the list of user IDs to whom the specified authorization is being granted. The authorization-ID list can also be the keyword PUBLIC, which grants authority to all users. Here are some examples that illustrate the GRANT command:

➤ All users are allowed to look at the DEALER table:
GRANT SELECT ON TABLE DEALER TO PUBLIC

➤ An application program can insert new records into the ADVERTISEMENT table:
GRANT INSERT ON TABLE ADVERTISEMENT TO PROG87

➤ A user known by the ID TERM 14 is allowed to access the view DLRPHONES:
GRANT SELECT ON VIEW DLRPHONES TO TERM 14

➤ Two users are allowed to change table definitions for the DEALER and SALESPERSON tables:
GRANT ALTER ON TABLE DEALER, SALESPERSON TO USER5, USER7

➤ An application program is allowed to delete SALESPERSON records:
GRANT DELETE ON TABLE SALESPERSON TO PERS000

When the DB2 database is installed, the system administrator is given total control over all resources. He or she may grant authority to or revoke authority from any other individual, including DBAs, by means of the GRANT statement. Of course, the resources and capabilities available to the system administrator include many options besides those just described.

The GRANT statement contains an optional clause: WITH GRANT OPTION. When used, this clause enables the grantee to give others the same capabilities over the same resources. Thus one can pass along authorization to others. Consider this example:

GRANT SELECT ON AD-COPY TO MURPHY WITH GRANT OPTION

This gives Murphy permission to read the AD-COPY table and allows her to authorize other users to do the same.

In addition to the explicit authorization conveyed by the GRANT command, the creator of a construct is automatically given full authority WITH GRANT OPTION over that construct, and this cannot be revoked unless the construct itself is deleted from the database.

If authority is revoked (by means of the REVOKE command), it has a cascading effect; that is, the specified privilege is revoked not only from the named authorized ID but also from anyone else to whom that authorized ID granted this privilege. Suppose that User A were granted the authority to read a table with the GRANT option and subsequently granted that privilege to User B. When User A is transferred to another department and his authority to read the table is revoked, User B's authority stemming from the GRANT is also automatically revoked. The following illustrates this sequence of events:

1. DBA:
   GRANT SELECT ON TABLE PRODUCT TO USERA WITH GRANT OPTION
   (User A can now read the PRODUCT table.)

2. User A:

GRANT SELECT ON TABLE PRODUCT TO USERB

(Users A and B can now read the PRODUCT table.)

3. DBA:

REVOKE SELECT ON TABLE PRODUCT FROM USERA

(Neither User A nor User B can read the PRODUCT table.)

➤ RELATIONAL IMPLEMENTATION USING DB2

This section discusses the implementation of KDK's application using DB2. A summary of KDK's database design appears in Figures 15-29 and 15-30.

First we create the database using interactive DB2 commands, and then we illustrate several on-line queries that product managers might execute. Finally, we present an application program that produces one of the standard reports that the PMs need.

CREATING THE DATABASE STRUCTURE

The interactive DB2 statements to create the database structure (KDKICB) presented in Figures 15-29 and 15-30 are shown in Figure 15-31. As you can see, the statements are straightforward. Having completed the design earlier, we need only specify the format of each table and column using DB2.

Keep in mind that this database will be used for reporting only—it will be neither updated nor altered. It is a snapshot of corporate operational data downloaded from the mainframe database to be analyzed by the product managers. All updates are made to the operational data in a carefully controlled environment. Therefore, other than authorizing each PM to access (SELECT) the tables, no other authority is granted. No one needs to alter, delete, or update any of the data. Because all the PMs are given access to all the columns in all the tables, no views are necessary.

EXAMPLES OF INTERACTIVE QUERIES

Figure 15-32 shows four sample queries that could be made against KDK's database. The first lists the names of dealers who shared advertising with KDK during the month of March. The DB2 word DISTINCT eliminates duplicate names from the list. Although the name of a dealer who shared more than one ad with KDK should appear several times in the list, we will print it only once.

➤ FIGURE 15-29

Summary of Relations for KDK Appliances

INVOICE	(Number, Date, Total, Salesperson.Number, Dealer.Number)
LINE-ITEM	(Invoice.Number, Line-item-number, Product.Number, Quantity, Extended-price)
DEALER	(Number, Name, Address-1, Address-2, City, State/Province, ZIP/Postal-code, Telephone)
SALESPERSON	(Number, Name, Region)
PRODUCT	(Number, Name, Description, Price)
AD-COPY	(Ad-name, Agency, First-run-date)
ADVERTISEMENT	(Publication, Date, Ad-name, Cost, Share-percent, Dealer.Number)
PRODUCT-AD	(Ad-name, Product.Number)

► FIGURE 15-30

Table Descriptions for KDK's Database

```
INVOICE
    Number                  Char (4)
    Date                    Numeric YYMMDD
    Total                   Numeric 9999.99
    Salesperson.Number      *
    Dealer.Number           *
LINE-ITEM
    Invoice.Number          *
    Line-item-number        Numeric 999 positive integer
    Product.Number          *
    Quantity                Numeric 999 positive integer
    Extended-price          Computed numeric 9(6).99
DEALER
    Number                  Char(4)
    Name                    Char(45)
    Address-1               Char(25)
    Address-2               Char(25)
    City                    Char(15)
    State/Province          Char(2)
    ZIP/Postal-code         Char(10)
    Telephone               Char(10)
SALESPERSON
    Number                  Char(4)
    Name                    Char(20)
    Region                  Numeric 9
PRODUCT
    Type                    Numeric 9
    Number                  Char(5)
    Name                    Char(25)
    Description             Char(50)
    Price                   Numeric 99999.99
AD-COPY
    Ad-name                 Char(15)
    Agency                  Char(30)
    First-run-date          Numeric YYMMDD
ADVERTISEMENT
    Publication             Char(10)
    Date                    Numeric YYMMDD
    Ad-name                 *
    Cost                    Numeric 9999.99
    Share-percent           Numeric 999.99
                            E.g., 30% is 30.00
    Dealer.Number           *
PRODUCT-AD
    Ad-name                 *
    Product.Number          *
```

*Definitions for foreign keys are shown in the foreign relations.

This example uses the subquery technique. Recall from Chapter 9 that subqueries allow us to narrow the scope of our search through the database by qualifying one level of query with another. Reading from the bottom up, the first example in Figure 15-32 begins by building a list of numbers for those dealers who shared with KDK the cost of advertising during March. Then, moving up to the next SELECT statement, it extracts the dealers' names from the DEALER table for all whose numbers appeared in the first list. Finally, the DISTINCT option causes the DBMS to eliminate duplicate names.

The second example in Figure 15-32 also uses the subquery technique, only this time it is more complex. Once again we interpret the statement by reading it from the bottom up. We begin by building a list of product numbers for refrigerators (Type = '5'). Then we build a list of invoice numbers that contain line items for any of those products. Next we extract the dealers' numbers for all of those invoices occurring in March, and finally we build a list of dealers' names, eliminating duplicates. This is the list of dealers who purchased refrigerators during March.

Interactive DB2
Statements to Create
Tables for KDK's
Database

```
CREATE    TABLE         INVOICE
          (NUMBER                     CHAR(4)          NOT NULL,
          DATE                        DECIMAL(8)       NOT NULL,
          TOTAL                       DECIMAL(7,2)     NOT NULL,
          SALESPERSON-NUMBER          CHAR(4)          NOT NULL,
          DEALER-NUMBER               CHAR(4)          NOT NULL)
CREATE    TABLE         LINE-ITEM
          (INVOICE-NUMBER             CHAR(4)          NOT NULL,
          LINE-ITEM-NUMBER            DECIMAL(3)       NOT NULL,
          PRODUCT-NUMBER              CHAR(5)          NOT NULL,
          QUANTITY                    DECIMAL(3)       NOT NULL,
          EXTENDED-PRICE              DECIMAL(8,2)     NOT NULL)
CREATE    TABLE         DEALER
          (NUMBER                     CHAR(4)          NOT NULL,
          NAME                        CHAR(45)         NOT NULL,
          ADDRESS-1                   CHAR(25),
          ADDRESS-2                   CHAR(25),
          CITY                        CHAR(15)
          STATE/PROVINCE              CHAR(10),
          ZIP/POSTAL-CODE             CHAR(10),
          TELEPHONE                   CHAR(10))
CREATE    TABLE         SALESPERSON
          NUMBER                      CHAR(4)          NOT NULL,
          NAME                        CHAR(20)         NOT NULL,
          REGION                      DECIMAL(1)).
CREATE    TABLE         PRODUCT
          (TYPE                       CHAR(1)          NOT NULL,
          NUMBER                      CHAR(5)          NOT NULL,
          NAME                        CHAR(25)         NOT NULL,
          DESCRIPTION                 CHAR(50),
          PRICE                       DECIMAL(7,2)     NOT NULL)
CREATE    TABLE         AD-COPY
          (AD-NAME                    CHAR(15)         NOT NULL,
          AGENCY                      CHAR(30),
          FIRST-RUN-DATE              DECIMAL(6))
CREATE    TABLE         ADVERTISEMENT
          (PUBLICATION                CHAR(10)         NOT NULL,
          DATE                        DECIMAL(6)       NOT NULL,
          AD-NAME                     CHAR(15)         NOT NULL,
          COST                        DECIMAL(6,2)     NOT NULL,
          SHARE-PERCENT               DECIMAL(5,2),
          DEALER-NUMBER               CHAR(4))
CREATE    TABLE         PRODUCT-AD
          (AD-NAME                    CHAR(15)         NOT NULL,
          PRODUCT-NUMBER              CHAR(5)          NOT NULL)
```

The third illustration in Figure 15-32 extracts data from several tables in order to give the user the desired results. Product names and descriptions come from the PRODUCT table. Advertisements, which are dated, are stored in the AD-VERTISEMENT table. But advertisements are not directly associated with any product—they are associated with advertising copy by means of the Ad-name column. Similarly, products are associated directly not with an advertisement but with advertising copy by means of the Ad-name column in the PRODUCT-AD table.

We begin by joining the PRODUCT-AD table and the ADVERTISEMENT table, matching on Ad-name. Then we extract unique (distinct) product numbers, but only for advertisements that ran in March. Finally, we extract from the PRODUCT table the name and description for each product number we have identified.

The fourth example of a query in Figure 15-32 begins by building a view (the join of two tables) and then selecting total sales figures from the view. The view is made up of sales data for Product 94605, taken from the INVOICE table (date)

➤ FIGURE 15-32

Sample Interactive DB2 Queries Against KDK's Database

1. List the dealers who participated in shared advertising during the month of March:
    SELECT DISTINCT NAME FROM DEALER
    WHERE DEALER. NUMBER IN
    SELECT DEALER-NUMBER
        FROM ADVERTISEMENT
        WHERE ADVERTISEMENT. DATE BETWEEN 19990301 AND 19990331
2. List the dealers who purchased refrigerators (product type = 5) in March:
    SELECT DISTINCT NAME FROM DEALER
    WHERE DEALER. NUMBER IN
        SELECT DEALER-NUMBER FROM INVOICE
        WHERE DATE BETWEEN 19990301 AND 19990331
        AND INVOICE. NUMBER IN
            SELECT INVOICE-NUMBER FROM LINE-ITEM
            WHERE LINE-ITEM. PRODUCT-NUMBER IN
                SELECT NUMBER FROM PRODUCT
                WHERE TYPE = '5'
3. List the products that were advertised in March:
    SELECT NUMBER, NAME, DESCRIPTION FROM PRODUCT
    WHERE PRODUCT. NUMBER IN
        SELECT DISTINCT PRODUCT-NUMBER FROM PRODUCT-AD
        WHERE PRODUCT-AD. AD-NAME = ADVERTISEMENT. AD-NAME
        AND ADVERTISEMENT. DATE BETWEEN 19990301 AND 19990331
4. Print the total sales for product #94605 for the month of March. Then print it for the month of April:
    CREATE VIEW PRODUCTSALES
        (DATE, PRODUCT, EXTENDED-PRICE)
        AS SELECT DATE, PRODUCT-NUMBER, EXTENDED-PRICE
            FROM INVOICE, LINE-ITEM
            WHERE LINE-ITEM. INVOICE-NUMBER = INVOICE. NUMBER
            AND LINE-ITEM. PRODUCT-NUMBER = '94605'
    SELECT SUM (EXTENDED-PRICE)
    FROM PRODUCTSALES WHERE DATE BETWEEN 19990301 AND 19990331
    SELECT SUM (EXTENDED-PRICE)
    FROM PRODUCTSALES WHERE DATE BETWEEN 19990401 AND 19990430

and the LINE-ITEM table (product number, extended price). Having established this subset of the larger base tables, we can ask DB2 to calculate the two sales totals by invoking the SUM built-in function in the SELECT statement. Two SELECT statements are needed, of course, one for each month.

APPLICATION PROGRAM EXAMPLE

Figure 15-33 presents a COBOL program that prints the report shown in Figure 15-3(c), entitled PRODUCT SALES SUMMARY BY REGION. In this section we examine the COBOL program, noting the placement of DB2 commands. Although this example is written in COBOL, SQL can also be embedded in PL/I, FORTRAN, C, and assembler language programs.

Looking at the WORKING-STORAGE SECTION of the DATA DIVISION, we find the definition of those variables that will hold data values as they are retrieved by DB2 from the database. These variables are defined following the SQL message BEGIN DECLARE SECTION. Notice that each SQL statement is surrounded by the precompiler keywords EXEC SQL and END-EXEC.

Within the DECLARE SECTION we have defined a sale record, made up of six fields. Later, in the PROCEDURE DIVISION, the data for this sale record can be found in four different database tables. The words END DECLARE SECTION signal the end of the DECLARE SECTION.

The next instruction in the WORKING-STORAGE SECTION directs the precompiler to copy SQLCA into the COBOL program. Again, this is a list of parameters shared by the DBMS and the application program. The most important field in SQLCA is SQLCODE, as described earlier.

The remainder of the WORKING-STORAGE SECTION defines the work areas and report formats to be used by the program. These are normal COBOL entries that are not affected by the need to use DB2.

In the PROCEDURE DIVISION we find a mixture of SQL statements and ordinary COBOL instructions. The first sequence of instructions in the PROCEDURE DIVISION defines a cursor (C-1) that will be used to retrieve data from the database. The SELECT statement on which the cursor operates is lengthy, but it is easily understood. To print the report seen in Figure 15-3, we need a set of sales records containing product numbers, names and descriptions, prices, quantities sold, and regions, which are found in several different database tables.

The SELECT specifies a join of four tables. The join conditions are specified in the where clause that starts

WHERE LINE-ITEM.INVOICE.NUMBER = INVOICE.NUMBER, etc.

Finally, the ORDER BY clause specifies that the rows (records) should be made available to the program sorted by region number within product number.

➤ FIGURE 15-33

COBOL Program to Produce PRODUCT SALES SUMMARY BY REGION Report

```
IDENTIFICATION DIVISION.
PROGRAM-ID.   DB2-EXAMPLE.
ENVIRONMENT DIVISION.
CONFIGURATION SECTION.
SPECIAL-NAMES.
       (special names go here)
INPUT-OUTPUT SECTION.
FILE-CONTROL.
       SELECT    (SELECT statements for nondatabase files go here)
DATA DIVISION.
FILE SECTION.
       FD           (FDs for nondatabase files go here)
WORKING-STORAGE SECTION.
*
*      DECLARE VARIABLES FOR USE WITH DB2
*
       EXEC SQL   BEGIN DECLARE SECTION    END EXEC.
   01  SALE-RECORD.
       05  PRODUCT-NUMBER            PICTURE X(05).
       05  PRODUCT-NAME              PICTURE X(25).
       05  PRODUCT-DESC              PICTURE X(50).
       05  QUANTITY-SOLD             PICTURE S999          COMP-3.
       05  UNIT-PRICE                PICTURE S9 (5) V99    COMP-3.
       05  SALE-REGION               PICTURE S9            COMP-3.
       EXEC SQL   END DECLARE SECTION       END EXEC.
*      REQUEST DB2 TO COPY INTO COBOL PROGRAM
*      DEFINITIONS FOR DB2 COMMUNICATIONS AREA.
*
       EXEC SQL   INCLUDE SQLCA            END-EXEC.
*
*      DEFINE NON-DATABASE VARIABLES
*
   77  PRODUCT-NUMBER HOLD           PICTURE X(5).
   77  REGION-HOLD                   PICTURE X.
   77  SUM-UNITS-THIS-REGION         PICTURE 999           COMP-3 VALUE 0.
   77  SUM-UNITS-THIS-PRODUCT        PICTURE 99999         COMP-3 VALUE 0.
   01  PAGE-HEADER-1.
       05  FILLER                    PICTURE X(24)      VALUE SPACES.
       05  FILLER                    PICTURE X(31)
           VALUE 'PRODUCT SALES SUMMARY BY REGION'.
       05  FILLER                    PICTURE X(25)      VALUE SPACES.
   01  GROUP-1.
       05  FILLER                    PICTURE X(16)
           VALUE 'PRODUCT NUMBER:'.
```

(a)

Having established the cursor, we now have a conceptual pseudofile that contains all the newly constructed sales records in the desired sequence. The rest of the program follows ordinary sequential file-processing logic, testing for two control-level breaks (one on region number and the other on product number).

First we open the output report file, and then we issue SQL statements to prepare the database data to be processed:

OPEN C-1

We use the cursor to retrieve the first database row in the sale pseudofile,

FETCH C-1 INTO :SALE-RECORD

placing the data values into the fields we defined in the DECLARE SECTION. The word SALE-RECORD is preceded by a colon (:) to help the precompiler determine

► FIGURE 15-33

(Continued)

```
          05   PRODUCT-NUMBER-OUT        PICTURE X(05).
          05   FILLER                    PICTURE X(59)      VALUE SPACES.
     01   GROUP-2.
          05   FILLER                    PICTURE X(16)
               VALUE 'DESCRIPTION:'
          05   NAME-OUT                  PICTURE X(25).
          05   FILLER                    PICTURE X(39)      VALUE SPACES.
     01   GROUP-3.
          05   FILLER                    PICTURE X(16)      VALUE SPACES.
          05   DESCRIPTION-OUT           PICTURE X(50).
          05   FILLER                    PICTURE X(14)      VALUE SPACES.
     01   GROUP-4.
          05   FILLER                    PICTURE X(16)
               VALUE 'PRICE:'
          05   PRICE-OUT                 PICTURE $(6).99.
          05   FILLER                    PICTURE X(55)      VALUE SPACES.
     01   COLUMN-HEADERS.
          05   FILLER                    PICTURE X(30)      VALUE SPACES.
          05   FILLER                    PICTURE X(24)
               VALUE 'REGION                UNITS SOLD'.
          05   FILLER                    PICTURE X(26)      VALUE SPACES.
     01   REGION-TOTAL-LINE.
          05   FILLER                    PICTURE X(32)      VALUE SPACES.
          05   REGION-OUT                PICTURE X.
          05   FILLER                    PICTURE X(13)      VALUE SPACES.
          05   UNITS-SOLD-OUT            PICTURE ZZ9.
          05   FILLER                    PICTURE X(31)      VALUE SPACES.
     01   PRODUCT-TOTAL-LINE.
          05   FILLER                    PICTURE X(36)      VALUE SPACES.
          05   FILLER                    PICTURE X(08).
               VALUE 'TOTAL'
          05   TOTAL-OUT                 PICTURE ZZZZ9.
          05   FILLER                    PICTURE X(31)      VALUE SPACES.
     PROCEDURE DIVISION.
          EXEC SQL
               DECLARE C-1 CURSOR FOR
               SELECT PRODUCT. NUMBER, PRODUCT. NAME,
                    PRODUCT. DESCRIPTION, LINE-ITEM. QUANTITY,
                    PRODUCT. PRICE, SALESPERSON. REGION
               FROM PRODUCT, SALESPERSON, LINE-ITEM, INVOICE
               WHERE LINE-ITEM. INVOICE. NUMBER = INVOICE. NUMBER
                    AND INVOICE. SALESPERSON. NUMBER = SALESPERSON. NUMBER
                    AND LINE-ITEM. PRODUCT. NUMBER = PRODUCT. NUMBER
               ORDER BY PRODUCT. NUMBER, SALESPERSON. REGION
          END-EXEC.
          OPEN OUTPUT REPORT-FILE.
          EXEC SQL   OPEN C-1              END-EXEC.
```

(b)

➤ FIGURE 15-33

(Continued)

```
            EXEC SQL   FETCH C-1 INTO :SALE-RECORD     END-EXEC.
            MOVE PRODUCT-NUMBER TO PRODUCT-NUMBER-HOLD.
            MOVE SALE-REGION TO REGION-HOLD.
            PERFORM ISSUE-HEADERS.
            PERFORM PROCESS-AND-FETCH UNTIL SQLCODE = 100.
            EXEC SQL   CLOSE C-1 END EXEC.
            PERFORM ISSUE-REGION-TOTAL.
            PERFORM ISSUE-PRODUCT-TOTAL.
            CLOSE REPORT-FILE.
            EXIT PROGRAM.
   *
       PROCESS-AND-FETCH.
            IF PRODUCT-NUMBER NOT EQUAL PRODUCT-NUMBER-HOLD
            THEN PERFORM ISSUE-REGION-TOTAL
                 PERFORM ISSUE-PRODUCT-TOTAL
            ELSE
                 IF REGION-NUMBER NOT EQUAL REGION-HOLD
                 THEN PERFORM ISSUE-REGION-TOTAL
                 ELSE NEXT SENTENCE.
            ADD QUANTITY-SOLD TO SUM-UNITS-THIS REGION.
            ADD QUANTITY-SOLD TO SUM-UNITS-THIS-PRODUCT.
            EXEC SQL   FETCH C-1 INTO :SALE-RECORD     END-EXEC.
       ISSUE-REGION-TOTAL.
            MOVE SUM-UNITS-THIS-REGION TO UNITS-SOLD-OUT.
            MOVE REGION-HOLD TO REGION-OUT.
            MOVE REGION-TOTAL-LINE TO (printer record goes here).
            PERFORM WRITE-LINE.
            MOVE 0 TO SUM-UNITS-THIS-REGION.
            MOVE SALE-REGION TO REGION-HOLD.
       ISSUE-PRODUCT-TOTAL.
            MOVE SUM-UNITS-THIS-PRODUCT TO TOTAL-OUT.
            MOVE PRODUCT-TOTAL-LINE TO (printer record goes here).
            PERFORM WRITE-LINE.
            MOVE 0 TO SUM-UNITS-THIS-PRODUCT.
            MOVE PRODUCT-NUMBER TO PRODUCT-NUMBER-HOLD.
            PERFORM ISSUE-HEADERS.
       ISSUE-HEADERS.
            MOVE PAGE-HEADER-1 TO (printer record goes here).
            PERFORM WRITE-NEW-PAGE.
            MOVE PRODUCT-NUMBER TO PRODUCT-NUMBER-OUT.
            MOVE GROUP-1 TO (printer record goes here).
            PERFORM WRITE-LINE.
            MOVE PRODUCT-NAME TO NAME-OUT.
            MOVE GROUP-2 TO (printer record goes here).
            PERFORM WRITE-LINE.
            MOVE PRODUCT-DESC TO DESCRIPTION-OUT.
            MOVE GROUP-3 TO (printer record goes here).
            PERFORM WRITE-LINE.
            MOVE UNIT-PRICE TO PRICE-OUT.
            MOVE GROUP-4 TO (printer record goes here).
            PERFORM WRITE-LINE.
            MOVE COLUMN-HEADERS TO (printer record goes here).
            PERFORM WRITE-LINE.
       WRITE-NEW-PAGE.
            (instructions for printing line at top of page go here).
       WRITE-LINE.
            (instructions for writing a line go here).
```

(c)

that SALE-RECORD is a program variable and not a database term. This FETCH SQL statement effectively reads the first sale record from the pseudofile.

The next instruction sequence saves the product number and region values in work areas and writes the first set of report headers. Now the program is ready to process the first record. The program starts the loop called PROCESS-AND-FETCH and remains in this program loop until no more "sale records" are left in the database (UNTIL SQLCODE = 100). When that eventually happens, the program closes the cursor, releasing those resources to other users of this database, and terminates the program normally.

Within the main program loop, PROCESS-AND-FETCH, we find only one SQL statement. The last command in the loop is

FETCH C-1 INTO :SALE-RECORD

This instruction, like an ordinary COBOL READ, reads the next sequential row from the pseudofile, replacing the one just processed. As we mentioned, the loop is executed until all appropriate data has been retrieved from the database. The remaining COBOL paragraphs contain no SQL statements. They are used simply to format and produce the SALES SUMMARY report and would be no different if a sequential input file had been used.

Note that because KDK database is being used exclusively for analyzing data, no database changes are illustrated. If changes in the table data were made in an application program, either the COMMIT SQL statement would be invoked whenever a change were to be made permanent (perhaps after each valid record update) or the ROLLBACK SQL command would be invoked if the program discovered an error partway through an update. Also, a COMMIT would automatically be invoked when the program terminated. However, COMMITs are unnecessary in this sample program because it does not update the database.

➤ SUMMARY

KDK Appliances, a manufacturing company, needed to analyze sales data from its operational database. The most effective and least disruptive way to do this was to download sales data from the operational database onto a smaller mainframe. Then the snapshot of the operational data could be studied by product managers so that they would have the data they needed to make timely decisions and to plan marketing strategies. KDK Appliances chose Database2 (DB2) as its relational database management system.

After identifying the various objects that the product managers needed, we developed a relational database design. First we drew a set of object diagrams and then converted them to relation diagrams. With the design completed, we turned to the database management system DB2 for implementation.

DB2 is an IBM product used to process relational databases on large computers operating under MVS. DB2 uses the language SQL to define, access, and manipulate data and to grant authorizations. SQL statements can be issued interactively or be embedded into application programs written in COBOL, PL/I, FORTRAN, C, or assembler language.

DB2 allows users to define various database constructs such as tables, views, table spaces, indexes, index spaces, data bases, and storage groups. Users—both on-line end users and application programmers—refer only to tables and views. The database administrator, or someone performing other system functions, is concerned with physical database storage and organization and thus deals with other DB2 constructs as well.

Database constructs can be defined, modified, and deleted, and DB2 includes SQL statements to perform all those functions.

SQL data manipulation language as implemented in DB2 contains all the relational functions studied in Chapter 9. In addition to reading a database, we can insert records, update stored data, and delete rows from a table. The SQL statements for these four functions are SELECT, INSERT, UPDATE, and DELETE.

When SQL statements are embedded in an application program, the entire program must first be processed by the DB2 precompiler. The precompiler finds all SQL statements (indicated in COBOL by the keywords EXEC SQL ... END-EXEC) and translates them into equivalent host-language instructions. It builds database request modules, stores them on disk, and inserts call statements into the program to access them. Thus the application programmer needs to know little about the inner workings of the database management system, as the precompiler effectively shields the programmer from it.

In order to process a multiple-row query, the application programmer needs to define a cursor, a pointer that acts on a SELECT statement. Although the SELECT statement does not actually generate a file, you can imagine that a cursor defines a pseudofile in which DB2 will store the rows it retrieves. Then the set of retrieved rows can be processed one at a time, as if in a sequential file.

DB2 handles any problems of concurrent processing by using locks on portions of a database. Shared locks allow multiple concurrent access to the same data. But if any application needs to modify data, DB2 acquires an exclusive lock. No other application can access data that has an exclusive lock on it. When the lock is released, all applications have access to the updated data. The exclusive lock ensures the integrity of the data.

DB2 can lock either table spaces (which might include several tables) or pages (which contain tables or parts of tables). Locking pages causes less interference with other concurrent users but costs more to administer. Trade-offs like these are common in information processing.

DB2 logs all database changes before they are committed, or written, to the database. Database modifications that are not yet committed can be eliminated by issuing the ROLLBACK command. This might be necessary if a processing error is detected or a system failure occurs. The system log enables DB2 to recover data in the event of a system crash, by applying all before-images of the database since the latest checkpoint and then all after-images of the committed transactions (that had been logged). Any transactions in progress at the time of the crash must be restarted.

➤ GROUP I QUESTIONS

15.1 Why did KDK Appliances decide to download only its sales data from its operational mainframe computer?

15.2 Why does the INVOICE in the downloaded data contain fewer fields than does the actual invoice used for operational processing?

15.3 What is the purpose of the PRODUCT-AD relation?

15.4 Describe two modes of DB2 access.

15.5 Define *table, view,* and *base table,* and describe their relationships with one another.

15.6 How can a view be used to make the database more secure?

15.7 Which database constructs are referenced by users and application programmers?

15.8 Describe the relationship among data base, storage group, table space, page, index space, table, and index.

15.9   Write the DB2 SQL statement that creates a table, an index, and a view. Assume that the table contains CustomerName, Address, and AccountNumber. Build an index on AccountNumber, assuming that the view presents unique customer names.

15.10 Show the DB2 statement to add a CustomerAge column to your answer to Question 15.9.

15.11 Write the DB2 statement(s) that would add these records to the customer table in your answer to Question 15.10:

Mike Thompson, Madison, 456, 45

Paula Hand, New Haven, 722, 20

Karen Munroe, Gales Ferry, 076, 27

15.12 Show the DB2 statement that drops the table, index, and view defined in Question 15.9.

15.13 Explain the role of the DB2 precompiler.

15.14 How does the precompiler know which instructions are SQL instructions and which belong to the host language?

15.15 Explain the role of the cursor in DB2 processing.

15.16 Explain the difference between a shared lock and an exclusive lock.

15.17 Why is an exclusive lock required when the data is going to be modified?

15.18 What two lock sizes are supported by DB2? What is the advantage of each over the other?

15.19 What is the purpose of the COMMIT statement? Of the ROLLBACK statement?

15.20 How does DB2 handle deadlock?

15.21 Explain how DB2 can recover from a system crash and from damage to the database.

15.22 Explain the role of the GRANT statement. How can GRANT authority be given to another user?

15.23 Explain the role of the REVOKE statement. What is the cascade effect of REVOKE?

➤ GROUP II QUESTIONS

15.24 Locate a company that is using DB2. Determine how long it has had the system, why it chose DB2, and how well DB2 has worked out. Does the company use DB2 interactively, is it used in application programs, or both? Do users develop any on-line inquiries using DB2? If possible, obtain a copy of an application program, and explain the meaning of each embedded SQL statement. How does DB2 identify the application program as an authorized user? How often does the company back up its database? Does it copy the entire database, or does it back up only those pages changed since the previous backup? Has this company ever had to recover the database? What problems, if any, did it experience? Has performance ever been a problem? If so, what did the company do to improve it? Explain whether you believe that DB2 has been an effective DBMS for that company.

15.25 Locate a company that uses a mainframe relational DBMS other than DB2, and answer Question 15.24 for this DBMS.

The Hierarchical and Network Data Models

The hierarchical (DL/I) and network (CODASYL DBTG) data models preceded the relational model, and they were at one time the workhorses of the database industry. Today, DL/I lives on as the basis of an IBM DBMS product called IMS. Large manufacturers in particular use IMS to manage substantial and important operational data bases. The CODASYL DBTG model was the basis for several DBMS products, the most popular of which was IDMS. You may find uses of such DBMS products today, but they will be limited. The DBTG model is primarily important as part of the heritage of database processing.

➤ LIBRARY EXAMPLE

We will use a case that involves the processing of library data to illustrate the nature and use of the hierarchical and network data models. The objects to be stored and processed are illustrated in Figure 16-1. This design contains composite objects 1:1, 1:N, and M:N compound objects and association objects. COPY is a composite object because it contains Due-date as a multivalued nonobject attribute. The 1:1 compound objects are STUDENT and VIDEO (students are allowed to check out only one videocassette at a time). The 1:N compound objects are PUBLISHER and TITLE. The M:N compound objects are AUTHOR and TITLE, because an author can write many books and a book can be written by many authors. The association object is COPY, which documents the relationship between a TITLE and the STUDENT who checks it out.

A relational design for these objects is shown in Figure 16-2. Note that there is one relation for each object and multi-value attribute. The names of the relations are slightly different from the object names in order to differentiate the

Six Objects Used by a University Library

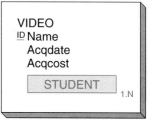
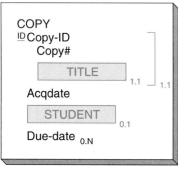
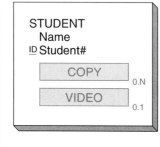

Relational Design for the
University Database:
(a) Relations for the University
Library Database and
(b) Relationship of University
Database Relations

TTLE (Name, <u>Call#</u>, *PUB.Name*)

PUB (<u>Name</u>, Address, Salesrep, Phone)

AUTH (<u>Name</u>, Affiliation)

CPY (<u>Copy#</u>, *TTLE.Call#*, Acqdate, *STU.Student#*)

DUE-DATE (*<u>Copy#</u>*, *<u>TTLE.Call#</u>*, <u>DueDate</u>)

STU (Name, <u>Student#</u>)

VID (<u>Name</u>, Acqdate, Acqcost, *STU.Student#*)

TA-INT (*<u>TTLE.Call#</u>*, *<u>AUTH.Name</u>*)

(a)

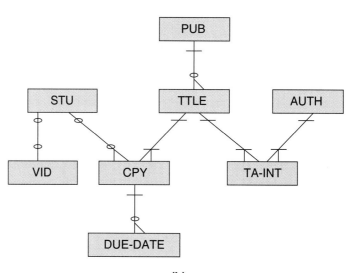

(b)

two. In addition to these six relations, the relation DUE-DATE represents the repeating group in the COPY object, and the intersection relation TA-INT represents the M:N relationship between TITLE and AUTHOR.

➤ DATA LANGUAGE/I

IBM and North American Aviation jointly developed DL/I in the 1960s as an outgrowth of data processing needs in the aerospace industry. DL/I is a language for processing a database, and its most popular implementation is IMS, or Information Management System, which for years was IBM's primary transaction processing-oriented DBMS (DB2 has now taken over this role). Actually, IMS is both a communications processor and a database management system, so it would be more correct to say that DL/I is implemented in IMS/DB, which is the database portion of IMS. DL/I uses hierarchies (trees) to represent relationships, which means that the users' objects must be transformed into tree representations before they can be processed using DL/I.

In DL/I terms, fields are grouped into **segments,** or the nodes of tree structures. Remember from Chapter 6 that a tree is a collection of records and relationships in which each record has at most one parent and all relationships are one to many between parent and child. (Throughout this discussion, we use the DL/I term *segment* rather than record or row.) DL/I refers to a particular tree structure (a collection of related segments) as a **data base record.** (*Data base* is two words in DL/I.) Since DL/I concerns only hierarchies, any network relationships must be transformed into hierarchies before they can be processed.

A sample STUDENT data base record is sketched in Figure 16-3. The forked line notation used throughout this text is not part of DL/I notation but is used here for consistency. Each STUDENT segment has Name, Number, and Address fields. Also, under each STUDENT segment are a variable number of JOB HISTORY and CLASS segments. An occurrence of the STUDENT data base record is shown in Figure 16-4.

In DL/I, a **data base** is composed of data base records, which can be occurrences of the same record type or of several different record types. For example, a DL/I data base could consist of occurrences of the STUDENT data base record in Figure 16-3 and the FACULTY data base record in Figure 16-5. The data base would comprise all occurrences of each data base record type. Figure 16-6 summarizes the DL/I data structures.

Data base records are defined by means of a **data base description.** In the DBMS product IMS, a set of assembly-language macro instructions indicates the structure of each data base record. (Note that this is different from the relational language SQL we examined earlier. SQL includes both data definition and data manipulation statements, whereas DL/I is for data manipulation only. This re-

➤ FIGURE 16-3

STUDENT Data Base Record

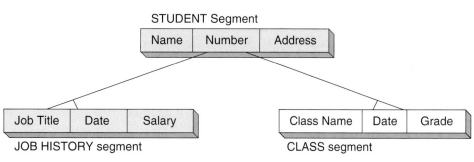

STUDENT Segment

| Name | Number | Address |

| Job Title | Date | Salary |

JOB HISTORY segment

| Class Name | Date | Grade |

CLASS segment

➤ FIGURE 16-4

STUDENT Data Base Record Occurrence

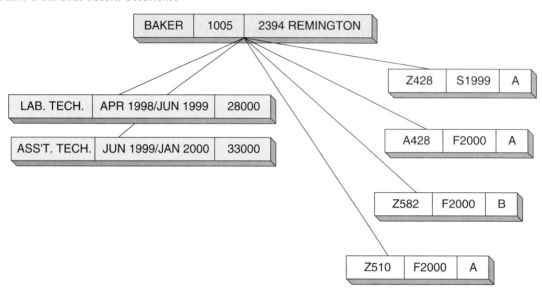

➤ FIGURE 16-5

FACULTY Data Base Record

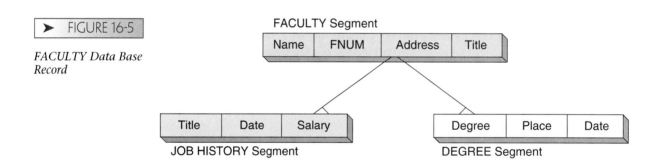

➤ FIGURE 16-6

Summary of DL/I Data Structures

Data Structure	Description
Field	Smallest unit of data.
Segment	Group of fields; segments must be related by hierarchical structure; each segment has a sequence field used for logical ordering.
Data base record	Hierarchically structured group of segments.
Data base	Collection of data base record occurrences of one or more data base record types.

➤ FIGURE 16-7

Description of Data Base for STUDENT Data Base Record in Figure 16-3

```
                  ⎧  DBD     NAME=STUDB
   STUDENT        ⎪  SEGM    NAME=STU, BYTES=61
   segment        ⎨  FIELD   NAME=SNAME, BYTES=30, START=1
   description     ⎪  FIELD   NAME=(NUM, SEQ), BYTES=11, START=31
                  ⎩  FIELD   NAME=ADDR, BYTES=20, START=42

   JOB HISTORY    ⎧  SEGM    NAME=JOBHIST, PARENT=STU, BYTES=47
   segment        ⎨  FIELD   NAME=JOBTITLE, BYTES=30, START=1
   description     ⎪  FIELD   NAME=(JDATE, SEQ), BYTES=15, START=31
                  ⎩  FIELD   NAME=SALARY, BYTES=6, START=46

   CLASS          ⎧  SEGM    NAME=CLASS, PARENT=STU, BYTES=10
   segment        ⎨  FIELD   NAME=(CNAME, SEQ), BYTES=5, START=1
   description     ⎪  FIELD   NAME=CDATE, BYTES=5, START=6
                  ⎩  FIELD   NAME=GRADE, BYTES=1, START=11
```

flects DL/I's age, as it was developed before having a convenient means of defining data was judged important.) Figure 16-7 depicts a portion of the data base description for the STUDENT data base record in Figure 16-3. The format of this description is unique to IMS.

Each segment description is headed by an SEGM macro that names the segment, shows its total length, and gives the name of the parent if there is one. The first segment, or **root,** has no parent. Each field within a segment is represented by a FIELD macro that indicates the field's name, length, and starting position in the segment. One field in each segment is designated as the **sequence field** and is used to order the occurrences of a given segment type. The order is a logical one; although it may appear to the application program that the segments are in order of sequence field, the physical ordering of the segments may be different.

In Figure 16-7, the STUDENT segment is named STU and is 61 bytes long. The STU record is composed of an SNAME field in bytes 1 through 30, a NUM field in bytes 31 through 41, and an ADDR field in bytes 42 through 61. (Because DL/I uses uppercase letters, all names are spelled in capitals.) The sequence field for STU segments is NUM.

JOB HISTORY segments are called JOBHIST and are composed of JOBTITLE, JDATE, and SALARY fields. CLASS segments are called CLASS and have CNAME, CDATE, and GRADE fields.

The data base description is assembled and can be stored in object form in a library to be called into main memory when needed. Consequently, each application programmer need only reference the data base description to have it copied into his or her program.

DL/I REPRESENTATION OF THE LIBRARY EXAMPLE

Since DL/I represents and processes only hierarchies, all data base designs must be transformed into hierarchical designs. This is done by transforming any network relationships into multiple hierarchies with data duplication and then removing the data duplication by placing pointers to the source data in any duplicate segments. This process is illustrated in this section.

The relational design in Figure 16-2 is not a hierarchy because two relations, CPY and TA-INT, have more than one parent. We can transform this structure into hierarchical structures by creating two trees for each path from

FIGURE 16-8

Representing Hierarchies for DL/I Processing: (a) Logical Data Base Records for the Relations in Figure 16-2 and (b) Physical Data Base Records for the Relations in Figure 16-2

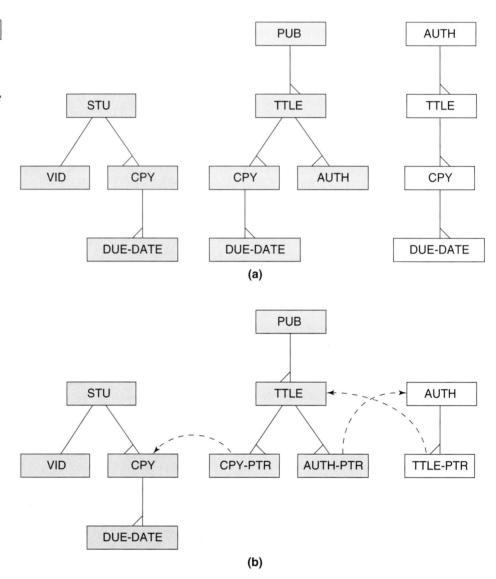

(a)

(b)

the parent to the child, for a total of four trees. This has been done in Figure 16-8(a) (only three trees appear because the middle tree in this figure holds two of them).

Consider this process for the CPY relation first. Since both TTLE and STU are parents of CPY, we need to construct one tree for each of them. Thus you see in Figure 16-8(a) the STU/CPY/DUE-DATE tree (part of the left tree in that figure) and the PUB/TTLE/CPY/DUE-DATE tree (part of the middle tree). STU also has a child, VID, which we can add under STU without causing a problem, thereby completing that tree.

Now consider the TA-INT relation in Figure 16-2. The purpose of TA-INT is to represent many titles for a given author and many authors for a given title. Thus we want a tree with AUTH as parent and TTLE as child and a tree with TTLE as parent and AUTH as child. This representation is also shown in Figure 16-8(a). AUTH/TTLE/CPY/DUE-DATE is shown as a separate tree. The TTLE/AUTH relationship has been represented within the PUB/TTLE/CPY/DUE-DATE tree by adding the AUTH relation under TTLE. Figure 16-8(a) therefore shows four trees (two for each of the relations that have two parents), but two of them have been combined under the common parent TTLE.

The trees in Figure 16-8(a) have considerable data duplication. For example, the CPY segment appears in three different places. Since duplicated data not only waste file space but also can cause data integrity problems, we want to eliminate them. This can be done by storing the data in one place and storing pointers to the data in the other places. This is what is done with DL/I and what is illustrated in Figure 16-8(b).

DL/I divides a data base into physical and logical constructs. The terms physical data base (PDB) and **physical data base record** (PDBR) are used to describe the data as they exist in data storage. The terms **logical data base** (LDB) and **logical data base record** (LDBR) are used to describe the data as they appear to the application programs that process them. LDBRs differ from PDBRs in either of two ways. An LDBR may be a subset of a PDBR, or an LDBR may contain portions of two or more PDBRs and represent tree structures that are not present in the PDBRs. The trees sketched in Figure 16-8(a) are LDBRs, as they represent data as they appear to an application program. Conversely, the trees sketched in Figure 16-8(b) are PDBRs; these are the physical data structures that are created on disk.

DL/I Data Manipulation Language

DL/I processes data in segments; DL/I statements can retrieve, update, insert, and delete segments. Unlike SQL, which can be used interactively or be embedded in application programs, DL/I statements must be embedded in application programs. DL/I has no interactive query language. (Keep in mind that DL/I was one of the earliest data base languages, used exclusively for transaction processing by information systems professionals and not by end users.)

Using DL/I, the application programmer defines an input/output (I/O) work area that is shared by the application program and the DBMS product. To insert or update a segment, the application program places new data in the work area; the DBMS takes the data from there to modify the data base. When the DBMS retrieves data from the data base, it places it in the work area for the program to access. System status data, such as completion flags and error flags, are also placed in the work area by the DBMS so that the application program can examine them.

The DL/I syntax that is presented in this section represents functions that are embedded in application programs. The specific form of the functions depends on the language used and hence we present a generic form here. To understand these commands, consider the LDBR in Figure 16-9, which is based on the PUB/TTLE/AUTH-PTR/CPY-PTR PDBR in Figure 16-8(b).

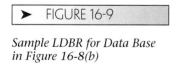
➤ FIGURE 16-9

Sample LDBR for Data Base in Figure 16-8(b)

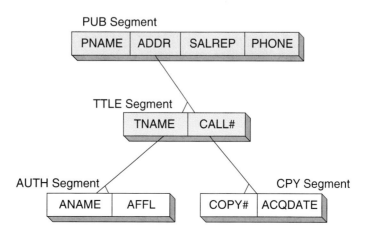

FIGURE 16-10

*Two Occurrences
of the LDBR in
Figure 16-9*

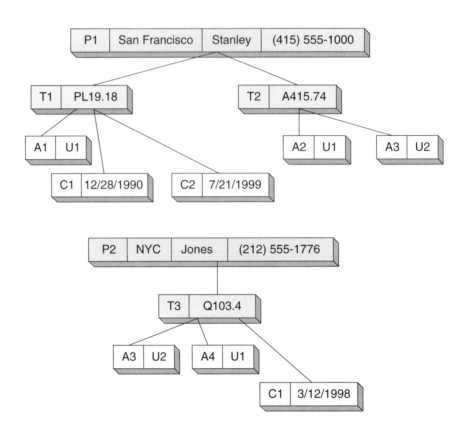

GET UNIQUE (GU) GET UNIQUE (GU) is a command used to read a particular segment into the I/O work area. For example, the statement

GU   PUB(SALREP = 'JONES')

causes the first PUB segment with the SALREP value of JONES to be placed into the I/O work area. Thus, if the occurrences in Figure 16-10 are the first ones in the data base, the segment P2,NYC,JONES,(212)555-1776 will be placed in the work area. The following statements cause the first AUTH with name A3 of TTLE T2 to be placed in the work area:

GU   PUB
        TTLE (TNAME = 'T2')
        AUTH (ANAME = 'A3')

If no such segment exists, the DBMS will set an appropriate return code in the work area.

The DBMS searches for the desired segment by starting at the first occurrence of the LDBR, at the first T2 occurrence of the TTLE segment (assuming that there could be more than one), and at the first A3 occurrence of the AUTH segment (again assuming that there could be more than one). The order of the segments is determined by the sequence fields in each segment (see Figure 16-7). For this LDBR, assume the following sequence fields:

SEGMENT	SEQUENCE FIELD
PUB	PNAME
TTLE	TNAME
AUTH	ANAME
CPY	COPY#

To find the first occurrence of AUTH A3 in TTLE T2, we examine the segments in the following order: P1 (PUB) segment, T1, T2 (TTLE segments), and, finally, A2, A3 (AUTH segments). The segment read into the work area is A3.

The qualifying data after the GU command are called a **segment search argument** (SSA). In general, an SSA is the name of a segment, which may be followed by a condition. As shown, there can be one SSA for each segment in the hierarchical path for the segment to be retrieved.

GET NEXT (GN)   GET NEXT (GN) is a command used to read the next segment. Next implies that there be a current segment to start from, so it is necessary to indicate a current segment before issuing a GN command. For example, the statements

```
GU       PUB
          TTLE (TNAME = 'T1')
GN       TTLE
```

cause the first TTLE segment in the data base with TNAME field equal to T1 to be placed in the I/O work area. This establishes a current position. (There most likely would be some program instructions to process that segment following the GU command, but we have omitted them.) The GN statement reads the next TTLE segment. For the occurrence in Figure 16-10, the T1 segment is read first, followed by the T2 segment. If a subsequent GN TTLE command is executed, the DBMS will attempt to find another TTLE segment under the current PUB segment. There is none for this occurrence, so it searches under the next PUB segment (P2) and reads the T3 occurrence of TTLE.

A third execution of GN TTLE causes the DBMS to look for the next TTLE segment. Because there are no more in the P2 occurrence of PUB, the DBMS searches the next LDBR occurrence for a TTLE segment and, if it finds one, places it in the work area. The search will continue to the end of the data base if necessary. If no TTLE segment remains in the data base, appropriate status data will be set.

When the GN statements are executed, the DBMS selects the next occurrence of the segment named. If there is no such occurrence under the current parent, the DBMS will switch to the next parent. The application program may need to know, however, when the DBMS selects a segment from a new parent. For example, if the second GN TTLE statement is executed as discussed in the preceding paragraph, the program may need to know that a new PUB segment has been retrieved.

To provide this information, when a segment is read, data regarding the path leading to the segment is placed in the work area. IMS places the *fully concatenated key* of the retrieved segment in the work area. This key is the concatenation of all sequence fields of segments leading to the segment, along with the sequence field of the segment. For example, the fully concatenated key for the A4 AUTH segment is P2 T3 A4. After the second GN TTLE command is executed as described, the DBMS returns the key P2 T3, and the application program can detect the new PUB segment by means of the change in PUB sequence field in the key. Now consider another example. The commands

```
GU       PUB
          TTLE(TNAME = 'T1')
GN       TTLE(CALL# > 'P')
```

cause the T1 TTLE segment to be read, followed by the next TTLE segment with a call number starting with a letter beyond P in the collating sequence. Consequently T3 is read next. The important point here is that sequential retrieval can be either *qualified* (with a condition after the segment name) or *unqualified* (with no condition).

Another type of sequential retrieval command requests the next segment regardless of its type. For example, the commands

```
GU      PUB
        TTLE(TNAME = 'T1')
GN
```

cause the T1 segment of TTLE to be read, followed by the A1 AUTH segment. A subsequent GN command reads the C1 CPY segment.

As an aside, this LDBR does not include DUE-DATE segments (or, as sometimes expressed in DL/I, this LDBR *is not sensitive to* DUE-DATE segments). When the GN commands are executed, no DUE-DATE data is presented to the application program; the DBMS automatically skips it. IMS never presents to an application any data to which the application is not sensitive.

GET NEXT WITHIN PARENT (GNP)   GET NEXT WITHIN PARENT (GNP) is a command that sequentially retrieves segments under one parent. When all segments under that parent have been read, end-of-data status is returned to the program. For example, when the commands

```
GU      PUB
        TTLE (TNAME = 'T1')
GNP     TTLE
GNP     TTLE
```

are executed, the T1 and T2 segments of P1 are read. The second GNP command does not return data; rather, it causes the end-of-data status flag to be set. Contrast this with the statements

```
GU      PUB
        TTLE (TNAME = 'T1')
GN      TTLE
GN      TTLE
```

Here, the second GN command retrieves the T3 TTLE segment.

GET HOLD COMMANDS   GET HOLD UNIQUE (GHU), GET HOLD NEXT (GHN), and GET HOLD NEXT WITHIN PARENT (GHNP) operate like their Get counterparts except that they inform the DBMS to prepare for a change in or deletion of the retrieved segment. They are used with Replace and Delete commands. When the program replaces or deletes a segment, it first issues a Get Hold command for the segment. DBMS retrieves the segment and "holds" it; then Replace or Delete can be issued.

REPLACE (REPL)   Replace is used to modify data within a segment. For example, the commands

```
GHU     PUB
        TTLE (TNAME = 'T2')
```

(here the application program changes TTLE data)

```
REPL
```

cause the DBMS to retrieve the T2 TTLE segment and replace it with the changed data. (In this and several following examples, the program processing is in lowercase letters. Syntax is dependent on the language used and is omitted.)

The following instruction sequence sets the acquisition date of titles to 1/1/1998.

```
GHU       PUB
          TTLE
          CPY
DOWHILE data remain
          Set ACQDATE = '1/1/1998'
          REPL
          GHNCPY
          END-DO
```

The GHU command obtains the first CPY segment; GHN obtains subsequent ones.

DELETE (DLET)   Delete operates in conjunction with the Get Hold commands in a manner similar to Replace. The commands

```
GHU       PUB (PNAME = 'P1')
          TTLE (TNAME = 'T1')
          AUTH (ANAME = 'A1')
DLET
```

delete the A1 segment under T1 and P1 from the data base. When a segment is deleted, any subordinate segments are also deleted (including ones invisible to the application). Thus, the commands

```
GHU       PUB (PNAME = 'P1')
          TTLE (TNAME = 'T1')
          CPY (COPY# = 1)
DLET
```

delete not only the C1 copy segment under T1 and P1 but also all of the DUE-DATE segments under that copy. Therefore, any subordinate segments to which the application is not sensitive are deleted.

Deleting invisible data is dangerous and not recommended. In order to prevent it from happening, the data base administrator, data base designers, and application programmers must communicate clearly with one another and establish and enforce standards. They also should review the designs. Otherwise, application programmers may write application code that appears to them to be correct but that in fact is causing errors—errors that the programmers could not know might exist.

INSERT (INSRT)   Insert is used to create a new segment. For example, the statements (instructions to place new AUTH data in I/O work area)

```
INSERT    PUB (PNAME = 'P1')
          TTLE (TNAME = 'T2')
          AUTH
```

insert a new AUTH segment into the data base. Since the AUTH sequence field is ANAME, the new segment is logically inserted in order of that field. For example, if the new value of ANAME is A4, the new AUTH segment will be inserted logically as the last AUTH segment under the T2 parent.

SUMMARY OF DL/I DATA MANIPULATION COMMANDS   Figure 16-11 summarizes the DL/I data manipulation commands, all of which operate on the logical structure of the data as seen by an application program. Since the physical

Summary of DL/I Data Manipulation Commands

Name	Function
Get Unique (GU)	Retrieve a particular segment.
Get Next (GN)	Retrieve the next segment.
Get Next within Parent (GNP)	Retrieve the next segment under a particular parent.
Get Hold Unique (GHU) Get Hold Next (GHN) Get Hold Next within Parent (GHNP)	Similar to preceding commands but used to obtain a segment to be modified or deleted.
Replace (REPL) Delete (DLET)	Used in conjunction with Get Hold commands to modify or delete a segment.
Insert (INSRT)	Insert a new segment.

structure of the data may be quite different from the logical structure, the DBMS must translate the logical activity into actions on the physical data structures. The application is independent of the physical structures and is freed from maintaining them.

➤ THE CODASYL DBTG MODEL

The CODASYL DBTG data model was developed by a group known as the CODASYL (Conference on Data Systems Languages) Data Base Task Group (hence CODASYL DBTG). The CODASYL committee is best known as the group that developed the standards for COBOL. The CODASYL data model evolved over several years, and several transaction-oriented DBMS products are based on it. Today, however, those DBMS products are nearly unknown.

Several reasons account for the decline of the DBTG model. First, it is complex and incohesive. For example, a statement in a schema definition can combine with a seemingly unrelated operation in an application program to produce strange and unexpected results. Consequently, designers and programmers must be very careful when building DBTG databases and applications. Second, the model has a decidedly COBOL flavor to it, and this similarity has been an issue in organizations in which COBOL is not the language of choice. Furthermore, the development of the CODASYL database model was heavily politicized, and so the committee had to contend with the tendency to include everyone's favorite idea. Finally, in fairness to this model, it originated very early in the history of data base technology. Although it incorporated many important concepts, mistakes were also made. Indeed, some people believe that the model was developed too soon—before the essential concepts of database technology were known and had been explored.

CODASYL DBTG DATA DEFINITION LANGUAGE

The 1981 version of the CODASYL model provides three different types of database view. The **schema** is the complete logical view of the data base, the entire data base as viewed by the database administrator or other humans. A **subschema** is a view of the database as it appears to an application program. A sub-

➤ FIGURE 16-12

CODASYL DBTG Program/Data View Relationships

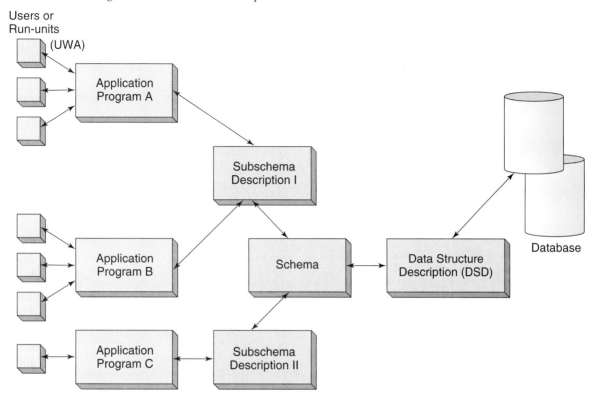

schema is a subset of the data base and is also allowed to have records that are constructed by joining records in the schema. This is similar to a DB2 view composed of relation joins, as discussed in Chapter 15. The **data structure description** is the third type of view, and it maps schema records, fields, and relationships to physical storage. It is the view of the data base as it appears in physical storage. Because data structure descriptions were introduced in a later version of the model, they were never used, and we omit them from the discussion here.

As shown in Figure 16-12, users interact with the data base by means of an application program (no interactive query language exists). One or more users can execute a single program. Each user has a **user working area** (UWA) that contains data base and control data for a particular user. The execution of a program by one of the users is called a **run-unit.** Figure 16-12 shows three run-units for Application Program A, and the application programs view the data base through a subschema. The programs may share subschemas, or each may have its own.

DATA DEFINITION CONSTRUCTS

Data base designers use the basic data definition constructs in CODASYL DBTG to define schemas and subschemas. The three fundamental building blocks are data-items, records, and sets.

DATA-ITEMS   A **data-item** is a field that corresponds to an attribute or column in the relational model. Data-items have names and formats, and examples are Name, Character 25; Address, Character 40; Amount, Fixed 6.2. Although data-items come from domains, the domain concept is not recognized by the DBTG model.

➤ FIGURE 16-13

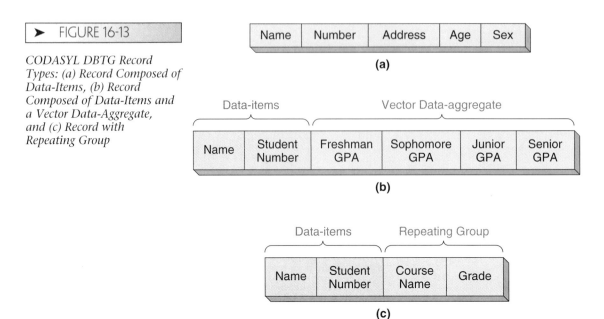

CODASYL DBTG Record Types: (a) Record Composed of Data-Items, (b) Record Composed of Data-Items and a Vector Data-Aggregate, and (c) Record with Repeating Group

RECORDS A **record** is a collection of data-items, and Figure 16-13 shows several examples of DBTG records. Unlike the relational model, this model allows **vectors,** which are repetitions of a data-item (like GPA in Figure 16-13[b]), and it allows repeating groups, such as the data-items Course Name and Grade in Figure 16-13(c). Although such repeating groups are allowed, they are unnecessary and generally not recommended. Repeating groups were developed to represent composite objects, but a better way of representing them is with two record types and a set.

SETS A **set** is a one-to-many relationship between records. Sets have *owners* and *members.* The owner of a set is the parent, and in Figure 16-14, ACCOUNTING is the owner of one set, and MARKETING is the owner of another set. Members of a set are the children in a one-to-many relationship. In Figure 16-14, Jones, Parks, and Williams are the members of the set owned by ACCOUNTING.

Figure 16-14 shows two occurrences of a general structure representing instances of a one-to-many relationship between the DEPARTMENT and FACULTY records. Figure 16-15 is a generalized representation of this relationship. The general structure, such as the one in Figure 16-15, is called the *set,* and examples of the structure, such as those in Figure 16-14, are called *instances,* or *occurrences,* of the set.

To define a set, we specify a set name and identify the type of record that will be the owner and the type (or types) of the records that will be the members. For example, in Figure 16-16, the set STU-MAJOR has MAJOR owner records and STUDENT member records; the set ORDER-ITEM has ORDER owner records and

➤ FIGURE 16-14

Two Occurrences of DEPT-FAC Set

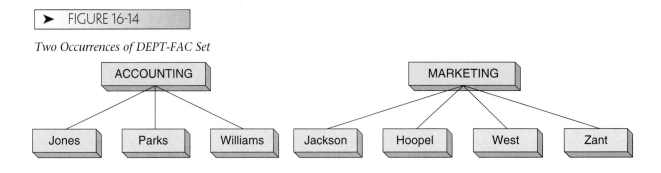

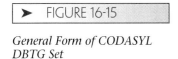

General Form of CODASYL DBTG Set

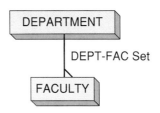

ITEM member records; and the set STU-HISTORY has STUDENT owner records and CLASS-GRADE member records.

The DBTG model has specific rules regarding set definition. First, a set can have only one type of record as owner, but one or more record types can be members. Figure 16-17(a) shows the set ACTIVITY: The owner record is CLUB, and the member records are PROFESSOR and STUDENT. Figure 16-17(b) shows two instances of this set, in which both PROFESSOR and STUDENT records are members of the SKIING and BOWLING clubs.

According to the DBTG model, a member record can belong to only one instance of a particular set; that is, a record may not have two parents in the same set. This means, in Figure 16-17, that Professor Guynes can have only the SKIING parent record; he may not have BOWLING as well. Furthermore, Professor Pipkin can have only the BOWLING record as a parent and not SKIING as well. If faculty members are allowed to belong to more than one club, a DBTG set cannot be used to represent this relationship. In fact, if faculty members were allowed to belong to two clubs, this would be an instance of an M:N relationship.

Although a record cannot have two owners in the *same* set, a record may have two owners if they are in *different* sets. For example, a professor may have one ACTIVITY owner and one JOB-TITLE owner. Figure 16-18 extends Figure 16-17 to allow this possibility. Professor Guynes, for example, has both SKIING and FULL PROFESSOR records as parents.

These restrictions on set membership mean that a set can readily be used to represent 1:1 and 1:N relationships and can directly represent composite objects, 1:1 and 1:N compound objects, association objects, and any hybrid objects that do not include an M:N compound object. M:N compound objects cannot be represented because M:N relationships cannot be represented directly with DBTG sets. The characteristics of sets are summarized in Figure 16-19.

A Schema Definition for the Library Database

Figure 16-20 presents a schema definition for the library database design shown in Figure 16-2. The schema definition has two main parts. The first concerns the definition of record structures, and the second, the definition of sets.

DEFINING RECORDS   Examine the definition of the PUB record in Figure 16-20. The first statement declares that values of PNAME must be unique. Following that, the data-items are described. Notice the CHECK statement that enforces the domain constraint that PNAME may not be null.

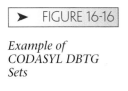

Example of CODASYL DBTG Sets

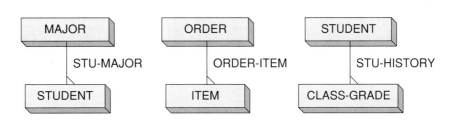

Set with (a) Two-Member Record Types and (b) Example Occurrences of Them

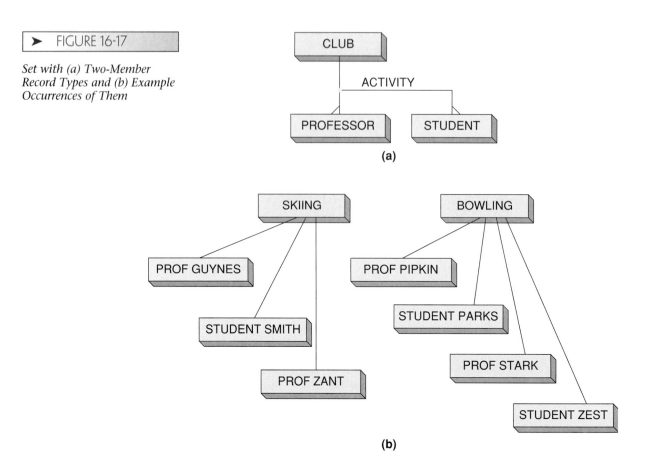

(a)

(b)

Example of Two-Owner Record in Different Sets: (a) Record Belonging to Two Different Sets and (b) Instance of This Set Structure

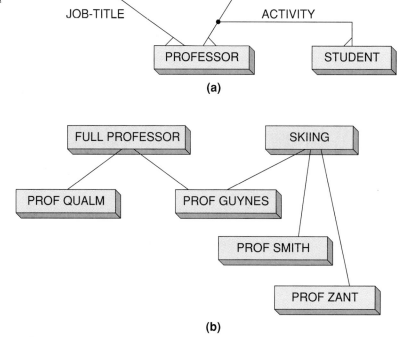

(a)

(b)

➤ FIGURE 16-19

Summary of Set Characteristics

- A set is a collection of records.
- There is an arbitrary number of sets in the database.
- Each set has one owner record type and one or more member record types.
- Each owner record occurrence defines a set occurrence.
- There is an arbitrary number of member record occurrences in one set occurrence.
- A record may be a member of more than one set.
- A record may not be a member of two occurrences of the same set.

➤ FIGURE 16-20

Definition of Library Schema

```
SCHEMA NAME IS LIBRARY
    RECORD NAME IS PUB
        DUPLICATES ARE NOT ALLOWED FOR PNAME
        PNAME                       TYPE IS     CHARACTER     10
                                    CHECK IS    NOT NULL
        ADDRESS                     TYPE IS     CHARACTER     25
        SALPSN                      TYPE IS     CHARACTER     20
        PPHONE                      TYPE IS     FIXED         10

    RECORD NAME IS TTLE
        DUPLICATES ARE NOT ALLOWED FOR CALL#
        DUPLICATES ARE NOT ALLOWED FOR TNAME
        CALL#                       TYPE IS     CHARACTER     8
                                    CHECK IS    NOT NULL
        TNAME                       TYPE IS     CHARACTER     50
                                    CHECK IS    NOT NULL
        PNAME                       TYPE IS     CHARACTER     10
                                    CHECK IS    NOT NULL
    RECORD NAME IS CPY
        DUPLICATES ARE NOT ALLOWED FOR CALL#, COPY#
        CALL#                       TYPE IS     CHARACTER     8
                                    CHECK IS    NOT NULL
        COPY#                       TYPE IS     FIXED         2
                                    CHECK IS    NOT NULL
        ACQDATE                     TYPE IS     DATE

    RECORD NAME IS AUTH
        DUPLICATES ARE NOT ALLOWED FOR ANAME
        ANAME                       TYPE IS     CHARACTER     30
                                    CHECK IS    NOT NULL
        AFFILIATION                 TYPE IS     CHARACTER     30

    RECORD NAME IS TA-INT
        DUPLICATES ARE NOT ALLOWED FOR CALL#, ANAME
        CALL#                       TYPE IS     CHARACTER     8
                                    CHECK IS    NOT NULL
        ANAME                       TYPE IS     CHARACTER     30
                                    CHECK IS    NOT NULL      7

    RECORD NAME IS STU
        DUPLICATES ARE NOT ALLOWED FOR STUDENT#
        STUDENT#                    TYPE IS     FIXED         10
                                    CHECK IS    NOT NULL
        SNAME                       TYPE IS     CHARACTER     30
        SPHONE                      TYPE IS     FIXED
```

```
RECORD NAME IS VID
        DUPLICATES ARE NOT ALLOWED FOR VID#, VCOPY#
        DUPLICATES ARE NOT ALLOWED FOR STUDENT#
        VID#                        TYPE IS      FIXED          5
                                    CHECK IS     NOT NULL
        VCOPY#                      TYPE IS      FIXED          2
                                    CHECK IS     NOT NULL
        VNAME                       TYPE IS      CHARACTER      40
        STUDENT#                    TYPE IS      FIXED          10

RECORD NAME IS DUE-DATE
        DATE-DUE                    TYPE IS      DATE
                                    CHECK IS     NOT NULL

SET NAME IS PUBLISH
        OWNER IS PUB
        ORDER IS SORTED BY DEFINED KEYS
        MEMBER IS TTLE
        KEY IS ASCENDING TNAME

SET NAME IS T-A
        OWNER IS TTLE
        ORDER IS SYSTEM DEFAULT
        MEMBER IS TA-INT
        CHECK IS CALL# IN TTLE = CALL# IN TA-INT

SET NAME IS A-T
        OWNER IS AUTH
        ORDER IS SYSTEM DEFAULT
        MEMBER IS TA-INT
        CHECK IS ANAME IN AUTH = ANAME IN TA-INT

SET NAME IS COLLECTION
        OWNER IS TTLE
        ORDER IS BY DEFINED KEYS
        MEMBER IS CPY
        KEY IS ASCENDING COPY#

SET NAME IS CHECKOUT
        OWNER IS STU
        ORDER IS LAST
        MEMBER IS CPY

SET NAME IS VCHKOUT
        OWNER IS STU
        ORDER IS LAST
        MEMBER IS VID

SET NAME IS HISTORY
        OWNER IS CPY
        MEMBER IS DUE-DATE
        ORDER IS LAST

SET NAME IS TITLE-SEQ
        OWNER IS SYSTEM
        ORDER IS BY DEFINED KEYS
        MEMBER IS TTLE
        KEY IS ASCENDING TNAME
```

The definition of TTLE is next. Here, two different statements declare that both TNAME and CALL# are to be unique. Since these statements are separate, they imply that the value of TNAME and the values of CALL# each must be unique. This is different from declaring that a composite group is unique. An example of composite data-item uniqueness can be found in the definition of the next record, CPY, in which the DUPLICATES statement declares that the composite (CALL#, COPY#) must be unique.

The remaining record definitions are similar, although one unusual statement appears in the definition of VID. In this record, STUDENT is required to be unique. Since a set is defined with STU as the parent and VID as the child, this relationship would normally be one to many, as the same value of STUDENT could appear in many different instances of VID. With the declaration that STUDENT must be unique, however, the same STUDENT can appear in only one VID record. This declaration therefore turns what would normally be a one-to-many relationship into the one-to-one relationship required in the design.

DEFINING SETS   In Figure 16-20, one set is defined for each one-to-many and one-to-one relationship shown in Figure 16-2. The first set, PUBLISH, represents the relationship between PUB and TTLE. The owner record of this set is PUBLISH, and the member record is TTLE. The records in the set are to be maintained in sorted order of TNAME, defined by two statements in the set definition. The first, ORDER IS SORTED BY DEFINED KEYS, indicates that the order is to be kept by a value of one or more data-items in the member record. The particular data-item is then identified by the statement KEY IS ASCENDING TNAME.

The remaining sets also are defined in Figure 16-20. The sets T-A and A-T represent the M:N relationship between titles and authors. The order is SYSTEM DEFAULT, which means that the application developers are not concerned about the order of the member records in the set. Other statements are similar to those for PUBLISH, except that these sets include a CHECK clause. Consider the set T-A. The CHECK clause in this set definition tells the DBMS to enforce the constraint that the values of CALL in TTLE and TA-INT must match.

SUBSCHEMAS FOR THE LIBRARY DATA BASE

To illustrate the definition and use of CODASYL DBTG subschemas, we consider two subschemas for the library data base. Figure 16-21(a) shows the structure of the PURCHASE subschema, used by application programs in the purchasing department. The second subschema, BORROW, is shown in Figure 16-21(b). BORROW is used by the checkout desk when books are lent.

PURCHASE SUBSCHEMA   The general format of a subschema description is shown in Figure 16-22. Each subschema description has three divisions. The TITLE DIVISION contains the name of the subschema; the MAPPING DIVISION contains alias descriptions; and the STRUCTURE DIVISION indicates the records, data-items, and sets in the schema that are present in the subschema.

Figure 16-23(a) has a subschema description for PURCHASE. In the MAPPING DIVISION, the record TTLE is renamed BOOK, and the record DUE-DATE is renamed BORROWED. In addition, the set HISTORY is renamed USES, and the data-item DATE-DUE is named USE-DATE. The application program that accesses this subschema must use these aliases rather than the names in the schema description. AD is a keyword that stands for *alias definition*.

The RECORD SECTION of this subschema redefines the PUB record to omit the ADDRESS data-item. All the data-items in BOOK, CPY, and BORROWED should be part of the PURCHASE subschema. Finally, in the SET SECTION, the sets PUBLISH, COLLECTION, and USES are declared to be included in PURCHASE. SD is a keyword that stands for *set definition*.

BORROW SUBSCHEMA   The subschema BORROW is defined in Figure 16-23(b). The structure of the description is the same as that for PURCHASE. BORROW includes the BOOK (alias for TTLE), BORROWER (alias for STU), CPY, and DUE-DATE records. The sets included are COLLECTION, CHECKOUT, and RETURN (alias for HISTORY).

 FIGURE 16-21

*Sample of Subschema
Structures: (a) PURCHASE
Subschema and (b) BORROW
Subschema*

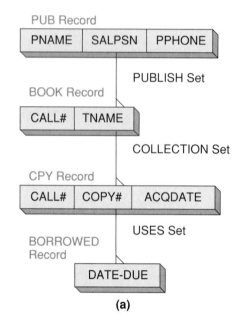

(a)

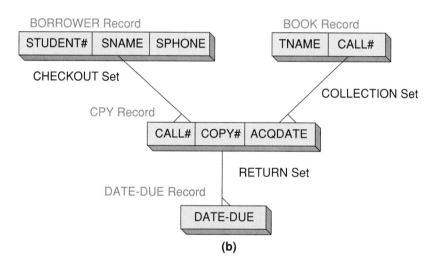

(b)

CODASYL DBTG DATA MANIPULATION LANGUAGE

Most CODASYL DBTG data manipulation commands have two steps. First, a FIND command is issued to identify the record to be acted on. The FIND command does not read or otherwise process the indicated record; it simply identifies a record for the DBMS to locate. After a record has been identified, a second DML command can be issued to perform an operation on it. Typical patterns are FIND, GET; or FIND, MODIFY; or FIND, ERASE.

The only DML command that does not follow this pattern is STORE. Since this command inserts a new record into the data base, there is nothing to be found before it is executed.

As we stated, every DBTG run-unit (a particular user connected to a particular program) has a user working area (UWA). The records in the subschema are stored in the UWA. For the PURCHASE subschema, there are four records in the UWA: PUB, BOOK, CPY, and BORROWED. For the BORROW subschema, they are BOOK, BORROWER, CPY, and DUE-DATE.

➤ FIGURE 16-22

Format of Subschema Description

```
TITLE DIVISION.
 (subschema name)
MAPPING DIVISION.
ALIAS SECTION.
 (alternate names for records, sets, or data-items)
STRUCTURE DIVISION.
RECORD SECTION.
 (records and data-items that are to appear in the subschema)
SET SECTION.
 (sets to appear in the subschema)
```

➤ FIGURE 16-23

Example Subschema Definitions for Library Data Base: (a) PURCHASE Subschema Definition and (b) BORROW Subschema Description

```
TITLE DIVISION.
SS PURCHASE WITHIN LIBRARY.
MAPPING DIVISION.
ALIAS SECTION.
AD      RECORD TTLE IS BOOK.
AD      RECORD DUE-DATE IS BORROWED.
AD      SET HISTORY IS USES.
AD      DATE-DUE IS USE-DATE.
STRUCTURE DIVISION.
RECORD SECTION.
01      PUB.
        05                      PNAME       PIC X(10).
        05                      SALPSN      PIC X(20).
        05                      PHONE       PIC 9(10).
01      BOOK ALL.
01      CPY ALL.
01      BORROWED ALL.
SET SECTION.
SD      PUBLISH.
SD      COLLECTION.
SD      USES.
```

(a)

```
TITLE DIVISION.
SS BORROW WITHIN LIBRARY.
MAPPING DIVISION.
ALIAS SECTION.
AD      RECORD TTLE IS BOOK.
AD      RECORD STU IS BORROWER.
AD      SET HISTORY IS RETURN.
STRUCTURE DIVISION.
RECORD SECTION.
01      BOOK.
        05                      TNAME       PIC X(50).
        05                      CALL#       PIC X(8).
01      BORROWER ALL.
01      CPY ALL.
01      DUE-DATE ALL.
SET SECTION.
SD      COLLECTION.
SD      CHECKOUT.
SD      RETURN.
```

(b)

DBTG DML FOR SINGLE-RECORD PROCESSING   The following examples show how FIND is used in conjunction with other commands to process the data base. The commands are shown in pseudocode form, and the particular syntax of each depends on the language in which they are embedded and on the particular implementation of the DBTG model.

Suppose we want to read the BORROWER record for STUDENT 150. The following commands will do this:

```
MOVE "150" TO STUDENT# IN BORROWER
FIND ANY BORROWER USING STUDENT#
GET BORROWER
```

The FIND command sets the current records of run-unit, BORROWER, and CHECKOUT to point to the record for Student 150. Then the GET command places the record into the BORROWER record area in the UWA. GET always operates on the current record.

Suppose we want to read all the CPY records for a book with the call number R726.8.L:

```
MOVE "R726.8.L" TO Call# IN CPY
FIND ANY CPY USING Call#
DOWHILE DB-STATUS = 0
    GET CPY
    (process CPY data)
    FIND DUPLICATE CPY USING Call#
END-DO
```

DB-STATUS, a DBNS-supplied return variable, is used here to control the loop processing. This code assumes that the DBMS will set DB-STATUS to a value other than zero at the end of data. A more sophisticated (and appropriate) algorithm would examine the value of DB-STATUS to ensure that no other condition or error had occurred. The first FIND specifies that ANY record can qualify, and the next FIND specifies DUPLICATE. This keyword means that the desired record must have the same value of CALL that the current record of CPY contains.

To illustrate the elimination of records, suppose we want to delete all CPY records for books having the call number R726.8.L:

```
MOVE "R726.8.L" TO Call# IN CPY
FIND FOR UPDATE ANY CPY USING Call#
DOWHILE DB-STATUS = 0
    ERASE CPY
    FIND FOR UPDATE DUPLICATE CPY USING Call#
END-DO
```

The logic is similar to that for the GET, except that the ERASE command is used in this example. Also, the words FOR UPDATE are added to the FIND command. These keywords inform the DBMS that an update is to occur, and, accordingly, the DBMS locks the record for the run-unit. This is similar to the DL/I GET HOLD commands described in the previous chapter.

To illustrate the modification of records, suppose that the BORROWER with STUDENT# of 150 changes her name to WILLIS:

```
MOVE "150" TO STUDENT# IN BORROWER
FIND FOR UPDATE ANY BORROWER USING STUDENT#
GET BORROWER
```

```
IF DB-STATUS = 0
    THEN MOVE "WILLIS" TO SNAME IN BORROWER
        MODIFY SNAME
    ELSE do error processing
END-IF
```

In this case, the MODIFY statement indicates that only the SNAME data-item has been changed. If no data-item is listed, the DBMS is to assume that the entire record (or this subschema's view of it) has been changed.

To create a new record, we first build it in the UWA and then issue a STORE command. The following statements insert a BORROWER record into the data base:

```
MOVE "2000" TO STUDENT# IN BORROWER
MOVE "CALBOM" TO SNAME IN BORROWER
MOVE "5258869" TO PHONE IN BORROWER
STORE BORROWER
```

After the STORE command, the new record is the currents of run-unit, BOR-ROWER, and CHECKOUT.

PROCESSING MULTIPLE RECORDS WITH SETS   Sets are used to process records by relationship. Three commands are used to insert and remove records from sets, and then several different formats of the FIND command are used to process the records in sets.

The DBTG model provides three commands for processing set members: CONNECT, DISCONNECT, and RECONNECT. The first command places a record into a set; the second removes a record from a set; and the third changes the set membership.

```
MOVE "R726.8.L" to Call#
MOVE "2" TO COPY#
FIND ANY CPY USING CALL#, COPY#
MOVE "150" TO STUDENT#
FIND ANY BORROWER USING STUDENT#
CONNECT CPY TO CHECKOUT
```

The first FIND command establishes copy 2 of R726.8.L as the current record of CPY. The second FIND then establishes Student 150 as the current record of the CHECKOUT set. The copy is then placed in the set with CONNECT.

DISCONNECT operates in a similar fashion. The current member record is removed from the current set. The following commands take copy 2 of R726.8.L from the set owned by Student 150:

```
MOVE "R726.8.L" to CALL#
MOVE "2" TO COPY#
FIND ANY CPY USING CALL#, COPY#
MOVE "150" TO STUDENT#
FIND ANY BORROWER USING STUDENT#
DISCONNECT CPY FROM CHECKOUT
```

SET MEMBERSHIP AND ERASE COMMANDS   If a record owns a set occur-rence, special considerations will apply when the record is deleted. The applica-tion program can request that all children (and children of children, and so forth) be erased when the record is erased, or it can be more selective.

Suppose we want to delete a BOOK record and all of the CPY and DUE-DATE records that pertain to this book. The following statements can do this for the book whose call number is Q360.C33:

```
MOVE "Q360.C33" TO CALL#
FIND FOR UPDATE ANY BOOK USING CALL#
ERASE ALL BOOK
```

The keyword ALL in this ERASE command directs the DBMS to erase all CPY records (and all DUE-DATE records belonging to the set owned by CPY).

If ALL is not specified in the ERASE command, the result will depend on other considerations that are beyond the scope of this discussion.

USING SETS FOR RECORD RETRIEVAL   Once records have been placed in sets, set membership can be used to retrieve records by relationships. Suppose we want to process a view of the STUDENT object that contains both BORROWER and CPY records. Say we want to retrieve the call numbers of all the books on loan to Student 400. The following statements do this:

```
MOVE "400" TO STUDENT#
FIND ANY BORROWER USING STUDENT#
FIND FIRST CPY WITHIN CHECKOUT
DOWHILE DB-STATUS <> 0
    GET CPY
    (process CPY record to display CALL#)
    FIND NEXT CPY WITHIN CHECKOUT
END-DO
```

The first FIND command establishes the current records of both BORROWER and CHECKOUT. The next FIND command sets the current of CPY to the first record in the set owned by the BORROWER with STUDENT 400. The first record is then processed, and the next one is identified with the FIND NEXT command. In addition to FIND FIRST and FIND NEXT, this model also provides FIND LAST and FIND nth, where n is the ordinal position of the record in the set. This last option is useful only if the set members are ordered in some manner.

➤ SUMMARY

DBMS products based on the hierarchical and network data models were created during the earliest years of database processing, and their importance lies in the existing databases whose structure is based on them. Almost no new databases use these models. Their chief importance to you is in maintaining existing applications or converting databases to the relational model.

The sole surviving hierarchical data model is the IBM language DL/I. The most important network model is the CODASYL DBTG data model, of which the DBMS product IDMS was the most important implementation.

DL/I uses terminology substantially different from that of the relational model. In DL/I, a row or record is called a segment. A segment is a group of fields. One field in the segment is designated as the sequence field; it is used to logically order the segments. A tree is made up of several related segments. An instance of a tree is a data base record (DL/I spells data base as two words). Data base records are defined by means of a data base description. A data base is composed of data base records of one or more types.

DL/I is hierarchical. Because the segments in a data base record can have at most one parent, in order to represent networks (relationships in which a child has more than one parent), the network must be decomposed into trees with data duplication. This duplication is then eliminated through the use of pointers or other data structures.

DL/I uses the term *physical data base record* (or PDBR) to refer to physically stored data and the term *logical data base record* (or LDBR) to refer to application views of data. An LDBR differs from a PDBR in one of two ways: It may be a subset of a PDBR, or it may contain portions of two or more PDBRs. An application view is a set of one or more LDBRs.

DL/I statements to retrieve, modify, insert, and delete segments must be embedded in application programs; thus, DL/I cannot be used interactively. DL/I data base requests are carried out by issuing subroutine calls from the application program.

Basic DL/I commands are GET UNIQUE, GET NEXT, GET NEXT within PARENT, GET HOLD UNIQUE, GET HOLD NEXT, GET HOLD NEXT within PARENT, REPLACE, DELETE, and INSERT. Each of these commands operates on an LDBR.

The most significant network data model is known as the CODASYL DBTG data model, named after the committee that developed it. The most significant difference between the network data model and the hierarchical data model is that simple networks can be represented directly in the network model. Thus, it was an improvement over the earlier hierarchical model.

The DBTG model introduced the concepts of both a data definition and a data manipulation language for DBMS products. Unlike DL/I, which has no database definition facilities, products based on the DBTG model provide both languages.

A schema is a logical view of the entire database as seen by the database administration. A subschema is a subset of the database, like a view in the relational model. A subschema is the application program's view of the database.

All user interactions with the database are carried out by means of application programs (there is no interactive query language in the model). An application program can be run by one or more users. Each user has his or her own user work area for passing data to and from the DBMS.

The building blocks used for DBTG data definition are data-items (or fields), records (collections of data-items), and sets (a set is a one-to-many relationship between records). These building blocks can be used to represent all the object types we have discussed in this text: composite, compound, and association. When defining the database, it is easy to transform the relational database definition into the DBTG data base definition.

The DBTG model specifies a data manipulation language. Generally, the database is accessed in two steps: The first is used to identify the record to be acted on, and the second performs some operation. The DBTG FIND statement is used to identify a record. When executed, the FIND statement sets the value of one or more currency indicators.

DBTG commands are available to read, insert, modify, and delete database records. DBTG DML can be used to access and process individual database records and to process sets. The syntax shown in this chapter is generic; the exact syntax varies with the DBMS product.

➤ GROUP I QUESTIONS

16.1 Explain the difference in the nature of DBMS products based on the hierarchical, network, and relational models.

16.2 Define the DL/I terms *field, segment, data base record,* and *data base.*

16.3 What DL/I structure corresponds to a node on a tree?

16.4 How are DL/I data base records defined? Does DL/I include data definition language as well as data manipulation language?

16.5   Why must simple networks be transformed into trees before they can be stored for processing by DL/I?

16.6   How does DL/I eliminate data duplication?

16.7   What is the difference between a physical data base record and a logical data base record? In what two ways does an LDBR differ from a PDBR?

16.8   Describe the function of each of the GET commands. Give an example of each.

16.9   Describe the function of each of the GET HOLD commands. Give an example of each.

16.10 Describe the function of each of the REPL, DLET, and INSRT commands. Give an example of each.

16.11 Explain the relationship among user, run-unit, application program, subschema, schema, data base, and DBMS.

16.12 Define *data-item*. How are data-items related to domains? How are domains defined using the DBTG model?

16.13 Define *record* as used in the DBTG model.

16.14 Define the following terms and explain their purpose: set, owner, member, set occurrence.

16.15 Give an example of a set structure, and sketch two occurrences of this set.

16.16 Consider the following tree: School districts have schools, and schools have pupils (one record type) and teachers (another record type). Teachers have past assignments. Show a DBTG representation of this tree, and describe two occurrences.

16.17 Consider the following simple network: Fathers have children, and teachers teach children. Show a DBTG representation of this simple network, and describe two occurrences.

16.18 Consider the following complex network: Children have many hobbies, and a hobby is enjoyed by many children. Show a DBTG representation of this complex network, and describe two occurrences.

For Questions 16.19 through 16.22, provide pseudocode similar to that used in this chapter, based on the following model:

SALESPERSON with data-items NAME, AGE, SALARY

ORDER with data-items NUMBER, CUST-NAME, SALESPERSONNAME, AMOUNT

CUSTOMER with data-items NAME, CITY, INDUSTRY-TYPE

SET SALE with owner SALESPERSON and member ORDER

SET PURCHASE with owner CUSTOMER and member ORDER

16.19 Retrieve
   a.   Customer with name ABC CONSTRUCTION.
   b.   Order with number 12345.
   c.   All orders for customer ABC CONSTRUCTION.

16.20 Delete all orders for salesperson PARKS.

16.21 Change the industry type of ABC Construction to type J (assume that INDUSTRY-TYPE is a character data-item).

16.22 Store a new SALESPERSON record: The name is CURTIS, the age is 39, and the salary is 65,000.

➤ GROUP II QUESTIONS

16.23 Consider the following organizational chart:

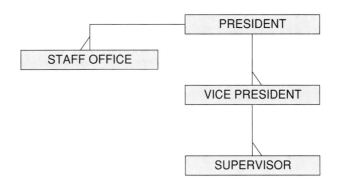

a. Sketch an occurrence of this structure.

b. What in this example constitutes a DL/I segment? A data base record? The total data base?

16.24 Sketch the hierarchical structure and logical pointers necessary to model the following data base records in DL/I:

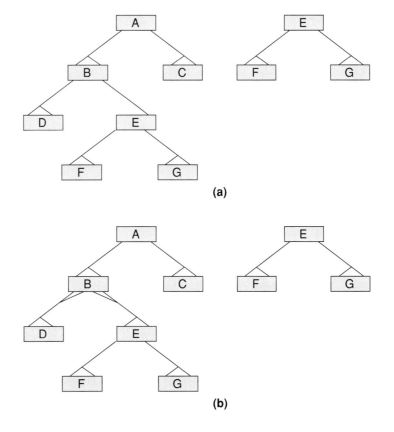

16.25 Assume that a data base consists of three separate PDBs, as follows:

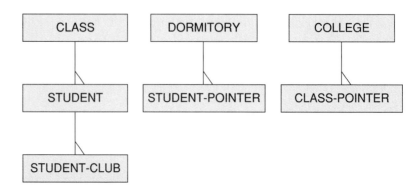

Describe the LDBR required to respond to the following requests:

a. Get the names of all students in a class taught by the College of Business.

b. Find the name of every student club that has at least one member living in Green Dormitory.

The data following Question 16.29 pertain to Questions 16.26 through 16.29. The sequence fields are underlined.

16.26 Describe the results of the following retrievals:

    a. GU   FACTORY

                  PRODUCT (COST = 40)

                  PART

    b. GU   FACTORY

                  WREHOUSE (NAME = 'W2')

                  DISTRBTR

    c. GU   FACTORY

                  PRODUCT (COST = 40)

                  PART(NUM-REQ = 24)

      GN   PART

      GN   PART

      GN   PART

      GN   PART

    d. GU   FACTORY

                  PRODUCT (COST = 40)

      GNP   PART

      GNP   PART

16.27 What will happen when the last GN PART statement is executed in Question 16.26(c)? How will the user be able to detect this?

16.28 What will happen if another GNP PART statement is executed immediately after those in Question 16.26(d)?

16.29 Show the DL/I statements needed to specify the following actions:

a. Delete the PRT6 24 segment under PRD2.

b. Delete all data concerning warehouse W3.

c. Delete all data concerning factory F1.

d. Delete all products costing more than $45.

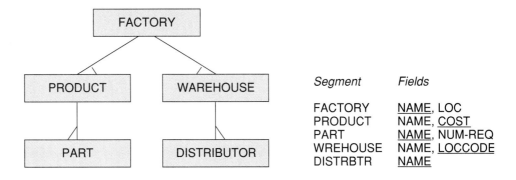

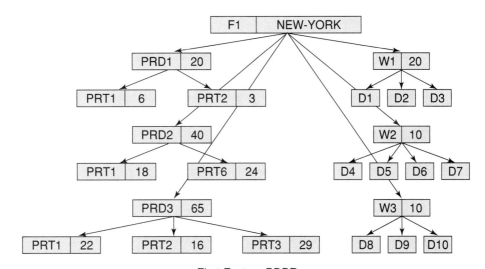

First Factory PDBR

16.30 Compare and contrast the DBTG model with the relational model. Which model is easier to understand? Which do you think would be easier to use? For what applications would the DBTG model be preferable to the relational model? For what applications would the relational model be preferable to the DBTG model?

16.31 Locate a company in your community that uses IMS. Interview its DBA and determine how the company uses its data base. Is it developing new applications for it? How is it putting this data on the Web? What plans does the company have for this data base? Talk to some of the people who work there, and find out how the schemas and subschemas are designed. If possible, get a copy of a schema, subschema, and application program, and compare them with the concepts described in this chapter.

PART

VII

OBJECT-ORIENTED DATABASE PROCESSING

This part consists of one chapter that addresses object-oriented programming and storage with ODBMS. It includes a brief tutorial on object-oriented programming and discussions both on the object extensions to SQL called SQL3 and on an object data management standard called ODMG-93.

This part supplements the discussions of OLE DB and ADO in Chapter 13. Whereas those chapters presented practical matters on using object interfaces to obtain database services, this chapter presents a more conceptual view on the rationale and purpose of object-oriented database processing.

Object-Oriented Database Processing

In the last 10 years a new style of programming, called **object-oriented programming (OOP),** has emerged. This new style has demonstrated such significant advantages over traditional programming that almost all new development at software vendors is done in OOP. In addition, many corporations have decided to standardize on OOP for their new application development.

As you will learn in this chapter, OOP is a radical departure from traditional programming. Because of this difference, file processing and traditional, relational DBMS products are difficult to use for object storage. As a result, a new type of DBMS—the **object DBMS (ODBMS)**—has been developed. While ODBMS have significant advantages over traditional techniques for object storage, most data in commercial systems today are in relational format. Organizations are reluctant to spend the time and money necessary to convert all of their file and relational data into ODBMS format. Furthermore, current ODBMS lack some features that are essential in the commercial environment. Hence, at present, ODBMS are not seeing widespread use. This may change in the near future, however, and it is important for you to understand the characteristics of ODBMS, their advantages and disadvantages, and the differences between ODBMS and traditional DBMS. We begin with a brief introduction to OOP.

➤ A SKETCH OF OBJECT-ORIENTED PROGRAMMING

Object-oriented programming (OOP) is a way of designing and coding programs. OOP is substantially different from traditional programming, as it entails a new way of thinking about programming structures. Instead of viewing programs as sequences of instructions to be processed, OOP views programs as sets of data structures that have both data elements and program instructions.

Another way to understand the difference between traditional programming and OOP is that traditional programming is organized around logic first and data second, whereas OOP is organized around data first and logic second. To design a traditional program to create an order, for example, we would first develop a flowchart or pseudocode of the logic of the ordering process. The data to be processed would be documented as a part of the logic.

When developing an object-oriented program to create an order, we would first identify the objects involved, say, ORDER, SALESPERSON, ITEM, and CUSTOMER. We would then design those objects as data elements and programs that are shared or *exposed* to one another. Finally, we would create a flowchart or pseudocode of the behaviors of the objects.

OOP Terminology

An OOP object is an **encapsulated structure** having both **attributes** and **methods.** The term *encapsulated* means that it is complete in itself; programs external to an object know nothing of its structure and need to know nothing of its structure. The external appearance of an object is referred to as its **interface.** The interface consists of the attributes and methods that are visible to the outside world. The encapsulated internals of an object are referred to as its **implementation.**

The *attributes*[1] of OOP objects are arranged in a particular structure, and they are quite similar to the attributes of semantic objects. Finally, OOP objects contain *methods,* or sequences of instructions that the object executes.

For example, an OOP object may have a method to display itself, one to create itself, and one to modify a portion of itself. Consider a method that modifies a CUSTOMER object. This method, which is part of the OOP object, is a program; to modify the OOP object, this program contains instructions to obtain data from the user or other source.

OOP objects interact by calling each other's methods. The CUSTOMER modify method, for example, invokes other objects' methods to obtain data, perform modifications on itself, and request services. These other objects' methods are called and may invoke yet other methods, and so forth. Because all the objects are encapsulated, none can or need to know the structure of any other object. This reduces complexity and promotes effective cohesion.

Many objects have methods in common. To reduce the duplication in programming, objects are subclassed from more general classes. An object, say O_1, that is a subclass of another object, say O_2, **inherits** all the attributes and methods of O_2. For example, an application may have a general class EMPLOYEE with two subtypes, SALESPERSON and ENGINEER. Methods that are common to all three object classes such as GetPhoneNumber are made a part of the EMPLOYEE class. The SALESPERSON and ENGINEER subclasses inherit those methods. Hence, when a program issues a call to GetPhoneNumber on either a SALESPERSON or an ENGINEER, the GetPhoneNumber method in EMPLOYEE is invoked. If the application requirements are such that ENGINEERs have a different way of providing phone numbers than other employees, then ENGINEER can have a special version of GetPhoneNumber as part of its class. That special version will be called when a program invokes GetPhoneNumber on ENGINEER. This characteristic is called **polymorphism.**

---

[1]The term *properties* is sometimes used instead of *attribute.* In the ODMG-93 standard, the term *property* is used instead of *attribute,* and *attribute* is used in a more restricted sense, as you will see. When reading the terms *class, type, property,* and *attribute,* pay attention to the context, as different authors use these terms slightly differently. Here we will use the terms in a way that is consistent with the source of the topic.

FIGURE 17-1

Sample of CUSTOMER Object

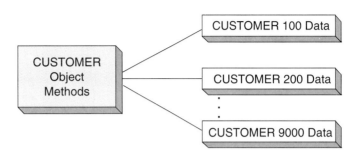

CUSTOMER Object Class

Object methods are stored once for each class
Object data is stored once for each object instance

Several terms are commonly used in OOP discussions. The logical structure of an object—its name, attributes, and methods—is called an **object class.** A group of object classes is called an **object class library.** And instances of objects are called **object instances,** or simply **objects.**

Objects are created by calling object constructors, programs that obtain main memory and create the structures necessary to instantiate an object. Object destructors are programs that unbind objects and free memory. Objects can be **transient** or **persistent.** A transient object exists only in volatile memory during the execution of a program. When the program terminates, the object is lost. A persistent object is an object that has been saved to permanent storage, such as disk. A persistent object survives the execution of a program and can be read back into memory from storage.

The purpose of an ODBMS is to provide persistent object storage. An object is both data and methods; this means an ODBMS, unlike a traditional DBMS, should store object programs as well as data. Since each object of a given class has the same set of methods, the methods need be stored only once for the class; in contrast, data items must be stored once for each object instance. Figure 17-1 illustrates this point. In point of fact, few ODBMS today provide method persistence, but this is likely to change in the future.

➤ OOP EXAMPLE

Figures 17-2 and 17-3 present a portion of an object-oriented interface and a sample method. To avoid details unimportant to this discussion, the code is written in a generic form that is consistent with object programming but is not in any particular object-oriented language. Consider this code to be something like pseudocode for an object program.

Figure 17-2 shows a portion of the interface of several objects used for order processing. Each object has a set of methods and attributes that it exposes. Every object has a constructor (Create) and a destructor (Destroy) method. Some of the methods take parameters; the Assign method of SALESPERSON, for example, takes a pointer to the ORDER object and a value of ZipCode as its parameters. Attributes that are marked with (R) may only be read; attributes marked (RW) may be read or written (changed).

The notation in Figure 17-3 on page 485 needs explanation. First, the braces { } represent remarks. They are used here to describe the function of program code that needs to be written but has been left out of this example for brevity or because it is unimportant to this discussion. The Dim statement is used to declare

➤ FIGURE 17-2

Sample Objects, Methods, and Attributes

Object	Methods	Attributes
EMPLOYEE	Create Save Destroy …	Number(R) Name(R) …
SALESPERSON (subclass of EMPLOYEE)	Create Save Destroy Assign(ORDER, ZipCode) …	TotalCommission(R) TotalOrders(RW) …
CUSTOMER	Create Save Destroy Assign(ORDER) Find …	Name(R) Phone(R) ZipCode(R) CurrentBalance(RW) …
ITEM	Create Save Destroy Find(Number) Take(ORDER, Quantity) Put(ORDER, Quantity) Find …	Number(R) Name(R) Description(R) Price …
ORDER	Create Save Destroy Print …	Number(R) Date(R) Total(R) CustomerName(R) SalespersonName(R) …

variables and their types, as it does in Basic. LineItem is declared as a structure having the data elements listed in the brackets [ ]. The exclamation point (!) is used as a separator between an object and one of its methods. Thus, CUS-TOMER!Find refers to the Find method of the CUSTOMER object. This character is pronounced "bang." A period is used as a separator between an object and one of its attributes. Thus, CustObj.ZipCode refers to the ZipCode attribute of the object pointed to by CustObj.

Two keywords are also used in Figure 17-3. **Nothing** is a special value of an object pointer that is used to represent a null value. In this figure, the expression

If CustObj = Nothing

means to compare the value of the object variable CustObj to the null object pointer. **Me** is an object pointer that references the object executing the code. When the code in Figure 17-3 is run, it will be run by an instance of the ORDER object, since it is an ORDER method. Me refers to the particular ORDER object that is executing the code.

The ORDER!Create method begins by obtaining data about the name of the customer placing the order; it is unimportant to our purposes how this value is obtained—it might be from a text box on a form. The Find method of CUS-TOMER is then invoked to find a customer having the given name and to set a pointer to the object that has been found. The particulars of how an instance is

Segment of an
Object-Oriented
Program

```
ORDER!Create method
Dim CustObj as object, SPObj as object, ItemObj as object
Dim OrderTotal as Currency, OrderDate as Date, OrderNumber as Number
Dim LineItem as Structure
        [
        ItemNumber as Number,
        ItemName as Text(25),
        ItemQuantity as Count,
        QuantityBackOrdered as Count,
        ExtendedPrice as Currency
        ]

        {Get CustomerName from some source}
        Set CustObj = CUSTOMER!Find (CustomerName)
        If CustObj = Nothing then
                Set CustObj = CUSTOMER!Create(CustomerName)
        End If

        CustObj!Assign(Me)
        Set SPObj = SALESPERSON!Assign(Me, CustObj.ZipCode)

        {Get ItemNumber, Quantity of first ITEM from some source}
        Me.OrderTotal = 0
        While Not ItemNumber.EOF

                Me.LineItem!Create
                Me.LineItem.ItemNumber = ItemNumber

                Set ItemObj = ITEM!Find (ItemNumber)
                {process problem if ITEM not exist}

                Me.LineItem.ItemName = ItemObj.Name
                Me.LineItem.Quantity = ITEM!Take (Quantity)
                If Me.LineItem.Quantity <> Quantity Then
                        Me.LineItem.QuantityBackOrdered = Quantity - Me.LineItem.Quantity
                End If

                Me.LineItem.ExtendedPrice = Me.LineItem.Quantity* ITEM.Price
                Me.OrderTotal = Me.OrderTotal + Me.LineItem.ExtendedPrice

                ItemObj!Save
                Me.LineItem!Save
                {Get ItemNumber, Quantity of next ITEM from some source
                assume the source sets EOF to true when there are no more}
        While End

        SPObj.TotalOrders = SPObj.TotalOrders + Me.OrderTotal
        CustObj.CurrentBalance = CustObj.CurrentBalance + Me.OrderTotal

        SPObj!Save
        CustObj!Save
        ME!Save
End ORDER!Create
```

found are encapsulated in CUSTOMER!Find, and we do not know how the selection is made, what happens if there is more than one customer that has that name, or other details.

The result of this operation is to set CustObj to either the value of a valid pointer to a CUSTOMER object or to the special value Nothing, which is the null pointer. If CustObj is null, then CustObj is set to a pointer to a new CUSTOMER object created by CUSTOMER!Create. As shown, the code assumes that a pointer to a valid customer object is returned at this point. In fact, CustObj should be checked again to see if it is null, but, for brevity, we will omit all such checking in the rest of this program segment.

CUSTOMER exposes a method Assign that is to be called to assign a CUSTOMER to an ORDER. Because of encapsulation, we do not know what the Assign method does, but we do call it and pass Me, the pointer to the executing object. In fact, in this application, the Assign method is an example of what is called a **callback.** ORDER!Create is giving a pointer to itself to CUSTOMER so that CUSTOMER can keep track of which ORDERs it has. One reason for doing this is that when a CUSTOMER object is to be destroyed, it can call all ORDERs that are linked to it before it departs. In that way, ORDER can destroy its pointer to CUSTOMER when that pointer becomes invalid. There are many other uses for callbacks, as well.

Next, ORDER!Create sets SPObj to a salesperson object. We are passing the value of the customer's ZipCode, so it would seem that ZipCode has something to do with how a salesperson is assigned to us. Again, because of encapsulation, we do not know how this is done, however. By hiding the allocation methodology, the SALESPERSON object is free to change its allocation method without disturbing this or any other program's logic. In fact, no code in Figure 17-3 would need to be changed if SALESPERSON.Assign started using phases of the moon to allocate salespeople!

The next section of code fills in line item values. Observe that the keyword Me is used to refer to local data items. (In fact, in most OO languages, Me would be assumed and would not be necessary; we put it here for explicitness.) At the start of each repetition of the While loop, storage is allocated for another line item in the method LineItem!Create.

The method ITEM!Take is used to withdraw items from inventory. Notice that the logic assumes that if a number of items less than the quantity requested was allocated, then the balance of the items has been backordered. Also, observe that the changed ITEM is saved after each line item has been processed. Also, unlike with CUSTOMER or SALESPERSON, no callback is issued to ITEM. This means that the ITEM objects do not know which ORDERs are connected to them. Apparently, for this application, it is unimportant for the ITEM objects to know which ORDERs are using their data.

The loop continues until there are no more items to be placed on the order. At that point, totals are adjusted in the SALESPERSON and CUSTOMER objects, and both of those objects and Me are saved.

The segment of code in Figure 17-3 is typical of object-oriented code, and it brings to the surface a number of important issues for object-oriented database systems. In particular, How are the objects to be made persistent?

➤ OBJECT PERSISTENCE

Figure 17-4 summarizes the data structures that exist after an ORDER has been created. In the order object, there are base order data, including ORDER.Number, ORDER.Date, ORDER.Total, as well as a repeating group for line items that have ItemNumber, ItemName, Quantity, a QuantityBackordered, and Extended Price. In addition, the base order data have a pointer to the CUSTOMER object assigned, a pointer to the SALESPERSON object assigned, and a pointer to each ITEM for each line item. These pointers are part of the ORDER object's data. To make this object persistent, all of this data must be stored. Further, although we do not know their structure, each CUSTOMER, SALESPERSON, and ITEM object

Sample Object Data Structures

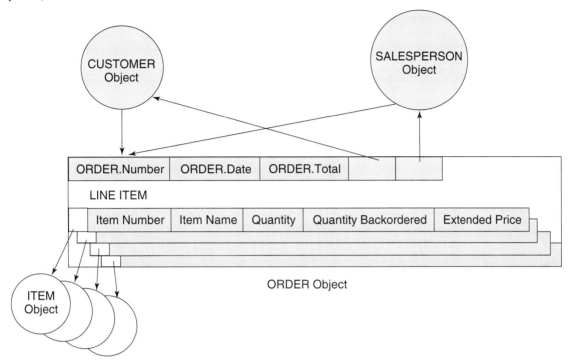

ORDER Object

must also be stored. The CUSTOMER and SALESPERSON objects are also storing a pointer back to ORDER as a result of the callbacks (!Assign methods) that were issued.

The pointers pose a particular problem. In most object-oriented languages, pointers are some form of in-memory address. Such addresses are valid only during the execution of the program; if the program terminates and is later restarted, the addresses of the objects will be different. Hence, when storing an object, the in-memory pointers need to be transformed into a permanent unique identifier that will be valid for the lifetime of the object, whether it is in memory or not. The process of transforming permanent identifiers into in-memory addresses is called **swizzling.**

Finally, recall that an object is defined as data values plus methods. Thus, to make an object persistent, we must save both the methods and the object values. Unlike data values, however, every object in a given class has the same methods, so we need to store the methods only once for all object instances in the object class. The requirements for object persistence are listed in Figure 17-5.

Objects can be made persistent using traditional file storage, a relational DBMS, or an ODBMS. We now consider each of these.

Tasks for Object Persistence

- Save object instance data values
- Convert in-memory object pointers to permanent, unique IDs (swizzling)
- Save object class methods

RecordNumber	RecordCode	Contents	Link
1	ORDER	ORDER 100 data	4
2	SALESPERSON	SALESPERSON Jones data	null
3	CUSTOMER	CUSTOMER 10000 data	null
4	LINEITEM	LineItem of ORDER 100 data	5
5	LINEITEM	LineItem of ORDER 100 DATA	null
…	…	…	…

Using a Fixed-Length File to Hold Object Data

OBJECT PERSISTENCE USING TRADITIONAL FILE STORAGE

Objects can be saved using traditional file storage, but doing so places a large burden on the programmer. Consider the data in Figure 17-4. The developer might decide to create one file to contain methods for all of the objects and a second file to contain the data for all of the objects. To do this, a generalized data structure will need to be developed to pack the methods and data into the files and to retrieve them when necessary. Figure 17-6 shows an example of such a file for storing just the data items. (Another will need to be developed to store the methods.)

To use such a file, the programmer will write code in the Save methods to pack and unpack object data in these records, to find objects on demand, to manage unused file space, and so forth. Also, the developer will need to devise and implement swizzling and de-swizzling algorithms. Further, there is a bootstrap problem. All methods are stored in files, including the methods that store and read methods. How is the method that reads the first method to be obtained?

All of these problems are surmountable; they have been solved in operating system file-processing subsystems for many years. But, that is just the point. Such programming is slow, tedious, risky, and difficult, and it has already been done for traditional file processing. Why should such programming need to be done one more time?

Because of these problems, traditional file storage is viable for object persistence only when the application has a few simple objects whose structure does not change. Few business applications fall into this category.

OBJECT PERSISTENCE USING RELATIONAL DBMS

Another approach to object persistence is to use commercial relational DBMS products. This approach places a smaller burden on the developer than traditional file processing, because basic file management issues like record allocation, indexing, space management, and so forth are handled by the DBMS. The data management tasks left to the programmer are to define relational structures to represent the objects and to write the code to interface with the DBMS to get and put objects and to swizzle pointers.

Figure 17-7 shows the tables needed to store ORDER, LINEITEM, CUSTOMER, SALESPERSON, and ITEM objects. We've seen this design before. The only new element is a table to store object methods; this table contains a memo field that stores the method code.

To get or put an object, the programmer needs to write code to access the DBMS and cause it to process the object data. In most cases, SQL statements are embedded in the Save methods in a manner similar to that shown for DB2 in Chapter 13.

Relational databases represent relationships via foreign keys. This means that the application programmer must devise some means to use foreign keys to make

FIGURE 17-7

Relations Needed to Store EMPLOYEE, SALESPERSON, CUSTOMER, ITEM, and ORDER Objects

EMPLOYEE (<u>Number</u>, Name,…)

SALESPERSON (*<u>Number</u>*, TotalCommission, TotalOrders,…)

CUSTOMER (<u>Name</u>, Phone, ZipCode, CurrentBalance,…)

ITEM (<u>Number</u>, Name, Description, Price,…)

ORDER (<u>Number</u>, Date, Total, *SALESPERSON.Number, CUSTOMER.Name…*)

LINEITEM (*<u>ORDER.Number</u>, <u>ITEM.Number</u>*, ItemName, ItemQuantity,

QuantityBackOrdered, ExtendedPrice,…)

METHODS (<u>ObjectName</u>, <u>MethodName</u>, MethodCode)

relationships persistent. The most common way of doing this is to code the creation of a unique ID in the object's constructor method. This ID could be stored in the object's base table and exposed as a read-only property. Objects that need to link to the object can save the ID value. This strategy creates the problem that when an object is destroyed, it must notify all objects that are linked to it so that they can remove the pointer to the soon-to-be-destroyed object and take other action as appropriate. This is one reason for having callbacks like those shown in the Assign methods in Figure 17-3.

Object thinking and design bury relationships in context. Thus, when an ORDER object assigns itself to a SALESPERSON, it is concerned only with its side of that relationship. If the ORDER wants to bind to many SALESPEOPLE, it does so. ORDER has no idea whether or not a SALESPERSON has a relationship to one or many ORDERs. Such knowledge is encapsulated in the SALESPERSON object and is no part of the ORDER logic.

This characteristic is either an advantage or a disadvantage, depending on how you think about it. Suppose that an ORDER can have several SALESPEOPLE and that a SALESPERSON can have many ORDERs. In database parlance, ORDER and SALESPERSON have an M:N relationship. Consequently, in the relational database world, an intersection table is defined to hold the identifiers of the ORDERs and SALESPEOPLE that are related to one another.

In the object world, SALESPERSON knows it has many ORDERs, and ORDER knows it has many SALESPEOPLE, but they do not know about each other. Hence, the data structures for carrying the relationship will be separated. ORDER will contain storage for many links to SALESPERSON, and SALESPERSON will contain storage for many links to ORDER. The sets of links will be isolated from each other.

Does this matter? No, not as long as there are no errors in the object processing. But there is risk because the object links are separate but not independent. If ORDER 1000 is linked to SALESPERSON A, then, by definition, SALESPERSON A is linked to ORDER 1000. In the relational DBMS world, since the relationship is carried in a row of an intersection table, deleting the row from one side deletes it from the other side automatically. But in the object world, the relationship could be deleted on one side but not on the other. Thus, ORDER 1000 might be linked to SALESPERSON A, but SALESPERSON A might not be linked to ORDER 1000. Clearly, this is an error and should not be allowed to occur, but it is possible if the relationships are defined from a purely object-oriented perspective.

Using a relational DBMS for object persistence is less work for the developer than using traditional file structures. There is still the need, however, for the developer to convert the objects into a relational design, to write SQL (or other code), to get and place the objects using the DBMS, and to swizzle. ODBMS are designed to accomplish these tasks.

➤ FIGURE 17-8

*Application
Development Work
for Object Persistence
for Three Alternatives*

ODBMS	Relational DBMS	Traditional File Processing
• Invoke ODBMS Save methods	• Convert memory addresses to permanent ID and reverse (swizzling) • Define relational data structures • Create SQL (or other code) • Embed SQL in program	• Convert memory addresses to permanent ID and reverse (swizzling) • Define file data structures • Create object persistence code • Invoke object persistence code • Pack and unpack objects into file structures • Find objects on demand • Manage file space • Other file management tasks

OBJECT PERSISTENCE USING ODBMS

The third alternative for object persistence is to use an ODBMS. Such products are purpose-built for object persistence and hence save the most work for the application programmer.

An ODBMS is designed to be integrated with an object-oriented language. Thus, no special structures, such as SQL, need be embedded in the application code. For the example in Figure 17-4, it is possible that the Save methods are, in fact, methods provided by the ODBMS. Hence, by invoking the Save method, the programmer has invoked the ODBMS.

Further, ODBMS products include a compiler (or are included with the compiler, depending on your point of view) that processes the source code and automatically creates data structures in the object database for storing objects. Hence, unlike with relational database or file processing, the object-oriented programmer need not transform objects into relation or file structures; the ODBMS does that automatically.

Finally, because ODBMS are designed for object persistence, some form of swizzling is built in. Thus, code like that in Figure 17-3 would be unaware of the problem. An object obtains a link to another object, and that link is a valid one, for all time. If the link takes different forms, the program is unaware of it.

This leads to a characteristic of ODBMS that is called single-level memory. With certain ODBMS, the program (hence, the programmer) need not know whether an object is in memory or not. If ORDER 1000 has a link to SALESPERSON A, then ORDER 1000 can use the exposed properties of SALESPERSON A without ever checking to see if those data are in memory or issuing a read or SQL statement. If SALESPERSON A is in memory, the ODBMS makes the link; if not, the ODBMS reads SALESPERSON A into memory and then makes the link.

Figure 17-8 compares the work required for each of the three alternatives for object persistence. Clearly, an ODBMS provides substantial benefit to the object-oriented programmer, so why are such products not in use everywhere? We consider that question in the next section.

➤ COMPARING ODBMS AND TRADITIONAL DBMS

At this point you can probably understand why it is difficult to give a short and specific answer to the question, What is the difference between a relational DBMS and an ODBMS? They have completely different paradigms. It's not that comparing these two is like comparing apples and oranges; it's more like comparing them is like comparing a wrench to a gallon of gasoline. They both involve automobile transportation, but in very different ways.

*ODBMS Advantages
and Disadvantages*

Advantages	Disadvantages
Integrated with programming language	Requires object-oriented programming
Automatic method storage (when available)	Little existing data in object form
User-defined types	Nonexistent (or poor) query and reporting tools
Complex data readily processed	Limited concurrency control and transaction management
Automatic persistent object IDs	Unproven performance
Single-level memory	Substantial change and learning required

To be able to answer the question, first consider the advantages and disadvantages of ODBMS, as listed in Figure 17-9.

ODBMS ADVANTAGES

The first advantage of ODBMS is that they are integrated with object-oriented programming languages. The programmer need not learn a programming language and then learn SQL. Using the language will automatically provide object persistence. Further, since ODBMS are designed for object-oriented programming, method storage and management are automatic.[2] In theory, a programmer can code an instruction that causes object methods to be invoked and the ODBMS will find the appropriate methods, load them in memory, and cause them to be executed. The programmer need not be concerned with the storage and management of object code.

Second, ODBMS provide for the definition of user-defined types. Unlike traditional DBMS products where the basic data types are hard-coded in the DBMS and are unchangeable by the users, with an ODBMS the user can encode any type of structure that is necessary and the ODBMS will manage that type. (The object-oriented language compiler will perform type checking, as well.)

Because of user-defined types and because relationships are defined in context, it is easy to define complex data in an ODBMS. There is no need to define 1:1 or 1:N or N:M relationships and create the appropriate foreign key structures as with the relational DBMS. Instead, the programmer defines the relationship in context, and the ODBMS creates the necessary data structures in the database.

Finally, ODBMS automatically create persistent object IDs and provide swizzling. This not only saves programmers work, but it also enables the ODBMS to provide single-level memory so that the programmer need not be concerned with whether or not an object is located in memory.

---

[2]Again, ODBMS vary widely in their support for method management. Some provide very little support, others provide more.

ODBMS DISADVANTAGES

The disadvantages of ODBMS are listed in the second column of Figure 17-9. First, using an ODBMS requires object-oriented programming. While there are substantial advantages to such programming, not every company or department is willing to make the shift, at least not all at once. There are billions of lines of perfectly good program code already in existence. Such code is written in traditional style, and many companies believe that transforming it to object-oriented code would not be worth the enormous expense.

Moreover, most organizational data are in either file or traditional database format. Converting those data to an ODBMS is also very expensive. And, as with code, there is no compelling reason to make that switch.

A third disadvantage is that ODBMS do not, today, provide effective query and reporting tools. The application programmer must code query and reporting capabilities into his or her programs. This is laborious and expensive. In addition, query and reporting requirements often change, and users may want to change the structure of queries and reports themselves. This is not feasible when the relevant code is buried in object-oriented programs.

In addition, ODBMS are immature concerning concurrency control and transaction management capabilities. The features and functions for defining logical units of work, for committing and aborting transactions, and for rollback and rollforward are either nonexistent or are primitive as compared to traditional operational DBMS products. Also, the performance of ODBMS in high-volume, transaction-oriented environments is an unknown. Companies are reluctant to make the conversion investment and then find the new applications are unworkably slow.

Finally, as you have seen, ODBMS involves a new paradigm for both programming and database management. Programmers and database designers must invest considerable time and energy to learn this new paradigm and become proficient at it. Such change is always slow and is resisted by many people.

ARE ODBMS BETTER THAN TRADITIONAL DBMS?

There is no cut-and-dried answer to this question. It begs other questions like, Better for whom? For which application? In which settings? For applications in which the data are new (or readily converted), in which the programs are being written in an object-oriented language, in which there are complicated data types, and in which query and reporting requirements can be met by application programs, and setting aside performance issues, ODBMS appear to have significant advantages to the application programmer. Hence, ODBMS will likely be important in the future, at least for a large class of applications.

At the same time, ODBMS products are, at least today, only for the skilled object-oriented programmer. This leaves many out in the cold. Whereas one might justify the belief that all programmers should become object-oriented programmers anyway, there is a large class of nonprogramming creators of personal databases who are successful with relational products. These people would be overwhelmed with the knowledge requirements of object-oriented programming and ODBMS. For them, traditional database products are likely to continue to be a better choice for a long time.

In the next five years, the application of ODBMS will likely grow at a substantial rate, especially for applications that have complex data requirements and limited need for query and reporting such as engineering, graphics, and scientific applications. At the same time, the use of traditional DBMS products will also grow even more dramatically, especially in light of intranets and the Internet. So unless you are an object-oriented programmer or work in a specialized industry, continuing to develop your skills and knowledge in relational DBMS technology and products appears to be a better investment at the present time.

Most likely, these two technologies will merge in the future. If this happens, it will be possible for people and organizations to migrate to ODBMS features without having to convert programs and data to the new format. Evidence of this merger appears in the work of two different standards committees. We conclude this chapter with a brief survey of these two standards.

➤ ODBMS STANDARDS

A number of groups have been working toward the definition of an object database standard that could be used as a basis for the construction of ODBMS products. We survey the work of two of those groups here. The first group is a combination of ANSI and ISO (International Standards Organization) committees that has focused on extending the SQL92 standard for object processing. The second group is a consortium of object database vendors and other interested parties that builds on another important standard in the industry, the Object Management Group's Common Object Model and Interface Design Language. As you might expect, the first standard begins with a database perspective and moves toward object thinking. The second standard begins with an object perspective and moves toward data management thinking. Both standards are important, and both will likely serve as the basis for a number of important commercial ODBMS. It is too early to tell whether one standard will dominate the other. Consider the SQL standard first.

SQL3

SQL3 is an extension to the SQL92 database standard that includes support for object-oriented database management. Both the ANSI X3H2 and the ISO/IEC JTC1/SC21/WG3 standardization committees have worked to develop the draft of the SQL3 standard that we will discuss here. This standard is very much a work in progress, and changes from this draft are likely. Furthermore, SQL3 is a standard for products and not a product itself. There are, at present, no commercial DBMS products that implement this standard. You should view this section more as a description of the likely evolution of relational DBMS products than as a description of specific product features.

SQL3 arises out of the tradition of database management and not out of the tradition of object thinking. The goal of the committees working on SQL3 has been to describe a standard that is upward compatible with SQL92. This means that all of the features and functions of SQL92 would also work with SQL3. Consequently, SQL3 both looks like and is a relational database facility with object features added to it, as opposed to a new object-oriented database facility.

Three groups of new ideas are incorporated in SQL3: support for abstract data types, enhancements to the definitions of tables, and extensions to the language constructs to make SQL3 computationally complete.

ABSTRACT DATA TYPES   An **abstract data type (ADT)** is a user-defined structure that is equivalent to an OOP object. ADTs have methods, data items, and identifiers. ADTs can be subtypes of other ADTs; inheritance is supported. Either SQL (with the new language extensions) or an external language such as C11 can be used to express the logic of ADT methods.

An ADT can be used in an SQL expression, or it can be stored in a table, or both. If the ADT appears in one or more SQL expressions but is not stored in any table, then the ADT is transient; otherwise, it is made persistent by its storage in a table.

► FIGURE 17-10

*Sample ADT
Definition in SQL3*

```
CREATE OBJECT TYPE employee WITH OID VISIBLE
        (name VARCHAR NOT NULL,
        number CHAR(7)
        salary UPDATABLE VIRTUAL GET with get_salary SET WITH change_salary,
        PRIVATE
        hiredate DATE
        currentsalary CURRENCY
        PUBLIC
        ACTOR FUNCTION get_salary (:E employee) RETURNS CURRENCY
        {code to perform security processing
         and return value of currentsalary if appropriate}
        RETURN salary
        END FUNCTION,

        ACTOR FUNCTION change_salary (:E employee) RETURNS employee
        {code to perform security processing
         and compute and set new currentsalary, if appropriate}
        RETURN :E
        END FUNCTION,

        DESTRUCTOR FUNCTION remove_employee (:E employee)
                                            RETURNS NULL
        {code to get ready to delete employee data}
        DESTROY :E
        RETURN :E
        END FUNCTION,
```

Figure 17-10 shows the definition of a sample ADT for an employee object type. The current syntax of SQL3 is shown in capital letters, and the developer-supplied code is shown in small letters. This specific syntax is unimportant, as it is likely to change. Instead, observe that this ADT, like an OOP object, has data items and functions (methods). The employee data items are: name, number, hiredate, currentsalary, and salary, a virtual data item (one that exists only as the result of a computation in a function). The functions are get_salary, change_salary, and remove_employee.

SQL defines two kinds of ADT: OBJECT ADTs and VALUE ADTs. An OBJECT ADT is an identifiable, independent data structure that is assigned an identifier called an **OID.** This identifier is a unique value that persists for the life of the object. If the programmer wants to be able to use the value of the OID to pass to other functions or to store in other tables, the expression WITH OID VISIBLE must be added to the first line of the object definition. This has been done in Figure 17-10.

OID values are pointers to objects; saving an OID value in a table saves a pointer to the object. This can be convenient, but it also creates a problem. When an ADT is destroyed, its OID is invalid, but that particular OID value may have been stored in rows of tables that are not even in memory when the ADT is destroyed. The SQL3 standard does not indicate what is to happen in this case. Apparently, programs are to be written to test whether an OID is valid before attempting to use it.

The second kind of ADT is a VALUE ADT. VALUE ADTs are not assigned OIDs and cannot exist except in the context in which they are created. If a VALUE ADT is created as a column in a table, it will be saved with that table. It will not be possible to refer to that ADT except through the name of the table. If a VALUE ADT is created in a function, then it will be transient and will be destroyed when memory for the function is released.

The code in Figure 17-10 defines the OBJECT ADT *employee* as a type. As such, the type name can be used in table definitions in the same way that SQL built-in data types can be used. In Figure 17-11, a table Dept is defined; it has a

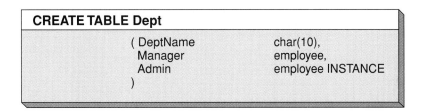

*Table Definition
Using the Employee
ADT*

CREATE TABLE Dept

(DeptName	char(10),
Manager	employee,
Admin	employee INSTANCE
)	

DeptName of type CHAR(10), a Manager of type employee, and an Admin, also of type employee. Thus, the ADT type is used as any other data type is used in a table definition.

When defining a column as having an ADT type, the keyword INSTANCE is used to indicate whether the object or a pointer to the object is to be stored. If INSTANCE is specified, then the object data is stored in the column. If INSTANCE is omitted, then a pointer to the object is stored in the column. If the ADT is a VALUE ADT, then INSTANCE is assumed.

In Figure 17-11, the manager column does not specify INSTANCE, but the admin column does. This means that each row of a dept table will contain a pointer to an employee in the Manager column and the actual data and methods for an employee in the Admin column.

The public data items of an object can be used in SQL statements just like regular table columns can be used. For example, consider the table in Figure 17-11 and the following SQL code:

SELECT   DeptName, Manager.OID, Manager.Name, Admin.OID, Admin.Name
FROM   Dept

When this code is executed, the DeptName, Manager.OID, Admin.OID, and Admin.Name would be extracted from the table. Behind the scenes, the DBMS would use the value of Manager.OID to find the instance of employee that it points to. The DBMS would then extract Manager.Name from that object and return it as part of the response to this SQL statement. The result would be the same as if all of the Manager object were stored in the table. Clearly, if the OID that is stored in the table has become invalid because its object has been deleted, then the DBMS will need to process this error in some fashion.

Consider the SQL statement

SELECT   DeptName, Manager.Name, Manager.Salary
FROM   Dept

To process this statement, the DBMS will need to access the Dept table, obtain the OID of the manager, obtain the instance of employee that is that manager, and then invoke the get_salary function in employee that materializes the virtual column salary. The get_salary function may perform security checking when it is executed and so the user may be asked to provide a name or password or perform other tasks before the DBMS receives a response from get_salary. Once get_salary has returned a value or an error code indicating that no value will be forthcoming, the DBMS can format the data for that Dept. Similar processing will need to be done for each row of the Dept table.

Private data items are private to the functions in the object. Hence, the following SQL is invalid:

SELECT   DeptName, Manager.currentsalary
FROM   Dept

The only way currentsalary data can be extracted from an employee object is through the function get_salary.

Values can be assigned to columns just like other SQL statements. Thus, the SQL expression:

```
UPDATE   Dept
SET      Admin.Name = "Fred P. Johnson"
WHERE    DeptName = "Accounting"
```

will set the name of the admin object that is instantiated in the Accounting department.

Since some objects are represented by pointers and not by data values, some surprising results can occur. Consider the following SQL:

```
UPDATE   Dept
SET      Manager.Name = "Fred P. Johnson"
WHERE    DeptName = "Accounting"
```

This statement does not change the employee assignment so that a different employee whose name is "Fred P. Johnson" is assigned to Accounting. Instead, it changes the name of the employee who is currently the manager. The *employee* name is changed; this means that any other table that references this employee object will also have its name changed. If no employee has yet been assigned to Manager in the Accounting row, this statement will generate an error.

In order to replace the manager of the Accounting department with a different employee whose name is "Fred P. Johnson," the Manager object needs to be set to the correct object instance. The following SQL will do this:

```
UPDATE   Dept
SET      Manager =
         SELECT   employee.OID
         FROM     employee
         WHERE    name = "Fred P. Johnson"
WHERE    DeptName = "Accounting"
```

Conceptually, this statement is correct. Whether or not it would actually work with a DBMS that implemented SQL3 would, of course, be up to the designers of the DBMS. As stated, since SQL3 is a work in progress and because no product yet implements it, consider the discussion here to indicate the direction of the industry, rather than a fixed, industry-accepted syntax.

The definition of ADTs gives SQL3 the ability to define, store, and manipulate objects. Two other changes to SQL are also proposed in SQL3. We consider them next.

SQL3 TABLE EXTENSIONS   SQL3 extends the definition of tables in several ways. First, SQL3 tables have a **row identifier,** which is a unique identifier for each row of a table. This identifier is the same as a *surrogate key,* the term we have used in prior discussions. Applications can use this identifier if it is made explicit by including the expression WITH IDENTITY in the table definition. Any table so defined is given an implicit column named IDENTITY. Values in the column can be used by the application, but it is not included in the results of a SELECT * expression.

Consider the table in Figure 17-12 and the next two SQL expressions:

```
SELECT   ProfessorName, Identity
FROM     PROFESSOR


SELECT   *
FROM     PROFESSOR
```

➤ FIGURE 17-12

Table Definition Using WITH IDENTITY

CREATE TABLE PROFESSOR WITH IDENTITY

(ProfessorName	char(10),
Phone	char(7),
Office	char(5)
)	

The result of the first SQL statement is a table with two columns; the first has the name of the professor, and the second has the value of the row identifier. The result of the second SQL expression is a table of three columns, which are ProfessorName, Phone, and Office.

The second extension to the table concept in SQL3 is the definition of three types of table: SET, MULTISET, and LIST. A SET table is a table with no duplicate rows; a MULTISET table may have duplicate rows and is equivalent to the table concept in SQL92. (This definition, of course, ignores the IDENTITY column, since with the IDENTITY column, no table has duplicate rows.) Finally, a LIST table is a table that has an order defined by one or more columns.

A third extension to the table concept in SQL3 is the **subtable.** A subtable is a subset of another table, called the **supertable.** A subtable inherits all of the columns of its supertable and may also have columns of its own. A table that has a subtable or a supertable has a row identifier defined implicitly. Figure 17-13 defines two types of professor: TENURED-PROFESSOR and NONTENURED-PROFESSOR. The columns of TENURED-PROFESSOR are ProfessorName, Phone, Office, and DateTenureGranted. The columns of NONTENURED-PROFESSOR are ProfessorName, Phone, Office, and NextReviewDate. Even though WITH IDENTITY is not specified for TENURED-PROFESSOR or NONTENURED-PROFESSOR, both have an IDENTITY column because they are subtypes.

Reflect for a moment on the logical consequences of adding both ADTs and subtypes to the table construct. Both ADTs and tables can have subtypes, and the two are not the same. ADT subtypes define one generalization hierarchy, and table subtypes define another. One hierarchy may be nested in the other or the reverse, or they may be disjoint, or they may partially overlap. SQL3 is open to the criticism of excessive complexity here, and it will be interesting to see how much of this complexity is actually implemented in DBMS products.

SQL LANGUAGE EXTENSIONS   According to SQL3, ADT methods can be coded in the SQL language itself. To make this capability more robust, language elements are proposed that will make SQL computationally complete. The proposed additions are summarized in Figure 17-14.

➤ FIGURE 17-13

Subtable Definitions

CREATE TABLE PROFESSOR WITH IDENTITY

(ProfessorName	char(10),
Phone	char(7),
Office	char(5)
)	

CREATE TABLE TENURED-PROFESSOR UNDER PROFESSOR

| (DateTenureGranted | Date) |

CREATE TABLE NON-TENURED-PROFESSOR UNDER PROFESSOR

| (NextReviewDate | Date) |

Proposed SQL3
Language Extensions

Statement	Purpose
DESTROY	Destroy an object ADT; valid only in DESTRUCTOR functions
ASSIGNMENT	Allow the result of an SQL value expression to be assigned to a local variable, column, or ADT attribute
CALL	Invoke an SQL procedure
RETURN	Return a value from a value computation in a procedure or function
CASE	Select execution path on the basis of alternative values
IF THEN ELSE	Allow conditional logic
WHILE LOOP	Allow iterative logic

To date, SQL has been a set-oriented language. SELECT statements identify a set of rows and operate upon them. The addition of the language statements in Figure 17-14 will change this characteristic. It will be possible to develop row-at-a-time logic within SQL itself. This change will make SQL more and more like a traditional programming language. This is necessary if SQL is to be used as the language for logic in ADT methods, but it also represents a change in the fundamental character of SQL.

ODMG-93

The Object Data Management Group is a consortium of object database vendors and other interested industry experts that has applied the ideas of another group, the Object Management Group, to the problem of object databases. The first report on ODMG was produced in 1993 and is accordingly referred to as ODMG-93. This heritage of this standard is object programming and not traditional relational database management. Hence, it is based on the object as the fundamental construct, rather than on the table as the fundamental construct as we saw for SQL3.

ODMG-93 is a definition of interfaces for object data management products. The implementations of the ideas in ODMG-93 may be quite different. An ODMG-93 product that is designed for C++ object data storage and manipulation might have a completely different implementation from a product that is designed for Smalltalk object storage and manipulation. The two products could be very different and yet still both implement the ODMG-93 interfaces.

Since ODMG-93 arises out of the context of object programming, a detailed description of it requires substantial knowledge of OOP. Such a description is consequently beyond the scope of this text. Instead, we confine this discussion to fundamental ideas behind the ODMG-93 report. Figure 17-15 lists five core concepts as described by Loomis.[3]

OBJECTS ARE FUNDAMENTAL   According to the ODMG Object Model, the object is the fundamental entity to be stored and manipulated. Unlike SQL3, in which the fundamental entity is a table and objects are stored in columns of tables, in ODMG-93 the object is the basic entity. The ODMG concept is more like

---

[3]Mary E. S. Loomis, *Object Databases, The Essentials*. Reading, MA: Addison-Wesley, 1995, pp. 88–110.

➤ FIGURE 17-15

Key Elements of the ODMG Object Model

- Objects are fundamental.
- Every object has a lifelong persistent, unique identifier.
- Objects can be arranged into types and subtypes.
- State is defined by data values and relationships.
- Behavior is defined by object operations.

the one we described for the object program in Figure 17-3. That is, the application program defines objects in and of themselves, and it is up to the ODBMS to make those objects persistent. No other structure, such as a table, is required.

According to the ODMG model, objects can be **mutable** or **immutable.** Mutable objects can be changed; immutable objects are fixed, and no application is allowed to alter the state of any immutable object. The ODBMS is required to enforce immutability.

EVERY OBJECT HAS A LIFELONG PERSISTENT IDENTIFIER The second fundamental concept in the ODMG object model is that each object is given a unique identifier that is valid for the lifetime of the object. Further, the identifier must be valid whether the object is stored externally or is in memory. The ODBMS is to perform swizzling transparently; the application program can use pointers to objects as if they are always valid.

The standard leaves the particular form of an object identifier open. Thus, different ODBMS vendors can use different means to specify object IDs. This means that object identifiers from different databases from different vendors are not necessarily compatible. For nondistributed databases, this is not likely to be a problem, since all of the objects in a given object database will have been created and stored by the same ODBMS.

In a distributed environment, the object identification problem is more difficult for two reasons: first, because object IDs in different ODBMS may have different formats, and, second, because object IDs are not necessarily unique across different databases. This issue is unaddressed by the ODMG-93 standard.

OBJECTS CAN BE ARRANGED INTO TYPES AND SUBTYPES The ODMG standard object model specifies that objects are arranged into groups by type. Objects are created to be of a given type. All objects of a particular type have the same data characteristics and behavior. Objects can be defined as subtypes of other objects. In this case, they inherit all of the data characteristics and behavior of their parent type. According to the standard, an object is created as an instance of a given type, and that instance cannot change its type.

The terms *type* and *class* are often used synonymously. According to Loomis, this is incorrect. An object class is a logical group of objects as defined in ODMG-93; such classes have subclasses that inherit from them. A type is the implementation of a class in a particular language. Thus, the class Employee is a logical definition of data and methods; it may have subclasses Salesperson and Accountant that inherit from Employee. An implementation of Employee in C++, for example, is called a type; implementations in C++ of Salesperson and Accountant are subtypes.[4] There may be another, different implementation of Employee in, say, Smalltalk. That implementation would be a different Employee type. Distinguishing between *class* and *type* helps to delineate logical definitions from particular implementations of those logical structures.

---

[4]*Ibid.*, p. 96.

Object classes (and hence types) can have properties. The ODMG standard specifies that each class has a name and uniqueness constraints as its properties. All of the instances of an object class are called the object's **extent.** Any attribute or combination of attributes can be declared to be unique over the extent. Thus, in Employee, EmployeeNumber can be defined to be unique, as could {FirstName, LastName}, and so on. Since uniqueness requirements apply to the entire extent and not to any given object instance, such requirements are class properties and not class instance properties. Thus, the name Employee and the requirement that EmployeeNumber be unique are class properties. EmployeeNumber itself, however, is a property of an Employee instance.

Since ODMG is a standard for an interface and not for an implementation, no attempt is made to describe how types and subtypes should be stored or manipulated. Rather, the interface simply indicates that objects should be stored and retrieved by class and that inheritance should be provided.

STATE IS DEFINED BY DATA VALUES AND RELATIONSHIPS   According to the ODMG standard, the state of any object is represented by its properties. Such properties can be either attributes or relationships. An attribute is a literal value or a set of literal values. DateOfHire and CurrentSalary are literal values. PastSalary is a set of literal values. A relationship is a property that indicates a connection between one object instance and one or more other object instances. Department is an example of a relationship property.

The ODMG specifies a set of operations that can be performed on relationships, which are listed in Figure 17-16. Operations are distinguished by the maximum cardinality of the relationship. This is done because in the case of a 1:1 relationship, the properties are single-value and no set of properties need be considered. In the case of a 1:N or N:M relationship, the number of elements in a property is plural; a set is created, and the program must be able to iterate over the elements of the set.

When objects have a relationship, the relationship must be made persistent when the object is made persistent. The standard does not specify how the relationship is to be represented and what means are to be used to swizzle the pointers among relationships. These issues must be solved when implementing an ODBMS, however.

BEHAVIOR IS DEFINED BY OBJECT OPERATIONS   The behavior of an object type is determined by its methods. All objects of a given type have the same methods, and objects of subtypes inherit those methods. If a subtype object redefines a method, then the redefinition will override the inherited method. If, for

➤ FIGURE 17-16

*ODMG Relationship
Operations*

Operation	Function
Set	Create a 1:1 relationship
Clear	Destroy a 1:1 relationship
Insert_element	Add an element to the many side of a 1:N or N:M relationship
Remove_element	Remove an element from the many side of a 1:N or N:M relationship
Get	Return a reference to an object in a 1:1 relationship
Traverse	Return a reference to a set of objects on the many side of a 1:N or N:M relationship
Create_iterator	Create a structure to process the elements of a set of objects obtained by a Traverse operation

example, Employee has method Get_Salary, and if Salesperson, a subtype of Employee, also has a method called Get_Salary, the local method will be used for Salesperson!Get_Salary operations.

Objects interact by invoking one another's methods. Sometimes this is expressed by saying that objects pass messages to one another, where a message is a string like Salesperson!Get_Salary that includes the name of the object type and the name of the method of that type. Messages can, of course, include parameters.

The purpose of an ODBMS is to make objects persistent. The ODMG standard indicates that objects include methods, so method storage and management would seem to be included in the functions of an ODMG-compliant ODBMS. In truth, current ODBMS vary widely in their support for method storage. Some ODBMS, in fact, provide no support whatsoever for method persistence. Others provide some support, but not support for versioning of objects.

Method persistence is important, and likely the capabilities of ODBMS in this area will be improved in the future. No application is static; requirements change, and object behaviors must be adapted. Furthermore, methods can change without changing the underlying data properties of an object. Without method management, two instances of an object could be based on two different versions of methods.

Consider an example. Suppose that an instance of a Salesperson class, say Salesperson A, is created and stored using a version of the Set_Salary method. Now suppose that the means of computing salesperson salaries changes, and the Set_Salary method is altered accordingly. At this point, Salesperson B is created and stored. Now, Salesperson A and Salesperson B would appear, in their data properties, to be equivalent, but they are not. Without method management on the part of the ODBMS, there is no way to determine that Salespersons A and B represent different versions of the Salesperson object.

This situation is no different from what occurs today with application programs in non-ODBMS environments, so proponents of ODBMS would claim that ODBMS has not made the situation any worse. This, however, seems to be a copout. If objects are defined to include data properties and behavior properties, then object persistence cannot be claimed to pertain to one and not to the other. Too much of the promise of object thinking is left on the table if ODBMS do not support method management as well as data management.

SEMANTIC OBJECTS AND THE ODMG STANDARD   Semantic objects are very close to the ODMG standard in terms of data properties. A semantic object can have either data attributes or relationship attributes. If the maximum cardinality of a data attribute is greater than one, a set of data attributes is created. Similarly, groups of either data attributes or mixtures of data attributes and relationships (hybrid groups) can be defined. If the maximum cardinality of such a group is greater than one, then a set having such groups as its elements will be defined. As we have discussed semantic objects in this text, they do not include behavior properties. They could be added by adding actions to semantic object diagrams.

➤ SUMMARY

Object-oriented programming is a new style of programming that has emerged in the last 10 years. It has substantial advantages over traditional programming, and many vendors and companies have standardized on it for their new applications. An object DBMS (ODBMS) provides for object storage. At present, ODBMS are not frequently used in commercial environments because most organizational data are in relational format. Also, ODBMS lack some essential features.

With object-oriented programming (OOP), programs are composed of objects that are encapsulated, logical structures that have data elements and behaviors. An interface is the external appearance of an object; an implementation is the encapsulated interior of an object. Objects can be subclassed; a subclass inherits the attributes and methods of its superclass. Polymorphism allows several versions of the same method to exist; the compiler invokes the proper version at execution time, depending on the class of the object.

An object class is the logical structure of an object; a group of object classes is called an object class library. Instances of an object class are called object instances or simply objects. Object constructors are methods that obtain memory and create object structures; object destructors unbind objects and free memory. Transient objects exist only during the execution of a program; persistent objects are saved to storage and survive the execution of a program.

Objects can be made persistent by using traditional file storage, using relational DBMS, or using ODBMS products. The use of traditional storage places considerable work on the application programmer and is feasible only for applications having a few simple objects whose structure does not frequently change. Relational DBMS can be used for object persistence, but the application developer must convert object structures to relations, write SQL, and develop swizzling algorithms. Using an ODBMS is the most direct and easiest means of object persistence.

The advantages and disadvantages of ODBMS are summarized in Figure 17-9. ODBMS appear to have significant advantages over relational DBMS for new applications written in OOP that have complicated data structures and limited query and reporting requirements. At present, relational DBMS appears to have advantages for other types of applications.

SQL3 is an extension to SQL-92 that provides for abstract data types (ADTs), enhancements to tables, and new features in the SQL language. ADTs, which are made persistent by embedding in tables, can be object or value; object ADTs have identifiers called OIDs. In SQL3, tables have a row identifier and can have subtypes. Three types of tables are defined: SET, MULTISET, and LIST. Figure 17-14 shows extensions to the SQL language proposed in SQL3.

The five basic elements of the ODMG-93 standard are that objects are the fundamental data structure, objects are given a lifelong persistent identifier, objects can be arranged in types and subtypes, object state is carried by data values and relationships, and object behavior is defined by object operations. Semantic objects as defined in Chapter 4 implement the ODMG standard for data attributes, but not for object behavior. Semantic objects as implemented in SALSA for the Desktop implement the ODMG standard for behavior and for data attributes, but not for types and subtypes.

➤ GROUP I QUESTIONS

17.1   Explain how object-oriented programming differs from traditional programming.

17.2   Why are relational databases more popular than object databases today?

17.3   Define an OOP object.

17.4   Define the terms *encapsulated, attribute,* and *method.*

17.5   Explain the difference between an interface and an implementation.

17.6   What is inheritance?

17.7   What is polymorphism?

17.8   Define the terms *object class, object class library,* and *object instance.*

17.9   Explain the function of object constructors and object destructors.

17.10 Explain the difference between a transient object and a persistent object.

17.11 Explain the difference in the notation CUSTOMER!Find and CUSTOMER.ZipCode.

17.12 What is the function of the keyword *NOTHING* in Figure 17-3?

17.13 What is the function of the keyword *ME* in Figure 17-3?

17.14 What is a callback, and why is one used?

17.15 What does the term *swizzling* refer to?

17.16 Briefly explain what tasks are required to use traditional file storage for object persistence.

17.17 Briefly explain what tasks are required to use a relational DBMS for object persistence.

17.18 Summarize the advantages and disadvantages of using an ODBMS for object persistence.

17.19 In what ways is an ODBMS better than a relational DBMS?

17.20 In what ways is a relational DBMS better than an ODBMS?

17.21 What is SQL3?

17.22 What is an abstract data type (ADT)?

17.23 Explain the difference between an object ADT and a value ADT.

17.24 What is an OID? How can one be used?

17.25 Explain what the DBMS must do when executing the following SQL on the ADT in Figure 17-10:

```
SELECT      DeptName, Manager.Phone, Admin.Phone
FROM        Dept
```

17.26 What happens when the following SQL is executed on the ADT in Figure 17-10:

```
UPDATE      Dept
SET         Manager.Name = "John Jacob Astor"
```

17.27 Code SQL that would need to be executed to change the instance of the manager of a department for the ADT in Figure 17-10.

17.28 What is a row identifier in SQL3?

17.29 Explain the differences among a SET, MULTISET, and LIST in SQL3.

17.30 Explain the differences among a subtable, a supertable, and a table.

17.31 What is ODMG-93?

17.32 List the five core concepts in ODMG-93.

17.33 What is the difference between a type and a class in ODMG-93?

17.34 What is the difference between a property and an attribute in ODMG-93?

17.35 What is an extent?

17.36 What are the properties of a class in ODMG-93?

17.37 In the ODMG standard, what values can properties have?

17.38 In the ODMG standard, what values can attributes have?

17.39 In the ODMG standard, what values can relationship properties have?

17.40 Why is method persistence important? Give an example of a problem that can occur when such persistence is not provided.

17.41 Explain how semantic objects conform to the ODMG standard and how they do not.

➤ GROUP II QUESTIONS

17.42 Compare and contrast object-oriented programming with traditional programming. Evaluate the two on the following criteria:

a. Ease of learning

b. Ease of use

c. Quality of code

d. Changeability of code

e. Data persistence

f. Representation of object (entity) relationships

For what types of applications do you think object-oriented programming should be used? For what types of applications do you think traditional programming should be used?

17.43 Contact a vendor of an ODBMS product, and evaluate that product's features and functions in terms of:

a. Object definition

b. Object storage facilities

c. Swizzling

d. Object relationships definition

e. Object relationship processing

f. Method storage and management

g. Object query and reporting

h. Concurrency control

i. Transaction management

j. Performance

Data Structures for Database Processing

All operating systems provide data management services. These services, however, are generally not sufficient for the specialized needs of a DBMS. Therefore, to enhance performance, DBMS products build and maintain specialized data structures, which are the topic of this appendix.

We begin by discussing flat files and some of the problems that can occur when such files need to be processed in different orders. Then we turn to three specialized data structures: sequential lists, linked lists, and indexes (or inverted lists). Next we illustrate how each of three special structures discussed in Chapter 6—trees, simple networks, and complex networks—are represented using various data structures. Finally, we explore how to represent and process multiple keys.

Although a thorough knowledge of data structures is not required to use most DBMS products, this background is essential to database administrators and systems programmers working with a DBMS. Being familiar with the data structures also helps you evaluate and compare database products.

➤ FLAT FILES

A *flat file* is a file that has no repeating groups. Figure A-1 (a) shows a flat file, and (b) shows a file that is not flat because of the repeating field Item. A flat file can be stored in any common file organization such as sequential, indexed sequential, or direct. Flat files have been used for many years in commercial processing. They are usually processed in some predetermined order, say, in an ascending sequence on a key field.

Examples of (a) a Flat and (b) a Nonflat File Enrollment Record

Enrollment Record

StudentNumber	ClassNumber	Semester

Sample Data

200	70	88S
100	30	89F
300	20	89F
200	30	88S
300	70	88S
100	20	88S

(a)

Invoice Record

InvoiceNumber	Item(s)

Sample Data

1000	10	20	30	40
1010	50			
1020	10	20	30	
1030	50	90		

(b)

PROCESSING FLAT FILES IN MULTIPLE ORDERS

Sometimes users want to process flat files in ways that are not readily supported by the file organization. Consider, for example, the ENROLLMENT records in Figure A1(a). To produce student schedules, they must be processed in StudentNumber sequence. But to produce class rosters, the records need to be processed in ClassNumber sequence. The records, of course, can be stored in only one physical sequence. For example, they can be in order on StudentNumber or on ClassNumber, but not on both at the same time. The traditional solution to the problem of processing records in different orders is to sort them in student order, process the student schedules, then sort the records in class order, and produce class rosters.

For some applications, such as a batch-mode system, this solution, while cumbersome, is effective. But suppose that both orders need to exist simultaneously because two concurrent users have different views of the ENROLLMENT records. What do we do then?

One solution is to create two copies of the ENROLLMENT file and sort them as shown in Figure A-2. Since the data are listed in sequential order, this data structure is sometimes called a *sequential list.* Sequential lists can be readily stored as sequential files. This, however, is not generally done by DBMS products because sequentially reading a file is a slow process. Further, sequential files cannot be updated in the middle without rewriting the entire file. Also, maintaining several orders by keeping multiple copies of the same sequential list is usually not effective because the duplicated sequential list can create data integrity problems. Fortunately, other data structures allow us to process records in different orders and do not require the duplication of data. These include *linked lists* and *indexes.*

ENROLLMENT Data Stored as Sequential Lists: (a) Sorted by StudentNumber and (b) Sorted by ClassNumber

Student-Number	Class-Number	Semester
100	30	89F
100	20	88S
200	70	88S
200	30	88S
300	20	89F
300	70	88S

(a)

Student-Number	Class-Number	Semester
300	20	89F
100	20	88S
100	30	89F
200	30	88S
200	70	88S
300	70	88S

(b)

► FIGURE A-3

*ENROLLMENT Data in
StudentNumber Order Using a
Linked List*

Relative Record Number	Student-Number	Class-Number	Semester	Link
1	200	70	88S	4
2	100	30	89F	6
3	300	20	89F	5
4	200	30	88S	3
5	300	70	88S	0
6	100	20	88S	1

Start of list = 2

A NOTE ON RECORD ADDRESSING

Usually the DBMS creates large physical records, or blocks, on its direct access files. These are used as containers for logical records. Typically, there are many logical records per physical record. Here we assume that each physical record is addressed by its relative record number (RRN). Thus, a logical record might be assigned to physical record number 7 or 77 or 10,000. The relative record number is thus the logical record's physical address. If there is more than one logical record per physical record, the address must also specify where the logical record is within the physical record. Thus, the complete address for a logical record might be relative record number 77, byte location 100. This means the record begins in byte 100 of physical record 77.

To simplify the illustrations in this text, we assume that there is only one logical record per physical record, so we need not be concerned with byte offsets within physical records. Although this is unrealistic, it simplifies our discussion to the essential points.

MAINTAINING ORDER WITH LINKED LISTS

Linked lists can be used to keep records in logical order that are not necessarily in physical order. To create a linked list, we add a field to each data record. The *link* field holds the address (in our illustrations, the relative record number) of the *next* record in logical sequence. For example, Figure A-3 shows the ENROLLMENT records expanded to include a linked list; this list maintains the records in StudentNumber order. Notice that the link for the numerically last student in the list is zero.

Figure A-4 shows ENROLLMENT records with two linked lists: One list maintains the StudentNumber order, and the other list maintains the ClassNumber order. Two link fields have been added to the records, one for each list.

When insertions and deletions are made, linked lists have a great advantage over sequential lists. For example, to insert the ENROLLMENT record for Student 200 and Class 45, both of the lists in Figure A-2 would need to be rewritten. For the linked

► FIGURE A-4

*ENROLLMENT Data in Two
Orders Using Linked Lists*

Relative Record Number	Student-Number	Class-Number	Semester	Student Link	Class Link
1	200	70	88S	4	5
2	100	30	89F	6	1
3	300	20	89F	5	4
4	200	30	88S	3	2
5	300	70	88S	0	0
6	100	20	88S	1	3

Start of student list = 2
Start of class list = 6

> FIGURE A-5

ENROLLMENT Data After
Inserting New Record (in Two
Orders Using Linked Lists)

Relative Record Number	Student- Number	Class- Number	Semester	Student Link	Class Link
1	200	70	88S	4	5
2	100	30	89F	6	7
3	300	20	89F	5	4
4	200	30	88S	7	2
5	300	70	88S	0	0
6	100	20	88S	1	3
7	200	45	88S	3	1

Start of student list = 2
Start of class list = 6

lists in Figure A-4, however, the new record could be added to the physical end of the list, and only the values of two link fields would need to be changed to place the new record in the correct sequences. These changes are shown in Figure A-5.

When a record is deleted from a sequential list, a gap is created. But in a linked list, a record can be deleted simply by changing the values of the link, or the *pointer* fields. In Figure A-6, the ENROLLMENT record for Student 200, Class 30, has been logically deleted. No other record points to its address, so it has been effectively removed from the chain, even though it still exists physically.

There are many variations of linked lists. We can make the list into a *circular list,* or *ring,* by changing the link of the last record from zero to the address of the first record in the list. Now we can reach every item in the list starting at any item in the list. Figure A-7(a) shows a circular list for the StudentNumber order. A *two-way linked list* has links in both directions. In Figure A-7(b), a two-way linked list has been created for both ascending and descending student orders.

Records ordered using linked lists cannot be stored on a sequential file because some type of direct-access file organization is needed in order to use the link values. Thus, either indexed sequential or direct file organization is required for linked-list processing.

MAINTAINING ORDER WITH INDEXES

A logical record order can also be maintained using *indexes* or, as they are sometimes called, *inverted lists.* An index is simply a table that cross-references record addresses with some field value. For example, Figure A-8(a) shows the ENROLLMENT records stored in no particular order, and (b) shows an index on StudentNumber. In this index the StudentNumbers are arranged in sequence, with each entry in the list pointing to a corresponding record in the original data.

> FIGURE A-6

ENROLLMENT Data After
Deleting Student 200, Class
30 (in Two Orders Using
Linked Lists)

Relative Record Number	Student- Number	Class- Number	Semester	Student Link	Class Link
1	200	70	88S	7	5
2	100	30	89F	6	7
3	300	20	89F	5	2
4	200	30	88S	7	2
5	300	70	88S	0	0
6	100	20	88S	1	3
7	200	45	88S	3	1

Start of student list = 2
Start of class list = 6

➤ FIGURE A-7

ENROLLMENT Data Sorted by StudentNumber Using (a) a Circular and (b) a Two-Way Linked List

Relative Record Number	Student-Number	Class-Number	Semester	Link
1	200	70	88S	4
2	100	30	89F	6
3	300	20	89F	5
4	200	30	88S	3
5	300	70	88S	2
6	100	20	88S	1

Start of list = 2

(a)

Relative Record Number	Student-Number	Class-Number	Semester	Ascending Link	Descending Link
1	200	70	88S	4	6
2	100	30	89F	6	0
3	300	20	89F	5	4
4	200	30	88S	3	1
5	300	70	88S	0	3
6	100	20	88S	1	2

Start of ascending list = 2
Start of descending list = 5

(b)

➤ FIGURE A-8

ENROLLMENT Data and Corresponding Indexes: (a) ENROLLMENT Data, (b) Index on StudentNumber, and (c) Index on ClassNumber

Relative Record Number	Student-Number	Class-Number	Semester
1	200	70	88S
2	100	30	89F
3	300	20	89F
4	200	30	88S
5	300	70	88S
6	100	20	88S

(a)

Student-Number	Relative Record Number
100	2
100	6
200	1
200	4
300	3
300	5

(b)

Class-Number	Relative Record Number
20	3
20	6
30	2
30	4
70	1
70	5

(c)

As you can see, the index is simply a sorted list of StudentNumbers. To process ENROLLMENT sequentially on StudentNumber, we simply process the index sequentially, obtaining ENROLLMENT data by reading the records indicated by the pointers. Figure A-8(c) shows another index for ENROLLMENT, one that maintains ClassNumber order.

To use an index, the data to be ordered (here, ENROLLMENT) must reside on an indexed sequential or direct file, although the indexes can reside on any type of file. In practice, almost all DBMS products keep both the data and the indexes on direct files.

If you compare the linked list with the index, you will notice the essential difference between them. In a linked list, the pointers are stored along with the data. Each record contains a link field containing a pointer to the address of the next related record. But in an index, the pointers are stored in indexes, separate from the data. Thus, the data records themselves contain no pointers. Both techniques are used by commercial DBMS products.

B-TREES

A special application of the concept of indexes, or inverted lists, is a *B-tree,* a multilevel index that allows both sequential and direct processing of data records. It also ensures a certain level of efficiency in processing, because of the way that the indexes are structured.

A B-tree is an index that is made up of two parts, the sequence set and the index set (these terms are used by IBM's VSAM file organization documentation. You may encounter other, synonymous, terms). The *sequence set* is an index containing an entry for every record in the file. This index is in physical sequence, usually by primary key value. This arrangement allows sequential access to the data records as follows: process the sequence set in order, read the address of each record, and then read the record.

The *index set* is an index pointing to groups of entries in the sequence set index. This arrangement provides rapid direct access to records in the file, and it is the index set that makes B-trees unique.

An example of a B-tree appears in Figure A-9, and an occurrence of this structure can be seen in Figure A-10. Notice that the bottom row in Figure A-9, the sequence set, is simply an index. It contains an entry for every record in the file (although for brevity, both the data records and their addresses have been omitted). Also notice that the sequence set entries are in groups of three. The entries in each group are physically in sequence, and each group is chained to the next one by means of a linked list, as can be seen in Figure A-10.

Examine the index set in Figure A-9. The top entry contains two values, 45 and 77. By following the leftmost link (to RRN2), we can access all the records whose key field values are less than or equal to 45; by following the middle pointer (to RRN3), we can access all the records whose key field values are greater than 45 and less than or equal to 77; and by following the rightmost pointer (to RRN4), we can access all the records whose key field values are greater than 77.

Similarly, at the next level there are two values and three pointers in each index entry. Each time we drop to another level, we narrow our search for a particular record. For example, if we continue to follow the leftmost pointer from the top entry and then follow the rightmost pointer from there, we can access all the records whose key field value is greater than 27 and less than or equal to 45. We have eliminated all that were greater than 45 at the first level.

B-trees are, by definition, balanced. That is, all the data records are exactly the same distance from the top entry in the index set. This aspect of B-trees ensures performance efficiency, although the algorithms for inserting and deleting records are more complex than those for ordinary trees (which can be unbal-

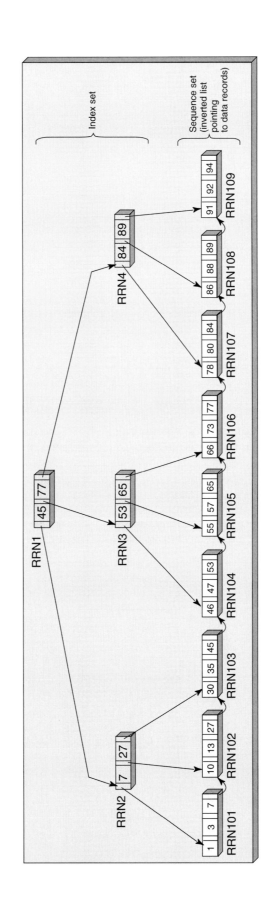

▲ FIGURE A-9

General Structure of a Simple B-Tree

➤ FIGURE A-10

Occurrence of the B-Tree in Figure A-9.

RRN	Link1	Value1	Link2	Value2	Link3	
1	2	45	3	77	4	
2	101	7	102	27	103	Index Set
3	104	53	105	65	106	
4	107	84	108	89	109	

.
.
.

	R1	Addr1	R2	Addr2	R3	Addr3	Link	
101	1	Pointer to 6	3	Pointer to 8	7	Pointer to 12	102	
102	10	· · ·	13	· · ·	27	· · ·	103	
103	30	· · ·	35	· · ·	45	· · ·	104	Sequence Set
104	46	· · ·	47	· · ·	53	· · ·	105	(Addresses of
105	55	· · ·	57	· · ·	65	· · ·	106	data records
106	66	· · ·	73	· · ·	77	· · ·	107	are omitted)
107	78	· · ·	80	· · ·	84	· · ·	108	
108	86	· · ·	88	· · ·	89	· · ·	109	
109	91	· · ·	92	· · ·	94	· · ·	0	

anced), because several index entries may need to be modified when records are added or deleted to keep all records the same distance from the top index entry.

SUMMARY OF DATA STRUCTURES

Figure A-11 summarizes the techniques for maintaining ordered flat files. Three supporting data structures are possible. Sequential lists can be used, but the data must be duplicated in order to maintain several orders. Because sequential lists

➤ FIGURE A-11

Summary of Data Structures and Data Organizations Used for Ordered Flat Files

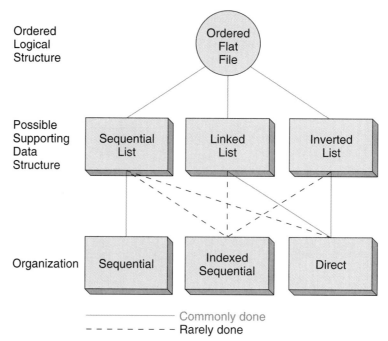

➤ FIGURE A-12

Occurrence of a Faculty Member Record

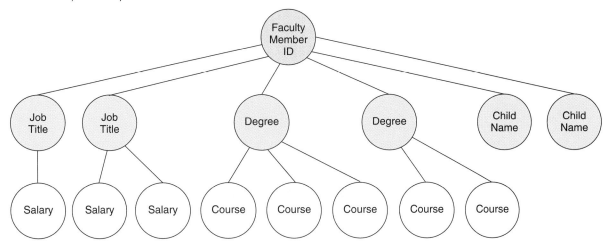

are not used in database processing, we will not consider them further. Both linked lists and indexes can be used without data duplication. B-trees are special applications of indexes.

As shown in Figure A-11, sequential lists can be stored using any of three file organizations. In practice, however, they are usually kept on sequential files. In addition, although both linked lists and indexes can be stored using either indexed sequential or direct files, DBMS products almost always store them on direct files.

➤ REPRESENTING BINARY RELATIONSHIPS

In this section we examine how each of the specialized record relationships discussed in Chapter 6—trees, simple networks, and complex networks—can be represented using linked lists and indexes.

REVIEW OF RECORD RELATIONSHIPS

Records can be related in three ways. A *tree* relationship has one or more one-to-many relationships, but each child record has at most one parent. The occurrence of faculty data shown in Figure A-12 illustrates a tree. There are several 1:N relationships, but any child record has only one parent, as shown in Figure A-13.

A *simple network* is a collection of records and the 1:N relationships among them. What distinguishes a simple network from a tree is the fact that in a simple

➤ FIGURE A-13

Schematic of a Faculty Member Tree Structure

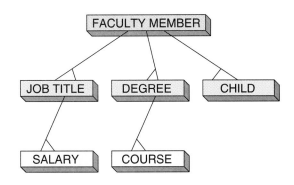

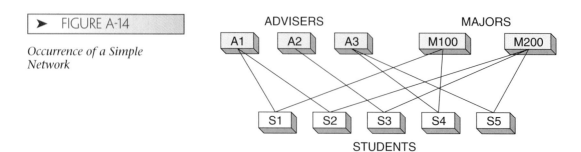

network a child can have more than one parent as long as the parents are different record types. The occurrence of a simple network of students, advisers, and major fields of study in Figure A-14 is represented schematically in Figure A-15.

A *complex network* is also a collection of records and relationships, but the relationships are many to many instead of one to many. The relationship between students and classes is a complex network. An occurrence of this relationship can be seen in Figure A-16, and the general schematic is in Figure A-17.

We saw earlier that we can use linked lists and indexes to process records in orders different from the one in which they are physically stored. We can also use those same data structures to store and process the relationships among records.

REPRESENTING TREES

We can use sequential lists, linked lists, and indexes to represent trees. When using sequential lists, we duplicate many data, and furthermore, sequential lists are not used by DBMS products to represent trees. Therefore, we describe only linked lists and indexes.

LINKED-LIST REPRESENTATION OF TREES   Figure A-18 shows a tree structure in which the VENDOR records are parents and the INVOICE records are children. Figure A-19 shows two occurrences of this structure, and in Figure A-20, all of the VENDOR and INVOICE records have been written to a direct access file. VENDOR AA is in relative record number 1 (RRN1), and VENDOR BB is in relative record number 2. The INVOICE records have been stored in subsequent records, as illustrated. Note that these records are not stored in any particular order and that they do not need to be.

Our problem is that we cannot tell from this file which invoices belong to which vendors. To solve this problem with a linked list, we add a pointer field to every record. In this field we store the address of some other related record. For example, we place in VENDOR AA's link field the address of the first invoice belonging to it. This is RRN7, which is Invoice 110. Then we make Invoice 110 point to the next invoice belonging to VENDOR AA, in this case RRN3. This slot holds Invoice 118. To indicate that there are no more children in the chain, we insert a 0 in the link field for RRN3.

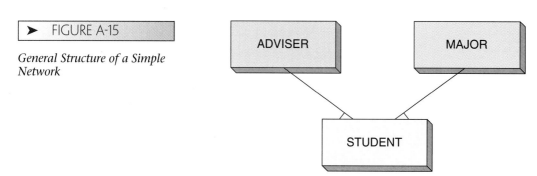

Occurrence of a Complex
Network

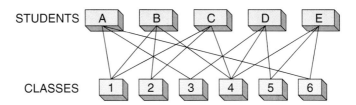

FIGURE A-17

Schematic of a Complex
Network

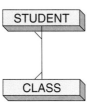

FIGURE A-18

Sample Tree Relating
VENDOR and INVOICE
Records

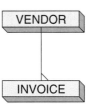

FIGURE A-19

Two Occurrences of VENDOR-INVOICE Tree

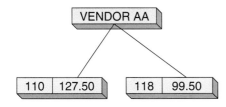

FIGURE A-20

File Representation of the
Trees in Figure A-19

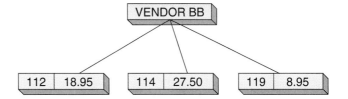

Record Number	Record Contents	
1	VENDOR AA	
2	VENDOR BB	
3	118	99.50
4	119	8.95
5	112	18.95
6	114	27.50
7	110	127.50

Tree Occurrences Represented
by Linked Lists

Relative Record Number	Record Contents		Link Field
1	VENDOR AA		7
2	VENDOR BB		5
3	118	99.50	0
4	119	8.95	0
5	112	18.95	6
6	114	27.50	4
7	110	127.50	3

This technique is shown in Figure A-21. If you examine the figure, you will see that a similar set of links has been used to represent the relationship between VENDOR BB and its invoices.

The structure in Figure A-21 is much easier to modify than is a sequential list of the records. For example, suppose we add a new invoice, say number 111, to VENDOR AA. To do this, we just add the record to the file and insert it into the linked list. Physically, the record can be placed anywhere. But where should it be placed logically? Usually the application will have a requirement like children are to be kept in ascending order on invoice number. If so, we need to make Invoice 110 point to Invoice 111 (at RRN8), and we need to make Invoice 111, the new invoice, point to Invoice 118 (at RRN3). This modification is shown in Figure A-22.

Similarly, deleting an invoice is easy. If Invoice 114 is deleted, we simply modify the pointer in the invoice that is now pointing to Invoice 114. In this case, it is Invoice 112 at RRN5. We give Invoice 112 the pointer that Invoice 114 had before deletion. In this way, Invoice 112 points to Invoice 119 (see Figure A-23). We have effectively cut one link out of the chain and welded together the ones it once connected.

INDEX REPRESENTATION OF TREES   A tree structure can readily be represented using indexes. The technique is to store each one-to-many relationship as an index. These lists are then used to match parents and children.

Using the VENDOR and INVOICE records in Figure A-21, we see that VENDOR AA (in RRN1) owns INVOICEs 110 (RRN7) and 118 (RRN3). Thus, RRN1 is the parent of RRN7 and RRN3. We can represent this fact with the index in Figure A-24. The list simply associates a parent's address with the addresses of each of its children.

Inserting Invoice 111 into File
in Figure A-21

Relative Record Number	Record Contents		Link Field	
1	VENDOR AA		7	
2	VENDOR BB		5	
3	118	99.50	0	
4	119	8.95	0	
5	112	18.95	6	
6	114	27.50	4	
7	110	127.50	8	
8	111	19.95	3	← Inserted Record

*Deleting Invoice 114 from File
in Figure A-22*

Relative Record Number	Record Contents		Link Field	
1	VENDOR AA		7	
2	VENDOR BB		5	
3	118	99.50	0	
4	119	8.95	0	
5	112	18.95	4	
6	114	27.50	4	← Deleted Record
7	110	127.50	8	
8	111	19.95	3	

*Index Representation of
VENDOR-INVOICE
Relationship*

Parent Record	Child Record
1	7
1	3
2	5
2	6
2	4

If the tree has several 1:N relationships, then several indexes will be required, one for each relationship. For the structure in Figure A-13, five indexes are needed.

REPRESENTING SIMPLE NETWORKS

As with trees, simple networks can also be represented using linked lists and indexes.

LINKED-LIST REPRESENTATION OF SIMPLE NETWORKS Consider the simple network in Figure A-25. It is a simple network because all the relationships are 1:N, and the SHIPMENT records have two parents of different types. Each SHIPMENT has a CUSTOMER parent and a TRUCK parent. The relationship between CUSTOMER and SHIPMENT is 1:N because a customer can have several shipments, and the relationship from TRUCK to SHIPMENT is 1:N because one truck can hold many shipments (assuming that the shipments are small enough to fit in one truck or less). An occurrence of this network is shown in Figure A-26.

In order to represent this simple network with linked lists, we need to establish one set of pointers for each 1:N relationship. In this example, that means one set of pointers to connect CUSTOMERs with their SHIPMENTs and another set of pointers to connect TRUCKs with their SHIPMENTs. Thus, a CUSTOMER record will contain one pointer (to the first SHIPMENT it owns); a TRUCK record will contain one pointer (to the first SHIPMENT it owns); and a SHIPMENT

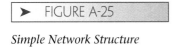

Simple Network Structure

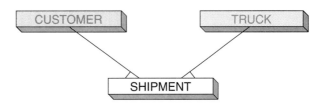

➤ FIGURE A-26

*Occurrence of the Simple
Network in Figure A-25*

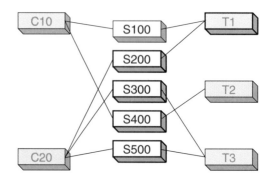

record will have two pointers, one for the next SHIPMENT owned by the same CUSTOMER and one for the next SHIPMENT owned by the same TRUCK. This scheme is illustrated in Figure A-27.

A simple network has at least two 1:N relationships, each of which can be represented using an index, as we explained in our discussion of trees. For example, consider the simple network shown in Figure A-25. It has two 1:N relationships, one between TRUCK and SHIPMENT and one between CUSTOMER and SHIPMENT. We can store each of these relationships in an index. Figure A-28 shows the two indexes needed to represent the example in Figure A-26. Assume the records are located in the same positions as in Figure A-27.

REPRESENTING COMPLEX NETWORKS

Complex networks can be physically represented in a variety of ways. They can be decomposed into trees or simple networks, and these simpler structures can then be represented using one of the techniques we just described. Alternatively, they can be represented directly using indexes. Linked lists are not used by any DBMS product to represent complex networks directly. In practice, complex networks are nearly always decomposed into simpler structures, so we consider only those representations using decomposition.

A common approach to representing complex networks is to reduce them to simple networks and then to represent the simple networks with linked lists or indexes. Note, however, that a complex network involves a relationship between

➤ FIGURE A-27

*Representation of a Simple
Network with Linked Lists*

Relative Record Number	Record Contents	Link Fields	
1	C10	6	
2	C20	7	
3	T1		6
4	T2		9
5	T3		8
6	S100	9	7
7	S200	8	0
8	S300	10	10
9	S400	0	0
10	S500	0	0

CUSTOMER Links   TRUCK Links

➤ FIGURE A-28

Representation of Simple Network with Index

Customer Record	Shipment Record
1	6
1	9
2	7
2	8
2	10

Truck Record	Shipment Record
3	6
3	7
4	9
5	8
5	10

two records, whereas a simple network involves relationships among three records. Thus, in order to decompose a complex network into a simple one, we need to create a third record type.

The record that is created when a complex network is decomposed into a simple one is called an *intersection record*. Consider the StudentClass complex network. An intersection record will contain a unique key from a STUDENT record and a unique key from a corresponding CLASS record. It will contain no other application data, although it might contain link fields. The general structure of this relationship is shown in Figure A-29. Assuming that the record names are unique (such as S1, S2, and C1), an instance of the STUDENT-CLASS relationship is illustrated in Figure A-30.

Notice that the relationship between STUDENT and the intersection record and that between CLASS and the intersection record both are 1:N. Thus, we have created a simple network that can now be represented with the linked-list or index techniques shown earlier. A file of this occurrence using the linked-list technique is shown in Figure A-31.

SUMMARY OF RELATIONSHIP REPRESENTATIONS

Figure A-32 on page 521 summarizes the representations of record relationships. Trees can be represented using sequential lists (although we did not discuss this approach), linked lists, or indexes. Sequential lists are not used in DBMS products. A simple network can be decomposed into trees and then represented, or it can be represented directly using either linked lists or indexes. Finally, a complex network can be decomposed into a tree or a simple network (using intersection records), or it can be represented directly using indexes.

➤ SECONDARY-KEY REPRESENTATIONS

In many cases the word *key* indicates a field (or fields) whose value uniquely identifies a record. This is usually called the *primary key*. Sometimes, however, applications need to access and process records by means of a *secondary key*, one that is different from the primary key. Secondary keys may be unique (such as a professor's name) or nonunique (such as a customer's Zip code). In

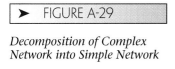

➤ FIGURE A-29

Decomposition of Complex Network into Simple Network

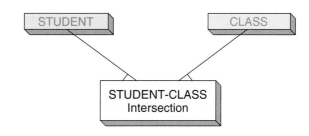

> FIGURE A-30

*Instance of STUDENT-CLASS
Relationship Showing
Intersection Records*

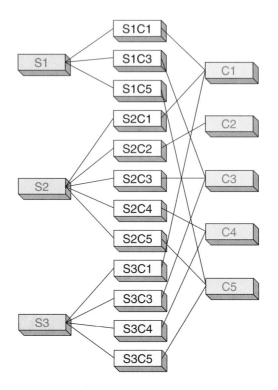

> FIGURE A-31

*Occurrence of Network in
Figure A-30*

Relative Record Number	Record Contents	STUDENT Links	CLASS Links
1	S1	9	
2	S2	12	
3	S3	17	
4	C1		9
5	C2		13
6	C3		10
7	C4		15
8	C5		11
9	S1C1	10	12
10	S1C3	11	14
11	S1C5	0	16
12	S2C1	13	17
13	S2C2	14	0
14	S2C3	15	18
15	S2C4	16	19
16	S2C5	0	20
17	S3C1	18	0
18	S3C3	19	0
19	S3C4	20	0
20	S3C5	0	0

Link Fields

STUDENT Links   CLASS Links

Record Relationships, Data Structures, and File Organizations

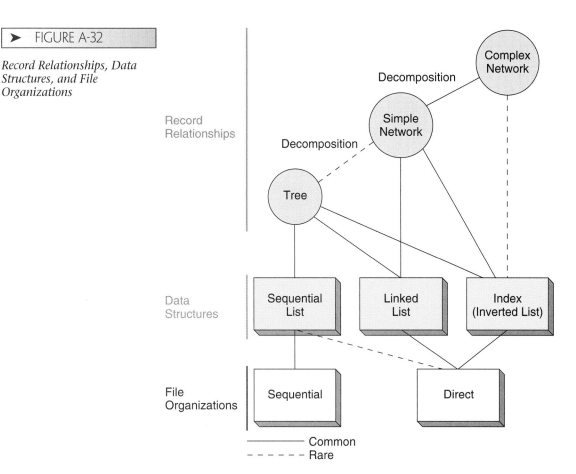

this section we use the term *set* to refer to all records having the same value of a nonunique secondary key, for example, a set of records having Zip Code 98040.

Both linked lists and indexes are used to represent secondary keys, but linked lists are practical only for nonunique keys. Indexes, however, can be used for both unique and nonunique key representations.

LINKED-LIST REPRESENTATION OF SECONDARY KEYS

Consider the example of CUSTOMER records shown in Figure A-33. The primary key is AccountNumber, and there is a secondary key on CreditLimit. Possible CreditLimit values are 500, 700, and 1000. Thus there will be a set of records for the limit of 500, a set for 700, and a set for 1000.

To represent this key using linked lists, we add a link field to the CUSTOMER records. Inside this link field we create a linked list for each set of records. Figure A-34 shows a database of eleven customers, but, for brevity, only AccountNumber and CreditLimit are shown. A link field has been attached to the records. Assume that one database record occupies one physical record on a direct file using relative record addressing.

CUSTOMER Record

➤ FIGURE A-34

Representing CreditLimit Secondary Key Using Linked List

Relative Record Number	Link	Account- Number	Credit- Limit	Other Data
1	2	101	500	
2	7	301	500	
3	5	203	700	
4	6	004	1000	
5	10	204	700	
6	8	905	1000	
7	0	705	500	
8	9	207	1000	
9	11	309	1000	
10	0	409	700	
11	0	210	1000	

HEAD-500 = 1
HEAD-700 = 3
HEAD-1000 = 4

Three pointers need to be established so that we know where to begin each linked list. These are called *heads* and are stored separate from the data. The head of the $500 linked list is RRN1. Record 1 links to record 2, which in turn links to record 7. Record 7 has a zero in the link position, indicating that it is the end of the list. Consequently, the $500 credit limit set consists of records 1, 2, and 7. Similarly, the $700 set contains records 3, 5, and 10, and the $1000 set contains relative records 4, 6, 8, 9, and 11.

To answer a query like, How many accounts in the $1000 set have a balance in excess of $900?, the $1000 set linked list can be used. In this way, only those records in the $1000 set need to be read from the file and examined. Although the advantage of this approach is not readily apparent in this small example, suppose there are 100,000 CUSTOMER records, and only 100 of them are in the $1000 set. If there is no linked list, all 100,000 records must be examined, but with the linked list, only 100 records need to be examined, namely, the ones in the $1000 set. Using the linked list, therefore, saves 99,900 reads.

Linked lists are not an effective technique for every secondary-key application. In particular, if the records are processed nonsequentially in a set, linked lists are inefficient. For example, if it often is necessary to find the 10th or 120th or *n*th record in the $500 CreditLimit set, processing will be slow. Linked lists are inefficient for direct access.

In addition, if the application requires that secondary keys be created or destroyed dynamically, the linked-list approach is undesirable. Whenever a new key is created, a link field must be added to every record, which often requires reorganizing the database, a time-consuming and expensive process.

Finally, if the secondary keys are unique, each list will have a length of 1, and a separate linked list will exist for every record in the database. Because this situation is unworkable, linked lists cannot be used for unique keys. For example, suppose that the CUSTOMER records contain another unique field, say, Social Security Number. If we attempt to represent this unique secondary key using a linked list, every Social Security Number will be a separate linked list. Furthermore, each linked list will have just one item in it, the single record having the indicated Social Security Number.

INDEX REPRESENTATION OF SECONDARY KEYS

A second technique for representing secondary keys uses an index; one is established for each secondary key. The approach varies depending on whether the key values are unique or nonunique.

➤ FIGURE A-35

Representing a Unique Secondary Key with Indexes: (a) Sample CUSTOMER Data (with SSN) and (b) Index for SSN Secondary Key

Relative Record Number	Account-Number	Credit-Limit	Social Security Number (SSN)
1	101	500	000-01-0001
2	301	500	000-01-0005
3	203	700	000-01-0009
4	004	1000	000-01-0003

(a)

SSN	Relative Record Number
000-01-0001	1
000-01-0003	4
000-01-0005	2
000-01-0009	3

(b)

UNIQUE SECONDARY KEYS Suppose the CUSTOMER records in Figure A-33 contain Social Security Number (SSN) as well as the fields shown. To provide key access to the CUSTOMER records using SSN, we simply build an index on the SSN field. Sample CUSTOMER data are shown in Figure A-35(a), and a corresponding index is illustrated in Figure A-35(b). This index uses relative record numbers as addresses. It would be possible to use AccountNumbers instead, in which case the DBMS would locate the desired SSN in the index, obtain the matching AccountNumber, and then convert the AccountNumber to a relative record address.

NONUNIQUE SECONDARY KEYS Indexes can also be used to represent nonunique secondary keys, but because each set of related records can contain an unknown number of members, the entries in the index are of variable length. For example, Figure A-36 shows the index for the CreditLimit sets for the CUSTOMER data. The $500 set and the $700 set both have three members, so there are three account numbers in each entry. The $1000 set has five members, so there are five account numbers in that entry.

In reality, representing and processing nonunique secondary keys are complex tasks. Several different schemes are used by commercial DBMS products. One common method uses a values table and an occurrence table. Each values table entry consists of two fields, the first of which has a key value. For the CUSTOMER CreditLimit key, the values are 500, 700, and 1000. The second field of the values table entry is a pointer into the occurrence table. The occurrence table contains record addresses, and those having a common value in the secondary-key field appear together in the table. Figure A-37 shows the values and occurrence tables for the CreditLimit key.

To locate records having a given value of the secondary key, the values table is searched for the desired value. Once the given key value is located in the values

➤ FIGURE A-36

Index for CreditLimit Key in Figure A-33

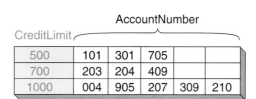

CreditLimit	AccountNumber				
500	101	301	705		
700	203	204	409		
1000	004	905	207	309	210

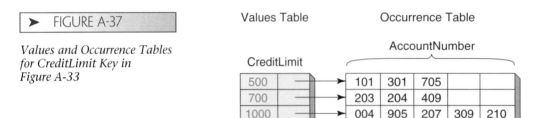

FIGURE A-37

Values and Occurrence Tables for CreditLimit Key in Figure A-33

table, the pointer is followed to the occurrence table to obtain the addresses of those records having that key value. These addresses are then used to obtain the desired records.

When a new record is inserted into the file, the DBMS must modify the indexes for each secondary-key field. For nonunique keys, it must make sure that the new record key value is in the values table; if it is, it will add the new record address to the appropriate entry in the occurrence table. If it is not, it must insert new entries in the values and occurrence tables.

When a record is deleted, its address must be removed from the occurrence table. If no addresses remain in the occurrence table entry, the corresponding values table entry must also be deleted.

When the secondary-key field of a record is modified, the record address must be removed from one occurrence table entry and inserted into another. If the modification is a new value for the key, an entry must be added to the values table.

The index approach to representing secondary keys overcomes the objections to the linked-list approach. Direct processing of sets is possible. For example, the third record in a set can be retrieved without processing the first or second one. Also, it is possible to dynamically create and delete secondary keys. No changes are made in the records themselves; the DBMS merely creates additional values and occurrence tables. Finally, unique keys can be processed efficiently.

The disadvantages of the index approach are that it requires more file space (the tables use more overhead than the pointers do) and that the DBMS programming task is more complex. Note that the *application programming* task is not necessarily any more or less difficult—but it is more complex to write DBMS software that processes indexes than it is to write software that processes linked lists. Finally, modifications are usually processed more slowly because of the reading and writing actions required to access and maintain the values in the occurrence tables.

► SUMMARY

In this appendix we surveyed data structures used for database processing. A flat file is a file that contains no repeating groups. Flat files can be ordered using sequential lists (physically placing the records in the sequence in which they will be processed), linked lists (attaching to each data record a pointer to another logically related record), and indexes (building a table, separate from the data records, containing pointers to related records). B-trees are special applications of indexes.

Sequential lists, linked lists, and indexes (or inverted lists) are fundamental data structures. (Sequential lists, however, are seldom used in database processing.) These data structures can be used to represent record relationships as well as secondary keys.

The three basic record structures—trees, simple networks, and complex networks—can be represented using linked lists and indexes. Simple networks can be decomposed into trees and then represented; complex networks can be decomposed into simple networks containing an intersection record and then represented.

Secondary keys are used to access the data on some field besides the primary key. Secondary keys can be unique or nonunique. Nonunique secondary keys can be represented with both linked lists and indexes. Unique secondary keys can be represented only with indexes.

➤ GROUP I QUESTIONS

A.1   Define a flat file. Give an example (other than one in this text) of a flat file and an example of a file that is not flat.

A.2   Show how sequential lists can be used to maintain the file in Question A.1 in two different orders simultaneously.

A.3   Show how linked lists can be used to maintain the file in Question A.1 in two different orders simultaneously.

A.4   Show how inverted lists can be used to maintain the file in Question A.1 in two different orders simultaneously.

A.5   Define a tree, and give an example structure.

A.6   Give an occurrence of the tree in Question A.5.

A.7   Represent the occurrence in Question A.6 using linked lists.

A.8   Represent the occurrence in Question A.6 using indexes.

A.9   Define a simple network and give an example structure.

A.10 Give an occurrence of the simple network in Question A.9.

A.11 Represent the occurrence in Question A.10 using linked lists.

A.12 Represent the occurrence in Question A.10 using indexes.

A.13 Define complex network, and give an example structure.

A.14 Give an occurrence of the complex network in Question A.13.

A.15 Decompose the complex network in Question A.14 into a simple network, and represent an occurrence of it using indexes.

A.16 Explain the difference between primary and secondary keys.

A.17 Explain the difference between unique and nonunique keys.

A.18 Define a file containing a unique secondary key. Represent an occurrence of that file using an index on the secondary key.

A.19 Define a nonunique secondary key for the file in Question A.18. Represent an occurrence of that file using a linked list on the secondary key.

A.20 Perform the same task as in Question A.19, but using an index to represent the secondary key.

➤ GROUP II QUESTIONS

A.21 Develop an algorithm to produce a report listing the IDs of students enrolled in each class, using the linked-list structure in Figure A-4.

A.22 Develop an algorithm to insert records into the structure in Figure A-4. The resulting structure should resemble the one in Figure A-5.

A.23 Develop an algorithm to produce a report listing the IDs of students enrolled in each class, using the index structure shown in Figures A-8(a), (b), and (c).

A.24 Develop an algorithm to insert a record into the structure in Figure A-8(a), being sure to modify both of the associated indexes in Figures A-8(b) and (c).

A.25 Develop an algorithm to delete a record from the structure in Figure A-34, which shows a secondary key represented with a linked list. If all records for one of the credit-limit categories (say $1000) are deleted, should the associated head pointer also be deleted? Why or why not?

A.26 Develop an algorithm to insert a record into the structure shown in Figure A-34. Suppose the new record has a credit-limit value different from those already established. Should the record be inserted and a new linked list established? Or should the record be rejected? Who should make that decision?

APPENDIX B

Using SQL Server 7.0

The disk enclosed with this text contains the Evaluation Edition of Microsoft SQL Server 7.0. This software can be used anytime after you have finished Chapter 2, although you will get the most from it after you have read through Chapters 6 and/or 7. This version, which can be run with Windows 95, 98, or Windows NT, requires a Pentium 166 MHz processor with 32 MB of RAM and about 120 MB of disk space. This program contains a license valid for 120 days, which should meet the needs of your class assignments.

In this section we will describe how to install this software using Windows 98. The process is similar for Windows 95, and is just slightly different for Windows NT.

INSTALLING THE EVALUATION EDITION

When you insert the CD-ROM into your computer, the self-running installation program will start and display the screen in Figure B-1. If you place the mouse pointer over the second button, the one labeled Install SQL Server 7.0 Prerequisites, a pop-up box will appear informing you whether or not you need to install Prerequisites. If you do, click on this button and follow the instructions. In most cases, especially with Windows 95 and 98, you should not need to install Prerequisites, and so you should start by clicking the third button, Install SQL Server 7.0 Components.

The screen in Figure B-2 will appear next. If you are running Windows 95 or 98, you should click the second button, Database Server—Desktop Edition. In this Appendix we will only be working with the Database Server, although you might want to install the OLAP services on your own after you have read Chapter 14.

Follow the standard installation instructions that appear. Once you have installed the software, click on the Start button and select Programs, Microsoft SQL Server 7.0, as shown in Figure B-3. The various elements of SQL Server 7.0 are listed in the rightmost menu. We will be most concerned with Enterprise Manager and Service Manager. You might want to use Books Online for additional help. Also, Query Analyzer can be used to execute queries against your database once you have created it.

FIGURE B-1

*First Installation
Screen*

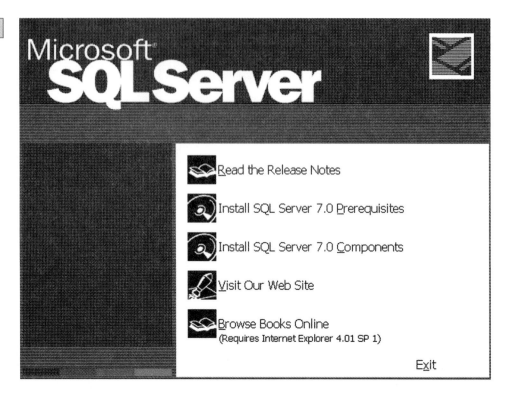

FIGURE B-2

*Second Installation
Screen*

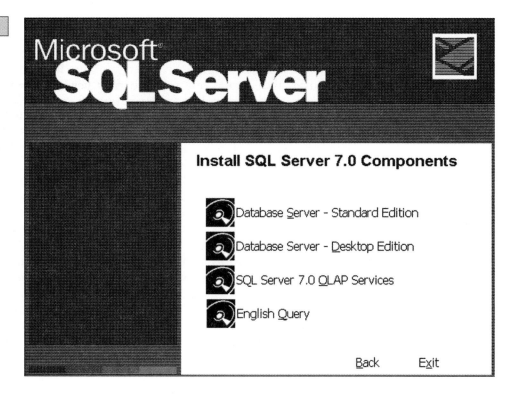

SQL Server 7.0 Programs

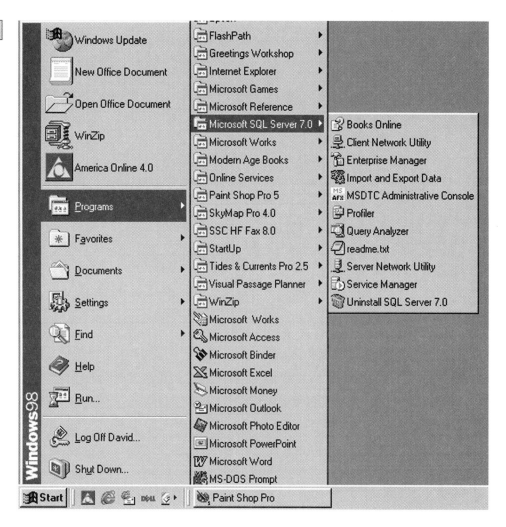

CREATING THE DATABASE

At this point SQL Server should already be running, but just to make sure that it is, select the Service Manager from the menu. Click the Stop button (red square) to close SQL Server, and then click the Start button (green arrow) to restart it. This may seem silly, but it will ensure that SQL Server is running correctly after the installation.

Next, go back to the Programs menu (from the Start button) and select Enterprise Manager. The screen that appears is similar to a File Manager display. Left click on the plus sign next to SQL Server Group, and the name of your computer should appear as a registered server. Left click again on the plus next to the name of your computer, and the list should expand to appear as shown in Figure B-4. There may be some delay as Windows starts the SQL Server 7.0 service.

If the name of your computer does not appear under SQL Server Group, then you may need to register your server manually. In this case, right click on SQL Server Group and select New SQL Server Registration from the pop-up menu. Follow the registration process; click Help if you need to.

Once you have the display shown in Figure B-4, you are ready to create a database. Right click on the Database entry in the list and select New Database from the pop-up menu. The window shown in Figure B-5 will appear. Enter a name for your new database. You can make other changes also, but they are unnecessary; in this figure, we have increased the size of the database to 3 MB.

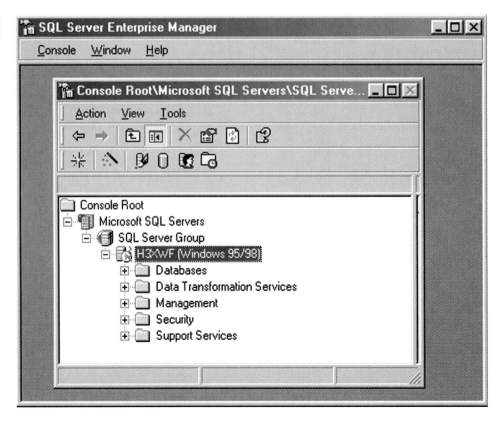

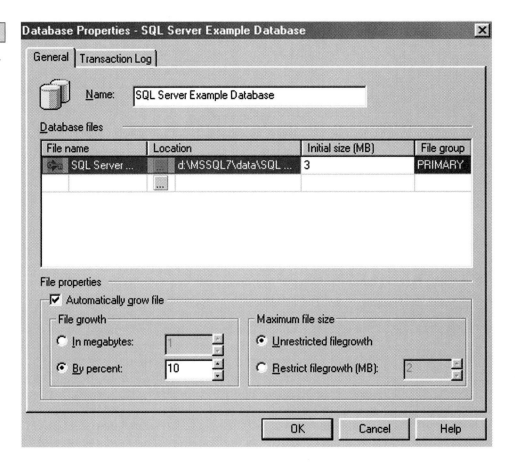

*Components of a
SQL Server Database*

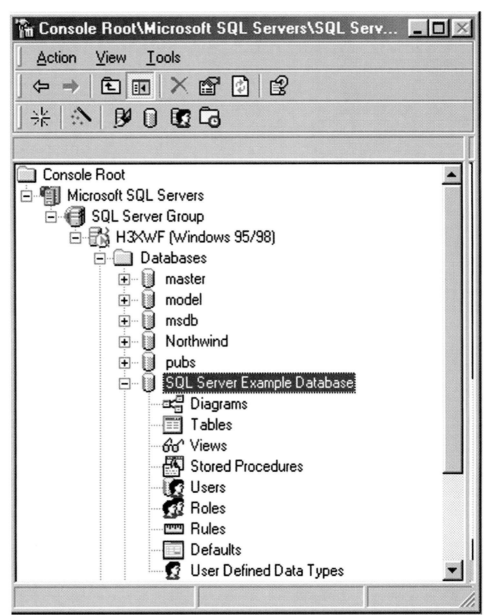

When you are done, click OK, and SQL Server will create the new database with the name you have entered. Here, we use the name SQL Server Example Database.

Once your database has been created, it will appear in the list of databases under the Database entry. Click on the plus sign next to your database and a list of database components will appear starting with Diagrams, Tables, Views, and so forth, as shown in Figure B-6.

CREATING TABLES

To create a table, right click on Tables and select New Table from the pop-up menu. A table definition display like that shown in Figure B-7 will appear. In this figure, we have created a table with a surrogate key attribute ID (called an identity column in SQL Server) and three other attributes FirstName, LastName, and Phone. In this display, nulls are not allowed for ID but are allowed for the other

➤ FIGURE B-7

*SQL Server 7.0 Table
Definition Form*

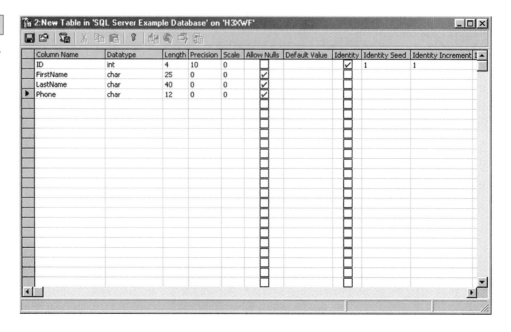

attributes. The Identity Seed specifies the starting value for the surrogate key, and
the Identity Increment specifies the amount added to the maximum ID when
creating a new key value. You can leave these at 1 and 1, as shown in this figure.

At this point, you can begin to see features and functions of SQL Server that extent beyond those of Access. We will just touch the surface of SQL Server in this appendix. See Books Online and go to www.microsoft.com/sql/ for more information.

Tables can also be created using a database diagram. Close the current window
and save the table under the name CUSTOMER. Now, right-click on the Diagrams
entry under your database and select New Database Diagram. Follow the instructions in the wizard to place the CUSTOMER table in the diagram. Initially, the
properties of the columns of your table will not be shown. To expose them, click
on the heading of the table, then click on the Show button (on the toolbar, to the
right of the magnifying glass). Select Column properties, and your table should ap-

➤   FIGURE B-8

*Creating a New
Table from a
Database Diagram*

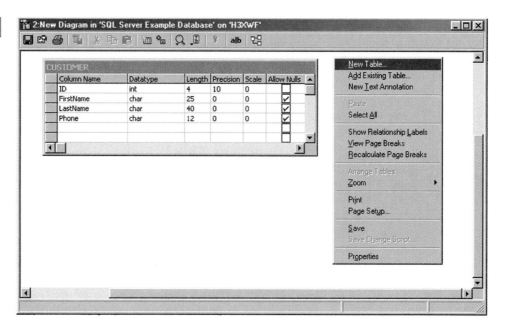

FIGURE B-9

Setting a Primary Key

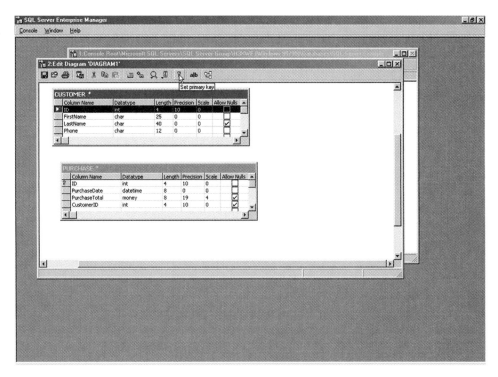

pear like the one in Figure B-8. You can create a second table by right-clicking inside the diagram workspace. The pop-up menu in Figure B-8 will appear. Select New Table, and create a second table like the PURCHASE table in Figure B-9.

At this point, neither table has a primary key. To set the ID column as the primary key, click on the ID column and then click on the Key button (just to the right of the Show button in the toolbar). A small key will appear next to the ID column as shown for the PURCHASE table in Figure B-9. In this figure, the user is in the process of establishing the ID column of CUSTOMER as its primary key.

CREATING RELATIONSHIPS

To create a 1:N relationship between CUSTOMER and PURCHASE, we first need to place the foreign key to CUSTOMER in PURCHASE. This can be done by adding a CustomerID column to PURCHASE and setting the properties of CustomerID to be the same as the ID column in CUSTOMER. Now, to create the relationship, drag ID of CUSTOMER on top of CustomerID of PURCHASE and drop it there. A dialog box like the one in Figure B-10 will appear. Click OK, and the relationship will be established as shown in Figure B-11.

ENTERING AND QUERYING DATA

There are many ways to enter data into SQL Server databases. We can use Microsoft Access or write application programs that use ADO or OLE DB. We can use import utilities or use still other options. For now, we need a simple way to add data and query it just to be certain that our tables are defined correctly and will behave as we expect.

An easy way to enter and view data is shown in Figure B-12. Find your database in the Enterprise Manager window, and click on tables. A listing of available tables appears in the pane to the right. Right-click on the CUSTOMER table, and select Open Table. Because the table has no rows, we can select Return all rows (if

*Defining a
Relationship with
SQL Server*

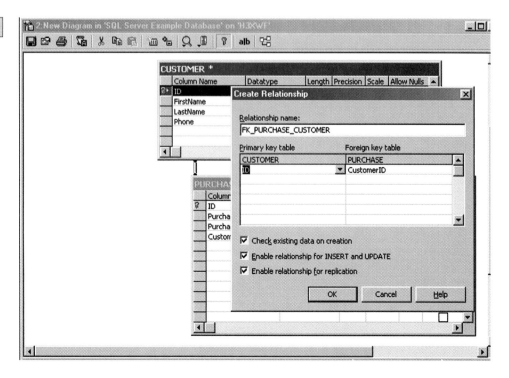

the table had thousands of rows, this would be slow and unhelpful, so the Return Top choice would be made). A window will appear showing the columns of the table. In Figure B-12, the user has keyed in three rows. Note that SQL Server supplied the values of ID because that was defined as an identity column. Close this window after you have entered a number of rows of sample data.

We can use the Query Analyzer to execute a SQL statement against this table (you will need to have read Chapter 9 to understand this example; skip this dis-

*Diagram with Two
Tables at a
Relationship*

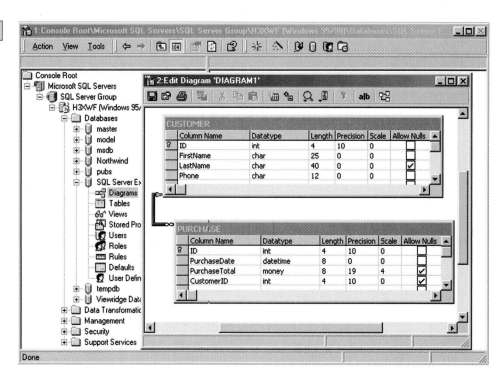

➤   FIGURE B-12

*Using the Open
Table Facility*

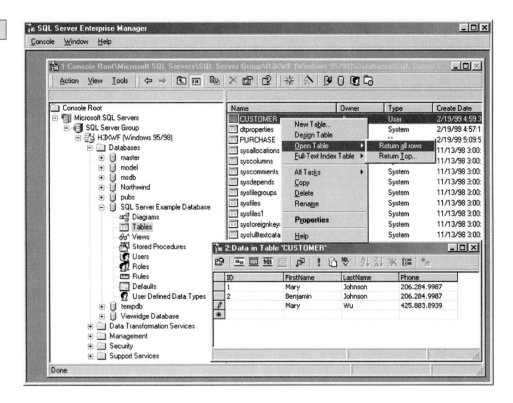

cussion if you have not yet covered Chapter 9). In the Enterprise Manager window, click on Databases and then select Tools/SQL Server Query Analyzer. In the window that opens, select your database from the list box labeled DB: in the toolbar of this window. Click on the button just to the left of DB: to expose the query results window. In the top window, key in any valid SQL statement against a table (or view) in your database. The example in Figure B-13 shows a query for

➤   FIGURE B-13

*Executing a SQL
Statement in the
Query Analyzer*

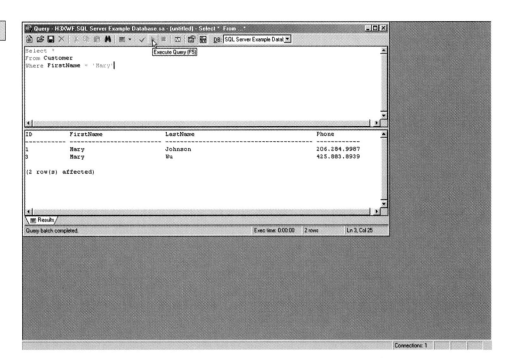

all of the columns of Customer where the first name is Mary. To execute this query, click the green forward arrow (next to the check mark in the toolbar). In Figure B-13, two rows appear as a result.

There are many other functions for Query Analyzer, as its name suggests. You can use it to check the validity of SQL syntax, to time queries, and more. Again, see Books Online or other SQL references for more information.

As an aside, notice the system tables that appear in the table list in Figure B-12. The table *syscolumns*, for example, has a list of all of the columns in your database. You can use Query Analyzer to query on any of these tables.

DEFINING RULES

SQL Server provides several facilities for defining rules on data values. Here we will show how to define a rule in the table definition. Click on Tables in the Enterprise Manager window under your database. In the listing of tables that appears in the right-hand pane, right-click on one of your tables, for instance, PUR-CHASE. Select Design Table from the menu that appears. In the Design Window, click on the second button in the toolbar (Table and Index Properties). A window like that shown in Figure B-14 will appear.

To define a rule, click on the New button in the group box labeled CHECK constraints for table and columns. Now key in a constraint. In Figure B-14, the constraint PurchaseTotal < 10000 has been entered. Close the dialog box and save the table definition, and the constraint will now be defined.

Because this constraint is defined in the DBMS, it will be enforced regardless of the source of the data—Access, ADO program, import, etc., as discussed in Chapter 10. Figure B-15 shows the results when a user tries to enter a PurchaseTotal greater than 10,000 in an Access 97 data entry form that is bound to this database. Clearly, this is an industrial-strength error message that would frighten most end users. The developer most likely would trap this error message in code and substitute a more friendly error message.

➤ FIGURE B-14

Defining a Check Constraint

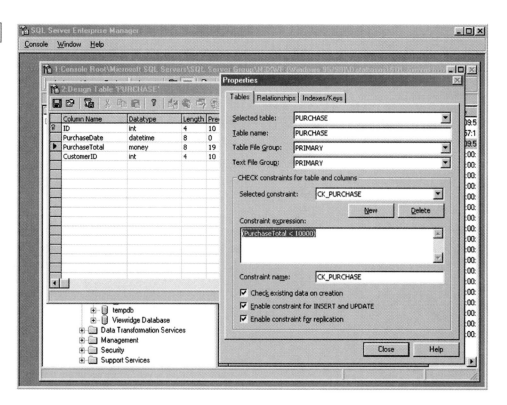

Check Constraint Error from ACCESS 97 Application

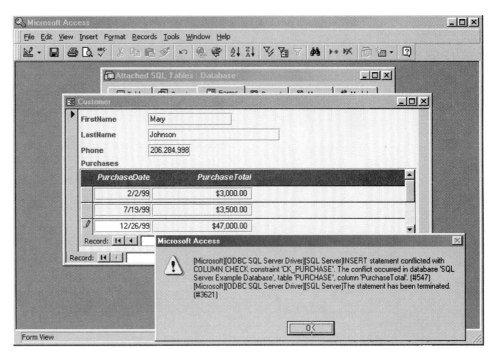

LINKING TO SQL SERVER FROM ACCESS 97

You can link to SQL Server 7.0 databases from Access 97. One way to do this to create a new, empty database in Access, then create an ODBC Data Source Name that points to your database, and then select tables from that Data Source.

To begin, open Access and create a new, blank database. From the File menu, select Get External Data/Link Tables. The window in Figure B-16 will appear. Go to the list box labeled Files of type and select ODBC Databases (the last item in the list) as has been done in Figure B-16. In the ODBC dialog box that appears, click New. In the Create New Data Source window, select the SQL Server driver (at the bottom of

Linking to SQL Server Via an ODBC Data Source

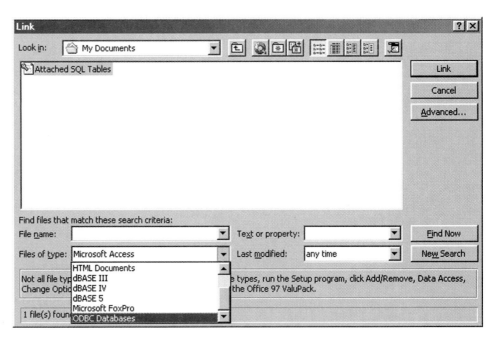

► FIGURE B-17

Specify Local Server When Creating the ODBC Data Source

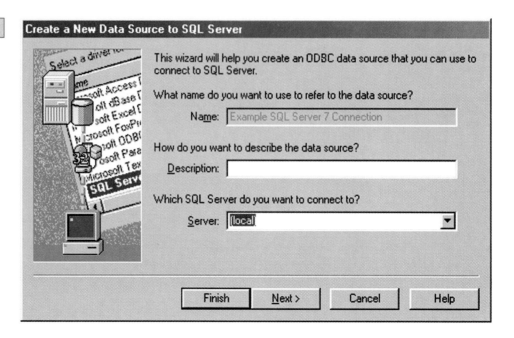

the list) and click Next. Type whatever name you want to use for your new ODBC data source in the text box that appears. Click Next, and then click Finish.

At this point, you will need to connect to SQL server. To help you, a wizard automatically will start in a window labeled Create a New Data Source. Type or select *(local)* in the Server text box as shown in Figure B-17. Click Next and enter a Login ID. Unless you have set up a new user, the only Login ID that will work is *sa* (for system administrator), so type that value in for Login ID (no password will be necessary). Click Next.

The next screen that will appear is shown in Figure B-18. Click the check box labeled Change the default database to: and then select your database from the list. Click Next and then click Finish. In the status box that is shown next, click Test Data Source. The test should complete successfully. If not, review this

► FIGURE B-18

Changing the Default Database to SQL Server Example Database

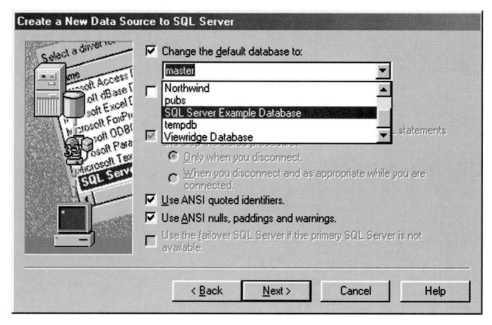

➤ FIGURE B-19

*Selecting
CUSTOMER and
PURCHASE Tables*

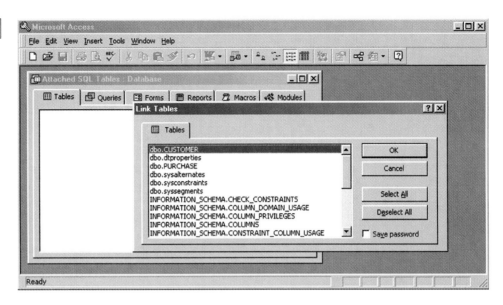

process to ensure that you have followed it correctly. If this test still does not pass, you will need to see your instructor for help.

After the test succeeds, click OK. Your new ODBC data source will now be shown in the Select Data Source window that was generated by Access. Select your new source and click OK. SQL Server will log you in (enter the Login ID *sa* again) and then present a list of tables as shown in Figure B-19. Click on dbo.Customer and dbo.Purchase and then click OK. As shown in Figure B-20, those two tables will now appear as attached tables in your Access database. You can use them like any other Access table.

➤ FIGURE B-20

*Access 97 Database
Linked to SQL Server
Tables*

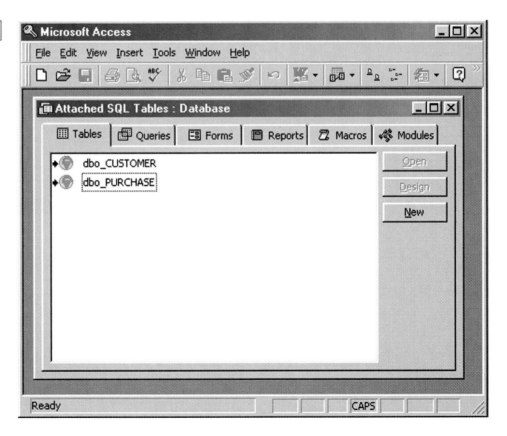

The form in Figure B-15 was generated by the Access Form wizard by including the columns of both these tables. If you defined the Check constraint in your SQL Server database, you will receive the error message in Figure B-15 when you try to enter a PurchaseTotal greater than 10,000.

LINKING TO SQL SERVER FROM ACCESS 2000

Microsoft simplified the process of connection to a SQL Server database when using Access 2000. Using it, you have only one dialog box to fill out to create a project that connects to your existing SQL Server database.

To do this, create a new database and select Project (Existing Database) in the initial dialog box. (If this choice is not visible, click on the tab labeled General.) Click OK, enter a name for your database, and then click Create. The dialog box in Figure B-21 will appear. Enter (*local*) for item 1, enter *sa* with no password for item 2, and click on the down arrow in item 3 to see the list of databases on your

➤ FIGURE B-21

Connecting to the SQL Server Database Named Example One Using Access 2000

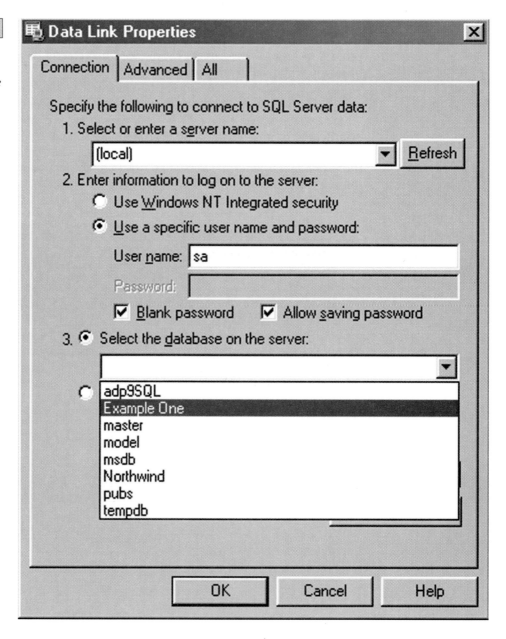

local SQL Server. Select your database from this list. Click OK. You now have an Access database that contains your SQL Server tables. These tables will be processed by Access 2000 like any other Access database, except that the SQL Server DBMS engine will be used instead of the Access local engine.

You can also use Access 2000 to create a new SQL Server database. To do that, open a new database and select Project (New Database). The process is similar to that shown for creating a SQL Server database using the Enterprise manager that was described previously.

CREATING SQL SERVER DATABASES WITH DBAPP

An easy way to create the structure of a SQL Server database is to use a product called DBApp from Wall Data. You can obtain a copy of that product by following the download instructions that you will find at www.prenhall.com/kroenke/. Download the software as described there. You then can create a semantic object model and generate a SQL Server database. See Appendix C for examples.

NEXT STEPS

Once you have completed the activities shown in this appendix, you should complete one of the exercises below. After that, there is much more for you to explore in SQL Server. If you are interested in Web applications, you could adapt the examples shown in Chapter 13 to use the SQL Server database you created in this appendix. An extension of that idea is to create a stored procedure and execute it from ADO in an ASP page. Other topics of interest include importing and exporting data as well as security and user management.

➤ EXERCISES

B.1   When SQL Server is installed, several example databases are installed as well. Find the database named *pubs* in the list of databases and click on it to display its contents. Click on tables. Open the *authors* table and display the top 100 rows. Now open the *titles* and *titleauthor* tables and display 100 rows for each of them. Create a database diagram, and place *authors*, *titles*, and *titleauthor* in it. Print the diagram, and explain the relationship of these three tables.

Using Query Analyzer, create a join of these three tables that displays the first and last names of authors, the titles of the books they have written, and the royalty percentage that they receive. Print the result. Repeat this query but only with display authors who live in California. Print the result.

B.2   Using a process similar to that shown in this appendix, use SQL Server to create the two table database for equipment checkout described in Chapter 2. Once you have created the database, use either Access 97 or Access 2000 to create the Equipment Checkout Form shown in Figure 2-6(b).

B.3   Use SQL Server to create the View Ridge database shown in Figure 10-3. Using the Open Table facility, enter sample data to the CUSTOMER and ARTIST tables. Use the surrogate key values generated by SQL Server to create several rows in the intersection table that represents customer/artist interests. Use Query Analyzer to create a join that displays customers and the artists in which they have an interest.

Working with Cyberprise™ DBApp

Cyberprise™ DBApp is a Windows 95, 98, or NT application that you can use to create semantic object models and transform those models into Microsoft Access or other DBMS databases. In addition, you can reverse engineer an existing database to create a semantic object model from it. Once you have done this, you can modify the model and DBApp will change the associated database schema (and data) accordingly. Finally, you can use DBApp to generate ASP pages to create, read, update, and delete semantic object views from any browser using pure HTML. For this last function, you will need to place the generated ASP pages on a Web server that is running IIS or the Personal Web Server with ASP extensions. A summary of these functions is shown in Figure C-1.

To obtain a copy of DBApp, go to www.prenhall.com/kroenke/ where you will find download instructions. Once you have downloaded the software, install it according to the instructions. There is no charge for using this product in conjunction with your database class. DBApp includes comprehensive documentation. Click Help and you will see the display shown in Figure C-2. You may want to supplement the discussion here with that documentation, especially the discussion in the "Learning to Use DBApp Developer" book that is shown open in Figure C-2.

CREATING A SOM MODEL

To create a new semantic object model (SOM), pick File/New from the menu or click on the new document button (the first button in the toolbar). DBApp will display the window shown in Figure C-3. Here you can choose a starter kit, which is a list of prebuilt models and domains. In this example, we will choose Generic, but you might want to use the others as well.

The next display will show a list of domains in a list on the left-hand side of the screen along with an empty design space on the right. To create a semantic

*Functions of Cyberprise
DBApp*

• To Create a SOM model:
Generate an Access 7 or Access 2000 database from the model.
Generate a SQL Server 7 database from the model (if you have installed SQL Server 7 from the enclosed CD).
Generate SQL statements to create or modify a database.
• To Reverse-Engineer an Existing Database:
Create a copy of the database and modify its schema.
Create a copy of the database, with data, and use modeling to modify the schema and data.
Create a copy of the database schema, without data, and use modeling to modify the schema.
Bind to the database and use modeling to modify the schema and data.
• To Generate a Web Application:
Create semantic object views.
Generate ASP pages for create, read, update, and delete actions from those views.
Generated pages can be placed in Microsoft Visual Interdev for customization.

➤ FIGURE C-2

*DBApp Help
Facilities*

➤ FIGURE C-3

Choosing a Starter Kit

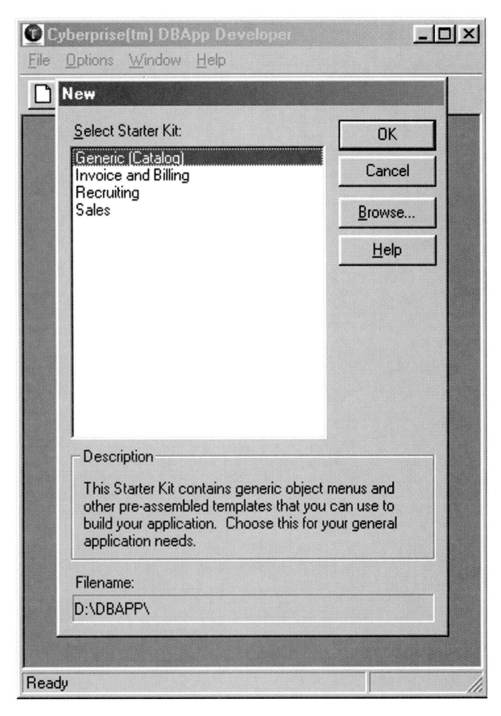

object, hold the left mouse button down in the design space and drag. A rectangle will appear. Release the mouse button and you will see the display shown in Figure C-4. At this point you can name the object whatever you want by typing in the open text box. Name this object STUDENT.

To add attributes to the STUDENT object, click on the Name domain in the left-hand list and drag and drop it into STUDENT. DBApp will create an attribute in STUDENT that inherits all of its properties from the Name domain. Click on Name in STUDENT and press the Enter key. Retype Name to be StudentName in the open text box in the semantic object.

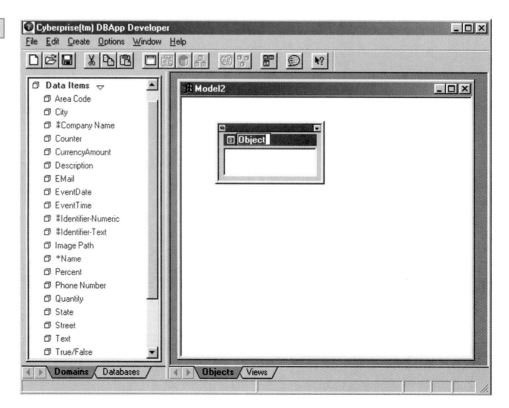

➤ FIGURE C-4

Creating and Naming a Semantic Object

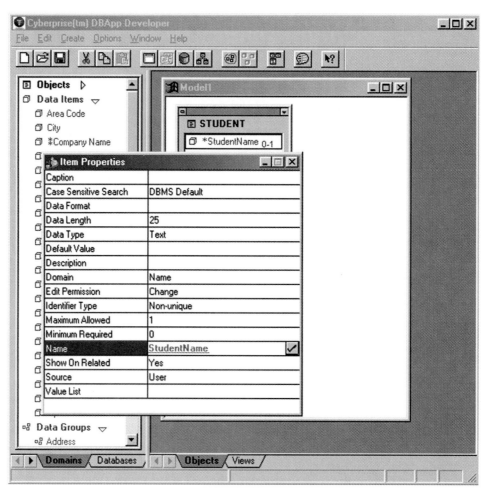

➤ FIGURE C-5

The Properties of StudentName

All domains and attributes (note that attributes are referred to as *items* in DBApp) have properties. To see them, right-click on Name in the domain list. DBApp displays the properties of the Name domain. Now, right-click on StudentName in the STUDENT object. DBApp will show the properties of the StudentName attribute as shown in Figure C-5. These properties will be the same as the Name domain except that the name of the attribute is StudentName. The fact that this property is shown in red means that it has been over-ridden from the property in its underlying domain. Close the property window. Press the 〈Ctrl〉 and Z keys simultaneously to undo the attribute name change. (As an aside, you can undo up to 30 steps of work with DBApp.)

To continue, drag Phone from the Data Group section in the domain list and drop it in STUDENT, just below Name. Click on the arrow next to Phone and it will open to reveal its contents, which are Area Code and Phone Number, as shown in Figure C-6. Drag and drop the Address group in the same way.

To continue with the model, create a second object in the design space by dragging another rectangle and name this second object CLASS. Drag Name and drop it in class. Also drag Quantity from the domain list and drop it in CLASS. Rename Quantity as CreditHours. If you examine the properties of Quantity, you will see that its Data Type is integer. If your school allows fractions of CreditHours, you can change the Data Type of CreditHours by right-clicking to reveal the property sheet and changing the data type to 7-digit Decimal Number.

To create a relationship between two semantic objects, click on the small icon just to the left of the word STUDENT at the top of the STUDENT semantic

➤ FIGURE C-6

Example of a Group Attribute

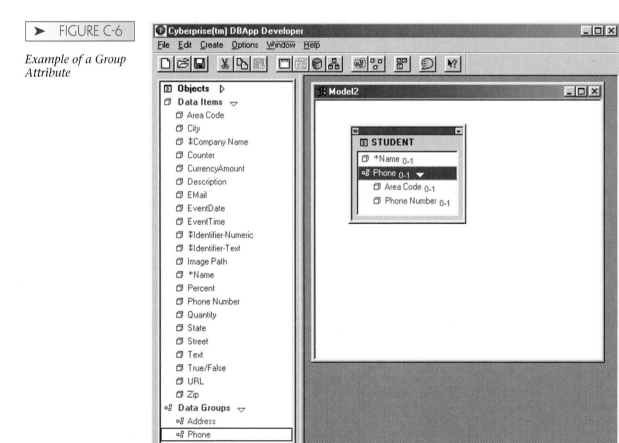

Creating a Relationship Between STUDENT and CLASS

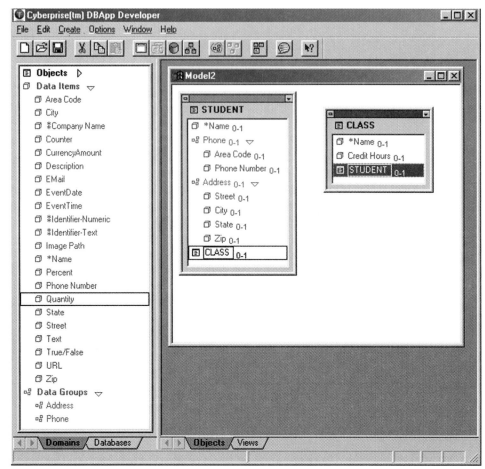

object. Drag this icon and drop it in CLASS, just below CreditHours. A relationship will be created between STUDENT and CLASS. Your model should now appear as shown in Figure C-7.

The cardinalities of the relationship can be modified by clicking on the 0-1 subscript of either the STUDENT or CLASS object link attributes. When you do this, the display shown in Figure C-8 will appear. Open the list box labeled Maximum allowed to find N. You can enter a specific number such as 7 if you would like. Doing this will have no impact on your schema, but it will cause the generated ASP pages to enforce this limit.

Continue with these operations to create a third object, ADVISOR, with the attributes shown in Figure C-9. To observe the consequences of domain inheritance, change the name of Phone in the domain list. Do this by clicking on Phone and then pressing the Enter key. Type Campus Phone as the new name of the domain. Notice that both Phone in STUDENT and Phone in ADVISOR have been changed to Campus Phone. These attributes inherit any change to their domain's properties.

You are now ready to generate a database. Since DBApp can modify your schema once you have created it, you do not need to be finished when you generate your first database. You can generate it as you go along if you like.

Click on the small disk in the toolbar (the ninth icon in the toolbar), or select Create/Database from the menu. Save your model under some convenient name; we used Example1 here. After the model has been saved, DBApp will display the window shown in Figure C-10. You can pick the DBMS to be used for the database from this list.

> FIGURE C-8

*Changing
Relationship
Cardinalities*

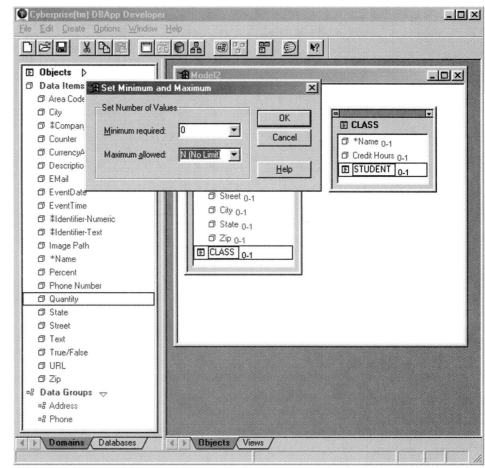

Because we had installed SQL Server 7.0 prior to this example, it appears in the list. To generate tables in a SQL Server database, click on SQL Server and then log in with SQL Server as discussed in Appendix B. Use the (local) server, enter *sa* for Login ID, and change the default database to be the one in which you want the tables placed. Here we used SQL Server Example Database, which was created in Appendix B. At that point, the tables necessary for the model were created by DBApp and placed into SQL Server Example Database. Figure C-11 shows the tables that were generated for the model in Figure C-9.

If you have not installed SQL Server but have installed Access, you can select it from the list in Figure C-10, and DBApp will generate an Access database.

You also can cause DBApp to display the SQL statements that it is about to execute before generating a database. To do that, select Create/SQL Text Only, and the SQL statements will be placed in a text file in a directory named SQL in the DBApp directory. You must do this before you generate your database; otherwise there is no SQL in the queue awaiting execution.

REVERSE ENGINEERING A SOM MODEL

In addition to creating new models, you can use DBApp to generate a model from all or part of an existing database. To do this, you first need to create an ODBC Data Source Name to the database you wish to reverse-engineer. In this example, we will use Northwind.mdb, a database that ships with Microsoft Access.

To set up an ODBC Data Source to Northwind, first open the ODBC Administrator by selecting File/ODBC Administrator from within DBApp. Select

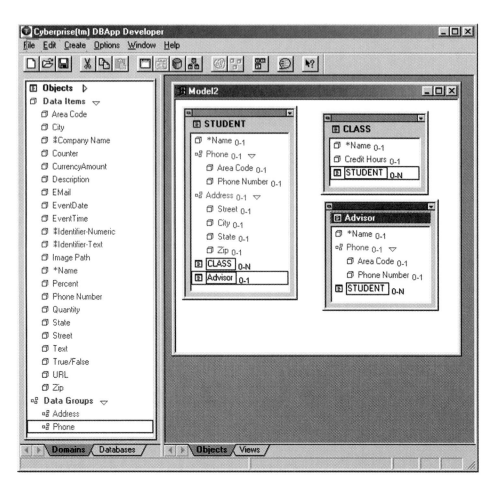

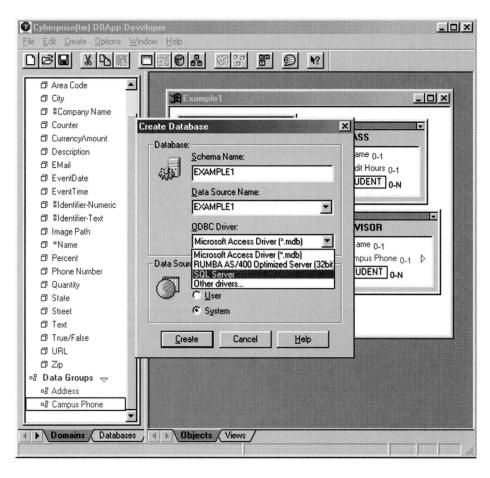

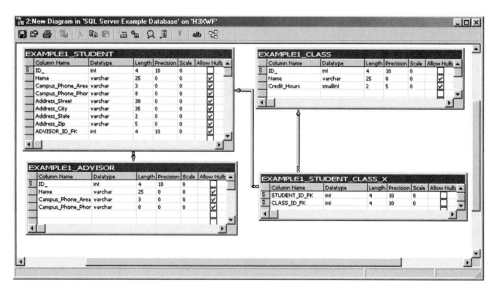

SQL Server Tables for the Model in Figure C-9

the System tab as shown in Figure C-12 and click Add. Select Microsoft Access from the list of drivers, and then click Finish. Enter a name for the data source (we used Northwind in this example), and click the Select button. Browse to the directory where Northwind.mdb is located. This location varies depending on how you installed Access. If you do not know where it is, use Windows Find to

Using the ODBC Administrator for Creating an ODBC Data Source

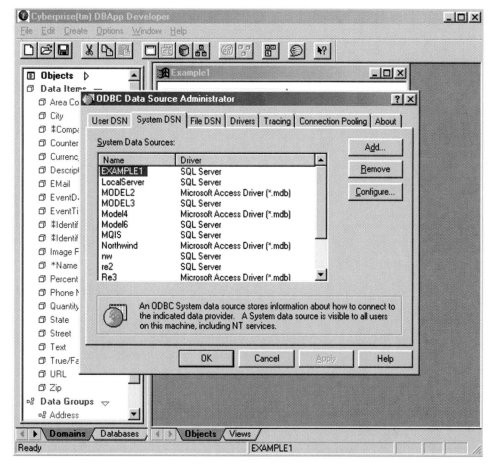

FIGURE C-13

Reverse Engineering
Northwind

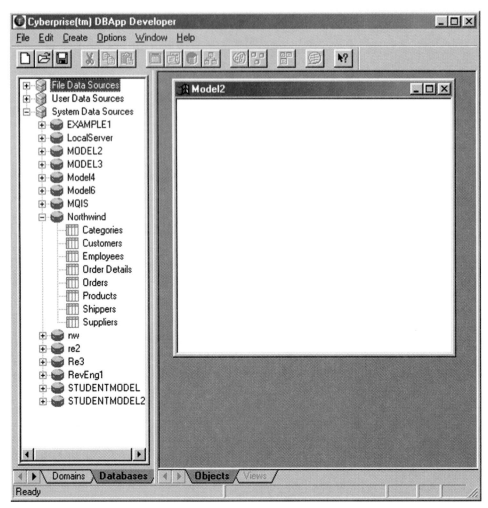

locate the file named Northwind.mdb. Go to that directory in the ODBC administrator and click OK.

Open a new model within DBApp. Look to the bottom of the domain list and click on the tab labeled Databases. DBApp will display a list of your File, User, and System data sources. Since we created a System data source, click there and look for the name of your data source. Click on the plus button to the left of it, and all of the tables in the database will be shown (as in the left-hand pane of Figure C-13). Drag the name of your data source (here Northwind) onto the empty design space in the window to the right. Save the model; we used the name RE1 for this example.

The dialog box shown in Figure C-14 will now appear. Click Help to find out about the various options. For now, select the last option, which will create a new database but not copy any data; it will set up the DBApp import files for copying later. You normally would use this option if you wanted to apply filters to copy only some of the data, but we will omit this exercise in this appendix.

DBApp now generates a database that conforms to the model. Select a DBMS from the list, and then click Create. The result of this action will be a model like the one shown in Figure C-15 along with a database that has a copy of the tables from Northwind. You now can make changes to this model and use DBApp to change the database structure.

We will use a different example to illustrate the copying of data and the changing of schemas. Close your model and open a new one. Click on the

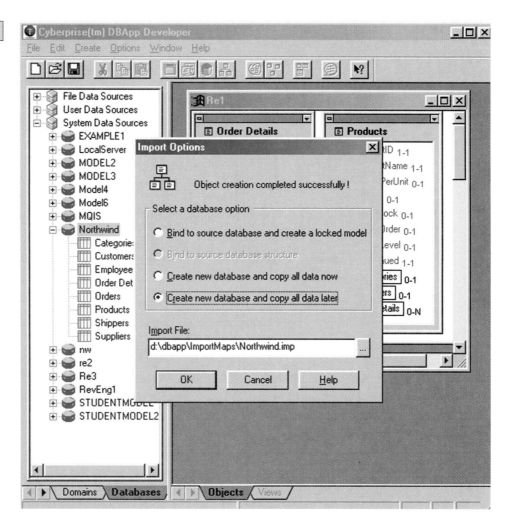

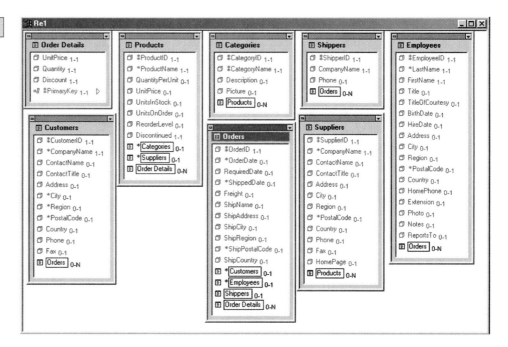

FIGURE C-16

Building a Two Table Extract of the Northwind Database

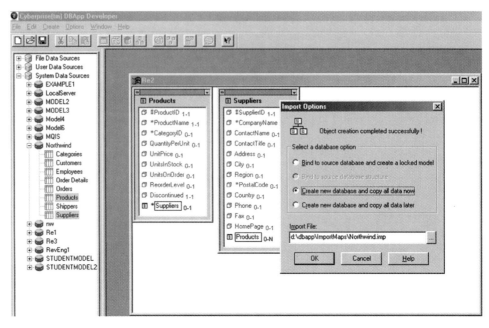

Databases tab and select System Data Sources. Click on Northwind to open the table list. Holding the ⟨Ctrl⟩ key down, click on Products and Suppliers. Drag those two tables onto the empty design space and drop them there. Save your model with a name (we used RE2), and select the third option, Create new database and copy all data now, as shown in Figure C-16. Click OK, then select your DBMS. We again used SQL Server in this example. You can use Access as well.

If you select SQL Server, you will need to log in three times: the first time via the ODBC driver to set up the connection, the second time just before creating the tables, and the third time when adding data to the tables. Use the Login ID *sa* as discussed in Appendix B. If you use Access, the process will be much simpler.

At this point you have a new database with data in two tables: Products and Suppliers. The two tables have a 1:N relationship as shown in the model in Figure C-17. Suppose that we want to make two changes. First, we want to have the possibility of multiple Suppliers for a product and, second, we want to be able to have many Contacts for a given Supplier. We will now make those two changes to the model and observe their consequence in the underlying database.

First, change the maximum cardinality of the Suppliers link in the Products object from 1 to N. Do this by clicking on the 0-1 subscript on Suppliers in Products and selecting N from the Maximum cardinality list in the dialog box that appears. This is the same process as described before.

Now, to allow for multiple contacts for a supplier, we will first create a group for Contact data and then set the maximum cardinality for that group to N. To create the group, hold the ⟨Shift⟩ key down, click on ContactName and then on ContactTitle. They both should be highlighted as shown in Figure C-18(a). Click on the group button, the one that looks like a pizza, in the toolbar. The mouse pointer is over that button in Figure C-18(a). Enter the name Contact in the dialog box that appears and click OK. You will now have a group containing ContactName and ContactTitle attributes. To allow for multiple contacts, set the maximum cardinality of the Contact group to be greater than one. Again, click on the 0-1 subscript of the Contact group and set the maximum cardinality. In Figure C-18(b), the maximum cardinality is being set to N. Click OK.

*Semantic Objects
Resulting from
Products and
Suppliers Tables*

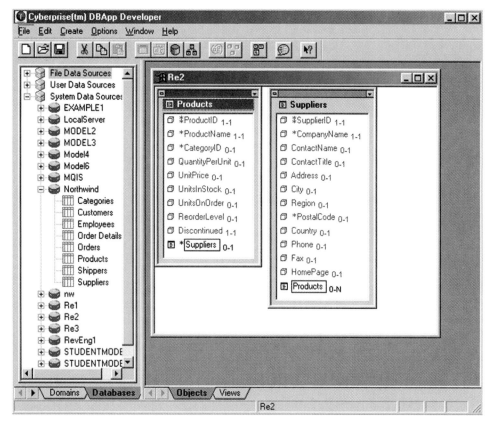

Before proceeding, consider what DBApp needs to do. Because the relationship between Products and Suppliers has been changed from 1:N to N:M, a new intersection table must be created. The database, however, has data so DBApp will need to move the data into the intersection table to preserve the relationship. Second, a new table will need to be created for the Contact data and all of the data moved to that new table. All of this will be done when you click on the database icon or Select.

Figure C-19 shows the SQL Server schema that was created by DBApp after these changes. Note that the intersection table has been correctly created and the new table, Contact, has been generated. Figure C-20 shows a portion of the data. Again, observe that the data has been moved correctly to the new tables.

This example shows the benefit of working at the level of a model rather than at the level of a database. Making these changes manually would have required at least several hours of labor.

PUBLISHING A DATABASE VIEWS ON THE WEB

In addition to schema creation and modification, DBApp can generate a series of ASP pages that will enable the user to create, read, update, and delete data in database views over the Web. (See Chapter 10 if these terms are unfamiliar to you.) These pages can be processed by IIS running on Windows NT or Windows 2000 and also by the Personal Web Server running on Windows 95 or 98. In the latter case, the components necessary for ASP page processing will need to be installed. See the documentation for Personal Web Server for more information.

The process of generating such pages is simple. First, create the views that you want to publish, then run the DBApp Web Publishing wizard to create the

➤ FIGURE C-18

(a) Creating a Contact Group (b) Setting the Maximum Cardinality of Contact

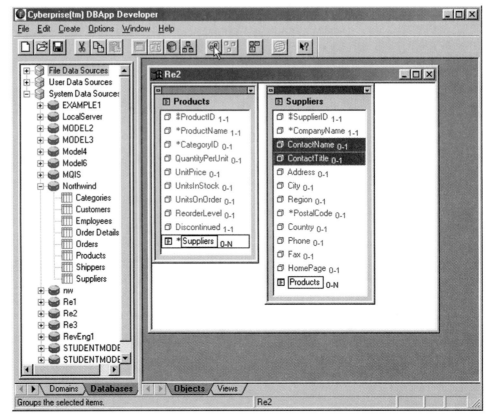

(a)

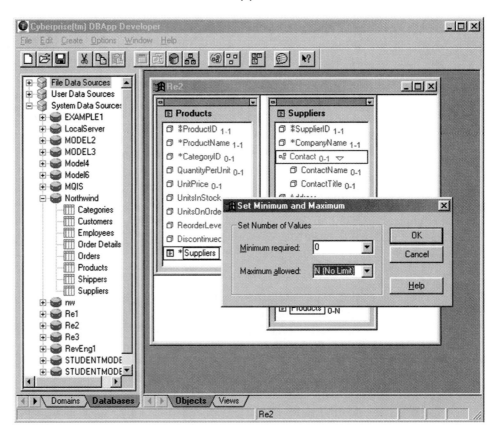

(b)

 FIGURE C-19

SQL Server Database Structure after Model Changes

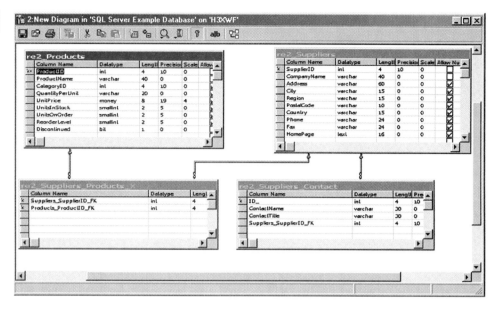

pages. Those pages need to be placed in a directory in which IIS or the Personal Web Server can find them. Because the pages use JScript, the directory will need to be marked for script execution. You can do this by modifying the properties of the application directory. Consult either the Microsoft documentation or the DBApp documentation for more information if necessary.

We will illustrate the page generation process using the RE2 model created in the previous section. Of course, you can use any model you want for this process. To generate a semantic object view, open the model you wish to work with (here, RE2.apm) and click on the View tab at the bottom of your design window. The left-hand pane now changes to display a list of views and objects.

 FIGURE C-20

Sample Database Data after Model Changes

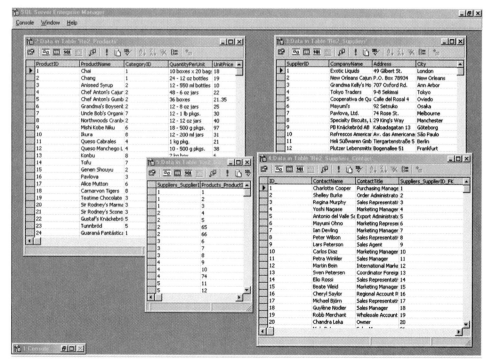

> ➤ FIGURE C-21

Initial Products Form and List Views

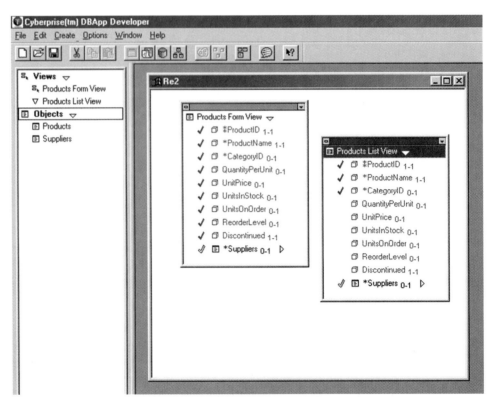

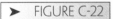

> ➤ FIGURE C-22

Modifications on the Products List View

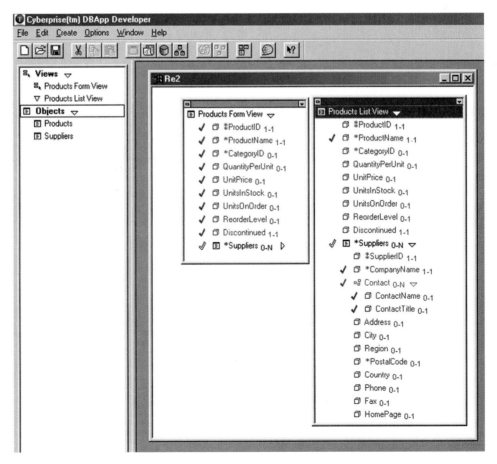

In the objects section, drag Products and drop it on the empty design space. Two windows will open in the design space as shown in Figure C-21. The Products List View is used to display a set of object instances. It is used most often to display the results of a query. The second view, the Products Form view, is used to enter and change data values. Only one object instance is shown at a time in a Form view.

Consider the List View first. A check mark next to an item indicates that the item will appear in the Web form. In this case, ProductID, ProductName, and CategoryID have been checked by default. Assume we do not want ProductID or CategoryID in our list view. To remove them from the view, double-click on their check marks; the check marks will disappear indicating that they have been removed from the view. Now, click on the arrow next to Suppliers to open it. This group represents the Suppliers object link in the semantic object view. Modify the check marks so that CompanyName and Contact will appear in the list view. Expand the Contact group, and your screen should look like the one in Figure C-22.

Now consider the Products Form view. Remove check marks so that only ProductID, ProductName, UnitPrice, UnitsInStock, and CompanyName (in Suppliers) are in the view. Your screen should look like the one in Figure C-23.

Follow a similar process for the Suppliers view. Add or remove whatever attributes you deem appropriate. One possible set of Supplier views is shown in Figure C-24. Now we are ready to publish the application on the Web.

To start the Web publishing wizard, select File/Publish Web Application. Save the model when asked to do so, then click Next. The views to be published are shown in the next screen. These are the ones we want to publish, so click Next

➤ FIGURE C-23

Modifications to the Products Form View

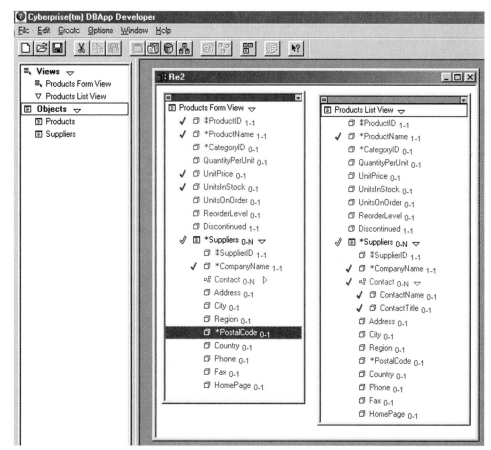

Final Set of Views

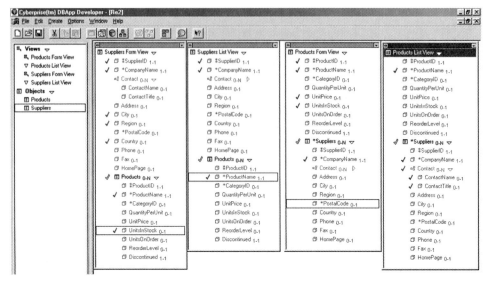

again. In the next screen, shown in Figure C-25, DBApp is asking which set of templates you want to use. Select the defaults by clicking Next again.

The wizard next needs to know in which directory to store the ASP pages. You should browse to the direction that you have set up with your Web publisher. Alternatively, you can use the directory that DBApp selects and then create Web publishing privileges for that directory. Either way, enter a valid directory here and click Next again. In the next screen enter Sample Application or some other title and click Next again.

In the following panel, accept the default selection not to register the application now. In the next screen, shown in Figure C-26, you can enter a default

Specifying the Views to Publish

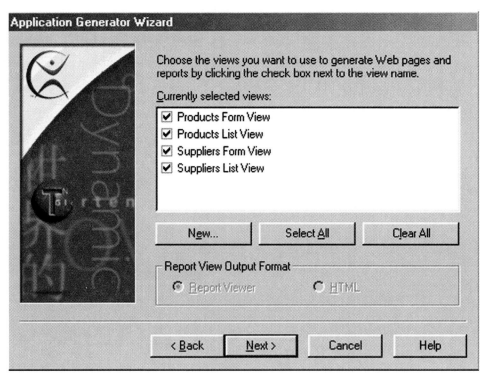

FIGURE C-26

Screen for Setting a Default User Name and Password

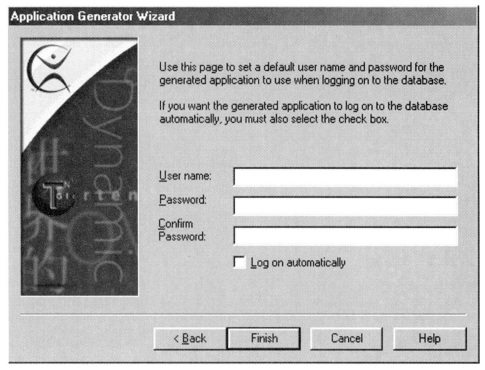

Login ID and Password. You would do this if you were creating an application that you wanted strangers to be able to access. Because we are not doing so, enter nothing and click Finish. At this point, DBApp will generate the ASP pages. When it is completed, it will ask if you want to open the Microsoft Web Publishing Wizard. Click No.

To run your generated application, open a browser and enter the directory into which you have placed your ASP pages, followed by the keyword *default.asp*. Thus, if you have placed your pages in the directory mywebs/apps/, then key the characters /mywebs/apps/default.asp into the address field of your browser and press ⟨Enter⟩. You may need to modify this text somewhat depending on how you have set up your Web server.

At this point, your browser should connect with the Web server and present a login page. If you are using SQL Server for your database, enter *sa* with no password or some other valid Login ID, and click Login. If you are using Access, enter nothing and click Login.

At this point you can use your pages to process your database. Select the Products page from the list box displayed, and click Query. You will see a display like that in Figure C-27. Since DBApp support query by form, you can enter search characters into this form. In Figure C-27, the user has entered >0 for UnitsInStock and New* in CompanyName. This user is searching for products for which there are more than zero in stock and in which the name of the supplier begins with *New*.

When the user clicks Search, the list view shown in Figure C-28 will be displayed. Notice that all of the products are supplied by companies whose names start with New. If the user now clicks on one of the products, that product will be displayed in the Products Form View. This has been done in Figure C-29. The pages generated here are very interactive, and you really need to create this application to gain an appreciation of them.

FIGURE C-27

Using Query by Form

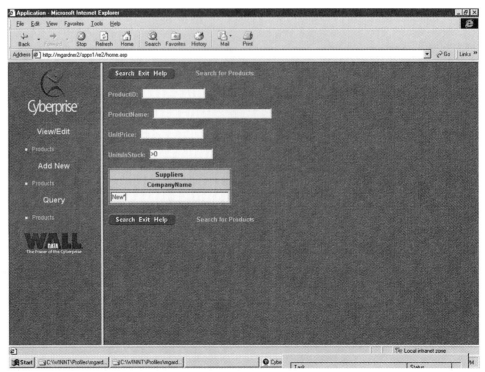

As an aside, reflect for a moment on what DBApp had to do to respond to this query. The filter on CompanyName applies to the Suppliers table, but the list view is based on the Products table. Furthermore, there is a N:M relationship between these two tables. This means that DBApp had to create a left outer join and an inner join across the intersection table to respond to this query.

FIGURE C-28

Results for Search in Figure C-27

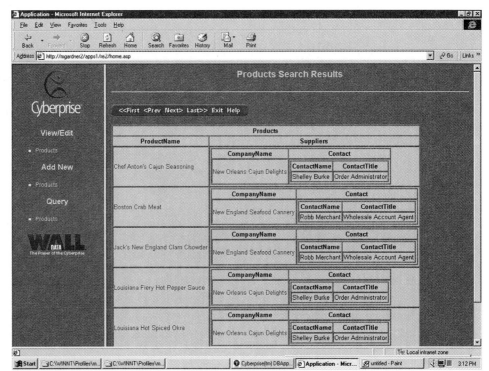

> FIGURE C-29

*Product Shown in
Products Form View*

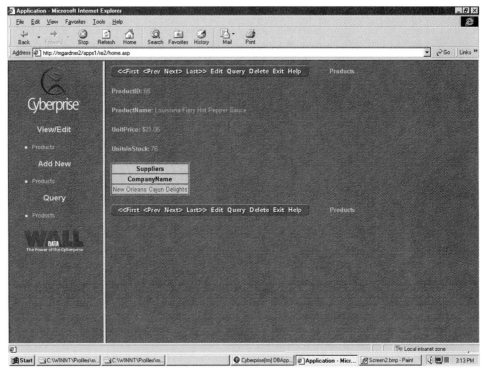

NEXT STEPS

There are many other features and functions of DBApp besides those described here. You should consult the DBApp help documentation for more information. A good place to start is with Applications/Development Process Overview. You can use DBApp to normalize non-normalized databases and spreadsheet data. See the normalization overview topic for documentation about that process.

> EXERCISES

C.1 Use DBApp to create the Highline University model described in Chapter 4. Create the model shown in Figure 4-13. Generate a database in either Access or SQL Server 7.0. Examine the resulting schema and explain how each table relates to the model. Change the model so that PROFESSORs can work in more than one DEPARTMENT. Regenerate your database and explain the changes that were made.

C.2 Use DBApp to create a model with an example of each of the following types of semantic object (see Chapter 4):

    a. Simple

    b. Composite

    c. Compound

    d. Hybrid

    e. Archetype/version

    f. Association

Generate a database from your model and examine the resulting tables. Explain how DBApp does or does not use the same design principles as described in Chapter 7.

C.3   Open a new model in DBApp and select the Recruiting starter kit. Examine the model and generate a database. Suggest ways in which you think this model could be improved. Make changes to the model and regenerate a database. Explain changes that were made in the database structure.

C.4   Complete Exercise C.1. Create a Form and List view for each of the objects and use DBApp to generate ASP pages for processing them. Place the generated pages in a directory for processing by IIS or the Personal Web Server. Open a browser, and use the pages to create sample DEPARTMENT, STUDENT, and PROFESSOR objects. Use the Web pages to link several of the objects. Open the underlying database, and examine the foreign key fields. Justify the foreign key values in light of the links that you made among the objects.

C.5   Install SQL Server 7.0 from the enclosed disk, if you have not already done so. Following the example in this appendix, create an ODBC System data source to the pubs database. You will need to pick SQL Server as the driver and follow the SQL server login process. Enter (local) for server, *sa* for Login ID with no password, and change the default database to pubs. Reverse engineer the publishers, authors, titles, and titleauthor tables, and create a new Access (use SQL Server if you do not have Access) database to copy data. Name your new database pubs2. Change the model of pubs2 so that a title can have more than one publisher. Regenerate the database and examine the changes. Open the title table in the pubs database and print the rows. Open the title table in pubs2 and print the rows. Also open the new intersection table in pub2 and print the rows. Explain the differences among these tables.

C.6   Create pubs2 as described in example C.5. Generate a view for publisher, author, and title. Be sure that your author view includes all of the titles for that author and that your title view includes the names of all authors for that title. Generate Web pages for these views. Use the Web pages to assign second and third authors to some of the titles. Close your Web application and examine the foreign key values in the database tables. Explain those values in light of the title/author additions you made.

GLOSSARY

Abstract data type: In SQL3, a user-defined structure having methods, data items, and identifiers; a version of an OOP object. Persistence is provided by binding the ADT to a column of a relation.

Abstraction: A generalization of something that hides some hopefully unimportant details but enables work with a wider class of types. A recordset is an abstraction of a relation. A rowset is an abstraction of a recordset.

Action/object menu: A system of menus in which the top menu refers to actions and the lowest menus refer to the objects on which those actions are taken.

Active Server Page: See ASP.

ActiveX control: An ActiveX object that supports interfaces that allow the control's properties and methods to be accessed in many different development environments.

ActiveX object: A COM object that supports a slimmed-down version of the OLE object specification.

ADO: Active data objects; an implementation of OLE DB that is accessible via both object and non–object-oriented languages; used primarily as a scripting language (JScript, VBScript) interface to OLE DB.

ADT: See Abstract Data Type.

After-image: A record of a database entity (normally a row or a page) after a change used in recovery to perform rollforward.

Anomaly: An undesirable consequence of a data modification used primarily in discussions of normalization. With an insertion anomaly, facts about two or more different themes must be added to a single row of a relation. With a deletion anomaly, facts about two or more themes are lost when a single row is deleted.

API: See Application Program Interface.

Application: A business computer system that processes a portion of a database to meet a user's information needs. It consists of menus, forms, reports, queries, Web pages, and application programs.

Application design: The process of creating the structure of programs and data to meet the application's requirements; also the structure of the users' interface.

Application metadata: Data dictionary; data concerning the structure and contents of application menus, forms, and reports.

Application plan: In DB2, a set of access paths for each SQL statement in an application program. It includes information about database tables' structures, available indexes, and data storage structures.

Application program: A custom-developed program for processing a database. It can be written in a standard procedural language such as COBOL, C++, or Visual Basic, or in a language unique to the DBMS.

Application Program Interface (API): A set of program procedures or functions that can be called to invoke a set of services. The API includes the names of the procedures and functions and a description of the name, purpose, and data type of parameters to be provided. For example, a DBMS product could provide a library of functions to call for database services. The names of procedures and their parameters constitute the API for that library.

Archetype/version object: A structure of two objects that represents multiple versions of a standardized item; for example, a SOFT-PRODUCT (the archetype) and PRODUCT-RELEASE (the version of the archetype). The identifier of the version always includes the archetype object.

ASP: Active Server Page. A file containing markup language, server script, and client script that is processed by the Active Server Processor in Microsoft IIS.

Association object: An object that represents the combination of at least two other objects and that contains data about that combination. It is often used in contracting and assignment applications.

Atomic: A set of actions that is completed as a unit. Either all actions are completed or none is.

Atomic transaction: A group of logically related database operations that is performed as a unit. Either all of the operations are performed, or none of them is.

Attribute: (1) A column of a relation; also called a column, field, or data-item. (2) A property in an entity or semantic object. (3) A data or relationship property in an OOP object. (4) In the ODMG-93 model, an implementation of an object property in an OOP implementation such as C++ or Smalltalk.

Authorization rules: A set of processing permissions that describes which users or user groups can take particular actions against particular portions of the database.

Axis: In OLAP, a coordinate of a cube or hypercube.

Band: The section of a report definition that contains the format of a report section. There normally are bands for the report heading and footing, page heading and footing, and the detail line of the report. There are also bands for group or break points within the report.

Banded report writer: A report writer in which the sections of the reports are defined by bands. Also see Band.

Base table: In relational implementations, the table from which relational views are defined.

Before-image: A record of a database entity (normally a row or a page) before a change used in recovery to perform rollback.

Bill of materials: A recursive data structure in which a part (or, in general, any element) can be both an assembly of other parts and a component of other assemblies.

Binary relationship: A relationship between exactly two entities or tables.

Bind: To connect a program variable or a GUI control to a column of a table or query.

Bottom-up database design: The design of a database that works from the detailed and specific to the general. Although this sort of design takes little time, it may result in a database that is too narrow in scope.

Boyce-Codd normal form: A relation in third normal form in which every determinant is a candidate key.

Branch: A subelement of a tree that may consist of one or many nodes.

Buffer: An area of memory used to hold data. For a read, data is read from a storage device into a buffer; for a write, data is written from the buffer to storage.

Built-in function: In SQL, any of the functions COUNT, SUM, AVG, MAX, or MIN.

Callback: An OOP design practice by which an object passes its identity to another object with the expectation that the called object will notify the calling object when some event occurs. Often the event is the destruction of the called object, but used for other purposes as well.

Candidate key: An attribute or group of attributes that identifies a unique row in a relation. One of the candidate keys is chosen to be the primary key.

Cardinality: In a binary relationship, the maximum or minimum number of elements allowed on each side of the relationship. The maximum cardinality can be 1:1, 1:N, N:1, or N:M. The minimum cardinality can be optional–optional, optional–mandatory, mandatory–optional, or mandatory–mandatory.

Cartesian product: A relational operation on two relations, A and B, producing a third relation, C, with C containing the concatenation of every row in A with every row in B.

Cascading deletion: A property of a relationship that indicates that when one row is deleted, related rows should be deleted as well.

CCP: Communications Control Program; a program that controls and administers transactions requests and responses in a teleprocessing system. The CCP routes transactions to the correct application programs and returns responses to the correct user terminal.

CGI: See Common Gateway Interface.

Check box: In a GUI environment, an element of the user interface in which a user can select one or more items from a list. Items are selected by clicking on them.

Checkpoint: The point of synchronization between a database and a transaction log. All buffers are force-written to external storage. This is the standard definition of checkpoint, but this term is sometimes used in other ways by DBMS vendors.

Child: A row, record, or node on the many side of a one-to-many relationship.

Child and twin pointer scheme: In DL/I, a technique used to represent segment relationships of a data base record in storage.

Child pointer: In the child and twin pointer scheme, the address of a child node.

Client computer: (1) A microcomputer on a local area network with client–server architecture. In a database application, the client computer processes database application programs. Requests for actions on the database are sent to the database computer. (2) In the three-tier architecture, a computer that hosts a browser for accessing a Web server.

Client–server database architecture: The structure of a networked computing system in which one computer (usually a microcomputer) performs services on behalf of other computers (usually a microcomputer). For a database system, the server computer, which is called a database server, processes the DBMS, and client computers process the application programs. All database activities are carried out by the database server.

Client–server system: A system of two or more computers in which at least one computer provides services for one or more other computers. The services can be database services, communication services, printer services, or some other function.

COBOL: Common Business-Oriented Language. The most widely used third-generation language for business applications.

CODASYL: Conference on Data Systems Languages. A nonprofit committee of vendor, user, and academic personnel that established and maintain the conventions for COBOL. The DBTG, or DataBase Task Group, developed a network model that was popular in the 1970s and early 1980s but is now being phased out.

Collection: An object that contains a group of other objects. Examples are the ADO Names, Errors, and Parameters collections.

Column: A logical group of bytes in a row of a relation or a table. The meaning of a column is the same for every row of the relation.

COM: Component Object Model; a Microsoft specification for the development of object-oriented programs that enables such programs to work together readily.

COM object: An object that conforms to the COM standard.

Command: A statement input to a database application by which users specify the activity to be performed. Contrast this with Menu.

Commit: A command issued to the DBMS to make database modifications permanent. Once the command has been processed, the changes are written to the database and to a log in such a way that they will survive system crashes and other failures. A commit is usually used at the end of an atomic transaction. Contrast this with Rollback.

Common Gateway Interface: A standard for defining forms and sending and receiving form data in HTML documents.

Communications Control Program: See CCP.

Complex network: A collection of entities, objects, or relations and their relationships, of which at least one of the relationships is complex (many to many).

Composite group: A group of attributes in a semantic object that is multi-valued and contains no other object attributes.

Composite key: A key with more than one attribute.

Composite object: An object with at least one multi-value attribute or attribute group. It is called a composite object because the key of the relation that represents the multi-value attribute or group is a composite key.

Compound object: An object that contains at least one other object.

Computed value: A column of a table that is computed from other column values. Values are not stored but are computed when they are to be displayed.

Concurrency: A condition in which two or more transactions are processed against the database at the same time. In a single CPU system, the changes are interleaved; in a multi-CPU system, the transactions may be processed simultaneously, and the changes on the database server are interleaved.

Concurrency transparency: In a distributed database system, the condition in which application programs do not know and do not need to know whether data is being processed concurrently. The DDBMS organizes update activities so that the results produced when concurrent processing is under way are consistent with the results that would occur if there were no concurrent processing.

Concurrent processing: In teleprocessing applications, the sharing of the CPU among several transactions. The CPU is allocated to each transaction in a round robin or in some other fashion for a certain period of time. Operations are performed so quickly that they appear to users to be simultaneous. In local area networks and other distributed applications, concurrent processing is used to refer to the (possibly simultaneous) processing of applications on multiple computers.

Concurrent update problem: An error condition in which one user's data changes are overwritten by another user's data changes. Same as lost update problem.

Conflict: Two operations conflict if they operate on the same data item and at least one of the operations is a write.

Consistency: Two or more concurrent transactions are consistent if the result of their processing is the same as it would have been if they had been processed in some serial order.

Consistent schedule: An ordered list of transaction operations against a database in which the result of the processing is consistent.

Constraint: A rule concerning the allowed values of attributes whose truth can be evaluated. A constraint usually does not include dynamic rules such as "SalesPersonPay can never decrease" or "Salary now must be greater than Salary last quarter."

CPU: Central Processing Unit; the portion of the computer hardware that processes arithmetic and logic instructions. The term CPU usually includes main memory as well.

CRUD: An acronym representing Create, Read, Update, Delete, which are the four actions that can be performed on a database view.

Cube: In OLAP, a presentation structure having axes upon which data dimensions are placed. Measures of the data are shown in the cells of the cube. Also called hypercube.

Currency indicator: In the CODASYL DBTG model, a variable that identifies the most recently accessed record or set. There are currency indicators for run-unit, record type, and set.

Cursor: An indicator of the current position or focus. (1) On a computer screen, a blinking box or underscore that indicates the position into which the next entry will be made. (2) In a file or embedded SQL SELECT, the identity of the next record or row to be processed.

Cursor type: A declaration on a cursor that determines how the DBMS places implicit locks. Four types of cursor discussed in this text are forward only, snapshot, keyset, and dynamic.

Data access language: See Data sublanguage.

Data administration: The enterprisewide function that concerns the effective use and control of the organization's data assets. It can be a person but more often is a group. Specific functions include setting data standards and policies and providing a forum for conflict resolution. Also see database administrator.

Data base: In DL/I, a collection of data base records.

Data consumer: A user of OLE DB functionality.

Data provider: A provider of OLE DB functionality. Examples are tabular data providers and service data providers.

Database: A self-describing collection of integrated records.

Database administration: The function that concerns the effective use and control of a particular database and its related applications.

Database administrator: The person or group responsible for establishing policies and procedures to control and protect a database. He (she or it) works within guidelines set by data administration to control the database structure, manage data changes, and maintain DBMS programs.

Database data: The portion of a database that contains data of interest and use to the application end users.

Data base description: In DL/I, a data structure that describes the structure of a data base record.

Data base record: In DL/I, a hierarchical arrangement of data segments. See logical data base record and physical data base record.

Data base request module: In DB2, a data structure that describes the SQL statements that need to be executed.

Database save: A copy of database files that can be used to restore the database to some previous, consistent state.

Database server: (1) On a local area network with client–server database architecture, the microcomputer that runs the DBMS and processes actions against the database on behalf of its client computers. (2) In the three-tier architecture, a computer that hosts a DBMS and responds to database requests from the Web server.

Data Definition Language (DDL):   A language used to describe the structure of a database.

Data dictionary: A user-accessible catalog of both database and application metadata. An active data dictionary is a dictionary whose contents are automatically updated by the DBMS whenever changes are made in the database or application structure. A passive data dictionary is one whose contents must be updated manually when changes are made.

Data dictionary and database administration subsystem: A collection of programs in the DBMS used to access the data dictionary and to perform database administration functions such as maintaining passwords and performing backup and recovery.

Data integrity: The state of a database in which all constraints are fulfilled; usually refers to intertable constraints in which the value of a foreign key is required to be present in the table having that foreign key as its primary key.

Data-item: (1) A logical group of bytes in a record, usually used with file processing. (2) In the context of the relational model, a synonym for attribute.

Data Language I: See DL/I.

Data Manipulation Language (DML): A language used to describe the processing of a database.

Data mart: A facility similar to a data warehouse but for a restricted domain. Often the data are restricted to particular types, business functions, or business units.

Data model: (1) A model of the users' data requirements expressed in terms of either the entity-relationship model or the semantic-object model. It is sometimes called a users' data model. (2) A language for describing the structure and processing of a database. See hierarchical data model, network data model, and relational data model.

Data owner: Same as Data proponent.

Data proponent: In data administration, a department or other organizational unit in charge of managing a particular data item.

Data replication: A term that indicates whether any portion or all of a database resides on more than one computer. If so, the data are said to be replicated.

Data source: In the ODBC standard, a database together with its associated DBMS, operating system, and network platform.

Data structure diagram: A graphical display of tables (files) and their relationships. The tables are shown in rectangles, and the relationships are shown by lines. A many relationship is shown with a fork on the end of the line; an optional relationship is depicted by an oval; and a mandatory relationship is shown with hash marks.

Data sublanguage: A language for defining and processing a database intended to be embedded in programs written in another language—in most cases, a procedural language such as COBOL, C++, or Visual Basic. A data sublanguage is an incomplete programming language, as it contains only constructs for data access.

Data warehouse: A store of enterprise data that is designed to facilitate management decision making. A data warehouse includes not only data, but also metadata, tools, procedures, training, personnel, and other resources that make access to the data easier and more relevant to decision makers.

DBA: See Database Administrator.

DBM: Database Manager. In a DDBMS, software that processes some portion of a distributed database in accordance with action requests received from distributed transactions managers (DTMs).

DBMS: Database Management System; a set of programs used to define, administer, and process the database and its applications.

DBMS engine: A DBMS subsystem that processes logical I/O requests from other DBMS subsystems and submits physical I/O requests to the operating system.

DBTG: (1) A subcommittee of CODASYL that developed the DBTG network data model. (2) A network data model that models data as records and record relationships as sets. Only simple networks can be directly represented. Although the DBTG network data model is fading in popularity, it still is in use on mainframe computers.

DB2: Database 2; a relational DBMS developed and licensed by IBM for use on mainframe computers.

DDBMS: Distributed database management system. (1) The collection of DTMs and DBMs on all computers that processes a distributed database (see Chapter 16). (2) A commercial DBMS product that has been modified to allow processing a distributed database.

DDL: See Data Definition Language.

Deadlock: A condition that can occur during concurrent processing in which each of two (or more) transactions is waiting to access data that the other transaction has locked. It is also called a deadly embrace.

Deadlock detection: The process of determining whether two or more transactions are in a state of deadlock.

Deadlock prevention: A way of managing transactions so that a deadlock cannot occur.

Deadly embrace: See Deadlock.

Definition tools subsystem: The portion of the DBMS program used to define and change the database structure.

Degree: For relationships in the entity-relationship model, the number of entities participating in the relationship. In almost all cases, such relationships are of degree 2.

Deletion anomaly: In a relation, the situation in which the removal of one row of a table deletes facts about two or more themes.

Determinant: One or more attributes that functionally determine another attribute or attributes. In the functional dependency (A, B) → C, the attributes (A, B) are the determinant.

DHTML: A Microsoft implementation of the HTML 4.0 standard. Key features are support for the document object model, cascading style sheets, and remote data services.

Difference: A relational algebra operation performed on two union-compatible relations, A and B, that produces a third relation, C. Each row in C is present in A but not in B.

Dimension: In OLAP, a feature of data that is placed on an axis.

Distributed database: A database stored on two or more computers. Distributed data can be partitioned or not partitioned, replicated or not replicated.

Distributed database application: A business computer system in which the retrieval and updating of data occur across two or more independent and usually geographically distributed computers.

Distributed Database Management System (DDBMS): In a distributed database, the collection of distributed transaction and database managers on all computers.

Distributed database processing: Database processing in which transactions data is retrieved and updated across two or more independent and usually geographically separated computers.

Distributed database system: A distributed system in which a database or portions of a database are distributed across two or more computers.

Distributed system: A system in which the application programs of a database are processed on two or more computers.

Distributed two-phase locking: Two-phase locking in a distributed environment, in which locks are obtained and released across all nodes on the network. See Two-phase locking.

DL/I: Data Language I. A data model developed by IBM in the late 1960s to define and process hierarchical databases. The IBM DBMS product IMS is based on DL/I. Although IMS is still in widespread use on mainframes, such databases are being replaced by relational databases.

DML: See Data Manipulation Language.

Document Type Declaration: A set of markup elements that defines the structure of an XML document.

Domain: (1) The set of all possible values an attribute can have. (2) A description of the format (data type, length) and the semantics (meaning) of an attribute.

Domain/Key Normal Form (DK/NF): A relation in which all constraints are logical consequences of domains and keys.

Download: Copying database data from one computer to another, usually from a mainframe or mini to a microcomputer or LAN.

Drill down: User-directed disaggregation of data used to break higher-level totals into components.

Driver: In ODBC, a program that serves as an interface between the ODBC driver manager and a particular DBMS product. Runs on the client machines in a client–server architecture.

Driver manager: In ODBC, a program that serves as an interface between an application program and an ODBC driver. It determines the driver required, loads it into memory, and coordinates activity between the application and the driver. On Windows systems, it is provided by Microsoft.

DSD: See Data Structure Diagram.

DSS: Decision Support System; an interactive, computer-based facility for assisting decision making, especially for semistructured and unstructured problems. Such a system often includes a database and a query/update facility for processing ad hoc requests.

DTD: See Document Type Declaration.

ECMAScript-262: The standard version of an easily learned interpreted language used for both Web server and Web client applications processing. The Microsoft version is called JScript, and the Netscape version is called JavaScript.

Encapsulated data: Properties or attributes contained in a program or object not visible or accessible to other programs or objects.

Encapsulated structure: A portion of an object that is not visible to other objects.

Entity: (1) Something of importance to a user that needs to be represented in a database. (2) In an entity-relationship model, entities are restricted to things that can be represented by a single table. Also see Existence-dependent entity, Strong entity, and Weak entity.

Entity class: A set of entities of the same type, for example, EMPLOYEE and DEPARTMENT.

Entity instance: A particular occurrence of an entity, for example, Employee 100 and the Accounting Department.

Entity-relationship diagram: A graphic used to represent entities and their relationships. Entities are normally shown in squares or rectangles, and relationships are shown in diamonds. The cardinality of the relationship is shown inside the diamond.

Entity-relationship model: The constructs and conventions used to create a model of the users' data (see Data model). The things in the users' world are represented by entities, and the associations among those things are represented by relationships. The results are usually documented in an entity-relationship diagram.

Entry-point relation: Used with regard to the relations representing an object. The entry-point relation is the relation whose key is the same as the key of the object it represents. The entry-point relation is normally the first relation processed. Also, the name of the entry-point relation is normally the same as the name of the object.

Enumerated list: A list of allowed values for a domain, attribute, or column.

Equijoin: The process of joining relation A containing attribute A1 with B containing attribute B1 to form relation C, so that for each row in C, A1 = B1. Both A1 and B1 are represented in C.

E-R diagram: See Entity-relationship diagram.

Exclusive lock: A lock on a data resource that no other transaction can either read or update.

Existence-dependent entity: Same as a weak entity. An entity that cannot appear in the database unless an instance of one or more other entities also appears in the database. A subclass of existence-dependent entities is ID-dependent entities.

Explicit lock: A lock requested by a command from an application program.

Export: A function of the DBMS, to write a file of data in bulk. The file is intended to be read by another DBMS or program.

Extent (of object): In the ODMG model, the union of all object instances. Attributes can be declared to be unique across an object's extent.

Extract: A portion of an operational database downloaded to a local area network or microcomputer for local processing. Extracts are created to reduce communications cost and time when querying and creating reports from data created by transaction processing.

Failure transparency: In a distributed database system, the condition in which application programs are isolated from failure.

Field: (1) A logical group of bytes in a record used with file processing. (2) In the context of a relational model, a synonym for attribute.

File data source: An ODBC data source stored in a file that can be E-mailed or otherwise distributed among users.

File-processing system: An information system in which data is stored in separate files. There is no integrated data dictionary. The format of the files is usually stored in application programs.

File server: In a local area network, a microcomputer containing a file that it processes on behalf of other microcomputers on the network. The term file server is normally used for the resource-sharing architecture. See Client computer, Client-server database architecture, Database server, and Resource-sharing architecture.

Firewall: A computer that serves as a security gateway between an intranet and the Internet. Firewalls monitor the source and destination of network traffic and filter it.

First normal form: Any table that fits the definition of a relation.

Flat file: A file that has only a single value in each field. The meaning of the columns is the same in every row.

Force-write: A write of database data in which the DBMS waits for acknowledgment from the operating system that the after-image of the write has been successfully written to the log.

Foreign key: An attribute that is a key of one or more relations other than the one in which it appears.

Form: (1) A display on a computer screen used to present, enter, and modify data. A form is also called a data entry form or panel. (2) A paper document used in a business system to record data, usually concerning a transaction. Forms are analyzed in the process of building a data model.

Forms generator: A portion of the application development subsystem used to create a data entry form without having to write any application program code.

Formula domain: A domain whose values are computed by an expression containing arguments that are themselves domains.

Fourth normal form: A relation in third Boyce–Codd normal form in which every multi-value dependency is a functional dependency.

Fragment: A row in a table (or record in a file) in which a required parent or child is not present. For example, a row in a LINE-ITEM table for which no ORDER row exists.

FTP: File Transfer Protocol. A standard Internet service for copying files to or from a remote server.

Fully concatenated key: In DL/I, a composite of the sequence fields of a segment and the sequence fields of all its parents. The root occupies the leftmost position in the concatenated key, and the segment occupies the rightmost position.

Functional dependency: A relationship between attributes in which one attribute or group of attributes determines the value of another. The expressions $X \rightarrow Y$, "X determines Y," and "Y is functionally dependent on X" mean that given a value of X, we can determine the value of Y.

Generalization hierarchy: A set of objects or entities of the same logical type that are arranged in a hierarchy of logical subtypes. For example, EMPLOYEE has the subtypes ENGINEER and ACCOUNTANT, and ENGINEER has the subtypes ELECTRICAL ENGINEER and MECHANICAL ENGINEER. Subtypes inherit characteristics of their supertypes.

Generalization object: An object that contains subtype objects. The generalization object and its subtypes all have the same key. Subtype objects inherit attributes from the generalization object. A generalization object is also called a supertype object.

Granularity: The size of database resource that can be locked. Locking the entire database is large granularity; locking a column of a particular row is small granularity.

Graphical user interface: GUI; an interface having windows, graphical symbols, pop-down menus, and other structures that are often manipulated with a mouse pointer. Popular graphical user interface products are Windows from Microsoft and the Macintosh System Software from Apple.

Group identifier: An attribute that identifies a unique instance of a group within a semantic object or another group.

Growing phase: The first stage in two-phase locking in which locks are acquired but not released.

GUI: See Graphical User Interface.

HAS-A relationship: A relationship between two entities or objects that are of different logical types, for example, EMPLOYEE HAS-A(n) AUTO. Contrast this with an IS-A relationship.

Hierarchical data model: A data model that represents all relationships using hierarchies or trees. Network structures must be decomposed into trees before they can be represented by a hierarchical data model. DL/I is the only surviving hierarchical data model.

Hierarchy: See Tree.

HOLAP: Hybrid OLAP using a combination of ROLAP and MOLAP for supporting OLAP processing.

Horizontal partition: A subset of a table consisting of complete rows of the table. For example, in a table with 10 rows, the first five rows.

Horizontal security: Limiting access to certain rows of a table or join.

Host variable: A variable in an application program into which a DBMS places a value from the database.

HTML: See Hypertext Markup Language.

HTML 4.0: A World Wide Web consortium standard for an advanced version of HTML. See DHTML.

HTTP: See Hypertext Transfer Protocol.

Hybrid object: An object containing a multi-value group that contains at least one object attribute.

Hypercube: In OLAP, a presentation structure having axes upon which data dimensions are placed. Measures of the data are shown in the cells of the hypercube. Also called cube.

Hypertext Markup Language: A standardized system of tagging text for formatting, locating images and other nontext files, and placing links or references to other documents.

Hypertext Transfer Protocol: HTTP; a standardized means for using TCP/IP for communicating HTML documents over networks.

ID-dependent entity: An entity that cannot logically exist without the existence of another entity. An APPOINTMENT, for example, cannot exist without a CLIENT to make the appointment. The ID-dependent entity always contains the key of the entity on which it depends. Such entities are a subset of a weak entity. See also Strong entity and Weak entity.

IIS: Internet Information Server; a Microsoft product that operates as an HTTP server. IIS requires Windows NT or Windows 2000.

Immutable object: In the ODMG standard, an object whose attributes cannot be changed.

Implementation: In OOP, a set of objects that instantiates a particular OOP interface.

Implicit lock: A lock that is automatically placed by the DBMS.

Implied object: An object that exists in the user's mind when he or she requests a report "sorted by x" or "grouped by x." For example, when the user requests all ORDERs sorted by OrderDate, the implied object is the set of all ORDER objects.

Import: A function of the DBMS, to read a file of data in bulk.

IMS: Information Management System; a transaction-processing system developed and licensed by IBM. It includes IMS/DC, a communications control program, and IMS/DB, a DBMS that implements the DL/I data model.

Inconsistent read problem: An anomaly that occurs in concurrent processing in which transactions execute a series of reads inconsistent with one another. It can be prevented by two-phase locking and other strategies.

Index: Overhead data used to improve access and sorting performance. Indexes can be constructed for a single column or groups of columns. They are especially useful for columns used for control breaks in reports and to specify conditions in joins.

Index space: An area of disk storage in which DB2 stores an index.

Information-bearing set: In the CODASYL DBTG data model, a set in which the relationship between records is not represented in the data values. The relationship, though not visible in the data, is recorded in overhead data created and processed by the DBMS. Contrast this with Non-information-bearing set.

Inheritance: A characteristic of objected-oriented systems in which objects that are subtypes of other objects obtain attributes (data or methods) from their supertypes.

Inner Join: Synonym for join.

Insertion anomaly: In a relation, the condition that exists when, to add a complete row to a table, one must add facts about two or more logically different themes.

Insertion status: In the CODASYL DBTG model, a rule that determines how records are to be placed into sets. Records can be placed automatically by the DBMS or manually by the application program.

Interface: (1) The means by which two or more programs call each other; the definition of the procedural calls between two or more programs. (2) In OOP, the design of a set of objects that includes the objects' names, methods, and attributes.

Internet: A worldwide, public network of computers that communicate using TCP/IP.

Internet Information Server: See IIS.

Internet mail service: A standard service of the Internet that provides personal E-mail.

Internet newsgroup: A standard service of the Internet that provides for public E-mail.

Interrelation constraint: A restriction that requires the value of an attribute in a row of one relation to match the value of an attribute found in another relation. For example, CustNumber in ORDER must equal CustNumber in CUSTOMER.

Intersection: A relational algebra operation performed on two union-compatible relations, A and B, forming a third relation, C, so that C contains only rows that appear in both A and B.

Intersection relation: A relation used to represent a many-to-many relationship. It contains the keys of the relations in the relationship. When used to represent many-to-many compound objects, it has no nonkey data. When used to represent entities having a many-to-many relationship, it may have nonkey data if the relationship contains data.

Intranet: (1) A private local or wide area network that uses TCP/IP, HTML, and related browser technology on client computers and Web server technology on serves. (2) Less commonly, any private LAN or WAN that involves clients and servers.

Intrarelation constraint: A restriction on data values in a relation. For example, in PART (Part, P-name, Units), the rule is that if Part starts with a 1, then Units must equal Pounds.

IS-A relationship: A relationship between two entities or objects of the same logical type. In reference to ENGINEER IS-A(n) EMPLOYEE, both of these entities are employees and are of the same logical type. Contrast this with a HAS-A relationship.

Isolation level: A declaration on a transaction that determines how the DBMS places implicit locks. Four types of isolation level discussed in this text are exclusive use, repeatable read, cursor stability, and dirty read.

IUnknown: An ActiveX interface in which one ActiveX program can call another, unknown ActiveX program. Once a connection has been established, the first program can use the Query Interface to determine what objects, methods, and properties the second program supports.

Java: An object programming language that has better memory management and bounds checking than C++; used primarily for Internet applications, but also can be used as a general-purpose programming language. Java compliers generate Java byte code that is interpreted on client computers.

JavaScript: A proprietary scripting language owned by Netscape. The Microsoft version is called JScript; the standard version is called ECMAScript-262. These are easily learned interpreted languages used for both Web server and Web-client applications processing. Sometimes written "Java Script."

JScript: A proprietary scripting language owned by Microsoft. The Netscape version is called JavaScript; the standard version is called ECMAScript-262. These are easily learned interpreted languages used for both Web server and Web-client applications processing.

Join: A relational algebra operation on two relations, A and B, that produces a third relation, C. A row of A is concatenated with a row of B to form a new row in C if the rows in A and B meet restrictions concerning their values. For example, A1 is an attribute in A, and B1 is an attribute in B. The join of A with B in which A1 < B1 will result in a relation, C, having the concatenation of rows in A and B in which the value of A1 is less than the value of B1. See Equijoin and Natural join.

Key: (1) A group of one or more attributes identifying a unique row in a relation. Because relations may not have duplicate rows, every relation must have at least one key, which is the composite of all of the attributes in the relation. A key is sometimes called a logical key. (2) With some relational DBMS products, an index on a column used to improve access and sorting speed. It is sometimes called a physical key.

LAN: Local Area Network; a group of microcomputers connected to one another by means of communications lines in close proximity, usually less than a mile. See Client–server database architecture and Resource-sharing architecture.

LDBR: See Logical Data Base Record.

Level: In OLAP, a (possibly hierarchical) subset of a dimension.

List box: In a GUI environment, an element of the user interface in which a list of choices is presented in a rectangle. The user moves the cursor to shade the item to be selected from the list.

Location transparency: In a distributed database system, the condition in which application programs do not know and do not need to know where data are located. The DDBMS finds data, wherever they are located, without the involvement of the application program.

Lock: The process of allocating a database resource to a particular transaction in a concurrent-processing system. The size of the resource locked is known as the lock granularity. With an exclusive lock, no other transaction may read or write the resource. With a shared lock, other transactions may read the resource, but no other transaction may write it.

Lock granularity: The size of a locked data element. The lock of a column value of a particular row is a small granularity lock, and the lock of an entire table is a large granularity lock.

Log: A file containing a record of database changes. The log contains before-images and after-images.

Logical Data Base (LDB): In DL/I, the collection of all the logical data base records in the data base.

Logical Data Base Record (LDBR): In DL/I, a hierarchy of segments as perceived by an application program. Such a structure may or may not exist physically; it may be taken from other structures using pointers and other overhead data.

Logical key: One or more columns that uniquely determine the row of a table or a record of a file; a synonym for a key. Contrast this with a physical key, which is a synonym for an index.

Logical Unit of Work: LUW; a group of logically related database operations that is performed as a unit. Either all of the operations are performed, or none of them is. A logical unit of work is the same as an atomic transaction. It is a term used with the DBMS DB2.

Look up: The process of obtaining related data by using the value of a foreign key, for example, when processing a row of ORDER (*OrderNumber*, Ord-Date, *CustNumber*, . . .), using the value of CustNumber to obtain the related value of CustName from CUS-TOMER (*CustNumber*, CustName, . . .).

Lost update problem: Same as Concurrent update problem.

LUW: See Logical Unit of Work.

Mask: A format used when presenting data in a form, Web page, or report.

Materialization: A database view as it appears in a form, report, or Web page.

Maximum cardinality: (1) The maximum number of values that an attribute may have within a semantic object. (2) In a relationship between tables, the maximum number of rows to which a row of one table may relate in the other table.

Me: In OOP, a special pointer to the current object instance. For example, Me.Name refers to the Name attribute of the current object.

Measure: In OLAP, the source data for the cube; data that is displayed in the cells. It may be raw data, or it may be functions of raw data such as SUM, AVG, or other computations.

Member: In the CODASYL DBTG model, a record type that is on the many side of a one-to-many or set relationship.

Members: In OLAP, the values of a dimension.

Menu: A list of options presented to the user of a database (or other) application. The user selects the next action or activity from a list. Actions are restricted to those in the list. Contrast this with Command.

Metadata: Data concerning the structure of data in a database stored in the data dictionary. Metadata are used to describe tables, columns, constraints, indexes, and so forth. Compare this with Application metadata.

Method: A program attached to an object-oriented programming (OOP) object. A method can be inherited by lower-level OOP objects.

Method: In OOP, a program attribute of an object.

Microsoft transaction service: See MTS.

MIME: See Multipurpose Internet mail code.

Minimum cardinality: (1) The minimum number of values that an attribute may have within a semantic object. (2) In a relationship between tables, the number of rows to which a row of one table may relate in the other table.

Mixed partition: A combination of a horizontal and a vertical partition; for example, in a table with five columns and five rows, the first three columns of the first three rows.

Modification anomaly: The situation existing when the storing of one row in a table records two separate facts or when the deletion of one row of a table eliminates two separate facts.

MOLAP: Multidimensional OLAP using a purpose-built processor for supporting OLAP processing.

MTS: Microsoft Transaction Service. An OLE DB service that coordinates transactions on distributed computers.

Multiple-tier driver: In ODBC, a two-part driver, usually for a client–server database system. One part of the driver resides on the client and interfaces with the application; the second part resides on the server and interfaces with the DBMS.

Multipurpose Internet mail code: A standardized list of symbols that indicate the type of a file embedded in an HTML document. Each MIME type code is associated with a program that processes files of that type. MIME types are defined for images, sounds, movies, etc. The code can be extended by adding new codes (and affiliated programs) to MIME code lists on clients and servers.

Multi-value attribute: The attribute of a semantic object that has a maximum cardinality greater than one.

Multi-value dependency: A condition in a relation with three or more attributes in which independent attributes appear to have relationships they do not have. Formally, in a relation R (A, B, C), having key (A, B, C) where A is matched with multiple values of B (or of C or both), B does not determine C, and C does not de-termine B. An example is the relation EMPLOYEE (EmpNumber, Emp-skill, Dependent-name), where an employee can have multiple values of Emp-skill and Dependent-name. Emp-skill and Dependent-name do not have any relationship, but they do appear to in the relation.

Mutable object: In the ODMG standard, an object whose attributes may be changed.

Natural join: A join of a relation A having attribute A1 with relation B having attribute B1 where A1 equals B1. The joined relation, C, contains either column A1 or B1 but not both. Contrast this with Equijoin.

Natural language interface: An interface to an application program or DBMS by which users can enter requests in the form of standard English or another human language.

Network: (1) A group of interconnected computers. (2) An intranet. (3) The Internet.

Network database application: A database application in which the clients use an HTML-based browser and the server includes both an Internet-style server and a database. The application could reside on either the Internet or an intranet.

Network data model: A data model supporting at least simple network relationships. The CODASYL DBTG, which supports simple network relationships but not complex relationships, is the most important network data model.

N.M: An abbreviation for a many-to-many relationship between the rows of two tables.

Node: (1) An entity in a tree. (2) A computer in a distributed-processing system.

Non-information-bearing set: In the CODASYL DBTG model, a set in which the child record type contains the key of the parent record type. The set ownership is implied by the value of the key in the child record instances.

Nonobject attribute: An attribute of a semantic object that is not an object.

Normal form: A rule or set of rules governing the allowed structure of relations. The rules apply to attributes, functional dependencies, multi-value dependencies, domains, and constraints. The most important normal forms are 1NF, 2NF, 3NF, BoyceCodd NF, 4NF, 5NF, and domain/key normal form.

Normalization: The process of evaluating a relation to determine whether it is in a specified normal form and, if necessary, of converting it to relations in that specified normal form.

Nothing: In OOP, a null object reference used to set an object pointer to null or test an object pointer to determine if it is null.

Not-type-valid document: An XML document that either does not conform to its DTD or does not have a DTD; contrast with type-valid document.

Null value: A value that is either unknown or not applicable. A null value is not the same as a zero or blank, although in most commercial DBMS products, null values are represented by zeros or blanks.

Object: (1) A semantic object. (2) A structure in an object-oriented program that contains an encapsulated data structure and data methods. Such objects are arranged in a hierarchy so that objects can inherit methods from their parents. (3) In DB2, a term used to refer to data bases, tables, views, indexes, and other structures. (4) In security systems, a unit of data protected by a password or other means.

Object attribute: An attribute of a semantic object that represents a link to an object.

Object class: In object-oriented programming, a set of objects with a common structure.

Object class library: In object-oriented programming, a collection of object classes, usually a collection that serves a particular purpose.

Object constructor: In object-oriented programming, a function that creates an object.

Object destructor: In object-oriented programming, a function that destroys an object.

Object diagram: A portrait-oriented rectangle that represents the structure of a semantic object.

Object identifier: An attribute that is used to specify an object instance. Object identifiers can be unique, meaning that they identify one (and only one) instance, or nonunique, meaning that they identify exactly one object instance.

Object instance: The occurrence of a particular semantic object, for example, the SALESPERSON semantic object having LastName equal to Jones.

Object-oriented Programming: A style of computer programming in which programs are developed as sets of objects that have data members and methods. Objects interface with one another by calling each other's methods.

Object persistence: In object-oriented programming, the characteristic that an object can be saved to nonvolatile memory, such as a disk. Persistent objects exist between executions of a program.

Object view: The portion of a semantic object that is visible to a particular application. A view consists of the name of the semantic object plus a list of the attributes visible in that view.

ODMG-93: A report issued by the Object Data Management Group, which is a consortium of object database vendors and other interested industry experts. The report applies the ideas of another group, the Object Management Group, to the problem of object databases. The first ODMG report was produced in 1993 and is accordingly referred to as ODMG-93.

OLAP: On-Line Analytical Processing; a form of data presentation in which data is summarized and viewed in the frame of a table or a cube.

OLE DB: The COM-based foundation of data access in the Microsoft world. OLE DB objects support the OLE object standard. ADO is based upon OLE DB.

OLE object: Object Linking and Embedding object. COM objects that support interfaces for embedding into other objects.

1:N: An abbreviation for a one-to-many relationship between the rows of two tables.

On-Line Analytical Processing: See OLAP.

OOP: See Object-oriented Programming.

Open Database Connectivity standard (ODBC): A standard interface by which application programs can access and process SQL databases in a DBMS-independent manner. ODBC was developed by a committee of industry experts from the X/Open and SQL Access Group committees and was incorporated as a part of Windows by Microsoft.

Optimistic locking: A locking strategy that assumes no conflict will occur, processes a transaction, and then checks to determine if conflict did occur. If so, the transaction is aborted. Also see pessimistic locking.

Option button: In a GUI environment, an element of the user interface in which the user can select an item from a list. Clicking on one button deselects the button currently pressed, if any. It operates like the radio buttons on a car radio and is the same as a radio button (see Radio button) but was introduced under a different name to avoid litigation among vendors.

Orphan: Any row (record) that is missing its parent in a mandatory one-to-many relationship.

Outer join: A join in which all the rows of a table appear in the result relation regardless of whether they have a match in the join condition. In a left outer join, all the rows in the lefthand relation appear; in a right outer join, all the rows in the righthand relation appear.

Overhead data: Metadata created by the DBMS to improve performance, for example, indexes and linked lists.

Owner: (1) In the CODASYL DBTG model, a record type that is on the one side of a one-to-many or set relationship. (2) In data administration, the department or other organizational unit in charge of the management of a particular data item. An owner can also be called a data proponent.

Page: A unit of disk storage. In DB2, a 4K block of contiguous disk space used to hold the database, data dictionary, and overhead data.

Paired attribute: In a semantic object, object attributes are paired. If object A has an object attribute of object B, then object B will have an object attribute of object A; that is, the object attributes are paired with each other.

Parent: A row, record, or node on the one side of a one-to-many relationship.

Partition: (1) A portion of a distributed database. (2) The portion of a network that is separated from the rest of the network during a network failure.

Partitioned table space: In DB2, a table space that holds data for exactly one table.

PDBR: See Physical Data Base Record.

PERL: The Practical Extraction and Report Language. An interpreted programming language developed by Larry Wall and originally for UNIX. PERL interpreters are now available for Windows and Macintosh. Often used for server programs on the Internet and on intranets.

Persistent object: An OOP object that has been written to persistent storage.

Pessimistic locking: A locking strategy that prevents conflict by placing locks before processing database read and write requests. Also see optimistic locking and deadlock.

Physical Data Base Record (PDBR):   In DL/I, a hierarchy of segments stored in data base files.

Physical key: A column that has an index or other data structure created for it; a synonym for an index. Such structures are created to improve searching and sorting on the column values.

Pointer: An address to an instance of a data structure. The address of a record often is in a directly addressed file.

Polymorphism: In OOP, the situation in which one name can be used to invoke different functions. Polymorphism in which the functions are distinguished by having different parameter sequences is called parametric polymorphism. For it, names are resolved by the compiler at compile time. Polymorphism in which the functions are distinguished by object inheritance is called inheritance polymorphism. Such names are resolved at run time by determining the type of object being invoked.

Pop-down list box: In a GUI environment, the list box that appears when the user selects an icon that represents that box.

Precompiler: A program that translates the database access commands of a particular DBMS product. Such commands are embedded in an application program normally written in a third-generation language. The commands are translated into data structures and calls to DBMS-processing routines in the syntax of the third-generation language.

Primary key: A candidate key selected to be the key of a relation.

Processing-interface subsystem: The portion of the DBMS routines that executes commands for processing the database. It accepts input from interactive query programs and from application programs written in standard or DBMS-specific languages.

Processing rights and responsibilities: Organiza-tional policies regarding which groups can take which actions on specified data-items or other collections of data.

Product: A relational operation on two relations, A and B, producing a third relation, C, with C containing the concatenation of every row in A with every row in B. It is the same as a Cartesian product.

Program/data independence: The condition existing when the structure of the data is not defined in application programs. Rather, it is defined in the database, and then the application programs obtain it from the DBMS. In this way, changes can be made in the data structures that may not necessarily be made in the application programs.

Projection: A relational algebra operation performed on a relation, A, that results in a relation, B, where B has a (possibly improper) subset of the attributes of A. Projection is used to form a new relation that reorders the attributes in the original relation or that has only some of the attributes from the original relation.

Property: Same as Attribute.

Proponent: See Data proponent.

Prototype: A quickly developed demonstration of an application or portion of an application.

QBE: Query By Example. A style of query interface, first developed by IBM but now used by other vendors, that enables users to express queries by providing examples of the results they seek.

Query Interface: An interface in Microsoft COM that can be used to determine the objects, methods, and properties supported by an ActiveX program.

Query/update language: A language that can be employed by end users to query the database and make changes in the database data.

Radio button: In a GUI environment, an element of the user interface in which the user can select one item from a list. Clicking on one button deselects the button currently pressed if any. It operates like the radio buttons on a car radio.

RDS: See Remote Data Services.

Real output: Output transmitted to the client of an information system, such as an order confirmation. When produced in error, such outputs cannot be changed by recovering the database. Instead, compensating transactions must be executed.

Record: (1) A group of fields pertaining to the same entity; used in file-processing systems. (2) In a relational model, a synonym for Row and Tuple.

Recordset: An ADO object that represents a relation; created as the result of the execution of a SQL statement or a stored procedure.

Recursive relationship: A relationship among entities, objects, or rows of the same type. For example, if CUSTOMERs refer other CUSTOMERs, the relationship *refers* is recursive.

Referential integrity constraint: The condition in a database in which all interrelation constraints are satisfied.

Relation: Same as a table; a two-dimensional array containing single-value entries and no duplicate rows. The meaning of the columns is the same in every row. The order of the rows and columns is immaterial.

Relational database: A database consisting of relations. Usually such a database is structured according to the principles of normalization, although in practice, relational databases contain relations with duplicate rows. Most DBMS products include a feature that removes duplicate rows when necessary and appropriate. Such a removal is not done as a matter of course because it can be time-consuming and expensive.

Relational data model: A data model in which data is stored in relations and relationships between rows are represented by data values.

Relational schema: A set of relations with interrelation constraints.

Relationship: An association between two entities, objects, or rows of relations.

Remote Data Services: A set of ActiveX controls and features that allow data to be cached on a client machine and formatted, sorted, and filtered without assistance from the Web server.

Replicated data: In a distributed database, data that is stored on two or more computers.

Replication transparency: In a distributed database system, the condition in which application programs do not know and do not need to know whether data is replicated. If it is replicated, the DDBMS will ensure that all copies are updated consistently, without the involvement of the application program.

Report: An extraction of data from a database. Reports can be printed, displayed on a computer screen, or stored as a file. A report is part of a database application. Compare this with a Form.

Report band: See Band.

Repository: A collection of metadata about database structure, applications, Web pages, users, and other application components. Active repositories are maintained automatically by tools in the application development environment. Passive repositories must be maintained manually.

Resource locking: See Lock.

Resource-sharing architecture: The structure of a local area network in which one microcomputer performs file-processing services for other microcomputers. In a database application, each user computer contains a copy of the DBMS that forwards input/output requests to the file server. Only file I/O is processed by the file server; all database activities are processed by the DBMS on the user's computer.

Retention status: In the CODASYL DBTG model, a rule that states whether or not a record must exist in a set. If FIXED, a record may never be removed from its original set. If MANDATORY, a record must be a member of a set once it is placed into a set. If OPTIONAL, a record may or may not reside in a set.

ROLAP: Relational OLAP using a relational DBMS to support OLAP processing.

Rollback: The process of recovering a database in which before-images are applied to the database to return to an earlier checkpoint or other point at which the database is logically consistent.

Rollforward: The process of recovering a database by applying after-images to a saved copy of the database to bring it to a checkpoint or other point at which the database is logically consistent.

Root: The top record, row, or node in a tree. A root has no parent.

Row: A group of columns in a table. All the columns in a row pertain to the same entity. A row is the same as a Tuple and a Record.

Row identifier: In SQL3, a unique, system-supplied identifier, a surrogate key. The row identifier can be made visible by stating WITH IDENTITY in the table definition.

Rowset: In OLE DB, an abstraction of data collections such as recordsets, E-mail addresses, and nonrelational and other data.

Run-unit: In the CODASYL DBTG model, the execution of an application program by a user. Several run-units may use the same application program concurrently.

Schedule: In a distributed database system, an ordered sequence of data requests.

Schema: A complete logical view of the database.

Screen: See Form.

Scrollable cursor: A cursor type that enables forward and backward movement through a recordset. Three scrollable cursor types discussed in this text are snapshot, keyset, and dynamic.

Second normal form: A relation in first normal form in which all nonkey attributes are dependent on all of the key.

Segment: In DL/I, a collection of fields that is a node in a data base record.

Segment search argument: An expression in a DL/I that indicates the segment or segments to which the command is to be applied.

Selection: A relational algebra operation performed on a relation, A, producing a relation, B, with B containing only the rows in A that meet the restrictions specified in the selection.

Semantic object diagram: Same as Object diagram.

Semantic object model: The constructs and conventions used to create a model of the users' data. The things in the users' world are represented by semantic objects (sometimes called objects). Relationships are modeled in the objects, and the results are usually documented in object diagrams.

Semantic-object view: The portion of a semantic object that is visible in a form or report.

Sequence field: In DL/I, a field that is used to order logically the segments of a given type under a given parent. The order can be ascending or descending.

Serializable: A condition pertaining to two or more transactions in which the results of the processing are the same as they would have been if the transactions had been processed in some serial manner.

Service provider: An OLE DB data provider that transforms data. A service provider is both a data consumer and a data provider.

Set: In the CODASYL DBTG model, a structure that represents a one-to-many relationship among records. The parent record type is called the set owner, and the child record type(s) is (are) called the set member.

Set membership: In the CODASYL DBTG model, the records that belong to a particular set instance.

SGML: Standard Generalized Markup Language.

Shared lock: A lock against a data resource in which only one transaction may update the data, but many transactions can concurrently read that data.

Shrinking phase: In two-phase locking, the stage at which locks are released but no lock is acquired.

Sibling: A record or node that has the same parent as does another record or node.

Simple network: (1) A set of three relations and two relationships in which one of the relations, R, has a many-to-one relationship with the other two relations. The rows in R have two parents, and the parents are of different types. (2) Any set of tables and relationships containing the structure defined in (1).

Simple object: An object that contains no repeating attributes and no object attributes.

Simple table space: In DB2, a table space that contains data from more than one table.

Single-tier driver: In ODBC, a database driver that accepts SQL statements from the driver manager and processes them without invoking another program or DBMS. A single-tier driver is both an ODBC driver and a DBMS; used for file-processing systems.

Single-value attribute: In a semantic object, an attribute having a maximum cardinality of one.

Slice: In OLAP, a dimension or measure held constant for a display.

SQL: Structured Query Language; a language for defining the structure and processing of a relational database. It is used as a stand-alone query language, or it may be embedded in application programs. SQL is accepted as a national standard by the American National Standards Institute. It was developed by IBM.

SQL3: SQL3 is an extension to the SQL92 database standard that includes support for object-oriented database management. Developed by both the ANSI X3H2 and the ISO/IEC JTC1/SC21/WG3 standardization committees.

Standard generalized markup language (SGML): A standard means for tagging and marking the format, structure, and content of documents. HTML is a subset of SGML.

Storage group: In DB2, a group of disk volumes on which database data is stored.

Strong entity: In an entity-relationship model, any entity whose existence in the database does not depend on the existence of any other entity. See also ID-dependent entity and Weak entity.

Subschema: A subset of a database that is processed by one or more applications. A subschema may also be called an application view; it is used primarily with the CODASYL DBTG model.

Subtable: In SQL3, a table that is a subtype of a second table, called a supertable.

Subtype: In generalization hierarchies, an entity or object that is a subspecies or subcategory of a higher-level type. For example, ENGINEER is a subtype of EMPLOYEE.

Supertable: In SQL3, a table that has one or more subtables defined on it.

Supertype: In generalization hierarchies, an entity or object that logically contains subtypes. For example, EMPLOYEE is a supertype of ENGINEER, ACCOUNTANT, and MANAGER.

Surrogate key: A column of unique values that is maintained by the application or the DBMS. This column is used as the primary key of the table.

Swizzling: In OOP, the process of converting a permanent object identifier into an in-memory address and the reverse.

System data source: An ODBC data source that is local to a single computer and can be accessed by that computer's operating system and select users of that operating system.

Table space: In DB2, a collection of one or more VSAM data sets, or files, used to store database data on magnetic disk.

Tabular data provider: An OLE DB data provider that presents data in the form of rowsets.

TCP/IP: Terminal Control Program/ Internet Protocol.

TelNet: A standard service on the Internet that allows a user to log on to a server from a remote computer.

Third normal form: A relation in second normal form that has no transitive dependencies.

Three-tier architecture: A system of computers having a database server, a Web server, and one or more client computers. The database server hosts a DBMS, the Web server hosts an http server, and the client computer hosts a browser. Each tier can run a different operating system.

Top-down database design: The design of a database that works from the general to the specific. The resulting database can serve an organization's overall needs; the danger is that it may never be completed. See Bottom-up database design.

Transaction: (1) An atomic transaction. (2) The record of an event in the business world.

Transaction boundary: The group of database commands that must be committed or aborted as a unit.

Transaction isolation level: See isolation level.

Transaction node: In a distributed database system, a computer that processes a distributed transaction manager.

Transform-oriented language: A data sublanguage such as SQL that provides commands and capabilities to transform a set of relations into a new relation.

Transient object: In OOP, an object that has not been written to permanent storage. The object will be lost when the program terminates.

Transitive dependency: In a relation having at least three attributes, R (A, B, C), the situation in which A determines B, B determines C, but B does not determine A.

Tree: A collection of records, entities, or other data structures in which each element has at most one parent, except for the top element, which has no parent.

Trigger: A procedure invoked when a specified condition exists in the data of a database. For example, when Quantity-on-Hand of an item reaches zero (or some specified amount), a procedure can be triggered to order more of the item.

Tuple: Same as Row.

Twin: A record or node that has the same parent as does another record or node.

Two-phase commitment: In a distributed database system, a process of commitment among nodes in which the nodes first vote on whether they can commit a transaction. If all the nodes vote yes, the transaction is committed. If any node votes no, the transaction is aborted. A two-phase commitment is required to prevent inconsistent processing in distributed databases.

Two-phase locking: The procedure by which locks are obtained and released in two phases. During the growing phase, the locks are obtained, and during the shrinking phase, the locks are released. Once a lock is released, no other lock will be granted that transaction. Such a procedure ensures consistency in database updates in a concurrent-processing environment.

Type-valid document: An XML document that conforms to its DTD; contrast with not-type-valid document.

Union: A relational algebra operation performed on two union-compatible relations, say A and B, forming a third relation, say C, with C containing every row in both A and B, minus any duplicate rows.

Union compatible: The condition in which two tables have the same number of attributes and the attributes in corresponding columns arise from the same domain.

Union incompatible: The condition in which either two tables have a different number of attributes or the attributes in corresponding columns arise from different domains.

Universal Resource Locator: URL; the address of a file on the Internet.

URL: Universal Resource Locator. Sometimes Uniform Resource Locator, but the meaning is the same.

User data source: An ODBC data source that is available only to the user who created it.

User view: A particular user's view of a database.

User working area (UWA): In the CODASYL DBTG model, the area of main memory that contains data values pertaining to a particular run-unit.

UWA: See User Working Area.

VBScript: An easily learned, interpreted language used for both Web server and Web client applications processing; a subset of Microsoft Visual Basic.

Vertical partition: A subset of the columns of a table. For example, in a table with 10 columns, the first five columns.

Vertical security: Limiting access to certain columns of a table or join.

View: A structured list of data items from entities or semantic objects defined in the data model.

Weak entity: In an entity-relationship model, an entity whose logical existence in the database depends on the existence of another entity. See also ID-dependent entity and Strong entity.

Web server: In the three-tier architecture, a computer that sits between the client computers and the database server and hosts an HTTP server.

XML: Extensible markup language; a standard markup language that provides a clear separation between structure, content, and materialization; can represent arbitrary hierarchies and hence be used to transmit any database view.

XSL: Extensible Style Language; a facility for defining the materialization of an XML document.

BIBLIOGRAPHY

INTERNET RESOURCES

Check these sites for recent articles about database topics:
CNet—www.news.com
Database Programming and Design—www.dbpd.com
Databased Advisor—www.advisor.com
Intelligent Enterprise—www.intelligententerprise.com
PCMagazine—www.zdnet.com/pcmag
ZDNet—www.zdnet.com

DBMS AND OTHER VENDORS

Microsoft—www.microsoft.com
Oracle—www.oracle.com
Perl—www.perl.com
Sun—www.sun.com
Wall Data—www.walldata.com

STANDARDS

ODBC—www.liv.ac.uk/middleware/html/odbc.html
ODMG—www.odmg.org
SQL3—www.objs/x3h7/sql3.htm
Worldwide Web Consortium—www.w3.org

BOOKS AND PUBLICATIONS

ANSI X3. *American National Standard for Information Systems—Database Language SQL*. ANSI, 1992.

Berson, Alex, & Stephen J. Smith. *Data Warehousing, Data Mining, and OLAP*. New York: McGraw-Hill, 1997.

Boumphrey, Frank. *Professional Stylesheets for HTML and XML*. Chicago, IL: Wrox Press, 1998.

Bruce, T. *Designing Quality Databases with IDEF1X Information Models*. New York: Dorset House, 1992.

Chamberlin, D. D., et al. "SEQUEL 2: A Unified Approach to Data Definition, Manipulation, and Control." *IBM Journal of Research and Development 20* (November 1976).

Chen, P. *Entity-Relationship Approach to Information Modeling*. E-R Institute, 1981.

Chen, P. "The Entity-Relationship Model: Toward a Unified Model of Data." *ACM Transactions on Database Systems 1* (March 1976).

Codd, E. F. "Extending the Relational Model to Capture More Meaning." *Transactions on Database Systems 4* (December 1979).

Codd, E. F. "A Relational Model of Data for Large Shared Data Banks." *Communications of the ACM 25* (February 1970).

Coffee, Peter. "No-sweat Database Design." *PC Week* (March 11, 1996).

Corning, Michael, Steve Elfanbaum, & David Melnick. *Working with Active Server Pages.* Indianapolis, IN: Que Corporation, 1997.

Embley, D. W. "NFQL: The Natural Forms Query Language." *ACM Transactions on Database Systems 14* (June 1989).

Eswaran, K. P., J. N. Gray, R. A. Lorie, & I. L. Traiger. "The Notion of Consistency and Predicate Locks in a Database System." *Communications of the ACM 19* (November 1976).

Fagin, R. "Multivalued Dependencies and a New Normal Form for Relational Databases." *Transactions on Database Systems 2* (September 1977).

Fagin, R. "A Normal Form for Relational Databases That is Based on Domains and Keys." *Transactions on Database Systems 6* (September 1981).

Fronckowiak, John W. *Microsoft SQL Server 7.0 Administration.* Microsoft Press, 1999.

Goldfarb, Charles F. & Paul Prescod. *The XML Handbook.* Upper Saddle River, NJ: Prentice Hall, 1998.

Goodman, Danny. *Dynamic HTML: The Definitive Resource.* Sebastopol, CA: O'Reilly and Associates, 1998.

Hammer, M., & D. McLeod. "Database Description with SDM: A Semantic Database Model." *Transactions on Database Systems 6* (September 1981).

Harold, Elliotte Rusty. *XML: Extensible Markup Language.* New York: IDG Books Worldwide, 1998.

IBM Corporation. *IBM Database 2 Concepts and Facilities Guide.* IBM Document GG24-1582.

Keuffel, Warren. "Battle of the Modeling Techniques." *DBMS Magazine* (August 1996).

Kroenke, David. "Waxing Semantic: An Interview." *DBMS Magazine* (September 1994).

Loney, Kevin & George B. Koch. *Oracle 8: The Complete Reference.* Oracle Press, 1997.

——. *Oracle 8 Handbook.* Oracle Press, 1997.

Loomis, M.E.S. *Object Databases, The Essentials.* Reading, MA: Addison-Wesley, 1995.

Maier, D., J. Stein, A. Otis, & A. Purdy. "Development of an Object-oriented DBMS." *Conference Proceedings from the Object-oriented Programming Systems, Languages and Applications.* ACM SIGPLAN 21 (November 1986).

Moriarty, T. "Business Rule Analysis." *Database Programming and Design* (April 1993).

Nijssen, G., & T. Halpin. *Conceptual Schema and Relational Database Design: A Fact-Oriented Approach.* Englewood Cliffs, NJ: Prentice-Hall, 1989.

Nolan, R. *Managing the Data Resource Function.* St. Paul: West Publishing, 1974.

Rogers, Dan. "Manage Data with Modeling Tools." *VB Tech Journal* (December 1996).

Soukup, Ron & Kalen DeLaney. *Inside Microsoft SQL Server 7.0.* Microsoft Press, 1999.

Thomsen, Erik. *OLAP Solutions: Building Multidimensional Information Systems.* New York: John Wiley and Sons, 1997.

Woelk, D., W. Kim, & W. Luther. "An Object-oriented Approach to Multimedia Databases." *ACM SIGMOD International Conference on Management of Data,* 1986.

Zloof, M. M. "Query by Example." *Proceedings of the National Computer Conference,* AFIPS 44 (May 1975).

INDEX